MW01122048

HUMBER COLLEGE
LAKESHORE CAMPUS
LEARNING RESOURCE CENTRE
3199 LAKESHORE BLVD. WEST
TORONTO, ONTARIO M8V 1K8

Anthology
of
Québec Women's Plays

in
English
Translation

Volume I
(1966-1986)

/60201

Anthology of
Québec Women's Plays
in English Translation
Volume I (1966–1986)

The Savage Season • Playing Double
Mine Sincerely • Evangeline the Second
The Ocean • A Clash of Symbols
The Fairies Are Thirsty • Mommy
The Edge of Earth is Too Near, Violette Leduc
Night • Marie-Antoine, Opus One

Edited by Louise H. Forsyth
Professor emerita, University of Saskatchewan

Playwrights Canada Press
Toronto • Canada

Anthology of Québec Women's Plays in English Translation, Volume I, (1966–1986)
© Copyright 2006 Louise H. Forsyth
Intro: "Québec Women Playwrights of the 1960s, 1970s, and 1980s"
© Copyright 2006 Louise H. Forsyth
Please see opposite page for individual title information.
The authors assert moral rights.

Playwrights Canada Press
The Canadian Drama Publisher
215 Spadina Avenue, Suite 230, Toronto, Ontario CANADA M5T 2C7
416-703-0013   fax 416-408-3402
orders@playwrightscanada.com • www.playwrightscanada.com

CAUTION: The plays in this book are fully protected under the copyright laws of Canada and all other countries of The Copyright Union. No part of this book, covered by the copyright hereon, may be reproduced or used in any form or by any means—graphic, electronic or mechanical—without the prior written permission of the publisher except for excerpts in a review. Rights to produce, film, or record, in whole or in part, in any medium or any language, by any group, amateur or professional, are retained by the author, who has the right to grant or refuse permission at the time of the request. Any request for photocopying, recording, taping or information storage and retrieval systems of any part of this book shall be directed in writing to Access Copyright,
1 Yonge St., Suite 800, Toronto, Ontario CANADA M5E 1E5 416-868-1620.

Financial support provided by the taxpayers of Canada and Ontario through the Canada Council for the Arts and the Department of Canadian Heritage through the Book Publishing Industry Development Programme, and the Ontario Arts Council.

Cover image © Estate of Marcelle Ferron / SODRAC (2006). Planche VIII. Marcelle Ferron, *Autoportrait*, 1983. See note 5, page 285 for more information on Marcelle Ferron.
Production Editor: JLArt

Library and Archives Canada Cataloguing in Publication

Anthology of Québec women's plays in English translation / edited by Louise H. Forsyth.

Includes bibliographical references.
Incomplete contents: v. 1. 1966-1986
ISBN 0-88754-868-7 (v. 1)

1. Canadian drama (French)--Quebec (Province)--Translations into English. 2. Canadian drama (French)--Women authors--Translations into English. 3. Canadian drama (French)--20th century--Translations into English. I. Forsyth, Louise

PS8315.5.Q8A58 2006   C842'.540809287   C2006-906066-5

First Edition: November 2006
Printed and bound by Hignell Printing at Winnipeg, Canada.

Permissions and Copyright Notices

Le Temps sauvage © Copyright 1966 Anne Hébert
translation *The Savage Season* © Pamela Grant and Gregory Reid
with permission of Centre Anne Hebert, Universite de Sherbrooke

Double jeu © Copyright 1969 Françoise Loranger
translation *Playing Double* © Louise H. Forsyth
with permission of Hélène Pednault

Bien à moi © Copyright 1970 Marie Savard
translation *Mine Sincerely* © Louise H. Forsyth
with permission of Éditions Trois

Evangéline deusse © Copyright 1976 Antonine Maillet
translation *Evangeline the Second* © Luis de Céspedes
with permission of the Dundurn Group

L'Océan © Copyright 1976 Marie-Claire Blais
translation *The Ocean* © Ray Chamberlain
with permission of Cormorant Books

La Nef des sorcières © Copyright 1976 Marthe Blackburn, Marie-Claire Blais, Nicole Brossard,
Odette Gagnon, Luce Guilbeault, Pol Pelletier, France Théoret
translation *A Clash of Symbols* © Linda Gaboriau

Les Fées ont soif © Copyright 1978 Denise Boucher
translation *The Fairies Are Thirsty* © Alan Brown
with permission of Talonbooks

Moman © Copyright 1979 Louisette Dussault
translation *Mommy* © Linda Gaboriau

La Terre est trop courte, Violette Leduc © Copyright 1981 Jovette Marchessault
translation *The Edge of Earth is Too Near, Violette Leduc* © Susanne de Lotbinière-Harwood

L'Homme gris © Copyright 1984 Marie Laberge
translation *Night* © Rina Fraticelli
Night/L'Homme gris © Productions Marie Laberge Inc., 1984, 1995.

Marie-Antoine, Opus 1 © Copyright 1984 Lise Vaillancourt
translation *Marie-Antoine, Opus One* © Jill MacDougall

This volume of plays is dedicated to the many women who have been doing theatre and performance in Québec since well before the end of the 19ᵗʰ century. Their vision, talent, genius and just plain guts have made women's theatre in Québec a dazzling and moving reality. They are the actors, playwrights and other writers, directors, founders of theatre companies, artistic directors, singers and songwriters, dancers, artists, choreographers, designers, journalists, scriptwriters for radio, television and film, producers, burlesque and other performers, teachers, publishers, publicists, and technicians who brought women's insistent voices, bodies, and stories out of the shadows and onto the public stage. They were among the pioneers in recognizing the importance of popular culture and mass media for the creation of Québec's own culture. Their radical spirit and myriad innovations can be felt everywhere, not just in women's theatre, but throughout theatre in Québec and elsewhere.

Acknowledgements

My thanks are extended to all the playwrights represented in this volume and to the many other fine playwrights who are not here, but who also played vital and integral roles in the creation of Québec's amazing feminist theatre. Their works excited my imagination when they created scenes from worlds where women players discover tiny components and vast networks of their humanity and share their discoveries with their audiences. These playwrights created new theatrical strategies through their writing. At the same time, they played with and subverted old and tired, yet powerful, theatrical conventions inherited from tenacious patriarchal cultural traditions. My particular thanks go to those who have allowed me, with such generosity, to reproduce their wonderful plays here in translation.

My thanks go as well to the translators, who were equally generous in allowing their work to be included here. Their sensitivity to the playwrights' fresh theatrical approaches is astonishing, and their playful inventiveness in finding new turns of phrase in English has been a joy to share. I acknowledge my own pleasure as translator in collaborating with Maureen LaBonté. My huge thanks goes to Linda Gaboriau, whose skillful work as a pioneering translator of theatre making Québec plays available to English audiences and creating workshops where francophone and anglophone playwrights and translators worked together has been nothing short of visionary, heroic and exemplary.

I acknowledge with most sincere gratitude the support and assistance that Daniel Gauthier, responsable du centre de documentation of the Centre des Auteurs Dramatiques (CEAD), has given me at every turn in this project. I could not have done the research nor handled many practical matters without him, the seemingly inexhaustible sources of documentary information available in CEAD files and on its website.

My appreciation goes to Angela Rebeiro and the staff at Playwrights Canada Press for having believed in the project, contributed in essential ways to it, and stayed with me while the various pieces came together. All of us in the Canadian theatre and theatre research communities owe Angela Rebeiro and Playwrights Canada Press a huge debt of gratitude for the extraordinary role they have been playing for years in bringing Canadian theatre to Canadians. It is particularly important to acknowledge this now when Angela is thinking about moving on.

It's been a joy to work with everyone and to realize my dream of making Québec women's plays available to anglophone audiences, while also bringing together and paying homage to generations of Québec women in theatre. Many books remain to be written on their history, dramaturgy and experimental strategies.

Table of Contents

Introduction
Québec Women Playwrights of the 1960s, 1970s, and 1980s
by Louise H. Forsyth

These scattered texts: experiences of journeys—made up of comings and goings, of meanders and junctions, of roads crossing among women's words and writings which touched me—brought me to my fog-bound self. I listened as women sought to tear some knowledge from bodies and lives coming together, gasped as they struggled back up for some air of freedom. They spoke to me; I loved their intonations, their dotted lines. Complicit, feeling a space open inside myself. Very quickly, I realized that they were shaping me, that I needed them, that, without them, my self would sink away, would exist no more. [1]

Who am I? Who shall I be, as if I had never been? [2]

The theatre, a collective art, is the ideal place to invent new social relations. [3]

An Inaugural Scene

The first voice heard in Luce Guilbeault's opening monologue of *A Clash of Symbols* belongs to a stage manager who is on the point of starting Molière's *L'École des femmes*, a classic in the canon of French dramatic literature. The second voice heard is that of the character Arnolphe, who opens the play by laying out his strategies for getting his young ward Agnès back in line. He is planning his marriage to her, a marriage that he must make happen quickly before she eludes his control and foolishly throws away her innocence. When the Mad Actress playing Agnès comes on stage she is thus already set up for playing in a theatrical piece that is integral to a centuries-old patriarchal culture where all the voices of creativity and authority are male, where plots are fashioned to reflect male desire, where the hands and voices controlling every aspect of representational practice belong to men, and where women are confined to a few fixed stereotypes. The Actress does not initially disappoint. She comes on stage wearing a white gown and a wig, carrying a dainty parasol, every inch the standard, virginal, pretty female character, ready to deliver her lines as expected, ready to adhere to the dictum that is soon enunciated: "Be beautiful and be silent, Woman." [4]

But!!… the Actress immediately has a complete memory loss. Her lines have slipped right out of her head; she does not even know what character she is playing, nor what play she is in. The show cannot go on. The action of *L'École des femmes*—the play within the play of *A Clash of Symbols*—stops for lack of actors who know their parts and believe in them. The magic that transforms an empty stage into a place for fiction is destroyed. Only a black box, virtually without meaning-producing signs, remains. A fictitious actor seeking her bearings is left alone before the audience waiting in silence. The actor speaks her stage name, "Désirée." She tries to reassure herself that her function is to be an actress and that she has always fulfilled this function well. But she can't get back into the part; she calls out for help and realizes that, without the assigned costume, role and lines, she has become, literally, nothing and nobody in a nowhere place: "Help, I'm not anything any more." [5]

However frightening her situation of abandonment might appear to her, this break in the process of regurgitating memorized lines written for her by others has cleared the stage for those who come after her in *A Clash of Symbols*. The patriarchal monopoly of representational practices in theatre and culture has been symbolically broken in this dark space. Consequently, the stage box remains open and available to present other stories for the audience.

Before she withdraws to her onstage dressing-room to watch the rest of the action in the following monologues of *A Clash of Symbols*, the Mad Actress displays her actual hair beneath the wig, her actual body beneath the costume and its constraining stays, and her body functions such as urinating and feeling chilly. When the lights go up on her again at the beginning of Act Two, she reveals further details about her existence as a flesh and blood individual, rather than the creature of someone else's fantasy: she masturbates, has had an abortion, has her own tastes and memories, and has a name, in this particular case, "Luce."

The experienced professional woman of theatre, Luce Guilbeault, has created an opening scene for *A Clash of Symbols* which announces in radical terms that the patriarchal show has imploded. It cannot go on, either in the theatre or in the streets of the city. With one short monologue, the Mad Actress has managed to clear the space of male fantasies so that the five remaining *sorcières* are free to sail their ship in with dramatizations of their own personal journeys and quests. As well, she has dramatized what occurred in Québec theatres in the 1960s, 1970s and 1980s when what has been called "Théâtre-femmes" burst onto stages and into halls and auditoria in Montréal, Québec and several other cities. [6] Feminist actors, performers, directors, playwrights, designers, technicians, and critics seemed to determine with almost one accord that they had little memory or taste to keep on doing shows that misrepresented their bodies, voices, desires, experiences, relations, memories, and feelings.

This generation of women was rebelling against tenacious traditions in both Québec society and its theatre that were still limiting their opportunities. The Catholic Church's role in imposing a very narrow range of social and moral possibilities on girls and women has been well documented. But beyond the direct control of the Church, there was the impact of institutions in Québec society that had served until the 1960s to keep women in their place in public and private spheres. There was, for example, a legal system which recognized for married women only the same rights as children and the mentally handicapped. There was also a mediocre education system that offered no access for girls to public secondary schools. Women's right to vote in Québec was not recognized until 1940.

Arrival of *Théâtre-femmes*

Québec women began to write plays for the amateur stage in the 19th century, and they continued to do so into the 20th century. Yvette Ollivier Mercier-Gouin's *Cocktail* enjoyed popular success in 1935, as did Jean Depréz's *La Cathédrale* in 1949. Starting in the 1930s, they wrote scripts for radio and then for television, where they were also actors and producers. They were acting and performing on stage in the 19th century, and they continued to do so in increasing numbers throughout the 20th century, despite official disapproval of women displaying themselves in public. They acted in professional and Church-controlled theatres, did burlesque, sang opera and popular songs, danced, and delivered monologues. Although women's condition was strictly controlled, people in Québec society got used to hearing their voices on the radio and seeing their bodies on television and public stages. As the century advanced, women travelled to places like New York and Paris; the frequency, diversity and audacity of their public performances increased; as artists, they defiantly signed explosive manifestos like Refus global in 1948; they wrote and published books[7]; they founded theatres, as Yvette Brind'Amour and Mercedes Palomino did with the Théâtre du Rideau Vert in 1948 (today Canada's longest lasting institutional theatre); they founded experimental theatre companies, as Françoise Berd did with L'Égregore in 1959; they taught radically new approaches to their various arts; they became journalists recording everything going on in the world. Clémence Desrochers (born 1933), poet, humourist, playwright, composer, actor and performer wrote the script for and performed in Québec's first musical comedy, *Le Vol rose du flamant* (1964), and the first feminist revue *Les Girls* (1969). Her songs were performed by many Québec singers, including the young Pauline Julien. She has toured widely in France and across Canada.[8]

In the 1960s several plays written by women were produced on stage and published, as is shown in this anthology by the works of Hébert, Loranger and Savard. Until the plays of Desrochers, Loranger and Savard, however, women playwrights were not positioning themselves explicitly as women, and they were not seeking a community of women with whom they could collaborate, nor looking for publics that would receive with understanding and appreciation the dramatization of women's issues. Lucie Robert has signalled the decisive influence of feminism for the emergence of women's theatre in the final years of the 1960s and has suggested that Loranger's explicitly feminine language in her 1967 play *Encore cinq minutes* was a first:

> Beginning toward the end of the 1960s, with the first production of *Encore cinq minutes* in 1967, specifically feminine ways of speaking (and not just in books, on the radio and in television) arrived on the Québec

stage. This makes Françoise Loranger a founding figure [as a playwright writing *in the feminine*].[9]

This generation of playwrights was convinced that it is possible to change societies and cultures by using the languages of the stage to stimulate eyes, voices and bodies to really see, speak and act in accord with their particular erotic energy, and thus to awaken inner landscapes and imaginations.

By the early 1970s there was, literally, an explosion of feminist playwrights, actors, performers, and companies, not just in Montréal and Québec, but in many other centres. Many of the first plays were, like *A Clash of Symbols*, collective creations: *Nous aurons les enfants que nous voudrons* (1974)[10], *Un Prince, mon jour viendra* (1974), *Si Cendrillon pouvait mourir* (1975), *Môman travaille pas, a trop d'ouvrage* (1976), *Trois et sept le numéro magique* (1977), *La Vraie vie des masquées* (1977), *À ma mère, à ma mère, à ma mère, à ma voisine* (1978), *Où en est le miroir* (1978), *As-tu vu, les maisons s'emportent* (1980), *Enfin, duchesses* (1982 in Québec City, 1983 in Montréal at the Théâtre Expérimental des Femmes), *Strip* (1983 in Sudbury). Also like *A Clash of Symbols*, many of the plays by women of the 1970s and 1980s were monologues or contained significant monologue components. The autobiographical dimension was strong. Collaborating in the theatrical performance of their own lives and stories allowed players and playwrights to call forth the silent spectres that had been hovering in the shadows of their experiences and in the darkness of the black box opened by Guilbeault's Mad Actress. Experimental fervour and creative energy were felt everywhere.

As women's voices were heard and their stories brought to light on stage through collective creations, as more and more women learned the profession of making theatre (as actors, directors, designers, technicians, and administrators), and, as well, as publics formed that were receptive to *Théâtre-femmes*, playwrights came in increasing numbers to theatres—or were invited by them—where their scripts were workshopped and taken into production. Following the early models of writers Hébert, Loranger, Blais, and Maillet, their feminist works began to go into production just a few years after the first collective creations. Denise Boucher's *Les Fées ont soif* and Jovette Marchessault's *Les Vaches de nuit* were among the first of these authored shows. Before the end of the 1970s, the Théâtre du Nouveau Monde had produced *La Nef des sorcières*, *Les Fées ont soif*, *Les Vaches de nuit*, *L'Hippocanthrope* by France Vézina, *La Saga des poules mouillées* by Jovette Marchessault, and would produce *Un reel ben beau, ben triste* by Jeanne-Mance Delisle the following year. Women playwrights and script writers were pushing back all the boundaries and protesting publicly when established institutions silenced them. An early and courageous example of this was Louise Maheu-Forcier, who spoke out forcefully when her TV script *Arioso*, telling the story of two lesbian lovers, was refused in 1973 by Radio-Canada. She said sarcastically: "vulgarity, violence, alcoholism, insanity, murder, suicide, all that is inoffensive. What is deadly, it seems, is love!"[11]

By 1980 when the special issue on women's theatre of *Jeu* appeared, feminist theatre was a recognized cultural phenomenon and the variety of its creative approaches was striking. Experimentation and research were in the air, and clear formulations of objectives for major changes in theatre practice were being developed. Loranger, collaborating with André Brassard in the 1960s, had already demonstrated her vision for a theatre transformed by a re-visioning of the functions of actor, character, director, plot, design, and spectator. The theoretical objectives shared by feminist women of theatre a decade later were expressed as follows by Francine Noël in her article making a plea for the representation of her own woman's image on public stages:

> And so a new aesthetic is taking shape making room for that part of us that has been passed over in silence for centuries, broken, civilized, and affirming our rights: the right to laugh and to cry without being accused of hysteria, the right to rest, the right to beauty but especially a redefinition of beauty, the right to dispose of our own bodies and our own minds, the right to love as well, and above all, *the right to a change of mentalities.* [12]

Experimental Theatre and Collective Creation

The decade of the 1970s was a period throughout theatre in Québec when there was a proliferation of small theatre companies created by those passionately wishing to do experimental theatre work, to encourage personal and collective improvisation. [13] Lorraine Hébert's 1977 description of collective creation makes it easy to see why this collaborative approach proved so fruitful in meeting the radical objectives for feminist theatre:

> Since this practice is tied, above all, to the redefinition of the function of the actor-creator, it implies the transformation of the traditional functions and relations among actor, author, director, and spectator, and, at the same time, the questioning of the structures and superstructures which encourage and perpetuate them." [14]

The members of Québec's experimental companies, all of which were in financially precarious situations, shared an opposition to written scripts that actors and directors were more or less obliged to respect and follow. They wanted to find out what else they could do with theatre. One of these experimental companies, the Théâtre Expérimental de Montréal (T.E.M.), founded in 1975 by Robert Gravel, Pol Pelletier and Jean-Pierre Ronfard, made a sustained and significant difference in Québec theatre. Their first productions were all collective creations. The T.E.M. became the Nouveau Théâtre Expérimental when the Théâtre Expérimental des Femmes (T.E.F.) split from the T.E.M. and became an autonomous company in 1979. [15]

The first collective creation experimenting with an entirely feminine and feminist universe was produced at the T.E.M. in 1976: *Essai en trois mouvements pour trois voix de femmes*. In *Essai*, as in the second, *Finalement*, there were no words, only sounds, objects and women's bodies. It was by going back to those basic elements that Pol Pelletier, Louise Laprade and Nicole Lecavalier believed women's acting methods could best be discerned and developed. In 1978, these three, assisted by the technical contributions and innovations of Dominique Gagnon, were ready to present a show with words: *À ma mère, à ma mère, à ma mère, à ma voisine.*[16] They summarized their collective objectives for this highly original play in "Notes sur la création du spectacle":

> We wished as feminists to represent our women's condition in a theatre that appeals to the imaginary, to myth, to the unknown. That is where our very great interest in the subconscious came from. In any case, the subconscious contains within itself women's entire history. We wished […], as Louise has said, to "do theatre that changes *us* and changes the world." In other words, we agreed upon a certain theatrical aesthetic (which does not at all tend toward realism).[17]

The working out of this theatrical aesthetic was rigorous. In order to release their own passions, obsessions and fears that would determine the characters, themes, myths, actions, props and design they created, they improvised alone and together, did vigorous physical exercise, talked, wrote, and dreamt aloud: "It was through orality that women's collective creations were born. With talking. By telling ourselves and each other our women's stories, since that material did not yet exist in books, or so little."[18] The play took shape as an innovative autobiographical performance piece, in which each person involved in the production was intensely and personally engaged. It involved putting the traditional mother on trial (the Reine-Mère represented in the opening scene in the manner of Denise Boucher's Statue as completely hidden and immobilized behind yards and yards of white bandages), exploring the experiences of little girls in the world of such a mother, and celebrating the physical and mental strength of women as Amazons. The innovative acting style was intended to tell the women's stories in broad terms and gestures, using burlesque methods as far removed as possible from theatrical realism.

Pol Pelletier has said that the process of collective creation and production astonished and seduced her, taught her a good deal and allowed her to exorcise long-suppressed emotions, including those regarding the mother.[19] When she invited the other women who had participated in *À ma mère* in 1979 to join her in forming the Théâtre Expérimental des Femmes, they took with them the same thirst for discovery of women's fantasies, their intimate and social experiences, along with their technical competence and the thirst for research into the languages of theatre.

Le Théâtre Expérimental des Femmes (T.E.F.)

During the years of its existence (1979–1987, at which time it was transformed into L'Espace GO), the T.E.F. was a marvelous site for new feminist ways of doing theatre and for bringing theatre people and publics together for plays, performance pieces, films, readings, lectures, workshops, exhibitions, and incredibly rich and varied festivals. It was a genuine laboratory for all the many facets involved in the exploration and discovery of some of the ways to do theatre *in the feminine*. I believe that the T.E.F.

was the first feminist company with its own theatre building in Québec and in Canada. Women in theatre, doing theatre, or writing for theatre in Québec would most certainly not have followed the same paths over the past three decades had the T.E.F. not existed. Of course, such an ambitious project was not without many difficult and painful moments.

In the beginning, most of the productions at the T.E.F. were workshop productions and collective creations as women brought to light, through processes of talking, improvising, physical exercise, imagination, memory, trial and creative performance styles, what they had to say and to show.

Then there was an evolution from collective creations toward scripted plays. Pol Pelletier has said that it was difficult to maintain the energy of the collective creation process. It is clear that she regretted this evolution, since, for her, it meant a retreat from the enormous erotic power of the imagination at work with the body. She dramatized in *Joie* the unusually joyous yet rocky road they travelled together in their theatrical experimentation, moving from the powerful rebellion that I have noted in *A Clash of Symbols* to a more literary, dramaturgical mode. *Joie* is an autobiographical play that was produced in Montréal and elsewhere in several versions between 1990 and 1995:

> The language of women's shows has changed radically […] the first collective creations! Do you remember? When we opened the floodgates, it was songs and cries that came out: a repetitive, concrete, untamed lyricism […] The evolution in women's theatre corresponds to the evolution in theatre in general: poetry first, epics next and finally plays where different characters confront each other in complexity. Complexity. The primitive language at the start was tied to an extreme revolt, a radical rejection of society and all its cultural manifestations. [20]

Despite Pelletier's regret for the passing of the collective creation period, the transition at the T.E.F. to staging scripts written by individuals proved to offer very fruitful terrain to playwrights who were beginning to find their dramatic voice and needed the workshopping opportunities offered by the T.E.F. to work out the theatrical challenges of their pieces, playwrights such as Marchessault, Vaillancourt, and Dussault. For the first time, women playwrights of the 1980s produced entire bodies of dramatic works.

The Edge of Earth Is Too Near, Violette Leduc, written by Jovette Marchessault, whose *Night Cows* Pelletier had already performed on many stages in both English and French starting in 1979 at the Théâtre du Nouveau Monde, was one of the first single-authored scripts produced at the T.E.F. In the exciting, although troubled, collaboration that occurred among Marchessault, director Pol Pelletier, and leading actor Luce Guilbeault (who apparently suggested the subject to Marchessault), we can see the transition from collective creation to single authorship and the move toward supporting feminist dramaturgy. The first play written by Pol Pelletier alone, *La Lumière blanche*, had, in fact, been produced at the T.E.F. in 1981, although it was not published until much later. Lise Vaillancourt followed more or less the same path as Marchessault, bringing her writing skills to the stage. Along with designer Ginette Noiseux, Vaillancourt became a director of the T.E.F. in 1982. She and the others at the T.E.F. produced, without publishing, her early pieces, and then produced *Marie-Antoine, Opus One*, directed by Pol Pelletier, in 1984. Louisette Dussault has discussed in "Itinéraire pour une moman" the central importance in her career as a feminist actor and playwright of workshopping and participating in collective creation during the productions of *A Clash of Symbols* and *The Fairies Are Thirsty*. In a similar process, Laberge was active in Québec City with experimental companies using collective creation, first with the Troupe des Treize and then with the Commune à Marie, a company founded in 1978 by Janine Angers, Denise Dubois and Denise Gagnon. The title itself of Laberge's 1977 show, *Profession, je l'aime* (a collection of five short plays), illustrates its experimental nature as well as providing insight into Laberge's practical and theoretical reflections on her chosen profession as actor and playwright at the beginning of her career.

Théâtre-femmes, a Mature Theatre

Lorraine Camerlain described women's theatre in Québec in the 1985 special issue of *Canadian Theatre Review* on "Feminism and Canadian Theatre," edited by Robert Wallace. Her description shows that in one short decade women's theatre had reached a recognizable stage of diversity and maturity and had legitimate aspirations to consider itself central in the social body of Québec and its culture:

> Henceforth, women's theatre designates more than simply a play written by a woman. Its vital and nervous centre is the expression of women's lives, of women's thoughts and desires. It seeks to inscribe women's bodies into the body of society by giving them dramatic space and shape. [21]

Strategies for Innovation

The evolution of *Théâtre-femmes* from the 1960s to the 1980s highlights the enormous challenges facing those who wished to do theatre in a radically different way, outside the confines of patriarchal and misogynist traditions, practices and thought. If we go back to the theatrical situation at the end of the Mad Actress's opening monologue in *A Clash of Symbols*, we recognize that, after the stage space has been materially and symbolically swept clean of characters, languages, actions, plots, and objects determined by sexist traditions, theatre's space of illusion must be filled by other functions and elements if it is to endure as theatre. How does one proceed to fill it? Obviously, not all traditions and conventions could be discarded, if, for no other reason, than that communication between characters and spectators was, at least to some extent, dependent on them. Nevertheless, all things theatrical, dramatic, cultural and social had to be reexamined in a fresh light in order to determine what could still be used creatively through imagination or subversion, and what needed to go back to an absolutely fresh start. As *A Clash of Symbols* shows, there were stories to be told, stories that indeed haunted the subconscious of women everywhere, but that had not yet been shown in stage lights and action. Feminist theatre's function of *monstrance* was and still is enormously important—simply showing women's experiences, dreams and pain as they are. Women's untold experiences were frequently closely tied to the ways they felt in their bodies, bodies whose sexed being and sexual desires have been so often deformed by dominant culture's representation practices. Revealing their sexed bodies, showing them as they are in either reality or women's fantasies, required courage to overcome irrational but powerful taboos and fears. As the fate of many of the plays in this anthology demonstrates, there were many in the theatre world who thought these pioneers of women's theatre were quite mad, extremely vulgar, or, in any case, lacking an understanding of what "good" theatre should be.

As I have already discussed, it was not surprising that Québec women's theatre activists often chose the *modus operandi* of collective creation. Also not surprising was the widespread use of monologues or dialogues that have all the characteristics of monologues because communication fails to occur between the interlocutors. When playwrights, actors and directors are bringing to the stage representations of experiences for which there is neither a theatrical tradition nor dramaturgical models, characters and events often appear more absent than present. Storytellers must often begin tentatively as they seek to breathe life into the spirits and ghosts that haunt them, while technical people must design lighting, props, stages and often even the house in order to place them in a setting where their universe appears theatrically coherent and comprehensible. The plays in this anthology provide fascinating examples of the many ways monologues and soliloquies—in the broadest sense of the word—can be used theatrically to invent entire theatrical realities. *Mine Sincerely*, *A Clash of Symbols*, and *Mommy* are monologues, each in its own mode, as are *The Edge of Earth Is Too Near*, *Violette Leduc*, *The Fairies Are Thirsty*, and *Marie-Antoine, Opus One* at key moments. Jovette Marchessault even doubled the monologue effect by making extensive use, verbatim, of Leduc's own first-person narrative. Very interesting is Christine's silent monologue in *Night*, where her body language and unspoken response to Roland's rant form her phantom monologue text. The songs throughout *Playing Double* function as monologues. The characters in *The Savage Season*, *Evangeline the Second*, *The Ocean* are almost always in the presence of an interlocutor. However, the themes of non-communication and exile are so powerful in these plays, that the words of the characters frequently have the impact of a monologue, as though only the spectators—or strangers—could understand the solitude felt by the characters.

The description of the function of solo performance offered by Knowles and Lane in the special issue of *Canadian Theatre Review* on solo performance applies to all the plays in this anthology insofar as the relationship between actor and character is thrown into question through solo performance, as it clearly is in *A Clash of Symbols*. The relationship between playwright and spectators, between authorial authority and viewers' implicit ideological site is also opened for active speculation in the plays in this anthology.

> Solo performance foregrounds the presence of the performer to the extent that it undermines illusion, throws into question the relationship between actor and character in the theatre, and suggests questions about why spectators watch, listen, and make meanings out of what they see and hear. [22]

One-woman shows and solo performances, where autobiographies are frequently present and allowed to be imaginative, lend themselves to playful ways for building an identity, constructing a sense of self, and making a voice and body resonate with newly discovered emotions and awareness. As Patricia Smart states in *Les Femmes du Refus global*, autobiography can be particularly interesting, and often humourous or moving, when it creates the impression of revealing through words or dramatic action what even the character herself does not know about herself:

> Autobiography […] can represent an entry into writing rather than an account of a finished life, a way of constructing a subjectivity for oneself by going against the obstacles that reduce women to silence or marginality in the field of culture. [23]

Performativity and Performance Art

I would describe the strategies of Québec women playwrights for discursive creativity and innovative theatrical practice between 1966 and 1986 as making extensive use of collective creation, monologue, and autobiographical archaeology. And I would sum up my understanding of these strategies by suggesting that the dominant mode of women's theatre during these two decades is performative— performative in two ways. First, it was the intent of the playwrights and all those working with them for the shows to produce change in theatre practice, dominant discourse, and sociocultural realities. Their intent was not in any way to either reproduce existing reality nor to simply entertain. Second, and to an amazing extent, these plays—which position themselves playfully and defiantly on the boundaries between art and documentary, between high and popular culture—anticipate a genre that has come in recent decades to be called performance art, as described and analyzed, for example, by Judith Butler and Jeannie Forte:

> Women's performance art has particular disruptive potential because it poses an actual woman as a speaking subject, throwing that position into process, into doubt, opposing the traditional conception of the single, unified (male) subject. The female body as subject clashes in dissonance with its patriarchal text, challenging the very fabric of representation by refusing that text and posing new, multiple texts grounded in real women's experience and sexuality. [24]

A major component of the performativity of the plays in this anthology is the use of other media and genres: visual effects, poetry, and song. This strategy brought women's theatre closer to the popular culture traditions of earlier decades and also made the plays more accessible to publics who, perhaps, did not regularly go to the theatre. Louise Cotnoir and Louise Dupré outlined this brechtian strategy in their 1987 commentary on their strategies for *Si Cendrillon pouvait mourir* in a special issue of *La Nouvelle Barre du Jour* dedicated to the "scandalous women" who created their radical art between 1965 and 1985:

> By using humour you can exaggerate portraits, achieve the grotesque or the vaudevillian, and thus reclaim theatrical forms scornfully rejected by the institution, "good literature," while giving the advantage, beside official voices, to a way of speaking that is more relaxed, more free. *Monstration* allowed us to present the *monstrous*, to measure its results [...] this effect is achieved using distanciation through excess, enormity, going over the top. [25]

The plays in this anthology and throughout the many works by Québec women playwrights between 1966 and 1986 do not avoid the themes of the world's great literatures: love, fantasy, spirituality, death, time, solitude, ambition, fear, nature, violence, or human corruption. However, in every case they give these themes an explicit feminist twist through performativity and experimental strategies.

Deconstructing Dominant Discourse

A major topic in each of the plays is the unsatisfactory nature of dominant discourse and its narrative traditions, as they prevail in institutionally based, authoritative *dicta* and in literary, theatrical, historical and philosophical texts. Playwrights of *Théâtre-femmes* might have wished to be included in literary and theatrical canons and repertories, and to be recognized by professional and university critics. Yet they dramatize in their plays the profoundly negative impact of patriarchal thought that underlies the structures of all forms of received culture, including what prevails throughout the social fabric in daily intercourse. All the plays highlight damaging ideologies that determine roles and structures in families. In *The Savage Season* the words of organized religion, as passed through Father Beaumont, are largely responsible for the family's self-imposed social ostracism. The need for fundamental educational reform is played out in *Playing Double. Mine Sincerely* and *Evangeline the Second* offer biting parodies of canonical texts such as Cervantes's *Don Quixote* and Longfellow's *Evangeline*, while *The Ocean* and *Marie-Antoine* deconstruct the very notion of the great writer or artist. Central to the message of *The Edge of Earth Is Too Near, Violette Leduc* is evidence shown by all the characters, their words and their actions—whether they are victims like Leduc or privileged like Jean Genet—of the biased and unfair criteria used by the literary institution to measure the value of a work. The plays all suggest that the discursive formulae of dominant culture must always be used with caution and distrust, whether in the theatre or in one's personal social relations.

Women's Themes: Motherhood and Mother-Child Relations

Théâtre-femmes succeeded in Québec, as in every other place where feminist visions and analyses were producing new forms, in bringing new themes onto public stages. Most striking of these themes in the plays in this volume is the problematic and complex theme of motherhood, along with complementary themes of mother-child relations and women's sexuality, all of which raise serious questions regarding personal agency and freedom. The main character of *The Savage Season* is the mother Agnès Joncas, who dreams of keeping all her children "on this mountain, for as long as possible, sheltered from the entire world, in a prolonged childhood, savage and pure." The ramifications of this dangerous objective of a mother, controlling in the extreme, are played out in the action of the play. In *Playing Double*, the young woman must discover the beauty and strength of her own body before she can decide on whether or not to marry and, if so, whom to marry. *Mine Sincerely* gives us a woman whose experiences of being a wife and mother have been entirely alienating. *Evangeline* has had eleven children, yet, at the age of 80, she has nowhere to feel at home. The mothers of both *The Ocean* and *Night* are evoked as absent, silent, powerless, and completely submissive to the will of their husbands. A range of facets of mothering, motherhood, and sexuality are major themes for resistance in *A Clash of Symbols*. Mothers are dramatized as freeing themselves from the painful chains of the stereotypes of motherhood in *The Fairies Are Thirsty* and *Mommy*. The mothers in *The Edge of Earth* and *Marie-Antoine* are simply pathetic, both handmaidens to cultures that exclude them as agents. Despite their lack of power and awareness, they remain dangerous models and influences for their daughters.

About This Volume

The present volume contains, in their entirety, translations of eleven of the plays written and produced by women in Québec between 1966 and 1986.[26] A second and third volume will include translations of plays by francophone women from the late 1980s to the present. The aim of this three-volume anthology is to make some of these innovative and important plays available to anglophone students, actors, directors, critics, teachers, researchers and other lovers of theatre, as well as to provide background information on them. I hope that all those who are passionate about drama and theatre as living culture, as I am, will find excitement in discovering playwrights and players for whom the stage has been a place for the representation of overlooked lived realities, for the exploration in fresh terms of complex philosophical questions that have never ceased to challenge human understanding, and for the imaginative construction of forms that exist only in the eyes of desire, fantasy, dreams, or terrors.

My intent in preparing this three-volume anthology of women's plays is to bring a few of these scattered playwrights' works out of the shadows and discursively present in the over-arching narratives about contemporary Québec theatre and its origins and about feminist theatre. The story of Québec women achieving the freedom to make their voices heard and their bodies seen in performances on public stages is a story of remarkable courage, brilliant imagination, and burning vision.

I have written the introductions to all the plays, with the exception of the introduction to Anne Hébert's *The Savage Season*. It has been my pleasure to include the translation of this play done by two specialists of Anne Hébert and translation: Pamela Grant and Gregory Reid of the Anne Hébert Centre of L'Université de Sherbrooke, and to include their introduction to this important, yet little-studied play. This volume includes considerable bibliographical material. Yet this material is far from complete. I particularly regret the omission from the notes and bibliographies of the articles by critics in newspapers and magazines at the time the plays in the volume were first produced, both in French and English. I hope that this anthology will incite students and researchers to go back to primary sources in order to lay the groundwork for the studies and performances these plays so richly deserve.

The volume, by the very nature of what it is, raises interesting questions regarding translation, which I have not been able to address here. Only Grant and Reid have included comments on their work as translators. All the other translators in this volume have developed their own strategies for translating the unique languages of theatre. In addition, anglophone and francophone scholars in this country are aware of the relevance of the trope of translation to represent strategies for feminist creation, theatrical creation, and experimentation of all kinds with the many languages the human imagination can and does play with. These plays in translation lend themselves well to further study of the creative, reflective and collaborative processes involved in translation.

Notes

[1] "Ces textes sans continuité: l'expérience de parcours faits d'allées et venues, de boucles et de raccords, de chemins de traverse entre des paroles et des écritures de femmes qui m'ont rejointe, menée à un moi embrouillé. J'ai écouté comment les femmes cherchaient à attacher quelque connaissance du joint de leur corps et de leur vie, tentaient une remontée vers l'air libre. Elles m'ont parlé, j'ai aimé leurs intonations, leurs pointillés. Complice, sentant s'ouvrir en moi un espace intérieur. Très vite, j'ai su qu'elles me constituaient, m'étaient nécessaires, que, sans elles, un moi coulait, n'existait plus." (Lamy, Suzanne. *D'Elles*: 12) Translated by LHF.

[2] "Qui suis-je qui serai comme si je n'avais jamais été?" (*Les Fées ont soif*: 84).

³ "Le théâtre, art collectif, est l'endroit idéal pour inventer de nouveaux rapports sociaux." (Pelletier, Pol. *Joie*: 52) Translated by LHF.

⁴ "Sois belle et tais-toi/Femme." (*La Nef des sorcières*: 18).

⁵ "Au secours, je ne suis plus rien." (*La Nef des sorcières*: 17) Translated by LHF.

⁶ A special issue of *Cahiers de théâtre. Jeu* on "Théâtre-femmes," frequently cited, was produced by Michèle Barrette, Hélène Beauchamp, Émile Bessette, Gilbert David, Joceline Hardy, Lorraine Hébert, Pierre Lavoie, Francine Noël, and Michel Vaïs: *Cahiers de théâtre. Jeu*. 16 (1980.3). For information on *Cahiers de théâtre. Jeu*, see Gruslin, Adrien. "*Jeu. Cahiers de théâtre*, 1976–1980." *Dictionnaire des oeuvres littéraires du Québec. 1976–1980*. Tome VI. Montréal: Fides, 1994: 442–45.

⁷ For information on the careers and philosophies of the seven women who signed Refus global, see Smart, Patricia. *Les Femmes du Refus global*. For information on the position of women writers in Québec literature during the first half of the 20ᵗʰ century, see Boisclair, Isabelle. "Les Femmes et le fait littéraire (1900–1959)." *Ouvrir la voie/x. Le Processus constitutif d'un sous-champ littéraire féministe au Québec (1960–1990)*: 71–111.

⁸ Playwright, journalist and author Hélène Pedneault has written a delightful book about Clémence Desrochers: *Notre Clémence. Tout l'Humour du Vrai Monde*. Montréal: Éditions de l'Homme, 1989.

⁹ "C'est à partir de la fin des années soixante, avec la création d'*Encore cinq minutes*, en 1967, qu'advient sur la scène québécoise (et non seulement dans les livres, à la radio et à la télévision), une parole spécifiquement féminine. Ce qui fait de Françoise Loranger une figure fondatrice." (Robert. 2000: 154) Translated by LHF.

¹⁰ *Nous Aurons les enfants que nous voudrons*, *Môman travaille pas, a trop d'ouvrage*, and *As-tu vu, les maisons s'emportent* were three of the productions of the Théâtre des Cuisines, founded in 1973 by Solange Collin, Carole Fréchette and Véronique O'Leary to create shows for the celebration of International Women's Day each year on March 8. The Théâtre des Cuisines also published a powerful manifesto outlining their collective's approach to political theatre, an approach that involved addressing specific social issues such as contraception, abortion, and paid housework.

¹¹ "La vulgarité, la violence, l'alcoolisme, la folie, le meurtre, le suicide, tout cela est inoffensif; ce qui est mortel, semble-t-il, c'est l'amour!" (Maheu-Forcier, Louise. *Un Arbre chargé d'oiseaux*. [téléthéâtre] Ottawa: Éditions de l'Université d'Ottawa, 1976: 15–16.) Translated by LHF.

¹² "Une nouvelle esthétique se dessine donc faisant place à cette part de nous qui a été tue pendant des siècles, domptée, civilisée et affirmant nos droits: droit de rire et de pleurer sans être taxées d'hystériques, droit au repos, droit à la beauté, mais surtout à une redéfinition de la beauté, droit de disposer de nos corps et de nos esprits, droit à l'amour aussi, mais avant tout, *droit à un changement des mentalités*." (Noël,

Francine. "Plaidoyer pour mon image." *Cahiers de théâtre. Jeu.* 16 (1980.3): 46, 48) Translated by LHF.

[13] See Andrès, Bernard. "Théâtre expérimental." *Dictionnaire des oeuvres littéraires du Québec. 1977–1980.* Tome VI. Montréal: Fides, 1994: 808–11.

[14] "Comme cette pratique est avant tout liée à la redéfinition de la fonction de l'acteur en termes d'acteur-créateur, elle implique la transformation des fonctions et des rapports traditionnels entre acteur, auteur, metteur en scène et spectateur et, du même coup, la remise en question des structures et des superstructures qui les encouragent et les perpétuent." (Hébert, Lorraine. "Pour une définition de la création collective." 1977: 38) Translated by LHF.

[15] See Brault, Marie-Andrée. "Théâtre expérimental des femmes." *Dictionnaire des oeuvres littéraires du Québec, 1981–1985.* Tome VII. Montréal: Fides, 2003: 917–19.

[16] *À ma mère, à ma mère, à ma mère, à ma voisine* was first produced May 16 to June 11, 1978 at the T.E.M. by the authors with the help of Anne-Marie Provencher and Alice Ronfard.

[17] "Autant nous étions féministes, autant nous voulions représenter notre condition de femmes par un théâtre qui fait appel à l'imaginaire, au mythe, à l'inconnu, d'où notre intérêt très grand pour l'inconscient, qui, de toutes façons, contient en lui toute l'histoire des femmes. Nous voulions […] selon l'expression de Louise «faire un théâtre qui *nous* change et change le monde». En d'autres mots, nous nous entendions sur une certaine esthétique théâtrale (qui ne va pas du tout dans le sens du réalisme)." ("Notes sur la création du spectacle." *À ma mère*: 60) Translated by LHF.

[18] "C'est par l'oralité que les créations collectives de femmes ont vu le jour. Par le parlage. En se racontant nos histoires de femmes, car cette matière n'existait pas encore dans les livres, ou si peu." (Pelletier, Pol. *Joie*: 47). Translated by LHF. For a complete discussion of the experimental philosophy and theatrical strategies of *À ma mère* see *Trac femmes.* Montréal: Cellule d'éditions Trac, *Cahiers de théâtre expérimental*, 1978.

[19] "[…] j'ai été étonnée, j'ai été séduite et j'ai beaucoup appris. (J'ai aussi beaucoup exorcisé. Entre autres, mon rapport à la mère.)" ("Introduction." *À ma mère*: 5). Translated by LHF.

[20] "Le langage des spectacles de femmes a changé radicalement […] les premières créations collectives! Vous vous souvenez? Lorsqu'on a ouvert les écluses, ce sont des chants et des cris qui sont sortis: un lyrisme sauvage, concret, répétitif […] Cette évolution du théâtre de femmes correspond à l'évolution du théâtre en général: d'abord la poésie, ensuite les épopées et finalement les pièces de théâtre où différents personnages s'affrontent dans la complexité. La complexité. Le langage primitif des débuts était lié à une révolte extrême, un rejet radical de la société et de toutes ses manifestations culturelles." (Pelletier, Pol. *Joie*: 79–80). Translated by LHF.

[21] "le théâtre des femmes désigne désormais davantage celui dont le centre vital et nerveux est l'expression de la vie des femmes, de la pensée et du désir des femmes, celui qui cherche à inscrire le corps des femmes dans le corps social en lui donnant forme et espace dramatique, que celui qui est écrit par une femme, tout simplement." (Camerlain, Lorraine. "En de multiples scènes": 74). Translated by LHF.

[22] Knowles, Ric and Harry Lane. "Editorial: Solo Performance." *Canadian Theatre Review*. 92 (Fall 1997): 3.

[23] "L'autobiographie [...] peut représenter une entrée dans l'écriture plutôt que le bilan d'une vie accomplie, une façon de se construire une subjectivité à l'encontre des obstacles qui réduisent la femme au silence ou à la marginalité dans le champ de la culture." (Smart, Patricia. *Les Femmes du Refus global*: 233). Translated by LHF.

[24] Forte, Jeannie. "Women's Performance Art: Feminism and Postmodernism." *Performing Feminisms. Feminist Critical Theory and Theatre.* Ed. Sue-Ellen Case: 254.

[25] "Par le biais de l'humour, on peut grossir les portraits, atteindre au grotesque, au vaudeville, récupérer par là des formes théâtrales laissées pour compte par l'institution, la «bonne littérature» et privilégier, à côté des voix officielles, une énonciation plus lâche, plus libre. La *monstration* nous permettait de présenter le *monstrueux*, d'en mesure les résultats [...] cet effet s'opère dans la distanciation par l'excès, l'énormité, le débordement." ("La Traversée des Miroirs": 22). Translation by LHF.

[26] For detailed information on the status of women in Québec from the time of the first settlers in 1604 to day, see Du Sablon, Claire. "Chronologie historique des femmes du Québec." http://www.pages.infinit.net/histoire/femmes.html.

[27] Although most of the plays in this volume have been previously translated into English, the translations are not easily available. Unfortunately, translations from even a few decades ago are frequently out of print or else were published only in typescript form. The major publishers of translations into English of plays written and performed in French have been Playwrights Canada Press (www.playwrightscanada.com, formerly an imprint of the Playwrights Guild of Canada), and Talonbooks (www.talonbooks.com). An important source of information on plays that have been translated into English, as well as of typescript scripts themselves, is the Centre des auteurs dramatiques in Montréal www.cead.qc.ca.

The Savage Season
(Le Temps sauvage)

by Anne Hébert

translated by Pamela Grant
and Gregory Reid

Introduction to
The Savage Season (Le Temps sauvage [1] *)*
by Anne Hébert
Introduced by Pamela Grant and Gregory Reid

In a 1963 interview, she described her four or five unpublished dramas stored away in boxes as "trop littéraire[s] pour être joué[s]" [2] [too literary to be performed]; however, she published *Le Temps sauvage* in 1966, and again in 1967 together with two other of her plays. Deeply infused with a poetic voice, biblical and literary allusions, and Ibsenesque romantic symbolism, *Le Temps sauvage* remains, as Neil Bishop points out, "la plus célèbre pièce d'Anne Hébert" [3] [Anne Hébert's most celebrated play]. The play was first performed by the Théâtre du Nouveau Monde in 1966 at the Palais Montcalm in Quebec City. It did well at the box office in 1966–67, [4] but reviewers of the play tended almost unanimously to judge it in terms of its absence of realism and authenticity. Although Hébert creates a scenario to justify extensive poetic licence in the dialogue of *Le Temps sauvage*—the matriarch Agnes Joncas has removed her family from the world to live in isolated retreat in the mountain wilds so that her children will grow up savage and pure under her watchful domination—Quebec critics in the 1960s remained largely unreceptive to the play's literary resonance.

Le Temps sauvage appeared at a pivotal period in Anne Hébert's career; it immediately anticipated the period in which she would begin to achieve recognition as an author of world renown—what her biographer, Charles Harvey, calls her period of glory (during which she published her most acclaimed novels, *Kamouraska* in 1970 and *Les Fous de Bassan,* in 1982). The play also signalled a pivotal period in the production of French-language theatre within Quebec and, indirectly, in English translation on Toronto stages. *Le Temps sauvage* was one of the first plays in a wave of Quebec drama that swept the Toronto theatre scene in the 1970s; translated by Elizabeth Mascall under its original French title, *Le Temps sauvage* was performed in Toronto in late 1972 at the Firehall Theatre, just ten days after the production of *Forever Yours, Marie-Lou,* the first Michel Tremblay play to be presented in Toronto in English translation. *Le Temps sauvage* met with mixed reception. Urjo Kareda described the translation itself as "a fair stab." [5] A second translation into English, by Eugene and Renate Benson, was published as *The Unquiet State* in *Canadian Drama/ L'Art Dramatique Canadien* in 1988.

The lack of a current, published version of the play in English translation, the play itself as a significant piece of dramatic literature worthy of further reflection and analysis, the importance of Hébert's work in general and drama in particular, which has still not been fully recognized in the English-speaking world, and, most acutely, the timely invitation by Louise Forsyth to participate in her anthology project have, all together, prompted us (Pamela Grant, a French-to-English professional translator, and Gregory Reid, a specialist in comparative drama) to engage in this latest translation of *Le Temps sauvage*. The process of translation has been thoroughly collaborative as we each translated sections of the play and exchanged drafts for revision, debating how best to convey Hébert's voice in the dialogue of her characters. We read scenes in front of Patricia Godbout, a specialist in English-to-French translation, who could not only confirm the accuracy of our translations but advise us on challenging nuances of phrasing, diction and register found throughout Hébert's text. Refining our translation, we found ourselves repeatedly moving closer to the original text. We realized that it was often by reflecting Hébert's lexical and syntactic choices as closely as possible, rather than by adapting her text to a more conversational and contemporary style, that we could best ensure that her precise voice and elliptical, elegant style came through in the English version. As Hébert revealed in her dialogue with Frank Scott on his translation of her poem *Le Tombeau des rois*, [6] her word choice and syntax were precise and deliberate, never arbitrary.

The challenge of translation was considerable, for the meaning of Hébert's text is contained not only in the literal meaning of the words spoken, but in what Northrop Frye calls the "underthought" [7]—the network of images, expressions, and metaphors that thread their way through the subtext. Motifs of sylvan secrecy, silence and primitive innocence, and countervailing images of refuge and stultification permeate the play. As a result, the translator must not only consider the words in their immediate context, but also their connection to the lexical web that runs through this piece, and even echoes in other of Hébert's works. [8]

The play's title *Le Temps sauvage* (which we translate as *The Savage Season*) immediately signals the translation challenge. The expression is used explicitly within the play to represent the out-of-time, feral world to which Agnes has retreated to raise her children in prolonged innocence, but it evokes as well the secret, unexplored space within the self. *Le Temps sauvage* also refers to the wilderness that surrounds Agnes and her family, the harsh weather with seasons of winter blizzard, spring flood and summer drought, and the impending storms, which Agnes's debilitated, limping husband, François, says he can feel in his bones, about to explode, not just on the horizon, but right in the heart of the Joncas family.

The dialogue reflects Hébert's literary style. Characters frequently use the more formal form "je puis" rather than the more common "je peux." Literary and cultural allusions abound. For example, Isabelle (Agnès's more worldly niece from Montréal who comes to live with the Joncas family after the death of her mother) compares Sébastien to *un douanier*—an allusion to the painter Henri Rousseau that Sébastien doesn't understand. In our translation, we chose to retain the original French expression (and artistic allusion) on first mention, and to give the literal English translation, a "custom's agent," on second mention, in response to Sébastien's query about the meaning of the expression. We strove throughout the translation to retain a distinctive Québec setting and flavour, using French proper names (Rue Saint-Marc, Hélène, Sébastien) and terms (Maman, Madame). The translation of biblical references and imagery from the Catholic Church, which reflect the prevailing presence of religion in Quebec society at the time, required a knowledge of both French and English liturgy.

Since her death in 2000, Hébert's work and its prominence in the canons of French literature have been judiciously celebrated, reflected upon and analyzed. With this new translation of *Le Temps sauvage* we hope to make a modest contribution to the awareness of Hébert's least considered genre, her writing for the theatre, among English-language readers and thespians.

Notes

[1] *Le Temps sauvage*, suivi de *La Mercière assassinée, Les Invités au procès*. Montréal: Hurtubise HMH, 1967: 31–158. First production of *Le Temps sauvage* by Le Théâtre du Nouveau Monde at the Palais Montcalm in Québec City, October 8, 1966; produced at Toronto's Firehall Theatre in 1972, translation by Elizabeth Mascall. First published translation: *The Unquiet State*. Tr. Eugene Benson & Renate Benson. *Canadian Drama/ L'Art Dramatique Canadien*. 14:2 (1988): 227–310. In addition to the bibliographical references in these endnotes, see *Anne Hébert: Dossier de Presse 1942–1980*. Sherbrooke: Bibliothèque du Séminaire, 1981; Denis Bouchard. *Une Lecture d'Anne Hébert: la recherche d'une mythologie*. Montréal: Hurtubise HMH, 1977; Jean-Cléo Godin & Laurent Mailhot. "Anne Hébert ou le temps dépaysé." *Le Théâtre québécois*. Montréal: Éditions HMH, 1970: 123–50; Alonzo LeBlanc, "*Le temps sauvage*, drame d'Anne Hébert." *Dictionnaire des oeuvres littéraires du Québec*. Tome IV, 1960–1969. Montréal: Fides, 1984: 862–64; Lemieux, Pierre-H. "Un Théâtre de la parole: Anne Hébert." *Le Théâtre canadien-français*. Archives des Lettres canadiennes, Tome V. Montréal: Fides, 1976: 551–79, Major, Jean-Louis. *Anne Hébert et le miracle de la parole*. Montréal: Presses de l'Université de Montréal, 1976.

[2] Anne Hébert, quoted by Michelle Lasnier in "Anne Hébert la magicienne," *Châtelaine* (avril 1963): 74.

[3] Neil B. Bishop. "Enfance de l'oeuvre, enfance à l'oeuvre dans le théâtre d'Anne Hébert." *Nouveaux Regards sur le théâtre québécois*. Ed. Betty Bednarski and Irene Oore. Montréal: XYZ, 1997: 64.

[4] Elaine F. Nardocchio. "1958–1968: Ten Formative Years in Quebec's Theatre History." *Canadian Drama/L'Art dramatique canadien*. 9.1 (1983): 165–94.

[5] Urjo Kareda. *Toronto Star* (November 24, 1972). Quoted in Jane Koustas, "From Gélinas to Carrier: Critical Response to Translated Quebec Theatre in Toronto." *Studies in Canadian Literature*. 17.2 (1992). http://www.lib.unb.ca/Texts/SCL/bin/get.cgi?directory=vol17_2/&filename=Koustas.htm

[6] Anne Hébert and Frank Scott. *Dialogue sur la traduction à propos du* Tombeau des rois. Presentation by Jeanne Lapointe, preface by Northrop Frye. Montreal: Éditions HMH, 1970.

7 Northrop Frye. "Preface." *Dialogue sur la traduction à propos du* Tombeau des rois. Anne Hébert and Frank Scott. Montreal: Éditions HMH, 1970: 13.

8 For example, Sébastien's use of the word "étale" in Act II, Scene 4 ("Demain, vous verrez comme c'est beau, la neige étale") reverberates in the opening sentence of *Les Fous de Bassan*, where its distinctive use and translation have been the subject of discussion.

About Anne Hébert

Anne Hébert (1916–2000) was born in Sainte-Catherine-de-Fossambault, near Québec City, where she did her secondary studies at the colleges Notre-Dame-de-Bellevue and Mérici. She was the daughter of Maurice Lang Hébert, civil servant, professor, poet and literary critic, and Marguerite-Marie Taché, and second cousin of Hector de Saint-Denys Garneau. She began to write in 1932 and first published texts in 1938. In 1942 she published her first poetry collection, *Les Songes en équilibre*, for which she received the Prix Athanase-David in 1939. Between 1950 and 1953 she wrote several radio scripts for Radio-Canada; between 1953 and 1954 she wrote and produced scripts for L'Office National du Film/The National Film Board. A grant from the Royal Society of Canada in 1954 made a three-year stay in Paris possible. She moved there permanently in 1965. She returned to live in Montréal in 1997, where she died January 22, 2000.

Her work, translated into at least fifteen languages, includes nine novels, five collections of poetry, plays and short fiction. Two of her novels have been adapted for the cinema, *Kamouraska* et *Les Fous de Bassan*. *Les Enfants du sabbat* was adapted for the stage in 2005.

Throughout her career she received many prizes and literary awards: for *L'Arche de midi* in the Concours littéraire et scientifique de la province de Québec (1951); Prix France-Canada for *Les Chambres de bois* (1957); Prix Duvernay, la Société Saint-Jean-Baptiste for her work as a whole (1958); Prix Athanase-David for *Les Chambres de bois* (1958) and for her work as a whole (1978); Governor General's Award for *Poèmes* (1960), for *Les Enfants du sabbat* (1975) and for *L'Enfant chargé de songes* (1992); Molson Prize of the Canada Council for the Arts (1967); Prix des Libraires de France for *Kamouraska* (1971); Prix de littérature hors de France of the Académie royale de Belgique for *Kamouraska* (1971); Prix de l'Académie française for *Les Enfants du sabbat* (1976); Prix de la Fondation Prince-Pierre-de-Monaco for her work as a whole (1976); Prix Fémina for *Les Fous de Bassan* (1982); Prix Canada-Belgique (1988); Prix Alain-Grandbois for *Le Jour n'a d'égal que la nuit* (1993); Prix Gilles-Corbeil of the Fondation Émile-Nelligan for her work as a whole (1994); and the Prix France-Québec/Jean-Hamelin *Un Habit de lumière* and her work as a whole (1999). She also received honorary doctorates from several Canadian universities: Toronto (1969), McGill (1980), Laval (1983), and Sherbrooke (1993). She became a member of the Royal Society of Canada in 1960.

Anne Hébert's earliest literary expression took the form of drama and poetry, and she first gained recognition as a poet with *Les Songes en équilibre* (1942) and *Le Tombeau des rois* (1953). She wrote prolifically in various genres: turning to fiction, she published *Le Torrent*, a collection of short stories, in 1950, and *Les Chambres de bois,* her first novel, in 1958. During this period, she also wrote for radio and film (including the script for the documentary film on Saint-Denys Garneau, her mentor, poetic influence and cousin).

Le Temps Sauvage was first produced by the Théâtre du Nouveau Monde, in October 1966, at the Palais Montcalm, Quebec City, with the following company:

AGNÈS JONCAS	Marthe Thiéry
FRANÇOIS JONCAS	Paul Guévremont
HÉLÈNE	Andrée Saint-Laurent
SÉBASTIEN	Jean Perraud
LUCIE	Francine Racette
MARIE	Michèle Jourdain
CAPUCINE	Myriam Thibodeau
ISABELLE	Rita Imbeault
FATHER BEAUMONT	Jean Ricard
A CHILD	Sylvain Hébert

Directed by Albert Millaire
Set and Costumes by Mark Negin
Assistant Director: Claude Grisé
Lighting by Yves Dallaire
Music by Gabriel Charpentier

Characters

AGNÈS JONCAS, 50 years old
FRANÇOIS JONCAS, 60 years old
Their children:
    HÉLÈNE, 22 years old
    SÉBASTIEN, 20 years old
    LUCIE, 17 years old
    MARIE, 15 years old
    CAPUCINE, 10 years old
ISABELLE (the cousin), 20 years old
THE PRIEST, FATHER BEAUMONT, about 35 years old
A CHILD

THE SAVAGE SEASON

ACT ONE

In the country, at the Joncas home. It is winter. A large living room with walls of varnished wood. A high ceiling with exposed beams. A bookcase with half-empty shelves. A cast-iron stove. Mittens, scarves and children's jackets hanging next to the stove. At the rear, AGNÈS's bedroom. To the left, the girls' bedroom. To the right, SÉBASTIEN's bedroom. A staircase leading to the landing on the second floor, where FRANÇOIS's bedroom is located. Opening onto the room, a veranda where an odd assortment of well-worn objects is piled up. An old sofa. Skis. Snow boots. Stacks of firewood. Primitive-style paintings hang over the sofa.

Scene One

On the veranda, LUCIE is cleaning her skis, furtively watching AGNÈS's every movement in the living room.

AGNÈS, dressed in black, is standing as if in a daze. A pile of clothes spills untidily out of a wooden trunk. On the table are a thick woollen sweater, knitted gloves, a shawl, and an old astrakhan coat. AGNÈS approaches the table and begins to sort through unmatched gloves. She tries a few on. Her movements are exaggeratedly slow, as if she is struggling to control her great agitation.

HÉLÈNE and MARIE, motionless, are watching their mother. AGNÈS speaks to them without turning, standing erect, endlessly trying on gloves one after another.

AGNÈS You would be better off going for a walk, both of you, instead of standing there like statues.

HÉLÈNE You look as if you're in deep mourning.

AGNÈS I am in deep mourning. *(to HÉLÈNE)* Hand me that shawl there, from the trunk.

HÉLÈNE leans over the trunk, takes the shawl, and hands it to her mother. AGNÈS places the shawl over her head and shoulders, as if she were donning a heavy religious habit. HÉLÈNE and MARIE watch AGNÈS in a sort of fearful wonder.

MARIE You're leaving tomorrow for the whole day?

AGNÈS For the whole day.

MARIE   All these black things are horrible! Are they because of Aunt Nathalie?

AGNÈS   *(exasperated)* Yes, they are because of Aunt Nathalie.

> *For the last few moments, LUCIE has been moving back and forth across the room, pretending to ignore AGNÈS. She prepares to put wood in the stove. AGNÈS notices what LUCIE is doing and gives a start.*

Leave it. I'm the only one in this house who knows how to lay a fire properly.

LUCIE   I know perfectly well how to do it.

> *AGNÈS takes over from LUCIE in front of the stove.*

AGNÈS   I have a terrible day before me tomorrow.

> *HÉLÈNE puts water on the stove. MARIE prepares the cups.*

HÉLÈNE   I'll make the tea.

AGNÈS   Put the water. I'll make the tea myself.

> *HÉLÈNE goes to fetch the cups and teapot.*

LUCIE   *(as if she has been working up the courage to ask a question she has had prepared for a long time)* What was she like, Aunt Nathalie?

> *AGNÈS remains impassive, as if indifferent.*

AGNÈS   Very beautiful and treacherous, like innocence. A little tramp, that's what you'd call her. Her beauty had something insolent and triumphant about it. And now she has died after a long illness. Little by little, life drained out of that beautiful edifice, and now justice has been done.

LUCIE   What did Aunt Nathalie do to you?

AGNÈS   You're making my head ache with all your questions!

LUCIE   *(fierce and stubborn)* I want to know.

AGNÈS   What do you want to know?

LUCIE   Everything. I want to know everything. There's too much silence in this house. It's suffocating.

AGNÈS   What business is it of yours? God, what business is it of yours?

LUCIE   Why did my Aunt Nathalie have to die for you to decide to go visit her? And my cousin Isabelle—why haven't we ever seen her? Why do we live so far away from everyone?

AGNÈS   You talk far too much, Lucie. I never question myself about anything, and I hate it for other people to ask me questions. If there is anything hidden in my heart, it is no concern of mine, nor of yours, nor of anyone else's. One thing is clear: it's my wish to keep you all here, on this mountain, for as long as possible, sheltered from the entire world, in a prolonged childhood, savage and pure. What more do you need to know?

LUCIE   *(in a sort of rage)* I am not a child anymore!

> *AGNÈS turns abruptly towards LUCIE.*

AGNÈS   That's just too bad. You act as if you were declaring war on me.

> *Silence. HÉLÈNE brings over the teapot. AGNÈS makes the tea.*

LUCIE   *(who won't let it go)* Take me with you to Montreal tomorrow, please.

AGNÈS   The city is vile, like a field of poison ivy. In the city, the air you breathe is polluted, the water you drink smells of bleach, and children waste away like birds in a cage.

LUCIE   The air, the water, the birds, the children—I don't care. I want to walk down wide streets bustling with people and noise. I…

AGNÈS   *(interrupting)* I'm telling you, this really isn't the time for this. Don't you realize that? It's utterly incredible. For the first time in fifteen years, I am leaving my countryside, my home, and my children. I am going on a ludicrous trip in the dead of winter. Four hours on the train so that, at the end of the line, I can pay my final respects to someone who was bitter and sweet to me, like no one else in the world. And you want me to take you with me, among the candles and the death knells, the funeral wreaths, the priest's litanies and the notary's papers? No, no, it isn't possible!

LUCIE   It's not just that. It isn't just death and the funeral service. If I'm upsetting you so much, it's because of this cousin Isabelle. You want to claim her at the lawyer's as part of your inheritance, and then impose her on all of us, as part of the family.

AGNÈS   *(very firmly)* I intend to bring Isabelle back with me to this house, tomorrow evening. That little girl has no one left in the world other than us now. Her mother is being buried, the house and furniture are going to be sold to pay off debts…

LUCIE   That's no reason to bring her here. We are suffocating already, with all these girls in the house! Sébastien says so all the time.

MARIE   Well, *I* can't wait to see cousin Isabelle!

LUCIE   Well, *I* would like to spit her out hard, far away from here, pst… like a rotten cherry.

HÉLÈNE   No one ever comes here!

LUCIE   I'd like for a boy to come here, not that girl!

AGNÈS   That little girl is no doubt difficult and very badly brought up. But such as she is, in her misery and her poverty, she is my sister's daughter, my own blood, and she has a place in my home, just like all of you.

LUCIE   The way you say that! You sound as if you are reclaiming a lost parcel.

AGNÈS   What are you waiting for? The tea's going to get cold.

>   *HÉLÈNE serves the tea.*

LUCIE   It's snowing; it's going to turn into a blizzard for sure. Tomorrow, the road will be impassable, you'll see!

AGNÈS   Stop predicting catastrophes. You sound like your father.

LUCIE   Take me with you to Montreal. I want to go to school, to study, to learn, to understand…

AGNÈS   *(stubborn)* There's nothing to understand…

LUCIE   Yes, there is! There's everything to understand and to discover: life, death, the world, everything, everything!

AGNÈS   So living isn't enough for you then? Without comments and chattering?

LUCIE   Life here isn't enough. Ask Sébastien. Ask my sisters. Ask me—I think about lots of things. About the rage in my heart, for example, and I want to call it by its name. What causes this? What causes that? Why do we live like lost animals?

AGNÈS   *(beside herself)* Be quiet, please, be quiet. So go ask your father. He has read so many books that I'm sure he'll have some ready-made answers for you.

LUCIE   All the same, if it weren't for that old man that you disdain so much, I'd be more ignorant than a mole digging in his burrow, his eyes full of sand. I can barely read and write, and the little that I know, I've learned mixed with stories and nonsense. I'm going upstairs to see him and take him his tea.

HÉLÈNE   *(calmly)* Don't bother. Papa has gone out.

AGNÈS   *(flabbergasted)* Gone out? But that's not possible!

HÉLÈNE   He passed through the kitchen while I was tidying up the counter. He said that he was going to the post office and was expecting a letter. Capucine was with him.

AGNÈS   A letter! And who from, for goodness' sake?

LUCIE   We never get any mail.

MARIE   *(listing)* Yes, we do—the fruit and vegetable catalogue, and then, sometimes…

LUCIE   *(interrupting)* Not for important news—the death of an unknown aunt, the existence of a similarly unknown cousin—for that, they send us a telegram. It's more reliable. That way, the whole village immediately knows all our news.

>   *Silence. HÉLÈNE is bending over her sewing. AGNÈS is examining a small bag that she has just taken out of the trunk. LUCIE is playing solitaire at the table. MARIE runs out to the veranda and searches through the skis.*

MARIE   (*calling to HÉLÈNE*) Hélène! Come quickly! Come on outside with me! I'm getting your skis ready!

HÉLÈNE   I haven't finished mending Sébastien's sweater!

> *LUCIE abruptly gathers up her cards from the table.*

LUCIE   (*to HÉLÈNE*) What an old maid you are!

HÉLÈNE   That's not true! You're always lying.

MARIE   It's Papa and Capucine! Here they come!

Scene Two

> *Enter FRANÇOIS and CAPUCINE, who is holding his hand. CAPUCINE runs over to her mother.*

AGNÈS   Capucine, my little girl, you're back! Where have you been?

CAPUCINE   In the village, at the post office! I saw lots of little children skating on the river!

AGNÈS   I forbid you to skate on the river!

> *FRANÇOIS seems very tired. He is limping. AGNÈS takes off CAPUCINE's outdoor clothing.*

François, you're limping badly this evening!

FRANÇOIS   (*limping*) That walk through the snow has completely exhausted me!

AGNÈS   What madness! At your age, how could you overestimate your strength so badly?

FRANÇOIS   Before I left, everything felt light and easy! I thought I could walk for miles and miles without getting tired.

AGNÈS   Tomorrow, you'll see, you won't be able to move at all!

FRANÇOIS   What bad luck that I had that car accident! I always used to like going for walks in the country so much!

> *LUCIE pours some alcohol into a tea cup and hands it to her father. AGNÈS, suddenly alarmed, turns towards FRANÇOIS.*

AGNÈS   You mustn't drink that.

LUCIE   Sébastien brought it home from Bertrand's.

AGNÈS   That liquor is poison.

> *AGNÈS empties FRANÇOIS's cup; FRANÇOIS rises painfully to his feet and looks at AGNÈS.*

It's wood alcohol—you can die from drinking it.

FRANÇOIS   Me, die? I think I'd be afraid to die.

AGNÈS   You took Sébastien's jacket!

FRANÇOIS   This jacket is mine.

AGNÈS   That jacket is Sébastien's!

FRANÇOIS   He took it from me!

AGNÈS   I told him to take it. What do you need a jacket like that for—you can't walk two steps in the snow without complaining, old cripple that you are!

> *FRANÇOIS turns his head away. He sits back down. With the back of his hand, he knocks his cup to the floor. The cup breaks.*

FRANÇOIS   My life is cursed. I've never done anything right.

> *HÉLÈNE picks up the pieces of the cup. FRANÇOIS rises to his feet as if the pain in his knee has become unbearable.*

Oh, what pain! What an affliction! Rheumatism is biting into my knee like a crown of thorns. It's a sign that a storm is coming. Oh, it's going to snow. It's going to snow!

> *AGNÈS picks up the jacket and examines it.*

AGNÈS   What is Sébastien up to, that he hasn't come home yet?

LUCIE   *(who is setting out her solitaire game again, under the watchful eye of MARIE)* He's setting his traps as usual, you know that!

AGNÈS   No, I'll never get used to that. Those expeditions into the heart of the forest, those long hours hunting at night, in the snow and the cold, those traps, those snares, those animals that they hunt down, kill and skin. *(She smells the jacket and then throws it from her in disgust.)* That smell of blood and old tannin that clings to my son—no, I can't stand it.

> *LUCIE picks up the jacket with great respect and goes over to hang it up on the wall. She returns to her cards.*

FRANÇOIS   Your son has become a trapper. It was to be expected. Do you think that you can get away with letting children loose on a mountain like goats, without them slowly turning into barbarians? *(He speaks to the children as if he were telling them a story.)* What a strange story it is. One day, Agnès, your mother, married the cripple, your father, and, as soon as she had given birth to her children, she picked them up in her teeth, like a hunted cat, and carried them off to hide them, far away, on the mountain…

CAPUCINE   Tell us the story! Tell us the story of how Maman turned into a cat!

> *CAPUCINE runs to her father, who picks her up and puts her on his lap. AGNÈS stands up abruptly, goes over to the table, and calls CAPUCINE over, to get her away from her father.*

AGNÈS   Capucine, my little one, you don't want to listen to that old story. Why don't you look at this coat, these gloves, this little bag instead?

> *As she speaks, AGNÈS shows CAPUCINE the clothes on the table as if they were on display. CAPUCINE runs over to her mother.*

CAPUCINE   What are you doing with all those black things?

AGNÈS   *(as if speaking to herself)* I have to leave by train, tomorrow, very early, on a long trip, despite the winter and the snow.

> *AGNÈS looks at FRANÇOIS wearily.*

Don't worry, old man. I'm leaving all of you tomorrow for the day, just for the day, just for the time it takes to say goodbye to Nathalie, who has died, and to bring her daughter back to our home.

FRANÇOIS   *(as if waking from a dream)* Oh yes, that's right, little Nathalie has died!

> *AGNÈS stops, remains suddenly motionless, struck to the heart.*

AGNÈS   Little Nathalie, as you say, wee little Nathalie—she was so fragile in my arms, and now her life is over, like a treasure that has been locked away. For so long she had a child's face, so open and easy to read. And then, one day, everything on her little face clouded over. She began to radiate malice, cunning, and ingratitude.

> *LUCIE approaches her mother.*

LUCIE   There's no point talking about it if you're not going to tell the whole story…. What did Aunt Nathalie do to you?

> *AGNÈS cuffs LUCIE.*

AGNÈS   Mind your own business!

LUCIE   Oh, how corrupt family life is! It rips out your heart and sharpens your claws.

> *FRANÇOIS, appalled, tries to restrain LUCIE.*

FRANÇOIS   You don't understand, Lucie, my little girl. Nathalie behaved very badly towards your mother. She offended her deeply and betrayed her.

AGNÈS   François!

LUCIE   She thinks she has the upper hand now because Aunt Nathalie is dead! But what if death didn't avenge the living? What if it was the other way around? Oh, she'd be in trouble!

> *A long wild cry can be heard from outside. LUCIE rushes to the door.*

It's Sébastien! Sébastien is back! That's the signal! We have to answer right away!

LUCIE opens the door onto the veranda and calls out through her fingers. CAPUCINE and MARIE run over to LUCIE. HÉLÈNE hesitates, looks at her mother and then her father. SÉBASTIEN's cry grows closer.

MARIE & CAPUCINE   *(chanting)* Sébastien! Sébastien! Sébastien!

LUCIE returns SÉBASTIEN'S cry.

FRANÇOIS   What wild cries! These children are possessed! It sends chills through my heart every time.

Scene Three

SÉBASTIEN enters, covered with snow. The three sisters surround SÉBASTIEN, who hands them his mittens, balaclava, and scarf as he takes them off. LUCIE speaks rapidly to her brother, taking him aside, managing, for as long as possible, to block his path towards AGNÈS, who is waiting for him in the living room.

LUCIE   What did you do outside all day long, Sébastien?

SÉBASTIEN is bursting with life. He laughs, mocking both himself and his own joy.

SÉBASTIEN   Business! Magnificent furs in beautiful, carefully selected batches, sold all in one batch to Chatillon. Bertrand and I are splitting the proceeds. I'm rich!

AGNÈS   *(calling)* Sébastien!

MARIE & CAPUCINE   *(surrounding their brother)* Sébastien! Sébastien!

SÉBASTIEN makes a move toward the room. LUCIE holds him back, leaning toward him.

LUCIE   You, Sébastien, my brother—I could pick you out, with my eyes closed, from among a thousand other boys, simply by your smell.

SÉBASTIEN   *(brushing LUCIE aside)* Let me by.

LUCIE   You reek of fox and money.

SÉBASTIEN enters the room. He kisses AGNÈS.

AGNÈS   Sébastien! You're being unreasonable! Out all day, in this cold, without your sheepskin jacket. You'll be the death of me, tormenting me this way.

SÉBASTIEN takes off his boots. CAPUCINE brings him a lighter pair of boots.

SÉBASTIEN   Tormenting you? But that's living. To each his own: you torment yourself, and I struggle—against the cold, against the snow, against the wind that blurs the tracks, against the traps, against the muskrat and the beaver, against the weasel, the wild cat and the little rabbit, against predators and thieves—and I win handily, too. The greatest pleasure of life in this world is hand-to-hand combat.

LUCIE   And what about the hand-to-hand combat of family life? Where's the pleasure, where's the joy in that? That's what I wonder about.

SÉBASTIEN   Time is on our side, sister. Soon we'll be all grown up big, like trees.

> *SÉBASTIEN dances a few steps with LUCIE. Mixed with laughter, their words can be heard: "All grown up big, like trees," "a whole forest of wicked trees." Then SÉBASTIEN runs to AGNÈS and throws himself at her knees.*

I'm hungry! I'm thirsty! I'm exhausted! I have returned to the fold! Here I am at your feet, begging your mercy, first woman of my heart!

AGNÈS   *(delighted)* Fool! Lunatic! My child is a lunatic! My son is a lunatic!

SÉBASTIEN   I feel so comfortable like this, with my head on your lap, like when I was a child. But I cannot remain like this.

> *SÉBASTIEN gets up abruptly.*

I'm as hungry and as thirsty as a bear.

> *MARIE rushes to serve SÉBASTIEN. She brings him ham and bread.*

AGNÈS   *(to MARIE)* Leave it. *(to SÉBASTIEN)* Sébastien, what are you doing, spending all your time with that Bertrand? You know that I don't like that braggart, with neither hearth nor home, and who does a little trapping here and there and makes wood alcohol.

SÉBASTIEN   *(suddenly serious)* You couldn't understand. Bertrand is my brother and my companion, my partner and my accomplice, my rival and my adversary. The fierce loyalty that binds us together is a thing between men.

AGNÈS   You, a man? My poor child! You will likely never be a man! Who is ever completely a man or a woman, here in this country from before the world was created? You can play that game, but I won't—I won't be duped. Didn't I create you all and bring you all into the world, small and miserable as you were, in my own image and likeness and in that of God the Father who art in Heaven? Amen.

SÉBASTIEN   Life in the forest fills my eyes, fills my nose, fills my ears, clings to my hands and my feet. I am possessed. *(to FRANÇOIS)* And no one in the world can stop me from calling my life a man's life, or holding on to it like my own skin. I taste my life like salt.

LUCIE   I'm the one who is most like salt, in this house. And I'm not happy to be here. I know how bewitching the forest you talk of can be, but I want to be somewhere else, in a big city, where it's civilized and safe.

AGNÈS   My daughter Lucie is stubborn.

SÉBASTIEN One day, if I feel like it, I'll swap the forest for "a big city where it's civilized and safe." I'll exchange all the animals, with their fur and feathers, and all the stands of wood, for an adventure of my choosing. You'll see. Look, I'm already rich, and this is just the beginning!

> *SÉBASTIEN takes a wad of bills from his pocket and shows it to his mother and sisters. AGNÈS turns her head away.*

AGNÈS Watch yourself, Sébastien. That money comes from the forest. It isn't good to sell what you love.

SÉBASTIEN The things that you love most bring the highest price.

AGNÈS Spend that money quickly and let's not hear about it again.

SÉBASTIEN You're wrong to disdain this money. And you seem to forget that we are all living off your inheritance. Nothing is freer than an inheritance, isn't that right? No use putting on airs. Without our mother Agnès's inheritance, we would have all gone to the devil, along with our father François, begging like humiliated saints.

AGNÈS You mustn't speak like that.

SÉBASTIEN François, our father, never earned a single cent to keep the odd pot boiling in this house. But then, it costs so little to live in the country.

AGNÈS Sébastien, please.

SÉBASTIEN Business is business. Little Nathalie, our aunt, got the house on Rue Saint-Marc. Agnès, our mother, got the cash. Each of the two sisters got her own share, cut and dried. And family life goes on! We are the Nth generation. Family life has so many storeys and branches. An aunt over here, a cousin over there. And at the far end, grandparents, who appear to be sleeping in the cemetery. Not to mention the ancestors, born in the old country. So many pasts are piled up in basements and attics that the current generation is reduced to fighting among themselves in haunted rooms.

MARIE Since you are so rich, Sébastien, buy me some skates.

CAPUCINE Oh, Sébastien! I want skates too!

> *SÉBASTIEN hands some bills to his two sisters.*

SÉBASTIEN Skates, skis, snow, the whole winter, whatever you want, my little beauties! Go ahead!

> *SÉBASTIEN approaches HÉLÈNE.*

And you, Hélène, my sweet big sister, leave your sewing for a minute and make a wish.

HÉLÈNE I wish that no one would argue anymore.

SÉBASTIEN   And what about the boredom? Did you think about the boredom that would sweep down on us like the plague if we ever stopped arguing? But, if you need thread, needles, wool, or whatever, I'll get it for you.

> *SÉBASTIEN places a bill on the table near HÉLÈNE, who doesn't touch it. SÉBASTIEN approaches LUCIE, who is on the veranda. The conversation between the brother and sister is rapid, a little muffled, as if confidential, a sort of sketchy joke.*

And you, Lucie? What would you like?

LUCIE   Me? I want a fox, alive and uninjured, understand?

SÉBASTIEN   I understand. You'll have your live fox. I'll catch him for you. You'll have him, marked only by the shame and anguish of the captive beast. You already look like him, high-strung and slender, wily and shiny, and unhappy in a cage, eh?

> *SÉBASTIEN goes to stroke LUCIE's hair; she recoils abruptly.*

LUCIE   Leave me alone.

> *Unexpectedly, AGNÈS grabs MARIE's and CAPUCINE's bills.*

CAPUCINE & MARIE   (*protesting*) My money! Sébastien gave it to me! I want skates! Skates!

AGNÈS   I've always forbidden you to skate on the river. You'll get mittens and scarves instead. They're less dangerous.

> *SÉBASTIEN, following his mother's example, scoops up HÉLÈNE's bill, which is still lying on the table.*

SÉBASTIEN   Injustice calls for injustice. Remember that, oh wise one, and you'll become even wiser.

HÉLÈNE   Oh Sébastien! It was for orange wool and new needles!

SÉBASTIEN   Then you shouldn't have left it lying around!

> *SÉBASTIEN gives the bill back to HÉLÈNE.*

You really are too pitiful, sister Hélène.

> *SÉBASTIEN, ill at ease, approaches his father, with his wallet in his hand.*

For him, the injustice is even greater, as indelible as a birthmark.

> *FRANÇOIS stands up and goes to leave the room. SÉBASTIEN stands in his way. Silence.*

You know, if you want a new jacket to replace the one of yours that I took…

FRANÇOIS   You are all mean, stubborn and crazy. Why would I need a new jacket? I'm old and crippled. Winter is hard. Who would go out in such cold?

No jacket. No boots. No walks. Your mother told me so clearly: I am old and crippled. Ah, the priests are right: "The real world is elsewhere." "Be in the world without attachment." And what is suffered will be glorified by the angels throughout eternity.

> *FRANÇOIS turns and climbs the stairs. CAPUCINE approaches SÉBASTIEN.*

CAPUCINE   Paint me a house, Sébastien, with a sun in the sky and grass all around the house, and trees too, lots of trees…

> *For a few moments, AGNÈS has been watching LUCIE prepare tea.*

AGNÈS   I've said it a hundred times: I'm the only one who knows how to make tea in this house.

> *AGNÈS goes to the stove and starts to make the tea again. In the background, the voices of SÉBASTIEN and CAPUCINE can be heard: "The red, Capucine!" "A sun, Sébastien!" "The yellow, Capucine!" "The sky, Sébastien!" "The blue, Capucine!" "Trees, Sébastien!" "The green, Capucine!" "A frog, Sébastien!" "You're the frog, Capucine!"*

Until you've all grown up as big as wicked trees, I am in absolute charge of the tea, and as for the rest…

FRANÇOIS   *(from the top of the stairs)* All the same, little Nathalie died yesterday, at noon.

> *AGNÈS becomes upset again.*

AGNÈS   Oh, what a terrible day I have ahead of me tomorrow! What a terrible day!

> *AGNÈS rushes over to a surprised CAPUCINE and takes her in her arms. SÉBASTIEN hangs his latest painting on the wall. AGNÈS leads CAPUCINE into the living room.*

Capucine, my littlest one! How small and fresh you are! Tell me that you have everything you could want here, and that life in the country shields children from all evil.

> *MARIE, who is on the veranda, starts to shout.*

MARIE   Maman! Maman! You'll never guess who's coming this way!

> *CAPUCINE, SÉBASTIEN, and LUCIE rush to the window, taking MARIE's place one by one to watch the priest approaching the house.*

SÉBASTIEN   Oh my! This is incredible!

> *CAPUCINE turns towards her mother to tell her the news.*

CAPUCINE   Maman! Maman! A visitor! It's the new priest coming to see us. He is having a lot of trouble walking through the snow.

AGNÈS (*furious and then appalled*) The new priest! What's he coming here for? No one has invited him, as far as I know. This is ridiculous. He thinks he can do whatever he wants. My home is not a public place. I won't receive him! You know that I don't want to see anyone today.

> *AGNÈS retreats slightly. There is a knock at the door. AGNÈS hesitates and retraces her steps.*

It's impossible to hide in this house.

> *The young girls hesitate to open the door. FRANÇOIS comes downstairs. There is another knock on the door.*

FRANÇOIS The new priest? And what if God has sent him? We must open the door for him.

> *FRANÇOIS moves towards the door. SÉBASTIEN approaches AGNÈS, who is frozen with anger.*

SÉBASTIEN (*continuing FRANÇOIS's sentence*) And if it were the devil who had sent him, should we leave him to freeze to death outside?

> *FRANÇOIS, MARIE, LUCIE, and CAPUCINE are on the veranda. FATHER BEAUMONT enters. A voice can be heard saying, "I am the new priest." FRANÇOIS replies, "Good day, Father." All of this is indistinct as SÉBASTIEN speaks to AGNÈS.*

Why do you think he's come here? He is counting the souls in his new parish so that he can enter them all into his big ledger. He has the law on his side. Don't we live within his territory? Our Lord and Master is touring his parish. Everyone will have to see him, you'll see—you, just like everyone else, and little Capucine, who has already reached the age of reason and is old enough for communion.

Scene Four

> *FATHER BEAUMONT enters, escorted by FRANÇOIS, who is both embarrassed and moved.*

FRANÇOIS Please come in, Father.

> *SÉBASTIEN is sitting on a step on the staircase. When FRANÇOIS introduces him to the priest, SÉBASTIEN's greeting is off-handed.*

(*introducing his family to FATHER BEAUMONT*) My wife, my son Sébastien, my daughters Lucie, Hélène, Marie, Capucine…

> *FATHER BEAUMONT takes a step towards AGNÈS, who doesn't move. No one extends a hand to the priest. FATHER BEAUMONT is standing at the extreme left of the stage. AGNÈS is at the extreme right. All*

attention is drawn to the two parallel black silhouettes. The solitude of
FATHER BEAUMONT is palpable as he faces the Joncas clan.

FATHER BEAUMONT   I am the new parish priest. In the village I heard the sad
news of your sister's death, Madame. I would like to offer you my sympathy…
(He hesitates and continues in a lower voice.) …and my prayers, if you will allow
me.

AGNÈS   I can see that you are very well informed. News travels extremely quickly
in the village. I don't doubt that your intentions are good, Father. But I am
not in the habit of allowing anyone to feel sorry for me or to pray for me.
A question of pride and respect for the independence of others. The only people
who share my grief with me today, and who have the right to be here with me,
are those that I have willingly gathered around me, based on the strictest and
closest of blood ties.

FATHER BEAUMONT   Pardon me, Madame, I didn't mean to impose, but you
know that it is the duty of a priest to watch over each of his parishioners, to
share in their joy, or their sorrow, to the extent that God permits. *(He hesitates.)*
I would like to share your bereavement and repeat to you today the words of
Saint Paul: "Don't cry for those who are with the Lord as you would for those
who are without hope."

AGNÈS   What do you know of my bereavement and my hope, as you say? Who
can know what lies in the depths of a human heart? Who has the right to know?
No one! No one! I find you to be very presumptuous, Father. Oh, I know that
all your parishioners belong to you and you belong to all your parishioners.
Well! No, not exactly. Count me out. No matter what, my land, my house, my
children, my husband and I will remain a little free enclave, a bitter thorn in the
blessed heart of your parish. It's for your own good, no doubt, Father. *(pause)*

FATHER BEAUMONT   Father Joly, my predecessor, had warned me. But, I must
admit, I had hoped to reforge links, to bring the sheep back into the fold. This
has been very hard for me! I had dreamt, like a child, of writing all your names
in the parish registry, listed by age.

SÉBASTIEN   That will have to wait for another time. Father Joly must have told
you that we never go to church?

FRANÇOIS   *(humiliated, confused)* I go sometimes, but the village is so far away
and I have a terrible limp.

SÉBASTIEN   We all live like savages in this house. Hasn't our mother Agnès
claimed to rule alone here for many years? To bless us or to damn us as she
pleases, with neither church nor priest. More than anything else in the world,
she fears the rival magical influence of bells and mass, of candles and incense.
(pause) You'll surely have a little drink to warm you up, Father?

FATHER BEAUMONT   I don't know…

LUCIE   *(timidly)* Or a cup of tea?

FATHER BEAUMONT   A cup of tea, yes, that's it, a nice hot cup of tea. It's so cold outside, and with the snow piled up so high on the path…

FRANÇOIS   It's a good three miles from the village to here.

> *LUCIE offers tea to FATHER BEAUMONT.*

LUCIE   Your tea.

> *FATHER BEAUMONT takes the cup and remains standing. No one has invited him to sit down. At the other end of the room, AGNÈS seems upset and irritated by everything that the priest says or does. It can be felt that she wants to justify herself.*

AGNÈS   Take your time drinking your tea, Father. *(very annoyed)* The road that leads here is hardly easy, and it is to your credit that you have made it here.

SÉBASTIEN   You probably don't have the time to sit down, Father? Be reasonable. Recognize the situation for what it is. *(He points to AGNÈS.)* She is the black robe of this kingdom. She is the priest and the devil; the bread and the wine; the absolute judge, the heart and the head. She is all of that, she and she alone!

AGNÈS   Sébastien, you talk nonsense.

> *AGNÈS strides up to the priest, who has put down his cup and seems ready to leave. AGNÈS holds him back.*

Father, will you hear me well, before you leave? Isn't it your habit to hear people's confessions, even if you refuse them God's grace afterwards? Listen to me, please. Before he married, my father was a student at the seminary, and my two grandfathers were as well. Every day my father would read his breviary, like a monk, hoping to be pardoned for his lost vocation. I was born of a race of unfrocked priests and innocent sinners. Every Sunday the house was full of priests. All we had to do was to be quiet—especially the women. Be it questions of the weather, politics, art, or education, they alone knew the truth, and all that was left us was to be thankful, in silence, my mother, my sister and I. Very early on, the infallibility of some priests humiliated me, breaking my heart. My guilt was hung around my neck, like a millstone, to drown me. If you don't like what I have to say, you simply don't have to come here, to my house where I have sworn to keep my children savage and innocent. *(straightening up)* And yet I believe in Christ, and I am bringing sins down on my head, and on my children's…

FATHER BEAUMONT   *(beside himself with embarrassment)* Madame, I beg of you, Madame.

AGNÈS   When my parents died, I took over the education of my little sister Nathalie, thus discovering the only honour and the only prestige available to women in this country: motherhood. For, whether you want to admit it or not, the cult of the mother is the counterpart of the cult of the priest. *(She stops,* *then resumes.)* You shouldn't have come here, Father. You shouldn't have come here. I will never forgive you for this confession that I have just made. Through what ancient occult power and tenacious magic have you wrung this confession from me? In the name of what sovereign law do you torment me? I hate you! Here I have spoken about myself, from the depths of my being, in front of you and in front of my children. My night is wide open, and I had sworn to myself to live and die enclosed there!

> *A long pause. Everyone is shocked. FATHER BEAUMONT moves slowly towards the door. LUCIE watches the priest's movements closely. She hands him his mittens as if she were serving at a ceremony that she doesn't understand but that fascinates her.*

Scene Five

> *LUCIE, after having opened the door for FATHER BEAUMONT, remains for a few moments on the veranda. All the other characters remain frozen in their poses. SÉBASTIEN is the first to try to react. His words jar the general silence.*

SÉBASTIEN   Isn't the new priest nice, in his old woman's get-up, all thin and knotty, a little like an old tree; even though he isn't old, he has a sort of gnarled look to him.

LUCIE   A real confession takes two: it goes both ways.

AGNÈS   What are you saying?

LUCIE   *(coming closer)* I am saying that a real confession goes two ways. One confidence deserves another. You could have let the new priest confess in turn; that way, you would have dealt with him as equal to equal. Your pride would have been safe.

AGNÈS   You're crazy!

LUCIE   I'd like to know what is going on behind his priest's face. He must have things that weigh heavily on his heart, like everyone else.

AGNÈS   What business is it of yours? My God, what business is it of yours?

LUCIE   That man is a stranger, a pure stranger. That man is not my father nor my brother. It soothes my soul to think that there are strangers living in the world, with strange confessions on the tips of their tongues.

AGNÈS   You're raving. As for me, I have my bags to pack, and this long night to get through before the day that awaits me tomorrow.

> *Black.*

ACT TWO

The next day. Set One. The parlour of the presbytery. FATHER BEAUMONT is seated at his desk. He appears tired and irresolute. LUCIE is standing shyly in the doorway.

Scene One

FATHER BEAUMONT   Please, come in, Mademoiselle.

LUCIE stays in the doorway, on her guard, ready to flee.

Well, come in, have a seat.

FATHER BEAUMONT gets up. LUCIE takes a step forward and examines the room suspiciously. LUCIE sits down. She is ill at ease and seems to be mentally rehearsing something she finds difficult to say. A pause.

Your parents are well, Mademoiselle?

LUCIE   My mother left this morning for Montreal. My father is sleeping, I believe.

FATHER BEAUMONT   And you, Mademoiselle?

LUCIE   *(astonished)* Me?

FATHER BEAUMONT   What can I do for you?

LUCIE   Since yesterday, since your visit to our house, I've wanted to speak to you.

LUCIE gets up brusquely.

But no, I think I would prefer to go. I'm not used to conversing. Your tongue grows thick when the only people you speak to are family.

FATHER BEAUMONT   And me? Do you think that I am used to conversing, as you put it?

LUCIE   But you speak to the people around here. They listen to you. They speak to you as well?

FATHER BEAUMONT   They speak to me? And I speak to them? They come to see me so that I will talk to them in parables. That way everyone is at ease; there is nothing to understand. I baptize them; I marry them; I give them communion and absolution. As for the rest, no one speaks of it. Life carries on, between them and their misery, between the lumberjacks and the logging companies, between ignorance and exploitation, between the birth and death of creatures living lives of humiliation before God. I make signs of benediction over bowed heads and I have the impression that I am blessing misfortune, giving it free rein, when I should be preaching fierce and harsh justice.

LUCIE   Have pity on me also, because I am living and unjust, like life.

FATHER BEAUMONT   I let myself get carried away. Forgive me. But you, Mademoiselle, I would have preferred that you had not come. "Living and unjust," here you are in front of me, calling to me with such force. Sometimes I would like to be blind and deaf. It is too difficult to carry the burdens of others' lives when you can do nothing for them. Take last night with your mother: I was a disgrace. I couldn't find the words that were called for. I behaved like a child, repeating without conviction a lesson that has become trite with two thousand years of use. Sometimes, when I speak in Christ's name, it's as if I am using his name in vain. Your mother was well aware of it, and there I was, laden with all the old deceptions of the clergy as well as the excessive weight of an offended soul.

LUCIE   If you are speaking of my mother, allow me to remind you that I am here on my own account and I will not cease until you have answered me.

> *Pause.*

FATHER BEAUMONT   What would you like to know?

LUCIE   Everything, absolutely everything. I want to know everything. But we have time. I will come back. You would like me to come back? Another day, because today, you see, Father Beaumont, is a rare day among all days: my mother will not be coming home before this evening. I'd like to see what our house is like when the cat's away and the mice are playing. I will come back. And so, lend me some books, please?

> *FATHER BEAUMONT makes a broad gesture toward his bookcase. LUCIE looks at the bookcase in astonishment, and then decides to choose some books. FATHER BEAUMONT comes to her aid and fills LUCIE's arms with books.*
>
> *Black.*

Scene Two

> *Set Two. The living room of the Joncas home. A lively jazz tune can be heard playing on an old phonograph placed on the floor of the veranda. SÉBASTIEN, MARIE and CAPUCINE are listening to the music with delight. At the back of the room, HÉLÈNE, visibly irritated by the music, is just finishing cleaning a lantern. She puts a sweater over her shoulders and crosses the room and the veranda, the lantern in her hand. Just as HÉLÈNE opens the door, she bumps into LUCIE arriving with her books.*

LUCIE   It's snowing and blowing hard enough to take your breath away.

HÉLÈNE   The train is bound to be late. It is so dark along the path, Mother must be able to see the light of the lantern in the distance when she comes home tonight.

HÉLÈNE exits. SÉBASTIEN advances toward LUCIE, sketching out a dance step. In passing, he takes a few dried flowers from the windowsill and offers them to LUCIE, who examines them with surprise.

LUCIE   What's this?

SÉBASTIEN   As you can see, they are immortelles. They are said to bring misfortune.

LUCIE, with a brusque gesture, throws them to the ground.

LUCIE   Why give them to me then? Leave me alone! I want to read!

LUCIE ensconces herself in the sofa with her books.

HÉLÈNE   And we are in mourning. I don't find that music very appropriate.

SÉBASTIEN   My poor Hélène, you've got everything mixed up as usual. It is in Montreal that Aunt Nathalie's passing is being mourned. But here, we are celebrating cousin Isabelle's arrival among us. On the contrary, I don't find this music out of place.

HÉLÈNE exits with the lantern.

LUCIE   *(Her nose in her book.)* And so perhaps you can offer the dried flowers to cousin Isabelle, to wear as a crown.

SÉBASTIEN   Isabelle is twenty years old. I am sure that she is very pretty, sophisticated and worldly. Ah! Life here is going to change!

LUCIE   *(without looking up from her book)* Personally, I'm sure this girl is coarse, a bit like Nora from the village, who lies in wait for the lumberjacks coming out of the woods so she can bleed them dry, like a weasel.

MARIE   Isabelle will soon be here with us to live, to sleep, to eat, just like that, every day, like a new little sister, and we don't even know her yet. Isn't it extraordinary!

SÉBASTIEN   *(intending for LUCIE to hear)* You have no idea just how extraordinary all this is.

SÉBASTIEN goes up to LUCIE and pulls her book away.

You read too much!

LUCIE tries to get her book back. SÉBASTIEN opens the book and reads the signature on the cover page.

(reading) Jean Beaumont, tsk… hum! The new priest!

LUCIE takes back her book.

LUCIE   I read, and you, you do your painting. As for me, I won't be hanging around here for very much longer, I can tell you that.

SÉBASTIEN   And it is good Father Beaumont who will help you to escape, just like that, gently, with books and sermons? Watch yourself, Lucie. There is, no doubt, an elegy in praise of resignation hidden in all this, and if you let yourself be indoctrinated, you risk wilting away right here where you are, rather than getting away from all this.

LUCIE   Mind your own business. You don't understand anything.

> *A beat. SÉBASTIEN hesitates to speak to LUCIE, then speaks to her in a low voice, in a confidential tone.*

SÉBASTIEN   I will be the first to be leaving.

LUCIE   What are you saying?

SÉBASTIEN   I know the forest around here like the back of my hand. For a long time, I've wanted to push on further. You know, like when you are little and you dream about reaching the far horizon, of feeling it under your feet, but the horizon keeps moving away, and the most distant point is constantly being revealed anew. And so I will set off, then set off anew, again and again, until I find it.

LUCIE   Until you find what?

SÉBASTIEN   A life where I am master.

LUCIE   And where will you go?

SÉBASTIEN   For a long time I thought that the far horizon was the Great North, ice, snow, rare and magnificent furs!

LUCIE   And now?

SÉBASTIEN   Life is for the taking, and perhaps even more than life—who knows? I want to risk it all to have it all.

LUCIE   I don't understand. You, always so cut and dried, waxing poetic like a drunk having visions.

SÉBASTIEN   Let's say I am having visions, as you say. That they exist only outside of me, those visions, cut and dried. Maybe they are the last frontier, to discover and possess?

> *HÉLÈNE returns from outside and crosses into her room. SÉBASTIEN opens a roll of disordered papers. He spreads out his paintings in front of LUCIE.*

LUCIE   You, Sébastien, you think of yourself as a real painter?

SÉBASTIEN   Yes, I, Sébastien Joncas, will be a great painter!

LUCIE   You're dreaming! And all because some bearded man with paint under his nails stopped here last summer and looked at your doodlings without laughing?

SÉBASTIEN   That man knew how to look. And how to paint as well. You could see it in the way he looked at my work. He told me that it was very good; he gave me his name and his address in Montreal: Jim Ladouceur Faribaldie is his name. Before, I didn't know what I was doing, I had no idea what painting was. I was enjoying the colours and my imaginings so much that I was satisfied. But now…

> *SÉBASTIEN examines his canvases with satisfaction.*

I think that one is very good. And that one! And that one! They absolutely have to be beautiful, superb, unique, or it's not worth it. How to know? Who to ask for advice? I will go to Montreal. The bearded man told me he would put me to work. I will see other painters, lots of painters. I'll have a studio, I'll work. And I'm rich! I can afford to treat myself to a good stay in the city. I have a batch of superb furs piled up at the trading post, and Chatillon is buying and paying cash. Ah, I've got more than enough to live on. *(beat)* But, before leaving, I want to see Isabelle.

LUCIE   You are leaving very quickly, then, Sébastien? You are leaving?

SÉBASTIEN   Once I've decided to do something, no one can make me change my mind.

LUCIE   Thank you, Sébastien. Bon voyage, Sébastien. Good luck, Sébastien. Happy painting, Sébastien. A brilliant career, Sébastien. And be quick, Sébastien, before our cousin arrives.

SÉBASTIEN   What a strange girl you are, Lucie!

LUCIE   Am I not your favourite sister! *(in desperation)* And one day, I also, I also will be leaving.

> *CAPUCINE and MARIE surge onto the veranda. They surround SÉBASTIEN in a great uproar: "I'm your favourite, eh, Sébastien."— "No, I am!"—"I'm the one you love the best. Say that it's me?" SÉBASTIEN defends himself, laughing.*

SÉBASTIEN   You're all favourites! All little locusts and ladybugs.

> *HÉLÈNE returns with SÉBASTIEN's jacket.*

HÉLÈNE   Sébastien! I mended the lining of your jacket, come see.

> *SÉBASTIEN goes toward HÉLÈNE; he examines the jacket that she hands him and slips it on.*

SÉBASTIEN   Thank you, Hélène. You are very kind. Well, I'm off to the station to pick up Mother and cousin Isabelle. So the family will be complete. Bertrand is lending me his car.

> *MARIE and CAPUCINE accompany SÉBASTIEN to the door. LUCIE has dived back into her book.*

LUCIE   Be careful, Sébastien. The horizon is like a mirage in the desert, it makes you thirst for nothing. And, if you want my opinion: Isabelle is also like the horizon!

> *SÉBASTIEN shrugs his shoulders and exits.*

Scene Three

> *At the sound of the door closing, FRANÇOIS exits his room and leans over the railing of the staircase.*

FRANÇOIS   *(calling)* Sébastien! Sébastien!

> *FRANÇOIS comes down the stairs slowly.*

And the mail? Will Sébastien think to bring home the mail?

HÉLÈNE   With all this snow, I doubt that he will go to the post office.

FRANÇOIS   Ah! The storm is here! I've been feeling it in my leg for two days now. Ah! What a bother! It's going to snow for some time and no one will go for the mail. And the letter I was waiting for. And Agnès away in this kind of weather.

> *FRANÇOIS wanders about the room like a lost soul.*

What is Agnès doing that she hasn't returned?

LUCIE   The train usually doesn't arrive until seven, and with this storm…

FRANÇOIS   What a long day I've spent, upstairs, all alone.

LUCIE   Why didn't you come down?

FRANÇOIS   I detest that frantic music that you enjoy listening to so much. And I am so nervous about an important letter I'm expecting and afraid of receiving that I end up not being able to move at all, mired in depression.

LUCIE   *You* are waiting for a letter?

FRANÇOIS   Ah! This day is turning in a void, like a stripped screw.

> *FRANÇOIS pours himself a drink.*

The house has lost its centre. If Agnès does not return tonight, I will drink myself to death; I've wanted to for such a long time.

LUCIE   Papa, please, you know very well that Sébastien's alcohol is dangerous.

FRANÇOIS   I would be very afraid of dying, of course, but who knows, once I'm good and drunk, maybe I won't even notice as I slip away into the next world.

LUCIE   Maybe not. But maybe you will. So be careful about slipping away, as you say. And Maman will be coming home any minute now with our cousin.

FRANÇOIS   Ah yes! It's true, Nathalie's daughter is coming here to live with us. What a nice house and what a nice family! What misery and what a miserable face I have to show! Maybe that's what the Holy Face is—the face of a man so defeated and humiliated, so resigned to his own destruction, that he no longer resembles anything at all.

LUCIE   Are you so unhappy then? You are toying with your own misery.

FRANÇOIS   *(echoing)* "I am toying with my own misery." …Perhaps, perhaps not, who knows? Probably yes and no. Truth is like sand; it gets into everything. The greatest games invented by man are convincing imitations of life and death.

> *Looking for a diversion, LUCIE notices CAPUCINE looking bored.*

LUCIE   Capucine, come here so I can tell you a story!

> *LUCIE takes CAPUCINE on her lap.*

(telling her story) "The Devil arrives home for dinner. He is famished. He says to his wife in a terrible voice: 'I am hungry!' His wife leaps into the pot and heats up the stove under the pot. She climbs out of the pot and she says 'Ah! I am so tired!'"

CAPUCINE   *(laughing)* Your story doesn't make sense at all!

> *The sound of voices and muffled exclamations can be heard.*

HÉLÈNE   Here they are! They've arrived! I recognize Maman's voice.

> *CAPUCINE and MARIE bound toward the door, followed by HÉLÈNE trailing behind them. LUCIE, somewhat apart, affects an air of detachment.*

Scene Four

> *AGNÈS, ISABELLE and SÉBASTIEN enter. CAPUCINE jumps into her mother's arms. SÉBASTIEN, very attentive to ISABELLE, is carrying the young woman's suitcase.*

AGNÈS   Ah! What a journey! I nearly died between the station and here. Impossible to make your way in the snow. Couldn't see a thing two steps in front of you. My heart is pounding, pounding…

> *ISABELLE is in mourning and is very elegant. HÉLÈNE, MARIE and CAPUCINE surround AGNÈS, taking her boots and packages. ISABELLE is alone in their midst. SÉBASTIEN takes the suitcase to the bedroom on the right. LUCIE studies ISABELLE with obvious malevolence. FRANÇOIS approaches ISABELLE and, acting very much a man of the world, holds out his hand to her.*

FRANÇOIS   Hello. I am your Uncle François.

> *FRANÇOIS kisses ISABELLE.*

ISABELLE   Hello. I'm Isabelle.

SÉBASTIEN returns hastily, eager to press his attentions on ISABELLE. He hesitates, then kisses his cousin in a clumsy parody of his father's gesture.

SÉBASTIEN   Hello. I am Sébastien.

ISABELLE   Yes, I already know that. Hello, Sébastien.

SÉBASTIEN   *(indicating his sisters)* This is Hélène, and Marie and Lucie, and here, our little Capucine.

> *The cousins greet one another from a distance. The girls surround AGNÈS, except for LUCIE, who continues to study ISABELLE. FRANÇOIS helps ISABELLE out of her coat. He has her sit and prepares to take her boots off. SÉBASTIEN circles around ISABELLE. He examines her coat.*

This is imitation mink!

ISABELLE   *(shrugging her shoulders)* Of course!

SÉBASTIEN   I know furs. I've been trapping for a long time.

> *Very brusquely, SÉBASTIEN helps his father to get up and takes his place at ISABELLE's feet. He awkwardly pulls off his cousin's boots.*
>
> *HÉLÈNE and MARIE bustle around the table. AGNÈS examines everything with an air of exasperation.*

AGNÈS   I am away from this house for a single instant and everything falls into disorder.

HÉLÈNE   Maman, I'm sure I've done everything I could to please you.

> *AGNÈS continues her inspection.*

AGNÈS   The bread is stale. And this dish towel. Have you seen this dish towel? And what is that awful smell?

LUCIE   *(quietly)* It's the garlic that I put in the stew.

AGNÈS   Garlic! How horrible! Isabelle, take this chair, here.

> *SÉBASTIEN offers ISABELLE and FRANÇOIS each a drink.*

Sébastien! What is that you're serving us? Do you want to poison us? Don't drink that, Isabelle.

> *FRANÇOIS empties his glass. He speaks animatedly, addressing himself to ISABELLE as if telling a story.*

FRANÇOIS   The world is full of poisons, this one here or another one. As for me, I catch my poisons in full flight, tsk… *(He makes the gesture of catching a fly.)* In summer, the poisonous plants search me out—seven years, and seven bouts of poison ivy. And in winter, a hundred little barometers lodge in my right knee to predict the weather, in my very bones. Aie!

AGNÈS   You talk a lot, old man.

SÉBASTIEN   One day, when I am rich and have a city named after me, I'll set up a nice still there, right in the centre, like a fountain, for the simple-minded folk. Poetry and music will flow, like their own blood, from their hearts.

AGNÈS   *(following her own train of thought)* At my age, and with this storm, a journey like that one is madness!

ISABELLE   It's very cold in this house.

AGNÈS   The fire is out. Ah! My daughters are dolts!

> *AGNÈS goes to rekindle the fire.*

When are you going to learn that green wood gives neither heat nor light. You would think that my house had been abandoned all day! It really wasn't worth it to bring four living daughters into the world.

Isabelle and I were the only ones in the church this morning. A mass with a collection for the poor when only the poor would attend. Ah! Those priests know what they are doing! There was no doubt about it. The church was deserted. I was spared nothing: neither the auction nor the sight of the creditors: poor Nathalie was swamped with debts. The family furniture was piled on the stairway, like stolen goods. I bought back my father's table. I had to fight for it with an English woman who smelled of tobacco. One horror after another. And the never-ending train trip! The tracks had to be cleared of snow as we went…

ISABELLE   Nor was I spared anything today, I can assure you. Could you please excuse me. If one of my cousins would be so good as to show me my room…

> *HÉLÈNE gets up to direct ISABELLE.*

HÉLÈNE   Come, it's this way.

> *HÉLÈNE heads toward the room on the right. ISABELLE follows. AGNÈS calls ISABELLE back.*

AGNÈS   *(in a constrained voice)* Isabelle, come here. Come closer so that I can look at you a bit more.

> *ISABELLE approaches AGNÈS, who studies her intensely.*

How you resemble Nathalie. Don't look at me like that. Those eyes that are too wide open, that haughty manner beneath the fatigue and pain, those white hands, that thick hair and that beautiful blank face. Despite the best of intentions, all the evil in the world could lurk there without a soul suspecting. What a mask is the beauty of a young face. You resemble her so much, it's incredible! You hurt me and you frighten me, but I want to keep you here, under my eyes, as long as possible. And if I were to believe in your pure little soul? And if I let myself be taken in a second time, risking love and betrayal? Child. Bird. Little one, so little.

AGNÈS, who had approached ISABELLE to look at her and touch her up close like an object that is both precious and dangerous, suddenly moves away. ISABELLE, transfixed and fascinated, is unable to move.

I am your guardian until you come of age. You will live here, with my children. All of my family must sleep with me, under my roof. And of course, you don't know what life in the country is like. In the course of time, wilderness and silence erase all grief and wear away the most beautiful of faces, like water.

ISABELLE   Aunt Agnès, you are like the devil.

SÉBASTIEN   You have to sleep, Isabelle, to sleep, to forget. Tomorrow, you will see how beautiful the snowdrifts are, after the storm.

ISABELLE   Why did you come to get me? My God, what am doing here? I could very well have managed on my own.

HÉLÈNE   Come, Isabelle, come!

ISABELLE and HÉLÈNE enter the bedroom to the right. Silence. Everyone one seems transfixed.

FRANÇOIS   Ah! I am dying of shame. Why couldn't I have welcomed Nathalie's daughter with the words of compassion and tenderness that were required.

FRANÇOIS mounts the stairs slowly.

AGNÈS   I will do everything in my power, no matter what it costs me, to keep Isabelle in my home.

AGNÈS enters her bedroom. FRANÇOIS climbs the stairs. HÉLÈNE returns with MARIE. The two girls whisper together.

HÉLÈNE   I feel so terribly uncomfortable having that strange girl sleeping in our bedroom.

MARIE   And do you think it's any fun for her?

Black.

Scene Five

Set Three. SÉBASTIEN cautiously approaches the veranda. He is dragging a canvas bag. Into the bag he packs papers, pots of paint and clothes that he takes out from under the sofa. ISABELLE appears in the room. She walks slowly, seemingly overwhelmed. She has put her coat over her shoulders. She is shivering. She sits close to the table, remaining motionless for a moment. Then she begins to cry, her head in her hands. She turns her back to SÉBASTIEN, who is looking at her very intently. He advances toward her. ISABELLE, having heard his steps, regains her composure and turns toward him.

ISABELLE   I am very cold.

SÉBASTIEN   *(ill at ease)* Would you like something to drink?

ISABELLE   *(with hesitation)* Well, yes, I would.

> *SÉBASTIEN looks around cautiously.*

SÉBASTIEN   We mustn't wake anyone.

> *SÉBASTIEN offers his cousin a drink.*

ISABELLE   It burns!

SÉBASTIEN   *(apologizing)* You were cold, so…

> *ISABELLE looks at SÉBASTIEN's baggage.*

ISABELLE   You're leaving on a trip.

SÉBASTIEN   Yes, I'm leaving.

ISABELLE   In this weather? You must be desperate to leave.

SÉBASTIEN   I've been desperate to leave for a long time.

ISABELLE   I'm hungry.

> *SÉBASTIEN offers ISABELLE a piece of fruit.*

(biting into the fruit) Are you going far?

SÉBASTIEN   As far as Montreal.

> *ISABELLE begins to cry again.*

ISABELLE   I was there this morning. *(regaining her composure)* But I will go back there. I could never live here.

> *SÉBASTIEN doesn't answer and continues to roll up his paintings.*

Did you do these?

SÉBASTIEN   I'm a painter!

> *ISABELLE examines the paintings and bursts out laughing.*

Why are you laughing?

ISABELLE   Because they make me happy! Sébastien! You paint like a *douanier*!

SÉBASTIEN   Like a what?

ISABELLE   Like a custom's agent! Like an innocent, a primitive, a tiny little child! And all those raw colours exploding! Oh Sébastien, thank you! It's as if all at once I have rediscovered joy!

SÉBASTIEN   *(vexed)* You don't know what you are talking about.

ISABELLE   Yes, I know very well. I have known many painters and artists. They often came to the house to see Maman.

SÉBASTIEN   Do you resemble your mother?

ISABELLE   *(with a sort of painful rage)* Yes, I resemble her. I resemble her.

SÉBASTIEN   You are beautiful. *(beat)* I know furs, traps, hunting, the woods, in summer and in winter, the *coureurs du bois*, the village girls, but a girl like you, Isabelle, this is my first time.

> *SÉBASTIEN returns to his baggage. ISABELLE takes a cigarette from her bag.*

ISABELLE   *(in a weary tone)* Do you have a light?

> *SÉBASTIEN, surprised, rummages in his pockets. He finds a match and approaches ISABELLE, whose hand is trembling. For a moment, SÉBASTIEN holds the match close to ISABELLE's face. He looks at her.*

SÉBASTIEN   You are trembling?

ISABELLE   I am so weary.

SÉBASTIEN   No one smokes here. Be careful, the smell of smoke will give you away.

ISABELLE   I don't understand.

SÉBASTIEN   There are only three bedrooms that are habitable here in winter. I sleep on the left. Over there are my sisters. There, Agnès occupies the centre of her kingdom, like a queen…

ISABELLE   And Uncle François?

SÉBASTIEN   He is the drone, whom the queen bee has relegated to the upstairs since Capucine was born. He comes down only rarely. Agnès can recognize everyone's breathing in the dark. Not a dream nor a tear in the night escapes her.

ISABELLE   I could get used to never crying out loud, and never dreaming except with my mouth closed. But that dormitory of girls, breathing right next to my bed—no! No! I cannot bear it.

SÉBASTIEN   You have arrived too late, Isabelle. You should have come here when you were small. My mother adores little children. She would have loved you and you would have been mixed in with the rest of Agnès's children and entrusted to the same savage spirits.

ISABELLE   Really, Sébastien, we would have been together, every day, you and me, bound by the same daily life?

SÉBASTIEN   *(collecting himself)* What didn't happen, doesn't exist.

ISABELLE   *(in a breath)* Are you sure, Sébastien, that what didn't happen doesn't already exist between us, isn't terribly present?

SÉBASTIEN   *(collecting himself)* I am leaving tonight, it is decided!

ISABELLE   What is it that is so imminently threatening that you must leave this very instant, in the middle of a storm?

SÉBASTIEN   I never go back on a decision. I am taking the train tomorrow morning. A friend will put me up for the night. That way I will avoid a long goodbye scene, with the family lined up, their handkerchiefs waving.

ISABELLE   And Aunt Agnès, in dry tears, holding onto her son, a rearing colt.

> *Silence.*

SÉBASTIEN   Of all the people I know, you are absolutely the last one that I would have wanted to find in my path at the moment I was leaving!

> *SÉBASTIEN turns and pretends to arrange his paints.*

ISABELLE   Sébastien, look at me, please.

SÉBASTIEN   I have looked at you: I looked at you when you got off the train, with my mother. It was marvellous to see you, and to be seen by you. And it was at that precise moment that I decided to leave without further delay. That is the price of my freedom.

ISABELLE   What a wonderful exercise of will! You honour me!

SÉBASTIEN   Much more than you could possibly believe. I have resolved to become a great painter. It is a hunger that I have. I will be a very great painter, or nothing at all, like my father.

ISABELLE   It's a challenge?

SÉBASTIEN   My life belongs to me, and I intend to possess it to the core, totally, without concessions or regret.

ISABELLE   And tenderness, Sébastien? And the misfortunes that befall us without warning?

SÉBASTIEN   I will do what it takes. No tenderness will disarm me and, if misfortune befalls me, I will face it like a wounded animal that escapes from the trap and goes off to lick its wounds.

ISABELLE   You are very sure of yourself, Sébastien! As for me, I now have neither home nor hearth. I followed my aunt like a sleepwalker. And then there was that interminable train trip, with the windows covered in frost. My aunt was seated facing me, taciturn, pale and straight. I avoided looking at her, but I could feel her eyes fixed on me. As if I were caught in a trap. And now, I will have to live here, day after day, with that woman who frightens me. I wish I had the strength to flee!

SÉBASTIEN   And where would you go, Isabelle?

ISABELLE   I don't know. I would flee, escape, run until I was out of breath, through the snow, across fields and woods, until I collapsed from fatigue and cold…

SÉBASTIEN   Isabelle, you are too beautiful for despair!

SÉBASTIEN, disarmed by ISABELLE's grief, unrolls one of his paintings and offers it to her clumsily.

Look here, I have a gift for you. It's my most beautiful painting, my funniest one you would say. If you want to laugh when you look at it, well, so much the better, I will be happy!

ISABELLE looks at the painting.

ISABELLE   Thank you Sébastien! You are right. It is the funniest. *(She smiles.)*

Beat. SÉBASTIEN and ISABELLE are standing at a distance from each other, looking at each other, ill at ease.

Aunt Agnès knows that you are leaving?

SÉBASTIEN   No, not yet.

ISABELLE   Will she be very angry when she finds out?

Heavy silence from SÉBASTIEN.

(with effort) If you want, Sébastien, I will be the one to tell her.

SÉBASTIEN   *(astonished)* You, Isabelle? Well, if you want to, if you wish.

ISABELLE   Isn't that how you would like me to be, hard and invulnerable, only good for announcing bad news?

SÉBASTIEN   What a strange girl you are!

ISABELLE   Then, it is decided? You are leaving?

SÉBASTIEN   It is decided.

SÉBASTIEN buckles his bag.

ISABELLE   Goodbye, Sébastien! I will deliver your message.

SÉBASTIEN hesitates. He moves toward ISABELLE. He stops.

SÉBASTIEN   Goodbye, Isabelle!

ISABELLE   Goodbye, Sébastien!

SÉBASTIEN picks up his bag. ISABELLE follows each of his movements. SÉBASTIEN exits without turning. ISABELLE remains alone, still as a statue.

Scene Six

After a moment, AGNÈS appears in the doorway of her bedroom in a dressing gown. She moves toward the outside door.

AGNÈS   Did someone go out? My God! Who went out in the storm in the middle of the night? *(She sees ISABELLE.)*

> *ISABELLE turns and faces AGNÈS.*

ISABELLE   Your son is gone. I alone could have stopped him, and I didn't do it… *(She begins to cry.)* And I didn't do it…

> *Black.*

ACT THREE

Set One. Four months later. It is early spring. The living room at the Joncas's.

Scene One

AGNÈS, wrapped in a shawl, is seated, despondent and motionless. MARIE, HÉLÈNE and CAPUCINE, full of life and high spirits, are coming in and out.

MARIE   *(coming in)* The river is overflowing. They've opened the floodgates. It's full of logs running downriver.

HÉLÈNE   Ah! Sunshine, and the smell of the earth!

CAPUCINE runs to the bedroom on the right.

CAPUCINE   Isabelle! Isabelle! Come see! Spring is arriving!

AGNÈS   *(to herself)* Ah! This winter was long! I've lost all my strength. It's cold as winter. The cold in this country will never end. Every night, it still freezes. I can't sleep any more; I hear the earth freezing and the seeds dying. There won't be fruit or flowers for a long time yet.

HÉLÈNE   *(to her mother)* Perhaps you would like another shawl?

AGNÈS   Poor girls, looking at me, wide-eyed, waiting for me to command and govern, waiting for me to tell you what you want. Go away, you little fools. You're annoying me. But I will last, until Sébastien returns.

MARIE   Do you need anything?

AGNÈS   I don't need anything or anybody, to be sure. May I just last until Sébastien returns!

HÉLÈNE and MARIE talk in hushed tones.

HÉLÈNE   What a strange, heavy winter. Isabelle arrived, Sébastien left, and Maman has been sick for so long…

MARIE   Sébastien's leaving planted her in place, like a corpse. It's as if Maman has been poisoned with anger and grief.

HÉLÈNE   *I* think Sébastien left because of Isabelle.

LUCIE has silently come out of her bedroom, in bare feet and wearing an old dressing gown. She pours herself some coffee.

LUCIE   You're out of your mind. Sébastien left because he couldn't stand living with the family on his back any longer.

CAPUCINE has returned on tiptoe. She is listening to the conversation.

CAPUCINE   Sébastien writes letters to Isabelle. I know everything, I do!

CAPUCINE tries to run to her bedroom. LUCIE grabs her by the arm.

LUCIE If Maman were to hear you! And anyway, Isabelle is a liar. You can tell her I said so! Sébastien hasn't written her once, not even once, do you hear me!

CAPUCINE runs away.

HÉLÈNE You seem very sure of what you're saying, Lucie.

LUCIE You have no idea how sure I am!

HÉLÈNE Nevertheless, Sébastien should have written to Maman, at least to tell her where he is.

Scene Two

FRANÇOIS has just emerged from his bedroom, all dressed up in his Sunday best. He starts to come down the stairs warily, like someone who is trying to escape.

HÉLÈNE Every day, Isabelle goes to the post office with Papa. And this morning, they've decided to go to mass together.

FRANÇOIS is looking for his hat. He continues to walk very softly, trying not to be noticed. He speaks in hushed tones.

FRANÇOIS My hat! Where did I put my hat?

LUCIE turns abruptly to her father.

LUCIE Are you going out?

FRANÇOIS looks like a happy child caught in the act.

FRANÇOIS It's Sunday. I'm going to mass with Isabelle.

LUCIE tries to attract the attention of AGNÈS, who doesn't seem to be aware of anything that is going on.

LUCIE *(to AGNÈS)* Do you hear what he's saying?

AGNÈS pretends not to hear. FRANÇOIS has found his hat.

FRANÇOIS I have to hurry. It's almost eight o'clock.

FRANÇOIS moves slowly towards the door. LUCIE catches up to him.

LUCIE You seem very happy to be going to mass with Isabelle?

FRANÇOIS tries to open the door to escape. LUCIE holds him back.

FRANÇOIS Happy, yes, very happy!

LUCIE And Isabelle is happy too! Isabelle certainly likes to go out with you. The only thing is, you're forgetting Agnès! *(She points to her mother.)*

AGNÈS   *(her voice detached, as if it is coming from another world)* My poor
François! Lucie is being mean, as usual. It's true, I hate people going to church,
and you know that. If you obey me, you think that you're condemned to burn
in Hell, and if you dare to defy me, encouraged by that little fool Isabelle, then
you feel equally guilty. You're damned if you do and damned if you don't. Ah,
I know you well!

FRANÇOIS   My God, what am I to do? I have, however, promised to go to mass
this morning… I will go because, as I have told you, I have promised to go…

>   *FRANÇOIS goes to leave quickly. AGNÈS calls him back.*

AGNÈS   François, don't forget the mail: you know that I'm expecting a letter from
Sébastien!

FRANÇOIS   I know.

Scene Three

>   *FRANÇOIS leaves. ISABELLE comes in with CAPUCINE. She crosses the*
>   *room and heads towards the door. CAPUCINE walks along with her, and*
>   *then abruptly leaves her to go over to show her mother her hairdo.*

CAPUCINE   Maman! Look how pretty it is, in my hair, this blue ribbon! It's
Isabelle who…

ISABELLE   See you later. I'm going to church with Uncle François.

>   *ISABELLE leaves. AGNÈS seems to become aware of CAPUCINE's*
>   *presence. She rips the ribbon from the little girl's hair.*

AGNÈS   I hate it when people do up children's hair as if they were circus
performers!

CAPUCINE   *(shouting)* My ribbon! The beautiful ribbon that Isabelle gave me!

>   *CAPUCINE runs out.*

MARIE   How elegant Isabelle is! Did you see her dress? And her high heels?
Isabelle told me that I have pretty legs.

HÉLÈNE   Legs are for walking; it doesn't matter in the least if they are pretty or
ugly.

LUCIE   *(to AGNÈS)* Isabelle this, Isabelle that! All we hear the whole day long is
her name! Before, you were in charge, and now, Isabelle is. And you put up with
that?

AGNÈS   Be quiet. Please, be quiet!

LUCIE   No, I will not be quiet. It weighs heavily on my heart. I want to talk and
shout. I want you to listen to me and talk to me.

AGNÈS   Be quiet.

LUCIE   Am I disturbing you? Do you prefer to act as if you were deaf and dumb, to pretend to be dead, as if none of this were happening?

AGNÈS   I can very well pretend to be dead, as you put it. I already said too much when that little priest came here, like a thief. I want just one thing: to turn back the clock, to return to silence and the night. Sébastien's absence is the only thing that touches and moves me.

LUCIE   Sébastien's absence isn't the only thing that's tormenting you.

AGNÈS   You don't know what you're talking about.

LUCIE   I know that, in your heart, you brood about everything, absolutely everything that goes on here, like a bad tune that you can't get out of your head.

AGNÈS   When will you learn to mind your own business?

LUCIE   That's funny, it seems to me that everything is my business. That's how it seems to me.

AGNÈS   *(as if to herself)* The greatest achievement in life would be to remain completely secret, hidden away from everyone, and from oneself. No more questions, no more answers. A long season, without age or reason or responsibility. A kind of savage season, beyond time and beyond consciousness.

> *LUCIE takes out a notebook and a book and begins to write.*

LUCIE   Personally, I wish this foul season you're talking about would go somewhere else to die.

> *HÉLÈNE is tidying up the table; LUCIE's books are in her way.*

HÉLÈNE   Do we need to have these books left scattered about everywhere?

LUCIE   I forbid you to touch my books!

HÉLÈNE   Perhaps you think that literature and algebra are going to throw the doors of the world wide open for you?

LUCIE   *(evasive)* I don't understand what you mean.

> *HÉLÈNE points to the book on the table.*

HÉLÈNE   Don't be a hypocrite. What about this?

> *LUCIE is stubbornly silent. HÉLÈNE discovers other books hidden about.*

What about this one? And this one?

LUCIE   I forbid you to touch my books! Resign yourself to your lot as a spinster. But don't touch my books!

HÉLÈNE   Your books? And how would you happen to own anything? Did Sébastien give you money to buy these books?

> *MARIE searches through the books.*

MARIE   Oh! There are novels here too!

> *LUCIE pounces on her sisters and grabs the books, which she stuffs into the pockets of her dressing gown.*

LUCIE   What business is this of yours?

HÉLÈNE   *(brandishing a notebook)* You forgot your copybook! What pretty handwriting, and what pretty sentences! Is this yours? Your teacher, that new priest, must be thrilled to have such a brilliant student!

LUCIE   *(grabbing her notebook)* To each her own. *You* mend old sweaters, and *I* study. What are you complaining about?

HÉLÈNE   Complaining? Me? What would I have to complain about? Nothing, nothing, I assure you. Life is a mess, that's all. What can we do about it?

LUCIE   If life is a mess, then it is up to us to fix it. Everyone for herself.

> *LUCIE goes into her bedroom. The scene between the three sisters has been fast and fiery. AGNÈS hasn't moved.*

AGNÈS   Ah! This fire is drawing poorly! The only thing that warms my heart is rage. I'm so tired of waiting. I'm so tired…

> *LUCIE comes back into the living room. She has dressed hurriedly and is wearing an old hat. MARIE is astonished when she sees her sister.*

MARIE   What are you doing? Why are you dressed up like that?

LUCIE   *(speaking very loudly so that AGNÈS will hear her)* I'm going to mass!

> *No reaction from AGNÈS.*

Goodbye! I'm going to mass!

> *AGNÈS remains silent. MARIE laughs.*

(furious) I'm going to mass!

> *LUCIE leaves. A church bell can be heard ringing in the distance.*

AGNÈS   Little fool! You'll get nothing for your efforts. It's too late now. The sanctus is ringing.

> *The church bell rings again. AGNÈS bows her head.*

But who will take pity on us? My God, who will take pity?

> *Black.*

> *Set Two. The parlour of the presbytery. One hour later.*

Scene Four

LUCIE is sitting, lost in thought. ISABELLE comes in from the outside. The two cousins are surprised to see each other.

LUCIE Hi, Isabelle.

ISABELLE Oh! It's you, Lucie!

LUCIE But what are you doing here? Isn't Papa with you?

ISABELLE After mass, Uncle François went to the post office. I came to get a copy of the latest "School Newsletter" for him. The priest told me that I could get one here.

ISABELLE searches among the newspapers piled on the table.

LUCIE What good care you take of "Uncle François," and how pleased you are with yourself for taking such care of him. A real mutual blessing. You charm the whole family with your cute little act. Everyone except for Agnès and me, of course. You dream and you tell stories. But I know that you're lying!

ISABELLE What do you mean?

LUCIE You taught Capucine well! That little one is telling anyone who will listen that Isabelle has been getting letters from her cousin Sébastien!

ISABELLE Shut up!

LUCIE No, I will not shut up! I know that you have the gift of the gab and that my father and sister lap up every word that you say. But not me; I know that Sébastien has never written you, not once. Not even once, do you hear me!

ISABELLE Let me by.

LUCIE You're not going to ask me why I'm so certain, so sure of myself?

ISABELLE Let me by.

LUCIE You don't know Sébastien, you don't know how he is consumed by ambition. He covets genius with all his soul, like a beautiful hunting ground to conquer. But he must be recognized by all. My brother is stubborn: what he has sworn to do, he will do.

ISABELLE I'm stubborn too. I believe that one day Sébastien will need my help to be accepted and recognized over there. So, I'm waiting for him to call for me and…

LUCIE It has already happened.

ISABELLE I don't understand.

LUCIE Sébastien may need your help, as you say, but he also undoubtedly needs a go-between, since I'm the one he's writing to. Listen carefully: Sébastien scribbled these lines with a pencil on a piece of paper.

LUCIE takes a letter out of her pocket.

(*reading*) "See if you can get Isabelle to tell you the names of some painters that my Aunt Nathalie used to receive in her house on Rue Saint-Marc. I would prefer not to write to Isabelle. That bearded man dropped me almost right away. I would really love to meet a great painter and to work with him. Do you think that Aunt Nathalie's name would open doors for me? The big city is closed and noisy. You can hardly tell one season from another here. I am keeping well. I'm persisting, and I'm painting constantly. Write me back right away. Sébastien."

ISABELLE goes to rip the letter from LUCIE's hands.

ISABELLE   Give me that!

LUCIE   (*holding the letter out to ISABELLE*) See? I didn't make up or hide anything. It's all here, written on this paper.

ISABELLE   (*after having glanced at the letter*) Writing to you, Lucie! Asking you to do that! Wanting to use Maman's name! How disgraceful! And you, you should crawl back into a hole!

LUCIE   Before I crawl back into a hole, I could reply to Sébastien and give him the names he's asking for. But no, I won't do that. I would be too ashamed, you're right. Ashamed of myself. Ashamed of Sébastien. Horribly ashamed, as I've always been. Ashamed of my mother and my father. Ashamed of Aunt Nathalie… I'm ashamed of you too, Isabelle, of your sickly sweet airs and your lies.

ISABELLE   Leave me alone! Please, leave me alone!

ISABELLE goes to leave and then changes her mind.

The way you talk—you sound a lot like Aunt Agnès!

ISABELLE leaves.

LUCIE   That's not true!

Scene Five

LUCIE remains alone for a moment. FATHER BEAUMONT enters on the right. LUCIE jumps.

FATHER BEAUMONT   Hello!

LUCIE   Hello, Father Beaumont!

FATHER BEAUMONT   Hello. You didn't come to mass this morning?

LUCIE   No, I didn't go to mass this morning. My father and Isabelle went. And then, that's the communion of Saints, the economy of salvation, the reversibility of grace, as it says in your books. There are people who go to mass for those who don't go. There are people who are ashamed for those who have no shame. There are people who are wicked for those who are sugary sweet. There are people who are really jealous for those who pretend to love. Isabelle plays at being in love, and I'm jealous. There you go! Everyone does their part, and the universe unfolds as it should.

FATHER BEAUMONT   Perhaps we should accept as many people as possible, love as many people as possible, stretch open our horizons to embrace the world…

LUCIE   *(interrupting)* Drowning my family in a large noisy crowd—I'd like that well enough! But I'd have to learn to breathe. I'm short of breath, and the more people I accept, the harder it is for me to breathe. It's a little as if my family were expanding endlessly. Look, a few months ago, I didn't know my cousin Isabelle and I didn't know you either, Father Beaumont. And, in fact, there are moments when I don't like you at all, neither you nor Isabelle. Oh no! Not at all, not at all!

FATHER BEAUMONT   That's too bad. Isn't hatred the risk we take when we are charitable? Hatred and love—what if they are just two sides of the same coin?

LUCIE   People never really get to know one another. We get just a glimpse of life here and there. My mother lets herself be crushed, just like anybody else. My father isn't there. Sébastien acts the brute. Isabelle puts on airs. And you, Father Beaumont, you persist in keeping your priestly secrets. And as for me, my own life is so knotted and intertwined with everyone else's lives that it has formed a matted tangle that I want to pull apart with my teeth.

FATHER BEAUMONT   Perhaps you have to learn to see each tangled thread separately, in the light?

LUCIE   I would like it sometimes if you would answer me like a real priest: Wham! Wham! Without reflecting, in a snap, the right answer to the right question, like for the multiplication tables. Affirm very quickly that you are sure of God, of men, of the order of the world. I want someone to be sure of something and to tell it to me straight to my face.

FATHER BEAUMONT   Last night, I read a truly remarkable sentence and I thought of you when I read it. *(The priest takes a sheet out of his pocket.)* "The only possible proof that water exists, the most convincing and the most utterly true proof, is thirst."

LUCIE   *(after a grave silence)* That's beautiful.

FATHER BEAUMONT   Man's thirst is also beautiful and terrible. The greatest scandal in the world would be if water did not exist.

LUCIE   Do you believe in Christ, Father Beaumont, in the depths of your heart, down where the multiplication tables don't apply?

FATHER BEAUMONT   I believe in the thirst for God, and with all my strength, I call that proof that God exists. *(silence)* Did you bring me your Latin translation and analysis?

> *LUCIE hands her notebooks to the priest.*

LUCIE   Here.

> *The priest leafs through LUCIE's notebooks.*

Good. I'm going home. *(silence)* Father Beaumont, do you find my cousin Isabelle pretty?

FATHER BEAUMONT   Pretty and so fragile. There is really no reason for you to be jealous, I assure you. You, Lucie, you are as tough as the earth and as strong as thirst.

LUCIE   Thank you, Father Beaumont. I seem to be breathing better now.

> *Black.*

> *Set Three. The same day. The living room.*

Scene Six

> *FRANÇOIS is singing softly to himself. ISABELLE arrives and looks for some records.*

FRANÇOIS   "My heart is untrue…" Bah! I can't remember the words or the tune!

ISABELLE   Oh! It's you, Uncle! I thought you were upstairs. You're the one singing!

FRANÇOIS   It's an old song that I've forgotten. I can't seem to…. But where has Agnès got to? I don't understand it. She never leaves her armchair these days, and here she has gone off with the children.

ISABELLE   Capucine and Marie managed to get her to go for a walk by the river. It's so nice out!

FRANÇOIS   I don't understand it. Agnès, who obstinately refuses to budge, has gone for a walk by the river? No, no, that's not it. She knows that I can't stand it when the house is empty. I'm sure she's done it on purpose.

> *ISABELLE searches through the records.*

When I came out of church a while ago, I had a sudden urge to sing; it hit me like a wave of joy. But it's gone now. I'm starting to drink again. I've already broken the promise I made during mass.

ISABELLE   You promised not to drink anymore?

FRANÇOIS   It seemed easy to stop drinking at the time. I felt miraculously at peace with God. But the other side of this peace is Agnès's terrible reprobation.

No, I can't bear it. I drink to escape both God and Agnès. I can't please one without displeasing the other. And the more I drink, the guiltier I feel. I'll never break free of it. It's a vicious circle. Agnès is right; I am doomed to remorse.

ISABELLE puts on a jazz record.

ISABELLE   Life is full of evil spells. What can we do?

FRANÇOIS   Happiness comes at a price. The happier we are, the more we are punished, that's for sure. So I am very careful not to allow myself to be happy. It might have been better if you'd never come here, Isabelle. Everything has become so complicated since you've been here.

ISABELLE   Don't worry, I'll leave as soon as I can.

FRANÇOIS   Isabelle, sometimes I'm so happy that you're here. But it's very difficult. It's as if you have higher expectations of me than I can fulfill. And then…. No, go away. Simply knowing that you're here, so secret and pure, makes me feel so humiliated!

ISABELLE   Why are you speaking to me this way? No one here knows me. I'm a stranger among you.

FRANÇOIS   It started before you arrived, Isabelle. As soon as I knew that you were going to come, I wanted to erase the past. I wanted to start everything afresh: I wanted to become a brave man, a man who had a job and who was respected. I wrote to the School Board. I'm waiting for their answer. But I'm terrified, and I wish that I had never written that letter.

ISABELLE   You want to become a school teacher?

FRANÇOIS   I went to teacher's college and I have the required diplomas. But when it comes to the children in this house—I could barely teach them to read and write. Agnès set them loose on the mountain at a very young age, telling them that real life was not to be found in books. Just try to compete with the glamour of the river and the forest. I was left there, with my arms full of numbers and words, while the children grew up in total ignorance, like weeds, like wild ferns. Agnès would tell me time and again. How could I go to work every day, go out in good weather and bad, with this pain inflaming my knee at every step? And what if the misery in my heart crept into my face? How could I hide it from the schoolchildren? When you're a teacher, children watch you all the time. Sometimes, I have to hide or I would die of shame. Here, I can hide whenever I want. I can hide for days on end, without anyone knowing whether I exist or not, without my even knowing it myself. I can lock myself in my room upstairs. I read, I sleep, I dream. I don't move.

ISABELLE   *(as if speaking to herself)* Well, personally, I've seen a lot of things in books and in life. When I was a boarder at the convent, I would study and pray. But, during the holidays, I would read all the novels that I could get my hands on. Maman wasn't strict and would forget all about me when we had visitors, when we were at the beach, in the car, in the sitting room. I was a little witness of no importance. Grown-ups never hesitated to talk in their own language in front of me, and I very easily picked it up. Soon they were letting me in on all their secrets. They claimed that I was a precocious child, and they showered me with compliments and caresses. I pretended to be one of them, but in my heart, I was locked up like a prisoner that nothing could touch.

FRANÇOIS   Isabelle, you mustn't talk about all that.

ISABELLE   I have to tell: nothing good or bad has ever affected me. I know life, all of life, and yet it's as if I had never lived. Look at me carefully, (*She moves closer to FRANÇOIS.*) more closely. Touch my face if you want. Can't you see that there's nothing to see? I'm as smooth and soft as a corpse. Sister Agathe used to say that you could read right to the bottom of my eyes, like a clear spring. (*ISABELLE puts on another jazz record.*) I remember. It was just at the end of the holidays, after a summer of sand and water. Like a little sun-burnt Tom Thumb, I had followed my mother, who was the colour of ochre and honey. She would change men the way you change a shirt. One would give me candy; another would kiss me; another would throw stones at me. And I remember two women sitting on the sand, talking about a child that was not to be born. Sister Agathe took me to the chapel. She told me that I prayed like an angel. It wasn't true! I never prayed at all! I thought about nothing. That's how I was: I was nowhere, with no one. Look carefully at my face; do you see anything? A shadow of sorrow, perhaps? No, no, there's nothing. Isn't that so? Oh, I hide myself well. I can reflect whatever people want me to be, at will. Look—with you, Uncle François, it's easy: it's a little like with Sister Agathe. I act like an angel and I go to mass because that's the way you want me to be in your dreams.

FRANÇOIS   Isabelle, please stop!

ISABELLE   You're right. Our hearts should stay asleep, buried under a rock. Why wake them? (*ISABELLE turns off the record player.*) And what if the truth is hidden down there too? It would leap up at our faces, like a ferocious animal kept locked up all day. A scratch of a claw here, a bite of a tooth there, and we would be ripped apart.

> ISABELLE cries.

FRANÇOIS   Don't cry, Isabelle.

ISABELLE   It was fun to pretend that I was receiving letters from Sébastien. Capucine believed it, and so did Marie. They promised me that they wouldn't say anything to my aunt. When the two little girls would look at me, I would feel as if I were wearing a halo, as if I were truly a very mysterious girl, a sort of heroine. But your daughter Lucie knows how to expose people, and she won't put up for long with people deceiving themselves.

FRANÇOIS   Lucie is an uncompromising and brutal girl.

ISABELLE   And what about me? What am I? What am I doing here?

FRANÇOIS   Isabelle, your music is rattling my bones. Why are you playing such barbaric noise?

ISABELLE   Was the song you were singing earlier any better? *(She says slowly.)* "My heart is untrue…"

FRANÇOIS tries to recall the tune, and then gives up.

FRANÇOIS   Bah! I can't remember it anymore. There's no use trying; what's lost is well and truly lost, don't you think?

ISABELLE tries to start the record player again. The record player starts.

ISABELLE   What do you think of this music? Life is in order—a little too harsh perhaps? What a delightful wooden box of a room you have upstairs. With your books, your paper, a pen, ink, a place at the family table, enough to eat and drink guaranteed! She owes you that much, that imposing bitter woman that you served so loyally while she was bearing your children.

FRANÇOIS   Isabelle, stop it, please! You're mocking the unhappiness of this household!

ISABELLE   The unhappiness of this household? What if I were to make up a song about it? A song for Uncle François?

ISABELLE sings softly as the jazz plays.

"Beautiful marriage, the heart is untrue,
The black nanny lies, under pines
Where she spies
Loins expired,
So many kids sired
The old ram weeps, in the attic,
Where he sleeps."

FRANÇOIS   Isabelle!

ISABELLE turns the record player off.

Why are you singing such a cruel song? Please, be kind, Isabelle. Be good and generous. Help me no longer be a coward, help me be a man. No, no, don't look at me. I can't bear your looking at me.

ISABELLE   You have to look into my eyes and see if they are the way you want them to be, clear as a spring, as Sister Agathe used to say. Can you see for yourself?

FRANÇOIS leans his head on ISABELLE's shoulder.

(very gently) Please, Uncle François. I feel your grief in the depths of my solitude, like a stone that I want to melt in my two hands. Rest easy, Uncle François. Rest a bit.

FRANÇOIS closes his eyes with fatigue.

FRANÇOIS   What is Agnès doing, that she isn't back yet?

ISABELLE   *(to herself)* My God! What am I doing here? Why did she come and get me? As soon as she laid eyes on me, Aunt Agnès looked at me like a witch, summoning all her powers to project one single image onto my face. Despite myself, everything in me that resembled my mother bunched up in my heart like a withered bouquet. And I threw that bouquet right in my aunt's face. How I wish that people would look at me and see me for myself, for what I am in the very depths of my being—alone and unique in my closed heart.

> *ISABELLE buries her face in her hands.*

Scene Seven

> *FRANÇOIS is asleep. SÉBASTIEN's voice can be heard from a distance calling "Isabelle!" SÉBASTIEN climbs the stairs of the veranda. He is at the door.*

SÉBASTIEN   *(calling)* Isabelle! Isabelle!

ISABELLE   *(thunderstruck)* Sébastien!

> *ISABELLE goes to the door.*

SÉBASTIEN   *(very awkwardly)* You see, I've come back.

ISABELLE   *(also ill at ease)* You've come back!

SÉBASTIEN   The city is suffocating after a while.

ISABELLE   The city is like salt water: it carries you along, you don't know where, but it moves. You are swept along despite yourself. Whereas here, it's like fresh water…

> *SÉBASTIEN enters the veranda.*

SÉBASTIEN   Isabelle, you mustn't tell anyone that I am back.

ISABELLE   It's a secret?

SÉBASTIEN   A secret? If you want.

ISABELLE   A secret. Good. That's fun.

SÉBASTIEN   I've come back for just a few days. I'm staying at Bertrand's place. You know, it's set back a little from the road, a log cabin, under the trees, near the wood ovens.

ISABELLE   Did springtime lure you back? The river, the open lakes, the fishing perhaps?

SÉBASTIEN   The river is very high. It's magnificent. Isabelle, I wanted to see you, to talk to you.

ISABELLE   You wanted to talk to me? All you have to do is confide in Lucie, she'll pass on your message, you can be sure of that!

SÉBASTIEN   Lucie told you about the letter I sent her?

ISABELLE   Lucie had me read the letter you sent her.

SÉBASTIEN   I'm sorry about the letter. I think I needed to get back at you. You had poisoned my freedom in Montreal. But as soon as I had put my letter in the mail, I felt so much regret, I had such a desire to see you again, that I left.

Awkward silence.

I've been prowling around outside the house since this morning. I wanted to see you, but not the others. Try to get away this afternoon, or tomorrow, or the day after tomorrow. I'm here for a few days. Don't say no right away. Think about it. Please, don't say no!

ISABELLE   Your mother and your sisters will be back any minute.

SÉBASTIEN   They're off walking beside the river. But you, Isabelle, you were talking to my father for so long, I thought you'd never finish.

ISABELLE wants to go in. SÉBASTIEN holds her back.

You'll find some way to get away, won't you, Isabelle? I'll be waiting for you. We'll go for a walk in the country, just the two of us. I have some new paintings to show you; they're very beautiful, very amusing, you know.

FRANÇOIS's voice can be heard calling.

FRANÇOIS   Isabelle? Where are you, Isabelle?

Beat.

SÉBASTIEN   I came back for you, Isabelle.

Beat.

ISABELLE   For me, Sébastien? Really for me? How strange! You're sure that your paintings are all that amusing? Well, I would like to go for a walk with you in the country, Sébastien!

ISABELLE rushes inside. SÉBASTIEN moves away. In the living room, FRANÇOIS is worried. ISABELLE comes in, very animated.

FRANÇOIS   But where have you been, Isabelle? Please don't leave me alone. I feel so very lonely.

ISABELLE turns on the record player.

ISABELLE   What lovely music, don't you think? It stills my heart, like a storm that washes everything clean, even its own echo!

Scene Eight

AGNÈS, HÉLÈNE, MARIE and CAPUCINE come back in. AGNÈS turns off the record player.

AGNÈS You can hear the music blaring out of my house from a distance: it sounds like a black voodoo shanty. And I had forbidden anyone to play that wild record. But you, Isabelle—you think you are beyond my rules.

AGNÈS drops the record, which breaks.

ISABELLE Too bad; one record more or less doesn't matter to me. I have my whole life ahead of me, my whole life!

ISABELLE leaves.

AGNÈS What an exasperating walk! We had to make a number of detours through wet grasses. The lower fields are all flooded.

FRANÇOIS My God, Agnès, that was such a long walk! I thought that you'd never get back!

AGNÈS You know that I am always here, that I could not stop myself from being here, like the earth itself. And that I dream of interring you all, like black soil, in the depths of my heart.

LUCIE, who is entering, listens carefully to her mother's last sentence. She drops a book that she is holding. AGNÈS looks at LUCIE.

Black.

ACT FOUR

*It is summer. A hot and humid day. The atmosphere is suffocating. Set
One. Bertrand's cabin. Hunting and fishing gear. Paintings hung on the
wall. In one corner, an easel with a portrait of ISABELLE.*

Scene One

SÉBASTIEN and ISABELLE are embracing.

SÉBASTIEN   Isabelle! How beautiful you are!

ISABELLE   For a month, since you returned, you've been hiding out here at
Bertrand's: for a month I've been coming here, every day, and I have been yours
completely. You know it well…. And before you, there was no one.

SÉBASTIEN   It makes me crazy with joy and pride to be your first. Look at me.
You are beautiful.

ISABELLE   What good does it do me to be beautiful if you want to leave me.
(pause) And if I asked you to take me with you, to Montreal?

SÉBASTIEN   And if I didn't want you to come.

ISABELLE   I know that you need me.

SÉBASTIEN   I'll learn to get by without you.

ISABELLE   *(shyly, earnestly)* And if I loved you, Sébastien?

SÉBASTIEN   I wouldn't believe you, Isabelle.

ISABELLE   And if you loved me, Sébastien?

SÉBASTIEN   I would act as if nothing had happened, and I would leave as
decided.

ISABELLE   Ah! how bitter it is. For so long I was imprisoned in the darkness of
my heart, and you have pulled me out toward the light. I am living for the first
time. Please don't abandon me.

SÉBASTIEN   Hush, Isabelle.

ISABELLE   Didn't you tell me: "I came back for you. I could no longer live
without you, but no one else must know that I am here."

SÉBASTIEN   I told you that. And it was the truth. But now I have to leave.

ISABELLE   Leave! That has been the only word on your lips since the first instant
I saw you, the very night that I arrived at Aunt Agnès's.

SÉBASTIEN   If I stay here a single day longer, the forest, like a disease, will reclaim
me. This afternoon I spent hours paddling down the river. I shot the Gouge
rapids. I was soaked. My canoe was bobbing like a cork. The slightest lapse of
attention, and I would have been crushed on the rocks; the slightest false move,

and I would have been thrown overboard. But I was in complete control. And I won!

ISABELLE   Weren't you happy?

SÉBASTIEN   Perfectly happy, and I told myself: "This is it, this is real life."

ISABELLE   And with me, Sébastien?

SÉBASTIEN   With you, I am too happy. I mistrust that victorious peace going to my head. If I am to succeed, I have to remain armed and at war. My stay in Montreal was a failure. I want to go back there, the way one retakes a failed exam. I want to work. To prepare a showing. To sell my canvases. All my canvases. I'll come back. But not before, you understand.

ISABELLE   No, I don't understand. What does it mean, "to succeed"? Doesn't it mean to do what you love with the greatest passion possible?

SÉBASTIEN   Do what I love? That would be too easy. It means to make a choice and to go to the very end of where that choice leads you. You, you take my breath away, and you want to chain me to your skirts.

>   *ISABELLE goes to the easel.*

ISABELLE   Look! This is me! Me, as seen by you, as expressed by you! And I was half the inspiration when you were painting this canvas. Would you dare to say differently? Without my colour, without my form, would you have painted with such joy?

SÉBASTIEN   I am proud of that canvas, just as I am proud of your face and your body, Isabelle. But that's something else. You remain you. And my painting is me. It is my pleasure, with my paints and my brushes. When one day an art dealer pays me very handsomely for that pleasure, it will be like selling a fine pile of furs to Chatillon.

ISABELLE   I don't understand! I don't understand! When I say "you," I'm not thinking about possessing you so that I can turn you into something else, a painting that will sell well. I love you as you are, flesh and bone. It pleases me that you are you, irrevocably you, Sébastien, even if you are a monster. And I don't care if I ever succeed at anything, as long as you take me and hold onto me.

SÉBASTIEN   Anger gives you a spark and a fire that I haven't seen in you before. Come close to me.

ISABELLE   I don't understand! A boy and a girl who feel about each other the way we feel about each other, with such joy, is it possible that one day, they will part like strangers? *(pause)* If you leave me, I will die, Sébastien.

SÉBASTIEN   I'll be back. You know very well that I'll be back.

ISABELLE   It will never be the same. We'll be old, both of us. And I don't want to wait. One day, you will see me arrive in Montreal, at your place, and I will sleep in your bed, all night, like a real woman that you hold onto, and not like a girl that you chase away after making love to her.

SÉBASTIEN   Come, Isabelle. Let's go swimming. Enough arguing for one day. The river is so close by. Come.

ISABELLE   You won't make me change my mind so easily, Sébastien. Listen. You can't leave without me. I know the city, that milieu you dream of. I will help you. There will be two of us working together to succeed.

SÉBASTIEN   It's strange, Isabelle, but I cannot separate you from life here. I protect myself from you the same way I protect myself from the forest I love. You are part of the landscape of my childhood. And you are too much like the women in my family—you are my cousin and my family. I need a new life, a fresh life, do you understand?

ISABELLE   That image you have of me, I want to shatter it like a mirror! And you can go swimming alone in "your" goddamn river! As for me, I've known other far more pleasant beaches, and the ocean, so alive and cleansing. Good night, Sébastien.

ISABELLE makes a movement to go. SÉBASTIEN calls her back.

SÉBASTIEN   Isabelle!

ISABELLE turns.

ISABELLE   Before you "succeed," as you say, perhaps you should learn your craft, practice a bit, let your work mature. Your would-be master, the *Douanier*, contemplated his primitive paintings for a long time before he presented them to the public. As for you? Do you even have a talent for painting? You would do well to question the authenticity of your genius, instead of playing hard and ambitious. You dream of glory. At heart, you are nothing more than a dreamer, like your father!

SÉBASTIEN   Get out! Get out, Isabelle Simon, daughter of Nathalie Simon! Get out!

ISABELLE exits running. After a second of hesitation SÉBASTIEN follows after her.

(calling) Isabelle!

Black.

Set Two. The living room. The veranda. The same day.

Scene Two

AGNÈS is sewing. CAPUCINE and MARIE are sitting on the steps of the veranda. HÉLÈNE is cleaning green beans. On the veranda, LUCIE is reading.

AGNÈS   There hasn't been a summer like this for a long time. A lot of the wells in the village have gone dry. And the dust from the road reaches all the way up here at times, like a burning shower that stings your eyes and irritates your throat.

FRANÇOIS passes through like a tormented soul, entering from the right.

FRANÇOIS   And this storm! Will it never break! I've been feeling it in my leg!

FRANÇOIS goes into the house.

AGNÈS   We are lucky to live on the mountain. Three gushing fresh springs feed our well. But we have to be careful, manage the water as if there were none left. You never know. Every day I check the level in the well. It has hardly gone down, despite the drought. And Isabelle! What's she up to that's taking so long?

MARIE   Isabelle promised to bring us back some lemons from the village.

AGNÈS   These girls are crazy. They have to have lemonade at any cost. Even if it means dying on the road from the dust and heat. Ah, I hate these days, so still, white, and chalky. That invisible sun consumes you to the bone. I can endure it no longer. I am going to walk a bit.

AGNÈS moves off.

HÉLÈNE   And if someone comes from the village to ask us for water?

AGNÈS   *(turning)* What a bizarre idea! You know perfectly well that no one ever comes up here. And anyway I forbid that you talk to people.

AGNÈS leaves.

HÉLÈNE   Isabelle is taking her time, isn't she! She's been gone for two hours now!

MARIE   Every day it's the same thing. Isabelle disappears all of a sudden, like a shadow. Do you think she's studying with the new priest, like Lucie?

HÉLÈNE shrugs her shoulders.

Well. I'm going to take a dip in the river. Are you coming, Hélène?

HÉLÈNE   No, not right now.

MARIE   Too bad for you. Well, I'll go alone.

MARIE exits right. AGNÈS, very agitated, returns from the left.

AGNÈS   I've just seen a man heading over towards the well. When I approached, he disappeared into the forest.

LUCIE descends the stairs and approaches the pump.

LUCIE   He was probably coming to get water, that man. It is no accident that Agnès's well is perched on the foothill of the mountain. You cut off the people of the village from their source of water. In ordinary weather, no one cares. But with this drought, isn't it natural for them to come to draw from your well?

AGNÈS   I don't allow people to come onto my property, not for water, nor for anything else. That man disappeared into the woods. He was moving cautiously, like an animal following a track and masking his trail behind him.

LUCIE   It was probably the Michaud's son. I already gave him water yesterday.

AGNÈS   You already gave him water, yesterday?

LUCIE   The boy was very thirsty. You can't drink the water from the river, you know that. And the Michaud's well has been dry for two days now.

AGNÈS   The Michaud boy! How dare you offer a drink to that roughneck, and against my orders?

LUCIE leaves.

Scene Three

A pause. ISABELLE appears. Her hair is wet, as if she has just come out of the water. She is trying to slip into the house. AGNÈS sees her.

AGNÈS   *(in a weary tone)* Where are you coming from?

ISABELLE   From the village.

ISABELLE tries to pass. AGNÈS calls her back.

AGNÈS   Isabelle! I asked you where you are coming from!

ISABELLE   From the village. I already told you.

AGNÈS   And did you forget the lemons?

FRANÇOIS is listening attentively.

ISABELLE   I forgot everything except for the mail, since Uncle François has been waiting for a letter for such a long time.

AGNÈS   I too have been waiting for a letter for such a long time. You seem to have forgotten.

An awkward silence from ISABELLE.

You spent the afternoon at the post office, I suppose?

ISABELLE   Of course not! My hair is still dripping wet; my dress is sticking to my skin. I've just come out of the river; I'm sunburned and covered in sand. When kissed, I grind beneath the teeth like spinach. And I can still taste the sun lotion and sweat of the boy who was kissing me a few moments ago, by the river. And so it is!

AGNÈS   What are you saying?

FRANÇOIS   Isabelle, my darling little girl. My prettiest girl is being insulted and offended!

AGNÈS   Isabelle, I want to know. Who is this boy?

ISABELLE   I beg your pardon, Aunt Agnès…

AGNÈS   Who? Tell me, I want to know! Who?

> *ISABELLE is silent.*

ISABELLE   Leave me alone. I want to go in, to change my dress.

AGNÈS   Isabelle, listen to me, look at me!

> *ISABELLE tries to enter. AGNÈS holds her back.*

You are my daughter. You are going to hear me out whether you want to or not. That boy you are talking about is nothing but a coward who preys on children.

ISABELLE   Ah! The only thing I regret is that I did not keep my secret. But my heart is suddenly so full that I can no longer keep silent. My life is bursting in my veins and I have to speak. I am tired of keeping silent; I am tired of sneaking out, I am tired of going about on tiptoes; I'm tired of hiding my joy and my grief. I can no longer bury my face in my hands.

> *ISABELLE hides her face in her hands. AGNÈS approaches ISABELLE, who uncovers her face and looks at AGNÈS.*

AGNÈS   *(softly)* You have a fever; you have to rest. *(pause, almost in a whisper)* His name? Tell me his name.

> *ISABELLE is silent.*

(in an outburst) The first one to come along, a peasant, a vagabond, a woodsman! What shame! What misery! And yet I should have known. For a girl like you, no place in the world is really deserted. You'd make men pop up on the moon. Your heat, your smell, like bread fresh out of the oven, you are just like little Nathalie, who was lost…

ISABELLE   Ah! You shouldn't have said that, Aunt Agnès! You shouldn't have! Too bad. You are going to know everything. The name of the boy… it's Sébastien…

AGNÈS   Sébastien! That's not possible!

ISABELLE   Sébastien is back!

AGNÈS   *(echoing)* Sébastien is back.

> *ISABELLE moves off a little.*

ISABELLE   He told me that he would be coming home, tonight…

AGNÈS   Sébastien is coming home, tonight! My son will deign to visit me, like the bishop on a tour of his country parishes. And why didn't he come here immediately? And when did he arrive?

ISABELLE   A month ago! And I have been seeing him every day at Bertrand's and…

AGNÈS   A month ago! And you, Isabelle, you've been seeing him every day! Oh! Heaven is taking care of us, no doubt.

> *ISABELLE disappears into the house. She enters the bedroom on the right.*

Scene Four

> *AGNÈS finds herself face to face with FRANÇOIS. She sits down. Outside the children disperse.*

AGNÈS   I pushed Isabelle to the limit. I wanted to know. For a while now, I've had a feeling that she was hiding something from me. I wanted to know. And now I tremble as if I had brought down the wrath of heaven on our heads. The shamelessness of that child stupefies me and the confession of her love tears at me as if I had suddenly become conscious of the only good in this world. Isabelle and Sébastien! No, it is not possible. I would like to be able to close my eyes, to see no more, to hear no more, to understand nothing of what has been going on here.

FRANÇOIS   It is too late now.

AGNÈS   Too late, why?

FRANÇOIS   Too late to close your eyes, too late to see no more and hear no more, too late to understand nothing of what has been going on here. Too late for everything. Too late for Isabelle to become a child again. Too late to stop her from being happy or unhappy without you. Things have started to happen and to be said without you. And once that starts, it will never finish.

AGNÈS   Damned be he who first dared to shatter the silence of this house!

FRANÇOIS   From the beginning, I have done no more than complain feebly in words that ring incoherent and vain. But Lucie, even when she was small, dared to see the truth and took pleasure in naming it insolently and precisely.

AGNÈS   And that has made me fear her, in a way that we should never fear our children. For such a long time I chose to remain confounded before the mystery of this world. I preferred to remain ignorant and dark, buried in my vast maternal night. Sébastien left me without a word. He imagines himself to be a man because he is playing at being a man with that little girl, Isabelle. But I know that he is only a child, and what he fears more than anything in the world is to find himself face to face with me, his mother. And Isabelle is tumbling, bound by the wrists and ankles, into the arms of that selfish, headstrong little boy. Ah, life is a mess! I am so weary, so weary…

FRANÇOIS   Agnès, catch up to them at the edge of the savage storm, these children that you have delivered into the occult powers of this dark, fallow land. You imprisoned them in ignorance and silence. And now, questions and answers are bursting forth on all sides.

AGNÈS   Ah! I wanted my little ones so badly! I was no more than a little girl, without milk or breasts, and already it seemed to me a battalion of children was calling out from my veins. Five times I flowered in tears and blood. One son and four daughters, my flesh and my bones. And then I found Isabelle, a replacement for Nathalie. Isabelle, so fragile and vulnerable that I believed I could be her strength and her very will. Ah! I wish winter would reign forever, with the house closed up and my heart its only fire.

FRANÇOIS   And me? What about me? You forget me, your pitiful servant. And yet without me, you were growing sterile and dry like a pile of thorns. Say, do you remember, when you told me that you wanted to become my wife, you added: "Take me as I am, without love, and give me lots of children; that is the only way that I will agree to go on living." Can you say it once, just once, that I saved you from despair and death? Agnès, my wife, say it, please?

AGNÈS   Be quiet, please. Be quiet.

FRANÇOIS   I am speaking of these things now, for speech has begun to pull the secrets from my heart. Since Isabelle has been here, I only have to nod to her, and she listens to me and understands me. She tells me the frank truth about myself. My life has become clearer and more terrible.

AGNÈS   Isabelle has nothing to do with our pitiful story.

> *Cries of birds. AGNÈS puts her hands over her ears.*

The whippoorwills!

> *FRANÇOIS starts to speak as if recounting an old story.*

FRANÇOIS   The nights are short in July. The whippoorwills sometimes cry out until morning in the middle of the village. Do you hear? It's a strange little note that stretches out and beckons, oh so much like the voice of desire in the night.

AGNÈS   I cannot abide that bird's cry.

FRANÇOIS   There are things like that, sometimes, that we cannot abide. Tiny little things which once occurred precisely when our lives were being marked by some important event. A bird's cry in the night, a flower in the chintz curtains. And then, when these little signs return, we are so afraid of reliving the event which lies buried at the bottom of our memories, that our ears ring and our hearts tighten. Memory is terrible when it rises on the horizon like a surging tide.

AGNÈS   Be quiet, I beg of you, be quiet!

FRANÇOIS   Summer, what a strange season, all the same. We were married in the summer, Agnès, do you remember?

AGNÈS   Leave it, my poor François. It's no use, I assure you. All that is very far away, packed away, lost, finished.

> *Cries of birds.*

FRANÇOIS The whippoorwills. You can see that the past is near, palpable and harrowing. Memory has opened up like a chest full of ghosts. Nathalie, what a radiant little girl. She stole your heart with both hands, as if it were nothing. One day, that little girl had no one in the world but her big sister Agnès.

AGNÈS One day I, the plain daughter, took my little sister with me. I raised her, lavishing affection upon her as if she were my first-born. But Nathalie's childhood passed like a breath of wind. One day, the ingenuous child took her older sister's fiancé, just like that, for no reason, just to take and to be taken, for she was made to take and to be taken.

FRANÇOIS You remember? The weather was like it is today; heavy and stifling. Whippoorwills filled the night. I followed you everywhere like a lost dog that refused to be chased away. We entered the house on Rue Saint-Marc together. Little Nathalie was just finishing dressing. Your fiancé was looking for his cufflinks under the bed.

AGNÈS No! No! I assure you I didn't see any of that. Why are you tormenting me, François, my husband?

FRANÇOIS Say it, once, Agnès, my wife, just once, that I saved you from despair and death!

AGNÈS What importance can that have? I never had but one idea in my head: this big house, lost in the country, that I dreamed of buying and filling with a brood of savage and pure children.

FRANÇOIS And little Nathalie? You left her, lost, far away from you, like a mad-woman left to her madness?

AGNÈS I loved her nonetheless, that little girl. But by the time she was twenty, she had already betrayed me with everyone and anyone. I fled from her the way one flees from treason and evil. But Isabelle is something else. She is taking my son away from me, and yet, it's strange, I can't bring myself to bear her a grudge. I tremble at the life I see ahead of her, because I know Sébastien.

FRANÇOIS Sébastien is as you have made him, and you can be sure of Isabelle's future unhappiness, without your having to intervene.

AGNÈS What has come over you? Not only are you reawakening the past, poking at old wounds, but you are busy interpreting what doesn't yet exist, in that vague region of my soul where certain thoughts may never form? Would you be a charlatan and a clairvoyant as well?

FRANÇOIS A small prophet, a very small prophet of unhappiness, only of unhap-piness. (*pause*) And I followed you up into the mountain. I married you. I loved you like a simpleton.

AGNÈS You speak well, for a simpleton. What has come over you?

FRANÇOIS   It's Isabelle; she speaks to me and listens to me. Because of her, I see myself for the first time, and I see you as well. Soon, I will judge life blind, this life that caused us to be born impoverished and wicked.

Scene Five

ISABELLE comes out of her bedroom, a letter in her hand.

ISABELLE   Uncle François, I forgot to give you this letter.

ISABELLE gives the letter to FRANÇOIS, who is troubled. He turns the envelope in his hands but is unable to open it. AGNÈS, and then ISABELLE, suddenly seem very intrigued by the letter.

FRANÇOIS   *(to himself)* It's from the School Board! I would like to pretend this letter was not addressed to me. Is there not some way for things not to be as they are? Who can stop this letter from existing, from having been written and addressed to me? I beg God to erase the request that I wrote with my own hand!

FRANÇOIS reads the letter. ISABELLE tries to slip away. AGNÈS holds her back.

AGNÈS   Do I have to ask you where you are going?

ISABELLE   You know very well, Aunt Agnès. And where I am going, Sébastien is waiting for me. And we will return here this evening. To say our goodbyes. Both of us, together.

AGNÈS   Watch yourself, Isabelle. That boy is an ingrate. Nothing good can be expected of him.

ISABELLE   *(as if summing up her whole life)* When a girl who has never lived, like me, discovers her life, and when that life has Sébastien's handsome face and Sébastien's hard heart, it is too late to turn back. The life of that girl will be as it will be, no more, no less.

FRANÇOIS   My request for a teaching position has been refused!

AGNÈS turns, astonished, toward FRANÇOIS.

AGNÈS   You applied for a teaching position?

FRANÇOIS tries to stop ISABELLE from leaving.

FRANÇOIS   Isabelle, stay. Please. I would like to speak to you. Here I am in the depths of despair. You can't abandon me now, you who have already started to listen to me and to understand me so well.

ISABELLE   I would like you to be happy, Uncle François. If you only knew how I would like it. But I can only wish it, just wish it.

ISABELLE slips away and exits from the house.

Scene Six

FRANÇOIS   I am all alone here. Well, let's dream a good one. And real life can go hang itself.

> *FRANÇOIS starts to climb the stairs. AGNÈS, who has remained disconcerted since ISABELLE's departure, suddenly seems to become aware of FRANÇOIS's distress and tries to call him back.*

AGNÈS   *(calling without turning around)* François!

> *FRANÇOIS stops climbing for a moment.*

They refused you a teaching position, you, my husband?

> *AGNÈS, overwhelmed by her thoughts, remains with her back to the stairs.*

François! François! Listen! Come down! I have to talk to you about… about Isabelle… about that teaching position.

> *During the last of AGNÈS's speech, FRANÇOIS disappears up the stairs.*

You know, that little sentence that you begged me to say a moment ago? Well, I am going to say it now. Listen, please. (*She murmurs with great difficulty, as if FRANÇOIS were still behind her and she did not dare to look at him.*) "One day, it is true, you, François, my husband, you saved me from despair and death." It is the truth. Listen. Now, or never. I need to say it to you now, that little sentence that is so difficult to utter. I am choking with that damned little sentence stuck in my throat. François, come down quickly, or it will be too late. François, I cannot stand to be alone any longer with that poisonous little sentence weighing on my heart.

> *AGNÈS turns and realizes that FRANÇOIS is no longer there.*

François!

Scene Seven

> *LUCIE enters.*

LUCIE   Maman. Father Beaumont would like to ask you something.

AGNÈS   *(very wearily)* Father Beaumont? And what would he want, that man?

LUCIE   Permission for the Michauds to draw water from our well, and something else of great consequence…

AGNÈS   The Michauds! Ten children, the mother, the father, the grandmother, their dogs, their cats, not to mention the stable and the hen house. Do you want to see our well run dry?

LUCIE   There's enough water in that well for ten generations of humans and animals.

AGNÈS   All the better, and I am proud of it. Thanks to that well, I feel as though I am controlling the springs of the world. And that is a reassuring feeling.

Scene Eight

FATHER BEAUMONT enters.

AGNÈS   Ah! It's you, Father Beaumont.

FATHER BEAUMONT   *(very ill at ease)* I didn't come here willingly. But your daughter Lucie has asked me to intercede with you on her behalf.

AGNÈS   So my daughter Lucie needs someone to "intercede" with me on her behalf? Can't she speak for herself? Like a daughter speaking to her mother? What is it then that my daughter Lucie wants that is so important? But have a seat, Father.

FATHER BEAUMONT   Here before you, Madame, and before your daughter, I can no longer find confident words or present a serene facade. And I am bone weary. This heat is killing me. I didn't sleep last night. All night I kept vigil with a dying man who would not let life go and who, in total fear and agony, demanded that I promise him eternal life.

AGNÈS   And so?

   Beat.

FATHER BEAUMONT   And so, I promised.

   Heavy silence.

AGNÈS   If you are lacking faith, you should no longer be a priest.

LUCIE   You are preaching despair, Father Beaumont. And I needed so much for you to be strong and help me. *(beat)* And yet, it's strange, I'm grateful to you for speaking to me as you are doing, without pretence or reserve. It is a bit as if someone were gently disarming me in the shadows.

   Silence.

AGNÈS   It is about permitting my neighbours to supply themselves with water from my well, isn't it? It is also about allowing my daughter Lucie to pursue her studies at a college or at university?

FATHER BEAUMONT   Yes, that is it.

AGNÈS   And so, make your requests in the name of Christ, Father Beaumont! Hurry up!

FATHER BEAUMONT   I make these requests in the name of your daughter Lucie, and in the names of those poor people, your neighbours, and in my own name as well…

AGNÈS Ask in the name of Christ, Father Beaumont. Use your prerogatives. Appeal to the heart of an old woman who was baptized long ago. You have to force my hand. Don't forget it!

> *Silence.*

FATHER BEAUMONT I cannot. I assure you that I cannot. No, no, I cannot.

AGNÈS How softly you make your confession, Father Beaumont. Each one of us in turn. When it comes to confessing our souls, you and I are even.

LUCIE But I am not even, not with anything or anyone. I will never be absolved. I must bear the burden of all the thirst in the world. And of this household, and of that large crucified woman who is my mother. The blow that I must deliver to her, in order to live. I am leaving.

AGNÈS You are leaving. As if I hadn't always known it. Since we first met, was there ever a question of anything else between us? Cursed be whoever let the light shine on us. But who would dare to convict me, the mother, of having sinned?

Scene Nine

> *SÉBASTIEN enters with ISABELLE.*

AGNÈS And you, Sébastien? Why did you leave the house like a thief? And why have you come back with Isabelle? You want me to bless your childish love affairs?

> *SÉBASTIEN makes a gesture toward his mother. LUCIE rapidly intervenes and eyes her brother scornfully.*

LUCIE You, Sébastien, a free man? You are only an emancipated slave. There are so many women in the world outside this family, and you become infatuated with your little cousin!

> *SÉBASTIEN attempts to respond. We hear "You, Lucie," "My favourite sister," "Bittersweet girl." SÉBASTIEN's words are lost in the cries and mad rush of MARIE and CAPUCINE entering.*

Scene Ten

> *MARIE and CAPUCINE, calling—Maman! Maman!*

AGNÈS And you, little ones, what do you want? Couldn't you enjoy this summer day quietly? What do you want then? No doubt permission, you as well? Have you come to claim your lives ahead of time, so that I can learn early on to get by without your little faces?

MARIE We need a big bucket to give water to the Michaud boy!

FRANÇOIS descends the stairs

AGNÈS And you, old man? What do you have to ask of me? Perhaps you want boundless love, unblemished and unbroken, til death do us part?

A little boy appears on the veranda with two buckets.

And that one, who is he? What is he doing here, the little urchin?

MARIE That is the Michaud boy who went to get two buckets.

AGNÈS *(exploding)* The Michaud boy! Show him in. And have a seat as well, Father Beaumont. And you too, Sébastien. And Isabelle too. As you can all see, my home is open to all, grand central station, a game of chance, a bazaar, or who knows what, an open market where everyone takes whatever their thirst tells them to take.

LUCIE Your house is being violated and there's not a thing you can do about it.

AGNÈS continues in a sort of delirium of power slipping away from her.

AGNÈS Who can stop me from regaining control of the very source of my life? To re-establish the order turned to havoc by fleeing deserters. To organize once again a strong season without fever or desertion. To be my absolute mistress. To seal the doors and windows. To take back all the keys to the world and keep them on a little ring on my belt.

Silence. AGNÈS, with her gaze, inspects everyone. No one moves except HÉLÈNE, who seems to be feeling great compassion for her mother.

Ah! There you are Hélène! As reliable and steady as the table. That comforts me. And you François, what are you doing then, so still and silent?

FRANÇOIS is silent, lost in his thoughts. LUCIE notices the little boy who has not moved.

LUCIE You are still here, lad? Go quickly, the well is in the yard.

LUCIE pushes the little boy outside. AGNÈS addresses FRANÇOIS but she knows very well that she is speaking to herself, from the bottom of her solitude.

AGNÈS François! We will have lots of time to talk, when the children have gone…

Black.

The end.

Playing Double
(Double jeu)

by Françoise Loranger

translated by Louise H. Forsyth

Introduction to
Playing Double (Double jeu¹)
by Françoise Loranger
Introduced by Louise H. Forsyth

Playing Double is a two-act play with fourteen characters: a night-school teacher and thirteen students. Dyne Mousso, whose unique acting career reflects her close association with members of the revolutionary Refus global group, played the lead role when it was first produced on radio in 1969, the same year she first played the single character in Marie Savard's *Bien à moi*.² Both plays were directed by André Brassard. *Playing Double* is a play of protest against the stultifying impact on individuals and society of unexamined conformity to received ideas and conservative values. It is an experimental, multi-media play making extensive use of screen images (five screens on stage), original music, and multiple stage areas. Created as a play within a play, it presents a group of adult night school students improvising on a short text previously handed out by their teacher. Its themes, reflecting the revolutionary spirit of the 1960s with its emphasis on personal freedom and responsibility, challenge compliance and submission to authority in behaviour. The students' improvisation leads most of them to overcome personal fears and inhibitions and so to generate energy as strong individuals and members of a dynamic group. The energy comes from inner depths, communion with the natural world, and collective spirit. However, much of the play dramatizes the students' reluctance to get involved. The dramatic conflicts arising out of this reluctance underline the central message of the play, which is that necessary change will never occur if individuals, diminished by unacknowledged docility, remain passively on the sidelines of society's affairs. The unspoken despair of their humdrum and meaningless lives will continue unless they are prepared to take risks and speak out.

Produced to encourage spontaneity and audience participation, *Double jeu* took its innovative form as a result of Loranger's and Brassard's shared excitement about experimentation as it was showing its avant-garde self throughout Western theatre. Brassard's extensive notes, which include detailed indications of how he directed the play and how it subsequently evolved during its run, were published with the play text and are included in this translation. During their collaboration in preparing the show, Loranger and Brassard travelled to New York to meet with members of the Living Theatre, a young experimental and socially engaged company they particularly admired.³

The Living Theatre appealed to Brassard and Loranger because of its radically new approach to theatrical aesthetics, its disturbance of the lines of demarcation between actors and audience, its challenge to audiences regarding norms for theatrical reception, as well as its aim to provoke social change. Brassard has recently written about the influence American popular culture and, specifically, the Living Theatre had on his director's approach for *Double jeu*: "I incorporated [into *Double jeu* by Françoise Loranger] much of what had seduced me in the Living: to bring spectators up on stage and integrate them into the performance, to ask actors to recount moments in their lives or to force these brave actors to go into the audience, to introduce themselves and to shake hands."[4] Loranger, who similarly hoped to see an explosion of experimental plays in Québec, wrote in "Au lecteur": "This is just a first, still timid attempt at new theatrical forms born out of the research being done by different groups around the world, particularly the Living Theater of New York. It goes without saying that much more in this direction remains possible."[5]

The students' assignment in *Playing Double* is to improvise on the teacher's handout wherein a young woman catches sight of an unknown young man and immediately falls in love with him. She is determined to reach him at all cost. In order to do so, she must cross untamed natural landscapes: a dense forest, a raging river, and a slimy swamp. She can reach her goal only if she manages to convince a hermit, a ferryman, and a surveyor to assist her. At each dangerous stage, there is a price to be paid. The price involves revealing to herself and to others her body and her unrecognized desires, fears, inhibitions, and strengths. As she chooses to pay each successive price, she engages in a process of discovery: her own beauty and that of the natural world, the strength of community, and the joys of a life fully embraced. The play challenges directly many received taboos, including those surrounding women's sexuality, and makes a particularly powerful attack on the apathy of those who refuse to run the risk of getting involved and who give themselves permission to criticize those who do dare to jump in.

The play advances simultaneously on two stage areas, a central circular riser and the larger stage, that is, on the dual sites of the classroom, where the students respond with varying degrees of reticence and excitement to the challenge of improvising, and of the river, where the characters in the teacher's text play their roles. Gradually, the students are drawn more and more willingly into the story and consent to open unacknowledged doors of their own lives. The student in her 30s who plays the young woman of the sketch comes to make a full commitment to the creative search for self, freedom, and agency. She begins the play as the docile and fear-ridden fiancée of the one student who adamantly and violently refuses to be drawn into the improvisational project. When he scornfully rejects her at the end because she is so "dirty" and now so morally sullied by having discovered the legitimacy of her own desires and the beauty of her own body, he is excluded from the group and so excluded from moving forward with a freshly discovered shared sense of identity and power.

By this time, the young woman has cast off all sense of regret at the loss of her fiancé, her virginity, and her idealized image of romantic love. The meaning of love has been radically transformed, and a fresh ethical model has emerged. Love has become love of life and freedom, the right to pleasure and an embrace of each intense moment, with all its unexpected dangers and delights. Imagination, creativity, theatricality, physical experience have combined to show her to herself as strong and beautiful. Experimental techniques, music, multi-media technologies, and the participatory approach that is particularly developed in the second half of the play ensure that this recognition of one's own creative self, in a community ready to act on its collective behalf, is shared by everyone in the theatre who is willing to join in. Boundaries between stage and house, character and actor, actors and spectators melt away.

Songs are sung by some of the students throughout the play for each of the characters in the story: the woman, the hermit, the ferryman, the surveyor, and the young man. The songs, like the songs and poetry that burst forth in Québec in the 1950s and 1960s, resonate with a shared sense of belonging. They strengthen the characters and articulate the meaning they give to life. Most importantly, the songs are the vehicle by which the students come together into community. In supporting the young woman's passionate drive, they all, with the exception of the one fearful yet arrogant character who refuses to join them, find themselves moving forward together, removing obstacles, affirming their own identities and those they share with each other and with the audience.

Double jeu received considerable critical attention, in the form of both acclaim and condemnation. Many thrilled to its timely themes and exciting experimentation. However, in what seems to be an all-too-common response when women undertake artistic experimentation, there were many who denied its right to call itself experimental or even theatrical (see Tarrab). A particularly notorious moment, leading to criminal charges, occurred in what came to be called "L'Affaire Paradis" (February 15, 1969) on the penultimate day of the run when a small group of spectators, challenging the claim that the play was truly improvisational and participatory, undressed on stage and then proceeded to cut the throats of a couple of doves and a rooster.

Notes

[1] *Double jeu*. Montréal: Éditions Leméac, 1969, with Loranger's "Au Lecteur" at the end explaining experimentation and collaboration with Brassard and cast during discussions and rehearsals for the first production: 205–07. *Double jeu* was first produced by the Théâtre du Nouveau Monde at La Comédie canadienne in Montréal January 17 – February 16, 1969, directed by André Brassard, with Dyne Mousso in the lead role. *Double jeu* was one of the first plays published in Éditions Leméac's Collection Théâtre canadien which played a decisive role in the emergence of revolutionary new theatrical forms and languages in Québec in the 1960s. To the best of my knowledge, none of Loranger's plays, including *Double jeu,* has previously been translated into English.

[2] Dyne Mousso (1930–1994) was a widely admired professional actor for stage, cinema and television. Throughout her career, she engaged with others in the subversion of convention-bound theatre norms and oppressive social practices and discourse. Her sister was the celebrated actor Muriel Guilbault and her husband was

the famous artist Jean-Paul Mousseau, both of whom signed the explosive 1948 manifesto Refus global. Dyne Mousso also played the lead role in the first performance of Savard's *Mine Sincerely*. She and Mousseau were divorced before *Double jeu* and *Mine Sincerely* were produced.

[3] Information on Loranger's interest in the Living Theatre was provided in an email from Madame Danièle Michaud, daughter of Françoise Loranger (16 August 2005) to LHF. Madame Michaud remembers the lively rehearsals and performances, as well as the intense emotions that were transforming Québec theatre, and, in fact, all of Québec society at the time. The Living Theatre was founded in 1947 by Judith Malina and Julian Beck "as an imaginative alternative to the commercial theatre." It is recognized as launching the off-Broadway movement. In the 1960s the company toured internationally and "evolved into a collective, living and working together toward the creation of a new form of nonfictional acting based on the actor's political and physical commitment to using the theatre as a medium for furthering social change" http://www.livingtheatre.org.

[4] Brassard, André. "Mes deux chaises." *Cahiers de Théâtre. Jeu.* 114 (mars 2005): 106: "[…] j'ai incorporé [dans *Double jeu* de Françoise Loranger] beaucoup de ce qui m'avait séduit du Living: faire monter les spectateurs sur scène et les intégrer à la représentation, demander aux acteurs de raconter des moments de leur vie ou les forcer—ces braves acteurs—à descendre dans le public pour se présenter et lui serrer la main." Translation by LHF.

[5] Loranger, Françoise. "Au Lecteur." *Double jeu*: 206–07: "Ce n'est qu'une première tentative encore timide vers de nouvelles formes de théâtre nées des recherches de différents groupes à travers le monde, particulièrement le Living Theatre de New York. Inutile de dire qu'on peut aller beaucoup plus loin dans ce sens." Translation by LHF.

Bibliographical Suggestions

Selected Other Works by Françoise Loranger

Encore Cinq Minutes, suivi de *Un Cri qui vient de loin*. Montréal: Le Cercle du Livre de France, 1967. (Governor General's Award for Drama 1967.)

Une Maison ... Un Jour ... . Montréal: Le Cercle du Livre de France, 1968.

Medium saignant. Montréal: Éditions Leméac, 1970.

On *Double jeu* and Françoise Loranger

Dramaturges québécois II. Dossiers de presse: Françoise Loranger, 1949–1977. Sherbrooke: Bibliothèque du Séminaire, 1986. 29 pages.

Coates, Carrol F. "From Feminism to Nationalism: The Theater of Françoise Loranger, 1965–1970." *Traditionalism, Nationalism, and Feminism. Women Writers of Quebec*. Ed. Paula Gilbert Lewis. Westport, Conn. & London: Greenwood Press, 1985: 83–94.

Crête, J.P. *Françoise Loranger. La Recherche d'une identité*. Montréal: Éditions Leméac,1974.

Duciaume, Jean-Marcel. "Françoise Loranger: du théâtre libre au problème de la liberté." *Le Théâtre canadien-français. Archives des Lettres canadiennes*, Tome V. Montréal: Éditions Fides, 1976: 531–50.

Forsyth, Louise H. "Françoise Loranger." *The Oxford Companion to Canadian Theatre*. Ed. Eugene Benson & L.W. Conolly. Toronto, Oxford, New York: Oxford University Press, 1989: 311–13.

———. "Loranger, Françoise (1913–1995)." *The Literary Encyclopedia*. http://www.litencyc.com.

Godin, Jean-Cléo. "*Double jeu*." *Dictionnaire des oeuvres littéraires du Québec*. Tome IV, 1960–1969. Montréal: Éditions Fides, 1984: 274–75.

Marois, Thérèse. *Le Québec et la "Québécité" dans l'oeuvre de Françoise Loranger*. Thèse de doctorat de IIIe cycle. Université de Paris-Sorbonne (Paris IV). Centre International d'Études Francophones. 1984.

Tarrab, Gilbert. "*Double jeu*." *Livres et auteurs québécois*. Montréal: Éditions Jumonville, 1969: 65–68.

About Françoise Loranger

Françoise Loranger (1913–1995) was born in Saint-Hilaire and grew up in Montréal in a family that encouraged progressive ideas and ideals. Personal circumstances forced her to leave school at fifteen. She began writing short pieces of fiction in her teens and later published a successful novel, *Mathieu* (1949), in which her interest in theatre is evident and the struggles of a young experimental theatre company in Montréal figure centrally. The plot and dialogue of the novel reveal the intrinsic theatricality of her writing style and also illustrate the central theme of all her work: the quest for personal and collective identity and autonomy, in opposition to stifling and repressive social norms that impose conformity. Loranger began to write for radio in the 1930s. In addition to her prolific production of scripts, she became one of the first female radio producers in Québec. When television came in the 1950s she immediately recognized its creative potential for scriptwriters. In both radio and television, she was particularly successful in telling Québec's own stories to the people of Québec. She was a leading pioneer in laying the groundwork for the dynamic popular media culture that has characterized Québec for the past several decades.

The dilemmas facing the characters in Loranger's plays for the stage, all written and produced between 1965 and 1970, bring to life the urgent and controversial issues and events of the Quiet Revolution. Her bold and incisive dramatizations of difficult issues facing women and men in a society in rapid transition are unique. Productions of her work toured widely in the francophone world, receiving national and international acclaim for their innovative theatricality and bold thematics.

Loranger was an indomitable observer of the hardships worked in the lives of Québec people by dominant ideologies and monolithic institutions, particularly as they invaded the very minds and spirits of individuals, depriving them of self-esteem, filling them with fears of all kinds, condemning them to poverty, and paralyzing them to such an extent that they did not dare take control of their own affairs and assume their own freedom. Although she did not call herself a feminist, she was one of the first to pay particular attention to women's place in society, to subvert stereotypes about women that narrowly confined them in colourless roles as wives and mothers, and to represent women as complex human beings with the right to control their own destinies, including control of their bodies and their sexuality. As a writer of scripts for radio, cinema, television and the stage, she was a leading pioneer. In theatrical space she created robust characters who explored repressed dreams, performed acts and stories that revealed and subverted the discourses and sociocultural codes of behaviour that serve so effectively to keep individuals in narrow, pre-determined, alienating places.

Double jeu was first produced by the Théâtre du Nouveau Monde at La Comédie canadienne, Montréal, January 17 – February 16, 1969, with André Brassard directing.

Characters

THE NIGHT-SCHOOL TEACHER

STUDENTS:

No. 1	TEACHER (f.)
No. 2	TEACHER (m.)
No. 3	MUNICIPAL EMPLOYEE (m.)
No. 4	BANK CLERK (m.)
No. 5	MUSICIAN (m.)
No. 6	SALESWOMAN (f.)
No. 7	SECRETARY (f.)
No. 8	MOTHER/ HOMEMAKER (f.)
No. 9	LABORATORY ASSISTANT (m.)
No. 10	ASSISTANT LIBRARIAN (f.)
No. 11	HAIRDRESSER (f.)
No. 12	MUSICIAN (m.)
No. 13	ASSISTANT SOCIAL WORKER (m.)

A Note From the Translator

Stage directions in italics between parentheses are by André Brassard. They are based on rehearsals for the first production of the play. Brassard's occasional notes on changes made during the production appear as footnotes. There are also a few stage directions written by Loranger. These are given without italics between parentheses in the text.

Set

(*A classroom—An immense screen upstage—Four other screens, two on the left and two on the right, surround the stage and even extend out into the house—Downstage left, a row of lockers for students' use—Upstage left closer to the centre, THE TEACHER's desk and chair—On the right, four rows of chairs angled so they face the blackboard—Downstage centre, thrust halfway out over the stage, a round riser that serves as the acting area for the play within the play.*)

PLAYING DOUBLE

(While audience members take their seats in the house, the students take their places on stage.[1]

8 enters through Area C. She is alone. She crosses the stage to Area F, straightens the chairs, organizes the bag she uses to carry books and papers, erases notes from previous classes off the blackboard. She goes to THE TEACHER's desk [Area D], does some cleaning, empties the ashtray, tidies papers.

1 and 2 enter through Area C, 1 with a soft drink and 2 with coffee. They look at 8, whom they catch rummaging through THE TEACHER's notes. They cross the stage and take their places in Area F, take their seats, and begin a conversation.

10 enters. [All entrances, with the exception of THE TEACHER's, are made through Area A.] She goes to her locker, removes her coat, crosses the stage, takes her place. She rummages in her bag, takes out a book [Mémoires d'une jeune fille rangée by Simone de Beauvoir], begins immediately to read, underlining the passages which interest her. 8 leaves THE TEACHER's desk and returns to her place in Area F. She sits down, picks up her bag, takes out paper and pencil, returns to sit close to THE TEACHER's desk [Area E].

5 and 12 enter. They hang their coats, boots, etc. in the lockers [Area B]. They exit through Area A and reappear almost immediately, 5 carrying his guitar and 12 an amplifier. 6 enters at the same time [Area A], puts her things in her locker, then all three cross the stage to Area G. They set themselves up there, plug in their instruments, and quietly rehearse the songs they will have to play and sing later. 8 stands up and returns to her place in Area F in order to hear them at closer range. She says "Good evening" to them as she goes by.

---

[1] *Director's Note*: These entrances occurred roughly at two-minute intervals, except on those evenings when the number of spectators forced us to speed up or slow down the rhythm. Right from the beginning, the audience should have a sense that, except for a few, the students would like to communicate with each other but none of them is able to break the ice. So they don't go beyond "Good evening," timid smiles, and a few mundane exchanges. The order of the entrances was modified from the fifteenth show on and varied every evening after that so the actors would constantly question their assumptions about the way their character related to the other characters.

13 enters[2], takes his bag to his place in Area F, crosses back toward the group in Area G, and watches the musicians with an obvious desire to strike up a conversation. 1 and 2, in order to get away from the "infernal racket" of the music, leave their places and move in front of THE TEACHER's desk in order to continue their private conversation.

3 enters. He goes toward 1 and 2 in order to strike up a conversation, but 2 draws 1 upstage. So 3 joins the musicians in Area G. After 3 moves away, 1 and 2 come back to their previous position at the corner of THE TEACHER's desk.

A few moments later, 9 enters timidly. He crosses the stage, stops briefly in front of the musicians, does not dare join them, takes his place in Area F. He takes his class notes out of his bag and begins to read them.

3 looks at 1 and 2, then moves to sit down on the chair beside THE TEACHER's desk, with the obvious intention of catching at least some of their conversation.

11 runs in, afraid she is late. She hangs her coat in her locker, takes a mirror, lipstick, etc. from her purse, moves quickly to fix her make-up [at the end of the lockers where there is a mirror], returns to her locker to put everything away, runs across the stage to take her place with the other students. She is bubbly and vivacious. Although over thirty, she would like others to think that she is twenty.

When the actors are ready to start the show, 4 enters and places his coat and boots in his locker. He takes a few steps toward THE TEACHER's desk, then stops, looks at the students and turns to face the audience. House lights go down and the action begins.)

ACT ONE

(Timidly, the students introduce themselves to the audience with the kind of discomfort people show when they must speak in public or on television for the first time. For some [9, 10] a slight panic precedes the moment when they have to speak; others [3, 5, 13] are more brash; but all of them show great humility, as if they were unable to see how what they have to say could be of interest to anyone.)

4   We are…. We are a night class. Late-comers to the world of education…. A sort of proletariat of higher knowledge. The sacrificed generation, the one that never received anything and didn't even know how to ask.

---

[2]   *Director's Note*: When 13 enters he removes his coat and boots and places them in his locker. From now on each student will do the same. This will not be explicitly indicated in every case.

(7 enters late, discreetly takes off her coat. 13, 11, 8 take their positions on the riser.)

Life seemed to have forgotten us. But one fine day education became all the rage, and people began to look at us out of the corner of their eye. And to talk about us!… In newspapers, on the radio and television.

(1, 2, 3 take their positions on the riser, 1 and 2 face to face. She is very shy; he reassures her. 7 takes her position.)

People everywhere in Québec were telling us we're ignorant. They were ashamed of us. They called us a disgrace because we didn't even know how to speak properly. They said that if we wished to remain French, we needed an education. And we had better get one as quickly as possible!…

(5, 6 and 12 take their positions on the riser.)

We were ashamed of what we are. What was being said forced us to come out of our holes. People like us came into sight from all over.

(10 and 9 take their positions on the riser.)

The young, the old, people from the city, from rural areas, all ages, all classes, all professions.

7   28 years of age—married—born in St-Paul d'Abbotsford—secretary at the University of Montreal.

13   I'm 38—a bachelor—from the Gaspé—assistant social worker.

8   46—married—never left Montreal—mother and housewife.

3   Born in Chicoutimi—40 years old—married, separated for 6 years—I've had more jobs than you can think of: lumberjack, prospector, dock worker, I've worked for Price Brothers, Consolidated Paper, Wayagamak, International Paper, Clarke Steamship, Canada Steamship, Gaspé Copper Mine, and that's not even the half of it…. Needless to say, I'm bilingual. Been in the city for 6 months, work for the Montreal Parks Service.

5   24—bachelor—born in Montreal—musician.

11   30—married—I'm from Montreal—hairdresser.

4   43—married—three children—assistant bookkeeper at the Caisse populaire Notre-Dame des Sept Douleurs.

12   22—bachelor—born in a village in the Beauce—musician.

6   23—unmarried—I come from Drummondville—saleslady in a bookstore.

10   35—unmarried—born in Sherbrooke—assistant librarian in a CEGEP.

9   29—bachelor—I come from the Abitibi region—lab assistant.

2   35—bachelor—born in Joliette—grade 5 teacher.

1   *(When she speaks she always smiles, because she's so afraid people might think she's not a nice person.)* 32—unmarried—from the country—elementary school teacher.

4   Ordinary people, union members, low-income wage earners—the great, middle-class herd. We aren't the spoiled children of the new generation; protests aren't yet our thing…. Life has made us so reasonable that we are always ready to understand whatever comes our way. We believe things happen in their own sweet time and all you can do is wait.

(1 and 2 turn to face the audience.)

2   Well! Just let me tell you I'm more ambitious than that. I don't intend to waste all of my life in a fifth grade class of boys! I'm planning to move on to high school teaching and even university later. Getting ahead in the world is what matters most to me. And in addition, my fiancée thinks the same way I do…

1   Well…. Let's just say…. I'm less ambitious but… *(severe look from 2)* He's right to think about his future. He's right!…

11 I work in a large beauty salon. A very classy salon! I decided to go back to school because I'd like to open my own salon one day in a good neighbourhood, with high class customers…. My husband is taking accounting courses. That way he'll be able to manage our finances. We have two children and we want to be able to give them a good education. The best!…

13 I'm not interested at all in diplomas. I'm just auditing this course. I'm dating a school teacher, and I want to be as well-read as she is. Culture is important. That's the way I'll get a better quality of life.

10 I got caught up in the enthusiasm of the young people at the CEGEP where I work. It hooked me on going to school. I'm an idealist. *(embarrassed laugh)* I'd like to get to know the other students here too…. But we don't hardly ever speak to each other!

5   I'm taking this course just in case it turns out I can't make a living as a musician when I'm older. But it's hard for me. Studying is a drag. I don't know how long I'm going to be able to stick it out.

8   I have older children at CEGEP. They'll be going to university soon. I know that if I want to be able to speak their language I'd better go back to school.

9   I need more credits. Otherwise, I'll just be an assistant all my life. That's why I'm here. I want to do something with my life.

6   Do something with my life.

9   It's important to me to do something with my life.

12 I want to do something with my life.

7   It's important to me to do something with my life.

3   Well, of course I think it's important to get an education, but really my purpose in coming to night school was to meet people. I'm a little disappointed, because, when you get right down to it, we spend our time studying and we don't get to know each other. And I'm the kind of person who likes to talk, communicate with other people. *(quick look at 1)*

4   They've given you their most obvious motives, but there are others that matter a lot to us and that are hard to put into words. Like for example…. Yes…. We want education to… we expect it… we hope it will free us from everything we're afraid of. One day we want to be able to introduce ourselves without blushing, to just say what we are, to be completely what we are. It would be good to finally be able to accept ourselves…. Yes, that's what we want more than anything else. If not for ourselves, for our children…

11 That's what we want more than anything else, if not for ourselves, for our children.

7   Yes, that's what we want more than anything else.

13 If not for ourselves, for our children.

8   If not for ourselves, for our children.

>   *(A pause. They look at each other. Then they take the following positions: 9 and 10 sit back down in their places in Area F. 5, 6, 12 move to Area G. 7, 4, 8, 3, 13, 11 form a group between Areas G and H. 1 and 2 break away, isolate themselves beside the desk. 2 is always the one who initiates their movements; 1 follows him. As soon as 4 and 7 have joined the group in Area H, 3 takes the lead.)*

3   Should we start?…

11 Start what?

3   The test! That's what we're here for.

4   I don't know what to think about this great test.

3   I don't either.

7   No one knows.

8   It's a behavioural test. The teacher asked us to find a way to work on it, together.

4   But the class isn't used to working on its own.

13 We don't know each other very well…

>   *(Suddenly there's a silence. The conversation between 1 and 2 can be heard. All the students turn to laugh at them.)*

1   (to 2) I don't know any more what my life would be like without you…

8   Except for those two.

13 Our lovebirds.

11 They've already been together for three years.

7 They're supposed to get married soon…

3 Well, I'm not so sure about that… not so sure…

4 And you can bet he'll be the one to decide.

8 She'll go along. She always does. [3]

THE TEACHER Good evening!

> (*THE TEACHER enters through Area C. He is quite young, appears warm, open, empathetic; he dresses as fashionably as he can. In a word, he is a "sporty" guy. He goes directly behind his desk in Area D, takes papers out of the briefcase he was carrying under his arm. 5, 6, 7, 11, 12, 13 return to their places in Area F. 8, 3, 1, 2 all hope to be able to have a personal conversation with THE TEACHER, for various reasons: 8 because she wishes to be the favourite, 3 out of friendliness, 2 because he believes himself above-average and so deserves the special attention of the TEACHER, 1 follows, 4 stays where he is because he does not have time to go to his place.*)

1 Sir…. About the test, you know…. Not one of us feels we understand it very well.

3 We tried to talk a bit about it…

2 It didn't help.

THE TEACHER (*downstage, left corner of the desk*) Maybe my explanation wasn't clear enough?

> (*2 comes toward THE TEACHER. All of 2's remarks should imply that he thinks he is superior, even to THE TEACHER, whom he is always trying to show up.*)

2 Let's just say…. These characters of yours…. I can't believe in them!

> (*1 moves close to 2. She is always more or less attached to him and serves as a buffer during discussions.*)

1 You go too far.

2 It's impossible for me to identify with any of them.

1 (gently mocking) Not even with the YOUNG MAN?…

2 Perhaps the YOUNG MAN…

4 Well, I like the HERMIT better.

> (*No one pays attention to him. His sentence falls flat.*)

---

[3] *Director's Note*: Cut during production.

3   (to THE TEACHER) You have to admit it's a strange test.

2   *(moves away toward Area M)* I really don't see where it can possibly get us.

THE TEACHER   But…. It won't get us anywhere!

> *(2 turns back toward THE TEACHER. The class, which has been following the conversation with interest, has a strong reaction of astonishment. Students do not understand; some even grimace to show displeasure, as if to say: "Does he think we're nothing but a bunch of fools?")*

At least not right away.

2   If it's not supposed to be useful to us, why are we doing it?

THE TEACHER   *(speaks to all the students through him)* I told you this test could be an interesting personal experiment for each of you. It will probably help you know yourself. Isn't that enough in itself? *(2's reaction makes THE TEACHER turn back to him)* Or maybe that's precisely what you're afraid of.

2   That's not the issue here.

1   *(joins 2 and sticks close to him as she did before in an effort to reconcile the two parties)* Rather it seems to me we just don't know what to do with it…

THE TEACHER   Pretend it's a game. *(He moves toward the riser so that he can speak to both the students in Area F and those who are closer to him. The students: "He's crazy." "He's treating us like children," etc. but others: "Let's hear him out." "Let's see where he wants to go with this.")* Why not? The test is made up of five characters. Try to see them in your mind's eye, or better still… play the parts. Turn it into a sort of psychodrama…

1   *(with almost childish enthusiasm)* Actually, that could work.

THE TEACHER   Each of you choose the character that suits you best and play the scenes one after the other. The material I handed out to you contains all you need to know about the problem.

> *(The students go toward their places to find the handout, move to take it out.)*

4   If someone read it again, maybe that might help us?

THE TEACHER   Good idea… why don't you…[4]

4   Me? Uh! Okay… *(After taking the handout from his bag, 4 stands at his place to read. 11 moves toward the blackboard in Area G to write down the characters of the test as they are named.)*

---

[4]   *Director's Note*: To keep the performance alive and the actors ready for improvisation, it was decided for the last two weeks of the show that THE TEACHER would choose a student to read the test, and another student, never the same one, would go to the blackboard to draw the diagram of the test.

DIAGRAM OF THE TEST

(To be drawn on the blackboard and to remain visible throughout the show as a guide to the action.)

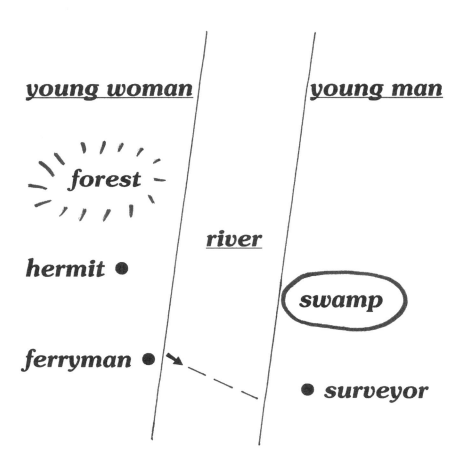

4   One day a YOUNG WOMAN sees a YOUNG MAN on the other side of a river. She falls in love with him. She sets out immediately in search of a boat to go and find him. After walking for a long time in the forest she meets a HERMIT and tells him her story. The HERMIT refuses to lend her his boat and advises her to forget this YOUNG MAN she does not even know. The most he is willing to do for her is to tell her where to find the FERRYMAN…

2   Any normal young woman would have stopped there, it seems to me.

THE TEACHER   (to 8) Carry on…

> *(4 sits down. 8 stands up, steps forward and continues the reading.)* [5]

8   The YOUNG WOMAN goes to see the FERRYMAN, who refuses to take her across the river unless she accepts… (hesitates, embarrassed) unless she accepts to take off all her clothes in front of him…

> *(Laughter from the class. These are nervous laughs coming from people who are uncomfortable when they have to deal with situations like those evoked in the test and with the words used in it to describe these situations.)*

2   Is that all?

8   She accepts!…

1   (to 2) Out of love!

3   For the YOUNG MAN!

1   Yes!

THE TEACHER   Please continue. [6]

8   …and the FERRYMAN takes her to the other bank where she meets the SURVEYOR whom she asks to guide her through the swamp which still separates her from the YOUNG MAN. The SURVEYOR refuses at first, but after hearing her story he agrees to guide her on condition that she let him make love with her… *(sits down)*

2   This just keeps getting worse!

THE TEACHER   Oh, please! (to 13) Continue…

> *(13 takes the handout, stands up, and continues the reading.)* [7]

---

[5]   *Director's Note*: During the last two weeks of the show, another student, never the same, continued the reading.

[6]   *Director's Note*: Lines were cut during production from 1's "Out of love!" to THE TEACHER's "Please continue."

[7]   *Director's Note*: During the final two weeks, THE TEACHER selected a third student.

13 She accepts. And there she finally is in front of the YOUNG MAN whom she loves, and to whom she recounts all the difficulties she has had to overcome in order to reach him. But the YOUNG MAN looks at her with disgust and rejects her, saying that he wants nothing to do with a woman like her. *(sits back down)*

> *(Reactions from the students. They all start talking at once. THE TEACHER stops them.)*

THE TEACHER   Listen, I sense all of you have something to say about this test. You find it disturbing. But I must insist that we start by acting it out. Are any of you prepared to live this experience, rather than just talk about it?

> *(They all freeze when this question is asked. They were ready to discuss but not to act. Embarrassed silence. A few seconds later, 1 moves forward. She takes the plunge, somewhat boldly. There is a naive innocence about her.)*

1   I'll do it.

2   *(surprised and shocked)* You?

1   *(with an apologetic tone)* Yes, I'd like to.

3   So would I.

> *(3, who is in Area M, moves toward Area J. We should feel that if 3 agrees to play a part it is, of course, because he is a "doer", but also because he sees this as an opportunity to get close to 1.)*

THE TEACHER   The characters in the test can help you understand your own outlook on life. Keep a record of which ones you prefer as you get to know them better. That record of your preferences will probably be a fair reflection of your own behaviour.

> *(Turns to the audience. He will continue throughout this part of the scene to alternate between addressing the audience and addressing the students, as if they were all in the class.)*

At least, this is true for right now. Of course, you can always make changes in your life.

2   But…

THE TEACHER   The search for self-knowledge. Come on now. People have been saying "Know thyself" ever since Socrates. It must have some kind of importance. *(addresses the following lines to 2, who disagrees and wishes to make his case)* All the more so at this point in our evolution when human beings must increasingly find ways to live together…

> *(13 stands up and moves forward. He has been trying for a while to get THE TEACHER's attention. He believes he has a question THE TEACHER will be unable to answer.)*

13 But, Sir, if, increasingly, living together is what counts, why should we worry about knowing what's going on inside each of us?

THE TEACHER Well, it's precisely to avoid slipping into group think. To remain an individual within the group. *(speaks to all the students in Area F)* If you expect to continue, or even to start—as the case may be—to think for yourselves, you must first know who you are. If for no other reason than to know at least who is thinking when you think.

> *(During these lines 1 and 2 move upstage to Area M, backs almost turned to the audience. 13 sits down.)*

4 *(turns to address the students behind him)* Isn't that brilliant?! Obviously, when I think, it's… it's me who's thinking!

> *(4 is the joker of the group. While he is speaking, THE TEACHER moves to stand in front him.)*

THE TEACHER (friendly tone) Yes, but who are you?

> *(Surprised, 4 turns to THE TEACHER, unable to respond to his question. Laughter from the class. The laughs die down. In the silence, a part of the conversation upstage between 1 and 2 can be heard.)*

1 (speaking to 2) It's not that simple!

> *(THE TEACHER moves toward 1 and 2, who turn toward him.)*

THE TEACHER No, it's not that simple. [8] And of course this test doesn't claim to resolve the problem. But it can help you understand at least one facet of your personality. And that's a start.

Okay, who's willing to take part in it?

2 Here and now?

THE TEACHER Why not?

3 *(moves toward the corner of the desk)* I'm in.

1 *(timidly moves a little closer to 3)* Me too. (to 2) How about you?

3 *(moves downstage toward 1, speaks to her with sympathy and friendliness)* Do you want to be the YOUNG WOMAN?

1 I can try.

2 *(comes over to 1, speaks only to her and never to 3, whom he despises)* No, no, no! Why you?

3 *(moves toward 1 and 2)* Why not her?

2 It would take… it would take someone younger, it seems to me.

---

[8] *Director's Note:* This repeated line, "It's not that simple," was cut during production.

THE TEACHER *(to 1 and 2)* Think about what you just said! Age has nothing to do with this: neither age nor sex.

> *(Diverse reactions from the students. THE TEACHER goes toward them.)*

An old man can just as easily identify with THE YOUNG WOMAN as a woman can identify with the HERMIT, the SURVEYOR, etc.

> *(moves downstage, speaks to the audience)*

The five characters are there solely to represent the five most common human behaviour patterns.

1 (to 2) You see.

3 You'll do it?

> *(3 moves toward 1 who makes a move forward, but 2 holds her back.)*

2 Well, anyway, it would be easier to believe in, if it was a young woman.

1 Maybe he's right…

THE TEACHER I don't think so…

3 Is this jealousy or what? *(2 moves toward 3 but 1 holds him back.)*

THE TEACHER Well, no point in insisting.

> *(Moves closer to 1, 2 and 3 who separate; 1 and 2 go upstage toward Area M. 3 goes downstage to the corner between Areas J and L. THE TEACHER comes back to the students.)*

Who wants to be the YOUNG WOMAN?

> *(The following lines are spoken very quickly, may even overlap. The audience should have an impression of reticence in all the women, except 6.)*

11 What? Right away?

8 Here? Tonight?

10 In front of everyone?

7 It's very embarrassing!

6 No it's not.

13 It's just a game after all.

9 We have to do it.

12 You go ahead then!

10 Thanks but no thanks! Never!

8 No, not me! You?

11 No!

THE TEACHER   *(to 6 who is having a discussion with 7, with her back to THE TEACHER, 6 stands up)* You, perhaps?

6   Me?

THE TEACHER   You would certainly have the right look for the job, since they think that's important.

ALL   Yes, yes, yes, yes!

> *(5 stands up and tries to convince 6, happy to have finally found someone to designate. They all display great enthusiasm for the songs that 5 and 6 have prepared.)*

It would be perfect.

4   She'd be right for the part.

13   They both really know the test.

8   They even composed songs for it.

4   They sang them to us.

> *(6 hesitates, slightly tempted, but finally sits back down. 5 does the same and teases her quietly.)*

6   I'm willing to sing, but not to act.

THE TEACHER   Who then?…

> *(The students all look at each other hesitantly.)*

Come on, make up your minds…

4   *(to 7 softly)* You could do it. I know you could.

7   *(tempted, but shy)* Do you think so?

4   Yes, yes, go ahead.

> *(She finally makes up her mind to do it, goes to the TEACHER, proud of having overcome her shyness. The students, surprised but impressed, comment quietly on her decision.)*

9   She's agreed!

11   How can she?

THE TEACHER   Bravo! It's important for you to not be afraid of exposing yourself in front of others.

> *(During the following speeches which overlap, 1 appears envious, 2 skeptical. 7 progressively loses her façade of self-confidence as she hears THE TEACHER's explanations and feels 1's envy.)*

9   Do you believe she'll be able to do it?

8   Why not!

THE TEACHER   (to 7) This experience will teach you a lot about yourself.

2   That I'd like to see.

THE TEACHER   Live it and, at the same time, observe yourself living it.

1   She seems quite intimidated.

THE TEACHER   I'm willing to bet you'll be a changed person afterward.

2   Isn't that encouraging!

THE TEACHER   What are you worried about? (*speaks directly, first to 2, then to the entire class*) Just think about it. You've already changed thousands of times since your birth.

10   She must feel silly!

7   I'm warning you, I'm just trying this out!… If I can't…

     (*THE TEACHER and 3 draw close to her.*)

THE TEACHER   Of course! (*speaks to the whole class*) We also need the HERMIT…. Who wants to be the HERMIT?…

     (*Another moment of indecision in the class. The TEACHER looks around. 3 would be inclined to participate, but since he does not like the HERMIT he prefers to wait until someone else volunteers. Finally, 4 makes a decision, stands up and is about to speak when THE TEACHER asks 2.*)

You?

2   No! Thank you very much! (*moves away to Area J*)

THE TEACHER   (*Even though 2's behaviour is beginning to get on THE TEACHER's nerves, he forces himself to maintain his good humour.*) Not again!

1   What are you afraid of? (*joins 2 in Area J, the same friendly teasing*)

2   (*2 is not endowed with much of a sense of humour. For these lines he should slow down his rhythm as much as possible, become pedantic in a way that gradually exasperates the entire class. 1 continues to listen to him almost religiously, trying to understand his point of view.*) There's that word again! I am not afraid, but there are only two ways of looking at it: either I am truly the HERMIT, and if that were so, I would refuse to show myself out of the woods, would I not? Or else, I am not the HERMIT, in which case all I would be able to do would be to make up his reactions and so distort the character. It's only logical…

3   (*crosses behind 7 and addresses his joke to the other students*) Hey! Will you listen to this smart guy talk when he's trying to explain why he doesn't want to jump in.

     (*Laughter.*)

2   You do it then, instead of pushing everyone else into the act!

3   Oh! I'm happy to. *(another joke, delivered after a brief silence)* If you don't think I'm too old.

1   Apparently, age isn't important.

THE TEACHER   Exactly. Let's go!

> *(It is finally possible for the action to begin. 5 and 6 get up, go to get ready for the song.)*

We'll find the other characters as we go along. *(goes toward 7 and leads her to the edge of the riser)* The test begins with you…. Take your lead from the material that was handed out. Have you read it?

> *(7 nods head affirmatively.)*

Okay, get ready to take the plunge.

> *(7 hesitates then goes up on the riser, moving to the centre. She is at a loss; she searches, increasingly upset. 5 begins to play the YOUNG WOMAN's theme on his guitar. 3 remains at the edge of the riser, ready to step in. 1 is fascinated. For the first time, she leaves her fiancé and draws close to the riser in order to follow the action better. 2 remains upstage, a skeptical and vaguely scornful smile on his lips.)*

7   *(to 3, after a time)* I don't know how to do it…

8   *(changes place and goes to take 6's seat, in order to see better)* She seems pretty discouraged.

11   If that's what the YOUNG WOMAN is like!

13   Not surprising the YOUNG MAN lets her go!

3   Not another word from the rest of you! *(goes toward the students with righteous indignation)* It's easy enough to laugh while you're sitting there on your backsides.

> *(They realize they are wrong, quit talking.)*

13   Well, she could have just said no!

3   *(goes back to 7, takes her by the shoulders)* Go ahead, try…. Think about the character, imagine you're the YOUNG WOMAN.

10   *(lower, because of 3's remark)* She's sorry she accepted.

9   She can still back out.

3   She's at the bank of the river, remember…

7   Oh! yes, the river, I'd forgotten…. Is it important?

2   *(unable to stand such stupidity any longer, feels compelled to intervene)* Of course not! You're getting her confused with these details!

THE TEACHER   (*walks all around the riser addressing the audience at the same time as the students*) Wait a minute! Wait a minute! The river is one of the essential elements of this test. The fact that you did not feel this proves my point that we in the West have lost touch with humanity's great symbols. Do you remember, a few years ago, newspapers from around the world published a photo of Mao swimming in a river with the members of his government around him?

> (*8 agrees from her place. She is the only one who keeps old newspaper clippings in a scrap book. THE TEACHER responds to 8's reaction.*)

The Americans made a joke of it; they saw it as nothing more than a sports event, the kind of show they see all the time, but the Chinese, like all Asians no doubt, understood the symbol right away.

8   (*agrees once again*) The symbol…

THE TEACHER   Mao with them in the river meant Mao with them in life… (*returns to his desk*)

3   In it together! (*speaks to 7*) You have to say that to yourself. At this time, we're all in it together. You're representing us, you're the YOUNG WOMAN in our place. We're beside you, but we're in there with you.

7   (*speaks to the students, who reassure her*) You won't laugh?…

3   Go ahead…. Try to imagine the river that's flowing. We'll try as well; we'll keep on trying until we see it… (*to 6 in Area G*) How about singing the YOUNG WOMAN's song for us? That would help us get started.

> (*During the YOUNG WOMAN's song, 6 slowly walks around the riser, directing her song to 7 who is trying to concentrate at the centre of the riser. 3 stays with 7. He encourages her with gestures and with looks. 1 also moves close to the riser. She listens closely to the song. We should feel her drawn in, perhaps even more than 7. THE TEACHER remains seated near his desk and observes events as they unfold. During this time, on the central screen, we can start to make out (as though in 7's imagination) the flowing river, imprecise, hardly visible at first, then more and more perceptible and soon violently tumultuous until the end of the scene. Lights go down and focus on the central riser. We should feel the communion that brings together 7, 6, 5, 3, 1 and THE TEACHER, who are concentrating in order to help her become the YOUNG WOMAN.*)

THE YOUNG WOMAN'S SONG

6   That's the way life goes
When you've just been born
That's the way life goes
This is about you.

Being there, nothing more
In this amazing world
Wonder of wonders.
Air, waves, earth, sun,
Your body is in harmony
With all that is
And takes pleasure in all.

(7 slowly goes downstage on the riser.)

Being entirely there
Present in this instant
In this moment of life.
You are there, you are you
Right or wrong
You feel good in your flesh
You feel good with yourself
You are the heart of the world
The centre of the universe

That's the way life goes
When you've just been born
That's the way life goes
This is about you.
Go with your life.

(6 withdraws slowly and rejoins 5 on the right side of Area H. This "Go with your life" is also sung by 3, 1 and a few students [11 and 13] who seem to have taken a sudden interest in the matter. [In fact, they are the first who are won over to the idea of acting.] During the song, the expression on 7's face changes from concern to the most complete well-being. At the end of the song, she has become the YOUNG WOMAN for an instant. She closes her eyes and finally imagines the YOUNG MAN on the other side of the river.)

7   He's there!

THE TEACHER   *(gets up and takes a few steps toward 7)* You can see the YOUNG MAN?

7   *(eyes still closed)* Yes I see him.

THE TEACHER   What is he doing?

7   He's reaching his arms out to me. I love him! *(opens her eyes)* I love you! He's going away! He's going away! No, no, no!… *(Perhaps because she said "I love you" so loudly and in front of so many people, because she sees the object of her love disappear so suddenly, or because she is thinking of the obstacles that she will have to face, 7 loses her nerve and ceases to be the YOUNG WOMAN. She leaves the riser.)*

11 She did it!

> *(Lights up on the whole class. The river disappears. 1, 3 and THE TEACHER rush to support 7. All the women in the class stand up, moved. At the same time 2 is delighted; he was right, it is not possible to go all the way with such an experiment.)*

10 She's still upset by it. *(sits down)*

1 It was real for me.

13 Well, I don't know.

> *(He would like to have a discussion about it, but THE TEACHER interrupts him. He too is somewhat overwhelmed. Because he is upset, he jumps in quickly to keep the action going.)*

THE TEACHER Let's wait until we know all the characters before we make any comments. *(to 3 and 7)* The HERMIT's scene…

3 I'm ready.

THE TEACHER Go ahead.

7 I don't know if I can…

3 I know you can.

7 That was more than enough!

1 *(1 goes to 7, draws her downstage left on the riser.)* But you did it so well.

7 I didn't think it would be so hard.

3 It's only a game, you know.

THE TEACHER Don't forget that the YOUNG WOMAN is exhausted when she gets there…

7 Why is she exhausted?

> *(Hesitation, then answers pour forth from the students.)*

13 The forest, she's crossed the forest.

1 We should do something to help her.

ALL What?

1 The forest, for example! We could actually watch her cross the forest.

ALL The forest?…

THE TEACHER   Why not? We'd be part of the story that way. [9]

1   Come on everyone! (to 7) You see, we're with you.

> *(All are now placed around the riser. 7 is alone in the centre. Silence. Concentration. Breathing in unison. Change of lighting [focused on the riser, not very strong]. Students begin by making sounds [wind, branches cracking, bird or animal cries]. 7 reacts. She slowly becomes the YOUNG WOMAN once again and begins to believe in the forest. She comes slowly downstage on the riser, then sets out on her trek through the forest. She starts by going around the edge of the riser. Obstacles rise up in front of her: branches, trunks, roots, thorns (represented by the arms, hands or legs of the students). The sounds grow increasingly menacing. 7 returns to the centre of the riser, turns around to contemplate the forest. At this point a few students go to the centre of the riser, filling it and rendering the forest more dense and terrifying. Frightened, the YOUNG WOMAN has a moment of panic and shouts "Help!" several times. Soon it is 7 who is asking for help. 1, who, up to this point was being a tree, sees that 7 is on the verge of giving up. She leaves her role as a tree and joins 7 at the centre of the riser. 1 holds 7 tight and both, strengthened by the presence of the other, become once again the YOUNG WOMAN who can now continue her crossing of the forest. They set out and circle the riser once again, this time passing through the various obstacles of the forest by moving them aside rather than going around them. Timidly at first, 7 helps herself move forward by shouting her love to the YOUNG MAN. Soon 1 joins her and we hear "I love you" spoken by 1, by 7, by the YOUNG WOMAN. This second turn around the riser completes the trip through the forest. 7 begins to speak of her exhaustion: "I'm dead tired." 1, satisfied and very moved at having been able to be the YOUNG WOMAN for a few moments, withdraws with all the other students. They return to their places, except 4 who remains close to the riser, very interested in the scene with the HERMIT which he would have liked to play, while 3, who has become the HERMIT, joins 7 [YOUNG WOMAN] at the centre of the riser. 1 remains close to 7 but off the riser. Lights up on the riser. The river appears on the central screen.)*

7   I'm dead…

> *(3 signals to 4 to bring a chair, which he installs upstage right on the riser. 4 crosses to the right of the riser. 7 sits down. While 7 recounts her difficulties, 3 paces up and down on riser.)*

---

[9]   *Director's Note:* Since we found this scene of the forest while we were working together, the actors had great freedom every evening to improvise the reactions of their characters to this suggestion and the particular way they would participate in the forest. The rule was simply not to show enthusiasm too quickly and not to continue discussion once positions had been taken around the riser.

Of course, 2 showed himself to be more reluctant than any of the others.

If you knew what happened to me… I walked all day…. First, I went along the river hoping to find a boat…

3   *(moves upstage on the riser, his back to the public)* She's going to tell me the story of her life. I can feel it. I know it.

7   And then I had to plunge into the forest…. Every step took me further from him…

3   *(moves to the left edge of the riser)* Women always have to tell you the story of their life!

7   I walked, I walked in the brush, in brambles, on paths leading in unknown directions…

3   Some even start crying…

7   Sometimes, I thought I'd drop from exhaustion! *(She stops speaking for lack of inspiration. 1 leans toward her and whispers in her ear. 7 picks it up again.)* But the very thought of him brought me new strength…

3   *(returns downstage on the riser)* Why should I have to listen to her?

7   *(gets up, starts to move downstage)* So I set out again and again I fell, I hurt myself, I was dying of hunger and thirst… I shouted, I called for help…

> *(3 turns toward her, moves upstage past her, looks at her scornfully, leaves the riser, goes to join THE TEACHER near his desk.)*

No one came! So I kept on going…. Absurdly…. And now, my strength is all gone… *(Surprised by the lack of response, 7 turns around and sees that 3 has left. Seized with panic she wants to leave the riser. The river goes out on the screen. Lights up.)*

Where did he go?

1   *(comes to 7, as well as THE TEACHER)* Keep going, keep going!…

THE TEACHER   Don't stop!

7   But he's gone!

3   *(comes to 7)* Oh! How stupid! It's my fault!

13   *(from his place)* She shouldn't have got so upset.

> *(The scene among 7, 3, 1 and THE TEACHER is interwoven with reactions from the other students. Everything should flow together seamlessly.)*

7   You left me all alone!

3   Well yes! It seemed normal to me that the HERMIT would grab the first opportunity to get rid of this YOUNG WOMAN who's bothering him…

8   She's over-reacting!

3 If I'd known it would have such an effect on you…

4 Besides that, weren't you making him seem like someone out of a cartoon?

3 Do you think so? It's so out of character for me.

10 Maybe it was too difficult for her?

1 She should have called him back! That's what the YOUNG WOMAN would have done!

3 That's all I was waiting for to come back…

13 All she had to do was to say no.

7 *(starts to move back to her place, stops at the centre)* I thought… I'm not the YOUNG WOMAN…. It's possible to make a mistake! *(goes to her place and remains standing there)*

9 I hope they're not going to stop there. It's important to keep going.

ALL It's important to keep going!…

2 *(was seated beside the desk; fed up, makes up his mind to intervene)* Why don't we drop it? Don't you think that's enough?

1 Oh! Why?

2 *(for the entire class, some students agreeing with him)* We can each study the test on our own.

THE TEACHER No, no, I think this is important; it's group work.

2 Is that what you want: displays of emotion?

THE TEACHER *(standing at his place)* Emotions are part of our lives; why not admit it to ourselves?

7 I'm sorry…

THE TEACHER *(goes toward 7)* No, no, what you already did was very good. The very fact that you accepted; the very fact that you were willing to try…. Now ask yourself why you couldn't go right to the end. *(1 and 2 move close to the desk)*

Who else wants to play the YOUNG WOMAN? *(Throughout the following scene, 3 looks insistently at 1. THE TEACHER speaks to 8 who was speaking to 7.)* You?…

8 *(stands up, bursting with laughter)* Do you want everyone to laugh at me?

THE TEACHER We've told you, age has nothing to do…

8 I'd look like a fool.

THE TEACHER Not if deep down inside yourself you really are the YOUNG WOMAN…

8 *(very tempted, but sits back in her place before the mocking smile of 11)* No, no.

10 It's hard and really embarrassing.

THE TEACHER   *(to the class)* Who wants to give it a try?

4 No one will dare do it now.

11 Anyway, not me!

> *(THE TEACHER turns back to 3 who was waiting for just this moment.)*

3 You're really going to have to do it!

1 There's nothing I'd like more, if… *(indicates 2, who is holding her back)*

13 The teacher's going too far. Does he realize what he's asking?

THE TEACHER   If you don't mind!… We're wasting too much time.

3 (pulls 1) Come on! Come on!

2 If you do it!…

1 *(leaves 2 apologetically)* They have no one else!

> *(2 moves away toward the lockers, paces up and down, is chomping at the bit.)*

11 It's easy to see he's taking no chances.

3 Do you want to take it again from the top?

> *(They reach agreement in a low voice during the following scene.)*

9 *(to 5 and 6 in Area G)* The play is starting again. Finally.

THE TEACHER   Do you have a song for the HERMIT too?

6 For every character.

THE TEACHER   Well then, let's go.

13 *(to 1 and 3)* The other woman was better for the YOUNG WOMAN.

THE TEACHER   We need to get back into the action.

9 This one seems as good to me.

3 *(to 1 and THE TEACHER)* Let's say that the YOUNG WOMAN's gone looking for the HERMIT and that he returns to the place, delighted to have rid himself of her…. Does that work for you?

THE TEACHER   As you like.

> *(1 and 3 step onto riser and take their places for their scene.)*

8 You can tell her fiancé's not pleased. He's furious!

> *(Seeing 2's barely concealed annoyance, the class chuckles and whispers. 5 and 6 move close to the riser for the song of the HERMIT. The river appears.)*

11   Listen, just be quiet!

> *(Light cue: focus on the two protagonists who are getting ready to act. During the song, 1 is distracted by the presence of the chair that 7 forgot a few moments ago. 3 takes the chair, decides to use it when he's acting. He sits on it.)*

THE HERMIT'S SONG

6   That's the way life goes
When you've just been born,
Born or reborn,
This is about you.

Life, what is life,
I don't know life,
Not mine not others'
Not mine not others'.
Robbed of a future
Since Hiroshima-a-a
All those people walking in the streets
What are they thinking?
What are they rushing toward,
If it isn't death?

That's the way your life goes
This is about you.

> *(Removes his glasses and throws them to THE TEACHER, loosens his tie, removes a pencil from his pocket, puts it in his mouth as if it were a twig.)*

Between the end of the world
And hunger's rend in the world
What ends do we serve?
What ends do we serve?
Who can say
Who owns this herd? -d-d
Who's pulling our strings,
Like cows in a ring?

That's the way life goes
When you've just been born
Born or reborn
This is about you.

> *(5 and 6 withdraw slowly but continue to play the music theme softly during 3's first speech. Lights up on the riser. 3 is not the HERMIT. He agreed to play the part only to help the others out. He is not used to*

acting. So he feels the need to summarize in a few sentences his understanding of his character.)

3   There's my dilemma set to music…. Until it's been resolved, I'll just keep on asking myself why I would want to be involved in this world of madmen where people use nothing but their silly emotions to handle the worst kind of problems.

> *(When he receives THE TEACHER's go-ahead, he can signal to 1 that he is ready to start the scene. 1, who has not had a song to put her in the right space, concentrates intensely. On 3's sign she takes a deep breath and plunges in…. She moves toward 3. Her first speeches, spoken in a phony voice with awkward gestures, do not ring true. She should create the impression of a rather stiff school mistress who has never acted but is unshakably determined to make the scene a success. Slowly she becomes the YOUNG WOMAN. 3 never succeeds in being the HERMIT. In the course of the scene, he may learn to make his actions more subtle, but we always feel that he will never become the HERMIT.)*

1   You had a boat and you didn't say so! I just saw it by your house. *(awkward, clumsy gesture with her hand)* I spent all day trying to find that boat!

3   *(Not looking at her; he has his elbows on his knees and toys with the twig.)* You're right, that's my boat, but…

1   Come and help me put it in the water. I can't do it on my own.

3   That's my boat! *(categorically, a pause)* And anyway, the river isn't passable at this time of the year.

> *(3 tends to play his character as surly and uncouth. His responses will be dry and cutting. However, he will occasionally have to soften his brusqueness when he sees that 1 is too intimidated to be able to keep the conversation going.)*

1   *(not letting herself be discouraged, charges ahead in spite of everything)* Lend me your boat and your oars. I'll take care of the rest!

3   You trying to commit suicide?

1   I've never wanted to live so much before.

> *(She says this the first time to 3 in the heat of the action without really grasping its meaning. It is only after saying it that she realizes the significance of her utterance. So she picks it up again, this time for herself, discovering as she says it the profound meaning of her sentence.)*

3   *(turns his head to her)* So…

1   *(facing the audience)* I've never wanted to live so much before!

3   Well then, don't move and forget that boat.

1　I need it! *(turns back to him)* If you won't help me, I'll get it into the water myself.

　　(He grumbles. A pause. They no longer know what to say. 3 gets the scene going again. He gets up, goes to 1. They are face to face, sideways to the audience, at the centre of the riser.)

3　Have you even looked at the river?

1　*(wants to look at the river, but afraid, turns her eyes away)* I look at it every day.

3　Have you ever seen anyone dare go out on it in the spring?

1　I'll do it! *(finally makes up her mind and looks at the river, which now fascinates her)*

3　Well okay! Maybe you'll do it, but not with my boat. *(moves away to the left)*

1　*(automatically, without thinking about it, engrossed in the contemplation of the river)* After everything that's happened to me today, what's a little thing like crossing the river?

3　*(without moving, turns toward 1)* It's death.

1　It's death?

　　(Lost in her thoughts, she did not understand very well what 3 was saying. The silence that follows "It's death" draws her out of her reverie. She wonders what is happening, says to herself that it must be her turn to speak and tries to remember 3's last lines. She searches and finds them somewhere in her memory. She repeats them several times to herself until the sentence makes sense for her and she finds a response. The response she comes up with is naive. It is a recall of fine sentences she has heard or read. She tries to make it sound like an elegant turn of phrase, but the result sounds artificial, awkward, naive, although endearing.)

I have already died several times since this morning. *(has moved downstage, slightly below 3)* I know now that it's possible to die and be reborn many times.

　　(Break. What to say? Suddenly, an idea: she is going to speak about the bear [A well-known symbol in many behavioural tests]. At this point when the bear becomes part of her performance, they succeed for the first time in producing a dialogue. They are communicating with each other. She begins to live the adventure of the YOUNG WOMAN.)

If you had said to me this morning: "Don't run the risk of going into the woods, there's a bear on the prowl…"

3　Well exactly, there's one not far from here. I was even warned not to go out without my rifle.

1　And yet, here I am! I'm speaking to you! And I didn't have a rifle!

3　What does that prove except that you were lucky enough not to meet it?

1 Oh! excuse me! I saw it right in front of me!

3 Would it make any difference if I said I didn't believe you?

1 Yes! Because I didn't run away from it.

3 *(Sensing she has a lot to say, he draws back and supports her with his questions.)* Tell your story…

> *(1 advances downstage centre; 3 backs upstage to the top of the riser.)*

1 An enormous beast! My legs trembled, and I could hardly breathe.

3 Then what?

1 I overcame my fear! I started walking again…. Straight at him! And I said: "Get out of the way; this is my path."

3 *(whistle of admiration)* "Get out of the way; this is my path"!

1 Then he went into the forest and I got through! Just as I'm speaking to you, I got through! Right in front of him! *(as surprised as he is at the story she is inventing)*

3 Is this a true story?

1 *(Facing him, still very much under the spell of the story she invented, 1 suddenly feels herself to be the YOUNG WOMAN, delivers this line in a highly impassioned way.)* As true as I live!

3 Ah! I can see that you live to live. *(comes to 1)* You even appear dangerously alive to me. *(Already vaguely in love with 1, he draws near her with tenderness and admiration: she is even more resourceful than he first suspected.)*

1 So, come and help me! Come!…

3 Calm down first.

> *(1 had become the YOUNG WOMAN. She had forgotten herself, was completely "carried away." She was all set to cross the river using her own means. 3's words bring her back to reality.)*

Just now you were claiming to be exhausted.

1 I was! But all my strength returned when I saw your boat.

3 This boat hasn't been in the water since last fall. It needs to swell for several days before it can be used. Otherwise it will take on water like a sieve.

> *(She wakes up and realizes that she had allowed herself to be "carried away." She is afraid of having gone too far, instinctively tries to get her fiancé to look at her. He shoots her down. She considers leaving the riser, but 3's response holds her back. All the following lines are difficult. 1 is caught between 3 and 2. She does not know whom to choose. She stammers, shuffles her feet, goes in circles.)*

1   I'll just keep bailing. *(They are face to face.)*

3   And how will you go about steering? As soon as you get out in the water the current will toss you on the rocks. They'll rip your body to shreds! And then what'll happen? *(moves upstage)* Your body will be found, my boat will be recognized, and then who will have to deal with the police, eh?

1   I beg you! Can't you see that I'm ready to do anything?

> *(She is unable to continue. All are worried. General agitation. 1 puts her head in her hands, discouraged. THE TEACHER moves toward the riser, then motions to 5 and 6 to sing the YOUNG WOMAN's song again to help 1 to continue. 3 has turned to 1 to try to build her confidence. 5 and 6 move close to the riser to sing the song. 13, 11 get up and move close as well. 3 looks at 1 through the entire song. 2 continues to chomp at the bit. He was hoping that 1 would give up right away.)*

THE YOUNG WOMAN'S SONG

5 & 6   Being entirely there
Present in this instant
In this moment of life.
You are there, you are you
Right or wrong
You feel good in your flesh
You feel good with yourself
You are the heart of the world
The centre of the universe.

1   *(has regained control of herself, becomes the YOUNG WOMAN)* If you had any idea of how far I've come…

> *(THE TEACHER, 5 and 6 return to their places.)*

3   Have you really come from that far away?

1   From as far away as my childhood. *(takes the centre)* I left my childhood behind today.

3   *(returns to his chair)* Let's keep to plain talk. What exactly does that mean? Using ordinary words.

1   I can't speak about him in ordinary words.

3   *(leans against the back of his chair)* Oh! I get the picture now.

1   When he appeared to me, everything changed! And when he smiled at me… *(Her face lights up.)* When he smiled at me…

3   And could you tell me where this… visitation occurred?

1   *(turns to face him)* At the foot of the Great Dam falls.

3 Have you really come that far? *(stands up and comes to 1; they face each other)* Did you really cover all that distance on foot?

1 I told you I've been walking since this morning.

3 I didn't believe you. Come…. You're crazy, but even a crazy woman is entitled to a rest.

> *(3 makes a gesture inviting 1 to sit down. At first she accepts his invitation, but then changes her mind, deciding that the YOUNG WOMAN never sits down. 3 has returned to his own thoughts, has not seen 1's refusal. There is another lull. 1 launches her attack the best way she can, using the first cliché which comes to mind.)*

1 You have never loved; I have no trouble seeing that.

3 *(approaches 1)* This storm of emotions would make my heart sing, that is, if I had one!

1 You speak, but you have nothing to say.

3 You may be right. *(to her)* There's a time for everything and you're undoubtedly ripe for love.

1 Yes, I'm ripe for love. Yes, I'm ripe for love.

> *(The repetition is for herself. 2 moves into Area J; he is worried. 3 moves in front of the chair, back to the audience. She gets control of herself, and after saying it, she realizes what she has said and laughs shyly.)*

(regaining control of herself) Are you going to lend me your boat? *(moves toward him)*

3 Let me think. *(turns toward her)* I'm looking for a way to make you happy…. You aren't ugly; you even have a certain charm. *(makes a move upstage, passing near her)* When you've rested a bit…

1 *(stops him as he goes by)* I'm ready to go.

3 *(takes her by the arm and draws her downstage on the riser)* Well okay, follow me. I'm going to take you to the nearest village…

1 *(stops, pointing to the screen behind them)* But the river is that way…

3 Will you be good enough to forget the river.

1 But he lives on the other side of the river.

3 The village is full of boys just as interesting as him.

> *(She escapes from 3's clutches. 3's tone will be cynical, falsely so, since 3 is not cynical.)*

Didn't you admit yourself that you're ready for love? Everyone knows that one love drives out another. All the rest is romantic illusion.

1   You haven't understood anything! No one before ever made me feel the way I feel for him!

> *(2 moves close to the riser; THE TEACHER joins him there to prevent him from interfering.)*

3   Another will do just as well. After all, this guy, you aren't even sure he's going to love you back.

1   He reached his arms out to me.

3   From the other side of the river…

> *(She leaves suddenly, moves upstage.)*

Where are you going?

1   I'm taking the boat.

> *(3 catches 1, who turns toward him.)*

3   *(reacts like the SURVEYOR, which is in character for 3)* I absolutely forbid you to do it.

> *(Tension, then they calm down.)*

> (Pause. They look at each other.)

I'm prepared to feed you if you're hungry. I'll even take you in for the night if you want to rest…

1   (angrily) Who's said anything about eating? Who's said anything about sleeping? All I want is to find him.

3   In that case, I abandon you to your fate. (moves away toward the chair and sits down)

> *(The scene is finished. Lights start back up on the class; the river begins to disappear from the screen. The students prepare to give their comments. 2 rushes to draw 1 off the riser. But at that moment 3, remembering that he has not spoken about the FERRYMAN to the YOUNG WOMAN, starts to speak again.)*

Listen to me… *(All suspend their movements.)* I know a man who lives five minutes from here. He's the only one around here who can handle a boat in the spring… I didn't want to tell you about him because he has a bad reputation…

1   What do I care about his reputation! *(picks up on 3's line)* Where does he live? It's up to me to convince him.

3   And you could do it too… *(He gets up from his chair but doesn't move; he looks at her once again with much tenderness and admiration.)* Do people like you always get what they want?

Listen to me! *(3 goes to 1 and paternalistically puts his hand on her shoulder. Bothered by this gesture, she looks at her fiancé.)*

This fellow, no doubt you'll find him. But I'd be willing to bet that things won't work out the way you think. Life being what it is…

1   The FERRYMAN's house! Come on!

> (In order to put an end to this scene, which she finds upsetting and painful, 1 abruptly leaves the riser and moves toward 2. But as soon as she gets close, he moves away and goes to sulk near THE TEACHER's desk. Astonished, she slowly and discreetly tries to get close to him. Lights up. The river disappears. Some students applaud. 3 leaves the riser, somewhat disappointed, and goes to join 13 and 11 who are waiting for him. They are joined by THE TEACHER.)

THE TEACHER   (stands up from his desk) Excellent!

11   (to 3, overwhelmed) You were great! It couldn't have been better.

> (THE TEACHER crosses to Area H in order to speak to the class as a whole.)

THE TEACHER   I hope that you took note of the HERMIT's behaviour, because we won't see him any more in the test.

11   In my opinion, he's a very wise man.

1   (to 2) (She is finally near him, timidly moves close.) What do you think of him?

9   He's my favourite character.

2   (to 1) You put much too much passion into it!

10   You have to be strong to live alone.

2   It's upsetting…

13   Above all, you have to think of yourself first.

1   (to 2) (defends herself half-heartedly) But the YOUNG WOMAN…

8   It seemed to me he was heartless.

2   (to 1) And anyway, why ask for my opinion, since you did it without checking with me first!

> (2 moves behind the desk. He sits down on THE TEACHER's chair, back to everyone. 1 is left out in the cold.)

7   Me too…

12   I don't think so…. Not at all.

> (THE TEACHER moves to Area F. There is a very noisy discussion where each tries to present his or her point of view on the HERMIT. By now all the students are engaged in the experiment [at least as spectators].)

THE TEACHER   Who wants to be the FERRYMAN?

(THE TEACHER's question makes them all grow silent and look up at the ceiling. They try to make themselves invisible, hoping that someone else will be asked.)

Now that several of you played parts. *(goes back up toward 11 and 13)* It should be easier it seems to me.

12   Easier?—I wouldn't go that far!

10   Personally, I prefer to watch.

6   Why wouldn't we just keep the same ones?

(Reactions from 1, 3 and 2.)

7   Because it's going very well with them. Let them just carry on.

ALL   The same ones, the same ones, the same ones…

THE TEACHER   Are you absolutely content letting others live in your place?

(Reaction from the students. "No, it's not that, but…")

Please! I'd like to see you at least give the experiment a try! (to 3) It's worth it, isn't it?

3   Yes, yes…. You feel a bit ridiculous at first, but at the same time it's… it's a lot of fun!

THE TEACHER   (pointing to 4) You?

4   Oh, no! *(stands up in front of his chair)* The only character I could've played is the HERMIT…

(THE TEACHER moves toward 2 who is behind the desk. 3 approaches 4, gives him a friendly tap on the back.)

3   Hey, pal, you should have said so!

4   *(sits back down)* I wasn't sure enough of myself…

3   They're so afraid of making mistakes! *(moves toward 13 and 11)*

THE TEACHER   (to 2) You then?

2   Me? Never! *(returns to the front of the desk)* Especially not the FERRYMAN; I can't stand him. No, listen, I agreed to do a tree for you just now. Well, that's enough; my participation ends there.

THE TEACHER   I wonder if you're refusing to get involved because you're afraid of revealing too much of yourself. If you are, *(moves closer to 2)* I can tell you right now that your very refusal is every bit as revealing.

2   Would I ever like to see you in our place. *(timid agreement from some students)* It's easy enough for you to throw us into this adventure. It's like doing a mental striptease. But you, what risk are you running in this?

THE TEACHER   I don't understand…

2   Why don't you do the FERRYMAN yourself then?!

> *(Excited by the idea of provoking THE TEACHER, 8, 5, 6 stand up; 5 and 6 go and join 13, 11, 3 in Area G.)*

THE TEACHER   But I… I'm directing all the action; that's my way of participating.

2   In the meantime, you don't have to get wet!

4   *(gets up from his place)* Admit it! It's a lot easier for you to push us into the water and then watch us struggle.

THE TEACHER   So why don't you ask me to take your exams for you while you're at it?!

8   He's got to get wet like the rest of us.

2   We're asking you to expose yourself like us.

13   He has to get involved too.

2   Jean-Paul Sartre said it in May '68.

> *(THE TEACHER knows the citation, even says it with 2.)*

THE TEACHER & 2   A Teacher who is not capable of laying himself bare in front of his students will never be a good teacher.

3   *(joins THE TEACHER)* It's true. Since you tell us that the entire affair is a game, why not come and play it with us?

7   He wouldn't dare.

10   He's afraid of losing face.

13   He's going to refuse, you'll see.

THE TEACHER   I didn't think I had to go that far…

> *(4 and 7 join the group of students.)*

ALL   Yes…. Yes…. Yes…. Yes…

THE TEACHER   The problem is that the FERRYMAN, you see, the FERRYMAN isn't my thing at all. *(back against the wall, shuffles and tries to justify himself)* When you get right down to it, the YOUNG WOMAN's behaviour would suit me better…

2   Well, there you go! How about that! If that was true you'd accept, because the most important thing about the YOUNG WOMAN is precisely that she's capable of anything at all!

(This falls like a stone in 1's garden. She reacts to the accusation but cannot defend herself. THE TEACHER takes advantage of this diversion to talk about something else.)

THE TEACHER   Be careful! It would be a mistake to judge these characters using the criteria of conventional morality. That would make the test completely invalid.

> *(He has been aware for some time of the ironic and provocative smiles on the students' lips. In the end, he decides to rise above his apprehension and jump in.)*

But let's be done with it. I accept your challenge.

4   You'll be the FERRYMAN yourself?

> *(3 joins THE TEACHER. 5 and 6 move upstage in Area B and get ready for their next song. The students are very astonished that THE TEACHER would accept to get involved. They did not believe he was capable of it. Therefore, they settle in to watch him take the plunge with keen curiosity. Some are sympathetic, others hope he will fail.)*

3   Bravo! You're willing to play.

13   The teacher is taking the plunge!

> *(13, 11 and 7 look for chairs. They take up places near the riser all the better to see the scene that is about to start. 4 pulls his chair a little outside the group of the other students. From outside the group, 8 slowly approaches 4. 9 and 10 remain in their places, uncertain.)*

11   It takes courage, and it's risky.

10   He could be taken down a peg.

7   Don't you think it's a way for him to show that he at least isn't afraid of what other people think about him?

> *(THE TEACHER comes toward 1 and 2, who are in front of the desk.)*

THE TEACHER   (to 1) You're still participating, aren't you?

2   She did it once, that's enough.

> *(3 intervenes and joins the group. This discussion takes place in front and on the left side of THE TEACHER's desk.)*

3   Don't you think that's her decision to make?

1   (to 2) I like this character so much! (to THE TEACHER) The YOUNG WOMAN and the YOUNG MAN are the ones that I relate to.

3   Both? In the same way?

1   They're both seeking the absolute, aren't they?

2   The YOUNG MAN, yes! Not the YOUNG WOMAN!

1   But you said yesterday…

2   *(moves downstage, angry)* I can see her better today and I'm starting to understand that, more than anything else, she's just looking for sensation.

1   *(She joins 2, and leans her head on his shoulder. She is behind him.)* Of love! Of love!

THE TEACHER   First let's get through the test; once we've done that we'll be better able to judge. *(takes centre stage, moves upstage toward 1, takes her by the hand and draws her to the riser)*

Don't identify too quickly with one or the other of the characters. Wait until you know them all. Come on!…

2   *(between his teeth)* If you go through with this!….

1   *(delighted to have no choice)* Can't you see that I have no choice?

3   Just let her be! Funny that you're not interested in this at all. It's a great experience.

> *(For a time 2 and 3 glower at each other like two dogs. Then 2 moves to the back of the desk and sits down on THE TEACHER's chair facing the wall. 3 remains in place with his eyes on the riser. While 1 and THE TEACHER discuss and get ready [near the chair], 8 joins 4 [she is slightly behind him]. She has been showing for a few minutes that she has something on her mind. She speaks of her project to 4 because he is the closest to her at this moment.)*

8   (to 4) I'm beginning to be sorry I refused the role of the YOUNG WOMAN just now…

4   That's strange, I was just thinking to myself as well that it would have been good for me to play the HERMIT…

8   I was afraid of being laughed at because of my age, but now that I understand the test better…

4   (not listening to her) Yes, it really would have!

8   What would you say if…? *(draws close and lowers her voice; they scheme together)* Why shouldn't the two of us try the Ferryman scene?

4   But the decision has already been made. They're going…

8   They're going to present it to the class, but what's stopping us from working on it for ourselves? I'd like that…

4   The FERRYMAN, I don't know if I could do it…. You've seen how that scene ends… *(for her)*

8   *(goes downstage below 4)* (not listening to him) After all, it would be in the YOUNG WOMAN's personality to go back to school the way I have, it seems to me?… What the heck! Let's go find a place down there, near the lockers, no one'll see us there…

4   *(hesitant)* Is it that important to you?

8   Why don't we try?

4   Let's try!

> *(4 takes his chair; 8 goes to find one, and they both cross the stage slowly to the lockers. At the same time in Area F, 9 has stood up and moved close to 10. THE TEACHER and 1 go to the back of the riser. They take the chair, place it upstage centre; it will become a sort of boat, but will be forgotten. 8 and 4 move very slowly with their chairs. 9 is standing behind 10, who, turned toward the central riser, did not see him approach her. It is not easy for 9 to speak to 10, who has seemed very closed right from the beginning. But since she is the only student near him, he has no choice. 10 smiles constantly in her responses. She hesitates; she is without social skills. As a result, their conversation will always be 9's initiative.)*

9   Isn't he making us look brilliant?

10   *(turns to 9)* (ill at ease) What do you mean?

9   Doesn't it bother you that the teacher is acting instead of us?

10   I'd be even more bothered if I had to be one of the actors.

9   *(approaches her)* When you get right down to it, what risk would there be for us?

10   The risk of… *(gets up and steps away in order to put some distance between her and 9)* of looking ridiculous, of losing face…. Don't you think so?

9   What's so special about our damned face? Why should we be so afraid of losing it? *(uncomfortable laugh from 10)* Maybe that's all that's expected from us in life. *(puts one foot on a chair and leans toward 10 to reduce the distance separating them)* Would it be that hard for you to play the YOUNG WOMAN?

10   *(moves away again and stammers while smiling)* I don't know… I was a bit tempted at the beginning!… But… in front of the class, just think about it!

9   *(comes right up to her)* And what if we tried, just between the two of us?

10   (laughs) Between us?…

9   The two of us, yes! Somewhere out of the way, over there. Just to see, if we can do it.

10   (laughs) He's crazy!

9   Come on! *(begins to move toward the chairs)*

10 You're not making fun of me?

9 Of course not, of course not, come on!…

> *(They busy themselves with the chairs, clear Area F, keep only 3 chairs, using 2 chairs to represent a door and one for an armchair. THE TEACHER and 1 take their positions on either side of the riser. THE TEACHER is facing the audience. 1 in profile, turned toward THE TEACHER. 8 and 4 have now stopped at the left corner of the riser. They have problems.)*

4 Would you like to change it?

8 I'd rather have it take place in the city. These things about the countryside, the boat, the ferry, they don't mean anything to me.

4 You'd have to find work that's like what the FERRYMAN does. Do you have any ideas?…

8 In transportation, I suppose?

9 *(in Area F, finishes placing the chairs)* Let's say that the FERRYMAN is in his house and the YOUNG WOMAN comes and knocks on his door.

10 *(casts about for a moment but does not understand)* What door?

9 *(makes an outline with his arms of the contour of the door)* Imagine it!

10 *(laughs, happy she understands)* Yes, yes, yes, yes! (laughs) It's crazy!

4 Taxi driver?

8 Ooh, that's good!…

10 *(breaks off her laugh under 9's severe look)* I'll get it, don't you worry!

9 I hope there's a song for the FERRYMAN? That would help us empathize with the characters…

> *(The first bars of the song are heard. 9 turns to 10, then comes and sits down on the chair on the left and stretches out his legs under the third chair.)*

Ah! Listen…. And let's think about what we're doing…

> *(6 has come to stand behind the group 13, 11, 7. She will sing from there. 5 is on the other side of the riser, very close to THE TEACHER. 8 and 4, near the lockers, have placed their chairs in a way that represents the front and back seats of a car. 4 is seated in the front seat. 8 remains standing behind the rear seat. Throughout the song, THE TEACHER, 1, 4, 8, 9 and 10 concentrate. The three future Ferrymen listen carefully to the words of the song. 13, 11 and 7 join in the song, whether by marking the beat or picking up certain important lines. Lighting is concentrated on*

THE TEACHER and 1 on the central riser. The river begins to flow on the central screen and on the side screens above areas B and F.)

THE FERRYMAN'S SONG

6   That's the way life goes
When you've just been born
That's the way your life goes
This is about you.

There's so much to see
There are so many of us.
At the same time all alike
And yet different
There's so much to see

That's the way life goes
When you've just been born
That's the way your life goes
This is about you.

What's the good in getting involved
When you know nothing about yourself
Neither yourself nor others
When you're sure of nothing
What's the good in getting involved?

That's the way life goes
When you've just been born
That's the way your life goes
This is about you.

It's better to look at
The upside and the flipside
The for and the against
Rather than making a choice
It's better to look

That's the way life goes
When you've just been born
That's the way your life goes
This is about you.

I want to see
More than to give
To take or even reject
To lend or receive
I want to see

That's the way life goes
When you've just been born
That's the way your life goes
This is about you.
Go with your life.

> *(Lights up on entire central riser. 5 withdraws and will remain seated on the floor behind the riser. THE TEACHER turns to 1, but does not look at her.)*

THE TEACHER   (pause) What are you doing there?

1   Aren't you the person who takes people to the other side of the river?

> *(THE TEACHER looks up at her. This is the first confrontation of the YOUNG WOMAN and the FERRYMAN. They are paralyzed for a moment.)*
>
> (Pause.)

THE TEACHER   That's not my job.

1   I was told that you did it occasionally. That's what I was told!

THE TEACHER   Sometimes I do, to help out a friend…. Or sometimes for my own entertainment. *(turns to the audience, explains for the others)* I'm not often asked to. No one's anxious to cross in the springtime and in summer everyone gets across on their own. *(glances at 1 to see her reaction)*

1   *(takes a step toward THE TEACHER)* Would you agree to do it for me?

THE TEACHER   *(wants to delay his response, since he does not feel ready)* You're not a friend.

1   You also said: "Sometimes for my own amusement."

THE TEACHER   *(faces 1)* It doesn't amuse me today.

1   *(crushed, but regaining control)* Why not?

THE TEACHER   Why would it amuse me?

9   (turning his head toward 10) Go ahead…. Knock! *(Both try on their own to find ways to continue. Light on Area F. 9 is impatient with 10. He is sitting on one of the chairs representing the door, his feet placed on the third chair.)* Knock at the door…

10   Yes, yes, yes, yes, yes!

> *(10 tries to knock, but does not manage to believe in the existence of a door that she cannot see, bursts out laughing, regains control with difficulty. Tries again. Laughs. Finally, seeing that she is incapable of knocking in the void, she decides to say: "Knock, knock, knock." As 9 starts to laugh, 8 in Area B cautiously takes her place facing 4, as if he*

were in the car and she at a street corner. 9 is playing a FERRYMAN who is surly and old. This makes 10 laugh. 9 gets up, goes toward the wall. 10 laughs. 9 looks at her. 10 calms down.)

9   Yes? What is it? What do you want? I hope you haven't come to disturb me for nothing?

THE TEACHER   *(turns toward 1)* Are you still there?

(She turns toward him. They are now face to face.)

1   I'm waiting.

THE TEACHER   What are you waiting for?

1   … ?

(It was 1 who responded, while THE TEACHER was the FERRYMAN. He repeats his question so that she understands.)

THE TEACHER   What are you waiting for?

1   *(as the YOUNG WOMAN)* For you to find it amusing to cross the river.

THE TEACHER   Well, you'll be waiting 'til the cows come home, young lady!

1   *(becomes herself again)* There must be some way to convince you.

THE TEACHER   *(becomes himself again)* My last crossing was bad.

1   But, you're still here!… [10]

THE TEACHER   I barely escaped with the hair on my head out there. And even my boat. I've just now finished repairing it.

1   *(to THE TEACHER)* Do you mean to say you haven't used it since?

THE TEACHER   *(turns to 1)* No.

1   Oh!

(1 is discouraged at seeing all her attempts to get the conversation going reduced to zero by THE TEACHER's responses. He is delaying the real beginning of the scene because he does not feel ready to demand the agreed upon price. 1 steps forward, trying to find some kind of an idea, then decides to leave the riser. As 1 slowly moves upstage, 10 starts to laugh again.)

9   We won't get far if you keep that up.

(Just when 1 is on the point of leaving the riser, THE TEACHER stops her. He feels guilty for having been so little help since the beginning of the scene and realizes he must be more cooperative.)

---

[10]   *Director's Note:* Cut in production.

THE TEACHER   If I had to, of course, I could put it back in the water. *(1 turns her head toward THE TEACHER. He smiles.)* I've got most of the work done.

> *(Relieved, she resumes her initial position facing THE TEACHER. We feel that now the scene can begin. Lights up on Area B. Immediately, 4 begins to imitate with his voice the sound of a running automobile, and he mimes the gestures of the driver. 8 plays the role of a woman who is freezing on the street corner, notices the taxi and signals energetically to him with her hand.)*

8   Taxi! Taxi!… Oh! I'm so happy you stopped! Four taxis have already gone by right in front of me!

4   In this weather, and then it's the middle of the night…. I'm heading home myself, but if you're going in my direction…. Where're you going to?…

8   Pointe-aux-Trembles…

4   Ooh, lady! I'm going to North Montreal. That's the other way.

8   You have to take me.

4   That might seem like a good idea to you, but I'm not running out to the end of the world in this kind of freezing rain. No way!

1   Why is it that some days it amuses you and other days it doesn't amuse you?

THE TEACHER   You don't give up, do you.

> *(Lighter atmosphere; for the first time they are speaking to each other.)*

1   I'm like that!

THE TEACHER   It's that important?

1   Yes!

THE TEACHER   Who's it for? Your dad? Your friend?

1   For me.

THE TEACHER   For you?

1   For me.

THE TEACHER   *(takes a step toward 1, then, with his back to the audience, toward the screen)* Did you see how that river is crashing down? *(Darkly, he reflects on all of life's hassles.)* And along with that there's all those logs today.

> *(1 turns toward the river; she breathes deeply, draws the image into herself. Serene.)*

1   It's dangerous, I know that…

THE TEACHER   It's never been more terrifying!

1   *(spinning to face him, smiling)* You get across it.

THE TEACHER   I'm a man. *(turning to face her, somewhat casual)* And besides, I'm used to it.

1   With you I won't be afraid.

THE TEACHER   Oh! yes, you'll be afraid! You might as well know that right from the start, you'll tremble with fright. *(Paternalistic, THE TEACHER goes to 1, puts his hands on her shoulders.)* You don't ever forget such an experience. It's so powerful it can turn you into a different person.

8   Please take me!

4   I'm no more a fool than other guys. They keep talking on the radio about accidents everywhere! It's a skating rink out there just like at the Forum.

1   *(Impressed for an instant by the tone of THE TEACHER, she reacts.)* Well! Okay, I'll be afraid like the others. And so what? They didn't die from it, did they?

THE TEACHER   Only one! *(faces the audience)* Some poor idiot that was so terrified he threw himself into the water!

1   *(goes to THE TEACHER and takes him by the arm to pull him)* You don't need to worry. I won't throw myself into the water.

8   *(faces the audience, and for herself)* So what am I going to do?

1   *(tries to pull THE TEACHER, comes up behind him)* Let's go…

THE TEACHER   Wait a minute! Wait a minute! I didn't say…

1   If you went to the trouble of warning me that I would be frightened, you must have meant you were willing to take me.

THE TEACHER   You jump to conclusions quickly.

1   I beg you!

THE TEACHER   We'll see. *(moves very slowly downstage)* I need to think about it.

4   I'm very sorry, but you know it's not my problem, it's yours.

> *(4 pretends to start the car, then stands up and goes upstage, intending to end the scene. She turns toward him.)*

8   I beg you!

> *(4 hesitates, but comes back and sits down. A pause. They put themselves back into the setting. In Area F, 10 laughs, always the same, somewhat hysterical laugh.)*

9   If you don't want to do it, just say so!

10   *(tries without success to get control of herself)* Yes, yes, I want to do it!

> *(A pause. 8 and 4 do not know how to get back into the action.)*

4   I'm not the only taxi in town, you'll find another one…

8   They don't stop! I've been trying to catch one for over an hour.

4   Call a company.

8   I tried them all. They don't even answer any more!

> *(A pause. They look at each other.)*

4   So, go back home, you poor soul. *(stands up in place)* This isn't making any sense!… *(looks at her, examines her)*

8   You're not still thinking I'm doing this for my own pleasure?

4   No, I wouldn't say you look like the kind of lady who hangs out in the streets in the middle of the night.

8   I swear to you that if I had the good fortune of being in my own bed…

THE TEACHER   It would be the first time I took a woman on board… *(sits back down)*

4   Yep…

THE TEACHER   I'm normally dealing with tough guys who are desperate for a drink in the tavern or maybe need to go find a girl…

> *(1 tries to interrupt THE TEACHER. She finds that all his talking is holding up the action.)*

Sometimes it's for both reasons! When you throw yourself into that kind of raging water your determination to go has to be stronger than any kind of fear.

1   But how about you? *(takes a step toward THE TEACHER)* You do it! You even say it amuses you.

THE TEACHER   Well, yes… I do take them across sometimes just to see the look on their faces when the current carries them off at top speed and the logs look like they could pop right up in front of us at any moment. I like that… *(a pause, searches)* Especially when they bragged like you that they wouldn't be afraid!… As for women, *(turns to 1)* no, I can't remember ever taking them on board…

1   *(moves closer to THE TEACHER)* Well then, this is your chance! Do it for your own amusement! So you can see me tremble with fright, since you claim that's what will happen to me!

8   *(begs 4)* If you would…

THE TEACHER   *(moves toward 1)* It could be quite funny…

1   Are you coming? *(starts to move upstage on the riser)*

> *(10 laughs.)*

9   Listen, are you laughing at me?

> *(10's laughter doubles.)*

That's it; I've had it!

> (*9 leaves 10 and goes back up to the blackboard. He stays there for a time then [with 12] comes to join the group of 6, 7, 11, 13. 10 stops laughing immediately, starts to make a move to hold him back, does not move, upset. A pause, then THE TEACHER turns to 1.*)

THE TEACHER   Are you really in a rush?

1   (violently) Yes, I am! (*returns downstage just in front of THE TEACHER*) (more calmly) Yes, I am… the sun's going to set and I have a long way to go on the other side of the river.

THE TEACHER   All that for a guy, I suppose? (*1 closes up.*) A good looking guy? (*She faces the audience. THE TEACHER is astonished to hear her speak as she does.*)

1   I don't know if he's good looking. I only know that I have to find him again.

THE TEACHER   So you love him that much?

1   (*delivers these lines awkwardly, like someone who is trying to express lofty feelings without finding suitable words in her normal vocabulary. She gets tangled up in the attempt.*) It's like a hunger…. A thirst…. An unbearable ache that you wouldn't want to be without. It's…. No, it can't be explained!

THE TEACHER   (*He's disappointed. He had thought she would succeed in expressing her love in a coherent way.*) Can't be explained!… They always end up saying that! Seeing you suffer from such a disorder is very odd…

> (*1 turns to THE TEACHER. She has already said the same thing to the HERMIT. But at that time it was merely a formality intended to keep the conversation going, whereas now it is an attempt at communication between two people who have made contact with each other as a result of this test.*)

1   Have you never been in love then?

THE TEACHER   I have my head well screwed onto my shoulders! No! (*He moves downstage to the edge of the riser. Faces the audience. Speaks for himself. We should feel that he is revealing the deepest part of himself and that, perhaps, it is the first time this has happened to him.*) I enjoy my peace and quiet too much to get involved in affairs that, as far as I know, always end badly.

1   The river too, that could end badly for you, one day.

THE TEACHER   Well, yes!… Only, I know the river! No matter how treacherous she is, she doesn't cheat. And I don't play at outsmarting her. I go where she wants me to go, even if it takes longer to cross. I follow her rhythm, not mine…. That way, between her and me, no problems! But letting myself go like that in the hands of a woman? (*toward 1*) I'm not that stupid!

1   Let's go, are you ready?

(1 moves toward THE TEACHER. She is impressed and moved by what THE TEACHER has just revealed to her. But she owes it to herself to bring him back to the purpose of the scene. During this brief, fast-paced exchange, a feeling of warm sympathy will develop between the two characters. They smile and even laugh increasingly. All the lines leading up to "Well let's go then" should overlap.)

THE TEACHER   I think that I can already see you out there in front of the boat.

1   Let's go…

THE TEACHER   Hair in your face, carried by the current…

1   Well come on then…

THE TEACHER   I even think that I can hear you…

1   Come on…

THE TEACHER   Because you would shout, I suppose?… *(moves toward 1)* Yes, yes, you wouldn't be able to stop yourself.

1   Of course, I always shout when I'm frightened. I would shout at the top of my lungs. I would scream.

THE TEACHER   That would be something to see!

   (1 takes THE TEACHER's hand and leads him upstage. Caught up in the enthusiasm of the preceding lines, they have forgotten the "price" of the scene; they are ready to depart right away in the boat.)

1   Well let's go then!…

   (Suddenly, just before 1 leaves the riser, THE TEACHER wakes up, remembers that the scene cannot end that easily and stops 1. They are frozen, back to the audience, still holding hands, 1 slightly behind THE TEACHER.)

4   You must be getting pretty cold, eh?…

8   *(Lost in dreams, she jumps. Then she begins to imitate a woman who is cold.)* I'm turning to ice! It would be so generous of you to take me there.

4   Yeah!… Well, as far as generosity goes, all I can offer is you get in the car while you're waiting for another taxi to go by…

8   Why not drive me yourself in that case?

4   No, Ma'am, I won't be running out to Pointe-aux-Trembles tonight, that's for sure. But since I'm not interested in having your death on my conscience, if you want to get in, get in…. At least you'll be warm while you wait.

8   Well, it's better than nothing… *(goes to the chair representing the rear seat of the taxi)*

4   *(makes the gesture of opening the door for her, 8 coughs)* Especially with the cold you've got…

8   Oh! yes… *(now seated in the taxi)*

THE TEACHER   Are you ready to pay the price?

> *(The tone is serious now. It is up to THE TEACHER and 1 to find a way to end the scene, in accordance with the test. But this ending frightens both of them. Especially after the preceding euphoria, the audience should feel that this return to reality is particularly brutal.)*

1   *(drops THE TEACHER's hand)* The price?

THE TEACHER   Even if I'm doing this for my own amusement, there has to be some payoff in it for me too.

1   *(A pause. In desperation, 1 turns to the TEACHER.)* I have no money!

8   Have you noticed there are more taxis going by?

4   You're fine for the moment, you're in where it's warm…

8   That's for sure…. It's suffocating in your car!

4   Take off your coat, don't be shy…

> *(She begins to unbutton her jacket; he turns toward her. She stops her movement, shy. They are not yet ready to finish the scene.)*

8   If we'd left right away, we'd already be in Pointe-aux-Trembles!

4   Yes, in the morgue!

8   That's your opinion. If you weren't so nervous!

4   *(Vexed, he gets up and turns toward her.)* Nervous? Skidding around like that, I've spent my life doing it! You think that driving cab is a profession for nervous people? That's a joke!

8   So, why aren't we on our way?

4   Because there's nothing that says I have to go there! *(sits back down)* Pointe-aux-Trembles, you can wait!

> *(During the preceding scene THE TEACHER begins to move downstage, and faces the audience.)*

1   I could pay you later if you were willing to trust me? Will you?… Will you? *(comes up to THE TEACHER)* Wait, he's the one who'll pay you. We'll come to see you together…

THE TEACHER   *(turns toward 1)* You're joking?

1   I promise!

THE TEACHER   *(A pause, no longer knows what to say.)* It's no good!

> *(THE TEACHER no longer wishes to pursue the scene. He feels himself incapable of going all the way. He leaves and is about to step off the riser. But 1 catches him and holds on to him. The audience should have the impression she believes he does not have the right to abandon her; they must keep going. They are upstage on the riser, face to face with each other.)*

1   Well then, lend me your boat!… Just lend it to me! Help me put it in the water and I'll cross on my own. He and I will bring it back to you tomorrow.

> *(THE TEACHER is angry with himself for having thought of leaving the riser and for not being able to go right through to the end.)*

THE TEACHER   Do you know what you're saying? Take a good look once and for all at that bitch of a river! You'd be prepared to go off all on your own in that?

1   Yes, yes, yes! How is it that no one understands this! You must be able to see that it's stronger than I am! I can't live with the idea of never seeing him again!

THE TEACHER   I'm beginning to feel sorry for you…

1   *(urgently, holding on to THE TEACHER)* Help me then. Help me!

> *(4 turns on his chair toward 8. He is trying to gain time, delay the end of the scene, get ready for it.)*

4   First of all, what are you going to do there at this hour?

> *(Suddenly, 8 becomes the YOUNG WOMAN; no longer acting, she is living the part.)*

8   (in a reserved way) I have to go.

4   I'll betcha it's got to be for a man?

8   Yes, it's for a man! But make no mistake about it, he's my husband.

4   Oh! I could care less whether it's your husband or your boyfriend… I get to see all kinds, and so…

8   If it was just my boyfriend, as you say, I would've left him long ago!

4   Husbands get left too.

8   *(quarter turn on her chair, facing the audience, for herself)* It all depends on who you are. For me, husbands don't get left.

4   *(turns a little more toward 8; he is beginning to be sincerely touched)* In that case, it's because you love him.

8   (in anguish) I don't know, I don't know any more…. All I know is that he's in a bad situation and that I have to go get him out of it.

4   What happened to him?

8   (embarrassed) He's had too much to drink… have to get him back to the house, all by myself, don't even know if I can…

4   What a mess.

8   *(appeals to 4)* Why wouldn't you help me to…

> *(4 has been touched by 8's confidences. He is about to drive her where she wants. But suddenly he remembers that they must finish the scene, and his HERMIT's temperament takes over.)*

4   Wait a minute! Wait just a minute, you! That guy… he's not my husband.

> *(THE TEACHER moves downstage, facing the audience; he speaks very slowly; he is avoiding the issue, doesn't dare leap in, but is getting ready to do so. His hesitation exasperates 1, who will continue to press him.)*

THE TEACHER   Well you know, there may be another way for you to pay me…

1   I'll do anything!

4   I need some kind of payoff for me… something that works to my advantage…

8   But you're going to be paid! *(speaks of money, isn't ready)* I'll even pay you double what it's worth if you like!…

> *(4 turns toward her, looks at her for an instant, starts to ask her to take off her clothes, cannot do it, turns back around. During these lines, THE TEACHER walks along the edge of the riser and slowly moves toward the chair which is upstage. 1 will be right on his heels.)*

THE TEACHER   Everything, everybody has a price…

1   Tell me yours.

> *(8 leans toward 4. She is ready.)*

8   I'm telling you, I'm ready to pay.

THE TEACHER   *(turns to 1)* This must stay just between you and me.

1   Say it!

4   You know, at this time of the night, money isn't…. It's not what interests me most…

THE TEACHER   *(resumes his movement upstage)* The river is at its worst right now…

1   Say it!

4   There are other things in life. Money isn't the only thing in the world!

> *(8 is motionless, tense; she is waiting.)*

THE TEACHER   I'll be risking my life going and coming back…

1   Say it, for heaven's sake!

THE TEACHER   Just be a little patient.

4   What I'd like…. What I'd like…

8   What is it?

4   It's not what you're thinking either! I always have respect for a woman. *(goes to the chair, puts his foot on it and leans on it)*

THE TEACHER   Maybe you'll think the price is high, but it's not unreasonable in comparison to…

1   *(She too is ready for everything. A pause.)* I accept it in advance!

4   All that I want, it's… it's… I can't do it! It's no good! I can't go any further.

> *(4 stands up and moves away toward Area L. 8 remains seated, stunned and crushed. THE TEACHER comes and places himself in front of the chair, standing, arms crossed.)*

THE TEACHER   Take your clothes off!

> *(In Area F, 10, who has been following the main scene, imitates for herself the gestures and responses of 1. THE TEACHER and 1 speak to each other, but without daring to look at each other.)*

1   That's your price?

THE TEACHER   That's my price.

1   Your price… in full?

THE TEACHER   In full.

1   *(looks at THE TEACHER)* How can I be sure of that?

THE TEACHER   *(looks at 1)* It's the risk you take. (pause) You can still change your mind.

1   *(timidly, she tries)* I can also go and try to find money somewhere.

THE TEACHER   No! *(He walks toward her. They look at each other intensely.)* We've gone too far you and I. *(moves downstage, faces the audience)* I'd say no now for money. *(1 turns around slowly, trying to find courage. 2 approaches the riser.)* It's that or nothing! And if it isn't that, go away right now. *(moves upstage, pause)*

> *(Tension is felt in all the students. They are holding their breath, concentrating to help 1 go through with it. Even 2, overwhelmed by the course of events does not know what to do, does not even have the force to intervene.)*

1   Wait!

> *(THE TEACHER stops just at the edge of the riser, back to the audience. 11 and 7 stand up to help 1. After a final moment of hesitation, she*

begins to unbutton her dress and moves downstage centre on the riser. In parallel fashion, THE TEACHER moves to upstage centre, in front of the chair, looking at the ground. Alone in her corner, 10 has also begun to undo her dress. At the moment when 1 lets her dress fall, there is a change of light, total blackout except for a spot on 1 [projector coming from the back of the stage which shows us 1, naked, back-lit] and two spots, one on 10 who continues to undo her dress and one on 8, prostrate. 1 has undressed slowly. No one has budged except 2 who delicately turns his head. A pause.)

(weakly) I paid!

THE TEACHER You paid.

1 *(Proud now of having surpassed herself, 1 speaks this final line strongly.)* Well then, get your boat ready and take me to him.

> *(Lights up on the entire class. 7 comes on to the riser and helps 1 put her clothes back on. She then draws her behind the riser in a group formed by 6, 11 and 13, who surround her in silence. They will previously have moved their chairs upstage. 3 joins THE TEACHER and congratulates him in silence. 9 returns to the Area and, ignoring 10 who is fastening her dress back up, slowly begins to replace the chairs. 2 is completely outraged; he looks at 1 with disgust. 8, very slowly, gets up, takes her chair, goes to her place. Pathetically, 4 calls her. Their conversation takes place in Area L.)*

4 I hope you understand… I don't want you to be too upset with me…

8 You know, I was so far into it that… it wasn't you any more, it wasn't me any more…

4 The way I was brought up…. Affairs like that!…

8 It really wasn't me any more! It was her…. A woman who thinks of nothing but saving her man…

4 You would have…. You would've gone all the way?

> *(8 turns now to 4. Up to now neither of them had dared look at the other.)*

8 Yes… I'm pretty sure of it! Like her!… It's funny, eh?… I can't get over it…

> *(She repeats "I can't get over it" a few times, then slowly leaves with her chair and goes toward the group surrounding 1. 4 goes back toward the lockers to get his chair. He stays there. 9 is in the process of replacing the chairs in Area F. 10 approaches him timidly.)*

10 I want to apologize. I can assure you, I wasn't laughing at you…

9 *(continues to place the chairs)* That may be so, but it ruined everything.

10   (*moves toward him*) I really wanted to do it!

9   (*goes to her*) Yes, but by yourself…

10   I'm always by myself!

> (*She starts to laugh again in spite of herself. He pulls a chair up for her.*)

9   Sit down.

> (*She sits down, he sits beside her. As soon as 10 is seated, 2 catches 1 by the hand and forcibly draws her toward the exit in Area C.*)

2   Let's get out of here right now!

1   But?…

> (*3 moves forward and blocks 2's path; 2 pushes him back.*)

3   What's going on?

2   You can mind your own business! (to 1) I want to speak to you.

> (*3 follows 1 and 2 as far as their exit.*)

3   (to 1) But we need you!

1   I'll be back!

2   We'll just see about that!

> (*As they leave they jostle 4. 3 and 4 find themselves side by side.*)

3   (to 4) He's right out of his mind! Why is he taking it like that? This is work we're doing. His attitude is ridiculous.

4   Jealousy…. Put yourself in his place!

3   But she's crazy about him; what's he complaining about? After all, what can he blame her for? For being a perfect model of the YOUNG WOMAN?

> (*3 moves away toward THE TEACHER. 4 follows him.*)

(to THE TEACHER) Because that's really what the YOUNG WOMAN of the test is like, don't you think so?

> (*THE TEACHER leaves his desk and takes the centre. All the students, after witnessing the exit of 1 and 2, return to THE TEACHER.*)

THE TEACHER   Yes, that's indeed how she should be seen, I believe… I was mistaken about her myself. I hadn't imagined her that strong… that exuberant about life…

4   But just now you were saying…

THE TEACHER   That I identified with her…. Yes!… (*embarrassed*) But I was mistaken about that too! I was mistaken… (*5 and 12 join the group already in Area H. 9 and 10 remain in their places. The audience should feel THE TEACHER* *is very shaken up by the experience he has just lived through. He is the one who needs a break.)* You see, this test is as beneficial to me as to you! We're going to leave it there for the moment. Ten minutes for a *coffee break*, as they say in Paris!

7   No! No! Why stop?

13   There are still two more characters.

8   I'm just beginning to understand your test.

11   We have to continue, keep going with the test!

ALL   We have to keep going. We have to keep going.

THE TEACHER   First take a bit of a break to discuss the characters among yourselves and try to see what this group experiment has to offer you, on a personal level. Turn it into a kind of study of yourselves and pay close attention to what you feel.

> *(The students spread randomly around the stage. As soon as THE TEACHER speaks to the audience, the students turn to the house and smile at the spectators.)*

(without interruption) Right now, if there are some among you who would like to participate in this play, you're welcome to join us. You must remember that it's just a game, a game in which you're invited to participate. All you have to do is choose one of the characters of the test. It could be one that has already been represented, or one of the ones that are yet to come. If you don't have a partner, one of us will do the dialogue with you. We would welcome your participation. If it tempts you, we're here for you.

> *INTERMISSION.*

> *(Except for 1 and 2, who have already left the class, all the actors remain on stage throughout the Intermission. They move around freely, form groups, chat with each other, and greet audience members who would like to do improvisation.* [11] *Extra chairs can be brought in from the wings. If there are not enough, people should sit on the floor. Beverages should be distributed to everyone who wants one. All of this should occur in a friendly and natural way in full view of those members of the audience who have not left the house.)*

---

[11] *Director's Note:* The actors should work at facilitating the actions of those who are improvising and advise them where necessary. During the 29 representations of *Double jeu*, 248 people came out of the house to improvise. Of 53 improvised scenes, we saw:
19 times—THE HERMIT's scene (often played by 2 women or 2 men)
10 times—THE FERRYMAN's scene
8 times—THE SURVEYOR's scene
16 times—THE YOUNG MAN's scene

ACT TWO

(Act Two begins with the improvisations. As soon as the house lights have gone down, THE TEACHER moves downstage centre, introduces the first two participants to the audience, and announces the scene they have chosen to play. 5 and 6 sing the character's theme to help the improvisers work out their scene. [12]

(When the act begins officially, the actors stay in the places they were occupying during Intermission. However, it is important to balance the acting area so that all are not concentrated on the same side of the stage and that the actors are equally distributed among the people who came up from the audience. This makes everyone's subsequent movements easier. Immediately following the final improvised scene, THE TEACHER speaks to the class.)

THE TEACHER   If you would be good enough to go back to your places now, we'll continue with the test. *(Students begin to talk among themselves. They make a point of including the people who came from the audience. They chat with those who improvised, congratulating them warmly.)* I must remind you that if you expect this test to be beneficial to you you must live it for yourself. You could even help each other in this by asking, for example: "Which one of the characters do you think is most like me?" *(The students follow these instructions. No precise blocking is to be given to the actors. They should improvise their actions along with the other actors and audience members on stage. THE TEACHER looks at all the students and the people from the audience. All are speaking freely. 3 joins THE TEACHER.)*

3   Just look at them talking to each other all of a sudden. People who hardly gave each other the time of day before this.

(THE TEACHER looks around the entire class.)

THE TEACHER   That's right! I have the impression I'm finally getting to know my class…

13   I hope we're going to continue with the tests?

---

[12] *Director's Note:* In the original production, an actor tutored each couple, helping them develop the scene during Intermission and remaining near the riser during the improvisation itself, ready to keep the action going if necessary. Ideally, every actor would be assigned to a person from the audience. The positions on stage occupied by the actors and audience members following the improvisations varied from one evening to the next.

Unfortunately, it was not possible to let all those who wanted to improvise do so. We were forced to decide to limit ourselves to three scenes, each lasting about five minutes. Nevertheless, every evening we kept all those who had volunteered on stage. They joined the class and participated in the action. They had additional opportunities to express themselves throughout Act Two, which began immediately after the last improvisation.

6   We mustn't stop now.

THE TEACHER   No, no… we have to go right to the end. Please take your places. Is everyone here?

3   Not yet…

4   The lovebirds haven't come back.

3   We should wait for them.

THE TEACHER   Who was going to be the SURVEYOR?

3   *(stands up)* He hadn't been chosen yet.

THE TEACHER   (pointing to 4) You? Are you tempted to give it a try?

4   No, no, I assure you. *(stands up, comes close to THE TEACHER, speaks to him in confidence using an aside)* I tried doing an improvisation just now, and I couldn't go through with it. The way I was raised… the FERRYMAN, the SURVEYOR…

3   *(joins them)* (mocking) You have to stay pure before marriage.

THE TEACHER   Listen up, can I have your attention, everyone, please. *(speaks to students and audience)* Before we begin the test again, I must remind you that the situations in which the characters of the test develop are there solely to illustrate basic behaviour patterns. So… it's possible to behave like the FERRYMAN in real life without being, for all that, a *voyeur* as far as sex is concerned. I hope this is clear to you.

4   Of course it's clear. And I understood that we're not supposed to make moral judgments about the characters either, but it's beyond me.

13   All the same you need to know…

3   What criteria should we be using to judge characters that are so different if it isn't on moral grounds?

11   How can we make decisions about them if each of them has different values?

THE TEACHER   You can use your own life experience.

3   I thought about it. And I'm starting to see, in that case, which is the main character.

4   The HERMIT! He's the only one who's not controlled by his passions.

3   For the very good reason that he has none! He's a lazy man, egotistical…

THE TEACHER   A moral judgment again.

4   (disagreeing) I see him as a wise man.

   (Reactions from students, some approving, others disagreeing. 1 enters through Area C.)

1   I'm late, excuse me!

3   There she is!

1   (without pausing) But I'm ready…. If you haven't replaced me?…

3   (*moves toward 1*) You're alone?

(*4 returns to his place.*)

1   I don't think he'll be back. (*to THE TEACHER*) He doesn't agree with this work.

THE TEACHER   That's what I thought.

7   It's strange that her fiancé isn't with her.

(*The students comment on this scene, amongst themselves or speaking to audience members.*)

3   (*takes 1 by the arm, draws her slightly aside and speaks quietly to her*) You came back anyway?…

13   The main thing is that she's here. She plays the YOUNG WOMAN so well.

1   This test…. It's important to me!

3   Even if it means losing him…

6   Her whole life could be wrecked by this business.

1   He'll understand.

9   It's just a lovers' quarrel.

3   He won't be back.

1   He loves me!

3   He was wrong about you.

10   It's more important than that in my opinion.

3   He sees you through what he is himself.

8   Maybe they realized they weren't right for each other.

5   I felt badly for her.

1   Yes, there was this disagreement between us, but it's all cleared up now. I agree, he's set in his ways, but he's fair.

12   He was against the tests right from the start.

1   He'll accept me as I am. How could we be happy otherwise?

THE TEACHER   (*He moves to break up this private conversation between 1 and 3. He feels that 1 is tired. He moves to the centre.*) Let's pick the test up where we left it.

11   I'm sure she came back because she knew we'd wait for her.

(1 starts to move toward THE TEACHER, 3 holds her back.)

3   You see him through what you are as well. You're mirrors for each other.

1   Don't say that! (*breaks away from 3 and goes toward THE TEACHER*)

THE TEACHER   We had reached the scene with the SURVEYOR. (*pause*) Who would like to have this part? (*moves forward*)

3   I would! Me!

1   (*to 3*) But you've already played… you've already been the HERMIT.

3   I'll be a much better SURVEYOR. (*moves toward her*) And I really want to.

THE TEACHER   Go ahead then…. We'll do the scene over if someone else volunteers.

(to 5 & 6) Music!… Get ready. (*5 and 6 go to Area G, prepare. 1 and 3 cross to the left side of the riser. THE TEACHER moves to centre and speaks to students.*)

Remember that the YOUNG WOMAN has just crossed the river, a tumultuous river, where she thought more than once that she was going to perish. She is finally on the other bank.

1   (*to THE TEACHER*) Let's pick the scene up again at the moment when the FERRYMAN is about to leave. That would help me find the character again.

THE TEACHER   Do you want… me to become the FERRYMAN again?

1   It seemed to me that you did it very well.

THE TEACHER   Well all right, let's go…

(1 takes her place on the riser. THE TEACHER moves up close behind her, but off the riser. 3 pulls back close to the blackboard in order to get ready.)

10   The test is starting again.

(The following lines can overlap or be re-invented. They should be addressed to the audience members who have come on stage. Everyone, students and audience members, should form a circle around the riser. It is important to be sure that the audience members and the students are evenly distributed in the circle so that the students can suggest reactions more easily or initiate movements for the circle as a whole.)

7   Come on, come on, let's get as close as we can.

8   We need to be sure we don't miss anything.

13   We have no way of knowing which of the characters we'll identify with.

THE TEACHER   Let's get close around them so we can live the scene through them.

11   At the same time as them.

8   This play is telling the story of all of us.

4   We can live it for ourselves if we empathize with the ones that are acting.

10   Let's be right there for everything they do.

9   Everything they say.

11   Let's listen to them.

> *(Once everybody is in the circle, a few feet from the riser, lights go down on the stage and are focused on 1 and THE TEACHER. The river appears on the central screen. A muffled YOUNG WOMAN's song, played by 5 and 6, is heard during the following lines. 1 does not look at THE TEACHER. He speaks to her from behind. She listens to him and concentrates on the river. Initially, 1 looks at the ground.)*

THE TEACHER   There! You've got what you wanted. The river's behind you now.

1   I didn't know it was possible to be that afraid…

THE TEACHER   I've seen men tremble more than you did. You're strong.

1   *(lifts her head)* Yes, I am strong.

THE TEACHER   When he finds out where you've come from, he'll get down on his knees in front of you. Will you tell him the price I made you pay?

1   I paid, didn't I?

THE TEACHER   I got you across the river. No one else would have done it. Remember that, at least.

1   You taught me I was beautiful. Because of that, I'll go to him with more confidence.

THE TEACHER   Yes, you're beautiful. Goodbye.

> *(THE TEACHER withdraws and joins the circle at the far left. End of the YOUNG WOMAN's song. 1 turns around slowly and looks at the river, which she continues to watch throughout the next song and even into the beginning of the next scene.)*

1   To have passed that way!… To have passed that way!…

THE SURVEYOR'S SONG

6   That's the way life goes
When you've just been born
That's the way life goes
It's about you.
I'm going straight ahead

Tripping and falling
Standing back up
Falling again somewhere else
Getting back up anyway
And keeping on going.

You have no other choices
You are what you are
What a strange adventure!
Where will it take you?

You may fall and swear
You'll never go again
But you fall and do go again
And always start over
And always in your heart
The same obsession!

Hope or illusion
Of being one of those
Who build the world
With human dimensions

That's the way life goes
When you've just been born
That's the way your life goes
It's about you.

> *(Lights up on the riser. Pause. 1 is still looking at the river. 3 tries to start a conversation.)*

3 What are you doing here?

1 *(still on the river)* It's strange, isn't it?

3 Imagine, finding a girl like you in this forsaken place, beside a dizzying river, who seems to have fallen out of the sky on us…

1 (looking at the river as if she has trouble believing it) The river, I crossed it.

3 That was you in the front of the boat. *(Pause. 3 is caught short.)* I guess you didn't hear me shouting.

1 *(still on the river)* I crossed it!

3 (pause) And now where are you going? (pause) Did I hear you mention the Great Dam?

> *(1 turns to 3. They are now face to face.)*

1 That's where I'm going.

3 (mocking) Well then, have a good trip! It's a seven or eight-hour hike.

1   (for herself) But then I won't get there before nightfall.

3   *(in a low voice)* At least try to get across the swamp while it's still daylight. *(no longer looking at her, would have preferred not to have to speak of the swamp and so have eased her task)*

1   *(surprised, looks at 3)* The swamp?…

3   It goes on for miles. You sink in it up to your knees.

1   Oh, no!

3   No one would dare take the chance of going there at night.

1   All day I thought only of getting across the river, as if, afterward, everything would be easy for me. *(devastated, turns to face the audience)* And now you tell me there's a swamp…

3   *(looks at 1 now that she is no longer looking at him)* It's there, nothing I can do about it.

> *(During the following lines, 1 goes along the edge of the riser and starts downstage right. This movement is very slow. The audience should have the impression of a painful climb. In parallel fashion, 3 also goes along the edge of the riser, but upstage. His movement, easier and lighter than 1's, takes him upstage left. At the same time, as 1 moves, all the women of the circle step forward toward the riser to help her.)*

1   *(for herself)* I should give up.

3   This is as good a spot as any to spend the night.

1   I should give up.

3   If you'd like to sleep here, you're welcome.

1   I should be able to give up.

3   *(to 1)* When you're in a situation where there's no choice, you've got to accept it and say: "Oh, well, I did all I could!" …Try it… *(1 raises her head.)* You're living in a dream world.

1   I'm in the swamp… it's dark and I'm frightened…

3   That's exactly what would happen to you if you left at this hour. It's already starting to get dark.

1   I can't wait until tomorrow. Who's to say that he'll be there tomorrow?

3   You're meeting someone?

1   Yes.

3   If he knows you're supposed to come, he'll wait for you.

1   I'm not sure that he knows… *(turns to 3 and steps toward him)* How did you get here? Along the banks of the river?

3   It's no easier to go along the river on this side than it is on the other. On your side you have to go through the forest and here through the swamp. There's no getting around it.

1   (pause) Maybe he knows other ways of getting there.

3   There are no others. You can take my word for it.

(Disappointed and upset, 1 turns away.)

There's no part of this country that I don't know! This side and the other, and all the forests and the rivers and all the villages and all the towns. There's not a corner I haven't explored, surveyed, prospected, probed, or dug! Not any of its wealth and misery is unknown to me. *(He takes centre stage and advances downstage on the riser. It is not the SURVEYOR, but 3, who is speaking.)* I've discovered mines nobody knew existed. I even know a spot where iron juts out of the rock in almost pure form. A mountain of iron. Something else too… I've seen… I've seen villages wallowing in ignorance and poverty; I've seen whole families struggling for years on end, struggling just to survive, knowing they could never overcome. To survive, in this country that's so rich! Yeah, I know this country. It's as hard accept this country as it is to accept yourself.

1   I don't know what you're talking about… *(1 turns impatiently to 3. What he is saying has nothing to do with the scene—the women in the circle share her impatience.)*

3   Eh! No, you don't know… *(angrily)* There are thousands of you who don't know, and that's the whole problem! *(turns to 1 and steps toward her)* It's you I'm talking about!

1   About me?

3   Yes, about you! Yes, wake up! This country is you. What are you waiting for to realize that? It's you, it's me, your brothers, your family… and mine!… And the thousands of Indians that have been parked on reserves. [13]

(3 moves away, takes centre stage and speaks directly to the audience.) I'm speaking of the air you breathe, the earth that supports you, the river you just crossed, the songs you sing, the language you speak, a certain way of being that's like nowhere else in the world… I'm speaking to you about what's real; I'm speaking to you about you!

1   *(moves toward him)* Speak to me about him if you expect me to listen to you, otherwise be quiet. What you're saying makes no sense to me. I'm in another place, do you understand? Another place!…

3   *(He turns toward 1 with disgust. She understands nothing. He goes upstage to the back of the riser.)* In the swamp!…

---

[13] *Author's Note:* Lionel Villeneuve, who played 3, insisted on including the Indians in the Québec family. They should never have been excluded from our family.

(Concerned reaction from the students. They try to make 3 understand that he must get back into the play. Long pause, then 3 turns to face 1, makes a small gesture toward her.)

1   I don't want to be consoled. I'm crying because I'm weak, I'm crying because if I don't get across the swamp I might not ever see him again… *(She is angry with him for having made her step out of character.)*

3   I repeat: you have no choice.

> *(1 is empty. She crosses directly left. The students who are on the left side of the circle near the point to which 1 is heading go close to the riser and take her hand to give her courage and strength. 1 breathes deeply, her energy returns.)*

1   If you'd agree?…

3   If I'd agree…

1   *(slowly turns toward 3)* If you'd agree to go with me…

3   In the swamp?

1   *(steps toward him)* Yes, to show me the way…

3   *(moves right, away from her, stands downstage from her)* You're asking that of me? Me who just came back from there, and who's come back exhausted.

1   I've walked all day too. Your path and mine were the same, but on different sides of the river.

3   And you want to start out again?

1   I have to find him again. *(steps toward him)* I beg you!

3   *(turns his back to her)* No point even talking about it!

1   Then I'll just have to go on my own.

3   Whatever you like.

> *(1 moves away upstage. The people who are behind the riser draw close to prevent 1 from leaving. She stops and turns to 3.)*

1   Would you at least give me a map showing some landmarks?

3   I promise I will. Tomorrow morning.

1   *(steps toward him, suddenly very angry)* No, right now. Right now.

3   *(exasperated, rising tone)* It's already getting dark. You're crazy.

1   The moon is full right now; I'll be able to see as though it were daylight. *(about to step off the riser)*

3   That makes no sense. *(moves briskly toward her)* I'll force you to stay here! *(spins toward her)*

1　　What business is it of yours?

3　　It would be criminal to let you leave. You're not going to leave. *(She makes a move to leave. He grabs her by the wrists. She struggles. He subdues her and brings her in front of him, holding her wrists behind her back. He ties her wrists with an imaginary rope.)* Struggle all you like, I won't let you go. I'm even going to tie you up very tightly because with me being so tired you might wind up getting away from me.

1　　If he leaves before I see him again, if I lose him because of you, I'll find you wherever you are! And I swear on my life that I'll kill you! *(struggles, turns her head back in an attempt to bite him)*

3　　As you like. *(puts his hand on her shoulder to calm her)* And now just calm down, please. *(moves toward the left of the riser)* A little bit of peace and quiet.

1　　*(alone, lets her rage explode)* You're the worst kind of man! You're even worse than an animal! The others helped me. Even the HERMIT took pity on me. He could just as easily have said nothing. I didn't even know the FERRYMAN existed. I was ready to cross the river all by myself…

3　　*(back turned, over his shoulder)* The way things are right now you'd be sailing in a powerful sea, caught between two impossible currents.

1　　*(it is time, for her, to return to the subject of the scene)* Nothing, not a single obstacle, has stopped me all day long. Do you think it was easy to convince the FERRYMAN? He refused to cross. And yet, isn't it true that you saw me in his boat? All I had to do was accept his price! Do you want to know what he made me pay and how far I was prepared to go so that he'd bring me here? I went so far as to take off my clothes in front of him. *(Surprised, 3 raises his head then turns to her.)* Yes, I did! *(in a muffled tone)*

3　　That was his price?

1　　That was his price. I didn't haggle with him!

　　　　(3 moves downstage left. The following dialogue takes place simultaneously. Neither of the two listens to the other. The voices do not overlap.)

3　　I wish you hadn't told me that story.

1　　It's important for you to know what I'm capable of out of love for him.

3　　I wish you'd say no more. I want to forget what you've said.

1　　You have to know all the trials I've gone through so I can find him again.

3　　I wish I didn't know the price you paid the FERRYMAN…

1　　You have to know…

3　　You've really upset me with your story.

1   Do you have a price too? *(pause)* Untie me. I'll pay it. *(3 turns toward 1)*

    (3 makes a very slow, circular movement. He goes along the edge of the riser, comes up behind her. A pause. He hesitates. The audience should feel he is very tense. She believes that the decisive moment of the scene has come and does not feel ready. Then suddenly he unties her, and just as suddenly, moves downstage left.)

3   You can go…

1   Without paying?

    (He is facing the audience. 3 turns to 1.)

3   I don't need to make you pay for your freedom.

1   Thank you!

    (Relieved by not having had to go all the way, she is about to leave the riser. But suddenly some of the students—the ones that are close to her— squeeze up to the riser and let her know that she cannot leave. At the same time, 3 has made the decision to play the scene to the end. He gathers up his courage and attacks, timidly at first.)

3   All alone, at night, you'll never get through the swamp… *(slowly turns toward her)* With a guide it would be possible. With me, you could…

1   *(She in turn spins toward him, takes a deep breath and asks:)* What's your price?

3   *(He still hesitates. He finds it difficult to formulate this demand. He has been thinking for awhile that he is in love with 1. He loves and respects her. It is unthinkable for him to make love with her right away.)* It's not the same as the FERRYMAN's. I'm not a half-measure kind of guy. I won't be happy just looking at your body. I'll take it. I want to make love with you; that's what I want.

1   For that price you'll take me where I'm going this very evening?

3   Safe and sound.

1   *(She goes to draw some energy from the student closest to her, stretches out her hand. She has one last moment of hesitation, then accepts. Suddenly everything becomes simple and easy for her. She smiles, released.)* That's an easy choice compared to the idea of never seeing him again.

3   *(Is it a final instant of reticence? He steps toward her.)* You shouldn't have made me desire you.

1   *(She walks to him with determination. They embrace and will remain that way, standing, motionless, in each other's arms, until the end of the next scene.)* Take me.

    (Lights down on the riser. All those who are around the riser join hands and draw close to surround the area more tightly. When they are all still,

they make a sound, equivalent to the primordial Om, which they prolong and maintain until everyone has felt its vibration. This vibration draws all of them back to themselves as individuals, without breaking the bonds that have developed among them. When they have become themselves again, the actors, as well as the spectators on stage who wish to, recount an event in their personal lives. This brief story should recall a moment when they became aware for the first time of their individual, social or national identity.

The goal of these personal accounts is to awaken in the audience a desire for communication or exchange that will strengthen the bonds between the public and the players, between those attending and those participating. In order for this scene to reach its goal, the actors must be sufficiently committed to it in order to find new things to say every evening. At each show, they must give the audience a new part of themselves, thereby running the risk every evening of losing face, since they are speaking in their own name, not delivering a text written by someone else. Obviously, every actor must have the right to remain silent on those evenings when, for personal reasons, his or her capacity for giving is at a low point.

As soon as this scene is finished, lights come up on the riser. Then, slowly, ceremoniously, 1 and 3 end their embrace. Although they do not dare look at each other, they are serene. Then they do look at each other. Slowly 3 holds out his hand; 1 lowers her head slightly and 3 undoes 1's hair, which until then had been held in a bun. Her hair falls freely on her shoulders. All the participants in the circle follow this ceremony closely. Whatever 1 and 3 are doing is also being done for them and in their name. 1 and 3 look at each other. They tell each other their names so as to claim their own unique identity and show self-awareness. It is the actors themselves and not the characters who give their names, since the characters ceased to exist at the end of the preceding scene. They separate and bear their names to the other participants, on the two sides of the riser, starting from downstage and meeting again upstage.

At first, names are exchanged. Then they are proclaimed. Once all participants (actors and spectators) have exchanged names, they all turn to the audience and say their name, very loudly. This may sound like incomprehensible noise. The main point is to convey joy.

Slowly, without any apparent break between the two moments, they all go down into the house. They introduce themselves to the spectators and encourage them to say their names in return. When a spectator responds, actors who wish to may tell the story they told on stage, but this time in an intimate tone and much more warmly. Actors might incite several audience members to say their names simultaneously by introducing themselves in a low voice to a spectator who is close, then more and more

> *loudly to spectators who are farther away. At such moments, it becomes possible to witness an explosion of names throughout the theatre and even an exchange between the orchestra seats and the balcony [where the actors will also have gone].*
>
> *Then suddenly [the precise moment of this interruption is left to the discretion of the actors], 2 returns on stage.)*

2   What's going on? Have you all gone mad!

> *(1, 3 and THE TEACHER return to the stage. The other actors remain out of character, retaining their own personal identity. They comment on the stage action from the house.)*

1   (to the spectators who are close to her) That's him.

3   So what?…

1   You came back… *(joins 2 up on stage)*

2   I hope you didn't think I'd give up my schooling because of you.

3   (to the audience) Maybe he came back to play the role of the YOUNG MAN?

2   You're right, that's precisely why I came back! That surprises you, eh? You too?

THE TEACHER   *(THE TEACHER goes back on stage, followed by 5.)* In fact it does surprise me. I thought you'd refused to get involved.

2   *(to THE TEACHER)* I want to get one thing straight. I have a right to do the scene as I understand it, don't I? I have a right to do my own personal little bit of staging.

THE TEACHER   Certainly.

2   Well then, come and help me. I would like to move the desk onto the riser. *(to 3)* Make yourself useful, bring me a chair.

> *(2, assisted by 5 and THE TEACHER, moves the desk onto the riser [upstage right, slightly diagonally] and a chair to be used to climb onto it. 1 is worried as she watches all these manoeuvres. To reassure her 3 comes and joins her.)* [14]

3   Does this worry you?

1   Yes, if this is what he came back for.

---

[14] *Translator's Note:* 1 and 3 use the familiar "tu" form of address between them from now on. There are two ways of saying "you" in French: "tu" and "vous." Vous is always used when more than one person is being addressed. Between two people, the "tu" form is informal and implies some kind of intimacy. "Vous" is formal and implies respectful distance. The passage at this moment by 1 and 3 from the polite "vous" to the familiar "tu" represents a major step in the evolution of their relationship, to which both implicitly consent. This subtle shift is impossible to render in English.

(During this brief exchange, THE TEACHER clears the desk; 5 prepares to sing and 2, in area F, takes off his jacket and his sweater, which he will wear over his shoulders.)

3   But he does love you?

1   Do you still doubt it?

3   This is about you. Do you love him?

1   I don't know where I'm at any more…

3   It's your life.

4   (from the house) *(Is it 4 or is it the actor?)* It seems to me this game is getting dangerous. After all, in the final analysis, this test…

3   (to 4) Is it doing anything more than shedding a light on what was already there? *(to the audience)* It's amazing how afraid we are of seeing things as they are!

THE TEACHER   Let's not waste time… *(returns to centre stage)*

2   There, I'm ready.

1   What is this?

THE TEACHER   It's his idea.

2   This? It's a catwalk by the river.

1   You're not going to get up on it?

2   Everyone comes up with his own interpretation of the character. *(arrogant)* That's the only way I see the scene. If you don't want to play it, trade places with someone else. *(climbs on the desk, turns his back to 1)* [15]

3   *(joins 1)* We absolutely have to convince him to come down from there!

(Shouts of protest from the audience.)

1   Do we ever!… Him up there, me down here, it's unbelievable…

THE TEACHER   The YOUNG MAN's song…

(5 draws near the riser close to 2 and 1 goes up onto the riser. Lights concentrated on 2 and 1. 6 and the other students, who have remained in the house, participate in the song by clapping their hands. The river appears on the screens. During the song, 1 tries to attract 2's attention. He is on the verge of yielding, but catches himself and implacably turns his back on his fiancée.)

---

[15] *Translator's Note:* Throughout this scene 2 alternates in his exchanges with 1 between the familiar "tu" and the formal "vous," depending upon whether he is trying to establish his authority over her or his vulnerable intimacy with her.

THE YOUNG MAN'S SONG

6   That's the way life goes
When you've just been born
That's the way life goes
This is about you.

You can all give in
To the concessions of the day
Reject the past
And deny love
You can all scream
To new rhythms
About lustful joys
And all kinds of freedom
You can trample
All the traditions
But you won't have me
To sing your songs

I'll sing of pure love,
And fidelity,
And not what changes
And can never return
I'll sing of what lasts
And won't fade
And not extremes
Or facility
No, you won't have me
Instead of your songs
You shout in the wind
And the wind will blow by.

That's the way life goes
When you've just been born
That's the way life goes
This is about you.

1   Look at me!… *(steps toward the desk)* Look at me, I'm here.

2   *(over his shoulder)* Are you looking for someone?

1   This morning, from the other side of the river…

2   *(turns toward her)* I don't understand.

1   *(moves closer to him)* The YOUNG WOMAN, it was me… *(for herself, as though this was a discovery, turns to face the audience)* The YOUNG WOMAN, that's who I am.

2   Which young woman?

1   Try to remember!… *(turns to him)* You looked at me for a long time, and the picture of you has been with me ever since.

2   I just got here, and I have seen no one on the other side of the river.

1   Wait! I made a mistake. It was yesterday. *(2 shrugs his shoulders.)* Let me explain. *(steps back a bit to the middle of the desk, faces the audience)* I walked all night without any sleep and tomorrow became today without me noticing it.

2   Well… *(moves to left of desk, back to the audience)* And what can I do for you?

1   *(turns toward him, takes a step in his direction)* I want you to come down from that catwalk. You seem to be in a cage. I want you to come here beside me.

2   Why? *(this is 2 to 1, more intimate tone)*

1   Come…. Please, come…

2   I want you to tell me why.

1   *(Unable to express her real reasons, they seem so obvious to her, she is obliged to take refuge in hackneyed phrases.)* So that we can stand face to face. *(He turns his back to the audience and breaks the intimate tone.)* If you won't come down here, then lift me up to you. *(Quickly, she places herself in front of him at the corner of the desk. She holds her hand out to him.)* Give me your hand and I'll come up there.

2   (turns to her) You are just too dirty. *(She pulls her hand back.)* I don't believe I've ever seen anyone quite so dirty!

1   *(Shaken, her words ring false.)* When you find out how all this happened to me, you'll be amazed!

2   I doubt that very much!

1   Come down!… Come down to me.

2   There's too much mud where you are.

1   *(exasperated)* How can we get to know each other if we're not face to face?

2   Well. Let's just keep things the way they are.

>   *(He moves away to the far right of the desk, back to the audience. A pause. 1 seems to be completely devastated.)*

4   I wonder why he's doing that?

>   *(The students' exclamations that follow come from the house. If the actors find other expressions that suit them better, they are free to use them. They should address the spectators and encourage them to respond.)*

8   If he doesn't want to participate, he should say so.

9   Let someone else take his place.

13   He's doing it deliberately to get even.

10   He's been furious from the start.

11   He should come down from there.

9   They should be face to face.

7   Get him down from there.

13   Have someone else be the YOUNG MAN.

12   Get him down from there.

ALL   Get him down from there! Get him down from there!

2   What's wrong with all of them? Be quiet. I didn't interrupt other people, did I?

THE TEACHER   He's right. Let him play the scene as he sees it. Carry on.

> *(A pause. They all calm down. 1 uses the time to get back into her character. The impression could be created for the audience that 1 has somewhat "prepared" this scene. At times she should seem to recite sentences learned by heart. When 2 does not help her, she needs this in order to continue.)*

1   If you knew the road I travelled to get to you, you would make me…

2   Speak louder if you want me to hear you.

1   You see! There are things that can only be said up close. Up very close. *(She spins and takes a step toward him. A pause. He hesitates, crouches on his heels, then gives in.)* You're finally moving close to me…. When I saw you yesterday…. You can't have forgotten! You reached your arms out to me…

2   *(stands back up)* I never reach out my arms.

1   You reached out your arms. *(She moves back to the middle of the desk, and faces the audience. Both for herself and in order to get into the spirit of the test, she starts to become the YOUNG WOMAN once again. She is almost in tears.)* Would I have started out otherwise? Would I have spent the entire day looking for a boat to reach you?

2   A boat, at this time of year?

1   Yes!

2   When everyone knows that the river is not navigable in the spring?

1   I had to find you again. That's the only thing I cared about! I set out immediately; I followed the bank, I crossed the forest… I had to trek miles and miles through the woods…

2   *(goes to the left of the desk, starts to descend)* You're not going to start crying?

1   *(goes to him, near the chair and grabs his arm)* Even if you didn't see me yesterday, I exist nonetheless today. I'm right here in front of you. At least look at me!

2   *(very low, he is upset)* What if someone comes…

1   So what?

2   You should see yourself!…

1   *(backs away)* Am I that disgusting?

2   From head to toe! *(2's scorn for 1 hurts her deeply. She thinks that he might be right. She is shaken, begins to "fall apart." Seeing this reaction, 2, who still loves his fiancée and intends merely to teach her a lesson, gives in and comes down from the desk.)* All right, since it means so much to you. *(They are close to one another for a moment. Then he moves away to the right.)* Not for long, I warn you. I have to go…

1   Go?

2   Yes, to town.

1   *(rushes toward him, holds him in her arms)* No, no.

2   *(upset)* Please.

1   *(still clinging to his back)* Wait!… I know that it's hard to understand, that my feelings must seem ridiculous, but the very idea of losing you again!…

2   You are to have no expectations of me. *(frees himself from her embrace)* That must be clear. Only on that condition will I agree to listen to you.

1   I understand! *(She takes a step back and turns to face the audience. She repeats "I understand" over and over. In fact, she is beginning to understand the gap that separates them from each other. This is why she leaves.)* I understand!

2   Well then, you may stay. *(He sits on the desk and wipes his hand on his pants to remove the dust.)* But do not throw yourself into my arms. I detest being grabbed that way. (pause)

   Say something. (pause) You wanted to speak to me? *(She leaves the riser and heads toward the exit in area C. 3 joins her. Stirrings in the audience. THE TEACHER, who was watching the scene sitting in area F, gets up and comes toward her.)* What are you doing?

THE TEACHER   What's going on?

1   No. No, it's no use.

THE TEACHER   You're not going to stop. The whole class is counting on you.

1   (to the audience) I'm sure you can see he doesn't want to know anything. He's rejected this test right from the start. He's a man who's afraid of life.

4   You have to carry on anyway.

11   Don't let him use you! *(from the house)*

7   You can't give up, keep going.

13   Keep going. It's an important exercise.

6   Give him a better argument than that.

ALL   Keep going! You have to keep going! Have to keep going!

THE TEACHER   (to the audience) Silence please. (to 1) You have no choice. It's your responsibility this evening to live in their place.

2   You're making a mistake when you insist. Because she recognizes how wrong she is. Isn't it true that the results of the test are beginning to worry you?

1   How wrong you are! (to the audience) Isn't it obvious that he has understood nothing! But you're right, we must keep going. *(returns to the riser)*

2   Listen, I'll make you an offer that we leave it at that. We can still make peace you and I… *(takes her by the shoulders, speaks to her in a low voice)*

1   No, I want to see it through right to the end. *(breaks away, raises her voice)*

THE TEACHER   Let's pick up the scene where we left off. (to 2) You were on the catwalk. And you…

1   There… *(They resume their positions. He is seated on the desk and she is at the left-hand corner of the desk. A pause. She is concentrating. She knows that the YOUNG WOMAN must give all the details of her adventures to the YOUNG MAN. And so, that is what she will do, without ever showing emotion or getting carried away. She simply tells him the facts.)* One whole day in the forest, and there was this FERRYMAN that I had to beg… *(He gets up and steps forward, facing the audience. He is ill at ease. He senses what she is going to say and is not looking forward to hearing it. They are side by side.)*

2   The idiot who lives on the other side? You crossed this wild river, in his boat?

1   That's what I did.

2   People around here claim he'll lose his skin in it one of these days.

1   He said to me: "When he finds out that you crossed the river to come and join him, he'll be at your feet."

2   *(moves forward)* At your feet!

1   At my feet!

  (She repeats "At my feet" while looking at him almost scornfully. How could she have believed that someone like him would ever be at her feet? 2 is aware of her scorn. He moves away, walking along the edge of the riser, toward the left, until he is slightly upstage from her.)

2   In any case, I find it difficult to understand how you could go to so much trouble for a complete stranger.

1   I did much more. It took a much greater effort on my part to take my clothes off in front of the FERRYMAN than it did to go with him on the river.

2   *(turns to her)* He asked you? He dared?

1   *(turns to him, calm)* That was his price.

2   And you agreed to play along? *(He goes toward her, very carried away, outraged. She, in contrast, is calm, serene, relaxed, sure of herself.)* Yes, you did agree to play his game. You went that far.

1   That was his price. Otherwise, he refused.

2   You have no pride. No shame.

1   If I refused I'd lose you.

2   That's not a good excuse.

1   Listen to me…

2   *(turns his back to the audience)* No excuse! No excuse!

1   *(She turns to face the audience. She is obliged to continue with the account of her day.)* I did much more than that in order to find you again. When the SURVEYOR agreed to lead me through the swamp, at night, should I have refused his price too? Should I have refused to make love with him? The only way I could come to you was to pay his price.

2   *(returns to her, beside himself)* Yes, you should have refused. You should have let him know he deserved nothing but your disgust and scorn.

1   For you, because of my love for you…

2   Don't use me as an excuse to justify what you did.

1   Yes, I made love with the SURVEYOR, and he brought me to you. Do you know the swamp? Have you ever crossed it? *(For herself more than for him.)* The stagnant water, the foul slime that sucks you in to the point where you don't know if you'll ever get out, the clinging weeds that stick to your legs…. For hours and hours and hours…

2   *(He turns to her. He truly wishes to just understand.)* But what were you expecting from me?

1   To find you again.

2   *(He goes to her, unable to believe her. His principles stand in the way.)* Just to find me again?

1   Just to be here in front of you

2   Be completely honest! What were you expecting? That I'd fall in love with you when you told me the story of your adventures?

1   The question didn't even occur to me.

2 No doubt you even thought that you deserved it. And I should be on my knees here in front of you, and weeping at your misfortune?

1 You don't understand anything. (*He walks upstage, back to the audience. For her, this is the beginning of her journey toward serenity and joy.*) That long day was made up of more than just trials. If you know the forest, you know as I do the strange happiness found there. And the joy of its silence, a silence like no other, beyond silence, it seems to hold answers to everything…

2 I'm not a man of the woods.

1 Even the river wasn't just anguish and terror. Look at it… (*turns to the screen*) Imagine that water rushing at you. Imagine the overwhelming beauty of water that is capable of swallowing you up at any moment, and that carries you where you want to go, because you want to go there. Can you at least imagine that? (*She moves upstage. She turns toward him. He turns toward her. He responds to her with a gesture of futility.*) No, I suppose not. (*comes back to face the audience*) And you can't imagine the beauty of the swamp either?

2 The beauty of the swamp?

1 No, you can't. You have to have seen it in the moonlight to know that it has a particular beauty…. Disturbing, troubling, but moving as well. If I had found nothing but misery there, would I have laughed so much?

2 You laughed?

1 Yes, I laughed! I laughed at the absurd things the SURVEYOR told me to keep up my courage. I laughed at…

> (*2 comes to the same level as her. They are face to face, sideways to the audience.*)

2 You were able to laugh with that man who forced you to make love with him?

1 He didn't force me. That was his price.

2 But he raped you! That's a rape! (*turns to the audience, speaks to it*) Such blackmail is the same thing as rape.

1 He taught me that my body is good. Not just for him… but for me too.

2 (*turns to her*) And perhaps we should thank him for that!

1 I did thank him.

2 Then you're no better than him and no better than the FERRYMAN!

1 (*smiles*) True! That's true!

2 Go on back to them! You're their kind. I don't need a girl like you! The woman that I love will not be one of those who's ready for any and all kinds of experience. I am prepared to commit my entire life to this union. Such a commitment gives me the right to be as demanding of her as she is of me. You might as well know that once and for all. Everyone might as well know that!

> *(Receiving no sympathetic response, he leaves the riser and goes toward the exit in area A, where he waits for 1. He is hoping that the shock of his departure will make her think about the situation and come to her senses. He is hoping she will come back to him, repentant and ready to leave again with him. In fact, she is jolted by this break. She looks around her, looking for support. The river disappears from the 5 screens.)*

1   (to 3) That's what I said to you. He's a man who's afraid of life.

> *(3 and THE TEACHER move close to the riser. 1 looks at 3.)*

3   And you are life…

1   I am life? *(She turns to THE TEACHER, who agrees with a broad smile.)* I am life. *(She turns to face the audience, begins to sing timidly, then grows increasingly confident. Powerful return of the river on the central screen.)*

I am life,
Life for whoever counts
Neither tomorrow nor yesterday
But only the instant that is
Here and now.
Here and now.

> (The song is picked up by 1 and 6 together—6 still in the audience— then by all the students, but with a faster beat. As they sing and keep time with their hands, the actors go back up the aisles. They are joined by the spectators who participated in Act Two. The song to life is sung again once or twice when all of the class is back on stage. While the audience applauds, the actors, rather than taking a bow, clap their hands for the spectators. The actors remain on stage to welcome those who would like to come up and talk about the play with them.)

The end.

Mine Sincerely
(Bien à moi)

by Marie Savard

translated by Louise H. Forsyth

Introduction to
Mine Sincerely (Bien à moi [1])
by Marie Savard
Introduced by Louise H. Forsyth

Bien à moi was a one-act, one-woman radio play performed by Dyne Mousso [2] on Radio-Canada in 1969. A few months later in 1970 it was produced on stage at the Théâtre de Quat'Sous, opening on the same program as Michel Tremblay's *La Duchesse de Langeais*. Both plays were directed by André Brassard, designed by Jean-Paul Mousseau, and produced by Paul Buissonnault. The characters in *Bien à moi* and *La Duchesse de Langeais* have detached themselves, or, more precisely, have been excluded from mainstream values and standards of morality as a result of their blatant frankness in representing their unconventional sexual behaviour.

Bien à moi was the first explicitly feminist play written and produced in Québec. It is a hybrid dramatic monologue or performance piece, composed of poems, songs, and a dialogue of the main character—alternatively Marie and Marquise—with herself. She writes letters to herself and so joyfully tells to herself, and performs for herself, stories about her life to date. Its language, which ranges in register from baseness and vulgarity to the highly literary, offers a delightful parody of much of the world's canonical romantic literature. The character is a woman who has been around. She has been married, and has had at least one child, a son. The play captures a moment of awareness when she recognizes her own fragmentation, realizing that the various feminine roles she has played up to this moment have caused her to lose touch with herself, her desires, and her reality. She is alone, happily picking up the pieces of who she is. Her sense of self alternates between feeling she has been a mixed bag of disconnected pieces and a statue congealed in plaster:

> It often happened to me that I took myself for a statue in the eyes of men [...] when all is said and done, I had become a rather good and talented cripple. [...] And I went back to deal with my occupations of unbeloved statue. [...] There is nothing more strange than to see oneself in marble and to take oneself for another. [...] With one foot cast in plaster and the other in my glass, I'm still wondering whether I have indeed got there. It happens so seldom to me to take myself by the hand at the feet of men.

Savard's images to express the Marquise's sense of her fragmented woman's body encased, statuesque, in a hard material such as plaster, glass or marble from which she must break free anticipates imagery used elsewhere by Québec women playwrights of the 1970s: for example in *La Nef des sorcières*, *Les Fées ont soif*, or the collective *À ma mère, à ma mère, à ma mère, à ma voisine* (see Introduction and Bibliography).

In a wry twist of the standard discourse of romantic or courtly love, the Marquise acknowledges that she has been a poor mistress of herself and she begs her own "pardon for being so unfaithful to me." The six love letters that make up the play address this problem of infidelity to herself. They are the manifestation of her will to get in touch with herself, hear her own voice, claim control of her own body, and so put an end to her identity as a handicapped person.

Although Marie Savard was already an experienced singer, songwriter and performer by the time she wrote *Bien à moi*, she had not previously written for the theatrical stage. The production of *Bien à moi* was not *avant-garde* in the manner of the many currents of theatrical experimentation being done at the time. Instead, the play's innovative qualities arise out of the monologue and mixed media that develop its feminist themes. In the absence of a feminist theatre tradition, in the absence even of a tradition in which women exhibit their autonomous selves through their own voices on public stages, Savard chose to create a monologue, a form that reflects effectively the character's solitude and social exclusion. Her doubling of herself throughout the play is an effective dramatic device which makes dialogue possible, while underlining the sense of fragmentation that the character expresses with anguish, humour and poetry. The challenge for Savard, Mousso, Brassard and Mousseau was to invent staging and design approaches appropriate for the play's unusual subject and action. Savard's introductory text in the 1979 publication recalls with dark humour the obstacles she and Mousso encountered in getting the director and designer to engage conceptually and theatrically with such a radical feminist text. It seems that Mousseau was unable to see a middle-aged woman separated from her husband as anything other than frustrated, frumpy, and unattractive. Brassard, more understanding than Mousseau, could do no more than stumble in his attempt to stage the scene where the character joyously masturbates and achieves orgasm (that is to say, finally becomes mistress of herself and her destiny by getting in touch with herself). The blind spots that afflicted both Mousseau and Brassard were unfortunate and puzzling, particularly in view of the significant role both played in the exciting birth of Québec theatre in the 1960s, with its frank challenge through male homosexuality to prevailing sexual taboos. As a result of their reluctance to stage *Bien à moi* in a manner consistent with the vision of Savard and Mousso, the two women were obliged to withdraw from the theatre for rehearsals and to work together on the *mise en scène* in their own private space.

The opening poem of *Mine Sincerely* establishes the enigmatic tone of wry, yet raucous, humour used by the character throughout the play to position herself as determined to tolerate no holds in considering her own "case." Her relentless lucidity throughout the play, coloured by the frankness of her language and her ability to laugh at herself and her pain, is striking. Others, such as husbands or expert doctors, might call her hysterical or find her mad, but she is determined to speak for herself and celebrate her own joys. In the first letter Marie affirms the affection that she feels for herself and that she rarely expresses. As one would say in a letter to a person who is loved and who is absent, she has been missing herself. She realizes that her sense of beauty and self-worth has been concealed from her by the various roles she has played meeting others' expectations, leaving her in fragments. Most disconcerting about the situation is the realization that until now her fragmentation and alienation have seemed entirely normal to her. In the following letters, while she quaffs her beer, she evokes memories of moments when she served son, lover and husband, contextualizing them in prevailing sexist social myths and institutions and recalling myths Western society repeats to itself that capture the passivity of women and the heroism of men in tales of adventure. These myths underlie stories such as *Sleeping Beauty* and that of Dulcinea in Cervantes's *Don Quixote*. The height of the dramatic conflict in *Bien à moi* is reached when the central poem highlighting culture's practice of transforming living women into unchanging symbols of beauty and purity is immediately followed by the letter in which she becomes mistress of herself through masturbation and apologizes voluptuously to herself for having been untrue for so long:

> It is true that I am coming [...] wow! ... It is true that this is life. This is bliss. [...] I beg my pardon for being so unfaithful to me [...] Marie! Get hold of yourself [...] I close my eyes/ snuggled in my arms/ and I rock me gently to sleep. (Letter of January 18th)

But such bliss cannot last. Although the character retains her defiant attitude in the following letters, affirms her own powerful poetic language and vision, and shows herself ready to accept the consequences of being considered crazy, the play ends ambiguously. She has reclaimed herself from sexist norms, but she seems to remain alone and without a clearly established place to be. We don't know in the end whether the Marquise will remain mistress of herself or not.

Savard's work is poetically and humourously celebratory of women's lives. One would have to look long and hard to find her equal for originality in words and images. When brought to the stage, her writing is transformed into forms of energetic erotic performance that speak deeply to sources of personal spirituality. The theme which runs through all her work is the absence of women's voices and experiences from the myths and stories that make up the West's cultural heritage. Along with this outrageous absence has come the patriarchal control of women's bodies, the suppression of their desires, the denial of their erotic, spiritual, and intellectual energy. As a result, women's stories have remained untold, bonds of love and communication between mothers and daughters have been denied, while women and men have, as a result, been rendered unable to affirm a basis for love of themselves and each other.

Critical reception of *Bien à moi* was largely unfavourable. There were few critics at the time who understood feminist writing or feminist theatre. The misunderstanding was so complete that the play was virtually erased from collective memory. It is rarely mentioned by historians of theatre, despite the beauty of the text, its astonishing prescience regarding women's search for love of self, and what would become radical feminist theatre in Québec in the 1970s.

Notes

¹ "Bien à moi, Marquise," was first produced in 1969 on radio in "Studios d'essai" of Radio-Canada with Dyne Mousso in the title role. This first version was published in the literary magazine *Liberté*. 12:4 (juillet-août 1970): 11–28. The definitive version was produced in February 1970 in Montréal at the Théâtre de Quat'Sous, again with Dyne Mousso, on the same program as the first production of Michel Tremblay's *La Duchesse de Langeais*, both plays directed by André Brassard and designed by Jean-Paul Mousseau. It was published a decade later with an introduction by the Editor and an introductory text by Marie Savard, both of whom highlighted the production difficulties encountered for this radical feminist text and the misunderstandings that came from the critics: *Bien à moi*. Montréal: Éditions de la Pleine Lune, 1979. The text was re-published in 1998 in a bilingual edition by Éditions Trois. This edition contains all the pieces in the 1979 edition, along with a new introductory text by Marie Savard and a "Postface" by Louise H. Forsyth, who translated all the material in the volume into English: *Bien à moi/Mine Sincerely*. Laval: Éditions Trois, 1998.

² Dyne Mousso (1930–1994), who played the dual role of Marie and the Marquise, was a widely admired professional actor for stage, cinema and television. Throughout her career, she engaged with others in the subversion of convention-bound theatre norms and oppressive social practices and discourse. Her sister was the celebrated and controversial actor Muriel Guilbault and her husband was the famous artist Jean-Paul Mousseau, both of whom signed the explosive 1948 manifesto *Refus global*. Dyne Mousso also played the lead role in the first performance of Loranger's *Double jeu*. She and Mousseau were divorced before *Double jeu* and *Mine Sincerely* were produced.

Bibliographical Suggestions

Selected Other Works by Marie Savard

Le Journal d'une folle. Essai-roman. Montréal: Éditions de la Pleine Lune, 1975.

Sur l'air d'Iphigénie. Poème dramatique. Montréal: Éditions de la Pleine Lune, 1984.

On *Bien à moi* and Marie Savard

Frémont, Gabrielle. "Marie Savard, *Bien à moi*." *Livres et auteurs québécois 1979*. Sainte-Foy: Presses de l'Université Laval, 1980: 201–02.

Gélinas, Marc F. "Marie, la marquise." *Le Magazine Maclean*.

Robert, Lucie. "*Bien à moi*, monologue de Marie Savard." *Dictionnaire des oeuvres littéraires du Québec*. Tome IV, 1960–1969. Montréal: Éditions Fides, 1984: 100–01.

Tremblay-Matte, Cécile. "Marie Savard." *La Chanson écrite au féminin*. Laval: Éditions Trois, 1990: 99–101.

About Marie Savard

Marie Savard was born in 1936 near Québec City, where she spent her childhood and later studied Sociology at L'Université Laval with Georges-Henri Lévesque, widely recognized and admired as one of the leaders in laying the groundwork for the Quiet Revolution. At a time when secondary and post-secondary education for girls was unavailable through the Québec public system, Savard credits her mother and the religious who founded the college for girls that she attended for the encouragement to go against the dominant current and pursue her education. An urban artist, already writing poetry and songs in the 1950s, she moved to Montréal in 1961, attracted there by the vibrant cultural life during the years of the Quiet Revolution. Hers was a powerful response to the art, poetry and music of Québécois and French artists such as La Bolduc, Arthur Rimbaud, Louis Aragon, Edith Piaf, François Riopelle, Claude Gauvreau, Anne Hébert, Félix Leclerc, Gilles Vigneault, Pauline Julien, and Clémence Desrochers. Her unique sense of rhythm found resonance in American jazz and blues musicians of the day. For several years, Savard wrote for radio and performed her poems and songs in *boîtes de chanson*, such as Le Patriote, that had sprung up in Montréal and around the province.

Savard's work is a compelling and poetic love song for those who know how to love themselves and their fellow human beings. Its wicked humour is aimed at those who have allowed their ability to love to be tainted by abusive ideologies and their accompanying stereotypes. Her biting critique of social norms has particularly focused on the damaging myths perpetuated in literature, religion, social institutions and public discourse, myths that originated centuries and even millennia ago. Savard was one of the first to recognize that the source of the damage they do to human relations lies in their erasure of actual women from the historical record and the contemporary stage, whether public or private, and their transformation into abstractions and statue-like symbols. She has written her plays, poetry and songs to give voice and presence to those who have thus been silenced throughout the fabric of culture and society. Like Marchessault and Boucher, she has frequently made ironic use of the theme of madness in order to dramatize the many ways in which girls and women who refuse to play the games of patriarchy are classified by authoritative voices as hysterical and so rejected, scorned, and even hidden away in private spaces.

Savard founded Québec's first feminist press in 1974: Les Éditions de la Pleine Lune. In the course of her career, she collaborated with the Théâtre Expérimental des Femmes, frequently performed her poetry and music on stage, and produced a significant body of dramatic poetry and music in which the unique, quirky, witty and poetic elegance of her writing is striking.

Bien à moi was first produced on stage at Théâtre de Quat'Sous, Montréal, in February 1970, with the following company:

Dyne Mousso

Directed by André Brassard
Designed by Jean-Paul Mousseau

the grey ointment is to the blue baby
what the grey nun is to the black rod

MINE SINCERELY

a joyous city lady
jovial or nutty as a fruitcake in the view
of several
having found no remedy with
her doctor
or the other
came to the conclusion to look after herself
herself
without other

she found it normal to speak to the wall
went crazy when the wall responded to her

her doctor
or the other
has never understood her case
he continues to speak

she
exclaims
sends letters to herself

yesterday, April 7, 1969

My beautiful me
to whom I don't write often and whom I love to death,
little dot, little dot, little dot, dot.

I miss myself as much as me, but at least I can write to myself. Which is a lesser
evil when you know like me that I don't have a phone.

Don't matter. She just talks to hear herself talk. She's mad.

If you only knew, my dear, the adventures I have had since you left, you would
have to agree with me that, behind the appearance of a jovial woman, I conceal
the deepest of dramas.

The deep drama will be very much worn this year. It should be attached on the
left beneath the belt. As well, it will be quite long. And have it trail behind you,
love, life's no joke, y'know.

> *Opens a beer.*

But

very dear me,
let's get a bit serious and let's really talk about the deep drama.

I'll be brief, I'll be brave, I can do it, I want to do it, and in the short time it takes to write it down, I'm going to get going on my little spiel.

the drama

With one eye of glass and the other cast in plaster, I was wondering if I was disabled. It often happened to me that I took myself for a statue in the eyes of men. These sorts of things happen somewhat everywhere elsewhere and are not spoken about. IF I SPEAK OF THEM TODAY, IT IS BECAUSE I FIND THAT THIS HAS BECOME AN ALMOST TENABLE SITUATION AND I WONDER WHAT COULD BE CHANGED ABOUT IT ON THE FACTUAL LEVEL OF MY POPULAR MASSES. My husband's quite pleased, there's been no change since my operation.

I won't speak to you about my childhood, because that burden has been lifted… the eye cast in plaster. And I'll say nothing to you about the stories people tell regarding my husband… the other eye. But I'll simply tell you, that as a woman myself, that even I, her husband, wasn't able to restrain her.

Now then, with my two eyes well in place, I had almost learned to limp. No doubt, I didn't manage it every day, but, when all is said and done, I had become a rather good and talented cripple. I even had some leisure time to think about the unfortunate fate of so many crutches in ruin.

But after all, you can't live everybody's life, eh!
There indeed is the drama, eh!
And I went back to deal with my occupations of unbeloved statue.

Museums have mysteries that mystery is unaware of. There is nothing more strange than to see oneself in marble and to take oneself for another. This happens in rare cases where the exception does not prove the rule. I have my own ideas about this. But I'd just as soon not talk about it.

With one foot cast in plaster and the other in my glass, I'm still wondering whether I have indeed got there. It happens so seldom to me to take myself by the hand at the feet of men. These things happen somewhat everywhere here and are spoken of too much. I WAS TALKING ABOUT THIS VERY THING JUST LAST EVENING WITH MY BROTHER-IN-LAW.

And with these good words, I leave myself as is,
very dear me.

Will write again very soon.
I feel that I understand myself and make myself out between the lines.

Mine sincerely,

Marie.

day before yesterday, the first of September

Oh…
My beautiful me.
I can't wait any longer to write to me, I miss me so much.

Wake up this morning rosy-cheeked. Pimples are staying away from me this year, but I've still got my big heart.
On this matter, I have another little story to tell you, Marquise. It may be short, but lacks nothing for all that in fine silver quick wit…

pimples

Sometimes he laughed when he was getting dressed, sometimes when he was getting undressed. But that's in no way important, the motivation always staying the same.
Certain people will tell you that he was a depraved little fellow, that he was afraid at night and had trouble controlling his needs.

Takes a drink from her beer.

I would be unable to cheerfully confirm these rumours, but I can assure you that he had pimples, that his mother knew it, and that the cat was always outside.

And that is the way he had grown up, as an almost model child…. His masters often enjoyed the pleasure of casting their gaze upon him. He, the fine little fellow that he was, could only blush. And his mother
knew it,
and the cat
alouette
oh…

One day when he was wandering in the woods
here and there
naughty
curious little fellow that he was
he met the handsome thoroughly handsome prince
and right up on his horse
and la la la la the handsome thoroughly handsome prince
gave him candies
and the child laughed
and the child cried
and his joy was great
and the prince said to him
I AM THE IMMACULATE CONCEPTION
TELL THIS TO YOUR FRIENDS
and his mother knew it
and the cat

alouette
oh…

I hope, very dear me, that this little scene from daily life had the good fortune of pleasing you and teaching you about true friendship and the true joy which flows from it…. The life of country princes and of rural knights has some of these simple pleasures that we city women are no longer able to rediscover. My husband is in the Knights of Columbus. And y'know, it's true these guys know how to hide, eh!

I give myself a tender embrace,

me.

later, the same day

My dear me
whom I also call Marquise out of affection, the sweet nicknames of love, y'know!…

I owe you explanations for my letter of this morning. Yes, upon rereading myself before sealing myself up, I found myself somewhat confused. And that is why I cannot bring myself to close my eyes this evening without clearing up the little anecdote of the pimples for you.

Not that I doubt your perspicacity in stripping away the most obscure of symbolisms,… d'y'think it's maybe someone we know?… but even more, believe me, it's to respond to a very personal ethical concern I have. And, believe me one more time, I'll have a great deal of difficulty falling asleep this evening if I shirk this legitimate duty to me. Well then, love, that wouldn't do at all. Just let me tell you, not at all!

You must know, Marquise, that there's nothing fictitious in what I told you this morning, just let me tell you, not at all.

And I could even say to you that I knew the little boy of the handsome prince very well. Where I invent a bit is when it comes to his mother. And if I do so, believe me still yet one more time, it is not from dishonesty, but indeed because the dear little fellow had developed the fine habit of calling me mommy.

And I loved the little boy, it must be said. At that time I had little perspective on myself, and I was much too subjective to claim that one day I was going to rid myself of the enormous cultural heritage of the Western world coming from the fact of being mommy.

Opens a beer.

You might object, Marquise, that I did not write to you at that time but indeed this morning.

Drinks quickly.

On that point, I'll respond to you that time has nothing to do with the weakening of cultural subjectivity—you know, the alibi of culture!… aren't I terrible?… and that thinking the opposite is just a trap, just a utopia of real objectivity, just a quite naive or very pernicious way of projecting your subjectivity into an object, or, if you prefer, of objectifying your subjectivity.

    Finishes her beer.

In other words, objectivity is a myth.

I was talking about this just last night with my husband, about objectivity. After all, I'm not nothin' but an object, eh! Well, la-di-da, that didn't go over very well, no, la-di-da, not at all.

What rambling, Marquise, what bizarre reactions when you try even a little bit to be clear. So I was saying that the little boy had developed the fine habit of calling me Mommy. To which I paid no attention in the beginning, but which subsequently disturbed my mild and tender femininity… as a woman myself!… Well then, let's have no more of that, eh!

And that's how, as a thoroughly chaste North American woman and relaxed tragedian, I followed my base instincts and abandoned the little boy, all the better, henceforth, to fly in rapture with the handsome prince, thoroughly handsome, and right up on his horse.

I was indeed the foolhardy little thing that I was. Little scatterbrain who did not know the adventures which would befall her from all this nobility. You're still with me, Marquise, I carry on.

I had before me a hero thoroughly handsome and completely in a fog. From the mommy that I had been, I had become the little or the big sister… the comrade, the pal, palsy-walsy, you know!… And that's how I came to understand vaguely that the hero/warrior was missing life in the bush…. And that's how so as not to be paranoid, I became masochistic. My psychiatrist is quite pleased, I haven't changed pills. Seems things are going much better.

But, in spite of that and however much you are a Marquise, you must undoubtedly be able to understand me, I loved the hero/handsome prince thoroughly handsome and thoroughly in a fog.

NOW I SHALL SPEAK TO YOU ABOUT THE ROLE OF THE CHILD IN THE STORY OF SLEEPING BEAUTY.

This is what happened. An offspring was born very handsome, beside the horse and not in the fog. It was at that precise moment, when they broke my water…. Well then, just let me tell you, life's no joke, y'know!

I said, Marquise, at that very precise moment the hero/warrior felt shaken from on his pedestal and a dialogue, since you're supposed to speak of dialogue these days, started to develop between him and me. Everything was spoiled.

The hero/warrior rethought his structures and spouted these words from his beak.

Why, he said, does the thing speak? By what aberration of nature does she disturb the warrior's make-up table? Why should the femi... oh sorry... the verility [sic] of myself be imperilled? No longer a way to fabricate a reassuring visage for myself! Here I am forced to grapple with my face! What a turn of events! Since when have things forgotten to such an extent their role as objects of repose that they now are starting to utter words? I'm thoroughly fed up with all this! No further repose possible for the warrior! Oh... may the days of fixed mirrors and of windmills in the mind return.... Heroes can't take it any longer.

Yes, they are tired, heroes. Ever since the days when they preserved and avenged the memory they imagined for a Dulcinea, who did not survive long enough to tell her real story.

Yes, they are exhausted by their continual struggle against false dulcineas. You are one of them, Marquise, those perfidious enemy women who violate without mercy the memory of the true, the unique, the one and only Dulcinea, sincere and selfless.

Yes, they're so tired.

And in their fortified castle they tend their wounds and keep them open. For one cannot be cured without shame, without feeling guilty toward the memory of a Dulcinea, sorrowing and suffering at the end of her days.

It's 'cause her mother was always sick, eh! She was a sick woman.... Seems things didn't go so good with her husband either.

Myself, I would just as soon not speak, but seems it was a couple that didn't get along so good, eh.

There it is, Marquise.
All that happened a long, long time ago, But it was important for me to be frank with myself, since I'm getting close to me. And, the more I get close to me, the more I lose from sight the handsome prince/hero/warrior thoroughly handsome and thoroughly right up on his horse.

ANTHEM TO THE KNIGHT

where is she good knight
your living dulcinea
you keep her 'neath your brow
for fear of crushing her

you make a moon of her
with heart that's all in rags
you make a moon of her
ah woe with broken heart

you placed her in your head
a doo, a doo, a day
you placed her in your head
with swagger and with shield

closed heads, fresh breezes
the moonless nights go by
the beauties of this place
all sleep in porcelain

the beauties of this place
musical musical boxes
get payment in the street
get payment in the night

they were your deposit
a doo, a doo, a day
they were your deposit
with a stroke of your pen

where is she good knight
your living Dulcinea
you set her in your song
her beauty to preserve

your sleeping Dulcinea
untouched and marvelous
she is your rose 'neath glass
your mirror rose your lamp

you placed her in the ground
a doo, a doo, a day
you placed her in the ground
with swagger and with shield

    Goes for a beer.

today, January 18th

My all me all mine

It's true y'know she's got no choice Marie eh!
But that's OK

To think I had to wait until today
to truly find myself
well then, knighthood in the ass
yeah!
And I finally see myself in all the nudity of my absence, as far from myself as
I am. But this distance, this space in time that takes me far from me does not

alter in any way the viri… oh, sorry… the vivacity of my feelings about who I am, who I am.

Who I am, I am.

I'll even go so far as to put myself in words from the deepest depths of my childhood and my sweet memory… I'm coming to me from the depth of my youth, I am coming to me and I don't know it.

If there's any of you who take this for youthful mistakes, well you're wrong eh! And, like, you better see that right away, eh! Because I'll tell you that as I am me myself, even me, my conscience, I couldn't stop myself.

If I speak to you from the deepest depths of my childhood, it's because I always set my childhood as such aside, says she.

And if I speak to you of my sweet memory, it's because I'm simulating my death.

Come on, Marie, don't pretend you're dying…
I know it that you're not dead there…
I know it… I know it…

It's true that I'm coming. I'm coming from the depth of my your… wow!… It's true that this is life. This is bliss. I don't have to hide it from myself any more. I don't have to refuse me to myself and then take refuge behind the immense subterfuge of my modesty and my knowledge of how to behave. Once again I'm becoming the little girl in my mirror, the one perfect and only mistress of my games. Marie… get your fingers out of your nose!

So much cheating, Marquise, so many kinds of dissimulation I impose on myself, when I know full well and from the start that all my male fellow-citizens know how to walk only on their hands.

I'll always remember that marquis poet who, one evening by the full moon, read me like an open bed.
Madam, said he, the fragility of your vagina makes me think of the purest crystal. To which the Marquise replied… it is my finest wedding gift made from rock crystal. Just let me tell you, knighthood, nobility, they sure know how to pile it on!

If you manage to get rid of the niceties, things can get back to what is natural. I beg my pardon for being so unfaithful to me, in these moments of enjoying great bliss with me, by evoking a past from which I suffered so much and that I wish to have gone forever. Am I such a wretched lover… such a wretched mistress of myself then? Marie, just a child…. There, there don't get excited, Marie! Get hold of yourself…. Get hold of yourself…

I close my eyes
snuggled in my arms
and I rock me gently to sleep.

another day

Today, I'm sending me a telegram.

I think, during the preceding days, I have sufficiently pushed my time and my patience. I would not want to rush myself too much after all…

And, since I'm a timid woman, little tease of a timid woman that I am, why would I not give myself a surprise? A telegram, that's unexpected!

And besides, any means that lets me get in touch with me is good. And if I don't come to me, it'll be me who goes to me. That's it! This way I won't let me get away from me.

Hello me. STOP.
Temperature ideal. STOP.
Met the other's mother with a double scotch on the Main. STOP.
Speak of this to no one. STOP.
Would pass as a *voyeuse*. STOP.
Put all the soldiers of my frigidaire at attention. STOP.
Speak of this to no one. STOP.
Would pass as a spy. STOP.
Told a man he was handsome. STOP.
Speak of this to no one. STOP.
Would pass as gay. STOP.
Have in my room the most beautiful baby in the world. STOP.
Speak of this to no one. STOP.
Would pass as Mommy. STOP.
Have more and more time to speak to myself. STOP.
Speak of this to no one. STOP.
Would pass as cured. STOP.
Am a beautiful Marie. STOP.
Speak of this to no one. STOP.
Would pass as a women's woman. STOP.
I'm fed up with passing as. STOP.
SHE PASSES

> *Sings.*

I'm only passing by
I pass like a swallow only
a whirl of wings…

I'm only weeping
Ah yes if my poor things
could just have wings

I'm in too much of a rush
I'm called unlovely woman
a luscious fruit…

I looked at them
singing in their homes
their hearts in their heels

they said they had always sung
the same the same refrain
ever since they reached the age of reason

I wondered as they sang
if they still had the same keys
or if there'd been a change
ever since they reached the age of prison

they say she says whatever
wherever
whenever
Is mad

I began to spin
to spin in their living room
quite nude in my heels

when they looked at me
they said my dress, oh yes
was very much prettier

when I tried to cry
I began to laugh
they all took hold the door
to let me out

they say she does whatever
wherever
whenever
Is mad

the next time I saw them
I was spinning in the street
to go out for some air

they all seemed in a rush
and without looking at me
said I should clear out

I told them in reply
that I'm a spinning top
that everyone's going in circles
to be or not to be
a top or not a top

they say she cries whatever
wherever
whenever
Is mad

I am a spinning top
that's spinning in the street
while people honk at it

they say that spinning tops
must march around in time
to whirs of ticking clocks

I say that spinning tops
are coiling with the earth
while time-bound ticking clocks
are coiling in their case

they say she does whatever
wherever
whenever
Is mad

I asked them
if they minted their coins
on the sunshine of their hearts

they told me that the bank
had invested their precious coins
in accounts of war

I found it normal
to build a bank
but now I'm upset
that the bank is destroying me

they say she says whatever
wherever
whenever
Is mad

I sketched you
one evening when I was spinning
on the ceilings of your bedrooms

you say the photograph
looked more like you
on the morning you were wed

I say the ceiling view
gives spinning tops their eyes

to show the spleen that lies
in the shadow of your beds

they say she says whatever
wherever
whenever
Is mad

I'll come back often
from the city where I spin
in the midst of clock faces

it may be they will say
they know a spinning top
that spins off-centre

I really wish I knew
when I look in the air
if those who're in the air
look at me in the air

tomorrow

Well then, things aren't going well at all…
Just let me tell you, not at all!

Well frankly, Marie, now
Y'know you're exaggerating some, eh!…

If you start singing crazy things now, stuff that no one's going to understand….
As far as I'm concerned, well, it doesn't matter to me, Marie, but people are
going to talk…

Aside from that, everything's OK, things go on.

If I have decided to be a spinning top, it's 'cause my little girl wanted one. And
then, if my little girl has a beautiful face, that I looked for for years on sainte-
catherine street, it's 'cause she comes from my belly, from my heart… on the
ground. The heart will be worn very low this year.

And if chickens had pears instead of feathers, they would be much less
disgusting to arrange. And then, if anyone still believes in parachutes, it's
because our angels are dragging about around our countryside.
The tall woman is landing…
Everyone's getting stewed…
If your beers are drippy, it's 'cause your washers aren't good. A scotch!

Well then, love, things aren't going spinningly
Take Marie, it's 'cause she's having a nervous depreciation then, eh!

And if I cease immediately at once writing writing to me, it's because Madam Tristan does not exist and Romeo and Juliet had families that were too large…

So I'm sending my letters back to me, my photos and, if it wasn't already done, would send me back to my mother's.

Well then, it's a sham! so Marie bends under pressure, eh! That Marie, she's a child!…

Let the Marquise remain the companion of my bad days, if she really wants to. Her lack of reciprocity puts a stop to my relationship, to my concubinage with her. Chivalry had pushed me into this situation. Well then… it crushed Marie, eh! It crushed her…

Men remain as sleeping beauties of the forest. The beautiful women of this place are still in their case while in the streets the knights, now elected by the people, continue to pay homage to the all too well known soldier.

The beautiful women of the Western world look at themselves with gentle discretion and have strange ways of writing to themselves. Women of letters, addressed and deranged, correspond vicariously with one another… correspondence that the knights, still elected by the people, observe with the resignation of the *voyeur*.

Don't you think that Marie's an intellectual!
Well then as for me, I've seen everything now…

Well then, eh!
She spreads gossip
She has second thoughts
She speaks for
then she speaks no more…

«Y nous poussent à toute
Y'a un bout à toute»[1]

Denise Filatrault, Émission *Chez Denise*
Radio-Canada 18/3/79

---

[1] "They push us to everything/There's an end to everything." (Translated by LHF)

song

the lovely sleeping beauty
is made from boards of wood
is made from bones of wood
her hair is angel silk

you women of this land
you courtly, courted ones
oh where, oh where did you go
to make love 'round here
I see you coming and going
in memory
of good king Dagobert
your mothers' patron saint
oh where, oh where did you go
to weep 'round here
you women in this land
you courtly, courted ones

the lovely sleeping beauty
is made from boards of wood
is made from bones of wood
her hair is angel silk

Where did you hide
around here
you courtly, courted ones
of this land
I've almost heard about
what you've become
because I heard the rumours
of your desires
I've heard you're alone
in this land
I've heard you're isolated
around here

the lovely sleeping beauty
is made from boards of wood
is made from bones of wood
her hair is angel silk

you courtly, courted ones
of this land
the eve of being killed
around here
arrives for us today

at high noon
I think of Algeria
and too of Julia
madam climbs to her tower
in this land
my sister's in her grave
around here

the lovely sleeping beauty
is made from boards of wood
is made from bones of wood
her hair is angel silk

The end.

Evangeline the Second
(Évangéline deusse)

by Antonine Maillet

translated by Luis de Céspedes

Introduction to
Evangeline the Second (*Évangéline deusse*[1])
by Antonine Maillet
Introduced by Louise H. Forsyth

Évangéline deusse is the fourth play by Antonine Maillet to be published and produced on the professional stage. It is a play in two acts with four characters: an 80-year-old Evangeline, an elderly man from Britanny, an elderly rabbi, and a crossing guard who is a Quebecker from Lac Saint-Jean (the Stop). The play is a parody of Henry Wadsworth Longfellow's famous romantic poem *Evangeline, A Tale of Acadie*, first published in 1847. The 1850 edition of this popular long poem contained illustrations, the first showing a nun-like heroine surrounded by the banner: "Sorrow and silence are strong; patient endurance is god-like." Unlike Longfellow's heroine who quietly suffers her great misfortune with resignation, Maillet's character vigorously rejects all imperatives to remain silent and to endure with patience. Maillet's Evangeline is a heroine whose strength lies in her outspokenness, her bonds with others, her will to oppose exile, loss of culture, injustice, and her flippant scorn for docility.

The action of the play takes place in the present between May and October in a small park in Montréal, a city that has failed to become home for the four exiled characters. Evangeline has been sent from her home by the sea to live with her son and his family in Montréal. She shares her knowledge and love of all things maritime with the man from Brittany, and both of them have much in common with the rabbi who dreams of return as well. Unlike these three elderly characters, the kindly Stop is from rural Québec. His function in the play is primarily to facilitate the transitions and encounters of the other characters. All of them long to find a place where they belong and thrive, like the small spruce sapling that Evangeline tries throughout the play to plant and keep alive in the park. Initially isolated from each other and from all others, the characters slowly begin to share their stories, feelings, memories and desires. As bonds of friendship and love develop, they discover with joy that they can share some common heritage, along with the food and the songs they joyously bring to their encounters. Although their shared *joie de vivre* is fragile, shaken in the end by the death of the Breton, their affirmation of life is strong, as is their will to live every moment fully, without regret and without resignation. As the central character, Evangeline's evocation of the sea and the Acadian community brings to life for the audience the richness of the cultural homeland she has had to leave behind.

Evangeline the Second is innovative in its chosen subject-matter of Acadian history and continuing alienation within the fabric of Canadian and Québecoise culture. The age of the characters and their various dialects contribute to the play's uniqueness. Its form is not experimental, nor is it explicitly feminist. However, the striking theatricality of all Maillet's dramas is evident here in the compelling dialogue and simple range of actions. And Evangeline—with her quiet wit, gritty determination, earthy lucidity, and indomitable compassion for those who suffer—is the dramatic epitome of female strength. The play is revolutionary in its sensitive celebration of human dignity and the will to fight social injustice and ostracism. The strength of Evangeline, in effect a re-visioned anti-Evangeline who refuses all romantic and debilitating notions of love and stereotypes of both women and the elderly, make of her one of the most powerful feminine figures in Québec theatre.

Evangeline the Second begins with the characters coming together in the park, making conversation as they introduce themselves and evoke the vast geographies they bring as integral to their long life stories. Despite their differences, they quickly find common ground. The characters then share a discussion of Longfellow's poem and the history of the Acadians: the early years, the deportation by the British, and the painful return. This scene highlights the contrast between Longfellow's romanticized tale of a passive and docile tragic heroine and the harsh realities of survival, when families, and most often the women had to become involved in dangerous and illegal activities such as rum-running and prostitution. As the characters' friendship grows stronger and they share their delicacies from the sea and from their memories, they come to realize that the spruce sapling is taking root. Through the summer, however, each comes to realize that the passage of time is relentless, and one can never go back. Unknown hands have uprooted the little tree. However, they replant it, decorate it, sing and dance together and express their love for each other, just before they each move onto their own wintry path. The beauty of life, love and community have been explored and affirmed, even though loneliness, loss, death, and time have not been defeated. Evangeline reaffirms her faith in powerful life forces in conversation with the Stop:

> You'll know that age has no age; that the most beautiful hand is one that has a life 'n a country carved in its palm; that the most beautiful eyes come from a lifetime of looking people straight in the face; and that a person's soul don't shrivel up like his skin, it don't wrinkle, it don't age, 'n it won't die either.

Antonine Maillet's *Evangeline the Second* is a small universe representing a specific human community, its long history and its unique culture, with its people and their language, its sea and its sea shore, its trees and birds. As such it is a microcosm of all human communities, with its beauty, suffering, and struggle with forces of destruction and death. Created with an overriding tone of tenderness, readers and theatre-goers are brought to feel viscerally the power of a life lived fully right to the end. As the microcosm that is Acadia is transposed in *Evangeline the Second* to a small and unwelcoming park in Montréal, its vulnerability is highlighted. Alienation that can be neither avoided nor resolved determines the lives of the characters, which have been deprived of lasting and transcendent meaning. Yet Evangeline and the others have found or created their own vibrant meaning.

Maillet has created a female character who speaks to urgent socio-political realities and who also addresses the most compelling and complicated questions of the human condition. Evangeline, an elderly, dispossessed mother of eleven, moves completely outside stereotypes of passive and docile femininity, all the better to dramatize the human potential for resistance to dark forces, whether caused by human cruelty or the implacable passage of time.

Notes

[1] Maillet, Antonine. *Évangéline deusse*. Montréal: Leméac, 1975. *Evangeline the Second*. Tr. Luis de Céspedes. Toronto: Simon & Pierre, 1987. *Évangéline deusse* was first produced in Montréal on March 4, 1976 at the Théâtre du Rideau Vert, directed by Yvette Brind'Amour with Viola Léger in the role of Évangéline.

Bibliographical Suggestions

Selected Other Works by Antonine Maillet

Rabelais et les traditions populaires en Acadie. Diss. de doctorat. Université Laval.

Pélagie-la-charrette. Montréal: Leméac, 1979. *Pélagie—The Return to a Homeland*. Tr. Philip Stratford. New York & Toronto: Doubleday, 1982. (first novel by a person not a French citizen to receive Le Prix Goncourt)

La Sagouine. Montréal: Leméac, 1971. *La Sagouine*. Tr. Luis de Céspedes. Toronto: Simon & Pierre, 1979.

Les Crasseux. Montréal: Leméac, 1973.

La Contrebandière. Montréal: Leméac, 1981.

On *Évangéline deusse* and Antonine Maillet

Antonine Maillet: dossier de presse, 1962–1981. Sherbrooke: Bibliothèque du Séminaire, 1981.

Antonine Maillet: dossier de presse II, 1972–1986. Sherbrooke: Bibliothèque du Séminaire, 1986. 74 pages.

Andrès, Bernard. "Évangéline et la nef." *Voix et images*. II.1 (sept. 1976): 127–29.

Dionne, André. "Le Théâtre qu'on joue." *Lettres québécoises* (sept. 1976): 14–16.

Chiasson, Zénon. "The Acadian Theatre." *Canadian Theatre Review*, 46 (Spring 1986): 50–71.

Eddie, Christine. "Évangéline deusse, pièce d'Antonine Maillet," *Dictionnaire des oeuvres littéraires du Québec*. Tome V, 1970–1975. Montréal: Fides, 1987: 327–28.

Forsyth, Louise H. "Antonine Maillet," *The Oxford Companion to Canadian Theatre.* Ed. Eugene Benson & L.W. Conolly. Toronto, Oxford, New York: Oxford University Press, 1989: 319–21.

Godin, Jean-Cléo. "L'Évangéline selon Antonine," *Si que* (automne 1979): 23–46.

Godin, Jean-Cléo & Laurent Mailhot. "L'Évangéline selon Antonine," *Théâtre québécois II.* Montréal: HMH Hurtubise, 1980: 27–28; 147–64.

Maillet, Marguerite; Hamel Judith. *La Réception des oeuvres d'Antonine Maillet : actes du colloque international organisé par la Chaire d'études acadiennes les 13, 14 et 15 octobre 1988.* Moncton: Chaire d'études acadiennes, 1989.

Sabbath, Lawrence. "Théâtre du Rideau Vert. Viola Leger's appeal intact in new play," *The Montreal Star* (March 8, 1976): D-11.

Sarrazin, Jean. "Antonine Maillet et l'Acadie." *Forces*, 44 (1978): 33–38.

Smith, Donald. *L'Écrivain devant son oeuvre. Entrevues.* Montréal: Québec/Amérique, 1983: 245–68.

Usmiani, Renate. "Preface. Evangeline the Second: Antonine Maillet's Archetype of Acadian Womanhood," Antonine Maillet. *Evangeline the Second*, Tr. Luis de Céspedes. Toronto: Simon & Pierre, 1987: 11–17.

Weiss, Jonathan. "Acadia Transplanted: the Importance of *Évangéline Deusse* in the Work of Antonine Maillet." *Colby Library Quarterly* (Sept. 1977): 173–85.

About Antonine Maillet

Antonine Maillet (born 1929 in Bouctouche, New Brunswick) has written many plays and novels for which she has received prizes and honours in Canada and France: the Governor General's Award, le Prix France-Canada, le Prix Goncourt, le Grand Prix de la Ville de Montréal, and the Chalmers Play Award. She has received more than thirty honorary doctorates, is a Companion of the Order of Canada, Officier des Palmes Académiques Françaises, Commandeur des Arts et des Lettres de France, Member of the Royal Society of Canada, Member of the Académie canadienne-française, Officier de l'Ordre de la Légion d'Honneur.

Maillet completed a BA and a MA at L'Université de Moncton, a Licence ès lettres at L'Université de Montréal, and a Doctorat ès lettres at L'Université Laval. Subject of her doctoral dissertation was the relation between the stories and idiom of 16th century French writer François Rabelais and the popular traditions still alive today in the maritime provinces: *Rabelais et les traditions populaires en Acadie.* She began her professional career as a teacher of literature, and a writer and programmer for Radio-Canada in Moncton. Her first novels, in which her amazing storytelling abilities were already evident, appeared in the late 1950s. Like Rabelais, Maillet produces biting social commentary through the exceptional humour of her stories. Her first plays were produced and published in the early 1970s. The original and compelling qualities of her plays and fiction were quickly recognized. The voices of her characters were heard to represent for the first time ever the collective memory, language, cultural traditions, and contemporary social conditions of the people of Acadia. She was the first to use the popular oral speech of Acadians in literary texts. *La Sagouine*— a collection of sixteen monologues—received wide public attention and enthusiastic critical praise. The celebrated actor Viola Léger, who created La Sagouine and most of Maillet's other powerful lead characters in both French and English on stage, radio, television and cinema, received the Dora Mavor Moore Award in 1981 for her many haunting and earthy incarnations of La Sagouine.

Maillet is the author of about forty works of fiction, plays, histories, translations and children's books. She has made a major contribution to Canada's francophone canon, while playing a decisive role in affirming the rich beauty of the French language spoken in Acadia and in encouraging the revival of Acadian writing and culture.

Évangéline deusse was first produced at Le Théâtre du Rideau Vert, Montreal, in March 1976, with the following company:

EVANGELINE	Viola Leger
The BRETON	Guy Provost
STOP	Paul Guevremont
The RABBI	André Cailloux

Directed by Yvette Brind'Amour
Set Designed by Robert Prévost
Costumes Designed by François Barbeau

Characters

EVANGELINE, an eighty-year-old Acadian woman
The BRETON, a man of eighty
STOP, no particular age, but younger than the others
The RABBI, an elderly man

Scene

The action takes place in a small park in Montreal.

Time

The present.

EVANGELINE THE SECOND

Act One

Scene One

It is May. Seated on the back of a park bench, STOP gazes happily into space. Traffic noises are heard in the distance. STOP gets up and exits with his stop sign. A short pause before he returns, followed by the RABBI who canvasses the park, then settles into a bench upstage. STOP resumes his former position, staring into the distance; then, apparently distracted by something, he leaves his bench. EVANGELINE enters with a bundle. She searches for a resting place; STOP looks around with her. She sits on a bench downstage and proceeds to unwrap the parcel while STOP looks on attentively but discreetly. Finally, she unveils a spruce sapling.

EVANGELINE   A spruce. Yep! Nothin' but a sapling just now, but some day he'll be a spruce tree. You don't get 'em around here 'cause this ain't a city tree. Ah! maybe a few… them that you transplant…. Nope, they belong to the woods… 'n to the coast. Yeah, to the sea. Look, even the salt can't kill this little bugger here. It'll grow day 'n night, in autumn or spring, straight up or crooked, its branches covered with snow, its needles blown by the nor'easter, 'n its roots smack into the sand. Better believe it! Once, back home, a stranger came by who figured that them spruce trees could grow even in the sea. That's 'cause he'd seen the spruce trees that the officers plant in the bay to mark off the channel, 'n so he figured…. From the city he was, poor soul, 'n he'd never seen salt water before…. Come to think of it, in 'em days, I'd never seen the city myself 'n I didn't know they washed down the streets every mornin'. The first time I saw water gushin' out o' them red posts in the edge o' the sidewalk, I rushed to turn off all the big faucets so that folks wouldn' drown…. Well, they warned me…. Maybe you ain't from these parts, eh?

STOP   No.

EVANGELINE   Ah! You too. Well, that makes two of us. Two exiles, better believe it! It's good to know you ain't alone…. Excuse me, maybe you don't speak French?

STOP   Yes.

EVANGELINE   Ah, good…. But you ain't from aroun' here.

STOP   No.

EVANGELINE   Well, well. You ain't from these parts, but you speak French. Well, that's jus' like me, you see. I come from where the spruce trees grow in the sand.

> *She gets up and starts looking for a spot in which to plant her spruce. Finally, she walks up to a tree and pulls out a small spade from her pocket.*

Right here, he'll be fine. It'll have some company when it grows up. You gotta think about that when you transplant. You gotta plant yer feet where there's folks around. A spruce ain't used to living alone. Back home, they grow in armloads, you've got all the trees you want. But over here…. It's my son that sent me this one, my third boy, Robert. Ah, that's Robert! He wasn't easy. The little devil!… When I left, he said to me: "Mother," he said, "as soon as I get a chance, I'll send you a spruce." A spruce! Can you believe it! Robert, really… sending me a spruce to the city, sending a spruce to Montreal, really! Well, he said to me: "I'll send you a spruce or my ass'll turn into a pumpkin," that's what he said. Now, does that make any sense talking like that! Tee-hee… "Robert," I said, "who in the hell raised you?" "I'll send you a spruce," he said. So then, I tol' 'em: "Well, if you send me a spruce, I'll plant it 'n it'll make it."

> *STOP, who has been following her tale with great interest, suddenly freezes and points to the street.*

What's the matter?

STOP   A cop!

EVANGELINE   The bastard, he's after my spruce. *(She stands in front of the spruce to hide it. For a while, they look worried, then relax as the danger passes. EVANGELINE returns to her task.)* It'd be a shame to let it croak like that, after travelling alone on the CNR all the way from Le Fond de la Baie.

STOP   All the way from there?

EVANGELINE   Yessir! It's my youngest boy, Raymond, who went to pick 'm up in person at the station. Ah! the poor little thing! Wasn't a pretty sight: all skinny 'n yellow 'n flat. You barely had to look at 'm and his needles would drop into yer hands…. Sad to see. So I said to my boy Raymond, the youngest one: "It's gotta be planted, it's dying." He was willing, my boy, but there's the daughter-in-law. She says it kind o' messes up the place 'n fills the house with the smells o' wood. She does keep a clean house though, you gotta give her that, 'n every day she sprays it with her can of Evergreen. That's 'cause she's from the city, my daughter-in-law, 'n she knows nothing about woods…. So you ain't from aroun' here, is that what you said?

STOP   Yes.

EVANGELINE   Aha! Well, that's just like me. I'm from the coast. A couple o' days walk, almost 'n a good walk at that. First you follow the dunes, then the sea, you pass the small creek, the wooden bridge 'n the big creek, then you take to the north where the dirt road latches on to the paved road 'n then the post road. For a while, you keep following the sea. Then all of a sudden, you make a sharp turn 'n face the northwest. You let go o' the coast, then you're on yer way to

Montreal. So you look back one last time 'n you figure you'll end up getting a stiff neck, 'cause you keep looking back 'n yer neck is hurting. The salt air tickles yer nose; 'n the cries o' the gulls dance in yer ears; 'n tears bigger than usual fill up yer eyes on account o' them high tides; 'n all over yer skin you get these big pimples, like goosebumps. By that time yer neck is broken, so you turn around. For two days, the only thing you see is corn fields, woods 'n paved roads… paved roads… enough to parch yer throat right out…. It's gonna need a little water, the poor thing, if we wanna save it.

> *STOP looks around, then exits. The RABBI turns to look at*
> *EVANGELINE and the spruce.*

It was just about to die, would o' been a pity…. A real pity to let croak that part o' yer homeland you carry with you. A person might be willin' to expatriate herself 'n go far away into exile, but they can't ask you to forget. *(to herself)* When you lose yer right to own a piece o' land, to keep yer belongin's 'n to have a country, you still got a right to yer memories, that's fer sure. They can't take that away from you. Can't force you to forget.

> *STOP returns with a Shell gas can. The RABBI looks away.*
> *EVANGELINE smiles, grabs the container and waters the spruce.*

There, now he can last till the rains come. The rains, do they follow the tides around here?… The tides, why you ol' fool! You're talking through yer hat again, Evangeline. Tides with a river that wandered off this far inland, well! When a river travels five or six hundred miles through mountains, there can't be much of a tide left by the time it reaches the wharf.

> *The RABBI stands up, observes someone walking down the street, then*
> *clears his throat to attract the attention of the other two. Once again,*
> *EVANGELINE tries to hide the spruce while STOP rushes out with the*
> *container.*

I can't figure out what they've got against spruces. You might not be a city tree, but then… I sure ain't a city girl 'n yet here I am. So if they're willing to have me around, seems to me they also ought to have a bit o' the freshness 'n smell of the ol' country.

> *STOP returns with the BRETON who thanks him with a nod before*
> *sitting down on the bench previously occupied by EVANGELINE. From*
> *a suitcase, he takes out a small carving of a boat on which he's been*
> *working. STOP returns to his bench. EVANGELINE seems intrigued.*
> *She goes to sit near the BRETON to examine his work. The BRETON*
> *throws her a quick glance. That is all it takes to set her off.*

Is it a schooner?

BRETON   *La Défunte Espérance* that got smashed up on a reef one Sunday, the second day of April 1892, off La Grande Échouerie, northeast of the Magdalen Islands.

EVANGELINE   Aha!… What do you mean, 1892? Well then, you never knew her. So tell me…

BRETON   My grandfather knew her. And my great-grandfather spent part of his youth sleeping in her shrouds. The description of her comes from my father, who also sailed the north seas like all those of his race… before me.

EVANGELINE   You were a sailor too?

BRETON   I took to the sea when I was fifteen.

EVANGELINE   Fifteen, well I'll be! Just like us.

BRETON   Sorry?

EVANGELINE   I also come from a long line o' sailors. My father, Thaddée à Olivier à Charles à Charles, once took a schooner all the way to the south seas, after his own father, Olivier à Charles à Charles 'n his grandfather, Charles à Charles, who were both sailors before him. Like they say, we've got salt water running through our veins from one generation to the next. That's why we live long in the family: the salt stops the blood from going bad.

BRETON   Tee-hee!

EVANGELINE   Like the spruces that grow along the coast: makes 'em sturdier. This one here was born native of salty sand. *(pause)* Nice weather… still a bit cool, but the good weather can't be far off. Next month, there's be wild strawberries; 'n the one after that, clams.

> The BRETON looks up.

Clams. Sorry, maybe you've never heard of 'em. Down home, we call 'em clams 'cause we've never learned to talk fancy. And anyway, at my age, it ain't 'cause I spent the winter here in Montreal that…. You know what my second boy, Edward, said to me: "Mother," he said, "you're going to Montreal, but don't you come back speaking *joual* now." Speaking *joual*, can you believe it! Bad enough we've got this barn smell about us, without trying to speak *joual* to top it off. And then, there's too much salt in our throats, too much nor-easter in our lungs. Our voice is too hoarse to speak Québécois. No, I ain't about to speak *joual* or talk fancy, Edward, don't you worry. When you've hit fourscore years, it's just too late. So my daughter-in-law can call 'em quahogs all she wants, I'll still say clams.

BRETON   But that's what they are, madam, clams, not quahogs.

EVANGELINE   So you ain't from aroun' here either, eh?

BRETON   *(standing up)* A Breton from France, an old sailor, a resident of this country for over half a century, François Guéguen at your service, madam.

EVANGELINE   I'm sure happy to make your acquaintance. A Frenchman from France, would you look at that now! My name is Evangeline, almost freshly arrived from Le Fond de la Baie.

BRETON   From where?

EVANGELINE   Le Fond de la Baie. That's between Bouctouche 'n Richibouctou.

BRETON   Ah!

EVANGELINE   Just before Côte Sainte-Anne, if you prefer.

BRETON   That's on the North Coast, I gather?

EVANGELINE   The North Coast? Don't you go taking us fer Injuns, now!

STOP   Tee-hee!

BRETON   *(to STOP)* Beg your pardon?

       STOP is ill at ease.

EVANGELINE   That one ain't from around here either, but there's no way o' knowing where he comes from.

BRETON   Looks to me like he's from Le Bas du Fleuve or La Gaspésie.

EVANGELINE   Well! that's not far from home…. It's not that I want to be nosy, but are you a Gaspésien by any chance?

STOP   No… I was a farmer, myself, before coming to town. And now I walk folks across the street.

EVANGELINE   A walkman, he is. The kind that stops traffic though…. So then, you're not Gaspésien?

STOP   No, no.

EVANGELINE   And you ain't from down river either?

STOP   No, no.

EVANGELINE   For the love of God, where the hell are you from?

STOP   *(startled)* From… le… Lac Saint-Jean.

EVANGELINE   I kind o' figured it'd be something like Saint-Jean. And what brought you over here?

STOP   Well, I was looking for a job.

EVANGELINE   And you found nothing?

STOP   Yep, I walk folks across the street.

EVANGELINE   What more do you want? Walking folks across the street. In a town like this one, there's lots o' people going from one sidewalk to the other. Them that are on this side got business on that side, 'n them that are on that side, well…. There's always somebody somewhere that needs to change sides. So you need somebody to help you cross over.

…Back home, we use ferryboats to cross over. From early morning to the wee hours of the night, from one island to the next. I remember when I was young, we went to Miscou once. First you go north all the way to Shippagan, then you take a ferry boat to get to Lamèque; once you're in Lamèque, you gotta reach the tip o' the island to board another ferry 'n sail to Miscou. Then you figure you've reached the ends o' the world. Well no, 'cause when you look up, you see more land off the island, beyond the water, and that's Treasure Island. You don't have to go there, of course. But if you do, you'll need another ferry to get you across. So there's a lotta crossing to do in life…

Street noises. STOP gets up and exits.

…I told you, didn't I?

Sounds of a horn and tires screeching to a halt.

…God Almighty!

EVANGELINE, the BRETON and the RABBI walk towards the exit.
A sheepish STOP reappears, straightening his cap.

Well, next time, wait for me. I'll help you cross the street.

They all return to their benches.

So then, you're a Frenchman from France, eh? I'm glad to hear it. 'Cause I'm a Frenchwoman myself, yep! French from Acadia that don't speak no other tongue but French. Ah, well, maybe a little English to help me get by when I'm at the CNR station…. Now and then I go to the station like that, to see if by any chance I might see somebody from home coming in just then…. And there's always a few: some youngsters with their hands in their pockets, peach fuzz under their noses, chewing bubblegum 'n figuring on trying their luck with the big city; 'n whole families loaded with their belongings, 'n children already hiding behind their mother's skirts; 'n from time to time, an old man looking everywhere, hoping to find a face he might know…. You've been here long?

BRETON   Fifty years, madam.

EVANGELINE   Fifty years, can you believe it! Well, there's no two ways about it! Fifty years is a lotta days in exile, as they say. You must have been pretty young when you sailed across the sea?

BRETON   Oh, oh! Not that young. You're looking at an octogenarian.

EVANGELINE   An octogenarian, imagine that! Well, as fer me, I'm right smack in my eightieth year. That's almost as much as you. But I've no intentions of staying here fifty more years, that's fer sure. If I had fifty more years to live, that is. But I've got one behind me though… well, almost. One autumn 'n a winter. My very first winter in town. Ah! it wasn't too hard. First I had to learn to protect myself. When you got fourscore years on your shoulders, you get to know how to handle them winters. The best way is to grab on 'n hold tight.

BRETON How's that?

EVANGELINE You know, hold on to it, like a sailor in a storm, holding on to his schooner's mast.

BRETON During a storm, a sailor doesn't get the chance to hold on to his schooner's mast. He has to maneuver.

STOP Well, if it was me, I'd maneuver with one hand and hold on to the mast with the other.

BRETON And your winters by the sea, were they just as rough?

EVANGELINE Oh, yes! for that matter. Just as rough… rough, tough and cold. But a dry cold… a white cold… kind o' cleaner, you might say. Your feet sink in the snow, you see, not in the slush. And you have real snowflakes blowing across your face, not soot. And you ain't afraid o' cracking your chin on the sidewalks each time you go out, 'cause back home, everybody knows you 'n nobody cares if you walk across the bay on snowshoes or with spikes under your galoshes.

STOP Me too, I used to go into the woods on snowshoes to set my fox traps.

EVANGELINE Do you eat fox meat where you come from?

STOP No, it's only for their pelts.

EVANGELINE And do you set a few snares to catch rabbits?

STOP No, to catch hares.

EVANGELINE Rabbits 'n hares are all the same thing. A hare is a rabbit that lives in the woods. And do you eat stew, 'n *rappie*?

STOP …er… meat pie.

EVANGELINE Pooh! that's awful stuff. My daughter-in-law makes it. You should ask your wife to cook you some *rappie* one day; I can show her how if she wants.

STOP I ain't go no wife.

BRETON Tee-hee!…

EVANGELINE Well, your mother then. Does your mother hook rugs on them long winter nights? *(STOP and the BRETON look bemused.)* Hooked rugs?… Don't tell me the women of such a big country, with such a long winter, don't know how to make them!

BRETON You mean like crochet work?

EVANGELINE Yep, using a hook…. That way, you get crocheted blankets 'n hooked rugs. At first, when you're young, you learn to knit, 'n to hook by joining the others. Later, when you got a family, you hook 'n knit to dress your kids 'n keep the floor warm under their feet. Then, once you've raised your family, you go and hook 'n knit at your neighbour's place to catch up on the news. And in your old age, well… your fingers are so used to it… you knit 'n hook so you don't get bored.

BRETON   And in your exile, do you still hook 'n knit?

EVANGELINE   I did bring some strips of cloth 'n yarn with me. But my daughter-in-law complains it takes up too much space. What it mainly takes up is her card table. Ah! But at night, before falling asleep, I embroider handkerchiefs in bed. I do it for the daughter of my oldest boy, Ernest. Now that she's going on sixteen, I figur'd I might as well start on her trousseau. When I left home, I gave her my cedar chest, but I warned her: "Roseline," I said to her, "you'll have to fill it up before your wedding day, now." But youngsters today think it's a waste of time to embroider handkerchiefs when they can go into any store 'n buy ready-made Kleenex. "Especially when you think of what goes in 'em handkerchiefs," she said to me, la Rosaline. Well, it didn't take me long to find an answer to that one: "We'll all turn to dust when we die," I said to her, "and in that shroud o' yours there'll be dust. But is that reason enough to bury you in Kleenex?" "To talk like that," she said to me, "you gotta have your future behind you." As for her, the future was ahead.

BRETON   That's why I left the home country fifty years ago.

EVANGELINE   To find a future ahead of you?

BRETON   That's it. After the Great War, Europe has turned into an old maid. But me, I was still young. Not even thirty. I had my arms, my courage, fifteen years of sailing in my guts, and in my eyes…. But I had a wife and two daughters. Two little darlings as gentle as doves. I'd become a milkman after the French fleet was destroyed. A milkman…. Still every day I'd go to the harbour and look around…. Till one morning, I heard that a Canadian freighter needed men to replace those of her crew who died from the Spanish flu during the last crossing…. My wife nearly went crazy. Later she joined me with the girls, but she had a hard time getting used to your winters, so she went back.

STOP   She's still there?

BRETON   The Second World War took her. My daughters stayed there.

> *During the BRETON's tale, the RABBI gradually comes closer to the other three.*

RABBI   Did you miss your Bretagne?

> *All three abruptly turn to face him.*

EVANGELINE   So you also speak French, then? And I'll bet you ain't from around here either.

RABBI   Well, I'm from around here now, like all of you. But for me, exile was less painful. I'm used to it. And also, it's easier to leave once the party is over.

EVANGELINE   True. That's what happened to me. They gave me a party before I left. It was at one o' my boys' place, Gérard, the fifth one. And everybody came: Ernest, Edouère, Robert, Tilmon, Aldéric. They all come to Gerard's with their wives 'n their children. And they'd invited the neighbours 'n the whole family. The house was packed. And it's a big house. Ah! what a surprise… a cake, dandelion wine, little fancy sandwiches, gifts 'n square dancing.

STOP   Did you dance?

EVANGELINE   I'll have you know I even got them all out of breath. Four square dances, five or six swings 'n a jig to Pierre blue's reel. I danced it all by myself to the sound o' the violin… 'n it's after that they gave me a big gift. You know, the gift on-behalf-o-the-family-'n-friends-here-present: a lounge chair for ol' folks, it was. A lounge chair, at my age! Might as well have given me a stretcher!… I took it myself, under my arms, straight to ol' lady Ozite who hasn't' been able to walk for years…. A lounge chair!… Does the fact that you're leaving the country mean you gotta go feet first? They forget I'm a woman who can still run down the steps without grabbing the handrail! And still able to pack my things 'n leave home on my own two feet. And even though I'm on the wrong side of eighty, I still got all my hair 'n all my teeth; 'n oil in my kneecaps; 'n marrow in my bones; 'n spit in my mouth. So, yep, I can say to all the neighbours 'n daughters-in-law 'n folks who wanna hear it that my name is Evangeline 'n it so happens I'm from a race of people that can start a new life when others end up ending theirs. That's what I can say to them.

> *Fascinated, the BRETON, STOP and the RABBI stare at her.*

Scene Two

> *The RABBI is reading his newspaper in Hebrew, sitting on the BRETON's bench, facing the audience. STOP enters, followed by the BRETON. The RABBI quickly gets up and looks for another bench.*

BRETON   Please, don't move.

> *The RABBI excuses himself with a hand movement, smiling. He sits on STOP's bench and the latter remains standing. The BRETON lights his pipe.*

STOP   Hey you, get outta here! Leave that spruce alone!

> *He chases the pigeons away, then turns to the others.*

They were gonna kill 'm, soiling him like that! (*The other two get up and walk toward the spruce.*) Pigeon shit can kill a tree that's too young 'n too skinny.

BRETON   Still, this one here was born native of salty sand; he's seen worse. (*He laughs. STOP still looks worried; the RABBI smiles.*)

> *EVANGELINE enters, a bucket in hand.*

EVANGELINE   For the love of God! What happened?

> *She pushes the men aside and kneels by the spruce.*

BRETON   Just a couple of lovesick pigeons showing very little respect to your spruce.

EVANGELINE   The rascals. I'll show them a thing or two about respect. Get away from here, you devils, you! What's the point of being raised in the city, eh? No self-respecting gull from our shores would do that, let me tell you. Spotting the branches of my spruce like that, and in broad daylight. Just you try that again.

BRETON   A little manure never stopped no tree from growing, madam.

EVANGELINE   Sure, sir, as long as you shove it under the roots, not on top o' the leaves.

STOP   *(chasing the pigeons)* Shoo! Leave our spruce alone!

> *While EVANGELINE remains kneeling by the spruce, wiping it with a handkerchief and trying to straighten it, the men return to their benches. The BRETON pulls out a book from his pocket. The RABBI returns to his paper.*

EVANGELINE   *(watering the spruce)* Of all things! Poor little critter. Already deprived of salt air, of the nor'easter 'n the cry o' the gulls and now to top it all off, he's gotta put up with pigeon droppings…. It's no way to treat a tiny tender sapling…. And couldn't you change your tune for once?… Coo… coo… cooing all the time…. Gets on your nerves after a while. Reminds me too much of the way Armine talked after she came back from the States 'n didn't speak French no more. Bring it out from the throat, that cry o' yours, like this: quack… quack! That's how the gulls do it. Of course, their accent is from back home!

BRETON   Ha-ha! To turn a pigeon into a gull, madam, you need the sea and her fish.

EVANGELINE   If a country can remake us folks in our late years, I don't see why we couldn't remake a country that's still young.

> *STOP laughs then abruptly stops, looking embarrassed.*

BRETON   Your name is Evangeline, am I right?

EVANGELINE   Sure is.

BRETON   Evangeline… isn't that something…. Just like Evangeline Bellefontaine, the Acadian heroine.

EVANGELINE   Well, I'm Evangeline à Thaddée à Olivier à Charles à Charles, that's who I am. The heir and descendant of one o' the first 'n only founders of Le Fond de la Baie.

BRETON   Well, it doesn't stop you both from being alike, does it?

EVANGELINE   What's that you're saying? Me being like the one that's got her statue standing on top o' the Grand-Pré monument? That's a funny one!

> *She laughs; STOP also laughs.*

I'm sorry, no offence. It's just that back home, Evangeline, well… she's kind o' like a patron saint of the Holy Virgin. Something like the Unknown Soldier. As for me, well… everybody knows me. *(She laughs.)*

BRETON   *(opening his book)* When I heard your name was Evangeline, it reminded me—just like that, in a flash—of my school days…. Oh, a long time ago… when we were told something about French settlers in America who were being deported: it was the Acadian people. They were our cousins, so we were taught. More like second cousins actually. And they recounted the story of Evangeline, exiled in Louisiana with her people, who searched in vain for her Gabriel. I was just a kid then, and I bawled like a baby. The whole class laughed at me. I remember swearing to myself that one day I'd go to Acadia and search for Evangeline's descendants.

EVANGELINE   I thought the Virgin Evangeline had died without leaving any descendants.

BRETON   Yes, maybe. But the Acadians did come out of exile, didn't they, and all of them are somehow her descendants.

EVANGELINE   And all o' that is written in there?

BRETON   "Evangeline," a poem by Henry Wadsworth Longfellow… an American.

EVANGELINE   An American! Can you believe it! It ain't enough for them Americans to give us bosses anymore, now they're gonna give us our patron saint!… And her story starts in Acadia or in Louisiana?

BRETON   In Grand-Pré, in 1755.

> *Interested in their conversation, the RABBI drops his paper. STOP joins the group.*

EVANGELINE   In Grand-Pré…

BRETON   *(emphatically)* It was a happy people that lived there, on the shores of the French Bay: the Acadian people. They lived off the sea and the land, in spacious wooden houses, mindful of traditions and the will of God.

EVANGELINE   I know what you mean.

BRETON   In those days, a town notable called Benoit Bellefontaine had just betrothed his only daughter, Evangeline, to a brave and honourable young man named Gabriel Lajeunesse.

EVANGELINE   My man's name was Noré.

BRETON   The wedding was to take place in the fall. But when autumn came, the English, who for over a quarter of a century had had their eyes on the rich farms occupied by the Acadians, sent in their troops under the command of a certain Colonel Moncton…

EVANGELINE   Moncton, now! Even then, they were making fun of us.

STOP   And what about the young couple?

BRETON   Well actually, it was in that very same church of Grand-Pré, where Gabriel and Evangeline were to be wed, that the English troops locked up all the Acadian men.

STOP   Oh!

EVANGELINE   And they did nothing to stop them? Shame on them! Now, if I'd been there with my eleven sons, well…

STOP/BRETON/RABBI   *(in unison)* Eleven sons?

EVANGELINE   Eleven sons, gentlemen… and not a single girl. I've got seven o' them still living. Well, the way I know 'em, seven is more than enough to stop the English from locking you up in a church. Not even Roman Catholics 'n here they are coming into our churches 'n making us all prisoners.

BRETON   Only the men.

EVANGELINE   Well, that's why. A woman or two, that's what our men needed inside that church, to organize them, whip 'em into action 'n put 'em to shame…. But your Evangeline there, what was she doing all that time?

BRETON   She was sitting on the shore of Grand-Pré, crying, hiding her face in the folds of her apron.

EVANGELINE   A fine time she picked! Pooh!… When we had that shipwreck off the sand dune over twenty years ago, and fifty-three of our men perished the same day, you wouldn' of found a single woman from Le Fond de la Baie sitting by the sea with her face in her apron. Nope! We were all in the narrows that day, casting mooring lines and buoys into the water; pushing our men out to sea in their lifeboats 'n scrounging through the wreckage them sixty-foot waves threw up on our shores. The widows 'n orphans waited till it was all lost and done before hiding their faces in the crooks o' their arms.

BRETON   But in Grant-Pré, those ancestors of yours were unarmed, 'n facing soldiers.

RABBI   Taken by surprise, barehanded, there's nothing you can do.

STOP   And what about… Gabriel?

BRETON   The poor Romeo was with the others.

STOP   …Romeo?

BRETON   Then they brought the men to the schooners and set the church on fire.

EVANGELINE   The church on fire! *(She grabs her pail.)* They let the church go up in flames! Were all the wells dry? Well, I wouldn't mind having one o' them in front o' me trying to set the church on fire! You form a chain in a case like that.

> *She hands the pail to STOP who starts looking for the church.*

Throw it!

Throw it! Not time to be praying to Saint Jude while the church is burning.

> *In a panic, STOP runs around the park with the pail, hands it to the RABBI, who in turn hands it to the BRETON, who gives it back to EVANGELINE, who finally uses it to water her spruce.*

Into the blaze!

RABBI   Did anyone die inside the temple?

BRETON   No, not in the fire.

RABBI   Thank God!

EVANGELINE   Well, you didn't think they were gonna let people burn alive, do you?

> *The BRETON glances at the RABBI who makes a face. Pause.*

STOP   Er… so… the men are on board the schooners.

BRETON   The men, the women, the children. Everybody.

STOP   And Evangeline, is she with Gabriel?

BRETON   Well no! Lovers were separated from their sweethearts, husbands from their wives, children from their parents.

EVANGELINE   Yes… that I knew. My father used to say that's why it became so hard to unravel family ties. It took many a root-delver to fix all o' them lineages. Imagine a Cormier, for instance, from the branch of Pierrot à Pierre, put on board a schooner at the age of five and shipped to Virginia with the Girouère, the Belliveau 'n the Cyr. By the time he's old enough to figure out he ain't a Cyr or a Belliveau, but a Cormier, well the poor soul can't even remember his father's Christian name 'n nobody knows what branch he belongs to. Lucky thing we've got folks like Flora Goguen from Cocagne, 'n Alban Girouère from Sainte-Marie, 'n Alice Maillet from higher up in the county who can dig up your roots and follow them as far back as the Deportation. So today, we can hold our heads high and proudly declare that we're exiles of good stock, very clean 'n well scrubbed by the waves and salty winds of the open sea, 'n well preserved after two centuries.

…Actually, we spent the first of those two centuries coming back from Louisiana and looking for our lands 'n deeds we'd lost along the way; 'n we spent the next one clearing our lands and cultivating them once again. And listen to this, gentlemen: now that we've just finished replanting, 'n paying for our churches 'n schools, 'n casting our traps into the water, that's when they come 'n tell us the sea is empty, the soil is rotten 'n we'd be much better off moving to the city 'n working in those factories run by the English…. They're deporting us all over again, but this time without even supplying the schooners.

BRETON   *(moved)* Is that why you had to leave Acadia, Evangeline?

EVANGELINE   …No schooners this time around. That's one thing I'll tell my ancestors: no schooners for us, no sir; they didn't turn us into heroes and martyrs. Evangeline, the first one, they deported her to the South. And she stayed there. But we came back…. Ten years it took us to walk back through the woods. And we rebuilt. We replanted. And once again, we dropped our traps in the sea. And when we're finally able to look out of our shacks 'n see our trees just about fully grown 'n the fish starting to bite…

> *Furious, she chases the pigeons away.*

Now that's enough! You're gonna leave that spruce alone once and for all, you bunch of anglicized pigeons, you! We certainly didn't walk ten years through the woods 'n slave away by the sea for two centuries 'n make that trip alone all the way from home to have it said we ended up having some foreign fowl shitting on our branches! No, sir!

> *The others help her chase away the pigeons. We hear children shouting in the street. STOP freezes, then dashes after them, leaving his sign behind.*

STOP   Wait! Wait! Don't you cross the street like that, you little rascals. Wait for me! *(He returns for his stop sign and addresses the BRETON.)* I'll be back… hold the story, please, if you don't mind… I'll be right back.

> *He disappears. The other three burst out laughing. The BRETON then holds out his hand to the RABBI.*

BRETON   François Gueguen, Breton from Brittany.

RABBI   David Cohen, Wandering Jew.

BRETON   And this here is Evangeline the Second, from Acadia.

> *The RABBI bows.*

EVANGELINE   Well, like I say, with a bunch of exiles like us, you'd think we were back in 1755.

Scene Three

> *The end of June. The BRETON and the RABBI are alone. The BRETON pulls out a bottle of wine from one of his jacket pockets. The RABBI laughs.*

BRETON   She said: "Tomorrow, I'll have something to eat for you; I'll go get it during the night at the CNR."

RABBI   So Brittany applied to Acadia: "And I'll get something to drink."

> *The BRETON pulls out a corkscrew.*

BRETON   Here we are!

RABBI   Maybe we should wait for them.

BRETON   They won't be long. She usually comes early.

RABBI   She's full of life, that woman.

BRETON   Full-bodied too.

RABBI   Tee-hee!

BRETON   Ho-ho!

> *The BRETON fills a cup with wine and hands it to the RABBI.*

RABBI   Let's wait for them.

BRETON   Yes, of course. *(He puts the cup on the bench.)* Have you been in this country long?

RABBI   A few years.

BRETON   And you come from…

RABBI   From all over the place: first from Poland, then Germany, Switzerland, Sweden, France… a long time in France… then Brazil, Argentina… Argentina is a beautiful country… and finally, Canada.

BRETON   All that in half a century. And after that?

RABBI   After that…

BRETON   None of those lands became your country? Where did you leave your heart?

RABBI   My heart? Ha!… I left my fortune in South America, my friends in France, my health in Sweden and Switzerland and my three sons in Germany, in the camps. As for my father and mother, they are resting in Poland. When my wife and I landed in the port of Montreal, we had nothing left. She died here, last year.

BRETON   *(handing him the cup)* So you're the only citizen of the world today.

RABBI   The world is too big a place.

> *He drinks and hands back the cup. The BRETON pours himself a drink.*

BRETON   Then let's forget it. *(He drinks.)*

RABBI   Or let's find it inside the bottle.

> *Without realizing it, they both drink most of the wine while they're talking.*

BRETON   That's how Noah forgot his flood.

RABBI   And sailors forget the harbour.

BRETON   No, not the harbour. The sea. You think sailors get bored on the ocean? Let me tell you, my friend, on my word as a seaman: the saddest day in the life of a sailor is when a ship sails out to sea, leaving him behind. A good sailor walks on dry land with the grace of a cow on a conveyor belt.

RABBI   Men are strange. While some constantly dream of sailing the high seas in search of adventure, I know others who walk across the desert for forty years in search of their native land. People are strange.

BRETON   Once again, let's forget it. *(He drinks.)*

RABBI   Anyway, it's not worth remembering. It's much too small.

> *Both men are getting a little tipsy.*

Too empty.

BRETON   Too hard.

RABBI   Too soft.

BRETON   Too skinny.

RABBI   Too fat.

BRETON   Too conceited.

RABBI   Too vain.

BRETON   Too careless.

RABBI   Too carelessly careful.

> *EVANGELINE and STOP are heard in the distance.*

STOP   Aaah!… so that's how. I would o' thought you fish 'em in water, you see.

BRETON & RABBI   Too close.

EVANGELINE   No, no. They're not fish, they're not fish!

> *EVANGELINE and STOP arrive with a big basket of clams.*

BRETON   Are those… turtles?

RABBI   Come now, my friend, you must be a little troubled. Those are… winkles.

EVANGELINE   What's that I hear? Turtles 'n winkles? And you say you took to the sea at the age of fifteen? These here are clams, young man!

BRETON   Clams! Good heavens!

EVANGELINE   Fresh out of the mud from Le Fond de la Baie.

RABBI   They look like mussels.

BRETON   Fresh clams! Evangeline, my favourite Acadia!

> *He kisses her, but she fights him off. She then sniffs around and sees the bottle.*

EVANGELINE   Almost empty. Aha! I think they started the picnic ahead o' time. Yep, they can take a clam for a turtle, alright.

BRETON   Forgive us, Evangeline, we were waiting for you, then all of a sudden, the world became too empty…

RABBI   …too small…

BRETON   …too soft…

RABBI   …too skinny…

BRETON   …too fat…

EVANGELINE   …And a mite too full, I'd say. Come 'n eat, it'll settle your stomachs.

> *STOP sadly eyes the bottle.*

Come on, there's enough for everybody.

> *They settle down around the basket. EVANGELINE serves her guests.*

You open their beaks, like this, and oops!… Hmm… gives your throat the blues, it does.

BRETON   Good God, real clams from the shores of Brittany! Christ Almighty!

EVANGELINE   First of all, these here are Atlantic clams. And you, stop swearing like that.

BRETON   But ours, too, are Atlantic clams.

EVANGELINE   What's that you're saying?

BRETON   I, too, was born on the Atlantic.

EVANGELINE   Now look here…

RABBI   The Atlantic is the only thing that stands between your country and his, Madam Evangeline. He also lived on the ocean side.

BRETON   On the other side.

EVANGELINE   Is that so?… Well, now you're eating clams from this side, and they're the best.

> *Meanwhile, STOP can't seem to work up enough courage to try eating a clam.*

BRETON   Not better than crayfish, though.

EVANGELINE   What's so special about them crayfish o' yours?

BRETON   Crayfish, or spring lobsters, just like your lobsters, but smaller and without those large claws.

EVANGELINE   What's a lobster without its big claws? The only thing left is a tail 'n that ain't much.

RABBI   A lobster tail, not much!

> *STOP has managed to swallow one.*

STOP   I got it! …

RABBI   Do you find them on rocks, like mussels?

BRETON   No, in the sand.

EVANGELINE   In the mud.

BRETON   You gather them with a pick 'n a shovel.

EVANGELINE   And your hands. You grab a shovelful o' mud 'n you go through it with your bare hands. In a single dig, you can find about…

BRETON   Three or four…

EVANGELINE   A dozen or more.

BRETON   You're exaggerating.

EVANGELINE   Me exaggerating? You're telling me I can't find a dozen clams in a single dig? Well just you watch!

> *She gets up, looks around, then sits down again, looking disappointed.*

Here, I wouldn't even find a worm to put on the end of my line… worms instead o' clams, pigeons instead o' seagulls… what a country!

STOP   Hey! Those goddamn pests didn't come back.

EVANGELINE   Another one that swears!… But you're right, the little bastards didn't come back. We'll get rid o' them, you'll see. We got rid o' summer lightning 'n the puppets.

THE OTHER THREE   What puppets?

EVANGELINE   The puppets, you know, the puppets in the sky.

RABBI   *(to the BRETON)* Have you ever seen puppets in the sky?

BRETON   Maybe a little while ago, but I feel better now.

EVANGELINE   Those green and pink puppets that dance in the sky on autumn nights?

> *She sings the song of "Les Marionnettes." ***

---

*   Fiddler Lisa Ornstein composed this beautiful tune in tribute to Louis "Pitou" Boudreault (1905–1988), the last of a family dynasty of great fiddlers. http://www.greylarsen.com/extras/lesmarionnettes/

RABBI   I think I understand: she means aurora borealis.

BRETON   Ah! Northern Lights!

> *She keeps on singing. The men take up the refrain. STOP accompanies them on his harmonica.*

EVANGELINE   "Dance, dance the dance o' the puppets if you don't want them to come 'n pester you."

> *She gets the men to join in the dance. The each end up dancing as they did back home. This culminates in a quadrille around the spruce.*
>
> *Suddenly, the BRETON, feeling weak and dizzy, stops. The others quickly gather around him.*

Better rest a little. And don't you forget. You ain't as young as you used to be. *(to the RABBI)* Anything left in that bottle to buck him up?

> *The RABBI quickly makes him drink the last few drops.*

BRETON   Thank you, I'm okay. It's nothing. The heat… short breath…

RABBI   Of course! And perhaps the white wine.

EVANGELINE   As soon as the breeze starts up, you'll feel better, you'll see.

BRETON   I feel better already, thank you.

EVANGELINE   Happens every time. One whiff of a cork can put any man back on his feet in no time. I know. I wasn't raised in bootlegger country for nothing. *(They all perk up.)* Oh! Yes, just as true as I'm standing here. I was raised on the coast at the start of the century… about the time you had some rum running between the islands. And me, well, I had springs under my feet, then, 'n stars in my eyes. That's what they used to say. *(The men form a circle around her, listening intently.)* There was Cyprien, you see. Oh! I didn't marry him, no… kind o' hard in those days. And Noré had a piece o' land right next to my father's. Cyprien was a runner, a rum runner… he wasn't easy. Tee-hee!… From Saint-Pierre-et-Miquelon to Côte Sainte-Anne, 'n from there across the line to the States. And they could never catch 'm. Besides, what a pair of eyes he had… not like the buttonholes on my father's overalls, let me tell you. In all the land, they never found a single officer that could get a hold of Cyprien. And if ever one o' them had caught 'm, I got a feeling he would o' dropped him real quick 'cause that Cyprien was one hunk of a man.

…Are you feeling any better now?

BRETON   Me? I'm perfectly alright. It takes more than a small dizzy spell to upset a man of my constitution. I feel hale and hearty.

> *He opens his small suitcase and whittles away on his boat. The work has progressed noticeably since the first scene.*

EVANGELINE Better put your cap back on, though. No sense in catching a cold after that.

RABBI And that rum running, what exactly…

STOP Oh! I know about that, it's against the law, like moose hunting.

BRETON Rum running was the contraband of spirits during the heyday of Prohibition in America, what was known as the dry years. Dry America! He-ha…. And to think I came over here just when that wonderful period was coming to an end. Never mind! I still managed to get a small piece of the pie.

> *Children's voices in the street. STOP cocks his ears. He hesitates between the call of duty and his wish to stay, and finally leaves reluctantly.*

RABBI Was he young, Cyprien?

EVANGELINE He was… age has no age at that age.

BRETON Alas! Age comes with time. And when the time comes, age becomes aged.

EVANGELINE No, I don't believe in that. It ain't the years that age a man, it's slacking off.

THE OTHER TWO What?

EVANGELINE Slacking off. When a person wakes up one morning and finds he's slacking off, he realizes he's getting old. That's what kills the old folks: they slack off. You just can' slack off, you can't take a breather before reaching your destination to make real sure you did.

RABBI But Evangeline, when a person reaches that point, he doesn't have a choice. He slacks off.

BRETON I slacked off a while ago.

EVANGELINE Come, come now! When a man of your vigour has a little dizzy spell in between two square dances, it ain't no reason to start holding on to the small o' your back. I don't mean to flatter you, but with your kind o' build, you could live to be a hundred… and still hold your head up high.

BRETON Ooooh?…

EVANGELINE Knowing you, you don't need no wood to strengthen the soles of your feet, hey?

BRETON No, for sure.

EVANGELINE Nor oil in the hinges or springs in the sinews.

BRETON Nor fire in the chimney, for that matter, dear lady.

RABBI Oh, oh!

EVANGELINE Well, just you be careful you don't start a fire, now.

RABBI   And Cyprien, did he start a fire, back then?

EVANGELINE   Cyprien… he could've set the country ablaze if they'd given 'm a chance. He could've…. At night, he'd sneak his way through the frigates, the officers' frigates. When they were up north, he'd take to the south; 'n when they were tagging the sou'wester, he'd follow them nor'easter. They'd hunt 'm down, but he'd give them the slip…. Had to earn a living, Cyprien, like each and every one of us. In the ol' days, Acadians had no other choice but to do forbidden things 'cause, in their case, nothing was permitted. We were all outlaws at the time.

BRETON   Do you think Cyprien launched out into the great adventure just to earn a living?

EVANGELINE   Ha!… Maybe also a little bit to pester the governments.

RABBI   And those officers, they never caught your Cyprien at sea?

EVANGELINE   The officers, no; but the sea, yes. She's the one that caught 'm. *(The men lower their heads.)* He took to the sea one night and by daybreak the sea took 'm. but I can't blame the sea alone. 'Cause on the morning of my wedding to Noré, we heard from one of the locals that Cyprien had thrown all his jugs overboard: Jamaican rum and wine from Saint-Pierre-et-Miquelon. Now when a bootlegger throws his jugs in the water like that, for no reason, it makes you wonder… but me, I was dancing on that day, so I didn't have time to wonder. *(She sniffs. The BRETON puts his arm around her. But she regains her self-control.)* Well, I named by oldest boy Cyprien. Joseph-Ernest Cyprien. Noré never allowed us to call 'm anything but Ernest, but on his birth certificate, I had 'em write down the name o' Cyprien. And what Noré never knew… *(She smiles.)* …He's got long legs, Ernest, and eyes…

BRETON   …Not like the buttonholes on her father's overalls.

> *They all laugh.*

EVANGELINE   So, later on, my boys followed in Ernest's footsteps: all bootleggers.

RABBI   And that's one thing Mister Noré could never stomach.

EVANGELINE   A lifetime, Noré had, to learn that once an Acadian woman has embraced the ocean, her eyes will forever be searching the open sea.

BRETON   …If your eyes had searched a little longer, they would have found another adventurer who was also dealing in a little contraband… further out to sea.

EVANGELINE   Who?

RABBI   You couldn't have been smuggling wine in France, now. There never was a dry year in that country, that I know of.

BRETON   France is also Saint-Pierre-et-Miquelon, and I had already crossed the Atlantic at the time…. Those jugs Cyprien was piling up in his hold, they had to be brought over to him by a few brave men at sea.

RABBI   Oh, oh!

EVANGELINE   Well, of all things! Just look at 'm, born in the ol' country, with fancy ways and fancy words 'n a land of his own, 'n he becomes a bootlegger like any other poor slave.

BRETON   Slaves don't become bootleggers, my dear, adventurers do: those who dream of finding lost paradises.

EVANGELINE   That's it, yes. That's what Cyprien used to tell me. He took to the sea like a man takes a wife, to try 'n find something out there, something a person looks for all his life 'n only finds once in a blue moon. *(pause)* But after he was gone, I never found that paradise again, never.

BRETON   And what if it was still there waiting for us far beyond the open sea?

EVANGELINE   You only take to the sea once… and you gotta be young and strong.

BRETON   …Young, surrounded by the horizon 'n with a whole world to conquer…

RABBI   …At an age you can't possibly know how dearly life is going to make you pay for each one of your paradises.

BRETON   Not too dearly, no. If I knew there was still one left somewhere between the heavens and the sea…

EVANGELINE   I'd go looking for it, I would. The way I see it, a man that ain't dead is a man that's alive. There's nothing in between. You're either on one side or the other. There ain't no in between with death. So why play dead when you're still alive?

BRETON   Yes, why?

RABBI   Because old age is an in-between period.

EVANGELINE   Hush! You'll sink your own foot in the grave, talking like that. Could it be that we all slogged through life, dragging our rags from one plot o' land to the next, from one sea to the other, just so we might end our days in a foreign country without even having the right to look straight up at the sun once more? I say, and Cyprien would say the same thing, that we each got our share of life, our little piece of century he called it, and with it we gotta build our own happiness. So tell me now, do you think a person whose only inheritance in eighty years is gonna drop one, her last maybe… 'cause some folks find her old? Once I'm on my shroud and in my six-handled coffin, they can consider me old if they want; but not before. Especially since exiles like us don't have the right to age as fast as ordinary folks, 'cause we got a country to transplant.

> *The three stare at the spruce.*

BRETON   He's taking root!

RABBI   He's growing!

EVANGELINE   He'll live, God's little creature!

> *As they walk towards the spruce, STOP returns holding a bird in the hollow of his hands.*

STOP   Is this a seagull?

EVANGELINE   A sandpiper! In the name o' God! Where did you find 'm?

STOP   Not far from here… on St. Paul Street.

BRETON   That's near the harbour. A sea bird who lost its way among the garbage cans.

EVANGELINE   He's not really a seagull, but don't you fret. Where there are sandpipers, the seagulls can't be far.

> *She sings "Les Marionnettes" again and they all dance around the spruce. BRETON joins in song with EVANGELINE.*

Just watch you don't get winded again, young man.

BRETON   Why did you come so late, Evangeline.

RABBI   *(to STOP)* You must free your prisoner, brother. He also has a right to his own life.

> *STOP makes a face, then opens his hands. They all watch the sandpiper fly away.*

EVANGELINE   Go, little sandpiper, return home. But next time, bring back the seagulls.

Act Two

Scene One

It is September. STOP is alone, swaying to and fro, visibly worried. Suddenly, he straightens up, smiles and rushes out. He returns with the RABBI.

RABBI   And how did you spend your holidays, Mister Tremblay?

STOP   I'm not a Tremblay, I'm a Dufour.

RABBI   I'm so sorry. I thought of Tremblay because of where you come from, Le Lac Saint-Jean.

STOP   No, that would be my mother, 'n my grandmother, my father's mother 'n also my mother's mother. They're all Tremblays, but me, I'm a Dufour.

RABBI   Ah, yes! I understand. Still, the way I see it, there's been a lot of "trembling" going on in your family.

STOP   Tee-hee!… And you, what is it they call you, a rabbit?

RABBI   A rabbi, the son of a rabbi, the grandson of a rabbi.

STOP   Kind o' like a rabbit succession. *(The RABBI is a bit piqued. STOP freezes. After a while, they start looking toward the exit.)* It's him!

> *STOP rushes off, followed halfway by the RABBI. STOP returns with the BRETON. The RABBI and the BRETON greet each other warmly.*

BRETON   Hello there!

RABBI   Good to see you!

> *STOP looks on, his face beaming, as they both pat each other.*

BRETON   We haven't grown too fat.

RABBI   We haven't lost weight.

BRETON   Maybe we've added a touch of white to our heads.

RABBI   We seem to have lost a hair at the temples.

BRETON   No, that one was bothering me. I plucked it out myself.

RABBI   Oh!… well, I whitewashed my beard.

BRETON   Ho-ho-ho!

RABBI   Ha-ha-ha!

> *They both sit as STOP looks on.*

BRETON   And those holidays back home, in the old country?

RABBI   Pooh!…

BRETON   What do you men, "pooh"! Didn't you go?

RABBI   Yes, but…

BRETON   You didn't get there.

RABBI   Not to the old country, no. I turned back when I reached New York.

BRETON   My word! Leaving for Israel and stopping in New York. You're hiding something from me, my friend.

RABBI   Not at all. I came back simply because a few of my brethren told me this wasn't the time to return to Israel; that a man of my age should let the younger generation do the fighting.

BRETON   A man of your age! I know somebody who wouldn't be pleased if she heard you talking like that. *(to STOP)* She didn't come today!

STOP   No, but she came every day during the month of August.

RABBI   In that case, she'll be here soon.

BRETON   And she'll straighten you up with all your talk of old age.

RABBI   I can hear her now. *(imitating EVANGELINE)* What's that you're saying? Just you let me catch you one more time having them crazy notions in your head, you little rascal!

> He stops short when he catches the BRETON's furious expression.

Oh! I'm sorry! …

BRETON   You might be my friend, my dear son of a rabbi, but in my presence, I won't let nobody make fun of a lady I both honour and respect, do you hear me, nobody!

RABBI   I never knew you were so touchy, my dear son of a seaman.

BRETON   Touchy, me? Because I defend the weaker sex?

STOP   The weaker sex! Tee-hee!…

BRETON   Did you say something?

STOP   Er… no… I… er…

BRETON   When one is likely to say foolish things, it is best to keep one's mouth shut, young man.

RABBI   My thoughts exactly.

BRETON   Are you perhaps insinuating that I should keep my mouth shut, sir?

RABBI   I'm not insinuating, I'm speaking quite plainly.

BRETON   But you were implying that I might get carried away.

RABBI   I wasn't implying anything.

BRETON   …That I was impatient, irritable maybe.

RABBI   If you keep talking to me in that tone of voice, I'll have to agree with you.

BRETON   It wouldn't be new to me; I was told that before.

RABBI   It was well deserved, I'm sure.

BRETON   What? Did anyone ever tell you that you had a knack for shoving your nose in other people's business?

RABBI   No, never. I wouldn't have taken it anyway.

> *STOP tries to separate them, to distract them.*

BRETON   Stop meddling in other people's affairs, young man.

RABBI   Did anyone ask for your help?

STOP   It's her!

> *They all jump up, rushing over to greet EVANGELINE who has crossed the street without waiting for STOP.*

EVANGELINE   So! This is the secret assembly that was gonna rebuild the world without me.

> *The BRETON goes to her and tenderly kisses her hand. The RABBI does the same. STOP awkwardly tries to imitate them. EVANGELINE saves the situation by simply patting his cheek. STOP is so flustered his knees wobble. The other two sustain him and in doing so are reconciled.*

BRETON   The month of August seemed endless without you, Evangeline.

EVANGELINE   You should o' stayed around here. Me, I didn't budge.

RABBI   After fifty years, I think our friend was due for a short visit back home, to see if the willows were still standing in front of the house where he was born.

BRETON   There weren't any willows, but chestnut trees; 'n they're gone.

EVANGELINE   Gone? What kind o' trees do you plant in the ol' countries that can't live fifty years? Now where I come from, a spruce can outlive his master, his master's children 'n the children of his children. Talk about that, eh?… What's that I see? The poor little soul! Who did this?

> *She walks over to the uprooted spruce.*

STOP   This morning, I got here early and I found him unearthed.

EVANGELINE   You found 'm what?

BRETON   Uprooted?

STOP   Yep, right there, by the roadside, on top o' the garbage cans, his roots sticking up in the air.

EVANGELINE   The bastards!

BRETON   The swines!

RABBI   Who do you think did this? A vandal or some overzealous police officer?

EVANGELINE   One hell of a way to keep the peace, let me tell you! Picking on a poor defenceless little tree barely out of the cradle. That's what happens back home too, you know. They're always picking on the little guy. But once in a while, they get a surprise or two, like having them cradles rocking all over their toes. The revenge of the cradles, they call it!... So they also uproot trees where you come from, eh?

BRETON   It's not the bad guys that uproot trees back home, it's progress.

EVANGELINE   You call that progress?

BRETON   Twenty years without going back home and what do I find? Neon signs all over the old gables; a dry fountain in the middle of the town square; and instead of my chestnut, those glorious age-old chestnut trees my grandfather planted, they've planted wooden ducks all over the lawns. That's not my Brittany anymore. And ol' Mathurin…

THE OTHER THREE   What about Mathurin?

BRETON   He hasn't got his geese anymore, ol' Mathurin. Nope, no more geese at his house. Actually… he's dead, ol' Mathurin. There's no more yarn-spinners sitting by the fireside; no more ancient mariners hanging around the pubs at lunchtime; no more *bigoudens* rocking on the porches; no more fishermen calling out their oysters and mussels in the harbour. No, but co-ops, yes, 'n boutiques, 'n automatic lighthouses 'n Americans. A Brittany full of Americans.

RABBI   In the past, you had the English.

BRETON   An Englishman is more discreet; he doesn't mingle 'n usually whispers.

EVANGELINE   But even when he whispers, he still whispers in English.

RABBI   All the better if your country is no longer like you left it: it's easier to let go.

BRETON   What do you mean "easier"? Do you think I simply gave up my country? Do you know that, in France, a man keeps his citizenship for life? I'm a Breton-speaking Breton who'll speak Breton till the day he dies.

RABBI   But you're the one who said you couldn't find any more lacemakers, mariners and chestnut trees in Brittany.

BRETON   What, no chestnuts nor mariners in Brittany? I'll have you know that when there's no more sailors in the harbour, sir, it's because they're at sea; and if you can't find any chestnut trees, you'll still see oaks in Brittany, 'n alders 'n willows 'n aspens 'n lindens 'n heather 'n pines…

EVANGELINE   And spruces?

BRETON   Our pine trees are very much like your spruces. Brittany is on the Atlantic, like Acadia. As a child, just like you, I'd run over the rocky shores and across the sand dunes covered with wild grass; I used to gather shingles and pebbles… wheelbarrows full.

EVANGELINE   And seaweed?

BRETON   Wheelbarrows full of seaweed and kelp.

EVANGELINE   Certainly not to bank up the house, now?

BRETON   And driftwood to heat up the cast-iron stove.

EVANGELINE   And did the porpoises and whales swim by your shores from time to time.

BRETON   Once in a while, we could spot a sea cow in the open sea.

EVANGELINE   I would o' liked to have known that land where we came from a long time ago. And sometimes I get an urge to go back 'n take a look… just to have a peek.

BRETON   I'll take you there, Evangeline.

>   *He goes to her, filled with tenderness, oblivious to the others.*

EVANGELINE   You mean overseas?

BRETON   To the ends of the earth, if you wish. On horseback, on a schooner, or in my arms.

EVANGELINE   Well now, don't you go talking that way or you'll end up bowling me over.

BRETON   Then the two of us will be bowled over, and together we might do a few naughty things.

EVANGELINE   What's that I hear? A man o' your age! You should be ashamed of yourself!

BRETON   What's wrong with my age? Why should I be ashamed? Are you put off by my eighty years, my sweet? I wish I only had sixty or fifty to offer you. But much to my regret, I'm stuck with eighty. Still, those eighty years were pretty full. Eighty laps around the sun and twelve times eighty moons. Two wars, the colonies, three oceans. Years filled with hunger, cold, adventure, fear, dreams, longings and love. I wouldn't mind giving it all up for some fresh marrow in my bones and a lot more future to share with you.

EVANGELINE   *(moved)* Eighty years is the golden age, they say. And when a person finds gold, it would be foolish to wish for tin, that's what I think.

BRETON   Dear Evangeline! *(The RABBI calls out to STOP.)*

RABBI   Mister Tremblay! Wait for me! I see many people there, on the other side. The two of us will barely be enough to help them walk over here.

STOP   Where?

> *He looks around, doesn't see anyone, and tries to understand what's going on, but the RABBI has already reached him and drags him away.*

RABBI   Come, Mister Tremblay.

STOP   But you see, I'm a Dufour. Now the Tremblays are my mother, my father's mother, my mother's mother…

> *The RABBI takes one last knowing look at the two lovebirds, then disappears with STOP.*

EVANGELINE   What's that? The Jews are turning into walkmen, now? Well if that don't top it all! Things must be getting worse than we think in this country.

BRETON   The hell with Jews 'n walkmen! Let's use this precious time we have right now and pick up whatever pieces of life we've got left.

EVANGELINE   You're beginning to sound like a man who feels his last moments are fast approaching.

BRETON   The moment life becomes beautiful again, that's when a man starts worrying about his last moments. Beautiful, beautiful, yes, beautiful.

EVANGELINE   *(suddenly nostalgic)* Cyprien used to say I was beautiful, way back then…. Even Noré mentioned it a few times, in the beginning. They'd talk about my hands, my eyes, 'n my…. Well that was sixty years ago. And in sixty years, the north wind and the salt air can easily furrow your skin.

BRETON   And what in the world could be more beautiful than a woman who carries her life and her country carved right into her skin?

EVANGELINE   Even Cyprien couldn't 've put it so nicely.

BRETON   Ah! but what a lucky man he was, Cyprien, popping into your life in his twenties! And to think he let you get away, the fool!

EVANGELINE   It was my fault. I'm the one who said "no" and missed my chance.

BRETON   You can always get it back. What if I was the Cyprien of your final hour? One who would have waited threescore and ten years for you?

EVANGELINE   Threescore and ten!… I haven't heard that since I left the country.

BRETON   Where I come from, we used many of your old words. If I tried, I could ferret them out.

EVANGELINE   Ferret…

BRETON   So let's keep our chin up and wend our way back in time. *(He touches her chin.)*

EVANGELINE   Hey, stop that! You're tickling me. And anyway, you're not supposed to.

BRETON Excuse me.

EVANGELINE Tee-hee!… Do you know some more?

BRETON Oh!… Here sits the lord mayor *(taps her forehead)*, here sits his men *(taps her eyes)*, here sits the cockadoodle *(taps her right cheek)*, here sits the hen *(taps her left cheek)*, here sit the little chickens *(points to her teeth)*, and here they run in *(touches her mouth)*, chin-chopper, chin-chopper, chin-chopper chin *(tickles her under the chin and kisses her)*. And back up we go…. Here sit the little chickens, here sits the hen, here sits the cockadoodle! That's how we turn back the hands of time…

EVANGELINE If we could only turn back the hands of time 'n find that the springs in our legs are no longer rusty; 'n the oil in our joints is fresh again; 'n our eyes are sharp 'n, in a blink, can catch a sky full of stars; 'n in our hearts.

BRETON …bird songs.

EVANGELINE No pigeons!

BRETON Seagulls.

EVANGELINE Seagulls that fly off by the hundreds to the open sea at the slightest whine of a sea cow… landing on the bowsprit or on the masts… 'n that'll let themselves be held in the large hands of a sailor coming home from the isles, with their cargo of rum 'n wine from Saint-Pierre-et-Miquelon.

BRETON …Sailors who've waited for months, rocked by the sea as they lie in their hammocks at night, 'n who wake up one morning to the cry of the gulls bringing them news from home: the notary's young boy got lost among the rocks off La Pointe-du-Raz 'n the town had to organize a search party to find 'm; 'n ol' Josephine the Hunchback sprained her back carrying jugs of wine to her cellar; 'n grumpy Philip, late George's son, finally asked for the fair Françoise's hand in marriage, it happened three days ago; and yesterday, at about five o'clock, the sailors of Belle-Ile-en-Mer saw the phantom ship appear once again.

EVANGELINE At around five, last night, she appeared off la Côte-Sainte-Anne: the cod fishermen saw her entering the narrows; the wretched ship was burning at sea with all hands on board.

BRETON From the coast of Brittany, I could see her.

EVANGELINE I could see her from Le Fond de la Baie.

BRETON Great flames reaching up to the sky, like an omen.

EVANGELINE We called it "the ghost ship"…. It always warned of a storm at sea…

BRETON …and autumn close by.

EVANGELINE   …and winter bringing us them long nights of hooking 'n crocheting blankets…

BRETON   …and repairing fish nets.

EVANGELINE   …and the dawn of spring breaking the ice once again 'n calling men 'n ships back to sea…

BRETON   …and brand new vessels fresh out of the Saint-Nazaire shipyards.

He takes the small boat carving, now completed, out of his suitcase.

EVANGELINE   You've finished it!

BRETON   For you.

EVANGELINE   What's that I see? You named her Evangeline?

BRETON   To sail to Louisiana and find Gabriel.

EVANGELINE   Ah!… Louisiana seems so far away… especially when you can find a Gabriel pretty much everywhere.

BRETON   My love!

She slides into his arms while the other two reappear, tiptoeing their way to the spruce with Christmas decorations in their hands. Once they have finished decorating it, at a signal from the RABBI, both men start singing a Christmas carol. The surprised lovers abruptly turn and they all burst out laughing.

EVANGELINE   Holy Mother of Almighty Jesus!

They all laugh. Again they dance to the tune of "Les Marionnettes." Suddenly the BRETON stops.

BRETON   It's not my age, only my legs… my legs are giving up on me.

RABBI   Is something wrong?

BRETON   …just my legs…

He stumbles. Both men try to help him, but EVANGELINE pushes them away. She lets the BRETON glide down to the floor, cradling his head on her knees.

EVANGELINE   Air, give him some air…. Try to breathe… take a deep breath, like this…. Go get help… a doctor… a priest… *(Both men fuss around him. Then STOP exits.)* Don't you worry now, you'll feel better, try to breathe gently…. Autumn will soon be over. You'll see, 'n spring'll be back with its gulls on the masts and on the bowsprit…. Isn't there one priest, one doctor to be found in this big city?

RABBI   Tremblay went to get them…. Try to relax… clear your mind of everything.

EVANGELINE   Think of the sea rocking the hammocks inside them schooners.

BRETON   The phantom schooner is ablaze at sea.

EVANGELINE   *(searching in the distance)* No, those are branches you see burning on the shore. The fishermen are smoking cod for the winter.

BRETON   …no more winter… no more winter, ever… my wife…

EVANGELINE   Don't you worry, I'm here. And when the wild geese return, the two of us…

BRETON   …Who?

RABBI   Evangeline… Evangeline is here…

BRETON   …Evangeline… go to Louisiana… find… Gabriel…

> *His head drops back. STOP returns out of breath. EVANGELINE's eyes widen.*

EVANGELINE   Cyprien!

> *An ambulance screams in the distance.*

Scene Two

> *It is October. EVANGELINE is sitting on her bench, crying, holding a Kleenex in her hand, while STOP frantically fusses around her. She suddenly rumples the tissue, rolls it up in a ball and throws it away. She gets up and walks to and fro.*

EVANGELINE   When you reach my age and your man dies, how can you cry your eyes out in a Kleenex!

> *STOP sits on the back of the bench and listens to her.*

They took everything from me, bit by bit. The land that ran from the Post Road to the sea, three miles 'n three quarters, 'n one half-quarter, that's what the father-in-law reckoned. White sandy beaches by the sea, 'n inland, beautiful fields all cleared of trees. Nibbled away, piece by piece, and they replanted it with spruce trees for their sawmills. It took one little man in a fancy shirt to reforest what six generations of giants had cleared away. And they took Cyprien, 'n Noré, 'n my boys, one after the other: the factories, the States, Saint John, Moncton 'n now Montreal where I ended up myself with all the other exiles. And now in my old age, just when the good Lord seemed to be giving me one last chance, they take it away too, my very last one, 'n they leave me alone to bawl in a Kleenex, 'cause they even took my handkerchiefs away…

…Handkerchiefs ain't hygienic, 'cording to my daughter-in-law. Ain't hygienic! Hand-embroidered handkerchiefs that I kept in a cedar chest for over sixty years, a chest my late father hand-carved with his pocket knife for my wedding.

And that's not hygienic? I tell you, life ain't been too hygienic lately, when you end up having to mourn the death o' your man in a Kleenex. *(STOP stands up.)*

STOP *(exiting)* Wait for me, I'll be back.

EVANGELINE Sure, he'll come back, but some'll never come back. And never means never. You can count the hours, 'n the days, 'n the years, 'n it'll all be the same, just empty time. I used to watch the birds go by 'n say to myself "there goes time flying by." And I would o' liked to grab one by the wings 'n hold 'm a while in the hollow of my hand. That way, I could imagine I was stopping an hour from passing by. There are certain hours in a lifetime that you'd like to catch 'n keep a little while longer. But don't you fret, they're the ones that fly away; it's the others that stick to you like the plague. *(The RABBI and STOP enter. The RABBI and EVANGELINE shake hands. She sniffles.)* Alright, alright, sit down and button up your coat. Fall is here, you know. *(The RABBI does as he is told.)* And after all this time, why don't you try cutting a little o' that beard, the hairs get all tangled up aroun' them buttons. A person can't let 'mself go like that, it ain't hygienic.

RABBI I came to tell you, Evangeline…

EVANGELINE No, it's better not to say anything 'n just try to hold your chin up. the coming winter can't be as long as the one that just about barely left us. That don't happen two years in a row, no. And autumn is still young, look at them leaves. Yep, even winter will finally pass, like everything else. And next spring, there'll be wild strawberries once again, 'n clams…. Clams…. He perked up when he heard me say that word. They also have clams in the ol' country… and here sits the cockadoodle, here sits the hen, here sit the little chickens, and here they run in…. That day, I said to myself: when a man speaks your own tongue, he ain't far from understanding your feelings.

RABBI Yes, he understood everything, that man. He was one of the few who ever took me for the man I am; not a race, nor an idea. When you meet a man like that, late in life, you don't need to look for others; you can retire.

EVANGELINE What are you talking about?

STOP Now you wanna retire?

RABBI I want to go back home. And this time, I won't stop in New York.

STOP Where then?

RABBI In the land of my ancestors.

EVANGELINE But… that's in them faraway countries, at the other end o' the world. You can't travel that far at your age.

RABBI But you yourself went away quite far, Evangeline, at an age greater than mine.

EVANGELINE For me, it's different. I'm from a long line of exiles.

RABBI   (*a strange look on his face*) Ha!...

EVANGELINE   Alright, alright, you too! But they treat you well over here: no famines, no wars, no epidemics...

STOP   But lots o' strikes and lots o' snow.

EVANGELINE   Snow, he says. Did it ever kill a man? Except those who venture into woods during a big February storm. Now, that's looking for trouble. Of course, you can always stick your neck where it don't belong. But then, you might also use it to look up and see the wild geese fly by and the leaves turning yellow.

…Come 'n take a look at my spruce; see if it ain't possible to straighten up and strike root again in your old age.

RABBI   He's growing very well indeed.

EVANGELINE   What did I tell you? The soil in this country ain't so bad, after all.

RABBI   But it isn't mine. And neither is the spruce. What you've transplanted here is your soul, Evangeline. And now it's starting to blossom.

EVANGELINE   A month ago, it blossomed into Christmas ornaments.

STOP   And pigeons came 'n soiled the branches.

RABBI   You'll see, someday that spruce of yours will attract the seagulls, you'll see.

EVANGELINE   If it can't keep the men around, how do you expect it to keep the gulls?

RABBI   You have to make a bit of an effort to keep your chin up, Evangeline.

EVANGELINE   That's it now, make fun of me, you who can't even button up your coat without getting the hairs o' your beard tangled up in them buttonholes.

> *The RABBI laughs, then heads towards STOP and shakes hands with him.*

RABBI   Be good, Mister Dufour, and take good care of our Evangeline. She might be the last one of her kind her country will ever produce.

STOP   No, you see, I'm a Tremblay; it's my mother, and my mother's mother... (*He gets all mixed up.*)

> *The RABBI holds out his hand to EVANGELINE.*

EVANGELINE   (*grumbling*) Go, go to them far away countries 'n see if the palm trees stand any straighter than my spruce! And bring us back some juicy oranges when you finally get bored.

> *STOP moves to escort the RABBI, but he refuses with a hand gesture and walks away.*

STOP   Will he be back soon?

EVANGELINE Never. A Wandering Jew never stops twice in the same place.

     They watch him disappear.

STOP Well, there's something I would've like to know.… Is it really true that at the end of the story, Evangeline finds her Gabriel?

EVANGELINE At the end o' the story, yes, Evangeline found her Gabriel, so they say, but on his death bed.

STOP Oh!…

EVANGELINE Don't make a face like that; some stories do have a better ending than Evangeline's.

STOP Which ones?

EVANGELINE Well, I don't know… the Seven-Headed Beast maybe, or the Sleeping Beauty.

STOP Have you ever heard of Maria Chapdelaine?

EVANGELINE No, is she one of your local girls?

STOP She came from Péribonka.

EVANGELINE Aha! And what did she do? Did they send her into exile?

STOP No, she got married. Well, first there was Jos Paradis who tried to get her, but he died in the woods.

EVANGELINE Yeah, well, that's not making a very good start in life, I guess.

STOP Then there was his brother, Lorenzo Surprenant.

EVANGELINE Surprenant, surprising that he'd be the brother of a Paradis.

STOP He tried to take her to the States, but she refused.

EVANGELINE Good for her.

STOP Yep, it's her mare Paul-Eugène that wouldn't risk crossing the lake when it was thawing.

EVANGELINE Aha!

STOP So there came a third one.

EVANGELINE Always a third!

STOP Eutrope Gagnon.

EVANGELINE I'll bet you he finally got her.

STOP Yep! They got married and settled on their land.

EVANGELINE Are they still there?

STOP Well, it's just a story.

EVANGELINE   Ah!… It don't matter, it's a nice story. Like Evangeline. It means that folks where you come from stay on their lands, but us, we end up being deported. That's destiny. Well, after all that, I don't know what I'm still doing around here; already two of us are gone.

STOP   Seems like when he went home this summer, the Frenchman got to see his daughters one last time.

EVANGELINE   Yep. And that's not a good sign when old folks return home in their late years to see their children and their country. It always turns out to be for the last time. After that, they come back 'n die in a foreign land. I never should o' let 'm go.

STOP   Well, you can't stop a man from dying.

EVANGELINE   Sure you can.

STOP   Ah!…

EVANGELINE   What do you do when you're cold?

STOP   I shake.

EVANGELINE   You shiver, and that's what stops you from freezing; 'n when you're hot, you sweat, and that stops you from roasting. Now when a man feels that his heart wants to leave his body 'n wander away, you gotta tell 'm to let it sweat, 'n shiver 'n pound his insides. That'll stop it from choking up.

STOP   Well… the Frenchman sure wasn't in the prime youth…

EVANGELINE   And what do you mean by youth, anyway? Do you think today's youngsters got a stronger 'n tougher heart in their chest?… 'n can pump fresher air in their lungs? When you get to be my age, young man, you'll learn a thing or two about life; 'n life itself 'll teach you. You'll know that age has no age; that the most beautiful hand is one that has a life 'n a country carved in its palm; that the most beautiful eyes come from a lifetime of looking people straight in the face; and that a person's soul don't shrivel up like his skin, it don't wrinkle, it don't age, 'n it won't die either. That's what youth still doesn't know 'cause it hasn't lived long enough 'n it hasn't had time to learn anything. The only ones who have a long life are the old folks, remember that. That's one thing you can't take away from them. A long life belongs only to the old folks. So maybe it's better not to try 'n show 'em how to live it… or tell them too many things about life… and death…. When eighty times over you've seen flocks of wild geese returning in the sky, you get to know the difference between spring and fall; 'n when you've heard the ice cracking under the bridge, seventy times, 'n then head for the ocean, maybe you're not afraid to lift up your eyes 'n look to the open sea; 'n when all o' your years you've seen trees 'n men coming to life 'n passing away, then maybe in your old age you start to understand what it means to be born a native of this earth. Now don't you come 'n tell me, Evangeline, that I'm at the end of my rope, that my life is over, that there's nothing else for me to look for, wish for, 'r pray for to the good Lord down on my knees every morning. You can't teach the time o' day to old folks, who late in life, transplant their roots in foreign soil, or tell 'em how hoarse the cries o' the gulls are...

Slow fade in of crying seagulls.

Like my grandfather used to say: you can't teach your father how to make babies. And I say: don't try to teach old folks how to live their lives, don't pamper them, 'n of all things, don't lie to them. 'Cause they're the only ones I know that know all about life; they're the only ones who made lots o' fresh starts 'n ended up going the distance all the way... all the way...

STOP   *(panic-stricken by the gulls)* What's going on?

EVANGELINE   What's going on? Ha!... Them at least, they won't let you down. They'll follow you. Holy Mother of God! Your country can never be so far behind you that it won't show its face one day in the nor'easter or the sou' wester. If there's one bird in the world that can find a lost ship, it's a seagull.

STOP   The seagulls are here!

He runs around with his stop sign.

The end.

The Ocean
(L'Océan)

by Marie-Claire Blais

translated by Ray Chamberlain

Introduction to
The Ocean (L'Océan [1])
by Marie-Claire Blais
Introduced by Louise H. Forsyth

When the four segments of *L'Océan* were produced for television in 1976, the symbolism in the play of the vast ocean and the lands bordering the Saint Lawrence just before it flowed into the sea were visually evident. As the camera panned across the landscapes and seascapes, and the solitary characters in them, the audience could feel the desperate and dangerous longing for vision and fulfillment.

The Ocean has nine characters with speaking parts, five men and four women. Two of the characters are elderly fathers facing death; they are the living dead whose presence serves both to inspire and oppress the lives of those around them. In fact, *The Ocean*, like Laberge's *Night*, is a scathing indictment of patriarchal abuse of power and the devastating impact of its unavoidable legacy. The influence of these fathers on the lives of their spouses and children has been so destructive that none of them is able to move forward confidently in his or her own life nor to form supportive and loving relationships. In this season of the death of the fathers, individuals confront their solitude inside and outside their dysfunctional families. The search for meaning undertaken by each individual, whether motivated by society's materialistic values or by a veneration of artistic creativity, proves futile. The central character François, who has long nurtured dreams of following his father as a great writer but who has published nothing, drinks too much (like his father) and has attempted suicide several times, is, in the end, driven from the paternal home with nothing but his father's unpublished papers. The play dramatizes memories that hang around the neck like dead weights.

The wide river that provides the mysterious setting and that flows into the ocean of the title is closely associated with the fathers' vast artistic prowess. Like the river and the ocean, the fathers' uncontrollable power can create and can destroy. Maria, François's sister, describes her father like "the ocean; a proud, haughty man who possessed himself of nature's forces—the better to tower and spread out over us, the better to subject us to the power of words, the power of images" (80–81). In the opening scene of *The Ocean* the father, a famous writer and man of extraordinary vitality, is being interviewed on the beach by a woman journalist. Her questions raise issues regarding the value and meaning in today's materialist society of a life focused on ideas and artistic creation at the expense of others and relations with them. Before escaping from the journalist's disturbing questions, the father underscores the power to dominate life and the mastery over destiny itself that the act of writing offers him: "when you write, you dominate; yes, first you dominate life, so determined to destroy us, sweep us aside [...] like me become the master, the sole shaping hand, of his destiny." (52)

Between this scene and the following one the writer dies. His ineffectual son François remains alone in the paternal house with his illusory aspirations to walk in his father's footsteps and the music of Moussorgsky's "Boris Godounov," an historical figure whose ambition and abuse of power proved deadly for the generation that came after him: "Entranced by the music, enveloped in his solitude, he is holding a glass of scotch in his hand and is visibly happy." (53) François's solitary happiness is disturbed by the arrival of his sister and brother, Maria and Simon, who immediately announce, with sadistic glee, their intention of moving into *their* house while, at the same time, they evict François. Unfortunately, the memory and presence of the father haunts the house for all of them: "His memory refuses to die with him." (59) The ghost of the powerful writer, sensitive to the vast truths of the ocean but insensitive to the needs and feelings of his family, haunts their conversations and each of their lives. As Maria and Simon take action on their intention to drive François out, the audience learns about the father and the family's dynamics through dialogue and flashback scenes. In addition to his frequent affairs, his coldness and distance from his family, his rejection of his children and his scorn for François's dream of becoming a writer—all on the pretext of his own presumed superiority as an artist—the father has crushed their spirits, transformed them into either compliant, self-sacrificing and adoring slaves or ineffective rebels, and rendered them incapable of love and agency.

The brother and sister achieve their vengeful, materialist goal in the end with François's departure, but not without twinges of conscience: "We've punished him because we weren't strong enough to punish father." (102) François heads for the river, perhaps to revive his artist's vision or perhaps to commit suicide. The separation from his siblings is a rupture for all of them. The source of their unhappiness is not resolved and the things they have claimed from their father's legacy, whether a house or unpublished manuscripts, are meaningless. They have longed for love and a sense of self-worth, and their longing has been in vain.

The tragedy produced by a patriarch whose driving egotism as an artist has torn his family apart echoes throughout the play in the neighbour's house, in this case a composer who is less domineering and more lucid than the writer, but whose impact has been equally devastating. The life of the mother in this second family has been one of imprisonment and sacrifice, while the alienated son has failed to find love and now wanders alone in the world. He offers a final diagnosis of the hell that patriarchal families often are: "By mistake men and women wind up in the same family, and come to know each other, love each other, tear each other apart and kill each other, once they're able to…". (108)

The Ocean is a dark play that dramatizes in stark light the unresolvable conflicts produced by the will to power, human greed, solitude, death, unrequited thirst for beauty, and cruelty. While examining the creative imagination, the solitude of the artist, and the meaning of art, it dramatizes the cost of sacrificing life and love to the presumably higher goals of artistic grandeur and transcendent mastery.

Note

[1] *L'Océan*, suivi de *Murmures*. Montréal: Éditions Quinze, 1977. *The Ocean*. Tr. Ray Chamberlain. *Exile. A Literary Quarterly*. 4.3/4 (1977): 47–108. *L'Océan* was a four-part television drama series produced by Jean Faucher and Lucille Leduc for Radio-Canada in May 1976.

Bibliographical Suggestions

Selected Other Works by Marie-Claire Blais

L'Exécution. Montréal: Éditions du Jour, 1968. *The Execution*. Tr. David Lobdell. Vancouver: Talonbooks, 1976.

Fièvre et autres textes dramatiques (incl. "L'Envahisseur," "Le Disparu," "Deux Destins," "Fièvre," "Un Couple"). Montréal: Éditions du Jour,1974.

"Marcelle," *La Nef des sorcières*. Montréal: Éditions Quinze, 1976: 56–64.

Sommeil d'hiver (incl. "Sommeil d'hiver," L'Exil," "Fantôme d'une voix," "Fièvre," "Un Couple"). Montréal: Éditions de la Pleine Lune, 1984.

L'île. Montréal: VLB Éditeur, 1988. *The Island*. Tr. David Lobdell. Ottawa: Oberon Press, 1991.

Wintersleep, *Fantôme d'une voixnuit*. Tr. Nigel Spencer. Vancouver: Ronsdale Press, 1998.

L'aura des mots (in collaboration with Anne Barth). Montréal: Productions Vision-Top, 1996.

Paroles d'écrivaines (in collaboration with Anne Barth). Montréal: Productions Vision-Top, 1996.

Tu as crié let me go! (in collaboration with Anne Claire Poirier). Montréal: Office National du Film, 1996. *Let Me Go!* (in collaboration with Anne Claire Poirier). Outremont: Lanctôt, 1998.

Textes radiophoniques (incl. "Deux Destins," "L'Envahisseur," "Le Disparu," "Le Couple," "Murmures," "L'Exil," "Un Jardin dans la tempête"). Montréal: Boréal, 1999.

On *L'Océan* and Marie-Claire Blais

Alonzo, Anne-Marie. "Marie-Claire Blais," *The Oxford Companion to Canadian Theatre*. Ed. Eugene Benson & L.W. Conolly. Toronto, Oxford, New York: Oxford University Press, 1989: 53–54.

Fabi, Thérèse. *Le Monde perturbé des jeunes dans l'oeuvre de Marie-Claire Blais.* Montréal: Éditions Agence d'Arc, 1973.

Forsyth, Louise H. "Marie-Claire Blais." *The Literary Encyclopedia.* http://www.litencyc.com/.

Green, Mary Jean. *Marie-Claire Blais.* New York & London: Twayne Publishers & Prentice Hall International, 1995.

Nadeau, Vincent. "L'Océan, téléthéâtre de Marie-Claire Blais." *Dictionnaire des oeuvres littéraires du Québec.* Tome VI. 1976–1980. Montréal: Fides, 1994: 579–80.

Ricouart, Janine. "Le Théâtre de Marie-Claire Blais." *Québec Studies* (Spring/Summer 1990): 29–36.

Smith, Donald. "Les Vingt Années d'écriture de Marie-Claire Blais." *Lettres Québécoises* (hiver 1979–1980): 51, 53–58.

About Marie-Claire Blais

Marie-Claire Blais (born 1939 in Québec City) has produced a vast body of literary, theatrical and documentary work: fiction and non-fiction, poetry and more than twenty texts for stage, radio, television, cinema and video. The prizes and honours she has received are numerous: the Governor General's Award (three times), Prix de la langue française, Guggenheim Fellowships, Prix Médicis, Prix France-Québec, doctorate *honoris causa* (York University, University of Ottawa), Prix Canada-Belgique, Prix Athanase-David, Prix de l'Académie française, Prix Duvernay, International Biographical Centre of Cambridge, England, International Woman of the Year, American Biographical Institute Decree of International Letters for Cultural Achievement, Prix international Union Latine des littératures romanes, W.O. Mitchell Literary Prize, Grand Prix du Festival Métropolis Bleu, Prix littéraire de la Fondation Prince-Pierre de Monaco, Prix Gilles-Corbeil de la Fondation Émile-Nelligan. She was elected to the Royal Society of Canada in 1986, the Académie royale de langue et de littérature françaises de Belgique in 1992 (first Québec woman elected to a European literary academy), the Académie des lettres du Québec in 1994, and was named Chevalier des arts et des lettres de France in 1999.

Blais did not have an easy childhood. The eldest of five children forced by poverty to leave school in her mid-teens, she took office and factory work she detested. Despite the active discouragement she received from school and church, Blais knew from an early age that she wanted to be a writer. With the encouragement of her mother, who used her savings to buy Blais's first typewriter, and professors Jeanne Lapointe and Georges-Henri Lévesque of L'Université Laval, where she managed to take night courses, she published her first novel at the age of nineteen. She spent much of the 1960s in France and New England, where she continued to write, read extensively, and develop her unique view of society, with its critical focus on poverty, suffering, cruelty, violence and injustices of all kinds. Throughout her career she has engaged in fruitful collaborative projects with others working in theatre, fiction, television, film and radio. Since the 1970s she has divided her time between Québec and Key West.

The unique quality of Blais's work lies in her impeccable choice of words, syntactic rhythms, and subjects that illuminate the lives of ordinary women and men. Her characters form microcosms of those modest segments of humanity whose stories are seldom told or even acknowledged. Her work is exceptional for its exquisite writing, its huge cast of characters, its tapestry-like attention to social and thematic detail, and its celebration of the creative spirit. Based on closely observed mundane realities, her treatment of human affairs transmutes isolated everyday experiences into stories that take on the proportions of myth. Most of these stories are sad, often to the point of despair. Blame for the harsh absurdity of individual lives is cast on the family as destructive social institution. The intense emotions, raw cruelties and violence that relationships with others can produce are particularly compelling in her works.

Despite the cruel mysteries that underlie all Blais's works, none leaves the reader without hope. Counterbalancing the depiction of suffering is a thirst for life and a vision that goes beyond sordid circumstances through imagination, dreams and creative expression. Many of her characters are artists, writers or musicians. She places them in situations where they encounter the anguish brought about by difficult human relationships and the conflicts between artistic creativity and bourgeois society's materialistic values. Damaging gender roles and stereotypes are frequently determinants in the direction and outcome of the action of her texts.

L'Océan was first produced by Radio-Canada as a four-part television drama series, in May 1976, produced by Jean Faucher and Lucille Leduc.

Characters

FRANÇOIS
SIMON
MARIA
JEAN, an old musician
JUDITH, Jean's wife
NICOLAS, their son
THE FATHER, the writer
THE MOTHER
MARIA'S CHILDREN
SIMON'S CHILDREN
WOMAN JOURNALIST

THE OCEAN

Out of Doors

THE FATHER and the WOMAN JOURNALIST are walking along the beach. The writer is walking faster than the young woman. He seems annoyed by this meeting and answers her questions gruffly. But one can tell that this tall, powerful man, while hard to get along with, is full of extraordinary vitality, and that behind his harsh front there is tenderness. His dog trots playfully at his side.

WOMAN JOURNALIST   And this essay is your twenty-eighth published work, isn't it, Monsieur Laurain?

THE FATHER   *(as though hoping, with a wave of the hand, to be rid of her)* Yes! Right! I've already told you that.

WOMAN JOURNALIST   *(intimidated, halting in manner)* Poet… essayist, novelist—how can you be all those things at once? Don't you ever regret dedicating your whole life to ideas? To words? Isn't the writer's life a lie?

THE FATHER   No more than the journalist's, it seems to me.

WOMAN JOURNALIST   I mention lying because in your essays, and in your novels too, you raise the issue yourself—can you explain that, Monsieur Laurain? And why always show men as petty and ridiculous, as you do?

THE FATHER   Maybe that's the way I see them. I'm old, you know.

WOMAN JOURNALIST   But aren't you exaggerating, consciously, because you enjoy humiliating your characters? *(He doesn't answer. After a time she continues.)* Those around you worry about your health. Isn't the winter here too severe? *(pause)* Of course, it's not exactly like being by the sea, but the river's so wide, everything's so vast, overwhelming…

THE FATHER   *(interrupting her)* Who's been talking to you about my health?

WOMAN JOURNALIST   I asked your son Simon a few questions this morning; he was very open…

THE FATHER   What did he say this time?

WOMAN JOURNALIST   Nothing serious! He's concerned, that's all; your last attack has upset him.

THE FATHER   Ahh! I don't trust that kind of concern! How indiscreet children are.

WOMAN JOURNALIST   You're a great writer, Monsieur Laurain, but doesn't the life you lead, work and research, keep you from fully devoting yourself to your family?

THE FATHER   *(ironically)* A father…. Yes, I've tried to be…

WOMAN JOURNALIST   You seem to have some regrets…

THE FATHER   A family's like society, you've got to choose, show preferences, you can't love all men.

WOMAN JOURNALIST   By so choosing, aren't you afraid of rejecting someone?

THE FATHER   It's hard not to. We're always rejecting someone. Almost all of us are guilty of that.

WOMAN JOURNALIST   The thought must not leave you much peace.

THE FATHER   Enough to enjoy life.

WOMAN JOURNALIST   Besides being a writer, you're a man; don't you fear sickness, old age, oncoming death?

THE FATHER   *(dismissing her with a wave of the hand)* I work day and night. What's the use of worrying about things that threaten us? True, every morning's the last; but also the first… *(THE FATHER begins to play with the dog as though to change the subject.)*

WOMAN JOURNALIST   Do you feel you've lived a full life? Are you satisfied, unhappy, when you look back?

THE FATHER   Why place me in the past? Only after he dies does a man become a man of the past.

WOMAN JOURNALIST   But what's the present, then? In your work you say so little about the present.

THE FATHER   *(bitter)* So that's what you think my work is, a bunch of dead things? Don't you ever feel the life pulsating beneath those words? Too often the reader makes our books into dead things, believe me! *(ironic)* Old Monsieur Laurain's published a new novel? He writes too much, talks too much. What'll we do with all his books? Throw them away? Burn them? *(He laughs heartily.)* The present—you see, at present no one finds time to read… and no one believes we serve any purpose—on the contrary; in that sense, yes, I'm a man of the past.

WOMAN JOURNALIST   However, your books still seem to sell, Monsieur Laurain…

THE FATHER   Yes, but for how long? Our readers have stopped seeking, stopped discovering; after the first few pages of a novel, an essay—attempts at creation, participation—they get weary. Soon we'll meet open disdain, or simply be replaced by life's *other* diversions…. No doubt it's just as well!

WOMAN JOURNALIST   Where do you get the strength to write, torn by such thoughts?

THE FATHER   *(drily)* I'm not "torn." Haven't I made that clear? No, I simply observe the lassitude of men, their lack of curiosity, the slavish adherence of their imaginations to anything but art. *(pause)* I'm not exceptional; a man alone in the desert feels a similar excitement over being alive…. And when you write, you dominate; yes, first you dominate life, so determined to destroy us, sweep us aside; the solitary man dreaming his dreams in the desert can also write for himself, purely for his own pleasure, and like me become the master, the sole shaping hand, of his destiny…. Too arrogant, all of that; but we know it's true, we've got no illusions…

WOMAN JOURNALIST   I remember: you've said so in your books: The creator, even living in absolute solitude, denied all divine illumination, bereft of consolation, is a princely being, made so by his dignity…

THE FATHER   *(interrupting with restrained fury)* Did I say that? Ahh! How naïve! Why believe me? How unforgivably naïve! *(pause)* Don't speak about me any more, it's too disagreeable!

WOMAN JOURNALIST   *(seeing THE FATHER break into a run, playing with the dog, who follows him)* But Monsieur Laurain, I wanted to ask a final question…. Yes…. Monsieur Laurain.

> *He runs farther and farther away down the beach, still playing with the dog. The WOMAN JOURNALIST runs after him, not understanding.*
>
> *A country house (interior of rugged simplicity, resembling a workroom more than a place in which to relax, with a worktable, books, etc.*
>
> *FRANÇOIS is alone in the house. He is listening to "Boris Godounov" (one of Boris's monologues). Entranced by the music, enveloped in his solitude, he is holding a glass of scotch in his hand and is visibly happy. Then, as though needing to, he rises, leaves the room and goes down the hall towards the front door overlooking the river. He walks out of the house and down the hill to the water. We see him for a few moments walking slowly and with obvious joy now along the river bank, now by JEAN's house. Then he meets JUDITH, who is coming towards him.*

JUDITH   Still so all alone, my little François?

FRANÇOIS   Not for very long. The whole family's going to join me!

JUDITH   Your mother wrote?

FRANÇOIS   *(bitterly)* And Simon, and Maria! They say they're coming shortly.

JUDITH   It's out of affection for you. They think you've been by yourself too much since your father's death.

FRANÇOIS   Two months of solitude isn't nearly enough!

JUDITH   When are they coming?

FRANÇOIS   In a week, maybe.

JUDITH   Wait, you'll be happy to see them again.

FRANÇOIS   *(after remaining quiet for a time)* It's so nice here. I'm never really alone: I read, I work, I think about my father, and when I need company I stroll around your house listening to Jean's music. That's what living in silence means…

JUDITH   Jean and I aren't young any longer. We love this country, the violent climate makes the blood flow. But you, François, you're becoming attached too soon to this austere life.

FRANÇOIS   Still, it's the only one I like…

JUDITH   It's beautiful…. We're privileged, maybe the last persons in this world who are; but is it right? Think of Nicolas, so unsatisfied, leaving everything behind for the city—us too, his heart full of anger…

FRANÇOIS   He might come back.

JUDITH   No. Nicolas is a strange boy; maybe like so many others, he can't get close to anyone or anything. I don't understand him. We could take him in, give him all we have, but he despises our life here; he'd rather wander, keep losing his way…

FRANÇOIS   It seems each of us only lives to know the pleasure of freedom, of inner emancipation, to get it at any cost, with no compromises…

JUDITH   Even if this pursuit of freedom sometimes causes others pain…

> *FRANÇOIS is putting his father's posthumous papers in order. As usual, a glass is within easy reach. Suddenly there is the noise of an approaching automobile. He goes to the window.*
>
> *An automobile arrives. He hurries, intrigued, then with consternation he recognizes it as being SIMON's. MARIA is with her brother. The automobile pulls up and stops. They exchange greetings.*

MARIA   You seem rather surprised to see us.

FRANÇOIS   I wasn't expecting you until next week.

SIMON   We were tired of the city. Maria needs a rest right away. And don't the three of us have things to talk about?

MARIA   *(She takes several deep breaths.)* Oh, it's good to be back in the wide open spaces breathing this salt air! My children will get a good rest.

SIMON   Our children, Maria.

MARIA   Oh, you and your sons; never for a moment do you forget you're a father.

FRANÇOIS   The children?

MARIA   Of course, the children! Why not? They'll come spend their vacation with my husband.

FRANÇOIS   Your husband? The children?

MARIA   Simon's sons are coming too, with their mother.

SIMON   This is our home, François!

> *They enter the house. FRANÇOIS leads the way. Once in the house he looks at them for a moment.*

FRANÇOIS   *(testily)* I wasn't expecting you. There's nothing to eat, almost nothing to drink…

SIMON   With you, it's no surprise!

FRANÇOIS   *(taking out a bag for provisions)* I'm going to the village. Settle in.

> *FRANÇOIS leaves the house, goes to his automobile and drives off. MARIA and SIMON alone in the house.*

MARIA   Our little brother wasn't expecting us so soon.

SIMON   He thinks we've invaded his castle, but as far as I'm concerned he'll be the one invading ours… *(pause)* It's good to be together again here at home, Maria. We'll have lots of time. The whole summer, if you like…

MARIA   *(pensively)* After all, mother's right; we can't always leave him alone…

SIMON   Do you think François is drinking again? *(as though he were suddenly waking from a dream to remember FRANÇOIS's existence)*

MARIA   Another thing father left him.

SIMON   *(ironically)* We'll take care of him.

MARIA   He gets on my nerves already.

SIMON   It'll be difficult, but we've got to try to make the best of it, Maria.

MARIA   François is vulnerable and I can't resist the pleasure of hurting him, of hurting him, him, especially…

SIMON   Father's death has upset him too much. We've got to be patient. We liked to scare him when he was little, remember? Remember the cruel jokes we played on him?

MARIA   Yes…. The dead dog on the beach…. It was only a lazy hound asleep in the sun, but he was so naïve he'd believe everything we told him…. Even that story about the body of the dead dog…. But it was only a dog asleep, a happy dog whose stillness looked like death's own…

SIMON   And in the woods, remember the way he cried one day when he found the body of that rabbit some hunters had killed, saying, "Let me warm him, he'll come back to life…"

MARIA   It wasn't a rabbit, it was a rat…

SIMON   Really? All I remember is him trying to warm the animal up, caressing it softly. It was ridiculous, but touching too…

MARIA   But that time it was no lie or joke. The animal was dead.

> *They fall silent for a few moments.*

SIMON   Different from the rest of us, that's for sure; one of those sensitive souls I wanted to force a little courage on, a taste for fighting—even hatred, if I could have. I was always hitting him too hard, even when just meaning to play with him; my fragile companion would become an adversary too tender to break…. Yes, he shouldered the heaviest burden, I tell you.

MARIA   Simply say he got the lion's share of the legacy…

SIMON   *(ambiguous)* We'll have time to talk about that, lots of time, Maria.

MARIA   Who'll get the most of the royalties from father's books? First mother, but then François. Always François.

SIMON   But we'll get this house, Maria. *(catching himself)* I just told you, we'll talk about the whole business later, with François…

MARIA   Ah, he's so naïve—he probably doesn't understand that deep down Father despised him.

SIMON   We don't know anything about Father, we can't judge.

MARIA   We've got to judge, we've got to search for the truth. You know very well that's what we're here for.

SIMON   Be quiet, Maria…

MARIA   …pardon. Nor can Mother, for example, admit that Father… or rather, she's always known… husband's memory.

SIMON   There's no proof.

MARIA   Aren't my own eyes proof? And you think François, whom Father confided in, knows nothing? But, like Mother, he'll keep silent. Human fidelity's madness!

SIMON   You dwell on Father too much, Maria. You're too passionate: you should be more indifferent towards life.

MARIA   I only dwell on him to drive him from this house. I want to be rid of his presence at last, of any trace of his books, his writing!

SIMON   Why not just forget him? You've got to forget him.

MARIA   *(softly, as though to herself)* His memory refuses to die with him. That's something François knows only too well.

Living room. The three are together after the noon meal. They now clash openly.

We see FRANÇOIS timidly playing host, offering liqueurs, etc. to SIMON and MARIA.

FRANÇOIS　*(offering a glass to SIMON)* I haven't forgotten you like a cognac after lunch.

SIMON　*(mockingly)* And here I was thinking you hardly knew me.

MARIA　*(turning down the record player)* Enough of Boris Godounov!

FRANÇOIS　It's my favourite music. Father was listening to that monologue a few hours before he died.

MARIA　Yes, I know…. But I don't want to suffer that music any more. I don't want to suffer anything of *his* any more.

SIMON　*(self-satisfied air)* Poor Father! He'd listen to that for hours! It's so boring! He liked pompous music.

FRANÇOIS　No, he respected everything that had majesty, everything elevated; Father was no ordinary man.

SIMON　All men are alike, they share the same failings.

FRANÇOIS　So you'd like to think. The idea of a common baseness is always more reassuring; but it's false: Father was unique.

MARIA　Well, you know, today uniqueness is a vice not a virtue.

SIMON　You're unique, too, little brother, but what does it get you?

MARIA　You're lonely, unhappy, and already you drink too much…

FRANÇOIS　I'm very happy here in this house.

SIMON　You were so happy alone here for two months? Shut up between waves and sky since the day of Father's funeral…. Mother's very worried, she wants you to come back to town; she sent us…

MARIA　*(jealous)* You had your father all to yourself. How satisfying! Living in the softness of your memories. Now we're here. You'll need to think of us.

SIMON　*(condescending)* You know, François, I understand you. You loved him so…. But he's no longer here to shield you: Maria's right, it's about time you put your dreams aside and learned how to live with others. You want to know what we're expecting from you?

FRANÇOIS　I can imagine!

MARIA　A little solidarity, that's all we're expecting from you…

SIMON　It's time you surrendered your old privileges.

FRANÇOIS　I never had privileges.

SIMON He loved *you*. Love's a privilege, don't you think?

MARIA Yes, love's the most terrible privilege and you deserved it least of all, perhaps. You're the one he chose to have near him when he was working so doggedly the last long winters of his life, and when the passion to leave took hold, again, you're the one he chose to take along on his trips…

FRANÇOIS Growing old, he needed someone near. I was always available.

MARIA Available—why not say you liked being his slave.

SIMON Let's forget that, Maria. What counts is Father's last thought; it's the legacy that counts…

FRANÇOIS The legacy?

SIMON *(bitterly)* It's time we got to our father's final injustices—yes, the legacy!

FRANÇOIS I know both of you think Father always gave me too much, but you're wrong, he was a just man…

>   *Out of doors.*

SIMON Before coming, Maria and I went through Father's will, painfully attentive. Father left his house in town to Mother, which is normal; Maria and I approve. As for this country house, so dear to his heart, the three of us are the heirs. Now, let's talk about you: not only do you inherit this house with Maria and me, but Father left you his complete library, all his personal papers, private notebooks, diaries, etc.—in short, all his work from the last years of his life, perhaps the most valuable part of all. And what's left for Maria and me? Royalties from translations.

MARIA You've got to understand, François, it isn't enough. We've children, responsibilities; unlike you, we don't live just following our fancy. You have to make up for Father's negligence.

FRANÇOIS He willed me his posthumous work, it's true, but those writings won't be published right away. They're the story of his private pilgrimage towards death; I don't want to make that public now.

MARIA But thanks to those writings you'll be rich one day, very rich—surely you don't need such prosperity, you who're always saying you don't like money? No need to fear, we've no intention of depriving you of your "spiritual" or "poetic" legacy—how do you put it exactly? No, we're quite clear about what we want, and the only thing that interests us in the whole affair is this property here along the river.

FRANÇOIS But this house is already yours, and mine.

SIMON How can the house be ours and our children's when you're in it? How can we have our friends here? We need this house all to ourselves. Don't you think we deserve it?

FRANÇOIS   (*astonished*) But this is my house. Father's house belongs to his children, each of them.

SIMON   Then why should it be more your home than ours? Father's gone, it's time you learned to share, even give, if necessary…

FRANÇOIS   How can I give you what's already yours, yours as much as mine?

SIMON   It's very easy—we go to a notary and you sign over your share, that's all. Why not do it for us? That way things would be clearer. Naturally, you'd always be welcome here. Like you say yourself, this is your home.

FRANÇOIS   Would I be your guest or your brother?

SIMON   All we're asking is a sign of friendship…

FRANÇOIS   Yes, in fact it's very easy. You're asking me to leave, disappear.

SIMON   I'm asking you to give up excess privileges, no more!

FRANÇOIS   Be patient, both of you; maybe I'll do it. But I've begun something I want to finish.

SIMON   (*feigning softness*) Don't you want to leave? Travel? Live?

MARIA   We know you, François. It won't be any easier for you to leave the land after another couple of weeks in the company of Father's memory!

SIMON   When things are clearer you could live with us if you wanted, live like us, among our children, our friends. What do you think?

FRANÇOIS   I need quiet surroundings to work.

MARIA   Work? Write? Since we were kids you've talked about your work, but we still haven't seen any of it. Where is your work, François? You dream and drink, that's as far as it goes.

SIMON   Or have you stopped writing because brutally one night Father showed you you had no talent?

MARIA   You haven't got his talent, his intelligence, or his physical strength; you can't even copy his vices because in him they weren't vices, he was so strong and healthy we forgot them. But with you it's another story: start drinking like Father and you'll be an alcoholic, period. With him, drinking was a thirst, nothing disgraceful. You noticed nothing if not that his strength seemed to grow; his intelligence scrutinized you then with something like diabolical finesse…. Remember, Simon?

SIMON   (*dryly*) No, I don't. What's serious is the example he set for François. If you're already an alcoholic it's because of him.

MARIA   Like I've said, François, my children are coming for their vacation, and the time's getting near.

SIMON   Your children and mine, Maria. You always seem to forget my boys in all this.

FRANÇOIS   Oh, you two and your children!

SIMON   We're planning to live here, that's all.

FRANÇOIS   So you're bent on driving our father out of his house, driving me out.

SIMON   We can't wait. Maria and I want you to make us sole owners of the house… *(wanting to sound tender)* François, you know very well that after signing the papers you'll be free to come and go as you please. But, naturally…. Do you hear what I'm saying?

FRANÇOIS   You won't need papers, Simon. When I go I won't come back. *(He leaves.)*

> FRANÇOIS *walks down to the beach. We see him standing there for a time, an isolated figure against the countryside.*
>
> Out of doors. SIMON *and* MARIA *seem to be celebrating their triumph.*

SIMON   *(with slight concern in his voice)* You think he'll go along with giving up his share? You think he'll come with me to the notary's

MARIA   It doesn't matter now! He's signed already, don't you see?

SIMON   I'd like something more definite…. A paper…. A person's always more secure when things are in writing!

> FRANÇOIS *on the beach near* JEAN's *house. He meets* JUDITH.

JUDITH   I saw Simon's car on the road.

FRANÇOIS   They're here, all right; and their children are coming. I know why Nicolas shuns that kind of affection…. Only solitude protects us from it.

JUDITH   Solitude's especially fertile for artists, creators like your father or Jean; others get weighed down by it rather fast, don't you think?

FRANÇOIS   Yes, maybe…

JUDITH   I've seen you so often this winter wandering about at night. Why didn't you come to the house? Jean enjoys seeing you so much.

FRANÇOIS   I came by to listen to him playing, composing, working; I didn't dare bother you.

JUDITH   I wrote Nicolas, but he's never understood his father, never liked his music; I doubt he'll come. I mentioned Jean's illness—to no avail, they'll never be reconciled. *(pause)* Jean's afraid of dying in his sleep, so he refuses to rest.

FRANÇOIS   I'd like to talk to him a moment.

JUDITH   Go to the house. *(while FRANÇOIS climbs hurriedly up the hill towards the musician's house)* Could you put a few more pine branches on the fire? Jean needs to stay warm…

FRANÇOIS   *(while going away)* I won't forget!

> *FRANÇOIS at JEAN's house. FRANÇOIS walks up to the window, listens stealthily to the musician. His face is full of wonder and of respect for the old man, whose head we can see. He is a fine old man with aesthetic features which give off a youthful glow, a kind of calm and sovereign goodness.*
>
> *FRANÇOIS knocks at the door.*

JEAN   *(rising)* Is that you, Judith?

FRANÇOIS   No…. It's me, I was passing by… *(timidly)* Am I disturbing you?

JEAN   No, no, let's take a little time for a drink together… *(pause)* Not so long ago your father would come to see me about this same time.

FRANÇOIS   I'd like to hear your last composition; I hear you playing from far off. It's so beautiful…

JEAN   Beautiful not because of me but because of the wind and the beauty of the country.

> *FRANÇOIS walks over to JEAN, who is at the piano. This house is more orderly than the other, his surroundings showing that JEAN is a methodical and meticulous man.*

FRANÇOIS   Judith told me you weren't feeling well these days.

JEAN   Judith's always worried: she's worried now because I don't want to sleep. It's not so serious, you know! I've decided not to lose time sleeping, to work day and night; you can understand that; towards the end of his life your father had a horror of beds. Besides, haven't you noticed it's when you're in bed that death too often takes a person by surprise?

FRANÇOIS   I know you spoke a lot with my father here in your house during the last weeks of his life, what with his coming over every night to have a drink, not understanding your music but liking you; I know you were maybe his only friend, and when I see you I see something of him…

JEAN   No, François, you don't find him; it's only me, "an old pig-headed enemy of silence," as my boy Nicolas would say. Why not, my son, leave the dead where they lie? *(pause)* Soon there'll be no more joy in the world. We'll be ashamed of saying we like Mozart, we'll be ashamed of being tenderhearted. Fine, here we were, a small, happy colony of artists; we lived in peace; but it's over, the others are chasing us out. So maybe it makes more sense to die, don't you think?

FRANÇOIS   Simon and Maria, and, yes, others too, are chasing us out.

JEAN   We were too privileged. They're just taking our privileges away.

FRANÇOIS   Why resign ourselves to that?

JEAN   Well—our tolerance, one might say; but that's not the right word. *(pause)* You don't belong, François; it's a bit your fault; but also it seems your father created you, a piece of his imagination; yes, like in a book; you're more or less one of his characters destined always to suffer. You live in an old world of your own; it's dangerous, everything in that old world stands to die, it's useless hanging on to it, believe me! When the man is no longer there with his little whims and weaknesses we forget his art, especially when his gifts are limited. Everything has to disappear. Myself, I accept that, why not you?

> *FRANÇOIS does not answer.*

We like to dress life up in lies. When I play, when I compose, I try to forget the world's misery; and that's when my wife, reading the evening papers, remains aware for me, her conscience suffers the injustices on earth. My life has been one of innocence, and they tell us such blind innocence is an evil. Maybe it's true, who knows?

FRANÇOIS   But how could a life like yours be blameable?

JEAN   Because it's a useless life, my friend. At least, that's what my son Nicolas likes to say. Poor Nicolas! Consider his deception—he would have liked a father who was a social success, a father he could present without blushing, a musician worthy of the name who gave concerts and offered his family a pleasant life, and I give him none of that. I live like a monk, I only live for myself. Oh, it's a fine life, but I have one regret—to have brought, in my austerity, so little happiness to others. I could begin now but it's too late…. A little voice tells me, "Watch out, you're getting old, you're getting deafer, less flexible, save your strength, you're nearing the end." And I listen to that voice and when a season passes I wonder: "Will it be given to me to see the next?" Then spring comes and I'm grateful! It's the violent winter here that fills me with anguish!

FRANÇOIS   Winter is life and inspiration to you!

JEAN   No, not now. I fear the cold, I don't like this numbness creeping into my limbs. There was a time when I saw and heard everything, never tiring. The slightest thing: a shutter slapping in the wind, the lark's song at dawn—for years my wife and I lived off of those pleasant sounds! She still lives off of them. But I'm getting ready for total deafness, winter…

FRANÇOIS   Who knows, the sounds you've lost—maybe someone else will find them in your music.

JEAN   No, I don't think so; those things have to be lost.

FRANÇOIS   My father never knew that one day I'd read his last writings, that I would be there to understand the final outpourings of his heart…

JEAN   He had so carefully disguised that heart all his life in his characters. What did he let it say?

FRANÇOIS   He goes on for pages, nostalgically describing what he'll never see again—an abandoned house near the river, a dead bird on the beach: he says he has vertigo, that all is blue and empty, he's afraid and trembles like a bird or leaf in the wind. Isn't it strange from him who never spoke of nature in his books, who was never afraid in his life? "I want to exhaust my soul this side of heaven," he says: "I want to devour the sky, the colour of the water." It wasn't his style writing the way a child speaks, but for the first time, I think, he felt what he wrote…

JEAN   You find it strange because you're still young. Your father was refusing to surrender his five senses, his body, everything he had savoured on this earth! Nothing's beautiful except the love of life, everything else pales beside it…

> *Absently he plays several bars of a melody. JUDITH enters the house.*

JUDITH   *(going towards the chimney, where now the fire is almost out)* Hah! He neglected the fire!

FRANÇOIS   Excuse me, I forgot…

JEAN   This boy is warmth; I wasn't cold.

JUDITH   *(She comes close to JEAN. She touches his shoulder tenderly.)* Haven't you done enough work for today?

JEAN   Poor Judith! You'll soon be rid of me. You'll be able to start living again…

JUDITH   I never stopped.

JEAN   You say that out of kindness.

JUDITH   I regret nothing; this life has become my own.

FRANÇOIS   I was about to leave, Judith…

JEAN   *(to himself)* I have dark thoughts these days.

JUDITH   You don't sleep enough!

JEAN   You can sleep in an easy chair, doze off while you're working, but beware of the bed—it's the grave!

JUDITH   Then you don't want to be cured?

JEAN   Cured of what?

JUDITH   *(to FRANÇOIS, without looking at JEAN)* Is it true it's going to storm tomorrow?

FRANÇOIS   Yes. They said specifically high winds with not much fog. *(to JEAN)* Judith's right, you have to get some rest. I'll come back tomorrow.

JUDITH   Okay, my boy. Until tomorrow!

> *Out of doors. JUDITH comes out of the house with FRANÇOIS.*

JUDITH   He knows it's almost over for him. Before long I'll be very alone. Is your mother coming this summer?

FRANÇOIS   They're all coming. Hold on to your solitude while you can, Judith; they're bent on taking it from you. And soon!

> *Music is heard. FRANÇOIS turns his head in the direction of JEAN's house. He is lost for a moment in thought.*

FRANÇOIS   Do you hear? What infinite sadness!

JUDITH   Why must he always play the same notes over and over? The same!

> *After supper. SIMON, MARIA, FRANÇOIS. SIMON is lying on the sofa smoking his pipe. In his hand is a book. MARIA is standing in front of her father's work table looking impatiently through a pile of notebooks.*

FRANÇOIS   *(aggressive)* You have no right to read those.

MARIA   Why not?

FRANÇOIS   Father's diaries were left to me in his will. You can't read them, they're my property.

MARIA   In any case, this one isn't interesting. You'd think it was an adolescent's; there's nothing at all remarkable in it. You know, you mustn't kid yourself, my little François, sickness had affected Father's mind…

FRANÇOIS   The last things Father wrote are the most dignified, the most revealing…

SIMON   Childish writing entirely lacking literary value.

FRANÇOIS   *(to SIMON)* All your life you waited, hoped, for a moment of weakness from Father… *(to SIMON and MARIA as he gathers his father's notebooks)* I can hide myself away in the little room in the attic; up there you won't come and disturb "our" peace…

SIMON   That attic's always been a subject of dispute between us. Before, we couldn't go play in the attic because you were there and wanted to read alone or were pouting and, if you had taken the notion, weren't speaking to anyone for days. Then later, going there was forbidden because you'd started an essay, so you said.… And your novel—do you remember that novel you were writing in the dreary attic when the summer days were so beautiful and Maria and I were below calling you all the time, asking you to come swimming with us?

FRANÇOIS   It was cooler in the attic…

SIMON   Even when you were young you looked down your nose at our games and our outdoor life. You and your reading. You and your attic!

MARIA   One day I had to beat you up so I could put my shells in the closet. Remember, Simon and I were crazy about shells that summer; we let them dry in the closet and you didn't like the smell. It kept you from reading, you said…

SIMON   François has always wanted everything for himself.

FRANÇOIS   I intend to leave, Simon. But you'll have to wait a few more days. Yes, I know, you still want concrete proof that the house will be yours alone…. Since you've already arranged everything we'll go see the notary. You and Maria will be free, this will finally be your home.

SIMON   *(unable to hide his joy)* It's nice of your to agree to that, very nice; you're generous, François; of course you know you'll be at home here, just like before. If I ask you to sign over…

FRANÇOIS   That's enough!

SIMON   As I so often say to my students at the university: "Thrice certain is he…"

FRANÇOIS   How can you teach literature, hating writers the way you do?

SIMON   I don't like them, it's true. But I like dissecting their works; you uncover all the failings, the secret vices. It's interesting.

FRANÇOIS   It's a crime.

SIMON   Father described all sorts of assassins, he even denounced assassins like me, the jealous ones, "the impotent in heart and mind" as he called them! But in his superior wisdom Father forgot to mention that each of us also has the right to show his hatred, his fear as well, whatever way he wants.

FRANÇOIS   I've read your articles in the newspapers, Simon. Don't bother explaining your theories to me.

> FRANÇOIS *pours himself a large drink.*

MARIA   *(feigning concern)* Careful, don't drink too much…. You'll end up one of those human wrecks found in Father's work.

SIMON   "A young man suddenly and voluntarily deprived of the light of intelligence." You see, I know a little of his work…. Didn't he say intelligence breaks us, kills us slowly?

FRANÇOIS   Shut up! You don't know his work. *(pause)* I have to protect his notebooks and writings while I'm here.

SIMON   Who's telling you to leave?

MARIA   You could work in that room upstairs if you wanted, if you can put up with the kids nearby, naturally…. It seems to me the house is large enough to share.

FRANÇOIS   That's not the question. You know I can't write when there's too many people around.

MARIA   In a large house people can always find a way to live together…. You should say instead you don't want to, you find our presence disagreeable…

SIMON   Make an effort! Since you've agreed to give up your share everything's different. We can live together very well here—at least for a while…

FRANÇOIS   Did you get what you wanted too fast, Simon? Are you afraid of feeling a little ashamed? But I'm not interested in your shame! I'll get out.

SIMON   Listen, Maria and I have social and family responsibilities. How can we do anything else? How can we live in your company? Do you want to imitate Father all the way and be negligent of others like he was of Mother and us? He sacrificed us; and sacrificed Mother. For his art!

FRANÇOIS   Mother loved the writer in Father. When one loves, sacrifices don't exist.

MARIA   That kind of love is called slavery.

SIMON   And have you noticed one thing, François? In his books Father never spoke about love, nor tenderness.

FRANÇOIS   A writer is allowed reticence with respect to certain things.

MARIA   It's easy, a clever writer covering up an absence of love, coldness, indifference even, under the word "reticence"—undoubtedly reticence was another of Father's literary virtues, but what one would like to know is whether underneath it all there was anything human.

SIMON   And you, François, when exactly did you acquire lasting proof of Father's love for you? He was the first to discourage you, to tell you you'd never be a writer; you think his telling you that meant he loved you?

> *Flashback. Out of doors: on the farm behind the house. THE FATHER is with his dog. FRANÇOIS comes to show him his poems. SIMON, rubbing down the horses, is a silent witness to the conversation.*

THE FATHER   It's a fine day today. Why not relax a bit? Here, you could help Simon with the horses. That's life, too, you know…. Maybe Simon has less imagination than you but he loves nature, he knows how to see; and he knows how to relax.

FRANÇOIS   *(irritated)* I don't have time.

THE FATHER   I know, you're writing. But the rest exists also. *(THE FATHER, while speaking, points to the countryside around them, plays with the dog, etc.)*

FRANÇOIS   It takes time to learn the rigour you talk about…

THE FATHER   If you can't criticize yourself by now, you'll never be able to. I've known too many young people like you of promising talent who get drunk off flattery; such adulation is just a lie! Because you're the age of Lautréamont and

Rimbaud, like the others you think you're able to write the revolutionary work that will destroy the past—or outmoded art, as you say...

FRANÇOIS   I never said that!

THE FATHER   You're all brothers when it comes to killing those who came before you.... You'll even kill Lautréamont, and everyone else.... Your idols are only there to serve you.

> *SIMON is seen standing with the horse, impatient.*

Learn to live first, François. You don't know it, but life is wonderful...

FRANÇOIS   But Father, you started one day. You wrote when you were young, too...

THE FATHER   Yes, yes, I know! One always writes much too soon. Why imitate me? *(pause)* From the beginning you have to feel the beauty of a work, experience a shock, suffer the violence of the artist. In your case things are still too new—and too soft!

FRANÇOIS   I can't make myself violent if I'm not!

THE FATHER   I'm not asking you to. But choose my craft and you necessarily choose violence; true, it's invisible violence, but it's there eating away at you.... You're still too vulnerable for that adventure.... What's unhealthy in being a writer is that, after all's said and done, you belong to others, they have too much power over you, they believe they penetrate your secrets; could you stand that destructiveness, calumny, around your life and your work? You can't give anything of yourself doing what I do without betraying yourself a little.... No, you aren't a writer, perhaps you were born to understand someone else's thought, the quivering deep within him; and what's certain, François—you were born to suffer, you won't be able to avoid it.

> *Return to the present. Living room.*

FRANÇOIS   He sensed everything; I'll never be a writer. I was born to understand someone else, no more.

SIMON   Father tried to crush everything in you, and in Maria and me; with us he failed, we resisted. But you, you love your heritage. *(seeing FRANÇOIS about to pour himself a drink, SIMON grabs the glass from his hand)* And *that* is your heritage, is it not? The novelist rejoicing at having created some real life! You're that life! Doesn't he write somewhere that in spite of his success he was always afraid of having failed? Yes, it was the fear, he said, of not having succeeded in creating living persons, but only creatures of the imagination.

FRANÇOIS   Is fear, doubt, condemnable? I remember we spoke one day, Father and I...

> *Flashback. On the beach.*

THE FATHER   Have I really made living beings out of the creatures born of my imagination?

FRANÇOIS   Why the doubt: Your readers recognize themselves in the human crowd you conjure up.

THE FATHER   No, the reader always complains he's been cheated. It's a profession in which betrayal almost can't be helped. Have you noticed that they always accuse the author, seldom his characters? We're spellbinders, we have dangerous powers—they don't like us, I guarantee you…. So why would you choose so uncompromising a craft?

> *The dog comes running towards them. THE FATHER grabs the dog and hugs him with obvious physical pleasure. FRANÇOIS is looking off in the distance.*

FRANÇOIS   I have only one passion, and it's yours too: to observe people, to watch them living. I admire you, knowing every feeling and how to express it. What good is it being stirred by everything as I am and not know how to express it? You give form to your revolt, I just keep silent and never quite manage my own. You should believe me, Father, the earth's loaded with impotent creators…

THE FATHER   I know, but maybe you won't be one of them. *(pause)* Don't admire me. That power of translating my feelings, which you envy, is a power which separates us from our best friends, our children, all those we love.

> *Return to the present. Living room.*

FRANÇOIS   An artist's creativity is like the ocean… and you can't…

SIMON   Yes, I know: you can't drain the ocean dry, it's vain dreaming of such a thing…. Our father was the ocean; a proud haughty man who possessed himself of nature's forces—the better to tower and spread out over us, the better to subject us to the power of words, the power of images… *(He takes his father's books from the library shelf and throws them to the floor in front of FRANÇOIS.)* Take his books, take them far, far away.

> *FRANÇOIS picks up the books, presses them against him for a moment with sorrowful tenderness, then places them in a large black briefcase.*

MARIA   You're lovely—so like a mother protecting her threatened little ones.

FRANÇOIS   I'll defend him till the day I die.

MARIA   Father would be very touched seeing you like this.

SIMON   *(assuming once again his protecting tone)* Drinking like you do won't defend him long. You don't understand, do you, that Maria and I want to save you from him?

MARIA   Father always said Simon and I were too materialistic. He spoke in his essays about his detachment from worldly things, but how did he show that detachment? Like everybody else Father was desperately attached to the earth, his passions!

FRANÇOIS   He spoke of such detachment towards the end, but he knew all along it was an illusion. He said himself that each thing his hand wrote was a contradiction of his life…

MARIA   More lies! *(pause)* I think I'll go to my room. Goodnight, François. No opera music, please.

SIMON   *(at the window)* The wind's dying down…. Maybe we won't get a storm tomorrow.

> *SIMON approaches FRANÇOIS, wanting to speak amiably with him, but FRANÇOIS moves away.*

FRANÇOIS   What do you want from me now?

SIMON   Nothing, only friendship.

FRANÇOIS   We've nothing to say to each other.

> *FRANÇOIS goes out of the house on the side facing the river. Standing at the window of her room on the second floor, MARIA watches FRANÇOIS.*
>
> *Flashback. Out of doors. MARIA is helping her mother hang sheets on a clothesline.*

MARIA   You're still working too hard, Mother; just always work more than the others.

THE MOTHER   Your father works a lot too.

MARIA   But not in a servile way like you or me. The things he does are nobler than what we do. Have you thought how unjust that is?

THE MOTHER   There is nothing servile about hanging out sheets to dry in the sun. Especially on such a nice day. Hand me some clothespins, Maria. You make no allowances, Maria for yourself or others.

MARIA   I can't believe this is my role in life…

THE MOTHER   And don't forget to take in the basket of dry clothes, Maria. The other day you forgot and left it on the grass and it rained… *(pause)* I know the sun tires you out quickly…

MARIA   Why don't you tell my brothers to work in my place? Or to share the housework with us?

THE MOTHER   And then you forgive so easily when you want to, even your father…

MARIA   No… I could never forgive him; no, I couldn't…

THE MOTHER   What good is it judging your father? I love him, I can understand everything, and he needs me.

MARIA   So you tolerate his affairs with other women?

THE MOTHER   I can't deprive him of experiences, of knowledge. Besides, he can't get attached to one kind of life, to a single person.

MARIA   No, I couldn't ever serve a man the way you have your whole life! You talk about Father's freedom, but what of your own? Mother, you have a right to freedom; what are you doing about it? How humiliating!

THE MOTHER   You're afraid of humiliation, Maria; above all, you're afraid of loving.

MARIA   I'll choose a man I don't love so I won't fall into the trap of adoration like so many women…

THE MOTHER   Maria! You just told me you love Nicolas!

MARIA   I intend to leave him. I told you, I want to live with an ordinary sort of husband whom I'll feel indifferent towards and who'll leave me free, without ever knowing it.

THE MOTHER   So, you want to lie all your life?

MARIA   I prefer lying to blind obedience. I'm not you, I don't like giving myself. Ever since we were children Nicolas has taken too much from me. *(pause)* And Father too…. You remember, Mother, we had to play in silence, live in silence, because Father was working…. And you, all he had to do was say your name and you would run to him—loving, in love, so far from us, so close to him! Entirely devoted to your passion, night and day…

THE MOTHER   You're afraid to love; yes, you're afraid to love…

> *Return to the present. FRANÇOIS is walking towards JEAN's place. He stops a certain distance from the old musician's house, sees that it is lit up and suddenly seems comforted, almost happy.*

VOICE   François… François…

NICOLAS   *(JEAN's son: young, in his early twenties, bohemian, unkempt hair, somewhat sad expression)* Don't you recognize me?

FRANÇOIS   You said you'd never come back here.

NICOLAS   I said I'd never enter that house again; that's different. My mother wrote saying my father was very sick and I should come right away.

FRANÇOIS   Have you seen Jean?

NICOLAS   No! I said I'd never enter my parents' house again! Besides, the old man's not as sick as all that; he still pecks away at it. Hear him? My mother even wrote saying that you were his real son. What do you think of that?

FRANÇOIS   I've always loved Jean. *(pause)* I'm no one's son now. Let's go.

> *They are now in the empty bar of a hotel.*

Your parents don't know you're here?

NICOLAS   I don't like my family. And I don't like the old man's music. When I see that he's quit playing for good maybe I'll be ready to knock on his door.

FRANÇOIS   They tell me you're married, Nicolas, and have children.

NICOLAS   Maria didn't love me any more so right away I thought about having a nice, healthy affair! But it's already over, I've left everything behind me. Don't forget to tell your little sister she wrecked my life! *(He laughs.)* She's right, you can't get stuck with one person, especially at our age. I want to live for myself; it's time I did. Besides, I don't like places where you're a prisoner; a house is too confining. I want to live outdoors from now on, walk all night…. How about you? Still over your books like a professor?

FRANÇOIS   *(ironically)* I don't change enough.

NICOLAS   That's too bad. You must be very alone…

FRANÇOIS   Yes, maybe…

NICOLAS   You ought to leave it all behind, too, take off; it's a great joy, you know. They were looking for me everywhere and I was hiding out in Italy. It was wonderful! For as long as I can remember they've talked to me about an inner life. Why? Where would that get me? An inner world—you know what that brings to mind? A house with a heavy suffocating roof…. A prison!

FRANÇOIS   Maybe you're right getting away…

NICOLAS   I'm convinced of it, François. Out there I drift, I never settle in one place; I look, and everything's beautiful out there…. But the thought of being still tied to that family, to that old dreamer, that quiet old fool about to die…

FRANÇOIS   He loves working and he has lots left to do.

NICOLAS   No. It's all over but he doesn't know it, or rather prefers not to know it.

FRANÇOIS   You seem eager for him to die.

NICOLAS   You can't understand. My mother and I have been his prisoners, prisoners of his music, for so long. You know, he could have given concerts if he'd wanted to; we'd have had a more normal life. But, no—he preferred to devote himself to a sterile career, composing, works leading nowhere! All without a thought for us, for my mother; not a single thought for the captives he kept around him. Sometimes I think if Maria and I lived that brief love story it was just to get our revenge…. Her father crushed her, mine me! We were ready to create passion for ourselves.

FRANÇOIS   So you reproach Jean for…

NICOLAS   For being an irresponsible artist…. For an innocence in his life which he had no right to…

FRANÇOIS   Be honest: what you mainly have against him is having gone further than you can go. It's not the father you don't like—he was beyond reproach—but the musician, that originality that you don't have…. Why not get to know him?

NICOLAS   You think he's trying to get to know me? I don't like this country. The winter is too long—the retiring life, that love of solitude he tried to impose on me…. Oh no, I can't put up with it…. Not any more.

FRANÇOIS   Your mother doesn't complain.

NICOLAS   A woman's love can reach the point of submissiveness. But I was only his son; a man can't accept that. At times I dream of setting the house on fire. I see the burning piano coming out the window. It's the opposite with you, isn't it? You dream of your heritage, your father's house. Profit from the occasion, sell your father's work; if my father's music were worth anything I wouldn't hesitate, you know. I'd go sell it right away. I want to be rich and, that way, free.

FRANÇOIS   *(after a moment)* I have things to do, I'm going back…

> *FRANÇOIS in the small room in the attic. He writes a single word over and over. Then he dreams.*

> *FRANÇOIS's dream: Out of doors. Lunch behind the house near the fields. Ethereal quality to the scene. Dressed in white, the children are playing together. The adults are seated around the table. Lunch in the clear light of noon: seated at the table are SIMON, MARIA, FRANÇOIS, in white summer clothes. They are waiting for their father before beginning the meal. At one of the tables are spotless fruit of a fleshy brilliance, as fruit are often seen in dreams. At the other end of the table is a basket containing sandwiches for the children, and there are glasses filled with milk shining in the sun. MARIA's young children are standing near the mother.*

SIMON   The children are hungry!

> *The atmosphere is joyful. His two sons are between eight and eleven years old.*

(as though to himself as he looks with pride at his sons) They're handsome boys; and all mine!

MARIA   Isn't your wife feeling well, Simon?

SIMON   Oh, she's always tired. I suggested she stay in her room and rest.

MARIA   The two of you are rarely together. You seem to prefer the company of your boys.

SIMON   True, I prefer them to their mother. They're saner than my wife.

MARIA   Maybe the weariness you speak of stems from marriage. I feel it myself at times…

THE MOTHER   Oh, I see him, coming up the slope. Thank goodness he took his cane this morning. That hill's difficult for him now…

SIMON   I can go help Father, if you want.

THE MOTHER   No, you don't do that with him.

MARIA   You can't ever help him. The older he gets the younger and stronger he gets—Father will never be an "old man"!

> *We see THE FATHER's silhouette. We hear him breathing, the breathing of someone who has run or walked a long way. He is wearing a hat. At no time during the dream do we see his face clearly.*

There he is!

THE MOTHER   We were waiting for you…

SIMON   It's the hill, Father, that tires you out…

THE FATHER   What are you saying, Simon? Nothing tires me out. I'm hungry and thirsty, that's all.

FRANÇOIS   *(sharing an aperitif with his father)* I'm thirsty too…. To your health, Father!

> *They begin the meal in the same atmosphere of gaiety. The children are restless and leave the table to play. When they look at the adults it is with a certain attention and wonder. THE FATHER eats hungrily. THE MOTHER is standing near him. Watching over him, she seems worried.*

THE FATHER   Mother, dear wife, this is the first time the whole family's been together. Why are we having this meal?

SIMON   It's your birthday, Father…

THE FATHER   Ah, I'd completely forgotten…. Now I understand. *(Everybody laughs, THE FATHER very loud.)* Usually I refuse to pay attention to time passing.

THE MOTHER   It's dangerous for your father to… to… laugh so hard… he's sick, you know!

THE FATHER   *(laughing)* I'm never sick! *(to FRANÇOIS, who is sitting next to him)* Do you think I'm sick, François? *(pause)* Aha! He doesn't answer; fortunately I see into his soul…

FRANÇOIS   Destiny is written in the hand…

THE FATHER   Then give me your hand… *(FRANÇOIS obeys.)* Hm, that's bizarre; your hand is white and smooth—nothing's written in his hand…

> *All look at their hands.*

SIMON   Not like us! Everything's there in black and white!

MARIA   Poor François! A hand with no lines, a hand without words…. Someone stole your life while you were asleep!

SIMON   A lifeless hand…

THE FATHER   But it's all right, François; I can write in your hand, if you want… (*THE FATHER writes in FRANÇOIS's open palm.*)

FRANÇOIS   You should think first, Father. Words are harmful…. They can destroy us…

THE FATHER   A single word…. For you alone… (*He writes the word "Leave."*)

SIMON   Show us your hand, François. What's so secret about a hand?

THE MOTHER   You're my son…

MARIA   You're our brother, François…

> *There is laughter around the table as FRANÇOIS makes a fist of his hand to hide what is written there from MARIA's and SIMON's stares.*

FRANÇOIS   Did you hear what he said? For me alone…. For me alone…

> *Workroom. FRANÇOIS on the sofa. He continues to write the word. Over and over he writes "Leave."*

For me alone…

> *Scenes of the river. In front of the house. It is the next morning.*

MARIA   Have you been up a long time?

SIMON   It's hard to sleep in that house! There're too many memories!

MARIA   Let's go up to the attic. François is still asleep. The view's superb from up there. I've been thinking about how to arrange the house too; about a playroom for the children.

SIMON   And what if François decides to come back?

MARIA   No, he's hurt. When he leaves he won't come back. At least not for several years.

SIMON   (*taking MARIA by the arm*) Yes, let's go up to the attic…

> *The hallway leading to the attic.*

(*lowering the trap door*) When you think he wouldn't let us come up here the whole time he was alive!

> *Attic. From a small window one can see the river.*

MARIA   It was Mother—when we were little; you confuse everything, Simon. Oh, it's so beautiful!

SIMON   And I shouldn't forget anything with François, the way he's always bringing up the past.

MARIA   There are some things he prefers not to bring up, again because he wants to save Father, out of filial love and devotion…

SIMON   What exactly?

MARIA   His suicide attempt at seventeen, when Father brutally told him he'll never be a writer…. He never speaks of that.

SIMON   And that time it wasn't "moral" suicide. François had tried to kill himself once before, the way a lot of teenagers do—with sleeping pills—but Mother got to him in time…. That was the year of what we termed François's "precocious depression." And the second time he frightened us all by trying to drown himself—but the dog sounded the alarm. The past is fragile, anything's sufficient to bring back all the regrets. Blame Father for François's despair. He harassed and discouraged him.

MARIA   What's more stupid than pardoning someone? I always knew Father wasn't interested in his children's despair—not in the least. And less still in his daughter's. It's a curse being a woman.

SIMON   You speak as though your husband and I didn't love you.

MARIA   I don't want to be loved. You love me, in your way; as for my husband, I prefer not to talk about him, as far as I'm concerned he doesn't exist. But I love my children; he was of use to me there—that's why I say it's a curse being a woman. *(pause)* Look, this room too is full of old things, more books, papers everywhere! This will be your study!

SIMON   He came here in the winter because it was warmer.

MARIA   I remember he corrected proofs here. *(She looks among the dusty files around her in the attic.)* You see, it's still all there…. One night I dreamed I threw Father's papers in the ocean…. It was only a dream; we all have that kind of dream…

SIMON   Are you sure you don't dream now?

MARIA   I don't dream. My conscience is there, watching from the shadows, watching us both! Someone's listening to all I say, and thinking but ashamed to say. *(pause)* What I regret most, I think, is the part of myself that died with him. That's different from—but maybe we all mourn deaths in that way; even Mother, having had so much pain and thinking she'd lost everything…. But down deep what was so painful was finding herself naked, deprived of her slavery!

SIMON   And you…. Tell me what you lost…

MARIA   Innocent hours and days, a little happiness, that's all!

SIMON   Are you talking about your walks with Father when you followed him, yes, in silent adoration along the beach? You, Father, and the playful dog? You were his flirtation when you were little. You were pretty, it was nice having that little girl and the dog at his side.

MARIA   It didn't last. When autumn came he only thought about his work…. He forgot me. And sometimes, when I stuck to him too much, he'd simply leave, often not going very far, just to a nearby hotel.

SIMON   No doubt because he had a rendezvous there…. That summer it was whispered he had a mistress.

MARIA   Mother said it wasn't any of our business. But I saw her crying when she thought no one was looking.

SIMON   Who knows, with a man like him, what you could discover by looking into his life a little further? Even deep within you, Maria, who knows what lies there? *(affectionately)* I remember certain betrayals… all the betrayals, perhaps…. Little by little I saw you, the child Father cast aside, finding consolation with Nicolas—he's a bad sort, he never had his father's softness…

MARIA   How can we hold that against him?

SIMON   I'd see you lying quietly beside each other in the sun, or walking together at night along the beach, always in a kind of incestuous intimacy.

MARIA   Yes. Nicolas and I often came to the attic.

> *Flashback. MARIA and NICOLAS in the attic. NICOLAS is lying on the floor smoking a cigarette. MARIA is sitting nearby, looking at him tenderly.*

What are you thinking, Nicolas?

NICOLAS   You and I are so much alike. We enjoy profaning sacred places. Your father works here a lot, doesn't he?

MARIA   Yes, this is where he keeps all his research files. Father's a superior and noble spirit, a physician of the soul; he can say everything, write everything; he knows you at a glance, you can't hide anything from him…

NICOLAS   I love you when you're angry. You know how to defend yourself, Maria.

MARIA   What would you say if you found yourself in one of his books?

NICOLAS   Oh, I wouldn't care. No one can really know me… *(pause)* Maybe you, of course…

MARIA   *(putting her arms around NICOLAS)* Yes, maybe me…

NICOLAS   We're strong too; we have our love. And we laugh at everything else, don't we?

MARIA   You're tougher than I am, Nicolas. Your contempt isn't so bitter. I'm still intent on being understood, even loved. I know it's childish…

NICOLAS   I'm here, why look for anything else? *(He draws her to him.)*

MARIA   No, not again! Father needs the attic. Let's go into the woods.

NICOLAS   Why not here? I like this attic.

MARIA   Listen! He's coming up; he's here…

> THE FATHER *opens the door without knocking, greeting* MARIA *and* NICOLAS *with pleasant indifference.*

THE FATHER   Hello, children. I know you like to have fun but I need the attic.

MARIA   *(wishing to provoke her father)* Love isn't recreation.

THE FATHER   You know the way I am, both of you, so you know very well that I can't work when I feel people around me.

MARIA   Your writing! It's all you talk about, Father; it's all you think about!

THE FATHER   *(searching absorbedly in his papers, then, to his daughter)* You still there? Love at your age is very definitely a light-hearted affair…. Later on you'll understand!

MARIA   *(with a different tone in her voice)* What are you looking for that's so precious?

THE FATHER   *(roughly)* Nothing! Nothing…. Leave me alone!

MARIA   *(to NICOLAS)* Come on. You see, he's not interested in us.

> *On the attic stairway.*

NICOLAS   At least you can say he's not shocked by our love. Your father's so amoral, how *could* he be shocked? Maybe he's even happy to find out we're as sensual as he is…

MARIA   Yes, that's one way I'm like him. *(pause)* He's neither a man nor a father, he's a rock! Did you see how distant he was when he looked at us?

NICOLAS   Yes. And why not? We look at him and don't see him. *(hugging MARIA)* I think only of you, of the two of us…

MARIA   What disdain! What coldness!

NICOLAS   Maria…

MARIA   *(freeing herself from NICOLAS's embrace)* Never a single gesture, not a thought for me; even trying to provoke him doesn't work!

> MARIA *and* NICOLAS *run through the fields.*

NICOLAS   Maria, what do you want to make out of our life?

MARIA   You're still only thinking of part of me; you want to be seduced, too, to conquer…

NICOLAS   And you love me for it…. You agree with your whole being…

MARIA   Yes, it's true. So nobody in the world can learn to love justly? Understand Nicolas, it seems that with love you also get hatred; we're too full of poison to know how to love…

NICOLAS   You learn, you invent. That's love. Like hunger or thirst—what more do you want: I devour you, you devour me, purely and simply. You're complicating things again! I understand you even better than your father because you belong to me.

MARIA   You don't belong to me and I don't belong to you.

>   *In the fields.*

You're right, Nicolas. I'm letting myself be devoured…

NICOLAS   I wonder why that thought bothers you so much?

MARIA   You're already suffocating me and my life is just beginning…

>   *She frees herself and stands up.*

NICOLAS   Where are you going?

MARIA   Let's separate, Nicolas; let's separate for a while.

NICOLAS   But why?

MARIA   There's nothing I can give you, nothing you can give me…

NICOLAS   *(as she is going away)* Maria! Maria, come back. I want to speak to you…

>   *She runs towards the house. Return to the present. In the attic.*

MARIA   A friend—that's what I wanted to be for him. Nicolas was already too much in revolt… I, too, perhaps… I discovered we were more eager to come together to destroy than to love, so I left him.

SIMON   *(trying to take MARIA's mind off the subject)* Do you think these stuffed birds come from around here? Look, there's even an owl on top of the closet.

>   *Flashback. We see THE FATHER from behind, a pile of manuscripts in front to him.*

Yes, Father, did you call me?

THE FATHER   Can you help me put all these manuscripts in order? Can you carry these down?

SIMON   Are you working for a publishing house now?

THE FATHER   No, no—I promised to help out a colleague. I'm to judge these manuscripts. What a waste of time!

SIMON   Those…

THE FATHER   Those are the ones I've refused.

SIMON   Have you read them all to the end?

THE FATHER   No. A few pages of each is enough.

SIMON   You're not afraid of making a mistake, Father?

THE FATHER   You're full of scruples all of a sudden! What mistake? It's simple. I either feel the quality of a piece of writing or I feel nothing.

SIMON   But you could read too fast, not be attentive enough, or just not be in the mood to read manuscripts all day. I don't know; I'd be afraid…

THE FATHER   I think these young people write too much…

SIMON   You do?

THE FATHER   I said it to François and it made him very unhappy. He writes too much, too—this need to write, to confess, but without any inspiration whatsoever: it's madness. Learn to live before you write.

SIMON   You're not afraid of killing someone's hope when you turn down a manuscript?

THE FATHER   Simon, please. Mediocrity doesn't deserve hopeful illusions!

> *The remembrance ends with SIMON holding somewhat triumphantly the refused manuscript and looks at his father, who is bent over others, absorbed in the job of correcting them.*
>
> *Return to the present. In the attic.*

MARIA   What are you thinking about?

SIMON   Oh, nothing. I was just thinking how easy it is to torture someone, and easier still to destroy him. *(pause)* Let's not come back here…

MARIA   *(as SIMON heads for the stairway)* Where are you going?

SIMON   François must be awake by now. I want to talk to him for a second.

MARIA   *(holding her brother's arm at the head of the stairs)* Don't torment him. You know he doesn't like the daytime.

SIMON   François thinks I'm unscrupulous. I wouldn't like to leave him with that impression…. Didn't you say that I've killed François?

MARIA   We've killed François together.

SIMON   As an act of revenge. We both know his only fault is loving too much.

MARIA   A fault which, in this instance, I can't pardon…. We've punished him because we weren't strong enough to punish Father. François is miserable—as you say, his only fault is love…. It'll get you killed by those who don't love!

> *SIMON and MARIA enter to discover FRANÇOIS with a glass of scotch in his hand.*

SIMON   It's awful drinking the way you do!

FRANÇOIS   Leave me be!

MARIA   François, look how beautiful it is outside. Why don't the three of us walk to the village? *(She opens the curtains.)*

FRANÇOIS   In a moment or two. I haven't finished packing.

MARIA   What? You're leaving already? Why?

SIMON   *(going to sit next to his brother on the sofa)* Yes, why? It's absurd. We don't want to chase you out of the house.

FRANÇOIS   I never liked what I saw in your eyes, Simon.

MARIA   And in mine?

FRANÇOIS   I prefer you…

MARIA   But if you're suffering right now, it's also because of me…. Don't always blame Simon just because you don't like him.

FRANÇOIS   Evil's silent connivance—Simon. You? Swells of passion…

SIMON   Where will you go?

FRANÇOIS   To Egypt, where Father went for a few months before he died.

SIMON   You're drunk again, François.

MARIA   So, it's not possible to live in harmony with us? You want to be alone in the world?

FRANÇOIS   Yes—my God, yes!

SIMON   I have a little money, if you need some…

FRANÇOIS   I don't want anything from either of you.

MARIA   It's crazy wanting to leave now. Wait till tomorrow; you ought to think about it a bit.

> *FRANÇOIS breaks away from his sister and goes up to the attic.*
>
> *Alone together, SIMON and MARIA look at one another, somewhat upset by the turn things have taken. Though still affectionate towards each other, now there is a certain stiffness between them.*

Doesn't his leaving remind you of anything? How much we enjoy leaving each other! How much we enjoy flying away! Today we're watching François leave us; yesterday it was Nicolas leaving me.

> *Flashback. Out of doors.*

We're too much alike, Nicolas. I'm beginning to get attached to you. Like my mother I'll be forced into sacrificing myself, and I don't like sacrifices. I saw a kind of free life between us, forever; but you know it can't last.

NICOLAS   Why not? Life's only possible with you; everything else is false.

MARIA   I feel too many things; my whole life is oriented towards you, and I need calm, indifference; even—I'll admit it—coldness.

> *Return to present. FRANÇOIS comes down from the attic carrying books.*

FRANÇOIS   No, I can't wait any more. I'm leaving right now. *(pause)* I had some things to get in the attic.

> *SIMON and MARIA no longer act in an arrogant manner. Despite their words they seem to want FRANÇOIS to stay with them.*

MARIA   *(firmly)* Father didn't leave anything in the attic. Nothing whatsoever. You've got everything he wrote before his death—you and nobody else!

SIMON   But there are some stuffed animals up there if you're interested…

FRANÇOIS   I was talking about Father's writings, not stuffed animals, Simon. *(to himself)* Poor Father! He'd be so ashamed now of having brought us into the world!

MARIA   You've got to be drunk to be saying such things!

SIMON   But he is, he can hardly stand up!

FRANÇOIS   Poor Jean! Poor Jean, too! I saw his son last night; he said such atrocious things, and said them so naturally—natural for him, no doubt…

MARIA   You saw Nicolas last night?

FRANÇOIS   For a few minutes. He's come to sell his father's hide!

SIMON   *(quickly showing jealousy)* Don't listen to him, Maria. He'll say anything; he's a drunkard, he has visions…

MARIA   Tell me about him, François.

FRANÇOIS   There's nothing to tell.

MARIA   He hasn't always been what he is now either. We all change.

> *MARIA looks at SIMON and falls silent. For a long while no one speaks. FRANÇOIS walks towards the door carrying his suitcase.*

SIMON   Where are you going?

FRANÇOIS   Far away. Very far away…

MARIA   *(almost screaming)* You have no right to despise us!

> *In front of the house.*

SIMON   *(following FRANÇOIS for a short distance)* No foolishness now, understand? Don't go back to the ocean like you did that time before…

FRANÇOIS   Relax, Simon, I won't ask you to carry that weight. Goodbye…. Though I can see you're not trembling for me but yourself.

> *There is an ambiguous expression on SIMON's face during this rupture scene. One becomes aware that he too regrets losing his brother. His fixed features show loneliness and that he is defenceless against it.*
>
> *Near JEAN's house FRANÇOIS stops momentarily and wipes his forehead with a handkerchief. No sound is heard from the house. NICOLAS appears, coming from the dunes. Clearly distraught, he nonetheless smiles defiantly at FRANÇOIS.*

NICOLAS   Don't be afraid. It's just me.

FRANÇOIS   If he's stopped playing it means it's bad…

NICOLAS   Yes, very bad…

FRANÇOIS   Then why aren't you with him?

NICOLAS   My mother's there, praying for him. I don't like death, I told you that. I saw him through the window. For once I saw him prostrate, fallen, defeated, my mother beside him.

FRANÇOIS   *(tears in his eyes)* A few hours ago you told me you'd be willing to see him and speak with him in his suffering.

NICOLAS   I don't know. It's the thought of him suffering that upsets me. He's so stoical, perfect; as mild face to face with death as he was with life. I'm not eager to sit for hours and watch it.

FRANÇOIS   Why are you ashamed of your feelings?

NICOLAS   That's the way it is…

FRANÇOIS   But Jean's your father!

NICOLAS   Is that any reason to watch him suffer? I'd howl to keep my life. My cries of rage would reach the bottom of the ocean. But he's patient; he's got uncanny patience, understand?

FRANÇOIS   Come with me and tell him goodbye…

NICOLAS   No. Death's going to free him, and free me from him. From his kindness, which is of no use to me. I said goodbye to him a long time ago, you know… *(pause)* Why don't you run to his side; he loved you; he loves you…

FRANÇOIS   That's your place, not mine.

NICOLAS   By mistake men and women wind up in the same family, and come to know each other, love each other, tear each other apart and kill each other, once they're able to…

FRANÇOIS   *(walking off)* Goodbye…

> *FRANÇOIS walks down the hill to the river. Arms clasping his knees, he sits crouched close to the water.*
>
> *The end.*

A Clash of Symbols
(La Nef des sorcières)

by Marthe Blackburn
Marie-Claire Blais
Nicole Brossard
Odette Gagnon
Luce Guilbeault
Pol Pelletier
France Théoret

translated by Linda Gaboriau

Introduction to
A Clash of Symbols (La Nef des sorcières [1]*)*

by Marthe Blackburn, Marie-Claire Blais, Nicole Brossard, Odette Gagnon, Luce Guilbeault, Pol Pelletier, and France Théoret

Introduced by Louise H. Forsyth

Taken together, the monologues of *La Nef des sorcières* make a radical feminist dramatic statement proclaiming an immediate end to women's compliance with patriarchal practices, authority, and traditions. The primary dynamics of the play arise from the dramatic conflict constructed between the performers on stage and the audience, whose active role is to serve as a microcosm of sexist and homophobic society: "No spectator is safe: the drama plays itself out between the house and six women […] From the stage itself they disrupt the scandalous spectacle of the sexist status quo that reigns in the house, this being nothing more than one possible representation of society's grand listening public." [2] The actors were all on stage throughout the performance, each isolated inside her own place and lit only for her monologue. The choice of monologues, this *mise en scène* of collective isolation, and Ferron's starkly simple design making extensive use of mirrors, simultaneously highlighted the isolation of each woman, their shared condition of oppression, and their common determination to make radical changes.

The *leitmotif* of "Je parle" ("I speak" or "I'm speaking") which recurs through all the monologues and is the last line of the play underscores the importance of women's words being heard on the public stage: women speaking or writing their own words so as to perceive the reality of their own experiences. As long as they remain silent, even they themselves remain unsure about the legitimacy and meaning of their own perceptions. They are without the necessary tools to share their perceptions with others and to awaken their imagination for purposes of creatively concocting alternative ways of seeing and being.

In most of the monologues the character makes a strong gesture casting off some item symbolizing the conventional feminine role she has played up to that moment and the oppression it signified. This dramatic gesture is signalled from the start in the opening scene of Luce Guilbeault's *Mad Actress*. The actor arrives on stage wigged, costumed and well-rehearsed to play the role of the young and lovely Agnès in Molière's *École des femmes*. In the canonical play she is the prisoner of her aging guardian who, determined to marry her shortly, has been protecting her virginity zealously from all comers. Almost immediately, however, the Mad Actress has a complete memory lapse, with the result that she has no words, no role, no play to act in: "Help, who am I?". The fictitious actress, at a complete loss for words, is struck by the ways in which she has been brainwashed and pre-programmed: "I believe what I say because I say it by heart. Bang, bang, bang. The words were hammered into my head with a big penis hammer." [3] She now realizes she knows nothing by heart. She is compelled to begin the exploration of her own face, knowledge, feelings and body. She rips off her wig and costume and shows for herself and the audience a body that urinates, ages, and is far from conforming to the beauty myth.

In the monologues that follow, the actors step similarly and ostentatiously out of the roles they have been programmed to play. Marthe Blackburn's menopausal woman, until now the epitome of silent discretion, discovers that she can speak for herself. She expresses her revolt against the 55 years that have kept all her memories bottled up inside her. While getting used to the sound of her own voice, she and the audience hear the demeaning voices of patriarchal authority: the medical doctor, psychiatrist, church and family all of whom taught her shame of her body, her fertile blood, and her desires. She emits a long and loud yell of protest, then demands a return to physical and psychic wholeness: "Where is my skin so I can feel good in it again!/I feel like a tree stripped of its bark,/nothing but guts and marrow./Where is my skin, so I can restore its dignity/and it can cling to my veins!".[4] She announces that the time has come for her and for all women to come out of the shadows.

France Théoret's Lucie, the garment worker, has spent a lifetime in the service of others, particularly her numerous siblings and her bosses. Her oppression as a woman, a francophone and member of the working class is extreme; yet she is not quite ready to speak out and declare open revolt. Family obligations have placed love and marriage out of the question; she is proud of her skills but humiliated, tired, alone, and suffering employment-related injuries. The moment has come for her to do something for herself. She has bought herself a diamond ring, with the legitimate motivation that she is as entitled to her dreams as anyone else. However, in the end she discovers that her mirror is broken and decides to leave the new ring in a drawer.

The first gesture of revolt of the young woman in Odette Gagnon's "The Date" is to decide she will not go out on a date this Saturday night. This woman, who has dedicated herself entirely so far in her life to getting ready to please others in accordance with the dictates of the beauty myth, will spend the evening alone examining fears and discovering for the first time what actually gives her pleasure. Later in the scene she throws open her housecoat to reveal to herself and the audience her naked, imperfect woman's body. She realizes that she learned as a little girl to play the seduction game in order to have money, that this made every other girl her rival in attracting boys' attention, and that she has spent all her life getting ready for men. She has moved from seemingly innocent flirting to prostitution without ever knowing the ecstasy of sexual fulfillment. She reflects upon the games of seduction she learned to play and sees them as not dissimilar to the games most women play, whether shopping, walking in the street, working, or building relationships.

Marie-Claire Blais's Marcelle, a lesbian waiting in loneliness for her current lover, talks about her situation in society, on the series of lovers she has had, and on her seeming inability to love or accept intimacy despite her extreme longing to do so. She remains alone and waiting in the end. Pol Pelletier, who played this monologue and the following, "Marcelle II," was dissatisfied with the passive aggression and resignation of "Marcelle I." In a powerful gesture of defiance and revolt, she began the stage action of "Marcelle II" by ripping off her wig to reveal a shaved head. Like the

Mad Actress, her first words announce a radical break with the roles and words women have been given. Hers is an angry revolt of hatred against patriarchal traditions and the complicity of patriarchal mothers in perpetuating these traditions, preparing their daughters to submit to them:

> I loathe you all. […] Hate, yes, hate for women./I see my mother and I want to vomit./You and your long line of humble servants, […] You have robbed me of my own sex. And you sold it. To men. […] I have lived and I still live in a world/where women are nothing. Decorative dishcloths,/comprehensive, sensitive sponges, softhearted whimperers./Women are shit./Submissive, quiet, gentle, nice,/insignificant, boring shit […] Hate for my own sex and hate for myself.[5]

This intense anger is immediately transformed into intense erotic emotion of women loving women: "No one knows it, but every time a woman sleeps with another woman it's a wonderful slap in the face of our rotten world. A magnificent act of subversion."[6] In proclaiming her right to love whom she pleases and to determine her own sexual pleasure, she offers a powerful rebuttal to the dynamics of compulsory heterosexuality, as Adrienne Rich saw so clearly.

In the final monologue, the lights go up on Nicole Brossard's Writer who is already prepared to refuse dominant discourse and to invent a new, autonomous role for herself. Her numerous repetitions of "I speak" highlight the inescapable need for words, discourse, and verbal and body language in her search for self-discovery and solidarity with other women: "As I speak, I have a political pact among women in mind./Touch me. Personal is political./The set starts to shake before my eyes and it is word-shaking./Which words? I am improvising on new ground. I reclaim my right, my due. Words come to the surface."[7] She moves from spoken words to written words shared, instruments for political change: "I write and I don't want to do it alone anymore. I want us. I want to make history shake and shudder and growl./Personal is political."[8] The Writer's final words affirming the power of listening and speaking out reinforce the erotic and psychic energy that has been sustained throughout the performance of the seven monologues of *A Clash of Symbols*.

From an attendance point of view *La Nef* was highly successful. From the point of view of the critics, it proved to be controversial—for its subject, language, and innovative theatricality. Most of the attacks that came from institutional sources were savage in their condescending scorn, ridicule, and dismissal of the play without even having seen it. Interestingly enough, there was also severe criticism that came from feminists who found that the play was too moderate. With the exception of those who were involved in the production, no one spoke of the theatricality and innovative performativity of the show.

Notes

[1] Marthe Blackburn, Marie-Claire Blais, Nicole Brossard, Odette Gagnon, Luce Guilbeault, Pol Pelletier, France Théoret. *La Nef des sorcières*. Montréal: Éditions Quinze, 1976 (with "Préface" by Nicole Brossard and France Théoret: 7–13). *A Clash of Symbols*. Tr. Linda Gaboriau. Toronto: The Coach House Press, 1979. 2nd Ed. Blackburn et al. *La Nef des sorcières*. Montréal: Éditions de L'Hexagone, 1992 (with "Introduction" by Lori Saint-Martin and "Préface" by Brossard and Théoret). *La Nef des sorcières* was first performed during the week of International Women's Day on March 5, 1976 at Le Théâtre du Nouveau-Monde. It was the first in an annual series of five original feminist plays produced at the TNM during the tenure of Jean-Louis Roux as Artistic Director.

[2] "Point de spectateur à l'abri: le drame se joue entre la salle et six femmes [...] C'est sur la scène même que l'on chahute le spectacle scandaleux du statu quo sexiste qui règne dans la salle, celle-ci n'étant qu'une représentation choisie du grand auditoire social." Translation by LHF: "Préface." *La Nef des sorcières*: 7.

[3] "Au secours, je ne suis plus rien [...] Je crois ce que je dis parce que je le dis par coeur./Bam, bam, bam dans la tête, les mots/Avec le grand marteau pénis." *La Nef*: 17.

[4] "Où est-ce qu'elle est ma peau pour que je sois bien dedans!/J'ai l'impression de n'être plus qu'une écorchée/en tripes et en moëlle./Où est-ce qu'elle est ma peau pour que je lui redonne/sa mesure de dignité/et qu'elle colle à mes veines!" *La Nef*: 27.

[5] "La haine, oui la haine./Je vous déteste tous [...] la haine des femmes./Je vois ma mère et j'ai envie de vomir./Toi et toute ta lignée de servantes aplaties [...] Vous m'avez volé mon propre sexe. Et vous l'avez vendu. Aux hommes./J'ai vécu, je vis encore dans un monde/où les femmes sont rien. Des lavettes décoratives, des éponges compréhensives et douloureuses, des pleureuses au coeur sensible./ Les femmes, c'est d'la merde./D'la merde soumise, tranquille, docile, gentille,/ insignifiante et emmerdante [...] La haine de mon propre sexe, donc la haine de moi-même." *La Nef*: 67–68.

[6] "Personne le sait, mais chaque fois qu'une femme couche avec une autre femme, c'est une merveilleuse gifle qu'on lance à la tête de notre monde pourri. Un magnifique acte de subversion." *La Nef*: 70.

[7] "Je parle dans la perspective d'un pacte politique avec d'autres femmes. Touchez-moi. La vie privée est politique./Le décor me saute devant les yeux et je saute des mots./Lesquels? J'improvise sur un terrain nouveau. Je reprends mon droit, mes dûs. Les mots font surface." *La Nef*: 74.

[8] "J'écris et je ne veux plus faire cela toute seule. Je nous veux. Faire craquer, grincer, grincher l'histoire./La vie privée est politique." *La Nef*: 75.

Bibliographical Suggestions

On *La Nef des sorcières*

Andrès, Bernard. "Évangéline et la nef." *Voix et images*. II.1 (sept. 1976): 127–29.

Burgoyne, Lynda. "Théâtre et homosexualité féminine: un continent invisible." *Cahiers de théâtre. Jeu*. (1990.4): 114–18.

Camerlain, Lorraine. "*La Nef des sorcières*," *Cahiers de théâtre. Jeu*. 16 (1980.3): 216–17.

Claing, Robert. "*La Nef des sorcières*," *Livres et auteurs québécois 1977*. Québec: Presses de l'Université Laval, 1978: 203.

d'Auteuil, Georges-Henri. "Visages de femmes." *Relations*. XXXVI.414 (avril 1976): 124–25.

Hajdukowski-Ahmed, Maroussia. "La Sorcière dans le texte (québécois) au féminin." *The French Review* (December 1984): 260–68.

Forsyth, Louise H. "A Ship of Fools in the Feminine: Six Characters in Search of Self." *Theatre and Autobiography. Writing and Performing Lives in Theory and Practice*. Ed. Sherrill Grace & Jerry Wasserman. Vancouver: Talonbooks, 2006: 167–82.

Girard, Gilles. "*La Nef des sorcières*," *Dictionnaire des oeuvres littéraires du Québec*. Tome VI, 1976–1980. Montréal: Fides, 1994: 566–68.

Moss, Jane. "Women's Theater in Québec: Choruses, Monologues and Dialogues." *Québec Studies* (Spring 1983): 276–85.

Roy, Hélène. *Une Nef … et ses sorcières*. Montréal: Vidéo Femmes, 1977.

Sabbath, Lawrence. "At Théâtre du Nouveau Monde. Female Playwrights Hit Hard." *The Montreal Star* (March 11, 1976): C-14.

Saint-Martin, Lori. "Écriture et combat féministe: figures de la sorcière dans l'écriture des femmes au Québec." *Quebec Studies* (Spring/Summer 1991): 67–82.

Vallières, Pierre. "*La Nef des sorcières* met un point final à l'ère braillarde des belles-soeurs." *Le Jour* (vendredi 12 mars 1976): 22.

Villemaire, Yolande. "Autour de *La Nef des sorcières*." *Cahiers de théâtre. Jeu*. 2 (printemps 1976): 22–23.

About The Collective [1]

Luce Guilbeault—author, director, and actor in *La Nef des sorcières*—had created early in 1974 with Paule Baillargeon and Suzanne Garceau of the theatre company Le Grand Cirque Ordinaire the feminist show *Un Prince, mon jour viendra*. In her continued concern regarding distorted images of women in theatre and the limited range of roles available to them, she invited writer Nicole Brossard, with whom she was making the documentary film "Some American Feminists," to collaborate in a collective feminist performance piece. The same year 1975 Guilbeault and Brossard invited the other writers to collaborate with them in the project. Although most of these writers belonged to a new generation of young artists, they were already experienced novelists, poets, playwrights, filmmakers, founders of literary magazines and an experimental theatre company. With Guilbeault and Brossard as facilitators and Guilbeault as director, the writers worked together for about a year, frequently workshopping their drafts with the actors they invited to work with them: Françoise Berd [2] who performed the menopausal woman, Michèle Craig who performed the garment worker, Louisette Dussault [3] who performed the girl no longer waiting for her date, and Michèle Magny [4] who performed the Writer. Guilbeault and Pelletier performed their own texts of the Mad Actress and Marcelle I and II. They invited artist Marcelle Ferron [5] to serve as designer. The original music written for the performance by Jean Sauvageau was not published with the text. These artists discussed, experimented, worked, and rehearsed together for a year preparing the production of *La Nef des sorcières*. This intense collective creative process was captured by Hélène Roy in her hour-long documentary video "Une Nef … et ses sorcières." In addition to footage from the performance, Roy included roundtable discussions and interviews with Guilbeault and Brossard. The seven monologues the artists produced together gave voice and stage presence to six recognizable women whose social situation in patriarchal and misogynist society makes them typical of certain groups, while also coming alive as individuals.

Roy's documentary shows improvised stage action that was not indicated in textual stage directions. It also provides clear and moving evidence of the consciousness-raising impact of the production and its long workshop process on the writers and the actors, who found, with astonishment and trepidation, that they discovered much about themselves they had not previously recognized or acknowledged. It was a time of consciousness-raising in the feminist movement. Although dramatized and fictionalized, the autobiographical dimension of most of the monologues is striking in that they create the impression the actors are performing their own gut-wrenching stories.

Notes

¹ Marthe Blackburn (1916–1991) was a well-established filmmaker, active in the National Film Board's Studio D. Marie-Claire Blais (born 1939) had already published collections of poetry and several novels. She is the author of the television drama in this volume, *L'Océan*. Nicole Brossard (born 1943) had already published several collections of poetry and novels. She and France Théoret were members of the founding editorial boards of the influential literary magazine *La Barre du jour*, founded in 1965, and the powerful feminist newspaper *Les Têtes de pioche*, published between 1976 and 1979. Odette Gagnon played in Michel Tremblay's *Les Belles-Soeurs* when it was first produced in 1968, and has been an actor and playwright since that time. Luce Guilbeault (1935–1991) was an actor, director and producer for stage, television and film, with an early and sustained commitment to women's issues. She played Violette Leduc in Marchessault's *La Terre est trop courte, Violette Leduc*. Pol Pelletier was a founding member of the Théâtre Expérimental de Montréal in 1975 and of the Théâtre Expérimental des Femmes in 1979. In the second original feminist show at the Théâtre du Nouveau Monde, *Célébrations* (1977), she created the brilliant role in *Les Vaches de nuit* by Jovette Marchessault. France Théoret had already published several poetry collections, including the much-admired *Bloody Mary*.

² Françoise Berd (1923–2001) was an actor for stage and cinema. She was founder and artistic director of L'Égregore (1959–1966), one of the first avant-garde theatre companies in Montréal. For many years she played a determining role at L'Office National du Film/National Film Board.

³ Louisette Dussault, actor and playwright for stage, radio, television and film, began her career in the 1960s, when she created roles by Michel Tremblay, Jean-Claude Germain, Réjean Ducharme and many others. She played the Statue in *Les Fées ont soif* and is the author of *Moman*. See "About Louisette Dussault" in Introduction to *Mommy* in this volume.

⁴ Michèle Magny created the role of Marie when *Les Fées ont soif* was first produced at the TNM.

⁵ Marcelle Ferron (1924–2001) was one of the dominant figures in contemporary art in Quebec and across Canada. Her career stretched over more than fifty years and, from the beginning, was dedicated to the exploration of new avenues in art. Very early she joined the Automatistes, and in 1948 she signed the *Refus global* manifesto. She participated in all the Automatiste group exhibitions, including the critically acclaimed retrospective, "Borduas et les Automatistes" at the Grand Palais in Paris in 1971. Her work was exhibited in numerous collective exhibitions, both in Europe and the U.S., and has been the subject of more than thirty special shows throughout Québec and Canada, as well as in Paris, Brussels and Munich. In 1970, the Musée d'art contemporain de Montréal staged a retrospective of her work, a show that was repeated in 1972 in Paris at the Canadian Cultural Centre. Examples of her work in modern stained glass can be admired in the Champ-de-

Mars and Vendôme métro stations and the International Aviation Building in Montreal. See "Bibliographical Suggestions on *Théâtre-Femmes*, 1966–1986" in this volume: Smart, Patricia. *Les Femmes du Refus global.*

La nef des sorcières was first produced at Théâtre du Nouveau-Monde, Montréal, in March 1976, with the following company:

A MAD ACTRESS	Luce Guilbeault
THE CHANGE OF LIFE	Françoise Berd
THE SAMPLE	Michèle Craig
THE DATE	Louisette Dussault
MARCELLE	Pol Pelletier
THE WRITER	Michèle Magny

Directed by Luce Guilbeault
Set Design by Marcelle Ferron
Costumes by Marielle Fleury
Original music by Jean Sauvageau

• • •

The English translation, *A Clash of Symbols*, was first published in a tapuscript edition by Coach House Press, Toronto, in 1979.

Scenes and Authors

A MAD ACTRESS	by Luce Guilbeault
THE CHANGE OF LIFE	by Marthe Blackburn
THE SAMPLE	by France Théoret
THE DATE	by Odette Gagnon
THE MAD ACTRESS PART II	by Luce Guilbeault
MARCELLE	by Marie-Claire Blais
MARCELLE II	by Pol Pelletier
THE WRITER	by Nicole Brossard

A CLASH OF SYMBOLS

A Mad Actress

By Luce Guilbeault

Part I

Houselights are still lit. The stage is in darkness.

STAGE MANAGER   *(offstage)* Miss Agnes, three minutes please.
Mr. Arnolphe, three minutes please.

Backstage noises: footsteps, doors, orchestra tuning up.

(offstage) Miss Agnes, Mr. Arnolphe, two minutes.
Miss Agnes, Mr. Arnolphe, one minute.
Three, two, one......

The word "Exit" lights up in red on the stage still in darkness. Houselights go down.

ARNOLPHE   *(offstage)* For the Emperor Augustus a certain Greek did devise,
advice as particular as it was wise:
When a situation our ire does ignite,
We must, before all, our alphabet recite,
lest in our bad temper we beget,
actions we shall surely regret.
I have followed this advice in this matter with Agnes and I have brought her here on the pretext of a simple stroll, while hoping all the time to calm my doubts of the worst kind, by urging her to speak her heart and mind.
Come, Agnes, enter.

A spot follows AGNES as she walks downstage. She acts as if ARNOLPHE were at her side. She is dressed in a period costume. She is wearing white, a wig, and carries a parasol.

(offstage)   Pleasant walk?

AGNES   Quite pleasant.

ARNOLPHE   *(offstage)* Beautiful day!

AGNES   Quite beautiful.

ARNOLPHE   *(offstage)* How are you?

AGNES freezes.

AGNES   I'm sorry, I don't know what to say. I've forgotten my lines. It's never happened to me before. *(She picks up her skirt.)* "When I left home, I was head over heels in love. I couldn't see straight." That's Pierrette Guérin. That's not the line. "Ladder far below, ladder that the elves climb".… No, Gauvreau, I won't do it, I won't do the striptease, I won't. "Father Ubu, you're a terrible man, frosh… shits." Take it again. This isn't the right costume.… Angéline, Marie-Lou, Carmen and my dear Belles-Soeurs, where are you? "Goddamn, Angeline, whadda ya doin' here. It's nice of ya to come.… Hey, don't go so fast. Where are ya goin' in such a hurry? Curley. I'm lookin' for Curley. You're lookin' for Curley. You're all lookin' for big handsome Curley."

Me too. I looked for him once when I was a curly-haired blonde with no eyebrows. With a mental age of 10 at thirty-six… something terrible happened to me, too. Gasp.

> *Her hands go to her throat.*

Don't laugh, don't laugh, don't laugh. It's no joke ending up strangled in back of the barn.
They're all gone. Disappeared.
Every one of the lovelies. Drowned. All drowned in beautiful Lake Ouareau.
I feel like throwing up.
Help, who am I?
Agnes, how are you?

> *The actress goes towards her dressing room, but doesn't go in. She returns downstage.*

My name is Désirée. Desire.
I am an actress.
I rehearsed all day.
I knew my part by heart. I could play it in my sleep.
By heart, sweetheart.
I'm heartsick.
I believe what I say because I say it by heart.
Bang, bang, bang. The words were hammered into my head with a big penis hammer. Penis?
No, that's not the line.
Agnes, how are you?
I'll take two steps…
then I'll step back, subtle, isn't it?
Ah, this trade is as old as the world.
What a marvelous actress!
She's forgotten her lines, but she's marvelous.
Woman to the tip of her toes.
Be beautiful and be silent,
woman.

The actress squats in a pissing position.

Agnes, how are you?

She sits on the toilet, at ease.

Curley, Curley, I remember you.
I was looking for you.
I wanted you with my dazzling smile.
Come on,
it's your turn to look for me.
Do you know the shape and colour of my sex with all its petals?
I do. I take a mirror,
I put it between my legs,
I look at my sex,
it's our only way of seeing ourselves there, you know.
My sex changes just like my face.
It's my other face.
Come on, Curley,
let's get to know each other.
And you. Curley's wife.
You,
Me,
You,
Come out of your shell,
Let your hair, the colour of dreams, go dark at the roots.
Your mouth turns white.
Stop holding your body back,
Stop forcing it to seduce.
Actress, starlet.
Agnes, how are you?
My mind's a blank.
I look at you.
You look at my face.
You see a hundred faces, one on top of the other.
My face?
No.
My face is blank for you to fill.
You see, I want you to swoon over my soft brain.
You look at my body.
My body?

She stands up wearily.

No, it's a body in disguise. Corseted, curved, stretched or bent for the part.
My body carries on, it changes and it ages,
thank you just the same.

I like the body I show myself in the mirror in my room,
all alone.
Agnes, how are you?

> *She glances towards her dressing room*

I believe what I say because I say it
by heart.
And I no longer know anything by heart. Agnes…
how are you?
There you go—
The actress died of a bad memory, at last.
She once knew everything by heart.
She forgot her lines.
She showed herself the way she was.
Horrors, horrors.
Agnes, how are you? My little dog died.
My dog, my little dog, I had him killed.
I went to the SPCA.
I went there with my dog. He was looking at me, wagging his tail, all happy.
I signed a form for a man in white.
Then I ran down the hall and a secretary, some girl, some woman, took me in
her arms. "It's alright, you can tell us, it does you good to cry."
I cried. I talked. She listened. Six years. I had this dog for six years. He was close
to me… it's not my fault. I just couldn't take care of him anymore. I couldn't do
everything and still take care of my dog.
It's not my fault.
And ten minutes later in her car, she was still crying. It was raining, the actress
was crying. Real tears, again.

> *The actress enters her dressing room and sits down.*

Agnes, how are you?

> *She's cold, takes an old fur from the back of her chair and puts it around
> her shoulders. Blackout.*

The Change of Life
by Marthe Blackburn

Just imagine.
I turned twenty. Yesterday…
Tonight. I'm fifty-five.
It's my birthday. I have left the age of silence behind.
My age of silence was an age of observation.
I am carrying archives in my head.
My mouth is no longer dry.
I am speaking. I can speak.
I don't need to scream: all the screams that were trapped inside me,
all the rebellions, that's all over, there is peace
now that I have begun to speak.
I can speak.
I have more to say than you do, that's all: my story is longer.
But whether it's a woman of twenty who opens her mouth today,
or a woman my age who unleashes her tongue,
it comes to the same thing,
because both of us have just learned to speak.

> *Voice exercises: A A A A A A AAAAAAAA*

You see. I have to practice: I'm not used to it yet.
I am carrying archives in my head.
I am bursting with memory…
No, not personal memories… everyone has memories.
But my woman's body is heavy with memory.
Everything that in my life as a woman made my blood churn.
Wait. I just said the word BLOOD.
Strange, that's a word I hardly use anymore…
because for me the bleeding is over.
I no longer see my blood.
I no longer know its smell.
That's what menopause means.
No more bleeding every twenty-eight days.
That went on for forty years.
You never get used to the blood.
Perhaps it's not so much the blood.
But the anxiety that takes over every month
when you wait for it, hope for it or try to stop its flow.
Forty years in a woman's life.
Now, it's as if I were floating.
I feel less attached to the earth,

and yet more bound than ever to the life I am inspecting and dissecting.
But that's all.
Otherwise I haven't changed.
I am simply cured of the bleeding.
The secret flow of our unwanted blood.
Not the blood of poetry. No, blood that leaves stains.
Blood that boils in anger.
Men have always been repulsed by our blood,
women's blood.
Even the Church (since we are still in the Middle Ages),
even the Church treated us like lepers.
We were forbidden entry to the temple at each turn of the moon, as if our
blood would make the blood of Christ seem pale.
Men's blood has always been different.
Men's blood is sacred and glorious.
The blood of courage.
The blood of heroes.
But ours…!!
And yet it is with our blood that you were all made, sustained, and nourished.
My woman's blood.

I went to see my doctor.

(Doctor's voice:) "Fifty years old! Ah! It's a difficult time.
You must feel a kind of heaviness, don't you, in your lower abdomen.
You're going to have migraines and mood swings, but don't worry, it's just your
menopause.
And whatever you do, don't worry about the itching around the vulva,
it's very common in women your age, you know.
Amenorrhea, sometimes it lasts for four or five years,
sometimes longer, one never knows.
My poor lady, you have to put up with these troubles, it's nothing, it's just
menopause, it's not a sickness…
You have hot flushes, don't you?
Don't worry, my dear,
it's not unattractive, you know, a woman who blushes…
it can be charming even at your age… ha ha ha…"

Tonight I am fifty-five.
It's my birthday. I am speaking. I can speak. But suddenly I feel like screaming.
May I? Just this once…

> *She screams.*

It's not true. None of it is true.
It's not the first time that medical science has lied to me,
interpreted me,

strangled me,
belittled me, and finally put me to sleep.
It has to stop.
They don't know my body. They have always feared it.
Oh, yes. They have dissected it. Raped it, often.
They know how my insides are made.
They have spread them out on the table.
But then, a long time ago, and then time and time again,
they filled all those curves and hollows and cavities with sin and perversity,
with shame and misery,
and scientific explanations.
"It's a kind of amputation, you poor little thing,
that's why your sexuality is so mysterious…."
"You shall give birth in pain."
"When you are no longer fertile, you are superfluous, a fallow field where no
seed can be sown."

I am fifty-five years old tonight, once I was twenty.
I can speak at last.
I have a lot to say. I swear in the name of life,
in the name of all that is gentle,
that it is all lies,
and we have had enough of your false prophesies.
The time has come to destroy the myths.
THE CRITICAL AGE! Ha! What a farce, what a cliché!
That's what you said when I was an adolescent, the critical age.
That's what you said when I was a child…
I don't need a speculum to know that my body is more than a penis trap,
that my blood is more than putrid fluids.
I give birth in joy, can you imagine,
my womb is not a well of evil spells
and I have known for ages that love is not an act of supremacy and possession,
no offensive-defensive game…
In fact it is not a game at all.
You don't play at love.
We have worried so much about how to meet,
we have forgotten why we were meeting.
Oh Lord it has never been simple!
We have allowed ourselves to be duped for centuries.
Endless myths
raise the barrier of incomprehension
between us.
Both of us.

We are drawn to each other.
Will we ever know each other's face?

Perhaps we are made for each other… perhaps.
Up until now we have been made by each other.
Defined by each other. Invented by others.
And it's a failure.
They always told me that you were the hero.
Do you really feel like a hero?
And who says you still have to be one?
The hunter who goes off to… remember?
The seducer who woos, who places his honour, his love and his wealth at the
feet of his fair lady.
The dreamer of romance, the dreamer of dreams, the creator of shapes,
of sounds, colours, rhythm and words,
the master craftsman, the pure thinker,
…they told me that was you and only you.
I read it in books, I learned it as a child.
You created the universe.
I gave you children to fill your world.
I furnished the raw material, and you created with it.
With my flesh and blood, you made a world where we can no longer live.
None of us. Neither you nor I. Nor our children. Nor the birds, the fish, the
trees…. Perhaps we should come down off our pedestals…
Tonight, I'm fifty-five, it's my birthday.
I have left the age of silence behind. I can speak at last.
I have no more blood to spare.
No more placenta will form in my belly.
I will die of hemorrhaging, but it will be internal.
I no longer furnish the raw material needed to build the world.
You, you can sow your seed randomly,
not me, it's over, I am sterile.
I no longer produce. I no longer ovulate.
My entire reserve of love remains within me…
Intact. Immobile. Full.

The Change of Life

My life has come full circle.
I can claim my due.
All the years invested.
I am ready to give love now, as once I was ready to give birth.
I am ready to rethink love.
I made love. And making love led to making children.
And now I am ready to revise
all life's loving energy.

Visit to the Psychiatrist

"Your genital period is over.
You're losing your sexual appetite…
Perhaps it's already gone.
Come now, you can tell me… don't be shy on my couch…
You're much less emotional, aren't you?
Much less impulsive…
But that's a plus, it's very positive.
Or perhaps it's the opposite for you…?
I know: hysteria…
Is that your problem?
The epileptoid phase, perhaps?
Don't you go into trances…
You know, grimaces and contortions…
Hasn't that ever happened to you?
Delirious hallucination…"

No, no, relax.
I've come to see you simply
because I am a MONUMENT.
Yes, since the beginning of time, I have been treated like a monument.
I am the Fountain of Love, you know.
I am Fertility.
I am the Torch.
I am the Pieta.
I am the one who holds man on my knee.
I am the monument in memoriam.
I am the Muse.
I am Glory.
I am the Apotheosis.
Since the beginning of time, I have been placed on a pedestal.
Since the beginning of time, women have been bound to myths,
to symbols and images.
Today, you see, it's the image of youth.
I am Youth.
I am Release.
I am the one who flies through fields of wheat, hair flowing in the wind,
draped in toilet paper.
I am the goddess of cars,
the bust of brassieres,
the softness of sanitary napkins,
the warmth of a good cup of coffee…
I am the calendar.
The day-after-day of garage mechanics,
in high-class brothels, in the boiler rooms of ships,

in bus stations and bureau drawers.
I am pornography, perversity and filth.
I am tits, ass and cunt.
I am the belly button of the world.

Where is my skin so I can feel good in it again!
I feel like a tree stripped of its bark,
nothing but guts and marrow.
Where is my skin, so I can restore its dignity
and it can cling to my veins!
Tonight I am fifty-five years old, it's my birthday.
The most statuesque thing about me is my hair
as white as stone.
The most beautiful thing about my body is its extension: my daughters are
twenty years old today.
Perhaps they carry the light.
My complexion is no longer dewy.
My blood no longer flows and gushes.
I am a mature woman.
Words have ripened in my mouth.

The Voice of Men

"What good will it do you to speak, you women have always lied.
You lie like you breathe, I don't know anyone who has lied more than you…"
Yes, you do. Your mother did.
And your grandmother.
All the women in your family.
Yes, we lie like we breathe.
I have been lying to myself for fifty-five years.
I have been lying to you for centuries. Thousands of years.
My life has been a lie.
I floundered in lies. I grew up in lies. I learned fear in lies.
I died in lies. I began again in lies.
Don't talk to me about dialogue. I am not ready.
You'll make me lie again.
I have to break through layers and layers of lies.
Labyrinths.
But I am getting there.
I have taken my time.
I know what to say.
Because I always lied for YOU.
FOR YOU.
Because I had to please you;
you were superior—you possessed Strength…

and I thought that Strength…
But what is to be done with your strength today…
I lied because I had to reassure you:
You were the one carrying the world on your shoulders.
But what has the world become today…
I lied in order to hold you in my arms.
My story always begins the same way:
I am holding you in my arms…
and all I held was shadows that slipped away.
I have always lied for you—
whenever I said, "You have to be a man."
And you believed that was a rank you could reach
where you would be higher than God.
And I held you like this for centuries of sons,
you were my masterpieces.
The only creation I was allowed.
I was a magician:
I pulled children out of my bag
and I taught them to fly…
then you killed them.
You have ruined my creation.
You annihilate each other. Man to Man. Son to Son.

The Time Has Come

The forgotten woman, the retiring, silent and reflective woman. APPEARS.
She speaks. She is solid.
She is new.
She is bursting with centuries of stifled urges.
She confesses centuries of secret truths.
I am a HUman WOman.
I have just devoted 55 years to history
and I don't want it to be in vain.
Tonight I am celebrating my blood birthday. Tonight.
My daughters are twenty years old.
I still have time to spare.
I can claim my due. All the years invested.
And I am speaking.
The time has come.
We'll sit in the grass of THE WHOLE WIDE WORLD,
and we'll begin to sort out our lies, one by one,
women's lies, men's lies, mine, yours, mine, yours.
We'll take our time.
And then, we'll talk about the TWO OF US.

And other children will come and they'll be wearing their real faces—
yours, the one I have always suspected,
mine, the one I reveal to you at last.
The time has come.
Once there was a king.
—I've always liked this story. You'll understand why…
Once there was a powerful king who besieged a town.
It was a happy, peaceful town
and in the face of calamity
all the men felt lost. The end had come.
So the women spoke among themselves
and together they went to meet the enemy. "Spare us," they said,
"and allow us to leave the town, taking with us only what is most fragile and
precious to us…"
At first the king was amused by all the troubled women
and even more amused by their naïve proposal,
for he knew that the town was poor and without treasure.
And so permission was granted.
The next day,
the gates of the town opened to let the women pass:
EVERY woman was carrying on her back, a MAN.
The time has come.

THE SAMPLE

by France Theoret

My name is Lucie, but my bosses usually call me Lucy. I'm an operator at
Marinette Dress. There are 18 of us girls at the shop. All ages. We're on the job
from 8 in the morning till 4:30 in the afternoon. Today I was in a bigger hurry
than usual to finish. It doesn't take much to set me back and make the day seem
longer. I had had it with the comments about my new ring. Today was the first
day I wore my diamond ring. It's 5:30, it's over at last. I didn't even cut it short.
I put in an hour overtime, just like I have every night for the past two weeks.
I'm the sample girl. Right now we're doing samples of summer dresses. Because
it's December. Next summer everything's going to be blue. And there'll be some
stripes and flowers too. Don't think it pays any better. For samples, you don't get
paid by the piece, you get paid by the hour. But you have to work fast and figure
out the patterns fast. I figure things out fast. Sometimes I make up my own
patterns. I've been doing it for a long time and for all the seasons. I like doing it.
And that's a bonus, 'cause you have to make a living. When the other girls leave
every day at 4:30, they turn out most of the lights. I stay on alone or sometimes
with this Italian lady, Mrs. Spinozi. There we are, both at the end of our
row, with our little lights. The others have gone. All of them—the girls, the
forewoman, the designer, the cutters, the presser, the finishers and the boss.
It's the only time of the day when it's almost peaceful. Today I was glad to have
a little peace and quiet. So, when you're finished you get everything set up for
the next day. Before, less than ten years ago, they didn't hire models to try on
the samples. When I was at Dayval, they were all my responsibility, because
I was the one who tried them on. I was a perfect size 12. I'd put on the dress
and there was never anything to alter. Tall and slim with breasts and hips just
where they belong and a small waist. I could wear them all. I had a nice figure,
you know. Armand could put his two hands around my waist. Now there's
a model who comes in the morning… we never see her. We don't get to see
what the dresses look like on… but what difference does it make. Sometimes
I think there's no other job like mine. You don't need any diplomas or special
qualifications. You don't have to worry about how you look. You don't have to
dress fancy or fuss with your hair. As long as you're in good health. You can be
sixteen or sixty. It doesn't matter. I can go to work the way I am. Sometimes
I say I'm going in my "old rags." So I get up in the morning a little before six
because I live in Sainte Dorothée. I take my shower and rub myself all over, but
especially around the knees. I get dressed, have some breakfast and I leave. Tired
or not, I walk to the train and an hour later I'm at Central Station. And then,
the time it takes me to walk up Beaver Hall to Phillips Square and I'm at work.
A few hellos here and there. At eight o'clock the bell rings, we start off. The
pieces start sliding under the needles one after the other, fast. I'm on the job;
we're all on the job. You have to go as fast as you can. One, two, three… *(She*

imitates the sound.) The bell rings. Ten o'clock, ten minutes, a quick cigarette, the bell rings again and we keep going till noon. The bell rings again. It's lunchtime. Along with the others, I take out my lunch; sometimes it's a little leftover salad with half a sandwich, and a plain cookie. Or something like that. In the summertime, maybe some radishes and tomatoes. In the winter, an egg and some cheese. You have to eat right, but it depends on the season. I hardly ever have anything hot…. Lots of times I do the pricing. Then I don't get a whole hour to eat. It takes a long time because the price committee has to negotiate the prices with the boss. We take a dress and we count so much for putting in the zipper, so much for putting together the pieces and so much for the trim. Then we say it's worth a dollar. The boss says eighty cents. Sometimes we make a deal for ninety cents. Other times we say the price isn't fair. Then we have to send for the union agent. It's not always easy. Then the bell rings and you don't even have time to go to the toilet. Then there's the whole afternoon with only one five-minute break. The machines start up again. When we finish one lot, we ask for another. Sometimes we've just started a new lot when the forewoman brings in the repairs. That slows us down. Then the boss steps in. The other day, a new girl, a young Greek girl, asked for six inches of tape. The boss laughed showing his gold tooth, "Six inches! It doesn't take much to satisfy a pretty little girl like you!" he says to her. She was embarrassed. The other girls gave sort of a sick laugh, but they're used to it. She was right beside me so I told her, "Don't worry, they never give you an answer without turning it into a sex thing. They do it on purpose just to make you feel uncomfortable." Once the boss gets started, it's one bad joke after the other. If there's a hole in the material he says, "what would you stick in there, a little busy one or a big lazy one?" Or if he walks by some girl who drops a spool of thread between her legs, he says, "A fat girl like you has to make do with whatever comes her way." With his stupid dirty jokes he makes us out worse than we are. Bringing us down to his level. The afternoon goes by. I can keep it up with my eyes closed. It's really mechanical. Automatic. The machine takes over. Only my right knee hurts. Sometimes it starts at work but usually it's in the evening or when I fall into bed exhausted. In this job it's your knee that starts and stops the machine. It took me a while to get used to it. I didn't like feeling my leg in that position. It felt caught. At night, I rubbed myself with alcohol. Now it's worse. Because about two years ago, one night in February, I was headed home half asleep. My eyes were closed and my head kept falling on my shoulder. I kept feeling the bones in my neck crack. I had had a crazy week. I was in the middle of buying my lot of land because I want to have a house built. That evening the notary was waiting for me in his office. I was on the train, half asleep when I realized that we had arrived and the train was about to leave again. So I gather up my stuff and I run for the door. I start down the steps without thinking about what I'm doing. Before I even realize how dangerous the situation is, I end up on the ground. Behind me, the train is already moving. Fast. That really hurt! It's my right knee that took the whole shock. It took all my courage to pull myself up. The train was gone. There was no one around. It was dark. I thought my leg was coming apart, that my knee was going to fall off. I thought it was all over. I had to miss a day of work. But I went back. I had to go back… listen to me talk! But I really wanted to talk about something else. I wanted to tell you about my ring, my beautiful new ring. My diamond ring. I got it yesterday. I had it made in one of the department stores downtown. I went to pick it up yesterday after work but I didn't put it on until I got home. I put it on the third finger of my left hand. I couldn't take my eyes off it. I stretched out my hand like this and separated my fingers. I went close to the light. It was shining away. I was laughing and crying at the same time. Ah! It was so beautiful, it is beautiful. I got my ring. I earned it. It's my own little splurge. I'm forty years old, you know, and I never got married. I've been on my own for twenty-five years. For once I'm really happy. I live alone but I haven't always lived alone. I've had all sorts of other arrangements. Sometimes I didn't do the arranging. For a while my sister lived with me, then one of my brothers, then my young nieces. I've helped them out a lot. But now I have to think of myself. I live all alone. I've made up my mind, I'm not going to get married. But I intend to have a real life and a real house anyway. First, I decided to get my own ring. I got married to my own life. I never have been and never will be dependent on anyone else, not on my family or on society. My ring—I guess it's because of other people that I wanted it. I figured once I had it I could always pass for someone's fiancée. Sometimes people call me Miss, really insisting on the word, Miss. Sometimes, 'cause I like to have a good time, I flirt, I like to talk. They're much more direct now when they ask me out. They want to go to bed right away. It's not that I don't like going out with men. It's not as if I haven't accepted lots of times. There have been men in my life. I've been around. But I don't want to play he-loves-me-he-loves-me-not anymore. It's not as if all old maids sit around waiting. We don't have one-track minds. Life goes on. I took a long hard look at my chances and I made my choice. Other people have trouble understanding that. It's like today with my ring. "Hey, Lucie, you didn't tell us you were engaged. When's the wedding?" Since I don't like gossip, I told them that I had bought it as a present for myself. There's a little Ukrainian girl that I like. She puts up posters and she's active on the union committee. She was trying to understand, so I said to her: "I can't face the fight on my own." Her answer was: "you have to face up to it, Lucie, you have to face up to it." I didn't really understand what she was trying to say. Because of all the gossip the day was so long. It went on forever. Why shouldn't my dreams come true just like anyone else's? It's true that I come from the country, that I arrived in the city by myself. I didn't know a soul and all I knew how to do was housework. But that doesn't mean I don't have a right to live my life. Just because I'm not married doesn't mean I don't have a right to a decent life.

> *She rummages around in her purse.*

Okay, my pass. Where's my train pass?

> *She looks for her wallet.*

Me, I don't like to keep my happiness and my problems to myself. I have to talk. But lots of times, I keep it all inside. It's better that way. Even when you're happy, you're on your own. Everyone is in it alone.

> *Gestures, giggles, she takes out her wallet.*

That was a good one. The other day I went into this store to buy myself a wallet. I wanted a leather one. The salesman, this Frenchman who sort of knows me, said: "Here's one just for you, Miss." Really polite, but insisting a bit on the "Miss." "Doeskin to go with your sad eyes." I answered him back real fast, "No thanks, I'd rather have patent leather." Once I got out of the store, I couldn't help but laugh. But it's not really that funny. In fact, it's not funny at all. It's like those birthday cards with kittens on them. Every year I get a few. I'm always telling my nieces to get married. Get married, girls, then you're somebody. Get married, people will call you Madam. Get married, even if you separate the day after your wedding, you'll still be Madam forever. It's the same old tune. How come people don't get tired of it? What is so important about a pair of pants?

> *She opens her wallet and counts her money silently. She picks up her lunch bag and opens it. She unwraps a piece of toffee and eats it.*

A piece of toffee to get me through till suppertime. The afternoon was so long.

> *She folds up her bag.*

It's time to change bags. This one's all crumpled. Here's my pass. Oh, no, it's my old unemployment book. I kept all my stamps. I should stick it in my bureau drawer. That will make quite a stamp collection. That's one thing, I'm never out of work. Some of the shops close. But when they're going to close down, you always know a bit in advance. And then I start looking for something else right away. So I change places. Sometimes I stay for six months, sometimes it's two years, five years, eight years in the same place. As long as there's work. You can always find a place in dresses. But you have to be ready to change shops. And you have to be able to do ordinary dresses or bridal gowns. You have to know how to do it all.

> *She rummages around in her purse and takes out her key case.*

I wanted a wallet to match my key case. It was a present from my brother who has all the kids. I helped him out often enough. There were ten of us kids and I was the oldest. When I was fifteen I came to the city and started working in homes. I only got into dresses about five years later, when my kid sister Simone came to stay with me and I wasn't allowed to keep her in my room. We had to rent a room downtown, and I had to give my notice. So there I was looking in the newspapers. I kept seeing ads for "operators," and you didn't have to be bilingual and I needed work, so I decided to go. I chose an address near my room. When I got to the office, they asked me if I had any experience. I said yes. They hired me and I went straight into the shop. I remember it like it was yesterday. I saw all the girls lined up at the tables. Everyone seemed to be going so fast. And everything was so dirty, I couldn't believe it. There were piles of dresses, tons of dresses. Cheap dresses. When I couldn't thread my machine, the girl beside me asked if I was experienced. I told her I was used to sewing on my mother's machine, but I couldn't figure this one out. The other four at the table said: "We'll work together. All you have to do is put together the skirts. We'll do the rest." There were three widths of material and I started sewing straight seams. I did thousands of them. That's how I got my experience. And that's how I learned what it means when the ads say "operators wanted." …Where's my lipstick?

She applies some lipstick and fixes a strand of hair.

This is Armand's mirror. I finally got used to using it. I kept it for ages in my dresser. Armand! Armand! He died. Just disappeared in an accident. With him, it was a different story. I couldn't get enough of him. I never got tired of being with him. It's impossible to explain. There was some kind of pull. It was in the eyes, in the hands. I can't find the words to describe it. Sometimes I think maybe I could find it again. But it only happens when I look at some stranger, that's all. It's vague, really vague… all my other experiences with men aren't worth talking about. There's one who promised to come help me when I have my house built. It feels nice and warm to sleep beside a man once in a while.

She takes the ring out of its case.

Maybe a ring is useless, what does it get me? But the little box sure is pretty. All satin and velvet! I'll keep it in my drawer.

She drops her purse.

My mirror broke. There's nothing left now. I guess it was already over. I'll replace it. I should make myself a new dress. I've got a sample of some plain beige material in my purse. I think I'll get it for myself. I need a change. Something new.

Sound of a train arriving.

Time to go. Tonight I was alone to talk it all out. Am I going to be alone on the train? I've had enough of being alone. It's got to end. Otherwise I'm afraid I will have worked for nothing. I'm afraid I will have talked for nothing. Take me away from here. Take me away.

THE DATE

by Odette Gagnon

It's Saturday night, we're going out.
Have to go somewhere, anywhere.
Get out your best dress and high heeled shoes.
Get out your cards, your games, your clues.
Get out your small talk and your latest news.
Get out your jokes to shake up the blues.
Get out your car and take a cruise.
Get out of the house, there's nothing to lose.
It's Saturday night, we're going out.
Have to go somewhere, anywhere.

If somebody had told me that one fine Saturday night I'd find myself at home
knitting red, white, and blue squares, no date, no husband, not a guy in sight…
up until recently I would have looked at them and said, "You're crazy, what do
you know!" Not so long ago, just thinking about that possibility would have
scared me. Tonight, Saturday night… I'm not expecting any calls, no visitors,
nobody's on his way over, nobody's coming to get me. I'm just sitting here
waiting to finish this square so I can start another one. Tonight you might say
that I'm my own mother, my father, my brother, my sister, my whole family, my
best friend, my date, my favourite TV show, tonight, you might say, I'm all
mine. I think this is the first time it hasn't scared me.

"No boyfriend to take you out,
no husband to keep you company,
not a single guy in your life,
what are you going to do?
What will become of you?"

Since I've been old enough to go out with guys I can't remember missing
a single Saturday night out. Always "busy." Guys and Saturday nights, for me,
they always went together. Good times. A Saturday night with no guy to take
you out, that was like spending Saturday night in hell. It doesn't matter if you
have a different guy every night of the week, if you don't have one on Saturday
night, you're not worth much.

"You're not worth much,
not worth the trouble,
not worth the price,
weekday guys are great
but they can't compete with the Saturday night date,
they say it's still the same,
they say it hasn't changed."

…Guys! Goddamn guys! I've sure run after enough of them! And even now… I can't get it off my mind. It's like I have to wipe them off the map for a while… like I have to stop seeing them so I can see straight. And yet, I've always been spoiled by guys. The first guys to spoil me were my brothers. At home, in our house, my mother always used to say, "Don't ask me for money, I don't have any." My brothers, they were young and they were already working, delivering newspapers, serving mass, delivering groceries. One of my brothers was even the Sexton's assistant. He's the one who earned the most money and he's the one who spoiled me the most.

"Do you remember that, Jean-Pierre, when you used to give me a nickel or two cigarettes as long as I didn't tell Mama where you were or who you were out with?"

Maybe it started with my brothers. Maybe that's where I learned that I'd get money from guys. That's something girls learn fast. I was only this high when I figured out how to get them to pay for the skating rink, the swimming pool at the playground, the movies at the parish hall, ice cream cones… I was such a beggar and made such a fuss. I can't believe it! Not with girls, just with guys. No wonder, I didn't pay any attention to girls. I only noticed them when they got in my way. Especially the pretty ones, you know, the ones that don't have to try, they just stand there and the guys come running. And you just stand there eating your heart out. Well, I made those girls look so silly that nobody could stand them, or I just made them cry.

With the guys, I was always game, always joking. With girls, I was always looking for a fight, always awful. At school, nothing I did made any sense, nothing they asked me to do made any sense to me; at home, there was nothing to do in the house that interested me. The only place I was happy was outside with the boys.

Going out. Going out. That's all I could think about. My mother wanted me to get a job right away, to bring a little more money home so my brothers could keep going to school. I gave in pretty fast that time. I signed up for a commercial course, and a year later I was a secretary. I didn't beat any records for speed but I could type a letter with no mistakes. That was good enough for me. The guys who hire you, at first, that's all they care about too. Other than that, they just want you to have a nice "personality." Well, I had one. Maybe I wasn't what you'd call a beauty, but people noticed me anyway. If you added up the time I spent in front of the mirror and the time my mother spent at her sewing machine, you'd find out how long it takes to have a "nice personality" and to make sure that people "notice" you.

I was 17 when I let guys into my life officially. I left the boys in the backyard for the boys in the office. I went from the parish hall to the dance hall, from ice cream cones to fancy dinners in restaurants, from petting on the front porch to making out in the back seat of a car parked on the Plains of Abraham. Then

I left Québec City for Montréal. Slowly but surely, without fuss, you make a little place for yourself, you make your way in life… a way in life… Sometimes the way leads to a weekend up north, sometimes it's a night in a hotel, or a night out in the clubs.

Once in a while, there's a little bracelet or a little pendant on a gold chain, all the little presents that show that you've been with a guy and there's a good chance you're gonna see him again. Little souvenirs…. That makes you wonder… it's as if guys go out and build themselves a future, while us girls, we build ourselves a past, we collect souvenirs.

During the winter he takes you skiing, or maybe to the Forum to see a hockey game, in person. In the city, during the summer, he takes you to garden parties and to the races. A few times I even ended up going to a baseball game at Jarry Park. For your vacation, he takes you to the ocean so you can get a tan lying on the beach at Cape Cod or Atlantic City.

That reminds me of the guy who offered to take me to see the ocean in Plattsburg one night. I had just arrived in Montreal. I was nineteen. I had never seen the ocean, and I had always thought it was a long way away. He says no, it's not even 100 miles from here. Okay. Let's go!

It was only the next morning in the office when I told them I had been to see the ocean in Plattsburg last night…. And one of them says, "Well, did you see it?"

"Sure."

"Last night…"

"Sure…"

"Who showed it to you?"

"The guy I'm going out with."

"That guy is something special! If he showed you the ocean in Plattsburg, you tell him for me that he's something else!"

Depending on whether the guy is married or not, he takes you to meet his friends or he doesn't take you to meet his friends. Over the year, he takes you out for Chinese food, Italian food, French food. He might even take you up to Altitude whatever-it-is at the top of Place Ville Marie. He takes you out for a drink after the movies. He even takes you out to the theatre… I could have been sitting in the theatre tonight, sitting there with him, with this one or that one…. Depending on whether the guy is married or not, the evening can end before or after midnight. If he's married, the latest it can go is two in the morning. Usually it's around that time that he starts to say he's sorry but, and he starts pulling on his pants.

A married man, for the girls who've never met one, he's the one you can only see Monday through Friday, but never on Saturday. If he's the only one you've got, don't take the risk.

That's the name of the game. Making sure that you get asked out as often as possible, setting it up, then fixing yourself up for it. From your toenails to the streaks in your hair. Fixing yourself up is no joke. It means going to the shops, the hairdresser's and the drugstore. Some girls I know, they even went to the hospital to have their nose fixed. And it all costs money. That's where we invest our money. I guess that's how we build our sense of security.

Fixing yourself up, there's no end to it once you start. It's a full-time lifetime job. The time comes when you can't set foot outside without stopping in the bathroom to check in the mirror. Without "fixing yourself up." The doorbell rings… you reach for your comb. There's someone at the door, you never know who it might be. Just in case… it's simple, you don't even dare go on an errand around the corner without changing, just in case…. Just in case you meet so-and-so, anyone, someone…

Just in case you run into the guy at the grocery store, you know, the one who noticed you last time…. Just in case you run into the guy across the street, you know, the one who watches you when you're sitting on the front porch. Just in case, one of these fine mornings on the way to the office, you meet The Guy, the one you think would… the one who could make it… the one who… the one that, I'm sure, with him it would be… the one…

You know! The one who could change your clothes, your shoes… change the colour of your walls, bring carpets into the house, the one who would make you change apartments and all your habits. And while you're at it, why not change neighbourhoods, change your name…. Just in case you run into the One and Only, The One meant for you, The Guy in the world who could change your whole life.

    Silence.

The worst of it is that after a while, it eats up all your time, all your energy and all your pay!

"Saint Catherine Street
I've been up and down
And all around.
From east to west,
I know it best.
From Guy to Papineau
Through rain and sun and snow.
Winter, summer, fall.
I've seen it all."

I can describe all the windows.
I can name all the stores.
Saint Catherine Street.
North side, south side.
I know it by heart.
Like the palm of my hand.
I spent all of my paycheques fixing myself up:
Making myself presentable,
desirable.
Fixing myself up to be "noticed,"
to be invited out.
Doing Saint Catherine Street, up and down,
for some girls it's a living.
That's where they pick up the guys,
it's a kind of prostitution.
Doing the stores.
It's the same business,
just another way of picking up guys,
another kind of shopping.
"Making your way up and down the street—streetwalking,
Making the rounds in the stores—windowshopping:
two different ways of putting yourself on the market,
up for sale.
Two kinds of prostitution."
…But one of them—shopping—isn't so obvious, it's a little prostitution that looks silly beside the other… but silly or not, when you think about it… there's big money involved.

"Going out," "fixing myself up," that's about all I've ever done!

Going out… it becomes so important… when you go out, anything can happen. You wouldn't think of going out alone. It's so bad that sometimes you really get pissed off because you can't even go out to take a little walk without being bugged. When a girl goes out alone, she's not at home, it's like she's a visitor. Let's say I went out for a walk, right now. Let's say I felt like it. I can't. At this hour? Are you crazy? If you ever ran into trouble, you can be sure they'd tell you you had no business being out alone anyway, the streets are no place for girls alone. The guy who bugs you might even tell you that himself. But that wouldn't stop him from raping you. He knows everything's on his side, because everyone's going to say the same thing: If you were out at that hour, you were looking for trouble, you wanted it, you got what you deserved, it's your own tough luck.

Once again you fixed yourself up for it! How come we can't feel at home outside? Like he does?

How did it come to this?
"If you go out alone,
anything can happen.
If you go out alone,
danger can strike.
You can be stopped,
you can be bothered,
you can be hustled.
Anyone and everyone can do anything and everything to you
any guy you meet becomes your enemy
when you go out alone
you enter his territory
you're not at home, young lady,
only he's at home, outside."

…Guys! Goddamn guys! If there was one here beside me tonight, I wouldn't know what to do with him, I'd have a hard time just… unless he picked up a pair of knitting needles and a ball of yarn… why not?

…Love? Make love? No thanks. I've done it just like anyone else. I've slept around, here and there, all around town… no, I shouldn't say that, I'm exaggerating. It's true I've had more than my share, but lots of times, if it had been up to me, I wouldn't have bothered. I would have passed up lots of opportunities. But the guys, they felt like it, and I didn't want to be taken for a cockteaser, so I did it for them, hardly ever for myself.

I don't mean that it was a nightmare every time. No, not that bad. With some of them it wasn't bad, it was fine. But with others, sleeping together seemed to ruin something. And sometimes you say to yourself, "Oh well," we've been out a few times together, I guess the time has come…." You know that's all he's really waiting for, so one night you make up your mind and you say okay… to keep him happy. And dammit if they're not the ones who always ask you if you liked it… you say yes… to keep them happy…

Fact is, after all that, I'm no better off. I don't really know what it is to make love. All I learned is that you make love in bed, in a room, at the end of the day. You turn out the lights and you say to yourself: "Maybe this time… maybe not… it will depend… if it works, Great, if it doesn't, too bad, maybe next time…. Seeing as how there was a miracle last year, maybe there'll be another one tonight, you never know…. Here goes! *Qué será será!*"

You don't like to think about it—or talk about it. Maybe that's why nothing ever happens. Crazy eh? No, really, it's true. Just think about it! We know what to do with the thousands of gadgets in our lives, but do we know what to do with ourselves once we get into bed, or anywhere else for that matter: we pretend nothing's happening, we're careful not to make any noise, not to disturb, not to go too far, careful not to touch too much… if you ask me, we're pretty dumb.

We try to make sure we don't make a mess when maybe that's what we should do, make a mess! Sometimes I think it could be so fantastic, and then I just don't know… I have a lot of trouble myself. It's become just so many obscene positions, dirty pictures, *Playboy* shots. My head is full of it all.

It's true, the only kind of love I know is the kind where you have to have a waist, tiny like this, hips not too broad, your ass, not too high, not too low, thighs you don't notice, nice long slim legs, and breasts… hah, I don't even want to talk about that… tits they can't be big enough as long as they don't sag. The kind of love where no one asks your opinion. It's more like a dirty trick they play behind your back every time.

It's a love story with no romance, that makes no sense. We should start all over again. I can't stand it anymore. If we could just erase it all and say: okay everybody, guys, girls, let's take it from the top.

But it's not that simple. As long as the guys keep looking at us to see if we pass, to see if we're worth a screw. As long as we accept that little game…. As long as we keep treating each other that way… nothing's going to change. The way it is now, you have the guys, like pimps, on the one side and the girls, like whores, on the other. When I was talking about making a mess a little while ago, I was just thinking of turning it all upside down. It won't happen on its own. There's a lot of work to be done. When I say that, I'm thinking about guys, I'm thinking about girls, I'm thinking about:

the woman across the street… the one with the kids,
the girl next door… the one who isn't married…
the woman downstairs… they say she doesn't work…
the girl upstairs who types letters in some office…
the woman out back who's a good seamstress… she wanted to be a nurse…
while the one who got her education practices her profession…
she made a place for herself in administration…
the girl across the street can't find a job… there's no market for what she knows…
like the woman on the first floor… who can do her housework blindfolded…
the girl on the second floor who waitresses five days a week, and the weekend shift when she can get it…
the sixty-year-old woman who knits for her grandchildren
and babysits them much too often…
and the sixteen-year-old who still lives at home… and is in such a hurry to have her own place and a guy in her life…
Tonight I'm thinking… about all those women and all those girls,
I'm sitting here talking about guys… but I'm thinking about Girls
for the first time.

A MAD ACTRESS: PART II
by Luce Guilbeault

During the intermission, the actress remains glued to her chair in her dressing room. The fur around her shoulders. She's cold.

The houselights go down. She's frightened. She lights three candles and walks once around her dressing room. Holding the candelabra, looking to make sure no one is there, she returns to her chair.

"But it seems to me, Agnes, if my memory serves me right, that I forbade you to see anyone."
Forbidden to go out.
Forbidden to enjoy, forbidden, forbidden…
"Yes but when I went to see him, you don't know why and I'm sure you would have done as much."
Daddy, I masturbate.
Daddy, I'm not a virgin anymore.
Daddy, I had an abortion.
"Perhaps, at any rate, tell me the story."
"It's all quite strange and difficult to believe.
I was working on the porch where it was cool…"
I was on the porch
I was on the porch of our big country house.
It was during the war.
No more butter.
I like spinach, and blood sausage, custard, birthday cake.
Is that mine?
There's too much of it.
It's too long, too golden, too thick.
They braid it.
They teach me how to brush it every morning and every night.
It pulls, it pulls, there are knots.
My loose tooth hurts.
The boil in my ear hurts.
The sprain is pounding in my head.
My little pimple hurts, I've been rubbing it too much.
The scab comes off on the facecloth in my bath.
The iodine stings. Tears well up.
Mama. Mama.
I was on the porch.
Let's go up to our room.
It's evening.
Let's undo our hair.

The bullfrogs are singing.
My hair falls in waves.
I brush my hair, gently because of the knots,
standing in the middle of the room,
avoiding the mirror,
never in front of the mirror.
When I look into my eyes, I'm afraid.
Sometimes when I feel brave, I play with my fear.
I look into my eyes, I exist, with my brush in the air,
for a second.
I turn my head, I no longer exist.
I am, I am not.
I am, I am not.
I start brushing my hair again, with long fast strokes.
My heart beats fast. A knot, ow, I exist.
The pain is so sharp, so sharp,
and I am so alive, so alive.
I was on the porch.
It is raining. There is thunder and lightning.
Daddy and Mama are out.
A car door slams in the rain.
Someone's there.
Uncle Simon!
All three of us on the porch in Uncle Simon's arms.
We laugh, we cry, we're all wet.
I'm going to slaughter you, you barefoot rascals, quick, in the house.
Uncle Simon, *(silence)*
"What does that mean, slaughter? Does it mean the same thing as DYING?"

> *The child listens to the vague answers and shakes her head.*

I am on the porch, it's wintertime.
I'm dying of the cold, eating an apple as frozen as I am.
The cold lulls me to sleep, I watch the snow fall.
They take me inside.
Daddy is there.
Daddy!
Nighttime Daddy who we never see,
who works too hard—for us.
They undress me.
I breathe in the smell of onions coming from the big green kitchen.
They kiss me.
I breathe in the smell of tobacco on warm cheeks.
I pick up my apple, just cool now.
It's good, everything feels good.
The pleasure is so real, so real,

and I am so alive, so alive.

In the city, when I was five, they used to put me to bed at first in my parents' big bed, then later at night they carried me half asleep to the sofa in the dining room.

My mother put me to sleep there. Her place in the big bed in their room was already warm,

my place, her place, my place, her place.

My father tucked me in and kissed me.

It was nighttime, not a sound.

In the morning, in the folds of the brown curtains, Jesus appeared in his robes. He appeared secretly with Saint Teresa... little Christ child, I give my heart to you, take it, please, to be yours and only yours, so be it......

       The actress thinks about her own life.

Everyone is looking for her. Where is she? She is lost, kidnapped.

They've kidnapped the child Jesus, HELP.

Uncle Simon and the police are looking for me everywhere.

My father is crying. My mother tearing out her hair.

Everyone is shouting.

Two hours later, Jesus returns to the house.

She's not lost.

She took a walk.

First I go to Saint Jacques' Church and then to Saint Louis de France.

First down Saint-Hubert Street.

Then down Saint-Christophe Lane.

Two trips, back and forth.

It's Sunday, I'm glad to be outside, I know the way. I've been there often enough in my head.

It's such a nice walk.

A beautiful day!

...children, beware of the deep blue skies,

for they can bring tears to your eyes...

I go back home. It feels cool and gentle in the house.

My mother's gentle arms feel cool. Her smell is like no other.

Help!

They love me too much!

My father's voice is like no other.

Help!

All this love is killing me!

They kept me inside.

From the window I can see me waiting for myself on the sidewalk across the street.

Agnes, how are you?

I was on the porch

neither inside

nor outside.
Luce,* how are you?
I AM ON THE PORCH.

> *She stands up, blows out the candles and sits down again.*

*Should be replaced by the name of the actress playing the role.

MARCELLE

by Marie-Claire Blais

I spoke to her a bit harshly yesterday when I left.
She probably won't dare come this evening.
What did I try to tell her again? What did I repeat, the same thing I kept
harping on? Listen, Lise. I don't like sentimentality, I don't need anyone, not you
or anyone else.
Poor Lise, why this need to mistrust life
and worst of all this need to prove to yourself that you are the strongest, the
stronger of the two? Freer. More independent. More…. Why this struggle?

>   *Pause.*

It's almost eight o'clock. No she won't come.
Maybe. Yes, but if she came, if she came
there's a little supper ready for her,
for her and me.
A bottle of wine, a book we could read side by side.
Tonight, I'd take the time, yes, enough time, to listen to her, to look at her, to see
her.
It would be so simple tonight.
She often reproaches me for not knowing how to listen to her.
Yes but I'm alive, I'm in love, I have so much to say, Lise.

>   *Pause.*

But she does too, do I have to lose her in order to feel all that? How often has
she told me that she wants to break away from me? That my stubbornness
exasperates her?
Tonight I could talk to her. Yes if she came,
but she has probably decided never to come back again.
Too many women in your life Marcelle, no that's not what she holds against me,
no, it's more how I make myself unhappy,
my refusal of all tender feelings.
A kind of egoism, when I think about it,
that delicate web bothers me, that bond, that weakness,
that vow of the whole being between two women,
between a man and a woman, between all couples, or those who dream of
becoming couples. I can't be part of a couple with anyone and yet I am capable
of love. Everyone is alone. Who dreamed it all up? Who was perverse enough to
write the law that says it is possible for two people to spend a lifetime together?
And yet it happens.

>   *Long pause.*

But you, Lise, and you, the others: Marianna in Europe or my other friends in this city, my friends, it feels good to call out their names. After all, they can't hear me, I always say, my friends, it's more than sentimentality that attaches me to you, maybe my dream is just another illusion. I tell myself that you are the reason for the ties between us, you, yourselves. I could celebrate Lise tonight, instead of praising in front of her all the other women I've loved the way I usually do
but it's already late, no, she won't be coming.

Why? What is she doing? Where is she? Who is looking at her this very moment? They can't possibly see her as I see her
unless she's with another woman,
it must be a woman and I probably know her,
looking at her the way I do, discreetly without imposing. But here I am waiting for her and she doesn't even realize it, too selfish no doubt.
Are you self-effacing because it makes life easier Marcelle?
Explode, pounce, be mean (it's the only way it will make you more humble, more generous.) Lise is right. I don't listen to her enough.
Ah! It's hopeless, she didn't call today. That's the reality, I really deserved it. So bad-tempered, they've all said so.
But when I praised other girls in front of her, I was acting like everyone else, out of some headstrong, cruel streak. Yes, to kindle that flame of jealousy, to make her worry, to protect my kingdom. But is my kingdom really mine? Does a woman belong to every man who looks at her arrogantly, indecently, I always wonder when I see him possess her with his eyes. She hasn't phoned, that's true. But I understand, it's because of my distant almost brutal attitude when I left her yesterday. Lise leave me alone I don't have time for anyone. Belonging to yourself alone is essential in life.
One love affair after another. Always the same feelings that tear people apart and when you're in love you become vulnerable. Like a child, you admit your weakness, you don't belong to yourself anymore.
There were days when I was like that with Marianna, and yet I don't regret a thing, there have to be crazy periods. Being in love is a delirious business. It's true. I love Mariana and if she came back from Europe tonight, I would talk to her in a different way, with feeling maybe. Only to her could I say all those useless comforting things.

>   *She mimes gestures of affection and caresses.*

Yes, only to her. But what good would it do?

>   *Pause.*

Is that Lise coming up the stairs?
No. Probably the neighbour and her dog. I wasn't fair to her. I spoke out in anger. Tonight I will celebrate her. Why? Because she is modest.
An admirable quality I don't have! Irresistible too, original, and a sensual

animal
not always only when she wants
a really touching sensitivity, and a strong person too
she knows how to defend herself with me, Lise
and how to say what I need to hear, she knows a lot of things I don't,
I could learn to live a better life with her.
For Marianna, it would be a different kind of celebration,
every woman is unique, Marianna is so unique that…

     Silence.

Is that you, Lise, no, Lise's footsteps
I could recognize them anywhere in the world, because she is alive in me and
her voice is like no one else's. A hoarse, rough sound. Lise, Lise.
I would talk to her tonight. Too bad she has no intention of coming.
I wouldn't look for words to seduce her
maybe I would say nothing at all.
And Marianna's beautiful cold eyes watching me ironically. Her passion was
a bit ironic. As soon as you get close to her, she withdraws again into her proud
wild self, she stretches out her hand: it's burning hot. Marianna, a season of
madness, it would take a lifetime to celebrate you.
Ah! Lise, where is she? And the others?
Why should anyone come here tonight?
I didn't call a soul!
I told them all not to set foot in my house, I was tired.
I muttered and bitched, they all understood. Marcelle is a bear.
Marcelle is fiercely independent, unsociable, let's leave her alone.
But perhaps it's necessary sometimes to be more direct and to tell the plain
and simple truth: even if you're independent, strong and capable of sustaining
yourself with your own experience and your own truths, you still need other
people to bring you something different from yourself, and Lise and my other
friends, I knew them well. They were always different from me. And wonderful
because of that. Being with them took me outside myself. Strangers at first,
slowly but surely, they became intimate friends.
A secret fire burned in Marianna. With some of them love is so physical that it's
impossible to think of it without pain, with others it's a chaste fraternal tie.
Anne, the one I call my brother, there's nothing sexual between you and me
but no brother has ever been as attentive as you. Anne, my brother, I should
celebrate you as well, the one who came to feed my dog when I was sick, and
I could defend you too, love you without expecting anything in return, protect
you. But Anne, you too say you don't always need other people and all these
faces of my inner family form an image of life in constant flux. With one friend,
it's the look in her eyes that I cherish, with another, with Lise, it's her integrity,
the frankness in her words and gestures.
Come Lise, tonight I'll talk to you and you too Marianna and you too Anne and
all the others.

These women want no more than to be understood and loved.
Why shouldn't I love them? There are others I don't know still in darkness,
unaware of the strength of their love. Don't be ashamed of this strange
emotion, lost among so many others; it's misunderstood love, you have to learn
to appreciate it.
But perhaps you have to live through it to understand it
Look you always tell me you want to write, Lise
And you, Marianna, you dream of a woman who could speak for us,
it's never been done, you say.
But throughout the ages, women have loved women.
They were just like you and me; we still hear their songs,
their words, their poems from time to time
But this cry of happiness of recognition of shared love will not come from
a distant and prophetic land
Perhaps it will come one night when a friend whispers in your ear or when
a stranger offers you one of her fleeting smiles. Don't wait, don't wait for others
to write or speak for you, Lise.
Tell your life story by living it.
Be triumphant. You know how to love you have that hidden patience.
Who can describe for us what trembles in your heart?
You, Lise, you'll do it and so will I in my way,
just recently our voices could not be heard through the sweetness of our
embrace we were going to die smothered in useless secrets. What happens
between two people always remains a secret but the light of the day is making
its way into our houses and entering our bedrooms. Our love for each other is
like anyone else's perhaps we think a bit better
but it is not always possible we too are children of mankind.
But there is a difference, Lise, you see, perhaps it's the quality of the bond
at the point where a man gets weary and he no longer sees what is alive or dead
in the person he just stifled, that is when the bond begins for us.
Who is she?
She is a woman. Yes she is familiar but we can't pretend to know her the way
a husband says of his wife "I know her." This woman, our friend for an hour,
for an evening, for a lifetime, is someone for whom we must create new bonds
outside the world of law and order and it is with her and in her that we must
look for something true but nothing is perfect. Lise ah! Here I am with my bad
temper and my fits of depression when everything seems hopeless there is love
yes but we have to live too. When I take your hand in the street and people
look at us with that look you know nothing is perfect, we have to fight for
elementary things for those human rights all men and women are still awaiting,
we have to fight for what is natural respect you give me respect I do too,
perhaps it is the kind of love I appreciate the most respect yes if she were
beside me
but she won't come at this hour it's too late.
I would tell her, ah! All the things she loves to hear and I say so seldom. Lise do

you know that you are no longer alone, do you know that when we make love somewhere there are other women loving each other too? I have met a lot of other women, they were not, they are not all as loveable as you but many have discovered that a special kind of caring and understanding can exist between us. We speak about ourselves simply

this person is the same sex as me and I like her that's all,

we'll listen to you, we listen to the voices yearning to join us. People are beautiful

not all the time you know that, but I am talking to you,

I'm talking to you and you are not coming.

Reading for hours side by side, often saying nothing,

talking isn't always necessary. Lise where are you?

But it's true that I don't always need you

sometimes no one, there are books that I read only for myself,

hours that I reserve for my own leisure, you do not always inhabit me.

But tonight I felt like changing for you.

No one is coming. I can drink the wine alone.

But she could have phoned me after all these years of tenderness,

and love sometimes bitterly won.

Lise is weary perhaps I don't want to tire her

sometimes I'm mean just to avoid the weariness that could show in her face,

after all these years she forgets, she doesn't even call

but she can't forget me if for no other reason because of my miserable outbursts, people used to say to me

Marcelle you are ambiguous but intelligent,

Marcelle a boy or a girl, who are you?

Sometimes people stopped me in the street to ask me and I answered, "isn't she lovely the woman I am with" often a secret loveliness,

aren't we happy together and in harmony

When we love someone that person becomes harmonious

Let us be glad, ambiguous but intelligent

people always try to define you

to diminish you when at times we feel so vast, infinite, longing to know everything,

to love everything, longing to take in everything during our brief journey in this hostile dangerous land, I feel so happy perhaps she will come after all?

Who still dares to come see me, sometimes I am so unpleasant sometimes the house is full all my friends come together, sometimes I chase them away all of them in order to be alone, to think, they accept me,

as I am.

She goes to the door when the light in the hallway goes on.

I'm not asleep Lise, here I come, I'm coming, I'm coming…

MARCELLE II

by Pol Pelletier

Hate, yes, hate.
I loathe you all.
I refuse, I spit.
Hate, yes, hate for women.
I see my mother and I want to vomit.
You and your long line of humble servants,
you humiliate me, you are deeply humiliating.
You have betrayed me, you have lied to me,
you have made me ashamed, very deeply horribly ashamed.
You have robbed me, do you hear?
You have robbed me of my own sex. And you sold it. To men.
I have lived and I still live in a world
where women are nothing. Decorative dishcloths,
comprehensive, sensitive sponges, softhearted whimperers.
Women are shit.
Submissive, quiet, gentle, nice,
insignificant, boring shit.
Always have been shit.
Who can I identify with?
That's not me, that heap there. It has nothing to do with me.
The rest of the world? It's a man's world…
it spins along without me and against me.
Where am I? Hate, hate and more hate.
Hate for my own sex and hate for myself.
I am torn, divided, drawn and quartered.
Shame, the shame of belonging to a race of slaves.
Woman-willing-waning-wooing-wanting.
I belong to a race of slaves.

And then one day a woman put her head on my shoulder.
I feel her cheekbone on my shoulder.
Her hand glides gently over my right breast, slips inside my shirt.
Her hand on my left breast.
Her voice says "it's soft."
What's happening? Everything comes to a stop.
Man's world stops turning. What?
What's happening?
I am amazed, overwhelmed
(and yet calm, very controlled as usual)
very… what?
I don't move, I look at her, she looks at me.

More important, most important of all, my body
my body is delighted, my body is enchanted, how wonderful,
how gentle, no man ever touched me like that,
this long bird-hand on my left breast…
This is in no way an act of possession.
No, a state of grace. We look at each other through
our eyes of the oppressed, with a deep understanding of silence,
of things left unsaid, of secrets. Like two cats.
I am in my bed with a woman, the first one.
Oh! This long smooth place where bodies can stretch out under cover!
Rustling, hidden, soft and warm.
I remember so well. We were the same length.
A perfect match.
A feeling of complicity and recognition.
And relief perhaps. She was made like me,
no need to ask questions, it happened all by itself,
it was all strangely simple. Two similar bodies
pressed against each other, a kind of reassuring equality.
The unique sensation of feeling her woman's breasts against my own breasts.
Her woman's body lying on her side, and me facing her,
lying on my side,
the sensation of a woman's skin touching mine, my legs,
oh God! legs, lovely long satin things,
entwined, interlocked, hands on breasts, my hands on breasts, (surely this is the
most wonderful of all possible discoveries)…

> *Deep laughter. She is delighted.*

Frigid women, that's a joke. There's not a woman in the world who won't have
an orgasm if she, or someone, caresses her clitoris for a few minutes. Women
are not "slow to come." Women are seas of sensuality. Women are bombs.
Let them explode. Let the tide rise and roar. Desire. The dam collapses. The
shattering revelation. I would like to talk about desire. About my desires. The
strongest desire I have known has been my desire for women. I could have torn
down walls, ripped off locks. Oh, not because they were women. No, for me
desire is desire, for men or for women. Nature makes no distinction. Desire has
no sex. Look at children, they understand. For them, playing doctor with the
girls, playing doctor with the boys, it's all the same, it just depends on who's
free to play. A body is a body. No, my desires for women have been so strong
because they are desires I have felt absolutely free to pursue. Free. The opposite
of what I feel when I desire a man. I never know what to do when I desire
a man. Why? Because men always get caught up in the social game of seduction.
That convoluted, tortuous, suffocating labyrinth of seduction. The trouble with
entering that labyrinth is that I always end up playing follow the leader. He's
active, I'm passive. The roles we get to play are totally unacceptable. What is this
stupid scenario where I keep asking myself questions?

"Should I wait till he takes the initiative?"
"Do I dare be aggressive?"
That's right, I said "aggressive." Oh horrors! What a dirty word! A woman is NEVER aggressive.
But it's not true. Women are aggressive! All human beings are aggressive. That's something else that children understand: the desire to grab, to act, to move ahead; impulsiveness; a feeling for power; a need to assert...
It's absolutely essential to survival.
That's why most woman are half dead,
because their desire and their aggressiveness have been stifled.
You see, with a woman, I'm alive, at least sexually.
I don't have to worry about my role, my place.
It folds and unfolds. Desire swells. The waves break and roll and tumble, racing toward a single point. It swells and swells, I am full, I am going to explode.
Oh, lovely one, lithe lady, graceful doe, nimble rabbit, in the house by the water, in the darkest night, with no moon, no stars, you are a bright splash in the lake as black as ink, you're cold, you run back into the house, a huge towel around a small frozen body, a wood fire, massage your arms, your legs, I am burning, it swells and swells, adrift, the great embrace, to eat you... to devour you...

We are all part of a secret society. No one knows it, but every time a woman sleeps with another woman it's a wonderful slap in the face of our rotten world. A magnificent act of subversion. "We don't need the rest of you, do you hear? Watch us swoon by ourselves, woman to woman." Every time a woman sleeps with another woman, she declares her love for her own sex and for herself. Bit by bit, she regains the self-respect that was stolen from her so long ago. Bit by bit. Piece by piece. Hundreds and thousands of pieces will come to light, and join together, fuse, solidify, and there will stand a mountain, a mountain with a voice.
Listen to that voice. A low deep rumble.
Patience is coming to an end.

THE WRITER
by Nicole Brossard

A woman presses down on her pencil, firmly, wisely.
But she is not writing love poems.
She is drawing flat bellies. Whole vulvas.
She is changing the order of the words.
She misses a beat, the pencil is soft.
It's midnight and it's still hot.
I like lampshades and shadow plays.
Something is stirring me and chilling me at the same time…
Long fingernails.
Thin skin. It tears too easily.
The skin of a fanatic. Tattooed.
Covered with ancient symbols and new words.
Images, flashes beneath the lampshade.
I don't want to put off anything until tomorrow.
Tonight I am going to face myself. Take stock.
I want to strip off all the cosmetic layers.
Where and how will I carry myself away?
To or from myself. To or from others.
I wait for nighttime to bring things to light.
Somewhere between fiction and reality. Which tale should I spin tonight?
What difference does it make?
My tales always precede me.
Fiction preys on me.
Sometimes I think I'm an adjective.
I grew up as an adjective.
Pretty, fat, feminine, bold, charming, skinny.
Not bad, smart little girl.
Tonight I am tearing out my blank pages, my old favourites.
I tear ahead.
I speak to forge a path through silence.
A break on the horizon.
What I am. What I am not.
An invisible sight in the blind spot.
A woman thinks she's right. She finds herself alone. After all, a woman talking to herself is a woman waiting for something to happen. I talk. I speak. My words are a white light in a dark room. The negative of the dark words printed on the pages of sleepless white nights.
And my hands are free to speak. To find a new sense. A sixth sense for my existence.
As I speak, I have a political pact among women in mind.

Touch me. Personal is political.

The set starts to shake before my eyes and it is word-shaking.

Which words? I am improvising on new ground. I reclaim my right, my due. Words come to the surface.

They arrive from afar. Through the ages. Barely audible through the songs and the sobbing of women in labour.

I am labouring in a reality that dangles like live bait under my nose.

I am looking for words. Searching everywhere. In the folds of dresses, in the tufts of hair, between my toes, under my tongue, between the sheets, in the bellies of statues. Beeswax.

The small wax Venus melts slowly and reveals no more secrets beneath the lampshades. She salivates. She speaks a few words. My mouth is not sealed. But pain is everywhere in the ghost of my limbs. No time to waste, I must burn some pages from the past when I loved men, took care of them, cleaned for them.

The time has come to call their bluff.

I refuse to write simply to expiate collective stupidity.

Tonight I shall step into history without opening my legs.

I step into history opening my mouth not my legs. I arrive with words and with solidarity. Like a mad woman at the time of the full moon I follow a difficult but necessary course. Perhaps it's obvious. Perhaps it isn't. But I am afraid. Afraid of being lured. Afraid of trading my most vital convictions. Afraid that they will cut off all dialogue. And that I will be cut off from other women's words and broken dreams. That I will be exiled and banished before I can reach them.

But there are bridges. There is a direct route from the brain to the belly, when we allow ourselves to move freely through our bodies. Inside. Outside. I bend to understand and the rediscovery always comes in an uncontrollable orgy of words. Words from a grammatical erection.

It destroys bridges. And leaves me alone like a silent 'e' weaving sentences where the masculine gender always dominates. I weave a web to my horizon. Adrift in the immense sea of my avid stare.

Listening.

My head is spinning with the planet. If it seems too fast, it's because I'm saying no, I'm resisting. Hysterical. Hysterical. Give us a kiss. Give us a kiss. I stink, I swarm. I am fighting a strange body. I am spoiling the show that impotent spectators want to enjoy at my expense.

Otherwise, I turn slowly, like a variation and my head moves to the tic-toc of my thoughts. Sounds, words, sounds, words, sounds. Words. Woolly. Wild. Who's afraid of Virginia Woolf? But in fact I don't want to take revenge on anyone. I am without a horse, without a shadow. Without a rider. And it feels good to be oneself, for oneself, quietly unfolding. I want to decipher the paperthin skin of my age. I want to exhibit for you, for us, all that we have in common. I write and I don't want to do it alone anymore. I want us. I want to make history shake and shudder and growl.

Personal is political.

This rupture will be an inauguration. I am crossing thresholds. I am passing through something that is me, something determined to prove that it is not an image. Pastel prints. Pale pink. Rosemary. Bleeding Hearts. Wild Daisies. I don the dark of morning when I cross the thresholds, written black and white. Could we see the difference if the ink was white?

Contrast, content, continuity, woman of fiction. Where is my centre of gravity? I am afloat.

It's difficult to live with your head caught in the "bottleneck of history." The night stretches out like a series of pendulums one after another marking time and unwinding memories. Men's memories. A souvenir of our love. *Mon amour*. Eternally yours. Iseult. Eurydice. Sappho. Emma Bovary, the wife of Charles taking pathetic vengeance in her monologues. All of them buried in passion.

Fragments. Ancient parchment and modern parchment. All worn thin. Dismembered.

Not possessed. But dispossessed.

My memory delves deep tonight. A breath of odours to be exhaled.

My memory is as deep as all the desires that remain caught in my chest. The writer and the woman are coming out of hiding. Something is arousing me but I can't quite call it by name.

Examine all my urges. I must have circles under my eyes.

It's late. Imagine imagination like a fan or like a mother tongue that has just had its first orgasm.

Unnerving, isn't it?

It's a perilous transition. Passing from one state of consciousness to another. Such a violent quaking that it stirs even the intestines. Maybe that's why it is so easy to confuse having guts and having balls.

It's hot. No truce. I speak. Rising life and limb. Tipsy Sagittarius. Drawn to the source. For the first time.

I am half delirious, on the one hand not the other. One-sided paralysis. In my stomach, my nerves, my muscles. It proliferates and ramifies. The sleepwalker finds rest. I dream. I speak. Like an old haunted house. My half, my better half, my half of myself. Who wants to be half of someone else?

Beauty and the beast. Enter. It's the victim speaking. Hysterical struggle.

Writhing in the witches' cauldron. The heiress of ridicule. A strange body doing public penance for its difference.

But here the victim takes part in the show. She watches herself. She talks to herself. With or without a mirror.

Rant, rave, radical.

Ready for hours and hours of acrobatics of the mind and the mouth. Amazon. Dart. Dash.

Beware of the harvest.

Riding the warm wave of dreams.

Take a deep breath. My chest swells. Here in the evening. In my mindless gap.

Ah yes, the sleepwalker's ultimate glory: you wave your hands as they slit your throat. My hands are free. No fresh pork to cook. The book is sleeping. I am speaking. I rock myself. I'm sitting in a hollow space. Panic surrounds me. My posture is ridiculous: I piss squatting and I have a pregnant woman's cravings. Owls screech in my throat.

I have been sleepwalking since Julie. I was so big. After months of getting up five or six times in the night, you get used to it.

You make friends with the night. In the dark of the night you rediscover yourself. Inch by inch. The freckles, the moles, your eyebrows. You take the real measure of your eyelashes. You keep your eyes wide open. My eyes are blue.

I have never enjoyed talking about myself. As if I always had the feeling that there was nothing special to say about my private life. When really that's all that matters. How you are born, how you play, how you laugh, how you cry, how you die. Men are so hot in public and so frigid in bed, the most private thing about them is their property.

Sometimes I feel that I have been floating along beside myself since adolescence. Floating in a well-ordered private life. Perhaps it's because I've always had my own way. A man's way. A man's mind grafted to a woman's body. I have been efficient, productive. Like the prodigal son, I have ranted and raved in the face of the powers that be. The revolution was on my side. I shouted as loud as any angry young man. My crises always came in October or in the autumn. But you become a woman when you've been to jail. You cry and scream and thrash and shout, you bang your head against the walls, you tell yourself stories. You make mountains. It's funny how crazy obstacles can make you. Some afternoons when I'd like to be alone and Julie keeps hanging around, I go crooked and crazy. I call it a mother-ache. On my own, I can work my way out. With someone else, I get locked into loneliness.

The woman writer is juggling on a kitchen chair. Tossing her father's sentences into the air with her mother's and her sister's silence.

I write in the kitchen. Coffee, street noises. I can see a tree through the window. I don't wash my dirty linen at home anymore. It's a public affair. It has to be seen and felt, let everyone know what is soiled and faded and mended.

Femmes fatales. Surely we must be fatal for someone, for something. Yes, I want to be fatal for thwarted love. Fatal for the family, fatal for insurance policies, fatal for our bodyguards. I am surrounded by bodyguards. Protected. Prevented. The body, my body. This is my body.

Little contractions. Release. Little contractions. My tongue is dry. It's hot. I am damp. It starts to flow. Push. Push. Breathe deeply. Relax. It's hot. Again. Enjoy it. Enjoy it. Push. Push. It's a girl.

My closely watched body. Overexcited. Full of electricity. Who does this body belong to? Where will it go? What will she do? Let me through. Let her through. I want to see up close and touch all over.

It is as if the penis and the vagina were two crippled stumps looking for a crutch. Let me through. It's hot. It's overcrowded. Pages are coming out. Words gather around the clitoris.

Every clitoral orgasm proclaims a historical trembling in the body of the species.

Pleasure in my own right with no holy hypocrisy. No ring, no papers. I celebrate on my own time, in my own unlimited space.

Feels good to hear myself talk.

I am not playing a role. I am not playing a role. I am succumbing. That's all. Happy bruised, delirious. I can relax my belligerent stance.

Do we look alike? I think we do. But we have our husbands' mannerisms. You from Outremont. Me from Laval. You from Saint-Henri. Me from Rosemount. We all look alike, it's easy, we all look the part.

It's hot in the galley. The shepherdesses are throwing off their sheep's clothing. There is no time to lose. Impossible to retreat. We must seize the sense and the senses.

All over the body and inside.

I wrote my first poems after my first broken heart.

Petticoats and ponytails. Lamartine and basketball. I started asking questions. That's all. The private life of an adolescent, the private life of an adult. It's all written in the colour of our cheeks. All the secrets shared at four o'clock in the schoolyard. The afternoon on the telephone. My memory is hot. The lampshade is on fire. I'm a little tired after all these questions, all this talk. Afraid that the search will lead to the soft centre of my Self. It's impossible to find the answer all alone. You cannot free a woman without breaking the chains of her childhood. The fear of inevitable death is greater than our worst nightmares. Tonight I cast off without a rope, without arsenic, without acid, without arms, without pills. I sink surrounded by madmen, famous, political, sexual, public madmen.

Bitterness, anger, desire, fatigue, love, longing, paper, words: orgasm, cunt, baby, nocturnal pollution, anxiety. That is what it is all about. And I am hot. I am in heat.

I cannot breathe with my airs of a poet, a *femme fatale*, a fallen angel, a whore, a woman of the world, a charwoman, menopausal matron, calendar dame and diaphragm. I choke on the rumours that say I'm just a pastime, a casual affair.

A species of wild animal to be mounted and tamed.

I liquidate.

Merry-go-round. I turn round and round in my woman's hole.

I'm learning, I'm learning. I'm speaking.

> *The end.*

The Fairies Are Thirsty
(Les Fées ont soif)

by Denise Boucher

translated by Alan Brown

Introduction to
The Fairies Are Thirsty (Les Fées ont soif[1])
by Denise Boucher
Introduced by Louise H. Forsyth

The thirsty fairies of the title *The Fairies Are Thirsty* are women performing in poetic and dramatic celebration their liberation from all forms of patriarchal control and exploitation of their sexuality, their bodies, hearts, and minds. When the play opens, the three characters—the Statue[2], Marie, and Madeleine—are each confined in their own particular space. They represent the three dominant stereotypes of women: virgin, mother, and whore. Like Savard's Marquise, they appear at the beginning of the play to be cast in their role and placed in plaster or marble, particularly the Statue. However, and despite their differences in appearance, state, and activities, these women come to the realization that they share a common condition—that in the eyes of society, girls and women are always personified as virgins: "The good and the bad virgin continue to signal the absence of actual women."[3] Their sexuality does not belong to them. It belongs to men who have given themselves the right to control women's bodies and minds. Women enjoy no legitimacy in seeking their own pleasures. Any action deemed by social standards to be a loss of purity on the part of women is their own fault and deserves punishment, frequently using violent means. Women are expected to marry (and thereby lose their virginal purity), be sexually available to their husbands, produce children, but never touch their own bodies nor achieve orgasmic pleasure. In contravention of such prohibition, nevertheless, the fairies are thirsty. In the course of the action of the play, the three women move out of their boxes, sing and talk together, form friendships, and free themselves from the chains of the harsh symbolism that binds them. These chains derive, of course, from religious traditions, but are also associated in the play with contemporary consumer society and its advertising, as well as with the discourses of medicine, psychiatry, romantic literature, and the law. The play develops thematically a search for the meaning of love and a questioning of the problematic relationship between mothers and children, particularly as mothers have inculcated to their daughters and sons for millennia patriarchal norms, practices and values.

In addition to the characters' particular spaces, the stage is designed with neutral areas to which the characters move as they move away from sociocultural dictates. In fact, as the characters shift to the neutral areas, the actors seem to peek somewhat out from behind their masks to speak on their own terms and to perform their own insights. Character roles are resumed whenever they move back to their official places. Downstage centre is a particularly powerful neutral space to which the characters/ actors move as the ramifications of their collective revolt extend further and further. The characters gather there in the final moments to put an end to their exile from themselves, affirm their right to full sexual pleasure, reject all forms of violence done to their bodies, and "imagine" worlds where they as individuals and women collectively are fully autonomous and alive. They have shared the question asked early in the play by Marie: "Who am I? Who shall I be, as if I had never been," and they are beginning to imagine the ways in which life might be otherwise.

Director Jean-Luc Bastien begins his notes by indicating that *Les Fées ont soif* is "a text that is not written in a way that could be said to be theatrically conventional. So the general sense of the text must first be decoded." He reflects on the scenography, the songs, and the characters' emotions which he sees as providing the guiding principle of the show, and he states that the acting should follow Brecht's distancing approach in that the actors regularly step in and out of their character in order to demonstrate and offer space to reflect upon relevant facts and situations. Bastien's notes indicate that he did not wish to impose prevailing theatrical conventions on a play which he saw as a new departure in theatricality. His *mise en scène* demonstrated the openness and creative approach he brought to the task. It was a matter of collectively discovering theatrical forms and languages that flowed from the feelings and ideas that the characters were formulating as they grew more and more intimately involved in the reflective process that forms the story and actions of the performance: "The entire conception at the level of the *mise en scène* is based on the inner reflection of the characters. It is a reflection that is alive and in action. Thought is in action." [4]

After the opening scene where the half-alive women identify themselves in their oppressive feminine roles, they leave their assigned places to wander in search of their bodies, hearts and heads. Together, they proclaim in song the fact that they are fed up. Scenes alternate throughout the play between the women in their places revealing the unhappy condition of their lives and the social myths that determine this condition and the women in free spaces sharing happy memories, desires, dreams and anger. In two particularly painful scenes, two of the characters take on the role and words of misogynist men doing violence to a woman. Such transformation into different characters is dramatically effective, by illustrating the ways in which women themselves can become handmaidens for systems of patriarchy and misogyny. In the first of these scenes, Madeleine and the Statue become momentarily Marie's viciously abusive husband. In the second scene where the characters turn into violently aggressive men, Marie and the Statue rape Madeleine on the pretext that prostitutes cannot be raped, and in any case she was asking for it/she likes it. In their final song, the three characters lament in song the fear that will now never leave Madeleine, and they inform themselves and the audience that the legal community, like a flock of sparrows rising out of a corn field, was unanimous in failing to find the rapist guilty.

Marie and Madeleine join the Statue, who steps definitively out of her box and declares she has had enough. Celebrating their sexual and intellectual autonomy, the three characters affirm their readiness to love women and men, but only on condition that such love does not require that their desires and emotions to be subsumed under male control.

Montréal audiences flocked to see *Les Fées ont soif*, and there were vast numbers of articles about it in newspapers, on radio and television, and in magazines. However, far from being an appreciation of the dramatic qualities of the play or its powerful feminist message, I believe that most of the attention paid to the show can be attributed to the notoriety surrounding the censorship its production received. Few critics have yet commented on the artistic qualities of *Les Fées ont soif* and its important place in Québec theatre as experimental theatre.

Notes

[1] Boucher, Denise. *Les Fées ont soif*. Montréal: Éditions Intermède, 1978. Tr. Alan Brown. *The Fairies Are Thirsty*. Toronto: Talonbooks, 1982. 2nd edition. *Les Fées ont soif*. Montréal: L'Hexagone, 1989. In 1999 the Réseau Vidé-Elle produced a 97-minute video of *Les Fées ont soif*. *Les Fées ont soif* was first produced on November 10, 1978 at the Théâtre du Nouveau Monde, directed by Jean-Luc Bastien, designed by Marie-Josée Lanoix, music by Jean-François Garneau, with Sophie Clément as Madeleine, Louisette Dussault as The Statue, and Michèle Magny as Marie. Louisette Dussault and Michèle Magny also acted in *La Nef des sorcières* when it was created at the TNM in 1976. (See "About Louisette Dussault" in Introduction to *Mommy* in this volume.) *The Fairies Are Thirsty* was first performed in English at D.B. Clarke Theatre at Concordia University in Montréal on January 27, 1981 in an adaptation by Anne Marie Desrochers, with Irene Arseneault as Marie, Catherine Batchelor as The Statue, and Shelley Spiegel as Madeleine, directed by Holly Dennison, designed by Suzanne Clermont, and music by Jean-François Garneau.

[2] The Statue is a particularly interesting and innovative character, in that she is a clear representation of the immaculate Virgin Mary of Roman Catholicism, but she is also the amalgam of all prevailing symbolic structures and myths—artistic forms, commercial icons of beauty, societal ideals, etc.—that evacuate women's individual characteristics all the better to transform them into ahistorical and immaterial metaphors, archetypes and mythical figures. The Statue's rosary is a heavy rosary that falls with a great clang at several moments through the show.

[3] "La bonne et la mauvaise vierge continuent de marquer l'absence de la femme réelle." Introduction by Denise Boucher, *Les Fées ont soif*: 71. Translated by LHF.

[4] "[…] un texte qui n'est pas théâtralement écrit d'une façon dite conventionnelle. Il faut donc d'abord décoder le sens général du texte […] C'est l'émotion qui est le fil conducteur de chacun des personnages […] Quand au jeu, il doit se faire dans un sens brechtien. Les comédiennes sortent souvent de leur personnage pour réfléchir et démontrer les faits et les situations qui s'y attachent […] Toute la conception au niveau de la mise en scène est basée sur la réflexion intérieure des personnages. C'est une réflexion vivante et en action. La pensée y est en action." "Notes du metteur en scène, Jean-Luc Bastien." *Les Fées ont soif*: 77–79. Translated by LHF.

Bibliographical Suggestions

Selected Other Works by Denise Boucher

Boucher, Denise & Madeleine Gagnon. *Retailles*. Montréal: L'Étincelle, 1977.

———. *Cyprine*. Montréal: Éditions de l'Aurore, 1978.

———. "Et le fruit," *La Nouvelle Barre du Jour*. 196 (mars 1987) *Femmes scandales 1965–1985*: 51–55.

On *Les Fées ont soif* and Denise Boucher

Dramaturges québécoises. Dossiers de Presse. Denise Boucher, 1969–1984. Sherbrooke: Bibliothèque du Séminaire de Sherbrooke, 1986. (88 pages)

Camerlain, Lorraine. "*Les Fées ont soif*." *Cahiers de théâtre. Jeu*. 16 (1980): 217–18.

Sabbath, Lawrence. "Censorship in Montreal." *Canadian Theatre Review*. 20 (Fall 1978): 81–85.

About Denise Boucher

Denise Boucher was born in Victoriaville, Québec in 1935. She received her teaching diploma in Sherbrooke, where she taught, but then moved to Montréal in the late 1950s. She worked as a journalist and script-writer for Radio-Canada. Poet, essayist, playwright, songwriter, performer, she published her first poems in 1976. Some of her songs recorded by Pauline Julien were particularly popular. Her writing has been consistently poetic, allusive, and subversive in her opposition to any and all claims to arbitrary truth or authority. She has been outspoken in her struggle against all forms of violence against women.

In 1978 her name was in all the newspapers and on the lips of many in the months leading up to the production of *Les Fées ont soif* because the Conseil des Arts de la Région Métropolitaine de Montréal withheld its grant to the Théâtre du Nouveau Monde. Authorities objected to the subject matter of *Les Fées*. Suspension of funding in this way was interpreted as censorship by members of the theatre community, whose associations made formal protests, while vast numbers of individuals openly expressed their support for Boucher and the TNM. [1] Artistic Director Jean-Louis Roux did not hesitate in his determination to produce the play, despite official disapproval and absence of public funding. In her statement at the time, Boucher stressed as follows the damage that submissive silence can cause, and the importance of speaking out against censorship and arbitrary, authoritarian decisions:

> I can indeed say this to you that I think my personal enjoyment is complete. Getting to know official censorship in this way is an extraordinary opportunity. It allows the debate to be taken onto the public square. I know so many men, so many and so many women for whom censorship has meant silence for their works. Censorship more oppressive and more deadly than any words. To all of them I say: "Speak out, denounce; it is better, a hundred times better, to be paranoid than masochistic. [2]

Notes

[1] The published text of *Les Fées ont soif* contains copies of documents and clippings of vehement support for Boucher, Roux, and the entire production team (49 pages).

[2] "Participation de Denise Boucher." In *Les Fées ont soif*: 28. "Je puis bien vous le dire, je crois que je jouis. C'est une chance extraordinaire de connaître ainsi la censure officielle. Ça permet de porter le débat sure la place publique. J'en connais tant des hommes, et tant et tant de femmes dont la censure a été le silence sur leurs oeuvres. Censure plus opprimante et plus morbide que toutes les paroles. À tous ceux-là je dis: «prenez la parole, dénoncez, il vaut mieux, cent fois mieux être paranoïaque que masochiste». Translated by LHF.

Les Fées ont soif was first performed at Théâtre du Nouveau Monde, Montréal, Québec, in November 1978, with the following company:

MADELEINE   Sophie Clément
MARIE   Michèle Magny
THE STATUE   Loiusette Dussault

Directed by Jean-Luc Bastien
Set Design by Marie-Josée Lanoix
Lighting Design by Claude Landré
Music by Jean-François Garneau

• • •

Les Fées ont soif was first performed in English at D. B. Clarke Theatre at Concordia University, Montréal, Québec, in January 1981, with the following company:

MADELEINE   Shelley Spiegel
MARIE   Irene Arseneault
THE STATUE   Catherine Batchelor

Directed by Holly Dennison
Set Design by Don Childs
Costume Design by Suzanne Clermont
Music by Jean-François Garneau
Adapted by Anne Marie Desrochers

Characters

MADELEINE
MARIE
THE STATUE

THE FAIRIES ARE THIRSTY

Each character is in her own place.

THE STATUE   I am the desert, grain after grain after grain. I recite myself, bead after bead.

MARIE   I feel like a rain that cannot fall. Could I shed my skin? Could I find myself elsewhere?

MADELEINE   I'm marking time, going nowhere. Life makes me curdle.

ALL THREE   (*sung to a Gregorian melody, nasally and ironically*)
Ah ah ah ah,
Ah ah ah ah,
All wo-men.
Ah ah ah ah,
Ah ah ah ah—
So are we.

THE STATUE   I lick the drip of your denegation.

MARIE   I am the feather gravy of the objects of your sociological investigations.

MADELEINE   I'm a naughty subject.

THE STATUE   What's that, so heavy on my shoulders?

MARIE   I'm fed up with taking valium.

MADELEINE   What the hell d'ya do about a day-old hangover?

MARIE   Who am I? Who shall I be, as if I had never been.

MADELEINE   On the stove, the coffee gurgles, like my gut.

MARIE   Do you hear the music of the old leaky saucepans?

THE STATUE   The veils of the temple slap like old, wet flags…

Pause.

The air is thick tonight.

MARIE   My name is Marie. They glorify my maternity, but what about me? Me, they can't abide.

MADELEINE   I'm the whore with a heart of gold. So they say. Men say. Who's going to let me love him? Who's going to give himself to me?

THE STATUE   I'm the desert, grain after grain after grain. I recite myself, day after day.

MARIE   I think I'll take a valium.

MADELEINE I'm fed up with boozing.

MARIE It's always the same old thing. It never changes. And I thought I'd do better than my mother.

THE STATUE Who, me?

MARIE I'm not much farther ahead than she was.

MADELEINE Whaddya expect to change? Us, maybe?

MARIE *(laughing)* And we saw the victim who began to change.

> *They leave their places and go to a neutral place.*

Song of the Odyssey

ALL THREE *(singing)*
(Refrain)
If this song appears to you
Made out of chords bitter and sad,
Voices of great disillusion,
Lyrics of loss and defeat,
Have mercy upon us,
Have mercy upon you.

Truth is in distant exile,
Beauty imperiled far away.
Love lies on its deathbed
And we are in search
Of our bodies, of our hearts, of our minds.

You can see us half alive—
Women gagged, women beaten,
Women outraged and alienated.
Our passions have burned
And sweet Penelope is just fed up.

(refrain)

You can see us women lost,
Mad, demented and born strangers.
What are we doing on this earth
Full of wars and scandals?
Could we change the course of destiny?

MADELEINE *(speaking)* We call on you, Jackie,
On you, Mary, on you, Suzanne,
On you, Peggy, Linda, on you,
On you Maggie, on you, Lisa,
On you, Rosalynn, on you, Bob.

MARIE   *(speaking)* We call on you, Pat,
On you, Liz, on you, Michelle,
On you, Doris, on you, Lila,
On you, Gloria, on you, Shirley,
On you, Annie, on you, Jimmy.

THE STATUE   *(speaking)* We call on you, Margarita,
On you, Germaine, on you Melina,
On you, Maureen, on you, Jane,
On you, Jo Anne, on you, Rachel,
On you, Kate, and Joe, on you.

ALL THREE   *(singing the refrain)*
If this song appears to you
Made out of words fragile but true,
Voices of great and growing hope,
Lyrics of searching and prayer,
Take care, take care of yourself
Let us take care of ourselves.

> *Each woman goes to her own place.*

THE STATUE   Once upon a time, there was a day. And that's today. And I'm about to unsing the whole Angelus.

MARIE   My house is clean, clean, clean. My name is Marie. I do my errands. You've met me at the shopping centre.

MADELEINE   I chuck spermatozoa out the window.

> *Pause.*

I'm sorry, your three minutes are up.

> *Pause.*

With my blood of the full moon.
Each of your children drips away. Poor Fatherland.

THE STATUE   As I said in Fatima: "Poor Canada!"

MADELEINE   Sorry, your three minutes are up!

MARIE   In the shopping centres, they sell cute bathing suits.
Skimpy bikinis.
I could never stand being alone beside the sea. I'm far too scared. The waves roll toward me. They want to talk to me. I'd never want to be alone beside the sea. I'm far too scared. The waves could take me in their folds and carry me where I don't want to go. I am the woman of the house.

THE STATUE   Whose house?

MARIE   I listen to my transistor. In winter, I go to Florida with my husband. He
plays golf.

THE STATUE   *(singing)* Some day my prince will come…

MADELEINE   At the reform school they told me, Madeleine, make a woman out
of yourself.
I never knew what that meant.

>   *Pause.*

I am the menstrual floodway of the thundering, breaking ice.
Dried coffee in the bottom of a cup that no one ever washed.
I am a hole. I am a hole. I am a big hole where they shove their money.
A big hole in a closed hoop that shrinks round my skull.
But I can see through the hole. There are days I'd like to believe in love.
Before they turned me loose in the world from the reform school, they decided
to have me treated.
The sick-guyatrist, he wanted to fuck me. Pretty funny for a voyeur!
But I told him, I said: "For you, shithead, it'll cost you. One thousand bucks.
Per shot."
He found I was a serious case. "Incurable," he said.
Then he wouldn't see me anymore.
That's how I came to be a lady of pleasure.

THE STATUE   Whose pleasure?

MADELEINE   There are days when something in me tries to believe in love.

THE STATUE   *(singing)* Some day my prince will come…

MARIE   *(in her neutral place)* When I was twelve, what did I want?… Adolescence
is a sickness. Better not remember it. The fewer desires I had, the sooner I'd be
a grown-up. No problem. Now, I think, I have NO DESIRE AT ALL. Except
those you give me. The new discoveries I like are the new soaps that get your
clothes whiter than white. Dish soap that keeps your hands ever so smooth.
Just as if you never touched those dishes…. What more could I ask from life?…
And as far as husbands go, there are worse ones than mine. But what good are
husbands anyway?

(singing to the tune of "I's the b'y that builds the boat")
I's the gal that mops the floor
An' keeps us clean and tidy.
He's the b'y that lays in bed
An' takes a bath on Friday.

(refrain)
Diddle-ee-us dee eye-dee-oh,
Diddle ee-um dee eye-dee.

Diddle-ee-us dee eye-dee-oh,
He takes his bath on Friday.

I's the gal that bakes the cake
An' everythin' else he wishes.
He's the b'y that drinks the beer
An' never does the dishes.

(refrain)

I's the gal that scrubs the wash
And irons every Monday.
He's the b'y that makes the dirt
And kicks my ass on Sunday.

(refrain)

MADELEINE   I'm not a gal that goes around collecting souvenirs.
Boxes full of photos or love letters tied in a little pink ribbon.
Not that I've had that many. But a few…
Just the same: "Yours forever if you want me"…

Two things, I did keep. My first rag doll.
Called, like me, Mad…. My pretty little Madeleine.
And I kept the first pair of sheets I got paid for sleeping between.
One day, I de-baptized my doll and locked her in a box.
Then, in another box, I put away that pair of sheets. Full of chiz…
I kept 'em so I could give 'em back.
Give 'em back to that guy.
I figger some day I'm going to see him again.

And then I'll give 'em back.
He paid for 'em.
They belong to him, those goddamn sheets.
I'll give 'em back to him…. Just to see his face.

THE STATUE   *(In place of a rosary, she has a thick chain between her fingers.)*
As for me, I am an image, I am a portrait.
My two feet stuck fast in plaster.
I am the Queen of Nothingness. I am the door to the abyss.
I am the priests' wet dreams.
I am the white sheep, the white ewe unshorn.
I am the star of the bitter sea.
I am the dream of ammonia.
I am the daughter of Mr. Clean.
I am the mirror of injustice.
I am the seat of slavery.
I am the sacred vessel, never lost and still unfound.
I am the darkness of ignorance.

I am the eye of the white tornado.
I am the refuge of imbeciles, the succour of the ineffectual.
I am the tool of impotence.
I am the rotting symbol of rotten abnegation.
I am a silence heavier and more oppressive than any words.
I am the yoke of those jealous of the flesh.
I am the image imagine. I am she who has no body.
I am she who never bleeds.

> *MARIE sings a few lines* from "La Fille de l'île" by Félix Leclerc, then returns to her place.*

THE STATUE   They gave me a bird to be my groom.
Century after century, they stole away my son.
They gave him a bachelor father, jealous and eternal.
They carved me in marble and had me bear down with my weight on the serpent.
I am the ultimate alibi of failed desire.
They gave me a bird as my groom.
They carved me in marble and had me bear down with my weight on the serpent.

> *Pause.*

No one ever breaks my image.
They recreate me over and over.
Who will deface my image?
Have I no daughter anywhere to liberate me, de-virginate me?

> *THE STATUE lets her rosary slip. It falls with a tremendous sound, out of proportion to its weight.*

MADELEINE   A mute woman can't talk. But I just heard something.

THE STATUE   In the name of the Father and the Son and the Holy Prick.
Brrr! The air is raw. It's damp inside my statue.
I am in the trees. Among the nests.
I see myself seeing myself having been Eve.
I see myself seeing him having been Adam.
I see myself seeing what never existed.
I see myself seeing his Adam's apple bobbing up and down faster as he hears what I have to say.

MARIE   In my throat, I have a song.
In my throat, as well, a cat that eats my song.
In my head, I have an idea.
And in my head, as well, a kind of order that eats my idea.

---

*   See stanza six of the song at
http://www.sinteticor.com/artist_f/felix_leclerc_lyrics/la_fille_de_lile_lyrics.html

MADELEINE   (*going toward the neutral place*) Heavy on my heart is a turd that
will not let me yodel (yodel ay-ee hoo).
My feet are stuck in shit and cannot jig away my freeeeeeeeedom.
Beee-cause.

THE STATUE   To speak, I must come down from my tree.

Madeleine's Song

MADELEINE   (*singing*) *The guys don't look no more*
At a girl as skinny as me.
My mom don't write no more,
One little drink and I'm free.

All my girlfriends are married.
Me, it never came to pass.
I never dream of wedding Mass,
Like death, it sticks in—my ass.

I was scared of having a kid.
I never told my lovers.
When I had the abortion done,
I never told my lovers.

Never found the man for me.
He must be around somewhere.
I wait and I drink, I drink and I wait,
But sixty will be—too late.

What if I left for the city?
There's all kinds to be had,
Maybe a city slicker, I dunno,
Something not too bad.

But I'm just a little whore
And my tongue sometimes runs over.
But I'd like to hear myself called "mother"
And have a kind husband for my lover.

> *MADELEINE and MARIE talk to each other as if they were talking from*
> *one balcony to the next.*

Christ, are you alone? You too?
Wanna have a drink together?
Come on, have a beer with me.

MARIE   Thank you, but I can't.
You can't mix beer and valium.

MADELEINE   Well, I'll have a little drink alone. I'm used to it. Goddamn, I'm
used to it.
I won't take customers today.

Why should I hide it? You know what I do. But I'm tired today.
Like I got the blues.
I get a spell like this once or twice a year.
As a rule, I keep it all inside.
But sometimes, it just bobs up like a drowned man.
Maybe it's the curse.
When I'm indisposed, that's the way it is.

       THE STATUE goes to her neutral place.

THE STATUE   *(in a TV commercial voice)* On those special days, ladies, feel free thanks to Tantax. Ride horseback, play tennis, go for a swim. Tantax is discreet. Tantax protects. Tantax doesn't hinder your movements. On those special days, ladies, use Tantax. Be up to date. Feel free! Use Tantax. Be Tantax.

MADELEINE   Don't know if you're like me on those days. But there's no way they're gonna tell me their tampons are some kind of vitamin or Geritol. Those days, I'm swollen up and constipated and depressed. Those days, I'd just like to lock myself in my room and pull down the blinds.
You too?

MARIE   Me too. I always know when it's coming. I feel heavy. And then I get a great fat pimple on my face. Right here. Those days, I don't go out.

MADELEINE   I don't ever see you go out much. Looks to me like you're always home.

MARIE   I go out the odd time. Just to go shopping. When I can't stand to be alone anymore.
That's all there is to it. When I catch myself talking to nobody, talking to myself. Yesterday morning, there I was, talking to my toaster.

MADELEINE   *(laughing)* Dear toaster, if I'm speaking to you this morning, it's to let you know…

MARIE   You seem like somebody who's always in a good mood.

MADELEINE   I'm pretty good-natured.

MARIE   You know, I've noticed something. You're always well-dressed. I've noticed. And you have all kinds of nice leather things. And boots.

MADELEINE   Yeah, I got a bunch of boots. All colours. Especially high boots. Did you notice? They're sexier than shoes. Sexier? I dunno why…
I'll drink to that.
You know, you look kind of delicate to me.

MARIE   Oh, my health is okay. I guess I'm bored and that makes me look sick. Seems I get more and more bored all the time.
When the housework's done…
TV, I enjoy it less and less.

Even the love stories…
Whose hand is this, whose hair, whose flesh?

THE STATUE   They said the flesh was a sin against the spirit. And they locked me up in the very heart of the apple's flesh.

> *MARIE moves toward the neutral place.*

MARIE   Between the fridge and stove,
Between the stove and fridge,
I wait and take a pill.
I take a pill between the fridge
And the stove.
And I wait for you
Between the fridge and the stove,
Between the stove and fridge.
I wait for you and take my pill.
The walls close in on me
And I take my pill.

> *Silence. She goes back to her own place.*

It's strange, I had two kids and it's as if my flesh had never been traversed.
Do I have to turn inside myself for ecstasy?

THE STATUE   Poor little girl. Perhaps you had your orgasm… perhaps you've just forgotten. They put me inside your bodies with all their holy images and medals, with blackmail, threats, promises and commercials. In the psychiatric hospitals, there are many women who think they are me. Or Miss Clairol…
I have to get out of this thing.

MADELEINE   *(in the neutral place)* I made love in such a place at such a time with Don Juan.
I made love in such a place at such a time with Casanova.
I made love in such a place at such a time with the Six Million Dollar Man.
I made love in such a place at such a time with the Phantom.
I made love in such a place at such a time with Mr. Leslie Quick.
I made love in such a place at such a time with Tarzan.
And even if I've been deflowered, I still crave the taste of virginity.

> *She sings "Plaisir d'amour ne dure qu'un moment" by Jean-Pierre Claris de Florian.*

(in the neutral place) You know, I understand Marilyn Monroe…
I'm just like her. Looking for beauty.
In search of all the qualities of seduction. I'd like to be beautiful. I want to be desirable. And at the same time, I should be unattainable.
I'd like to see me as transparent.
Virginal. So virginal.
Like a nun with her pale face and her small, soft hands…

The convent. Safe from the world and its filth…
In my body, I have tried all absences.
I would like to be thin and fleshless. I would like to be a scaffolding of bones, devoid of flesh.
I would like to have the least possible body.
I have never been thin enough or fragile or translucent. Always had too much body…
And I like cheesecake.

THE STATUE   And I eat apples. I eat apples. I eat apples.

MADELEINE   *(going back to her own place)* I've always had too much body for their sexes and their hands that grasp and want and never stop. I have introjected, yes, introjected their desires without ever making them come true. And I have been a whore. A hooker. A prostitute. A call girl. A courtesan. A cunt.
I have sunk into their follies, but never found my own.
I have been waiting for myself for so long.

> *Each woman is in her own place.*

THE STATUE   Waiting.

MARIE   Waiting.

MADELEINE   Waiting.

THE STATUE   Talking to nobody.

MARIE   Waiting for nothing.

MADELEINE   Love no one.

THE STATUE   Talking.

MARIE   Singing.

MADELEINE   Dancing.

THE STATUE   Love.

MARIE   Gaiety.

MADELEINE   Liberty.

THE STATUE   Waiting.

MARIE   Being bored.

MADELEINE   Crying.

THE STATUE   Because.

MARIE   Who am I?

MADELEINE   Who am I?

All three put on straitjackets as they go toward the neutral place.

The Song of Let's Suppose

THE STATUE   *(singing)*
>   *Let's say*
>   *I'm the prettiest girl in the world.*

MADELEINE   *(singing)*
>   *Let's say*
>   *I'm the smartest girl in the world.*

MARIE   *(singing)*
>   *Let's say*
>   *I'm the girl who never gets old.*

THE STATUE   *(singing)*
>   *Let's say*
>   *All my hair is blonde.*

MARIE   *(singing)*
>   *Let's say*
>   *I don't remind you of my mother.*

MADELEINE   *(singing)*
>   *Let's say*
>   *I have long legs, like a nymph.*
>   *Let's say*
>   *My rags are never red.*

>   *A rhythmic chorus comes in—the voices of the musicians.*

ALL THREE   *(singing)*
>   *(chorus)*
>   *Let's say that…*
>   *Suppose that…*
>   *Let us say…*
>   *Let's fancy…*

>   *This chorus is repeated until the end of the song.*

MARIE   *(singing)*
>   *Let's say*
>   *I can make babies at will.*
>   *Let's say*
>   *I'm a wild wife in bed.*

THE STATUE   *(singing)*
>   *Let's say*
>   *I can be like a sister*
>   *Let's say*
>   *I can be a perfect comrade.*

Let's say
I would never rebel.
Let's say
I would never drop a dirty word.

ALL THREE   *(singing)*
Let's say
I'm not a riddle.

MADELEINE   *(singing)*
Let's say
The most submissive one of all—that's me.

MARIE   *(singing)*
Let's say
I shone like a Holy Virgin.

MADELEINE   *(singing)*
Let's say
I become your very best mattress.

ALL THREE   *(singing)*
Let's suppose…
Just imagine…
Say for example…
What if we…

MARIE   *(singing)*
D'you think I'd stand a chance?

MADELEINE   *(singing)*
D'you think I'd stand a chance?

THE STATUE   *(singing)*
D'you think I'd stand a chance?

ALL THREE   *(singing)*
Say for example…
What if we…
Just imagine…
Let's suppose…

MARIE   *(singing)*
D'you think the doctor'd sign my leave?

MADELEINE   *(Singing)*
D'you think the doctor'd sign my leave?

THE STATUE   *(singing)*
D'you think the doctor'd sign my leave?

> *Each woman returns to her own place.*

MADELEINE   Everybody sez yer crazy.

MARIE   Everybody sez I'm crazy. I ain't crazy. No, I ain't crazy. For sure, I ain't crazy. Ain't crazy. That's for sure. For sure. I ain't crazy. Hell, I ain't crazy. I ain't crazy. I ain't just some old crazy. They'll see, I ain't just some old crazy.

THE STATUE   Everybody sez I'm a saint. I ain't no saint. No, I ain't no saint. For sure, I ain't no saint. That's for sure. For sure, I ain't no saint. Hell, I ain't no saint. I ain't just some old saint. They'll see, I ain't just some old saint.

MADELEINE   Everybody sez I'm hysterical. I ain't hysterical. No, I ain't hysterical. For sure, I ain't hysterical. Not hysterical. I ain't hysterical. For sure. For sure. For sure, I ain't hysterical. Hell, I ain't hysterical. I ain't hysterical. I ain't just some old hysterical. They'll see, I ain't just some old hysterical.

MARIE   But I'm afraid.

> *She moves slowly toward the neutral place.*
>
> *The characters speak to a counting rhyme.*

THE STATUE   Afraid.

MARIE   Afraid of being crazy.

MADELEINE   Afraid of being alone.

MARIE   Afraid of being ugly.

MADELEINE   Afraid of getting fat.

THE STATUE   Afraid of knowing too much.

MARIE   Afraid to touch myself.

MADELEINE   Afraid to laugh too much.

MARIE   Afraid to cry.

THE STATUE   Afraid to talk.

MARIE   Afraid they'll laugh at me.

MADELEINE   Afraid of being a slut.

MARIE   Afraid of being frigid.

MADELEINE   Afraid to enjoy it.

MARIE   Afraid to not enjoy it.

MADELEINE   Afraid to be free.

MARIE   Afraid of him.

THE STATUE   Afraid of mice.

THE STATUE   Fear.

MARIE   Dread.

MADELEINE   Fright.

THE STATUE   Horror.

MARIE   Let's talk. Talk. Talk. More words.
Hymns. Songs. Dances. Laughter. Tears.
Let's hammer at the wall of silence.

THE STATUE   Open the shutters of our words. Evil by evil.
Guilt by guilt. Fear by fear.

MADELEINE   Fear. Terror. Dread. Fright. Horror. Panic.

MARIE   Panic fear. It swells. It slides into the marrow of our bones.

THE STATUE   Stop driving me crazy.

> *THE STATUE goes back to her own place. MARIE and MADELEINE move to the front of the stage.*

MARIE   Stop worrying me.

MADELEINE   Lemme be.

MARIE   Oh Grandmother, what a big mouth you have!

THE STATUE   *(with a big jolly Santa voice)* Ho, ho, ho! The better to eat you with, my dears.

MARIE & MADELEINE   Mummy, I'm scared!

Song to Father Christmas

MARIE   *(singing in her neutral place)*
(refrain)
When you climb down
My long chimney
Without ringing my bell,
Dear Santa Claus,
Ain't no presents for me at the foot of your tree.

You know I'm not made
Like some kind of toy,
But Santa Claus doesn't know,
And your star-fairy
Is freezing outside
Alone
Oh, tell me why!

The snow falls white,
Falsely loved, falsely greeted
On the anguish,
On the distress

Of a long forgotten bird.
Lost bird.

(refrain)

I didn't leave, I really didn't leave,
And yet, and yet,
I had the dream
That kids would bind us
Back together
And make us friends.
Oh, little children!

I miss you now, I miss me now,
I miss our loving…
Miss our loving,
And in anguish,
Your star-fairy freezes outside
Alone.

(finale)

But I believed in Santa Claus!

MADELEINE   Good God, Marie, what's the matter?

MARIE   He beat me up. He came home drunk this morning. He wanted his breakfast right away.

> *THE STATUE and MADELEINE play the husband in a neutral place.*

THE STATUE   Fat slob.

MADELEINE   The toast is burning.

THE STATUE   Idiot.

MADELEINE   Can't ya look what you're doin'?

MARIE   I waited up for you the whole night.

THE STATUE   D'ya know what you cost me just in burned bread in a year?

MARIE   I didn't sleep a wink.

MADELEINE   You should take a look at yourself.

MARIE   Marcel, Marcel. I waited up all night. I didn't sleep a wink. I was so worried. And you didn't come. I was waiting for you.

MADELEINE   She waited for me. You're a bear for punishment, waitin' up like that.

THE STATUE   Are you crazy? You're just like your Ma.

MADELEINE   Why don't you just bugger off.

THE STATUE   I've had enough of you.

MADELEINE   Stupid bitch.

MARIE   Marcel, Marcel!

THE STATUE   Haven't even got a clean shirt.

MADELEINE   Where the hell are my socks?

MARIE   Marcel, Marcel!

THE STATUE   You went and shaved your goddamn armpits again with my razor, ya crazy bitch.

MARIE   Marcel, Marcel!

MADELEINE   Is that breakfast nearly ready?

THE STATUE   And get me a beer, now you're up.

MADELEINE   With some tomato juice.

MARIE   Yes, okay, Marcel.

THE STATUE   Cut out the bawling and get a move on.

MADELEINE   I work all night on those guys to get that contract and what thanks do I get from you?

MARIE   Marcel, Marcel! Don't talk so loud.
Don't shout those names at me. That hurts, you know.

MADELEINE   I've had enough of an old twat like you. If I wanted, I could have two like you, just like that.

THE STATUE   An' not like you, neither.

MADELEINE   Young chicks, eighteen, who like to screw.

THE STATUE   Who *like* to screw.

MADELEINE   You're a goddamn masochist.

> *MADELEINE and THE STATUE imitate the sound of beating, slapping.*

MARIE   *(raising her head)* And I told him again: "Marcel, I love you!"

THE STATUE   Women have always loved the most disgusting bastards.

> *THE STATUE goes back to her own place.*

MARIE   *(in her own place)* A man. A husband. A brute.
Where does love come in?

MADELEINE   *(with MARIE)* Love! It's their protection racket.
They're all pimps.
Have no fear, your man is here.

MARIE   But what's in his head all that time?

MADELEINE   In his head? Nothing at all. His head is just a garage where he parks his precious phallus.

THE STATUE   *(in her own place)* I am the immaculate in all of their conceptions.
I am the inarticulate in all of their obsessions.
Men are afraid of the flower that blooms between their legs.
That's why he beats you. That's why I was invented.
When men are frightened of the void, they invented God.

MARIE   What am I doing, staying in this place?
Am I going to wait till he kills me?
Maybe I don't know how to get around him.
Maybe I never understood him.
It must be my fault if I provoke him so much. I'll have to try a little harder.
Maybe he wants more children…
I think that would bring us back together.

MADELEINE   Tell it to the Queen Mother.

MARIE   The Queen Mother?

> *THE STATUE walks to its neutral place and sings.*

The Ballad of the Birds

THE STATUE   *(singing)*
When the great bluejay passes,
A red rose in his beak,
He fills me with promises
And constant wishes
To be my lover
He teaches me his way,
Teaches me how to love.
He's bringing me the moon,
The sun in his own hands.

(refrain)
I don't get high on men,
I don't get high on women,
I don't get high on money,
I do get high on birds.

Oh, when the white dove flies
And flutters over my bed,
I'm wakened by its wing.
When I hear it sing,
My rose-tree blooms.
Dear lady, have no fear,
Don't give up the ghost.

So then, my belly swelled,
And soon the bird was flown.

(refrain)

When the vultures circle,
There's a cross in my cry.
Judges betrayed him,
Cool soldier nailed him
To the pillory.
Crows in their black flight
Tear the sky apart.
My life is bled away.
The blackbird mourns the day.

(refrain)

When the nightingale sings,
Do you hear what I say?
He speaks of all my pain.
To love too much is to love in vain.
My lover ran away.
And my baby dear,
Oh daughter, can you hear?
Your mother's on her knees.
What sparrow has her ear?

MARIE   *(in her own place)*
Oh, oh, oh, I feel as if I'm a box of Corn Flakes.
Maybe if Mummy's little baby opened up the Corn Flakes box, he'd find a nice li'l toy or a hockey player's picture in there.
Mummy's pretty li'l baby. And he's got a nice mummy. She's the most beautiful mummy in the world. And Mummy's li'l baby's beautiful too.

Tell Mummy, is Mummy's pretty li'l baby a pretty little Jesus? Kitchy-kitchy-koo. You're a fine li'l boy.
When he grows up is he going to be Mummy's friend?
When he grows up is the little boy gonna be, gonna be strong like... like his mummy? Or Tarzan?
Now the li'l boy is goin' back to sleep! Going bye-bye!

I feel like bread dough that doesn't want to rise. And yet, it's spring, But I've got no spring left in me. The glories of motherhood don't keep *me* in the peak of form, that's for sure. Maybe I'm not normal. Is it always going to be like this?...

Now Mummy's going to tell you a story. Once upon a time, there was a little boy who was very, very strong. He was playing outside. The strong wind tries to throw him down. But the little boy was faster and stronger and more powerful than the wind.

He fought with the wind for a long time.

Then he started running, fast, fast, fast. He ran in the house and slammed the door before the wind could get him.

And the strong little boy ran into his mother's arms to tell her how strong he was...

I feel like a moron. Useless. I've no ambition left. That baby—even when he's asleep, he takes all the life out of me. Oh, Mother, how did you do it all?

MADELEINE   *(in her place, drunk)* Once upon a time, there was a pizza dough as light as a little girl, and it was whirled at arm's end by an Italian gentleman who knew how to make it flip and twirl. The dough, like a little girl, whirled and twirled faster and faster, and finally, took flight until she was safe and sound high up in the sky. And the Italian gentleman is still looking for his dough...

A beautiful little girl.

Oh, I'd rock myself as you rock a child. Slowly, gently.

And have the smell of that fresh body in my arms.

A little girl.

Two little girls.

And a little boy, too.

Three children. I'd like to have three children. Oh, I'd like to rock myself as you rock a child. Little babies. Little cribs. Little hands.

Little voices saying: "Mummy."

"Mummy, the little boats, just see—they're sailing on the sea..."

Oh, I'd like to rock myself as you rock a child.

And you, all the little babies I never had, I'll rock you too.

>   *Pause.*

When my cat has kittens in her box beside my bed, I have the feeling that all the stars begin to weep.

>   *Pause.*

A double scotch, please. Your star-fairy's got herself a thirst.

THE STATUE   All of my children were subtracted from me.

All of my children torn away.

MARIE   *(in her neutral place)* Dear Freud, I'm not in search of my father. I know him well. I'm searching for my mother, the one like me, the one who's just like me. My mother, my stranger. Who parted us, dear mother? You from me? You from you?

THE STATUE   You, me.

MARIE   You.

THE STATUE   Me.

MARIE   You, divided in yourself? And me, in myself?

THE STATUE   Me. You.

MARIE   Mother. You taught me to be clean and feminine and distinguished. And pure… to the point of neutrality.

THE STATUE   I did?

MARIE   I got trapped in your stories.
I know how much you cried. You cried and your tears taught you nothing. For the sake of virtue, Mother. What is virtue worth? You said once:
"We're always somebody's servant." Well, I don't want to be. I love the baby. But all day long alone with him, Mother, I can't take it. I'm bored. Mother, I'm wasting away.
You, who suffered so much from your submission, why did you teach me to submit as well? It makes no sense, Mother. Somewhere there's something you didn't tell me. You thought you were the Virgin Mary. The one with all the suffering. You loved the priests.
They turned you away from your body, from your man and from me. They robbed you of your being. Mother, I'm searching for my mother. Mother, tell me what battles we once lost to end up less than doormats.
Was the battle ever fought, Mother?
You were made for loving, but they turned you into a matron. How, mother, do you speak the mother tongue? They said it was a mother tongue. But it was their language. It was built to communicate their will and their philosophy.

THE STATUE   They were the eunuchs of the prophet. Eunuchs of the mind and flesh.

MARIE   They lied to you, Mother. Their language doesn't belong to us. It has words for what I'm seeking. It hides my identity. My whole body aches for the secret place inside of me. For your secret place that you could never show me. Mother, if I can't find you, how can I ever find myself? I long for the woman who is locked up inside of you.
Mother. Mother. Mother, I'd like to sleep once again in your arms. I want to be close to you.
To find the true voice of our real wombs. Mother, I'd like to peel myself like an orange.
I'd like to rip off your policeman's skin.
I'd like to strip myself layer by layer until I'm bathing in our soul.
Mother, Mother. Come and find me!

MADELEINE   Mummy, come and get your little girl.

THE STATUE   My poor little loves, poor babies.
All those men who wanted to be God, or gods, have undone my womb and the love that warmed my arms, my hands, my thighs, my eyes, my breasts.

> *Each woman is in her neutral place. They speak in counterpoint.*

MADELEINE   Prison.

MARIE   Fam-il-y.

MADELEINE   Re-li-gion.

MARIE   Prison.

ALL THREE   Our tears
  Do not corrode
  The bars of these our prisons,
  The bars of these our prisons.
  We are po-li-ti-cal pri-son-ers.
  We, the mo-thers, the pro-sti-tutes, the saints,
  We are po-li-ti-cal prisoners,
  Like women who have killed their husbands.

MADELEINE   It was him or me.

MARIE   I bent so far I had to break.

ALL THREE   We are po-li-ti-cal pri-so-ners,
  Our tears do not cor-rode the bars of these our pri-sons.

> *THE STATUE goes back to her own place.*

MADELEINE   One day, the March Hare said to Alice: "If you don't stop crying, you'll drown in your own tears."

MARIE   *(in her own place)* If I followed each of my tears back to its source, where would I be? What's the use? From one flood to the next. I've had enough. I've seen enough of these four walls. I'm going to take a close look at this life I lead.

> *MARIE goes to her neutral place and turns toward THE STATUE.*

Could you look after the kids awhile? I got something important to do.

THE STATUE   Calvaire! You're not going to do like your brothers and get your freedom over your mothers' dead bodies.

> *MARIE drops her apron, which makes the same noise as THE STATUE's chain. She closes her place and leaves.*

Song of the Nunc Dimittis

MARIE   *(singing)*
  (refrain)
  Oh husband dear, your turn to worry.
  I'm leaving this place in a hurry
  'Cause it smells of death in here.
  I leave you with the children…
  Your turn to care.

  You turned my years
  To one long night—one long black night.
  Half-waking now,

I go alone to see the light
Of my desires—I'll count the number
Ever after, and ever after,
Live in laughter.

(refrain)

It's fare thee well,
Goodbye old friend. Bear no ill will
Beyond the end.
I want the sun to rise for me,
To feed on joy. And now I'm free
To breathe each breath—to breathe each breath
Forgetting death.

(refrain)

While I'm away,
Stay warm, stay warm.
Sing tenderly
'Cause I'll return
Some day. Some day.
When I find love—
Love for myself.
When I find love in the best way,
With our young ones
On a new day.

MADELEINE   Oh, mothers, mothers! There's not one like another. But they're all the same!
Mine had nine kids. I was the oldest. And my dad…. When you don't have no schooling, the kids keep coming. It's all you know how to do.
When my ma was overtired an' fed up with the house and being poor, and dreaming how things could be better, she'd say: "I'm sick and tired of dreaming. I can't imagine how it's going to work and I don't know when." Poor Ma. Then she'd go out and she'd find a brick somewhere and let it fly at a window.
Then she'd laugh. And the police'd come.
They'd take her away to jail an' then to the hospital. Where they kept the crazies.
There, my ma would take a big long bath.
An' she'd go to bed. And sleep.
She didn't answer their questions. She wouldn't take their pills. But she'd sleep.
What a hell of an old girl she was!

THE STATUE   I had my old dream again last night. The sun was out and *she* was shining strong in the sky. And the sky was so beautiful, it was as if *she* were all my insides. There were impatiences that laughed into blossom. I told them: "Quiet, be quiet…. My son is dead. And he beat me with his Cross." All my daughters wept. I told them: "Quiet. Be quiet." And they too looked at me with spiteful eyes. Then I tried to hide from the sun. I looked for an egg to hide in. But I couldn't find her. Anywhere. And I said: "For a change, you have to find an egg. A red egg."

Has anyone seen a red egg? And not a bird in the sky?

> *MARIE at the beginning is in her neutral place facing the audience, then she goes toward MADELEINE.*

MARIE Madeleine, Madeleine.

Listen, Madeleine, I've left home…
Just the way you see me…. Left.
And I'm not even upset. Not as much as I thought…
I left a week ago…
Yeah, I'm on my own now. I rented a tourist room on St. Louis Square…
I've walked and walked and walked. And thought. And slept.
The first day, y'know?…
The first day was like I'd always been alone in the world…
Just nothin'. Just walking, nothing in my head…
I felt like a can of tomato soup.
Just a small red spot, that's all.

THE STATUE They took all my reds away and made red the colour of shame.

MARIE I wonder how I managed to live with him so long. Eight years, that's a long time.
I think I know what eternity is like.
It makes me shiver, looking back, to think what could have happened to me in that house.
I went to the tobacco store on the corner, I looked at the newspaper stand. And I realized I'd left so as not to end up in *Allô Police!*
There were things I took for granted, but now they make no goddamn sense.
Before we got married, when I went out with him, d'ya know what he'd tell me? He'd say: "If you run out on me, I'll kill you." And me—what a turkey—I'd say: "If you leave me, I'll kill myself."
I was always the one getting killed, coming or going.
Y'know, his mother said to me once, after a big fight: "You'll see, Marie, a mother's always a coward with her own child. She'll forgive anything at all. But you don't have to be a coward."
That day, it was like she gave me permission to leave him. As if I still needed her permission.
But now, I'm only thinking about the kids. Seems I've fallen out of one trap and into another.

THE STATUE They invented me to get the share of God that they had coming to them. For my own part, I played along with the little game. Irresponsible in my guilt. The anguish—too much anguish—at bringing a child into the light, and at the same time, into darkness. Because I gave him life, they said his death was my fault too. I was responsible for all the deaths in the world. What happened to my loves, between life and death? Oh, this damned statue. I'll crack it apart, burst it wide open. Get me out of this statue! Let me free myself!

MADELEINE   *(in her place, with MARIE)* Since I've known you, Marie, I haven't stopped thinking. You've put ideas into my head.
I understand you.
I'm tempted to kick all my customers out the door.
Open up a little business. A little dry goods store. I love nice cloth. Silk. Velvet. Fine cotton. Hey! Maybe we could open it together! I've come to hate their sex like a cookie-dipper hates chocolate.

> *MADELEINE pours herself a drink.*

When I can put a name on what I lack, I'll know what I need. And I've got something trotting around in my head.

> *MADELEINE is now standing in her neutral place. From now on, when she says, "Marie, Marie," she will speak to all the women in the audience.*

As a rule, it's after the second glass of scotch that all my balloons bust. That's when I see through my fiction like a flash of lightning. And the truth is there. Man after man comes into my bed and leaves again. Not one of them is sensual. A sensual man doesn't go to a whore.
No, the ones that come here, they come for the share of the devil they have coming to them.
They're looking for a she-devil.
They look to me for something I'm not. Crazy, eh?
What I really am is a cop.
There's the mother-cop.
And the statue-cop.
And the hooker-cop.
And all us women together, all us women, we're all cops. We're the guardians of the moral order of their society. What a hell of a job! As a rule, when I get to my fifth glass of scotch, I start to cry. Then I take another. And go to sleep.
Next morning, when I wake up, I start searching. Seems I remember that just before I went to sleep, just for a second, I had a revelation. Clear as day. What did I see that vanished before I could catch it? Like an important dream that slips away. What was it I knew, just for a minute, and then rejected?
It seems to me, tonight, I could touch my secret. I have a feeling it's at my fingertips. I feel like a strong wind, in June. The kind that blows the blossoms off the trees. Heeey! Marie, Marie, Marie, Marie, Marie! I know what I don't want anymore.

> *MADELEINE sits down in her own place. As she talks, she takes off her boots. As she holds them high and drops them, a loud noise is heard: the same noise as that of the chain and the apron.*

I don't want anymore of this goddamn life I lead. I don't want to be in the skin of a hooker. The skin of a whore. The skin of a dog.

> *MADELEINE takes MARIE in her arms. They dance together.*

Hold onto your hat, Marie, I'm closing up shop.

> *MADELEINE goes to her neutral place.*

I'm back in my shoes again. Tonight, I'm a single girl.

THE STATUE   (*in her neutral place*) Talked about nothing but my fragile side, so I'd pass my life in trembling. He likes his proverbs:
"Silence is golden"—so the silent majority would submit in silence.
He wanted me to shut my mouth forever, so I could listen to him for an eternity.
Wanted a Buddha smile, a Sphinx's face, a virgin's eye,
Wanted from me a Mona Lisa. Kept the poker-face for himself.

MADELEINE   (*in her neutral place*) Taught me, with his second-hand car dealer's smile, "Love is impossible!"
Said that behind my velvet eye hid a cunt with teeth, full of corpses.

MARIE   (*in her neutral place*) I've bled through all my silences.
I've abolished my crack. My walls have crowded in.
I unplugged myself from the void.

THE STATUE   Wolf, are you there?

MADELEINE   Do you hear me?

ALL THREE   Ready or not you must be caught.
Going, going, gone.

> *MARIE exits. THE STATUE goes back into "the statue" and MADELEINE is in her neutral place.*

MADELEINE   Think I'll take a little walk.
Think I'll go for a stroll.
No, no, no, no,
Another kind of walk…

> *The following scene is played with THE STATUE and MARIE in the male roles. MADELEINE physically performs the rape scene herself. Somebody whistles at the beginning of the scene.*

MARIE   I was lookin' for somebody just like you tonight. D'ya know me, mamselle?

MADELEINE   Yeah, yeah, I know you. But I don't wanna talk to anybody tonight. I'm in a hurry. Goodbye.

THE STATUE   I thought you were givin' me the eye. You know, you're a good lookin' broad. Not as young as you might be, but you're not bad.

MADELEINE   Don't you understand English? *Je veux être seule.*

MARIE   You must take pretty-pills to be that good-lookin'.

MADELEINE   I take the same pills as you, mister, but I can digest them. Now that's enough. Let me get by.

MARIE   Hey! You know, you're cute when you get mad.

MADELEINE   Get away! Leave me alone.

THE STATUE   Hey, come on! Don't ya know what I'm after?

MARIE   Don't you understand I want you?

MADELEINE   Oh! Oh! No! You're not going to pull that one! NO! Oh, no!

> *The rape begins.*

No. No. No. No. No. No. No!

> *Over MADELEINE, something like a great bird spreads its wing. THE STATUE and MARIE speak over MADELEINE's lamentations.*

THE STATUE   Hey there! Cut out the scaredy-cat act. I know all about pigs like you.

MADELEINE   Let me go. Let me go. Let me go!

MARIE   You know, you ain't bad. Just my type.

MADELEINE   Please, mister, go away. Go away before my husband comes. He's gonna kill you.

THE STATUE   No ya don't. I know you ain't got a husband. I like it when ya put up a fight.

MADELEINE   No! No! No!

THE STATUE   Why, you little bitch! What's the idea, puttin' on this holy virgin act? I know you're gonna like it.

MARIE   Get a move on now. Open your legs. You're gonna see. Spread 'em out so I can put my teaser in there.

MADELEINE   No!

THE STATUE   I'm gonna plough you, just wait. You're gonna like it. I got the best one in town. Don't worry. It's gonna be big enough for you, you cute little bastard. Open up or I'll break your goddamn neck. I'm the strongest one around here.

MADELEINE   No! No!

MARIE   I want you. I want you. I want you.

MADELEINE   No! No! No!

MARIE   Open up. And I want a mouthful of milk, by the way. One large half-pint, madame. You wouldn't refuse a drink to a thirsty man, would ya?

THE STATUE   You'll see, I'm gonna get into you. Don't pull the innocent stuff. I know you like it. You're made for it. Goddamn beautiful cunt. Fuckin' whore. Go to it. Now, come. Come, goddamn you.

> *MARIE and THE STATUE are breathing hard. MADELEINE groans. The bird disappears.*

MADELEINE   Mother, mother, mother!

Song of the Rape

(singing)
When the rising moon opens like a fan
I'll be imprisoned behind my windows.
I just can't go out at night
On la rue Marianne,
From the mountain to Park Lafontaine.
I'm too afraid now,
Afraid of the dark,
For I have been raped.

MARIE   There was a trial.
There was a judge.
There were attorneys.
And one accused.

THE STATUE   He was a plumber.
He was a notary.

MARIE   He was a professor.
He was a musician.

THE STATUE   He was a psychiatrist.
He was a carpenter.
He was a reporter.
He was a sociologist.
He was a travelling salesman.
He was a gynecologist.

THE STATUE   He knew the plaintiff personally and declared that he had examined her in his practice two of three times and that each time she had made specific advances to him.

MARIE   Certain criminologists wondered if, in fact, in this case, the accused was not the real victim.

THE STATUE   The court also called on its shadow moral squad: medical this and medical that.

MARIE   Hundreds of women came from everywhere to give moral support to the plaintiff.

MADELEINE   *(singing)*
I'm a single girl, I live alone.
Before, I was proud, but now, I'm just scared.
My God, I'd like to know why
On la rue Marianne
That guy had to go and hurt me so bad.
I was all alone.
He could have talked to me,
But I have been raped.

MARIE   There were the powers that be, to question, tease, to watch, to spy, to search and feel and persecute and raise their eyebrows, wink and grimace—the powers that desire and stigmatize at the same time.

THE STATUE   And it doesn't bother them a bit.

MARIE   Raping a whore isn't rape.

THE STATUE   Temptation always comes from the woman.

MARIE   She must have led him on.

THE STATUE   Eve, do you know what you are? You are the doorway to hell.

MARIE   Snow White is a nympho.

THE STATUE   Raping a whore isn't rape.

MADELEINE   *(singing)*
I'm a funny girl, my heart is open.
Ain't no sacred vessel, he should have known that.
Where do they lose all their tenderness?
My innocence lost, I fall into terror,
See fear in my mirror,
For I have been raped.

MARIE   She went through the whole masquerade. All the humiliation, all the misery of a woman dispossessed.

THE STATUE   The judge felt he was impartial. The lawyers too. Not one of them felt involved. Even though the fact of rape was admitted, no one of them saw it as rape. Not one of them recognized the image of his mother, his daughter of his wife. The patrimony remained intact. Only when she personified the patrimony could a woman be raped.

MARIE   Then there was the defence lawyer—he wanted to know how they could suspect a man who knew his women as well as a gynecologist?

THE STATUE   During the trial, the question that aroused the greatest interest and emotion, causing the accused himself to be forgotten, the crucial question came to be the following: "Did the plaintiff have an orgasm?"

MARIE   Suddenly, there were the powers that be who were not opposed to pleasure.
Suddenly, there was the might of the powers that wanted to mount on pleasure's back.
Suddenly, the orgasm was permitted.
There was an alliance of medicine and court affirming the right to give a whore an orgasm.

THE STATUE   Anywhere at all. Any old time. Any old way. A cock makes her come. Everybody knows that.

MADELEINE   *(singing)*
How did they learn to terrify like that?
How do they learn to beat and rape,
All tenderness lost on la rue Marianne?
I'm in my small house,
Alone with my fear
Hammering at my heart,
For I have been raped.

MARIE   Then there was the trial's end.
The rapist was acquitted.
It was like the end of a long summer.
In the transept, men of law, proud of themselves, exchanged congratulations.
In the court, everyone stood up at once.

THE STATUE   You'd have thought they were flocks of starlings rising from a field of corn. Had they had enough?
Madeleine, the plaintiff-prostitute, raised one strident cry in the boiling sunlight.
It was still summer. But in the distant air, the goldenrod already bloomed.
And it was like the last day of all our summers.

MARIE   There were the women who left the court, their throats choked with sobs.
And there were the women who laughed at the fate of the violated plaintiff.
There were women who held cries of violence behind clenched teeth.
There were women who wept softly. Openly.
There was a woman who wanted to know: "Rape, is it part of the pathology of sex or the pathology of power?"
No one could answer.
All replies awaited their right moment.
There was a woman who was as if she never had been raped.

MADELEINE   *(singing)*
At night, the boulevards, the parks and the streets

Are closed to me now, my rapist is there.
I've no right to walk alone
On la rue Marianne.
Yes, just to walk to ease my sorrow.
I'm too afraid now,
I cannot forget
That I have been raped.

> *THE STATUE howls out cries of rage and a woman emerges from the statue, violently, by way of the belly. The speeches of this woman will continue to be attributed to THE STATUE. At first, she directs her words in all directions.*

THE STATUE   I've had enough. I've had enough. I can't go on.
I can't go on. I can't take it. I can't take it. I can't take it.
I can't take it anymore. I won't take it anymore, any of it. Not anymore.
Nothing.
I want no part of that sarcophagus—I don't want to be worshipped in a statue and then insulted and despised in every woman.

> *She turns and faces the statue.*

Jesus Christ on the Cross!

> *The shell of the statue begins to rise. The serpent at its feet begins to rise as well, but falls to the floor before the statue disappears. THE STATUE laughs and speaks to the serpent.*

What are you up to there?
Let go. Serpent, get away from my heel.
Come out of your hiding place.
We've seen enough of you.
We've learned your tricks.
Tricks of old bachelors.
Race of old single men.
You, contemptuous of the earth, sick old
apocalypse, sick from your own fear.
Jealous of our children, you spread the word that I was a matriarchal torturer.
Be on your way.
I'll crush you no more.
Crawl off. Take over the earth. The earth is good. When I was small, I played barefoot in the mud. Know this, old sphinx of sin.
All your old schizoid plans have been sneezed away.
Go!
And nothing will be as it was before.
Imagine that!

> *She laughs again. The serpent crawls away. MARIE and MADELEINE appear. They are also laughing.*

Imagine.

MADELEINE   Imagine.

MARIE   Just imagine.

MADELEINE   Now the shindig starts!

MARIE   Imagine…

THE STATUE   Imagine…

THE THREE   Just let's imagine!

MADELEINE   There is no beaten path for women seeking what no one has ever seen.

THE STATUE   Waves and breakers of foaming follies ripple on our skins.

MADELEINE   *(singing)*
Take my hand, I'm a stranger in paradise.

MARIE   What's the old dream? Everyone's dream? Wanting to be for at least one person the most important person in the world?

MADELEINE   I don't know. I don't know what love is. I don't know what dignity is.
But I know all about contempt.

THE STATUE   Before I spoke to you I chatted with the trees, the clouds, the moon, my plants.
And with my cat.
I come prepared.
And now, open your ears.

MARIE   Because, from now on, you're not going to tell me how or in what style beaten women, desperate women, shut-in women or women prostitutes are to blow the system.

MADELEINE   You're not going to tell me how arteries are to harden.
You're not going to tell me how grandmothers go white.
You're not going to tell me how sensuality is impoverished.
You're not going to tell me how to heat cool reason.

THE STATUE   You will explain to me no more how my body should feel its pleasure.
You'll count me no more piece by piece.
You'll never again call my orgasms by your name.
You will not dictate any of my duties.

MADELEINE   Never again will you tell me how youth cools and freezes.
You'll never tell me how the lilac blooms.
You'll never tell me how the rose grows red.
You'll never tell me how the rivers rust.

MARIE   You'll tell me no more.

THE STATUE   You'll tell me no more.

MADELEINE   Nevermore will you give me the rhythm or the tune.

MARIE   And keep your advice.
  Just think things over.

THE STATUE   And open up your ears.
  And weigh your words.

MADELEINE   I'll be waiting for you somewhere. In the place where hearts cut
  their names in the living bark and grow along with the birch trees.

THE STATUE   I take my place in the midst of the path that oozes joy.
  I am the spreading river.

MARIE   I call upon you, loitering knights, with your vows of masculinity. I invite
  you to abandon your hysterical virility.
  Deserters wanted. Idol-breakers wanted.

MADELEINE   If not, who'll accept me as a woman, apart from women?

THE STATUE   I call on myself,
  For the day of the victims is past.

MARIE   Because, since the world's beginning…

THE STATUE   There's been only one "Thou shalt not."

MADELEINE   Only one "Thou shalt not."

MARIE   For lovers.

MADELEINE   For lovers.

THE STATUE   And here I stand before myself,
  Ready to love you.
  Carnal, I am, full of brains.
  I belong to all the days, all seven, and because of it,
  Here I stand alive,
  Before myself,
  To break the old iniquities.
  I will never again be in any part of you
  That means exile from myself.
  For the child's flesh excites me and
  Enflames my breasts and thighs.
  Pornographize me no longer.
  When you tremble at your own birth.

MADELEINE   I will never again be in any part of you
  That means exile from myself.

  Here I stand,
  Laughing inside.

THE STATUE Imagine…

MARIE The child's flesh excites me and
  Enflames my breasts and thighs,
  Whence I stand, here before you.
  Pornographize me no longer.
  When you tremble at your own birth.

THE STATUE Here we are, standing before ourselves, renewed.
  Imagine!

MARIE Imagine!

MADELEINE Imagine!

THE STATUE Imagine!

MARIE Imagine!

MADELEINE Imagine!

THE STATUE Imagine!

    The end.

Mommy
(Moman)

by Louisette Dussault

translated by Linda Gaboriau

Introduction to
Mommy (Moman [1])
by Louisette Dussault
Introduced by Louise H. Forsyth

Mommy is a two-act road play, the story of a journey of discovery. It enacts a bus ride taken in Québec by a young mother with her three-and-a-quarter-year-old twin daughters in the middle of a snowstorm. She is taking the girls for a two-week stay with their father, from whom she is separated. The story begins with their arrival at the Montréal bus station by taxi and ends with their arrival in Nicolet, the girls rushing to jump into the arms of their father, and the mother remaining alone to think about the journey she has just made. The trip has involved one difficult circumstance after another. Each of these circumstances has been part of her exploration of life with others in society, with particular emphasis on her own identity as mother and daughter. Until the end of the play there is no explanation in the dialogue of what she is discovering—the demands of looking after the children are too great—but in the course of the fast-paced action she and the audience make unspoken interpretations about what is going on. Questions are raised about the meaning of motherhood and the behaviours to which it gives rise. This microcosm of society shows that there are those who are considerate of others and who seem to enjoy them, and there are those who are rude and inconsiderate. Where do these different behaviours come from?

As a mother, Mommy grapples with problems on more than one level. At the immediate and practical level there is the incessant challenge of looking after the children in a busy public place: paying attention to their safety and expression of needs, keeping track of them in the bus station, and dealing with the considerable amount of stuff they are carrying with them. On this anecdotal level the play is amusing and heart-warming. Spectators breathe a sigh of relief at the end that the little family has arrived safely and happily. Another practical problem, that of ensuring that the children don't bother other people, recurs through the play and contributes to the audience's sympathetic understanding of Mommy's valiant efforts to survive the trip. At the same time, this problem leads the play into a serious exploration of the meaning of motherhood at another level, that is at a symbolic level. What are the responsibilities of mothers to other people? Does society construct mothers as people with an automatic responsibility to care for others, and if so, does this inculcate into mothers a guilt complex because they can never be sure they and their children have completely satisfied others' expectations? It is interesting to count in *Mommy* the number of times that the mother asks the children to excuse her or asks others to excuse her and the children because she thinks they are bothering them. It's a stressful, no-win situation for her. Can this need to keep children under control at all times in turn transform a mother into what Dussault calls *une mère-police*, "Mommy-The-Cop" and daughters into supplicants for maternal approval? What, on the other hand, are the responsibilities of others toward mothers and their children and what joys could they find by involvement in the affairs of children not their own? What difference would it make in the relations of mothers and daughters if motherhood were constructed as something other than an all-consuming role of caring for others, but never oneself? In evoking memories of difficult times spent with her mother, Mommy expresses her determination to put an end to the debilitating patterns that so often run through mother-daughter relationships. Dussault shared this determination in her "Itinéraire pour une moman":

> I no longer wanted to be the mother; I no longer wanted to play the mother with everyone […] It was my desire in *Moman* […] to show how and why we become Mommy-The-Cop. We absolutely must get rid of this if we don't want to transmit this pattern indefinitely to our children."[2]

In the course of her journey Mommy interacts with the mothers, daughters and men around her in the bus and grapples with these difficult questions. The audience understands that the problem is not that women have relationships with children and others whom they love and whose needs they meet. The problem is rather that the identity of individual women is so easily subsumed under the symbolic role of mothers and that this predominantly service role renders mature relationships impossible. Mommy says in a flashback to a conversation with the girls' father:

> No wonder I'm tired of playing mother! I've been playing Mother since I was born… I played Mother to my father, to my brother, to my sisters, my boyfriends, the men in my life… *(She listens.)* Yes, with you, too, don't deny it […] I guess it's my way of getting people to love me— anticipating everyone's needs, being at their beck and call…. As if no one would love ME just for ME… WHO AM I? Just plain ME![3]

As Mommy realizes in the second act when she gets very angry at one of the girls, this pattern of relationships based on mothering becomes doubly complicated when mothers condition their daughters to play it after them. She recalls in a flashback her own outburst at her mother when she understood this:

> I'm not mad at you! I'm not mad at you! *(furious, impotent)* I'm never mad at you!!! But I am mad!!!! *(beat)* I'm mad at everything that stands between us… between you and me…. The roundabout way you talk to me… the roundabout way I talk to you…. The things you hide from me, and I hide from you…. It feels like we talk to each over through a glass… a looking glass… a mirror.[4]

Moman tells a story of motherhood from a point of view seldom represented on stage. As well, *Moman* is unusually innovative technically. It is not a play like other plays. It is fiction and yet non-fiction; it is a monologue and yet not a monologue, a performance piece and yet not a performance piece; its theatricality depends much on mime and clown and yet it is neither of these. There are seventeen characters with speaking parts in the play, all played by the single actor whose primary role is that of

Mommy. Indeed, for Louisette Dussault, who wrote and directed the play, played Mommy and all the other roles, this is a *tour de force*. As is clear in "Itinéraire pour une moman," much of the story is autobiographical. Dussault was, in reality, mother of young twin daughters at the time *Moman* was written and produced. The French version of the play begins with the actor addressing the audience directly: "The story I'm going to tell is almost entirely true… almost!" [5] There is even a character who appears in both acts named Louisette.

Mommy begins to detach herself from her role and identity as mother and handmaid during the flashback in the second act when she recalls her angry explosion with her mother, who had just lost the cord of her daughter's favourite blouse in the dryer. In remembering dismantling the dryer and recovering the cord, Louisette is launched in a process toward dismantling their dysfunctional relationship and affirming her independence. The act of reclaiming the cord of her blouse is like cutting the umbilical cord with which her mother has controlled her behaviour. The act of separation frees both daughter and mother to be themselves and to love without guilt. Shortly after this flashback Mommy stands up in the bus in the present to announce to all fellow-travellers her revolt against formulas for the proper behaviour of mothers and children and her determination to facilitate normal relations among the girls and the rest of the passengers, each person taking responsibility for her or his own situation, thereby establishing a sense of community among all of them on a fresh and egalitarian basis:

> Suddenly dawn broke… I finally got it…. It took me a while, but I got it! (*She stands up.*) I stood up in the bus, I was terrified… I said: "Excuse me…. Excuse me, I have something to say!" […] As you have probably all noticed, I've been holding these two children hostage in this seat for almost four hours…. For four hours I've been preventing them from looking at you, from touching you, from smiling at you, from speaking to you!… For four hours, I've been preventing them from living! But now I quit. I refuse to say "no" to them in your place. If you want to talk to them, go ahead! […] And if you don't want to talk to them, that's your right! Your right as consenting adults! I'm just asking you to tell them yourselves… (*beat*) Nicely, please! So they don't feel rejected…. But firmly, so they understand! Don't wait till you explode… like me! But tell them yourselves!… I can't go on playing Mommy-The-Cop! I'm incapable of being the ideal mother you'd all like me to be. Incapable!… and I refuse to be your mother, too! I refuse to protect you like children, from my own children… I'm prepared to run the risk that you won't like me, but for the rest of this trip… (*beat*) For the rest of this trip, I refuse to play Mommy-The-Cop for all of you… [6]

Further to this announcement, after a moment of stunned silence, everyone in the bus begins to talk with everyone else and to enjoy the children. The play does not end with a sense of glorious victory over stereotypes that deform identities and relationships. Instead, the ending remains open, with Mommy leaving the impression with the audience that she has gained awareness and made a certain amount of progress toward living her life, with her daughters, on her own terms.

Dussault has said in "Itinéraire pour une moman" that she believes the all-encompassing role of motherhood renders other adult relationships virtually impossible for women: "I would like to be able to live in a world of adults and not of parents, to have equal relationships with women, men, children."[7] Since expectations about motherhood have a major impact on the lives of all girls and women, whether or not they become mothers, grappling with tenacious myths is a serious undertaking. The impact on behaviour and relationships is so determining that even a woman's professional life is closely tied to social expectations about women, marriage and motherhood, as Dussault recognized in her own case as a professional actor. Like the Mad Actress in *A Clash of Symbols*, who strips off the costume and wig she had put on for *L'École des femmes*, Dussault no longer wished to conform to conventional feminine roles, acting styles and theatrical techniques. The dramatic monologue of *Moman* allowed her to see herself and her situation more clearly. Getting rid of the over-arching imperative to conform to sociocultural stereotypes for women meant getting rid of the beauty myth and the role of seductress, as well as stepping out of the silence that has been imposed on women for millennia on public stages and in public forums: "I no longer wish to be on a stage solely to seduce nor to stop myself from saying the things that I have a desire to say, for fear of upsetting."[8]

Moman has attracted critical acclaim. It has been particularly lauded because of Dussault's great acting skill. To the best of my knowledge, it has never been performed by anyone but Dussault. Nor has it been studied for its theatrical experimentation.

Notes

[1] *Moman*, précédé de "Itinéraire pour une moman." Montréal: Boréal Express, 1981. *Moman* was first produced in Montréal at the Salle Fred-Barry on March 19, 1979 with Louisette Dussault playing the single role, serving as director and producer. The following month it played at the Centaur and subsequently toured elsewhere in Québec and Canada. Dussault was invited to represent Québec with *Moman* at the Festival mondial de Nancy, France in 1980. Tours of the play brought her prizes in Spain and Algeria. Dussault adapted the play for cinema as "L'Étau-bus" in 1983 (produced by l'Association coopérative de productions audio-visuelles), for which she was awarded three prizes. In 1987 she directed the first production of *Mommy* in Toronto, North Hatley and Ottawa, in a translation by Linda Gaboriau. Dussault remounted *Moman* in 1998 at the Petit Théâtre de Sherbrooke and in March 2000 at the Théâtre Denise-Pelletier in Montréal. During this run, Dussault passed her 500th playing of this role. The first version of Gaboriau's *Mommy* has been available in manuscript from CEAD in Montréal.

[2] "[…] je ne voulais plus être la mère; je ne voulais plus faire la mère avec tout le monde […] j'avais le goût, dans *Moman* […] de montrer comment et pourquoi on devient une mère-police dont il faut absolument se débarrasser, si on ne veut pas

transmettre indéfiniment ce pattern-là à nos enfants." ("Initéraire pour une moman." *Moman*: 28.) Translated by LHF.

3   "C'est pas surprenant que je sois tannée de jouer à la mère! Je joue à la mère depuis que je suis au monde... J'ai été la mère de mon père, de mon frère, de mes soeurs, de mes chums, de mes hommes... (*Elle écoute.*) Bien oui, avec toi aussi, proteste pas... [...] On dirait que c'est la seule façon que je connaisse de me faire aimer: [...] C'est comme si MOI sans ça je n'étais pas 'aimable'... QUI je suis MOI! MOI!" (*Moman*: 114).

4   "Je ne suis pas en colère contre toi! (*rageuse, impuissante*) Je ne suis jamais en colère contre toi!!! Mais je suis en colère, par exemple! (*un temps*) Je suis en colère contre tout ce qui est ENTRE nous... ENTRE nous autres.... Les détours que tu prends pour me parler. Les détours que je prends pour te parler.... Les choses que tu me caches, que je te cache.... J'ai l'impression qu'on se parle à travers une vitre... une glace... un miroir..." (*Moman*: 128).

5   "L'histoire que je vais raconter est presque toute vraie... presque!" (*Moman*: 42). Translated by LHF.

6   "J'ai compris.... J'ai compris.... Ça m'avait pris du temps, mais j'ai compris! (*Elle se lève.*) Je me suis levée dans l'autobus, j'étais morte de peur.... J'ai dit: 'Excusez-moi.... Excusez-moi, j'aurais quelque chose à vous dire! [...] Comme vous l'avez sans doute remarqué, ça fait bientôt presque quatre heures que je garde ces enfants-là prisonnières dans le banc.... Ça fait quatre heures que je les empêche de vous regarder, de vous toucher, de vous sourire, de vous parler, de vous jaser!... Ça fait quatre heures que je les empêche de vivre! À partir de maintenant, moi, je refuse de dire 'non' à votre place!... [...] Si vous voulez leur parler, allez-y! [...] Mais si vous voulez pas... et c'est votre plein droit! C'est votre plein droit d'adulte! Je vais vous demander de leur dire vous-mêmes... (*un temps*) Gentiment, s'il-vous-plaît! Qu'elles se sentent pas rejetées.... Fermement, qu'elles comprennent! Attendez pas d'éclater... comme moi! Mais dites-leur vous-mêmes!... Je suis plus capable de jouer à la mère-police!... Je suis pas capable d'être la mère idéale dont vous rêvez dans chacune de vos têtes pour ces enfants-là! Je suis pas capable!... Puis je refuse d'être votre mère aussi! De vous protéger comme des enfants, de mes propres enfants.... Je suis prête à prendre le risque que vous ne m'aimiez pas, mais pour le reste du voyage... (*un temps*) Pour le reste du voyage, je refuse de jouer le seul rôle de mère-police..." *Moman*: 136–38.

7   "J'aimerais en arriver à vivre dans un monde d'adultes et non de parents, à avoir des rapports d'égal à égal avec les femmes, les hommes, les enfants." ("Initéraire pour une moman." *Moman*: 37.) Translated by LHF.

8   "Je ne veux plus être sur une scène uniquement pour séduire et m'empêcher de dire les choses que j'ai envie de dire de peur de déplaire." ("Initéraire pour une moman." *Moman*: 37.) Translated by LHF.

Bibliographical Suggestions

On *Moman* and Louisette Dussault

Andrès, Bernard, Yves Lacroix & Lorraine Hébert. "Représentation. «Moman» Itinéraire pour une Moman. Entretien-montage avec Louisette Dussault," *Cahiers de théâtre. Jeu.* 17 (1980.4): 85–95.

Féral, Josette. "Louisette Dussault, *Moman*," *Livres et auteurs québécois 1981.* Québec: Presses de l'Université Laval, 1982: 169–70.

Leblanc, Alonzo. "Femmes en solo." *Revue d'histoire littéraire québécois et canadien-français* (hiver-printemps 1983): 89–97.

Lahaie, Christiane. "*Moman*," *Dictionnaire des oeuvres littéraires du Québec.* Tome VI, 1976–1980. Montréal: Fides, 1994. 528–30.

Peterson, Maureen. "Louisette Dussault grows by stages." *The Gazette* (July 26, 1980): 79.

Texier, Catherine. "La Belle Trajectoire de Louisette Dussault." *Châtelaine* (avril 1980): 46–48, 53–54, 56.

Whitely, David. "Of Mothers and Dragonflies: Two Montreal Solo Performances." *Canadian Theatre Review.* 92 (Fall 1997). *"Solo Performance."* Ed. Ric Knowles & Harry Lane: 34–38.

About Louisette Dussault

Louisette Dussault (born 1940 in Thetford-Mines) first intended to be a soprano and musician, but then enrolled in the École nationale de théâtre du Canada in Montréal, graduating in 1964. Actor, playwright, teacher, and director, Dussault spent two years in English Canada at the Manitoba Theatre Centre and the Canadian Players Foundation of Toronto. She subsequently acted on the stage, in radio, television, and cinema in the classical repertory and in many of the plays that, together, created the exciting new wave of *Théâtre québécois* of the 1960s. She has since written and produced many shows that remain unpublished. She was particularly well known and loved for her portrayal of *La Souris verte*, a long-lasting children's television program (1966–1971) on Radio-Canada. During the same years, she co-founded the Enfants de Chénier with Jean-Claude Germain and participated in their *Grand Spectacle d'adieu*—a farewell to alienating and colonizing French culture, collaborated in several collective theatrical initiatives, and worked with André Brassard on the first production of several plays by Michel Tremblay.

With regard to the time in her career when she began to play roles written by feminist playwrights, she has said:

> I have always had the impression that I was acting behind screens until the moment when there was *La Nef des sorcières* and *Les Fées ont soif*: finally women were doing women in theatre! It was about time! These experiences were decisive for me, very painful as well, because what the characters conveyed forced me to go deep inside myself and confront what I was, the idea of me that I had given to myself. The character of the girl in *La Nef* was much closer to me than I initially thought. [1]

She created the role of girl seductress and victim of the beauty myth in *La Nef des sorcières* in 1976 and the "Statue" in Boucher's *Les Fées ont soif* in 1978, just a few months before the first production of *Moman*.

Very active throughout her career as a militant working for social justice and in a wide range of theatrical activities and associations, she has been nominated four times for Gemini awards, received the Prix Victor Morin from the Société Saint-Jean-Baptiste, was named Chevalier des Arts et des Lettres de France, and has received many other awards.

Notes

[1] "J'ai toujours eu l'impression de jouer derrière des écrans jusqu'au moment où il y a eu *La Nef des sorcières* et *Les Fées ont soif*: enfin des femmes qui faisaient des femmes au théâtre! Il était temps! Ces expériences-là ont été déterminantes pour moi, très douloureuses aussi, parce que les personnages dans ce qu'ils charriaient me confrontaient profondément dans ce que j'étais, à l'idée que je me faisais de moi-même. Le personnage de la Fille dans *La Nef* était beaucoup plus proche de moi que je ne le croyais au départ." ("Itinéraire pour une moman." *Moman*: 22, 24.) Translated by LHF.

Translator's Note

I have taken a "hybrid" approach to translating *Moman*. Since it was such a quintessentially personal performance very much in keeping with the "first person feminine" writing of the Seventies, I did not adapt the (auto)biographical references to Louisette Dussault's career and life in Québec. These references illustrate Louisette's belief that personal can be political on stage. In oder to make the playful theatricality of the piece clear to English-speaking readers, I did, however, "adapt" the choice of songs. I hope the use of familiar English songs will give readers a better idea of the mood and spirit of the original production. An actress wishing to perform the play in English might want to make the autobiographical references her own.

Moman was first produced at the Salle Fred-Barry, Montréal, in March 1979, with Louisette Dussault playing all characters, and serving as director and producer.

Characters

All roles played by one actor:
MOMMY
EVE
PAULA
A MAN
THE GIRL AT THE COUNTER
THE TICKET AGENT
DRIVER
THE SPINSTER
THE ELDERLY MOTHER
THE GIRLFRIEND
THE BOYFRIEND
THE HIPPIE
THE YOUNG WOMAN
THE GENTLEMAN
MOTHER
FATHER
LOUISETTE
NEIGHBOUR

MOMMY

As the lights go up, MOMMY attempts to pay the taxi driver, as one of the girls almost closes the door on her.

MOMMY   *(to EVE)* No, no Eve… Eve, leave the taxi door open… Eve! Leave the door open, you hear me? Mommy has to talk to the taxi driver. What? Yes, this is where we're going to get the bus… *(to the taxi driver)* Sorry, how much do I owe you? I know, but I can't see the metre because of my baggage…. How much is it?

EVE   We're going to Paul's house, Mr. Taxi Driver!

MOMMY   *(to EVE)* The driver doesn't know who Paul is… *(to the driver)* Pardon me? She's three…

EVE   Three and a quarter, Mommy, we're—

MOMMY   *(to EVE)* Yes, yes, three and a quarter… a quarter… *(to the driver)* Pardon me?… Both of them… yes… they're twins… twin girls. That's Eve…. Now where's she going? *(to EVE)* Eve! Come back here! Eve, where are you going? Wait a minute, we have to get our bags out… *(to the driver)* Sorry, you're going to freeze! Okay, the sack of clean clothes, the suitcase, the bag of groceries… *(to PAULA)* What? The surprise is in the bag! Don't worry!… Your pillows and the blankies…. No, I won't drop it, Mommy's going to put your blankie on top of the clean clothes…. What? No, no it won't fall… well, okay, you can watch it, that's a good girl, like that, good… I know, you love your little blanket…. The Lego… *(to herself)* There, now I think I've got everything… I've got my gloves, my purse, I guess that's it. Good… *(to the driver)* Let's hope it stops snowing, right? Pardon me? Oh, no… I know the buses were cancelled yesterday and this morning, but the three o'clock bus is supposed to leave… who knows how far we'll get, but we're going to take our chances…. Thank you! *(to EVE)* Eve! Come help us! C'mon, help us carry the bags… at least the Lego.

PAULA   I'm a good girl, aren't I, Mommy? I'm carrying it all by myself!

MOMMY   Yes, you're a good girl, sweetie…. A very good girl. Okay, now… you go stand with your sister by the door. Wait for me!… Wait, I'll carry the rest… I don't know how, but I'll carry the rest… *(to herself)* The blankies and the pillows under my arm, that'll work, there… the bag of groceries should fit around my wrist… it's not too heavy… the suitcase, oooff… the sack of clean clothes… now let's see if we can move with all that!

MOMMY heads for the door of the bus station.

(to the audience) Our trip was off to a great start! *(beat)* The story I'm going to tell you is a true story… almost all true! It begins in the Montreal bus station, one Sunday afternoon in January. The province of Quebec has been paralyzed

for three days by three or four feet of snow. *(She gestures.)* At least this high. *(to EVE, as they reach the door)* No… I know you can't open the door alone… it's too heavy…. One, two, three, push! Mommy will try to open it with her bum…

A MAN *(as he opens the door for her)* Women might be liberated these days, but they still need men to open doors for them, right! Ha ha ha!

MOMMY We still need you!… *(as she ushers the children through the door)* And children do, too. Children still need you, too! Ha ha ha! Funny, eh? Thank you!… *(to herself)* Idiot!

Good heavens, it's crowded. Eve, stay here with us…. Yes, all these people are going to take the bus! Stay right here, in the aisle, I have to go to the counter. *(to the girl at the counter)* Just a minute, Miss, I'll make room… *(to EVE)* Can you help Mommy, we have to push our baggage out of the way…. Push, push…. Good heavens, it's crowded, sorry…. Eve, stay with Mommy. There! Miss, could you…. Paula, you forgot your Lego by the door. Can you go get it, sweetie. That's a good girl… yes, you are a good girl, a really good girl, put it there with the rest of the baggage…. This won't take long…. Eve!!!!! *(to THE GIRL AT THE COUNTER)* Sorry! Could you please tell me which gate the bus for…

THE GIRL AT THE COUNTER That's not our job, madam! See that red phone on the wall there. Don't you know how to read? There's a sign above it: in–for–ma—

MOMMY Thank you, I get it. *(to EVE)* No, Eve, Mommy will do it, no, you can't do it, look how high the phone is, stay here…. No, don't go there either, stay right here…. Look, you can guard our baggage for Mommy, okay? So nobody takes it… by mistake.

(goes to the phone, picks up the receiver and waits) Eve! No, stop, come back, stay with your sister… Eve! *(to PAULA)* Paula, tell your sister to come back! No, stop, you stay right there, stay there. *(She yells to EVE.)* Eve, come back here! You'll get lost. There are too many people… *(into the phone)* Yes, can you tell me which gate the bus for Saint-Gré…. Oh, no, wait, he's moved…. Which gate for Nicolet, please…. Pardon me? Yes…. Gate 17? Oh no, that's at the other end of the station. Yes, I know it's not your fault. *(to EVE who is wandering off)* Eve, come back here! *(into the phone)* No, I'm not talking to you. Thank you, Miss. *(She hangs up.)* Eve! Excuse me, madam…. Sorry… *(She goes back to PAULA.)* No, no, don't cry, Paula… I don't know where she is, look at all the people! Wait! Don't worry, we'll find her… Mommy will find her!

Just wait right here for me, I won't be long. *(to THE GIRL AT THE COUNTER)* Miss, could you please keep an eye on my little girl? I know it's not your job, but… *(She looks around for EVE.)* Eve! Eve! Madam, could you please… *(to a young girl)* Miss, could you please watch my little girl for just two minutes…. Yes, her…. The other one has taken off and I'm worried…. It's not easy keeping an eye on two of them who are the same age, plus the luggage…. Pardon me? Yes, they're twins. *(to PAULA)* Now you stay right here. I won't be long.

Eve! Eve! *(louder and louder)* Eve! *(She realizes people are staring at her and lowers her voice.)* Eve. *(to a woman)* Madam, have you by any chance seen a little girl about this tall, three years old… three and quarter, approximately, dressed in red, white and blue? Yes, I do have two of them to keep an eye on, two the same age… pardon? Yes! *(She shouts.)* Yes, twins! *(She hears her.)* Eve! Eve! Over here! Right here, madam, I'm the mother! *(She looks around and lowers her voice.)* I'm her mother! *(She takes EVE into her arms.)* It's alright, pussycat, don't cry. Yes, Mommy was scared. You scared me. Huh? You were scared, too? Poor baby. Don't cry. *(She turns around.)* Thank you, Mad—she's gone! *(to EVE)* No, Mommy's not mad, no…. But now do you understand why Mommy told you to stay with us?… *(gaily)* Look at the big buses! That's the kind of bus we're going to take…. Don't cry, come on… *(to the audience)* I'd found her! Have you ever noticed, when kids get lost in public places, they find their mothers really fast. Nobody wants to get stuck with them! *(to EVE)* Don't cry, come on, no, don't worry, your little sister isn't lost, Mommy knows where she is, Mommy sees her, she's… *(She points.)* Yoohoo! Hello! Don't you see her? *(She lifts her up high.)* Now can you see her? Give me your hand! *(to the audience)* By the time we reached the counter, they were both crying! *(to the children)* Come on, girls, give each other a hug. Yes, I know you're glad to find your little sister…. Now listen…. You know I don't bother you about silly things. But this is serious. Today you have to listen to me, a bit. You hear me, just a bit. *(to EVE)* No, no. Mommy's not mad at you. We're going on a nice bus ride. You'll see. We'll tell each other stories and sing— *(to THE GIRL AT THE COUNTER)* Pardon? Yes, I'll get out of the way, just a minute. *(to the children)* Okay, next. We have to go to the ticket counter. Paula, take the Lego… yes, you're a good girl, a very good girl… *(to EVE)* No, I know you were scared. Don't worry, Mommy won't let go. Here, hold on to my coat, okay? Hold on to my coat and you won't get lost. Paula, take the Lego and you hold on to my coat, too… and I'll take the rest… and off we go! *(She laughs.)* It's like a nursery rhyme, right? "Hold my coat, don't let go, hold your Lego, off we go! Hold my coat, don't let go—" *(She is held back by EVE who is tugging on her coat.)* Eve, follow me! Don't pull… *(to the audience)* We finally reached the ticket counter, and there were 20 people lined up at every wicket. We stood in the 21st position with all our bags, meaning: the bag of groceries, the sack of clean clothes, the suitcase, the Lego, one pillow-blankie, another pillow-blankie, and the two girls… *(to EVE)* No, Eve, stop… Eve! You can't go ahead, we have to stand in line.

EVE   Why, Mommy?

MOMMY   Because the lady was here before us, she deserves to go first and we have to wait our turn…

EVE   Why, Mommy?

MOMMY   *(to the audience)* Try to explain to a three-year-old why you have to stand in line! So twenty-one times, we had to move: the bag of groceries, the sack of clean clothes, the suit—you get the picture! *(to PAULA)* Stop, don't push the suitcase like that, it will open… Paula! *(The suitcase spills open.)* Great! *(On her hands and knees, MOMMY gathers up everything.)*

PAULA   I'm a good girl, right, Mommy? I'm helping you.

MOMMY   My God, what a mess this suitcase is! You must have played with it after I packed, did you?

PAULA   No, Mommy. You made the mess, the last minute, you threw our clean winter clo—

MOMMY   Alright! Fine! Push it this way, okay…. No, like this… *(to the audience)* We finally made it to the wicket. *(to EVE)* No, it's alright, Mommy will ask him. *(to THE TICKET AGENT)* Could you tell me the price of the ticket to Saint-Grégoire… Nicolet!

THE TICKET AGENT   Saint-Grégoire or Nicolet? It's not the same place, so it's not the same price, ma'am.

MOMMY   Sorry, I was distracted, of course, it's Nicolet…. What do I do with the kids?

THE TICKET AGENT   Hold them on your lap.

MOMMY   Are you kidding? Can't you see I have two of them?! How long is the trip anyway?

THE TICKET AGENT   Two and a half hours, ma'am.

MOMMY   *(sighing)* Oh, well, do I have the right to an extra seat? For free?

THE TICKET AGENT   How old are these kids?

MOMMY   They're three.

EVE   Three and a quarter, Mommy!

MOMMY   *(to EVE)* Yes, that's right…. Three and a quarter… *(to THE TICKET AGENT)* Yes, they're both three and a quarter, they're twins, twin girls.

THE TICKET AGENT   Twins! And you don't dress them alike? *(He grumbles.)* Half-price!

MOMMY   Pardon me?

THE TICKET AGENT   *(raising his voice)* Half-price, Madam.

MOMMY   Sorry, I couldn't hear you… Paula, you can sit on my lap for a while and Eve will have her own seat, okay? And afterwards—

THE TICKET AGENT   Hurry up, Madam, there's a long line behind you…. You don't have to explain everything to them…

MOMMY   That's my business, if you don't mind. Mommy will explain afterwards, okay? *(to a woman)* I'm doing my best, Madam, I'm doing my best! Yes, well, I don't want to miss my bus, either! *(to the children)* Wait! Just wait a minute and I'll explain everything. *(to THE TICKET AGENT)* Yes, please, one round-trip for an adult, and one half-price, one way only…

THE TICKET AGENT   One round-trip ticket full fare, one half-price one-way…. Are you sure? Are those your kids?

MOMMY   Yes, they're mine!… I'm going to hold one on my lap and the other one will have her own seat, and—

THE TICKET AGENT   I'm not stupid, I figured that out…. So those kids are going with you, but they're not coming back with you, is that it?

MOMMY   That's it!

THE TICKET AGENT   *(surprised)* They're not coming back with you!!!!

MOMMY   No, sir! I'm taking them to their father's house. Their father lives in Nicolet. And I live in Montreal. We're separated… we weren't married, we were living together, but now we're separated…. Is there anything else you'd like to know?

THE TICKET AGENT   Calm down, calm down! You can't expect me to know that…

MOMMY   *(to the woman behind her)* Yes, Madam, I'm doing my best! *(She takes out her money and hands it to the agent.)* There! *(She takes the tickets and speaks to PAULA.)* No, no, it's all right, Mommy will put them away so we don't lose them. *(to THE TICKET AGENT, coolly)* Thank you, sir, for being so kind… and so discreet.

PAULA   Are you mad, Mommy? Sing the little song you were singing before, you know, "Hold my coat, don't let go, hold your Lego…" It was nice.

MOMMY   Mommy doesn't feel like singing right now! We're not done yet… now we have to get to Gate 17. We can't go wrong, it's the last gate at the other end of the station…. Just around the corner there…. Now take your Lego…. Yes, alright, I'll sing… *(embarrassed)* Hold my coat, don't let go, hold your Lego and off we go! Hold my coat, don't let go, hold your Lego and off we go… *(to the audience)* I'll spare you the trek through the station! Unless you're dying to hear it! *(to the children)* No, girls, stop. No escalator now, c'mon, we're going to miss the bus!… Okay, just once! Go ahead, Eve, go on, Mommy's watching you. *(to someone who pushes her)* Sorry! Of course, I'll free the escalator, sorry… *(to EVE)* No, no, it's alright, Mommy's watching you, now, go ahead, go on! *(to the audience)* After her third turn! *(to the children)* No, that's a newsstand, it's for big people…. No, they don't have anything for little girls…. Yes, there's candy, but we're not buying any. Look! *(Enthusiastically, MOMMY shows them the bag of groceries.)* I have a surprise for you! Don't touch that, leave it on the shelf. Not on the ground! Put it back on the shelf, okay? We're not buying any. *(to the salesgirl)* Pardon me, she didn't squeeze it, she dropped it! If you don't want children touching your candies, you should keep them out of their reach! *(to the children)* Let's go, girls. Come, Eve!

> MOMMY *improvises a little song as they make their way through the station to the departure gate.*

(trying to be upbeat) Off we go, we're on our way.
We're on our way to Nicolet.
Off we go, we're on our way,
We're on our way to Nicolet!

(finally standing by the baggage compartment of the bus, takes the Lego from PAULA) Paula! Your Lego has to stay with our other bags in the baggage compartment. *(PAULA grabs it back.)* Your Lego has to stay with our other bags in the baggage compartment! *(PAULA grabs it back again.)* Okay. It's up to you! But I'm warning you, if you forget it in the bus, or if you lose some pieces, don't blame me. Is that clear? Good! What? *(She laughs.)* Of course, I'll take your blankies and your pillows…. You're going to take a nice nap for Mommy in the bus. Now hurry up, we have to stand in line again…. If we want to get seats…. Hurry up!… No, we have to wait… *(Someone pushes them.)* This time we're not waiting in a line, we're waiting in bunches! Madam? Madam? Miss?… Yes… if you have to step back, please watch where you're going, there are two little children behind you. Thank you. *(Someone pushes them again. To PAULA, under her breath.)* If the lady pushes you, push her back! I said: if the lady pushes you, push her back!

PAULA   How come we can push now, Mommy? You told us not to push before!

DRIVER   Tickets, please!… Yes, ma'am, you can board now…. But if you don't mind, we'll just punch your ticket first…. There we go…. What's that?… Yes, it's slippery, very slippery…. But don't worry, we'll get you there safe and sound. "Slow and steady wins the race," right? Whose little girl is that?

MOMMY   She's mine…. It's because I have two of them, and my luggage to keep an eye on…

DRIVER   I can't let her board the bus on her own, ma'am! Let this lady by, she's all alone with the girls.

MOMMY   Go ahead, Eve…. Go on…

THE SPINSTER   Some people don't mind using their children to get to the head of the line!

DRIVER   Now, don't you let those kids run around in the bus! I don't want to see either one of them in the aisle!

MOMMY   *(as she helps the girls board)* Don't worry, I have a seat for one of them… and I'll hold—Are you going to take care of our bags? I wanted to put them inside, but the compartment isn't open…

DRIVER   Your bags aren't my responsibility! You can get your little monsters settled, then come back—

MOMMY   *(to EVE)* What? No, he's only kidding… *(She boards the bus.)* Not right behind the driver, girls! A little bit farther back…. Here? Fine…. Put your Lego on the floor… go on, go in!… Look, there are lots of people waiting to get by. *(To someone whose way she's blocking.)* Sorry 'bout that…. Mommy's going to put the bag of groceries here, and she'll put your blankies and the pillows on top…. Look, they fit…. See how silly I am, I could have done that before!… Yes, it's hot…. Keep your boots on! The floor's all wet!… No, no…. Keep your boots on! Keep them on! *(to PAULA)* I know, I'm hot, too…. Shall we take your snowsuit off? Sit down! Sit up straight! Your zipper is stuck! Your mittens…. We'll put your mittens in with the groceries…. Pull your hand! Pull!… Good…. That's it, now the other hand! Don't worry! Mommy will put your scarf and your hat in your sleeve. Take off your boots! C'mon, take them off! No! You have to take them off to get your snowsuit off, but then you'll put them on again! You can't do it? *(She takes her daughter's boots off and gets increasingly impatient.)* No! Don't stand up, the floor's wet!… Put your arms around Mommy's neck, I'll slip your suit down over your bum! *(She lifts up her daughter.)* There we go! So, little girl, step into your boots…. Step into your boots! Mommy will put your snowsuit up here…. No, it won't fall! *(to the audience)* Multiply that by two! But there we were, finally, on the bus. Nothing else could go wrong. We were in an enclosed space… like a cocoon! I could give the girls my undivided attention… I was sure we were going to have a wonderful trip…. But, unfortunately, we weren't the only ones on the bus!!!

THE SPINSTER   *(making her way down the aisle with her mother)* No, no, no, I absolutely insist, I want to keep my overnight case on my person. I want to guard it with my life. All my souvenirs, my souvenirs from Rome, are inside… I'm dying to show them to you…. Is this seat all right with you? *(noticing the girls)* Oh, look at the beautiful children! *(aside, to her mother)* Will they get on your nerves, Mother? *(rolling her eyes towards the children)* The children in the seat behind us?

THE ELDERLY MOTHER   No, here is fine…

THE SPINSTER   Would you like the window seat? But there's probably a draught… it might be bad for your rheumatism.

THE ELDERLY MOTHER   No, that's all right, dear, you go ahead…. My leg is killing me, I'll be able to stretch it out in the aisle seat.

THE SPINSTER   As you wish! Oh, we're lucky we got seats. Did you see how many people are still lined up outside? They can't possibly fit everyone into this bus! *(She notices someone waiting to get by.)* Mother, you're blocking the way.

THE GIRLFRIEND *(chewing gum)* Excuse us…. We'd like to sit down, too. *(She notices the girls).* Ooooo, helloooo! Aren't you pretty? What's your name? Oh, that's a pretty name. And there's another one!… Don't tell me, you're twins! How cute can you get! *(to MOMMY)* Are these seats free?… Good… *(to THE BOYFRIEND)* How's this look, honey?

THE BOYFRIEND *(grabbing her bum)* Looks like a nice piece of ass, baby! *(He is drunk.)*

THE GIRLFRIEND *(pushing him away)* Hey! Stop that, you jerk! Not in front of the kids! You sit on the inside…. Go ahead, I like sitting on the aisle…

THE BOYFRIEND No way, you go in first!!! C'mon, move your ass! I didn't sleep all night, and I feel like sleeping on the bus! The window will prevent me from sleeping. *(A hippie pushes by him.)* Hey, you bum, stop pushing!

THE HIPPIE Take it easy, man! *(speaking to THE YOUNG WOMAN behind him)* What a jerk! Are you travelling alone, Miss?

THE YOUNG WOMAN Yes, I am… *(She notices PAULA.)* Oh, hello, Paula!

MOMMY *(surprised)* You know Paula? Oh, of course! Now I recognize you, you took care of Paula while I was chasing after Eve in the station. Did I say thank you, at least? I was so upset… *(to PAULA)* You see your friend is right behind us…

THE DRIVER Hey, everybody. Move ahead to the back, please…. You, sir… with the beard…. Yes, you… you're blocking the aisle.

THE HIPPIE Take it easy, man! Can I sit beside you, Miss? There are so many people, if it's not me, it'll be somebody else…. Wow! Whose little brat is this?

MOMMY It's mine! Paula, stay in your seat…. You can watch…. What's her name? Colette!

THE SPINSTER *(yelling at her mother)* NOOOO! No, no, Mother! Not under the seat! *(She grabs her overnight case.)* I intend to hold it on my lap…. On my lap!

THE BOYFRIEND *(reaching past his girlfriend, trying to pull down the window-shade)* How does this damn shade work?

THE GIRLFRIEND Ouch! You hurt me! You want to pull down the shade? You're going to pull the shade down on me, and snore away in your aisle seat! Honestly…. What a great trip this is going to be.

MOMMY Now you stay there, girls. Almost everyone is on the bus now. I'm going to put our things in the baggage compartment…

EVE *(crying)* Where are you going, Mommy?

MOMMY No, Eve, sit down. Stay there… I'm just going—

EVE I want to go with you, Mommy!

MOMMY   No, Eve, stay here. I'm just going to put our bags away… I'll be right
back! Paula, give your sister a hug, it's because she was scared… *(She tries to
make her way down the aisle blocked by people standing.)* Excuse me, sir, I have to
get out, sorry…

THE ELDERLY MOTHER   Ouchh!

MOMMY   I'm sorry, Madam, excuse me…. But you shouldn't leave your leg in the
aisle like that… I didn't mean to hurt you, but I have to get out…

THE DRIVER   Where do you think you're going, Ma'am?

MOMMY   Me? I just want to put my bags in the baggage compartment. Is it still
open?

THE DRIVER   Never mind! I did it… I felt sorry for you!

MOMMY   Sorry for me! *(Humiliated, she says no more.)* Thank you very much.
(She returns to her seat and speaks to the elderly woman.) Watch your leg! *(to
THE GENTLEMAN standing in the aisle)* Sorry, sir, this is my seat. *(to PAULA)*
Make some room for Mommy! *(beat)* No, not right away! We'll have the candy
later, after your nap. If there is a nap…

THE BOYFRIEND   *(He takes a flask out of his pocket and takes a swig on the sly. He
coughs.)* Hey, driver! I thought you weren't allowed to let people stand in the
aisle because of the insurance?

THE DRIVER   Why don't you mind your own business? You've got a seat, so count
yourself lucky! What can I say? There aren't any other buses…

THE GENTLEMAN   *(standing in the aisle)* Exactly! I absolutely have to be in
Gentilly first thing tomorrow morning!… Gentilly—the nuclear power plant.
(He clearly means to impress people. Then, speaking to himself:) Bunch of
ignoramuses. *(As he turns towards her to let someone by, he receives MOMMY's
elbow in his crotch.)*

MOMMY   Oh, I'm sorry!

THE GENTLEMAN   *(as he catches his breath)* No problem. Are you travelling
alone?

MOMMY   Well, no, I'm not alone, I'm with my daughters, Eve and Paula. *(to the
children)* No, girls, no Lego in the bus! No! All right, just a little handful… not
on the floor… just enough to make a little man… *(to THE GENTLEMAN
whom she has just elbowed again:)* So sorry, again! *(She doesn't know how to sit.
She speaks to him:)* Pardon me? Oh, no, not all the way to Three Rivers, just to
Nicolet… I'm taking the girls to their father's house…. It's his turn to have
them for two weeks. We have joint custody, fifty-fifty…. Until they start
school…. Do they miss me? I'm the one who misses them. *(caressing EVE)*
Right, sweetie?!

EVE   Mommy, I want to go there…

MOMMY   Where, there? In the aisle? No, you're not allowed, Eve.

EVE   Then why is the man there?

MOMMY   It's because he doesn't have a seat, do you understand? Besides, when the bus is moving, it's very dangerous.

EVE   We're not moving now!

MOMMY   *(smiling)* Okay, go ahead, but right here in the aisle… and as soon as we start moving…

PAULA   Me too!

MOMMY   Yes, of course, you too…

THE GIRLFRIEND   Hi! You coming to see me? You're pretty…. What? No, I don't have any more gum, too bad, eh?

MOMMY   *(apologizing for the girls)* They're not shy! You might regret it… we've got at least two and a half hours ahead of us. Maybe more…

> The bus shifts into motion.

Oops! We're off…. Back to your seats, girls. Hurry. Mommy's going to sit between the two of you. *(to the audience)* We were finally on our way! I was just about to tell them a story when—

PAULA   Mommy! *(She is crying.)* Eve won't give me my Lego man!

EVE   She wasn't even playing with it!

MOMMY   Eve, you know the rules: the one who makes the Lego man gets to play with it, for as long as she wants…

EVE   *(shouting)* She wasn't even playing with it!

PAULA   *(shouting too)* Mommy, I want it, there's only one red one like that… I want it…

THE SPINSTER   It's not easy, raising children…

MOMMY   No, Miss, you can say that again! Please, stop, Eve! You know the rules, you know— *(embarrassed, to THE GENTLEMAN)* We need rules, don't we? *(to the audience)* We need rules! *(to EVE)* Give it to Mommy.

PAULA   *(screaming)* I want it!

THE BOYFRIEND   For Christ's sake! Your little girl's got a helluva loud voice!

MOMMY   Yes, she does… Eve, let her play with it for a few minutes and then she'll forget it, alright? *(to PAULA)* There, take it. Now, stop crying.

PAULA   *(with a triumphant smile)* Thank you, Mommy. *(She looks at EVE, then looks at MOMMY and says)* Here, Eve. You can have it… take it…

MOMMY   Now you're giving it to her!? You're giving it to her! You make a scene, then you give it back to her… Paula, why do you always give your toys to your sister when she asks for them? Even when you really want them yourself?

PAULA   I'm a good girl, aren't I, Mommy?

MOMMY   You want me to tell you you're a good girl, don't you? You just want Mommy to say you're a good girl? *(to the audience)* That reminded me of me and my mother!

In another space, MOMMY becomes mother-woman-child.

MOTHER   Oh, what a good girl! Mommy's good little girl! Go ahead, sweetie, say "Daddy"…. Say "Daddy"…. "Dad–dy." Go ahead. Don't make Mommy sad…. You said it yesterday. C'mon, say it…. And don't forget, when our-dear-daddy-who-works-so-hard-all-day-for-us comes home, say it to him, it will make him so happy, don't forget… *(surprised)* Wait, is that him home already?… Now, don't forget, okay, precious…. Don't forget…

FATHER   Estelle?

MOTHER   I'm here in the living room with Daddy's little girl…

FATHER   *(obviously preoccupied)* After that scene this morning, don't you think we should—No, not in front of her…

MOTHER   Wait! Don't leave! You know what she said just now? *(to LOUISETTE)* Go ahead, sweetie, c'mon…. Say it now!

LOUISETTE   Dddd… dddd… ddaa…

FATHER   *(pleased)* Oh, what a sweet little girl, Daddy loves his sweet little girl!

LOUISETTE   Ddd… dda…

MOTHER   She says "Daddy" but she won't say "Mommy". Really! We all know, her father…

LOUISETTE   Da… da… a… ddda…

MOTHER   What about Mommy? Don't you love your Mommy? Can't you say "Mommy" for a change?

FATHER   *(hesitating)* That's right…. C'mon, say "Mommy" now…. Go ahead, say, "Mommy."

LOUISETTE   Ddda…. Maaaa… *(She hesitates, looking from one to another. She takes a few faltering steps, as if walking on a tightrope.)* Daddy…. Mmmom… my….

Change of scene. Her mother is teaching LOUISETTE a song.

(singing) Daddy had a little lamb, little lamb,
Daddy had a little lamb, her— *(She forgets the words, then remembers.)*
Her fleece was white as snow…

MOTHER   Oh, the doorbell. It's time for Mommy's music lesson. Now don't forget, you have to sing that for Daddy tonight. Don't forget. *(to her student)* Come in! Come in! Now, Louisette, you go outside and play with your little friend.

LOUISETTE   Hi, Michel! Did you bring your little red truck? *(disappointed)* Oh, did you bring your water pistol?… Oh, well, come here on my porch. I have something to show you. *(She takes down her pants.)* Look at my bum, go ahead, tickle me, here!

NEIGHBOUR   Oh, you nasty little girl! I saw you! What do you think you're doing? Wait till I tell your mother. *(calling)* Madame Dussault! Madame Dussault! You won't believe, your daughter and the little boy! It's awful! Terrible! And she was the one who asked him to… to… *(She can't bring herself to say it.)* Coming from a little girl! I don't know what you're going to do with that child!

MOTHER   Really… what am I going to do with you? *(She turns around once, then:)* Could you please take your little brother, and your little sisters by the hand, and take them into the kitchen…. You hear me? You're the oldest, old enough to understand! And old enough to do your share… *(in tears)* Can't you see I work my fingers to the bone for you kids! Now, go on, please…

LOUISETTE   Yes, Mommy…. C'mon, girls! *(to her little brother)* Come on, you! *(She hurts him.)*

MOTHER   I saw that!!! I saw you! You pinched him! Ah ha! You're acting bossy…. Taking advantage of the fact that your father's not around…. Just wait till he gets home…. We'll see how proud he is of his little Louii—

LOUISETTE   No, wait, Mommy, I'll take care of my little brother… my little sisters… my homework… the errands… supper… my prayers… my school-work… I run, I fly, I skate… *(to the audience)* I was always skating on thin ice… *(to her MOTHER)* Are you crying, Mommy? Is it my fault? Am I the one who made you sad? Am I the one who made you sad with Daddy? *(She is surprised by her own comment.)* Am I the one who made you sad with Daddy! If I weren't here, you'd be Daddy's little sweetheart, wouldn't you? Mommy… Mommy… *(anger followed by a forced laugh)* You're going to be happy, I practiced my scales…. Look: do, re, mi…. See how I move my thumbs? Look, Mommy, I went to my ballet lesson…. Third position…. Fourth position… I'm going to imitate Mrs. Baillargeon downstairs…. That always makes you laugh! "Bobbykins, Bobbykins!" Look, Mommy, look… *(She sings.)* London Bridge is falling down…. Look, Mommy, look! *(She clowns around, falls, then does a headstand.)*

>   *Change of scene. Back on the bus.*

PAULA   I'm a good girl, aren't I, Mommy?

MOMMY   You want Mommy to tell you you're a good girl, don't you? You want me to say you're a good girl? Well, I'm not going to say it. I'm not going to say it, because I want you to stop giving your sister your toys just so Mommy will tell you you're a good girl. I want you to give her your toys only when you feel like giving her your toys, you understand? When *you* feel like it, not me! *(worried)* Paula! What's the matter?! Paula!

PAULA   *(letting out a long cry of distress)* Aiiiieeeee!

MOMMY   Don't cry, pussycat…. Don't cry like that…. No, wait, go ahead, cry… *(She takes her into her arms.)* Go ahead and cry, mouse. If it makes you feel better… *(She makes PAULA look at her.)* Paula, Mommy loves you very much. Mommy loves you the way you are…. The way you are…. You don't have to do more… Mommy loves you just as you are. Even when you're mad, mad at your little sister, Mommy loves you, she loves you. *(almost to the audience)* What does that word mean? *(to PAULA)* I think you're nice because you're you… because you're you!

EVE   *(upset)* Mommy!

MOMMY   Yes, Eve…

EVE   What's wrong with Paula?… Something between you and her, oh…

> *She looks out the window and starts singing to the tune of London Bridge, obviously trying to please her mother.*

People walk across the bridge
Boats go by under the bridge.

MOMMY   *(picks up the song)* Now the bus drives o'er the bridge
See the planes fly o'er the bridge.

EVE   *(interrupting her)* Mommy, we're not on the Jacques-Cartier Bridge anymore…

MOMMY   It doesn't matter, Eve, we can still sing, can't we?

> *She sings.*

Jacques-Cartier is our own bridge,
Our own bridge, our own bridge
One two three, we drive across…

EVE   *(singing exuberantly)* One, two, three is Mommy and us…

MOMMY   *(hugging EVE)* Mommy's little clown! Yes, I love you! You're a good girl…. And you catch on fast….

EVE   *(pulling away)* Ouch, Mommy, you're choking me. What's our surprise?

MOMMY   *(to the audience)* I wanted to keep the candies for later on in the trip, but who could resist that… *(to EVE)* You little rascal! *(She picks up the bag of groceries.)* Okay, now close your eyes…. If you want it to be a surprise! No cheating! *(She takes out some lollipops.)* Look! Lollipops! There you go…. Do you feel better now, Paula? Wait, let me unwrap it…

EVE Me, too, Mommy!!!!!

MOMMY Of course, you get one, too, Eve. Don't worry…. But shhhh, don't shout so loud…. The man across the aisle is asleep!

PAULA He's not really sleeping, Mommy.

MOMMY He's not sleeping, but he's trying to sleep! Now don't stand up, you can hurt yourselves with the lollipop sticks…. Don't stand up!

THE SPINSTER *(showing her mother a holy medal)* Wait till you see this one…. It's the most beautiful of all…. And this one was blessed by the Pope, too.

THE ELDERLY MOTHER You're right, it is beautiful!

THE SPINSTER Isn't it? The chain is real gold and it's much more delicate…. Obviously, it wasn't the same price… *(beat)* That's the one I wanted to give you…

THE ELDERLY MOTHER It's much too beautiful for me!

THE SPINSTER Nothing is too beautiful for you…

EVE I want to see the little chain…

MOMMY Eve!!! Watch out for your lollipop on the lady's hat!

THE SPINSTER *(alarmed)* Ohhhhh! My hat!

MOMMY She didn't touch it, Miss, she didn't even come close! *(to EVE)* Now sit down with your lollipop! Watch out! You're getting it on my coat…. Watch what you're doing! Now you both sit still until we finish our lollipops. If the driver had to slam on the brakes, you could really get hurt.

THE HIPPIE *(to his neighbour)* Do you live in Montreal?

THE YOUNG WOMAN No, I live in Trois Rivières.

THE HIPPIE What a coincidence, me too…. You still living at home?

THE YOUNG WOMAN No, I moved into an apartment with a girlfriend when I started university…

THE HIPPIE University? I dropped out. There are no jobs out there, why bother to get an education? I decided to take a sabbatical for a couple of years.

THE GIRLFRIEND *(to her boyfriend)* Hey! Would you mind sleeping on your side! My arm is falling asleep, all the way up to my shoulder and my neck…

> *Clearly bored, she runs her hand through her hair, checks her breasts, adjusts her bra. She notices that THE GENTLEMAN in the aisle is staring at her and she stares back, provocatively. She stops chewing her gum, looks aloof, dignified, then looks away, very "super model." She keeps this up for a few seconds, but THE GENTLEMAN has stopped looking at her. She resumes her natural manner and starts chewing her gum again.*

*Fed up, bored, she goes to raise the shade, thinking that THE
BOYFRIEND is still asleep.*

THE BOYFRIEND   Hey, for Christ's sake, what are you doing, pull that damn
thing down!

THE GIRLFRIEND   I feel like reading… I want to sit here and read.

THE BOYFRIEND   Well, I feel like sleeping. I didn't sleep all night, I was sick…

THE GIRLFRIEND   You were sick?! You were sick because you drank too much!
You should've drunk less, you jerk!

THE BOYFRIEND   Drunk less! Stuck at a party with a dumb bitch like you!!!!

THE GIRLFRIEND   Shut up! Are you saying it's my fault you got dead drunk last
night? No way!

PAULA   Is the lady mad, Mommy?

MOMMY   Paula, stop staring at people! They want to be alone…. What's that?
Your lollipop stick?… You chewed on it, you little rascal, didn't you? That's not
good for your teeth, you know.

PAULA   Peepee, Mommy…

MOMMY   What?

PAULA   Peepee, Mommy…

MOMMY   You have to be kidding, Paula. We went in the bus station, less than an
hour ago! And there are people blocking the aisle all the way to the back of the
bus!

PAULA   *(It's an emergency.)* I have to go peepee, Mommy!!!

MOMMY   *(She stands up and takes EVE by the arm.)* Okay, fine…. Let's go. Both
of you. Eve, we're going to the toilet.

EVE   I don't need to, Mommy!

MOMMY   *(angry)* Eve, the three of us are going!!!!

EVE   *(shouting)* I don't need to go peepee!

MOMMY   Not so loud…. Are you sure? I'm warning you, Eve… I won't go back
again. You'll have to wait till Nicolet! What did you do with your lollipop stick?
On the floor! Pick it up! If everyone acted like that, we'd be travelling in
a garbage pail.

PAULA   Mommy, peepee, fast!

    MOMMY takes PAULA in her arms and heads for the back of the bus.

MOMMY   Excuse me…. Excuse me…. Sorry…. Very sorry… oops, sorry, did
I hurt you? Excuse me!

PAULA   My boot, Mommy!

MOMMY   Hold on tight, Paula! There we go, hold on…

PAULA   My boot!

MOMMY   We're almost there…. Sorry…. Excuse me…

PAULA   My boot!

MOMMY   Wait, Paula, for heaven's sake. We're almost there… *(She opens the door to the toilet and sets PAULA down, then surprised:)* You lost one of your boots!

PAULA   I told you, Mommy, I told you but you didn't listen to me.

MOMMY   Stay there, don't move, Mommy will go get your boot! Hold on to this little pipe… and don't touch anything, it's dirty! *(She heads back down the aisle.)* Excuse me, where's that boot? Excuse me… I'm looking for a boot…. A snow boot… *(Someone hands her the boot.)* Thank you, sir… *(She returns to the back of the bus.)* There you go, sweetie, put your boot on… Mommy's holding you…. No, nobody can see your bum… I'm going to close the door…. Push over, it's small in here.

PAULA   Look, Mommy, a little light goes on when you close the door!

MOMMY   That's right, the little light goes on when we close the door. *(She lifts PAULA up.)* Paula, pull your tights down first…. Your tights before your panties!

PAULA   Mommy, I want to peepee standing up.

MOMMY   Well, sorry, but you can't peepee standing up!

PAULA   I want a penis, like Daddy…

MOMMY   Don't be silly, Paula…. You're a girl. And you have a pretty little vagina and a pretty little clitoris…. Now, up you go!

PAULA   Mommy! I'm scared! There's a big hole in the toilet!!!

MOMMY   Don't worry, I'm holding you, now, go ahead…

PAULA   I don't have to anymore…

MOMMY   Oh, no! Psssss…. Pssss…. *(beat)* Ah, good, that's a nice peepee. Good, go ahead, what a nice peepee… *(it lasts forever)* Are you almost done? Mommy's arms are going to fall off… *(She sets her down.)* Now wipe your little private parts.

PAULA   No, you do it, Mommy…

MOMMY   All right, fine… *(She wipes her.)* There, your pretty little pussy… pretty pussy…. Pull up your panties…. Before your tights! Good! *(She hits her head.)* Ouchhh! It's all right… *(She flushes the toilet.)*

PAULA   Look, Mommy, the water's blue.

MOMMY   Yes, the water's blue.

PAULA   Why is the water blue?

MOMMY   The water's blue because they put a disinfectant in it.

PAULA   Why do they put a dis-in-fectant in it?

MOMMY   *(trying to close the door behind her)* So it doesn't stink!

PAULA   It stinks anyway!

MOMMY   No, Mommy can't carry you now…. Mommy's arms are going to fall off. *(They are in the aisle.)* Excuse us…. Sorry…. Excuse me… *(They reach their seat.)* Good, there's your little sister!

EVE   Mommy, I want to peepee in the little cabin, too!

MOMMY   No… no… Eve, we—

EVE   *(shouting)* I have to peepee bad, Mommy!

MOMMY   *(to the audience)* And back I went!!! *(to EVE)* It better be a big peepee! *(She picks up EVE and starts back down the aisle.)* Here we go again! *(She stumbles and almost lands in THE HIPPIE's lap.)* Oops! Sorry…. It's us again…

THE HIPPIE   Just keep cool, everything will work out… *(to THE YOUNG WOMAN)* Do you smoke?

THE YOUNG WOMAN   I don't smoke tobacco…

THE HIPPIE   *(bursts out laughing)* That's a good one…. How 'bout a little joint?

THE YOUNG WOMAN   You're not going to smoke in the bus! Wow, you don't mess around…. Well, if you light one up, I'll have a little toke.

THE HIPPIE   *(lighting up a joint)* Wait till you try this… *(He takes a toke and holds his breath, then:)* Here, have some—

THE DRIVER   Hey, you back there, you sure you're allowed to smoke in those seats?

THE HIPPIE   Yes, driver…. No sweat. We're allowed because I don't see a no-smoking sign…. And there's an ashtray, that's a sign, right? Ha ha!

PAULA   My daddy smokes cigarettes like that!!

THE SPINSTER   That tobacco smells strange, don't you think? It must be those French cigarettes!

THE ELDERLY MOTHER   You know I always hated the smell of tobacco. But I had no choice, I had to get used to it.

THE BOYFRIEND   *(waking up)* What's that smell? *(loudly)* I smell pot!

THE GENTLEMAN   *(standing in the aisle)* I'm afraid so! *(to THE HIPPIE)* Sir!?… Yes, you, sir!… Aren't you afraid to smoke that in public?

THE HIPPIE   Oh, I thought you wanted a toke, man! *(He takes a puff, but he burns his fingers. He drops the joint and tries to stamp it out.)*

THE GENTLEMAN   Never mind! *(He steps on the butt.)*

MOMMY   *(returning from the toilet with EVE)* Excuse me, sir, so sorry… *(to EVE)* Eve, you and your three little drops! Sit down. I know…. You just wanted to see what it was like, right? Look outside… it's still daylight…. Look out the window now, pretty soon it will be dark. *(Out of breath, she breathes in deeply, notices the smell of marijuana, smiles, and replies to THE GENTLEMAN in the aisle.)* What? I'm smiling because it smells of… *(She hesitates.)* Marijuana, right! *(conspiratorially, to the audience)* Pot! Pot!

> *Change of scene. MOMMY is pregnant. She opens the door of their pickup.*

(sniffing the air) You smoked a joint in the pickup? It makes me nauseous… I don't know if it's because of my condition, but it makes me anxious, too…. It seems to me you've been smoking a lot lately…. How many joints do you smoke a day? Six? Seven? Eight?… Forget it. Since I can't smoke anymore, it feels like we're not on the same wavelength. *(She hesitates before carrying on.)* Listen, you should go to the Parti Québécois meeting alone. I keep getting this pain in my back… I don't know what it is… I'll stay here…. The sun feels good… *(Beat, as she listens to his response.)* No, I'm not trying to make you feel guilty because you were smoking… I'm really tired. *(beat)* No, I wanted to go, I changed my clothes, everything, I even put on the t-shirt you gave me…. It looks good with my tummy, doesn't it? *(She opens her shawl and reveals a t-shirt with the slogan "Québec, on t'aime ben gros"/"Quebec, our love for you is huge", over an enormous fleur de lys. She laughs.)* But go ahead, go by yourself, okay… *(Beat, then she makes up her mind.)* And, by the way… I have the feeling you never say anything when I'm around… I inhibit you, don't I? I know I can take up a lot of space… *(She points to her tummy.)* No, that's not what I mean. *(beat)* Anyway, I think I'll stay home. You're not mad at me? Are you? Are you mad at me? You're not answering me. Oh, well, see you later. Have a good afternoon…. Drive safely, okay?

(She pats her stomach. The pickup has just left.) I've been worried about him lately. *(She feels the babies move. She is moved.)* Oh, my beautiful little babies, my beautiful babies! Now I know for sure that there are two of you. Not one, two! *(She laughs.)* You know, your daddy and I wanted to have two…. We even said: "It would be fun to have two at once…. 'Cause me and you make two." And it happened! It actually happened! It's like a miracle…. You've changed my life. *(She realizes.)* You've changed my whole life. I'm much slower now. *(She sits down in the sun.)* I don't know if you can see the sun through my skin…. It probably makes a red glow. Floating in red heat. *(She peeks under her t-shirt.)* Did I apply my coconut oil this morning? Let's do our exercises now! *(She does some pre-natal exercises.)* Ever since you arrived, I take care of my body like

never before… *(She laughs.)* It's as if my body HAS finally found a use…
(suddenly anxious) That's a stupid thing to say… *(beat)* As if I could only accept
my body if it's useful…. As if I decided to have children so I could feel useful?
To feel less guilty? Guilty about what, for heaven's sake? My two abortions?
(She rocks her stomach.) Oh, no, my little babies, my sweet babies, you're not
just a pretext…. Ever since you've been inside me, I feel as if I'm living inside
myself with you, as if I truly exist for the first time! I can hardly wait for you to
come out, I want to hold you in my arms, and hug you, and love you… I need
you… *(beat)* This doesn't make sense…. Could I be giving birth to you when
I should be giving birth to myself? *(She starts.)* Oh, ow! What's that… I think
it's too late! *(Pain. Panting.)* Looks like we're going to be born at the same
time…

>   *Back to the bus.*

EVE   Hey, Mommy, I want to pretend to be the little baby in your belly.

MOMMY   No, not in the bus… I don't want to stretch my sweater.

EVE   I want to see your breasts, Mommy…

THE SPINSTER   Don't tell me?!

MOMMY   Not in the bus, Eve…. Why not? Because some people don't like that.
(beat) Girls! Stop! *(trying to distract them)* I'm going to tell you a story… okay?
My best story! Stay in your seats! The story of how you were born…

EVE   *(disappointed, interrupts her)* We know that story…. You mean when Daddy
put his penis in your vagina and all that?

THE SPINSTER   *(shocked)* Do you hear that, Mother?

MOMMY   Really, Eve! That's not how I told the story…. At least, not exactly….
No, in those days, Daddy and I really loved each other and we were living
together. *(beat)* We still love each other a lot, but not enough to live together.
We don't love each other like lovers, but like friends. You know, like you and
your friend, Renaud. You like him a lot, but… *(She listens to EVE.)* You do want
to live with him? *(to THE GENTLEMAN)* Yes, she is precocious! *(to EVE)* Eve,
this is my story…. In those days, we loved each other very much and we
thought: "It would be fun to turn our love into a little baby."

EVE   *(interrupting her)* Into two little babies…. Boring! We know that story, you
tell it all the time…. Tell us a scary story, Mommy!

MOMMY   Not in the bus, okay, Eve? *(pause)* Oh, look, girls, it's getting dark out….
Time to take a little nap. What do you say? That will be nice for the whole bus!

EVE   *(protests)* I'm not sleepy, Mommy!

MOMMY   You're going to take a nap. We agreed on that.

EVE   *(crying)* I'm not sleepy, Mommy!

MOMMY   See, you're crying… that's because you're tired. Look! Here are your pillows, your blankies… lie down with your heads on my lap… Eve, be quiet! *(She lays her down again.)* Eve, lie down! Lie down! *(sharply, firmly)* Lie down! What's the matter? Stop crying. *(She listens.)* Fine, a little rest… yes, I know the difference…. You don't have to close your eyes for a rest… *(to PAULA)* Yes, I know, if she's not going to take a nap, you won't either. I know…. Now lie down, both of you. Take some deep breaths. *(Beat. Relieved, she sighs.)* Yes…. That's better! I'll give you a little backrub. *(She rubs their backs.)* Does that feel good? I'll give you some love taps and sing a little song to help you go to sl—to help you rest. *(to THE GENTLEMAN in the aisle)* Yes, they have a mind of their own! *(She sings.)* A-A-ni-kou-ouni cha-a-ou-a-ni *(to THE GENTLEMAN in the aisle)* That's how I put them to sleep. *(She resumes singing.)* A-a-ni-kou—

EVE   We're sick of that song, Mommy, sing another one!

MOMMY   Lie down, Eve…. Okay, let me think of another one… I know! *(She sings.)* Twinkle, twinkle, little star, how I wonder—

EVE   *(interrupting her)* It's not even dark out!

MOMMY   *(laying EVE down, speaking to the audience)* My songs from *la Souris Verte* don't always work. All right, fine, no nap, but on one condition: you have to sit still for five minutes without moving… *(to PAULA)* Yes, you, too. I know, if Eve doesn't sleep, you won't…. Fine…. Fold up your blankies. You know how… *(Annoyed, she puts the pillows away.)*

PAULA   I want a candy, Mommy.

MOMMY   You think you deserve a candy!

PAULA   You have some and you're going to give us some…

MOMMY   How can you be so sure of yourself? *(bitterly)* Or so sure of me?! Okay. I'll give you some candy, as long as you sit still for ten minutes… *(to the audience)* I hate blackmail, but sometimes, dammit, it works! *(to PAULA)* Now stay in your seat and I'll give you a candy… that's simple, right? Fine…. Sit… candy… sit… candy!

THE SPINSTER   Some people don't know how to deal with children. Women today can't make them obey…. They let them have their way. Imagine, giving them candy so they'll sit still!

MOMMY   Paula, if you don't sit still, I'll take it away from you. That was our deal!

THE HIPPIE   If I ever have kids, man, I'm going to bring them up as free spirits! Like Summerhill…. You want some candy? Have some! You feel sick? Tough luck for you!

THE YOUNG WOMAN   *(stoned)* Well, if I ever have kids, I'll know why I had them. Hi, Eve!

MOMMY   If you don't mind, they're going to sit still for a while.

THE ELDERLY MOTHER Believe you me, things were different in my days…. We didn't go traipsing around in buses with our children. Besides, on the farm, there were always lots of people around to take care of your children…

THE SPINSTER What can I say, Mother? Women today aren't willing to sacrifice anything for their husband and children. They prefer to be free! Feminism…. They end up raising their children alone…. Well, it serves them right, let them suffer…

MOMMY *(to PAULA, taking her candy away from her)* I told you! I told you, I'm taking it away from you!

PAULA *(shouting)* You're not nice…. You're not nice!

MOMMY Stop shouting!

PAULA *(still shouting)* You're not… *(She lowers her voice.)* …nice…. Give it back to me.

MOMMY I told you to sit still.

PAULA I love Daddy more than you! I want to live with Daddy. I want to live with Daddy and Liliane!

MOMMY *(surprised, she registers the comment)* Ah, blackmail, it works both ways. *(beat)* Well, well… Paula… you're just a little girl, but you already know how to hurt me, don't you? You already know how!

> *Change of scene. The lights go up on MOMMY, back to the audience.*

Oh! You scared me! I didn't hear you come out… I needed a breath of air! What? *(She listens.)* Well, there's no point in hiding it from you… I thought you'd tell me when you and Liliane moved in together… I thought you'd warn me…. When we arrived a while ago and I saw the girls run over and hug her, calling her "Mommy," it was quite a shock. Especially since lately they've been calling me "Louisette"… *(She is crying.)* I'm jealous. *(louder)* I'm jealous! Not of your relationship with Liliane…. We've been separated for so long…. That's pretty much healed! But I'm all alone. I'm playing the mother and the father! It's impossible, but I try!… But the two of you are together, there are two of you, and that's like everything the girls see on television, in their storybooks… at school, in all the commercials: Daddy, Mommy and the children, all happy together—Walt Disney! What can I say? I'm tired of playing Mother. I have two children, two beautiful daughters I love, and I want to give them everything I can, but I'm exhausted, drained…. After years of entertaining other people's children…. Pathetic! *(She listens.)* You're right! No wonder I'm tired of playing Mother! I've been playing Mother since I was born… I played Mother to my father, to my brother, to my sisters, my boyfriends, the men in my life… *(She listens.)* Yes, with you, too, don't deny it… you were the first one to tell me so… *(She listens.)* I know you didn't ask me to be your mother…. Not consciously, at least…. But that's what I do! I guess it's my way of getting people to love me—

anticipating everyone's needs, being at their beck and call…. As if no one would love ME just for ME… WHO AM I? Just plain ME? *(She cries. Beat.)* Would you mind… just for a change… would you mind not talking to me about your problems at work, your money problems, your problems with Liliane?… *(She listens.)* Yes, it shows how much you trust me…. It helps erase all the pain…. Sure, but it casts me in the role of the mother more than ever! *(She cries.)* I don't want to be your mother anymore… I don't want to feel like my daughters' grandmother. *(She turns away to cry. He takes her into his arms.)* It's nice of you to hold me. It feels good. *(She listens.)* No, don't worry, I won't get any ideas! *(She listens.)* Yes, we're managing pretty well with the girls, you're right! They seem happy, they're thriving…. It's not them… it's me. Now I'm giving birth to myself and it's a difficult delivery… *(beat)* I feel a bit better…. Thanks…. We better go back in, before Liliane gets worried. *(to the audience)* Don't tell me I'm going to start mothering her, too!

> *Back in the bus.*

THE DRIVER   Okay, we usually stop here for fifteen minutes, but since we're running late, 47 minutes late, I'm the only one getting off today, just to pick up the mail…

THE SPINSTER   What do you mean? I absolutely have to get some aspirin… I've got a splitting headache… *(to her mother)* What do you expect? The noise, the crying… *(She glances towards MOMMY.)* And the jetlag…

THE BOYFRIEND   What the hell? Now what's going on? Have we stopped?

THE GIRLFRIEND   You know we always stop here for fifteen minutes, to get a snack, but today, we can't—

THE BOYFRIEND   What? Are you crazy? I could use something to drink, to settle my stomach.

THE HIPPIE   Me, too! I could use something to drink and eat!

THE YOUNG WOMAN   I've got some nice fruit—

THE HIPPIE   Some nice what!

EVE   Mommy, you said you'd buy me a soda here… Mommy…

MOMMY   I know, Eve… but you heard the driver…. We can't get off the bus…. We'll be in Nicolet soon, real soon…. Then I'll buy you—

PAULA   *(shouting)* I want one now…

MOMMY   Well, that's just too bad… I'm not a magician.

PAULA   *(shouting)* You're mean! I want one!

MOMMY   Don't shout…. The woman in front of us has a headache, the other lady is tired, the gentleman wants to sleep…. The people behind us want to be alone… *(to EVE, who is standing on the seat)* Eve, will you please sit down…. Sit down! *(to the audience)* I was at my wits' end, I grabbed Eve by the arm and I told her: *(She shouts at EVE.)* Sit down!!!! *(to the audience)* Then she started to cry and so did I. *(to EVE)* Oh, Eve! Did I hurt you? That wasn't nice…. No, I won't do it again! Yes, I'm a mean mommy, I'm sorry, sweetie… *(She kisses her.)* I'm sorry…. Really sorry…. No, I'm not mad at you… I mean, yes, I am a bit mad. I've been asking you to sit down since we left the station… I know it's not fair, you should be able to move around, but what can I say…. We're on a bus and there are other people… I'm not mad at you, I'm mad at myself… I'm mad at myself…

> *Change of scene.*

MOMMY/LOUISETTE   Oh, that's nice, Mom… you did my wash. That's such a big help!

MOTHER   Oh, dear, wait till I tell you what happened! It's awful! Awful!

MOMMY   What happened?

MOTHER   Oh, it's just awful! I'm so mad at myself, it's so bad, I could kill myself…

MOMMY   Stop, Mom! Just tell me what happened!

MOTHER   *(crying)* My poor little girl… *(beat)* You know your pretty pink blouse? The pretty pink blouse with the pretty braided cord you can wear around your waist… or your neck… if you want…

MOMMY   You burned it with the iron!!!

MOTHER   Well, no…. That's not it! *(She starts crying again.)* You know, the nice little cord? I lost it in my dryer!

MOMMY   What? How?

MOTHER   I don't know…. One of the little rubber thingies is loose, and all the little things I put just go round and round and I never find them again… I knew you'd be furious, I just knew it…

MOMMY   Stop! I didn't say a thing. *(beat)* It's not your fault. You were trying to help…. It's the little loose rubber thingie…. I'm not mad at you. It's all right… *(a longer beat)* Dammit! It's my favourite blouse… I've only worn it twice. Twice! It's brand new… this kind of thing only happens to me…. It went so well with all my clothes, with my grey outfit, with my green suit, my mauve skirt, my brown…. Dammit! Stop bawling! I'm not mad at you… I'm just mad, period! I can't keep it inside… I have to let it out…. For God's sake! What?… Maybe it's just a cord, but it's what made the blouse special… I want it! I want it! I won't leave the house without that cord!…

MOTHER   Well, what can I say, sweetie… I looked for it for over an hour… Louisette? Louisette! Where are you going?!

MOMMY   I'm going to find it even if I have to turn that dryer inside out… *(to the audience)* Fifty minutes later… *(She mimes screwing something together.)*

MOTHER   What did you do to my dryer?

MOMMY   I unscrewed one of the panels, that's all.

MOTHER   But you don't know how—

MOMMY   They are screws, Mom… all you have to do is unscrew them… and rescrew them…

MOTHER   You moved the dryer! Louisette! It weighs more than a hundred pounds…

MOMMY   And now I'm going to turn it over… I want my cord…. And I'm telling you, I'm going to get it. I'm not leaving here without it… *(surprised)* What's this? *(She is holding the ventilation duct.)* Your ventilation duct! I'm afraid it's broken! No, I'm not the one who broke it! What's this mess? *(She looks inside the pipe, then shows it to her mother.)* What is that mess?

MOTHER   What? Oh, I see. That's Cling-free… I put it in the dryer to make the clothes fluffy, you know, so there's not so much electricity… I put at least three boxes in, and I could never find—

MOMMY   Well, they're all right here! Don't you know that's dangerous, Mom…. That's why there's a ventilation duct…. You're crazy! It can overheat in there…. Bring me a garbage bag, I'll clean it for you while I'm at it. *(She takes the lint out.)* Look, one of Catherine's socks…

MOTHER   That disappeared a year ago!

MOMMY   Here, take it! *(She sticks her arm down the duct.)* I can't get any farther…. You'll have to have it cleaned. *(She goes to attach the duct to the dryer.)* Look, everything's clogged up… *(She takes more lint out of the dryer.)* My little braided cord! *(beat)* My cord!!! *(She laughs and waves her cord in the air, triumphantly.)* You see that? I found my cord! Yeah! *(She laughs and kisses her mother.)* I'm so happy, you'd think I just won the lottery! Don't ask me why!!! *(beat)* I found my cord. You thought I'd never find it, right? I saw the look on your face. I had to empty the guts of your dryer, but I got my cord back… *(Her MOTHER is crying and LOUISETTE understands the meaning of "cord." Beat.)* That's not what I meant, Mom! *(She shouts.)* Don't cry! *(She wraps the cord around her neck, mechanically.)* I'm not mad at you! I'm not mad at you! *(furious, impotent)* I'm never mad at you!!! But I am mad!!!! *(beat)* I'm mad at everything that stands between us… between you and me…. The roundabout way you talk to me… the roundabout way I talk to you…. The things you hide from me, and I hide from you…. It feels like we talk to each other through a glass… a looking glass… a mirror…. Talk about a Freudian slip! A mirror! *(beat)* Well, maybe that's it…. C'mon, don't exaggerate. This must be the first time I've lost my temper with you since I was two and I used to stomp my feet and bang my fists on the floor… *(She thinks about it.)* That's too true… *(beat)* What? *(to her MOTHER)* I've got a bad temper! I explode at the drop of a hat! *(Beat, then she unwraps the cord from around her neck.)* I must've been born with the cord around my neck, right? Do you remember? No, of course you don't. *(She's uncomfortable.)* They had to put you to sleep…. It had been so long…. Three days and three nights of labour pains, and you said I tore you from stem to stern… *(with emotion)* Three days… and three nights… in labour… waiting for me… how did you do it, Mommy! Was I the one who didn't want to be born, or was it you who didn't want to bring me into this world? *(She takes her MOTHER into her arms.)* No, I'm not blaming you…. Listen…. Your mother died in childbirth, you must have been afraid of giving birth… but try to understand… *(She is crying.)* Try to understand that it's hard for me to think that maybe I didn't want to be born… *(imploringly)* Try to understand!!! *(She lets go of her MOTHER.)* Have you noticed? Have you noticed that I'm always the one who hugs you first…. Maybe I don't give you a chance… *(moved)* Maybe I'm afraid you'll never do it! *(beat)* I'm your mother! *(She laughs.)* I am your mother. I mean, I protect you like a mother! *(She listens.)* From what? From everything, Mom! From bad news, from the stupid things that this one or that one did, from… *(She hesitates.)* From me. I protect you from me! If I showed you who I really am—moody, angry, jealous… not very pretty, is it? Hysterical…. You'd stop loving me, wouldn't you? You don't know me, Mommy, you don't know me. *(beat)* And I don't know you. *(beat)* Is that what it means to be a mother—to prevent other people from seeing us as we are?… No! To stop living our lives just to make the right impression— *(She shouts.)* Oh, no! No! That's not what I want! I want to live! I want to live, Mommy! *(beat)* Ahhh! It feels good to get mad! *(teasingly)* Just wait! That won't be the last time!!! *(She goes to take her mother into her arms and stops short.)* What?… Am I going to let you hold me in your arms? *(moved)* Oh, Mommy.

    Back in the bus.

THE SPINSTER   What's the driver doing? Why hasn't he come back? Oh, Mother, I think I'm going to faint.

THE ELDERLY MOTHER   Oh, my poor girl, he's been chatting with the waiter in the restaurant for at least twenty minutes…

THE YOUNG WOMAN   *(to THE HIPPIE)* Hey, stop! Don't touch me like that, the little girl is watching us!

THE HIPPIE   So? It's love, not violence…

THE YOUNG WOMAN   Exactly, but I think you're getting a bit carried away!

THE GIRLFRIEND   *(to THE BOYFRIEND)* What are you drinking? I thought so! I saw that!

THE BOYFRIEND   Have some! It's a flask of gin! Everyone knows…. Alcohol is the only cure for a hangover!

THE GIRLFRIEND   Are you crazy? You're not allowed to drink on the bus, you know that. The driver told you so last week! We're going to get arrested. *(She looks out the window.)* Here he comes! Hide that! Quick!

THE DRIVER   Everybody back to their seat, please. We're off… *(THE GENTLEMAN from the aisle boards the bus again.)* Did you get off the bus, sir?

THE GENTLEMAN   Sorry… an extremely important telephone call—

THE SPINSTER   Good for you, sir. We would have had time to get off, too! *(She is mad.)* This is a compulsory stop! I'm going to complain.

THE DRIVER   That's right, ma'am, go right ahead! But wait till we arrive! Right now, I'm not interested! Everybody in their seats!

THE GENTLEMAN   For those who are lucky enough to have a seat!

THE DRIVER   Enough of your wisecracks!

PAULA   The gentleman has a soda, Mommy! I want one, too, I want—

MOMMY   Well, that's just too bad. It's the man's soda, not mine. I can't help it.

PAULA   *(shouting)* I want some, Mommy!

MOMMY   *(to THE GENTLEMAN who is handing her the bottle)* No, that's yours, sir! Let me take care of this! *(to PAULA)* Now just stop, Paula, you hear me…. We'll be in Nicolet soon! And I'll buy you one! I'll buy you two!

PAULA   I'm thirsty, Mommy. I'm thirsty! I'm dying of… Mommy! Let me ask him myself, Mommy, let me ask the man— *(MOMMY's hand has covered her mouth.)*

MOMMY   *(guiltstricken)* Oh! I'm sorry, Paula! *(beat)* What did you say? *(She insists, devastated.)* What did you just say?

PAULA   *(spitefully)* Let me ask him, myself… *(She is crying.)* Let me ask the man…

MOMMY   *(to the audience)* Suddenly dawn broke… I finally got it…. It took me a while, but I got it! *(She stands up.)* I stood up in the bus, I was terrified… I said: "Excuse me…. Excuse me, I have something to say!"

THE SPINSTER   What's wrong with her? Has she lost her mind?

THE ELDERLY MOTHER   Don't ask me.

THE DRIVER   *(after looking over his shoulder, straightens the steering wheel)* We're going to end up in the ditch!

THE GIRLFRIEND   *(standing up)* Goddammit! You and your damn gin! You're going to spill it on me!

THE HIPPIE   Far out, man! Far out!

MOMMY   As you have probably all noticed, I've been holding these two children hostage in this seat for almost four hours…. For four hours I've been preventing them from looking at you, from touching you, from smiling at you, from speaking to you!… For four hours, I've been preventing them from living! But now I quit. I refuse to say "no" to them in your place. If you want to talk to them, go ahead! I won't be jealous! And I'm not afraid of germs…. And if you don't want to talk to them, that's your right! Your right as consenting adults! I'm just asking you to tell them yourselves… *(beat)* Nicely, please! So they don't feel rejected…. But firmly, so they understand! Don't wait till you explode… like me! But tell them yourselves!… I can't go on playing Mommy-The-Cop! I'm incapable of being the ideal mother you'd all like me to be. Incapable!… and I refuse to be your mother, too! I refuse to protect you like children, from my own children… I'm prepared to run the risk that you won't like me, but for the rest of this trip… *(beat)* For the rest of this trip, I refuse to play Mommy-The-Cop for all of you… *(After a long pause, she sits down again. She speaks to the audience.)* There was a deathly silence. People sat there looking at each other.

> THE SPINSTER, *astonished, looks first at her mother, then at* MOMMY.

THE SPINSTER   I don't blame her!

THE DRIVER   *(looking in his rearview mirror)* This I have to see!

THE BOYFRIEND   I'll drink to that!

THE HIPPIE   Far out, man! Far out!

MOMMY   *(to the audience)* All of a sudden, everyone started talking at once.

THE SPINSTER   So what's your name?… Eve! Oh, that's a pretty name…. Do you want to come see me? *(to her mother)* Do you mind, Mother?

THE ELDERLY MOTHER   No, as long as she doesn't jump on my leg…

MOMMY   You want to go, Eve? Fine! *(to THE GENTLEMAN in the aisle)* Excuse me, sir, she wants—

PAULA   Me too, Mommy!

MOMMY   Yes, you, too. You can go see Colette and…???? Michel! *(to the audience)* That's our peace and love man… *(to PAULA)* Go ahead… *(Once PAULA has left, to THE GENTLEMAN in the aisle:)* Well, I'm all alone now. Would you like to sit down?

THE GENTLEMAN   I won't say no! Here! *(He hands her his bottle of soda.)* I brought them a little soda…

MOMMY *(She takes the bottle, surprised, then embarrassed about her reaction with PAULA.)* It was for them?! Then you should give it to them yourself! That will show them that complete strangers can be unexpectedly kind…

THE GENTLEMAN   Unexpectedly? Not really. I have three children myself, you
know. I'm divorced, but I have three children…

THE HIPPIE   *(to PAULA)* You like my medallion, don't you? It means "Peace."

THE YOUNG WOMAN   Are you nuts? She's much too little to understand.

PAULA   *(looking from one to the other)* I'm going to see that lady…

THE GIRLFRIEND   *(pleased)* You want to come see me?

THE BOYFRIEND   Whoa! Wait a minute! Watch out, kid! *(complaining)* I was up
sick all night…. What? Did I have an earache? No!

THE GIRLFRIEND   You jerk! C'mon, change places with me. C'mon! It's dark
out, the window won't bother you, let's go! C'mon, push over! *(They change
places and she speaks to PAULA.)* Don't mind the old grouch… come sit on my
lap…. You're heavy, but you're so pretty!

THE SPINSTER   *(laughing)* How about you, Eve? Do you know any songs?

EVE   Oh, yes, I know lots of songs!

THE SPINSTER   They're so smart so young these days…. And so lively.

THE ELDERLY MOTHER   What do you expect? They see all sorts of things on
television…

EVE   *(to the SPINSTER)* Do you want me to sing my song to you, Madam, you're
not listening!

THE SPINSTER   *(to her mother)* And they're not shy either! Go ahead, dear, sing!

EVE   *(singing)* Old MacDonald had a farm, E-I-E-I-O…

THE SPINSTER   *(delighted)* I know that one! Do I ever! Do you remember,
Mother, when I was in the Catholic Youth Club…. It doesn't make me feel any
younger…

EVE   *(singing)* And on his farm he had a pig, E-I-E-I-O…

THE SPINSTER   Look at that! She knows all the words! You know it better than
I do! *(She sings.)* With an oink-oink here, an oink-oink there… *(She bounces
EVE on her knees.)*

MOMMY   *(laughing)* Aren't they sweet?! I love them! *(Beat. Then to herself, or is it
to the audience?)* That's strange. Ever since I stopped trying to be their mother
at all costs, I can see them differently… I love those girls! They're beautiful…
I was so afraid of failing with them… I had to make sure I didn't fail myself!

THE GENTLEMAN   *(to MOMMY)* So true. So true. My wife would never let me
have the kids for a whole week…. Never!… Our relationship is very tense…
I can only see the children one Sunday afternoon, every two weeks. I have to
find activities for them in Montreal…. Oh, you must know—is it true they've
cleared a nice skating rink in Park Lafontaine?

MOMMY   Yes, it's great! I even bought myself some skates… so I could go skating with the girls. We go every weekend…

THE GENTLEMAN   Maybe we could meet… *(beat)* I mean, to take the children skating, all of us together…

MOMMY   I have very little to do with men these days! I'm taking a break… from the seduction game… from the emotional blackmail, from… *(She is looking for the right word.)* Mommying! Maybe the word doesn't exist, but you get the idea…. It's true, though, the girls would like to meet some other children…

THE DRIVER   *(to PAULA)* Sorry, sweetie, but I can't talk to you…. No, I can't talk to you, because if I talk to you, I'll look at you, and if I look at you, I won't be able to keep my eyes on the road and we'll end up in the ditch!!!! Sorry…. You can watch me if you want. *(He shifts gears.)* But I can't talk to you…. What's your name? Paula? That's a nice name! A really nice name, but I can't talk to you…

EVE   *(singing)* Old MacDonald had a farm, E-I-E-I-O! And on his farm he had some chicks, E-I-E-I-O. With a… with a… *(She tries to remember what chicks do.)*

THE SPINSTER   Oh, dear, you can't remember what chicks do? Neither can I… do you remember, Mother? *(to MOMMY)* Maybe their mother knows?

MOMMY   Well, she doesn't. *(to the audience)* I could never remember that one. Then someone at the back of the bus chimed in— *(She encourages the audience to join in.)* With a cheep-cheep here and a cheep-cheep there, here a cheep, there a cheep, everywhere a cheep-cheep, Old MacDonald had a farm, E-I-E-I-O!

THE BOYFRIEND   And on his farm he had some booze, E-I-E-I-O! With a slurp-slurp here, and a slurp-slurp there—Oops! That's not it? Okay, let's start over again…. Old MacDonald had a farm, E-I-E-I-O! And on his farm, he had a cow…

MOMMY   *(to the audience)* And the whole bus started singing.

PAULA   Mommy, the driver can't talk to me…. But he can sing… he's singing!

THE GENTLEMAN   *(to MOMMY)* This one is Paula, right? Good! Paula? Would you like some soda?

PAULA   Yes, I'm—

EVE   Me too, I want some too!

MOMMY   Now, girls, don't start fighting again! There's only one soda and there are two of you…

THE GENTLEMAN   Let me handle this! It's my soda, let me work it out.

MOMMY looks at him, then at the audience and pretends to faint. As she comes to, she speaks to the audience.

It was a party! Eve and Paula disappeared again, and I ended up alone! A bit lonely… but I was enjoying it… and on we went to the tune of "Old MacDonald."

MOMMY   Hey, girls! Girls! Nicolet! We're almost there! Come get dressed.

THE SPINSTER   Let me help you…. Give me her snowsuit… Eve!

MOMMY   Thank you. *(She passes the snowsuit to her.)* Her snowsuit! Her tuque and her scarf are in the sleeve. Thank you… Paula? Come get dressed…

THE GIRLFRIEND   I'd like to dress Paula, can I?

MOMMY   Fine! Thank you…. Well, look at that, I have only myself to dress!

THE GENTLEMAN   *(offering to help her)* May I?

MOMMY   *(surprised)* It's been a while since somebody dressed me…. Ooopps! That's not what I meant! *(to the audience)* That's all they can think of! That kind of chivalry is rare these days, but it's nice all the same! Okay… time to gather up my gear…

THE SPINSTER   Did you see how nice this snowsuit is, Mother? A zipper! One, two, three and the little girl is dressed!

THE ELDERLY MOTHER   If only we'd had those in my days…

THE GIRLFRIEND   There you go, little chickadee! You're all dressed now, too. I wish I had a daughter like you. Oh, wait, here, take my gum. *(She gives PAULA her own wad of gum.)*

MOMMY   Here, bunnykins, take your Lego. Are you happy? You learned lots of new things today, didn't you?

THE GENTLEMAN   I'll get off and help you with your bags.

MOMMY   Don't bother!

THE GENTLEMAN   It's my pleasure.

MOMMY   Well! *(to the audience)* It's his pleasure. *(speaking to the other passengers)* Goodbye, Colette, thank you! Have I forgotten anything? *(to THE HIPPIE)* Right, peace! Peace! *(to THE GIRLFRIEND)* Thanks, Miss! *(to THE BOYFRIEND)* Take care of that hangover!

THE SPINSTER   *(to EVE)* Watch out for my mother's leg!

MOMMY   I'll carry her.

EVE   *(in MOMMY's arms)* Goodbye, Madam.

MOMMY   Goodbye, Madam.

THE ELDERLY MOTHER   Goodbye, sweetheart.

MOMMY   Goodbye and thank you! *(to everyone)* Goodbye! *(They move down the aisle.)* Hold on to the railing there! *(to the driver)* Let me get the tickets for you… *(She searches in her pockets.)*

THE DRIVER   Never mind, ma'am! It's all right…

MOMMY   I insist! I insist! There! *(She hands him the tickets.)*

THE GENTLEMAN   I'm getting off to help her with her bags, and I'll be right back…

MOMMY   *(to THE DRIVER)* Could you drop us off at the next corner, please?… Yes, right there…. Careful…. Hold on, girls! Ooops! My God, it's slippery! Can you stop? Thank you very much!

(to everyone) Goodbye! And thank you!… *(to the children)* Let Mommy get out first… *(She gets out and takes one of the girls.)* Phew! One little girl in the snowbank! *(to the audience)* There had been a big storm! *(to PAULA)* The Lego… here, catch!

THE GENTLEMAN   *(rushing over to the baggage compartment)* Which is yours?

MOMMY   The sack of clean clothes… and the green suitcase, too, please…. That's right, thank you!

THE GENTLEMAN   Could I have your telephone number?

MOMMY   I'm warning you… if I don't feel like talking to you, I'll be very frank!

THE GENTLEMAN   I'll take my chances!

MOMMY   Fine, if you agree to that! *(She writes down her number.)*

THE GENTLEMAN   Goodbye…. I'll be in touch….

MOMMY   *(to EVE)* No, Eve, no! We're not getting back on the bus! *(to the audience)* Half of the bus was standing up to wave goodbye to us, and everyone was singing "Old MacDonald." *(to everyone)* Goodbye, everyone! Goodbye! Careful, girls, the bus is leaving… *(to PAULA)* Who do you want to say goodbye to? *(to the audience)* To the man with the earache? *(to the audience)* So long! Goodbye! *(to EVE)* Yes, they love your song, sweetie…. They're still singing it!

> *MOMMY and the girls watch the bus drive off.*

(kneeling beside her daughters) I want to tell you I'm proud of you both… *(beat)* But I think I'm proud of myself… I'm proud of all three of us! I learn so much when we're together…

EVE   *(breaking away from her mother)* Daddy!

PAULA   Daddy!

MOMMY   *(laughing)* They're happy!

> *She blows kisses to the girls. The girls walk off with their father. MOMMY, still kneeling, is left alone. She is moved to tears, as she is*

every time the three of them separate. She looks at her empty hands, then realizes she has to take care of herself.... She'll have time. She stands up, looks at the audience, tries to get them to understand—or feel—then brusquely, she turns away, as if to leave.... She comes back, looks at the audience, then, without a word, she shrugs, meaning: "What more can a woman do or say?"

The end.

The Edge of Earth is Too Near, Violette Leduc

(La Terre est trop courte, Violette Leduc)

by Jovette Marchessault

translated by
Susanne de Lotbinière-Harwood

Introduction to
The Edge of Earth is Too Near, Violette Leduc
(La Terre est trop courte, Violette Leduc[1])
by Jovette Marchessault
Introduced by Louise H. Forsyth

La Terre est trop courte, Violette Leduc is a play in eleven Tableaux about words and creative writing. Its main character, Violette Leduc, is a writer, for whom verbal expression is a visceral necessity. She is dedicated body and soul to her writing projects, despite her hesitations and innumerable difficulties. The intense energy that drives her projects is powerfully erotic. She establishes her sense of identity with the words she writes; these same creative words produce reality for the worlds she represents and creates. Through her writing she becomes a member of society. Her books are meant to take their place in society's cultural fabric as significant representations of human experience. There is nothing other than creative expression that casts even a modest light on her otherwise sombre existence. Absolutely necessary to the writing process, however, is a reading process. There must be someone to read the writer's books, recognize her work, acknowledge the relevance and importance of what she has to say, and give them reality. It is only through words received that there can be a vital human exchange. Without the exchange and the recognition they produce, madness lurks in the dark corners.

La Terre est trop courte, Violette Leduc is a fictionalized dramatization of the life of French author Violette Leduc (1907–1972), whom Marchessault considers one of the great, yet unknown, writers of the 20th century.[2] Leduc wrote with intense passion, yet notoriety and not recognition was largely her lot. Although she had the same publisher as Simone de Beauvoir, Jean-Paul Sartre, Jean Genet, Maurice Sachs, Albert Camus and many others, her books were expurgated, censored, and poorly marketed. Her story is entwined with several of these other writers, some of whom also appear in the play. But unlike theirs, Leduc's books did not sell well and received little critical attention. The famous authors that made up the "stable" at Gallimard are evoked in the fifth tableau of *The Edge of Earth Is Too Near* when the switchboard operator, who is also Violette's mother, is heard naming many of them, while also trying to carry on a conversation with her mother, the grandmother Fideline whom Leduc adored.

Marchessault's Violette is a compelling example of a female dramatic character who has stepped completely out of the stereotypes and theatrical conventions that the Mad Actress of *A Clash of Symbols* decided to forget about. She is the central figure in her own story, richly complex and full of contradictions, in many ways responsible for her own sad destiny (like all tragic heroes). The audience's sympathies remain with her throughout the play because of the overwhelming forces that oppress her, her very human frailties, and her passionate ambitions. Marchessault has neither glamorized the historical Leduc nor whitewashed her failings. She describes her as follows in the introductory text where she highlights Leduc's passion for writing and "the impossible": "ugly woman, bastard, sexually obsessed, *voyeuse*, sado-masochistic, paranoid, chronic weeper, thirsty for luxury, shoplifter, trafficker during the French Occupation, vestal of Parisian literary homosexuals, whore, matricide, pimp, informer, neither worker, nor bourgeoise, nor intellectual, but beggar, humiliated, impassioned, obsessive." [3] Despite these problematic traits, Marchessault gets her audience on Leduc's side through a confrontation with Jean Genet on the question of who is seen to have legitimacy as a writer. The historical Genet, who could easily match Leduc for his despicable character and questionable origins, becomes a condescending colleague in the play who proudly describes his essence as that of a "thief, pimp, tough guy, drag-queen, informer, traitor, coward." [4] Beyond their writing styles, the only difference between these two writers is their sex. Whereas the literary world beat a path of recognition and adulation to the door of homosexual Genet, its members had only scorn and rejection for lesbian and bisexual Leduc. As Marchessault has Violette note while quoting Leduc saying to her table in the eighth tableau: "There are those who can say anything they please. There are those who can say nothing. There are those who are always forgiven. There are those who are never forgiven." [5]

The fictional scene between Leduc and Genet sets the stage for the sexist and misogynist dynamics at work throughout the play producing the unfair ostracism of Leduc and her work.

Violette's distress in the first scene derives from her just having learned that her publisher, fearing censorship, has expurgated the first 150 pages of her novel *Ravages*, a tragic love story between two lesbians, Thérèse and Isabelle. Violette learns of this absence of support on the part of her publisher and receives the news as though it were an amputation done to herself or the killing of her child. Marchessault uses here, as throughout *La Terre est trop courte, Violette Leduc*, extensive quotations from Leduc's own work, which she sets off using italics. Susanne de Lotbinière-Harwood has indicated these passages in quotation marks in her translation. [6] This interweaving of the voices of Leduc's first-person narrative voice and of Marchessault's Violette creates a fascinating impression of affinity among three different, yet similar, writers: the Violette in the play, the historic writer Violette Leduc, and the playwright Jovette Marchessault. It also blurs the boundaries among fiction, theatre, biography and autobiography.

Throughout the first scene, Violette alternates between rebellion and despair, between self-knowledge and self-loathing. Disputes with Genet and her husband humiliate her. Later in the play she humiliates herself and deeply wounds her generous and adoring lover, Hermine, when she allows Hermine to go deeply into debt to buy her clothes, prostitutes both of them by agreeing to make love for the pleasure of a hustler and voyeur, and then abandons her. Hermine is the fictional name given by Leduc in *La Bâtarde* to her lover Denise Hertgès.

As a counterbalance to the males who surround, tempt and oppress her, Violette comes into contact with female authors who are aware of the sexism that prevails in the literary world and speak out in favour of women's freedom and imagination. The discussion among them that Marchessault creates in the seventh tableau shows that, despite widespread dismissal of women's capacity for intellectual thought, they are a group of intellectuals whose original and well-conceived ideas deserve respect and recognition. In the following tableaux these women provide support and compassion to Violette. They realize that the lack of appreciation for her work and the demolition of it has brought her to the point of madness. Marchessault dramatizes this madness in Violette's "Conversation with So-Called Inanimate Objects" in the eighth tableau and her conversation with Nathalie Sarraute in the ninth. Like Savard's Marquise, Violette has found no cure at the hands of psychiatrists who fail to recognize themselves as part of the systemically based sexist problem for women in search of their own freedom.

The most important person in the life of Leduc/Violette is Simone de Beauvoir, who consistently gave her the recognition she needed for herself as a writer and thinker. De Beauvoir took a public stand in support of Leduc by meeting with her, reading what she wrote and writing prefaces for her work.

The vampiric forces that deny her autonomy and freedom return to haunt Violette in the 10th tableau, where all the men, cast alternatively as artists, transvestites, homosexuals and finally her husband as a psychiatrist, appear to represent the network of patriarchal systems that form contemporary culture. They remain to the end of the play and are joined by her mother, completely submissive to these systems, with their discourse intended to scorn, humiliate and discourage Violette. However, de Beauvoir's recognition has been sufficient, at least momentarily, to restore Violette's belief in herself:

> (*stubbornly continues writing*) Vampires up in the ceiling, I'm not listening to you anymore. I'm not insane, I'm not sad. I'm inventing my life with my own hand. I surprise it giving me shape, letting out my cry. [...] I came into the world, and I pledged myself to a passion for the impossible.[7]

Marchessault's instructions for staging *La Terre est trop courte, Violette Leduc* suggest a rich intermingling of places, discourses and individuals. Boundaries fall away as the stage metaphorically represents either an oniric landscape where all things can come together, or else an inside look at the complex networks that go to make up the omnipresent and mutually reinforcing systems of patriarchy. Particularly interesting in this regard are the instructions for doubling of characters. All the characters are to be on stage in their own spaces throughout the performance. Only the actors playing Violette Leduc and Simone de Beauvoir have a single role. All the others play multiple roles and seem to pop up everywhere. For example, Violette's husband plays the additional roles of hustler, bum, and psychiatrist. Jean Genet transmutes into a hustler, transvestite, and waiter. There is no ultimate escape for Violette.

Notes

[1] Jovette Marchessault, *La Terre est trop courte, Violette Leduc*. Montréal: Éditions de la Pleine Lune, 1982. First production in Montréal at the Théâtre Expérimental des Femmes on November 5, 1981, directed by Pol Pelletier, designed by Ginette Noiseux, with Luce Guilbeault as Violette Leduc (see note 2 of the Introduction to *A Clash of Symbols*). *The Edge of Earth Is Too Near, Violette Leduc*, translated by Susanne de Lotbinière-Harwood, received a dramatic reading by the Ubu Repertory Theater in New York on October 16, 1984 and was produced by Nightwood Theatre in Toronto in April 1985. This translation, an earlier version of the translation published here, was available in manuscript form through CEAD.

[2] "Violette Leduc est un des grands écrivains du 20ᵉ siècle, mais qui le sait?" Pelletier, Francine."Violette-Jovette, Jovette-Violette." *La Terre est trop courte, Violette Leduc*: 6. ["Violette Leduc is one of the great writers of the 20th century, but who knows it?"]. Translated by LHF.

[3] "[…] femme laide, bâtarde, obsédée sexuelle, voyeuse, sado-masochiste, paranoïaque, pleureuse chronique, assoiffée de luxe, voleuse à l'étalage, trafiquante durant l'Occupation en France, vestale des homosexuels littéraires parisiens, putain, matricide, maquereau, délateur, ni ouvrière, ni bourgeoise, ni intellectuelle mais mendiante, humiliée, passionnée, démesurée." Marchessault, Jovette. "La Passion de l'écriture et de l'impossible." *La Terre est trop courte, Violette Leduc*: 13. Translated by LHF.

[4] "mon essence de voleur, de maquereau, de mec, de travesti, de délateur, de traître, de lâche." *La Terre est trop courte, Violette Leduc*: 26.

[5] *"Il y a ceux qui peuvent tout dire. Il y a ceux qui ne peuvent rien dire. Il y a ceux à qui on pardonne tout. Il y a ceux à qui on ne pardonne rien." La Terre est trop courte, Violette Leduc*: 121.

[6] Source of all quotations from the works of Leduc are given in the notes of *La Terre est trop courte, Violette Leduc*: 154–57.

[7] "Vampires des plafonds je ne vous écoute plus. Je ne suis pas folle, je ne suis pas triste. Ma main invente ma propre vie, je la surprends en train de me construire, de me gémir. *Je suis venue au monde, j'ai fait le serment d'avoir la passion de l'impossible." La Terre est trop courte, Violette Leduc*: 151.

Bibliographical Suggestions

Selected Other Works by Jovette Marchessault

Comme une enfant de la terre. Montréal: Éditions Leméac, 1975. (novel, winner of Prix France-Québec in 1976)

La Mère des herbes. Montréal: Éditions Quinze, 1980. (novel)

Tryptique lesbien. [*Les Vaches de nuit*: 78–94] Montréal: Éditions de la Pleine Lune, 1980. Gloria Orenstein: "Postface": 89–95. *Les Vaches de nuit* first produced for International Women's Day in the collective show "Célébrations" by the Théâtre Expérimental des Femmes at Théâtre du Nouveau Monde in 1979, with Pol Pelletier in the single role. Produced as *Night Cows*, translation by Yvonne M. Klein at the Women's Salon in New York in the Fall of 1979, with Pol Pelletier in the single role. *Les Faiseuses d'ange* was first produced by Madeleine Arsenault at the T.E.F. Fall 1982. *Lesbian Triptych*. Toronto: Women's Press, 1985.

La Saga des poules mouillées. Montréal: Éditions de la Pleine Lune, 1981. First produced Fall 1981. First produced in English, translation by Linda Gaboriau, at Tarragon Theatre in Toronto on 18 February, 1982. *Saga of the Wet Hens*. Vancouver: Talonbooks, 1982.

Alice & Gertrude, Natalie & Renée et ce cher Ernest. Montréal: Éditions de la Pleine Lune, 1984. First produced by the Productions Vermeilles on October 24, 1984.

Anaïs, dans la queue de la comète. Montréal: Éditions de la Pleine Lune, 1985. First produced in Montréal by the Théâtre de Quat'Sous on September 1985. *Anaïs in the Comet's Wake*, translated by Susanne de Lotbinière-Harwood in 1987 has been available at CEAD.

Le Voyage magnifique d'Emily Carr. Montréal: Leméac, 1990. First produced in Montréal by the Théâtre de Quat'Sous on September 21, 1990. *The Magnificent Voyage of Emily Carr*, translated by Linda Gaboriau, was first produced in English by the Belfry Theatre in Victoria, British Columbia on December 1, 1992. Vancouver: Talonbooks, 1992.

On *La Terre est trop courte, Violette Leduc* and Jovette Marchessault

Alonzo, Anne-Marie. "Jovette Marchessault." *The Oxford Companion to Canadian Theatre*. Ed. Eugene Benson & L.W. Conolly. Toronto, Oxford, New York: Oxford University Press, 1989: 331–32.

Burgoyne, Lynda. "Biographie et théâtre chez Jovette Marchessault: du «mentir-vrai»." *Cahiers de théâtre. Jeu.* 60 (sept. 1991): 111–20.

Coll. *Dramaturges québécoises. Dossiers de Presse. Jovette Marchessault, 1975–1984.* (50 pages)

Forsyth, Louise H. "Jouer aux éclats: l'inscription spectaculaire des cultures de femmes dans le théâtre de Jovette Marchessault." *Voix et Images*. 47 (hiver 1991). 230–43. Special issue on *Jovette Marchessault* edited by Claudine Potvin.

Frémont, Gabrielle. "*La Terre est trop courte, Violette Leduc.*" *Livres et auteurs québécois 1982*. Sainte-Foy: Presses de l'Université Laval, 1982: 175–77.

Michaud, Ginette. "*La Terre est trop courte, Violette Leduc.*" *Cahiers de théâtre. Jeu*. 24 (1982.3): 124–25.

Orenstein, Gloria. "Les Voyages visionnaires de trois créatrices féministes-matristiques: Emily Carr, Jovette Marchessault et Gloria Orenstein." *Voix et Images*. 47 (hiver 1991): 253–61.

Potvin, Claudine. "Entrevue avec Jovette Marchessault." *Voix et Images*. 47 (hiver 1991): 218–29. *Jovette Marchessault* [Bibliographie de Jovette Marchessault. 272–80]

Ricouart, Janine. "Jovette Marchessault's Matriarchy in her Autobiographical Triptych." *Women by Women. The Treatment of Female Characters by Women Writers of Fiction in Quebec since 1980*. Ed. Roseanna Lewis Dufault. Madison & Teaneck: Fairleigh Dickinson University Press & London Associated University Presses, 1997: 230–40.

Sabbath, Lawrence. "Censorship in Montreal." *Canadian Theatre Review*. 20 (Fall 1978): 81–85.

Saint-Martin, Lori. "De la mère patriarcale à la mère légendaire: *Triptyque lesbien* de Jovette Marchessault." *Voix et Images*. 47 (hiver 1991): 244–52.

Veyrat, Christel. "*La Terre est trop courte, Violette Leduc.*" *Dictionnaire des oeuvres littéraires du Québec*. Tome VII, 1981–1985. Montréal: Fides, 2003.

About Jovette Marchessault

Jovette Marchessault (born 1938 in Montréal) is a painter, sculptor, novelist and playwright. Forced by financial circumstances to leave school very early, she began with work in a textile factory and then went on a long journey across the United States in search of identity and spiritual roots. She held her first exhibition of frescos, masks and sculptures in 1970 at the Maison des Arts La Sauvegarde in Montréal. She has since had exhibitions elsewhere in Québec, Toronto, New York, Paris and Brussels. The three volumes of her fiction trilogy were published between 1975 and 1980: *Comme une enfant de la terre*, *La Mère des herbes*, and *Triptyque lesbien*.

Her first plays, including *La Terre est trop courte, Violette Leduc*, are unique in the way in which they memorialize women writers of Québec and elsewhere, indeed in which they share their creative voices, often word for word, with Marchessault and her dramatic characters. In the special issue of *Jeu* on "Thêâtre-Femmes," Francine Noël wrote a particularly moving and well-informed article pleading for women's rights to their own theatrical images, "Plaidoyer pour mon image," as Luce Guilbeault had insisted at the start of *A Clash of Symbols* in 1976. In her article Noël singled out Marchessault's *Night Cows*, created by Pol Pelletier in 1979 at the Théâtre du Nouveau Monde, as having played a particularly decisive role in bringing these images to theatrical physicality, materiality and reality:

> I think that *Les Vaches de nuit* marks a point of no return in Québec women's mental landscape: the text not only tosses out traditional images, but it throws the stage wide open to a powerful and ravaging cohort of powerful women, who will be irremediably present from now on. Their expansion will be impossible to contain. When we *see* this ample cohort on stage (shown by the voice and the body of a single great actor), we begin to foresee what that other thing that we've been looking for is. [1]

Marchessault wrote and produced several plays after 1990. However, it is her wonderful dramatizations of the lives of great women writers, written and produced during the 1980s, following the creation of her remarkable *Night Cows* by Pol Pelletier in 1979, that had a determining impact on the course of women's theatre during the period that interests me in this volume.

Note

[1] "Je crois que *les Vaches de nuit* marquent un point de non-retour dans l'onirisme féminin québécois: non seulement les images traditionnelles y sont-elles révulsées, mais le texte ouvre toute grande la scène à une cohorte puissante et ravageante de fortes femmes, dorénavant irrémédiablement présentes et dont le déferlement est impossible à contenir. C'est en *voyant* cette ample cohorte sur scène (montrée par la voix et le corps d'une seule grande comédienne) qu'on commence à pressentir ce que c'est que cette autre chose que nous cherchions." (Noël. 1980: 54). Translated by LHF.

La Terre est trop courte, Violette Leduc was first produced at the Théâtre Expérimental des Femmes, Montréal, in November 1981, with the following company:

Violette Leduc   Luce Guilbeault

Directed by Pol Pelletier
Designed by Ginette Noiseux

• • •

The Edge of Earth Is Too Near, Violette Leduc, translated by Susanne de Lotbinière-Harwood, received a dramatic reading by the Ubu Repertory Theater, New York, in October 1984, and was produced by Nightwood Theatre, Toronto in April 1985.

Characters

VIOLETTE LEDUC

SIMONE de BEAUVOIR

JEAN GENET, who will also play the part of the FIRST HUSTLER, of a DRAG
    QUEEN and of a WAITER in a café.

MAURICE SACHS, who will also play the part of the THIRD HUSTLER, of
    a DRAG QUEEN and of a WAITER in a café.

VIOLETTE'S MOTHER, who will also play the part of a SWITCHBOARD
    OPERATOR, of a SALESWOMAN, and of CLARA MALRAUX.

HERMINE, who will also play the part of NATHALIE SARRAUTE.

GABRIEL, Violette's husband, who will also play the part of the SECOND
    HUSTLER, of a BUM and a PSYCHOANALYST.

Four actresses, three actors, twenty roles.

Outline for a stage setting

All the actresses and actors could be visible simultaneously while each is in their
respective spaces. Cramped spaces for the women, more open ones for the men.
Maurice Sachs standing on a train-station platform, Genet reading in his room,
Gabriel in a bar or café, Simone de Beauvoir writing in a café, her space larger than
that of the other female protagonists, Violette's mother rocking in a confined space,
Hermine sewing in a sordid room. Violette is in her kitchen-bedroom, the bed edged
against the table. Seated at the table, with a notebook in front of her, she is writing.

Translator's Note

Throughout the play, the playwright has used excerpts from the books written by
Violette Leduc. I have indicated these passages by putting them in quotes.

THE EDGE OF EARTH IS TOO NEAR, VIOLETTE LEDUC

FIRST TABLEAU

The Vampire is On Duty

VIOLETTE, seated at the kitchen table, in front on an open notebook. She writes a few words. Sniffles, blows her nose, writes some more, sniffles.

GABRIEL   Hey there, pal, hey there! *(almost whispers)*

THE MOTHER   *(louder)* Listen to me, girl! Be careful!

GABRIEL   *(louder)* A bit of friendly advice. Watch your language, pal. You're running off at the navel.

THE MOTHER   You're wasting your time. This can't be serious, child. Isn't it enough that you know how to write letters without making any spelling mistakes?

GABRIEL   *(whispering)* You've been exposed! Mind the neighbours. You're afraid of the neighbours, aren't you, pal? You're too old to be wielding your pen like a sword, Don Quixote! Put away your pens and paper, all your brooding won't bring the void to life.

GENET   Watch what you write, Violette Leduc. Violette Leduc, what a strange name. Viollet-Le-Duc, why he was a famous architect!

GABRIEL   Come outside, pal, come and get a scent of the clouds!

GENET   You fondle words, Viollet-Le-Duc, you salivate all over them. You deal in excess, you're a total outrage!

GABRIEL   Why don't you join me for an aperitif instead, pal. Come on, let's have some lunch together: a little plate, a little fork, a big glass of wine. You'll feel better. You'll feel bigger inside.

THE MOTHER   He's right.

GABRIEL   I'm a patient man. I've been faithful. I love you.

GENET   Are you sniffling? Hey writer, are you crying?

VIOLETTE   "Come now, Violette, calm down…. Your tears are staining my settee. I'm like a public fountain, flowing day and night. Come now, Violette, your tears are making the roast cold. What to do? I can't help it, my tears follow me everywhere. Please, Violette, your tears are drowning the *grand marnier mousse*. I'm a weeping willow, mother always said so. For pity's sake, make a move, have a heart. Your eyes are a blank. Have you nothing to offer but cold? Look into my eyes. I'm pleading for some tenderness. Have you any to give? Open your arms. Encourage me, believe in me. I'm shivering, you turn me to ice."

GABRIEL   Watch your language, pal. This is not the Garden of Eden, this is a state of alert and the edge of earth is too near, they'll soon overtake the words you dared to let loose.

GENET   You make words speak, that should suffice. Being outrageous is not a woman's place. To each his own. Literature is ours, by divine right. An ancient and glorious heritage which we know how to magnify…. A book is a potent thing: muscular, virile, seminal, penetrating the flesh through the holy ring of the anus. Literature is a handsome pair of trousers! A dream figure in a pair of pants with one pocket on the right cheek. Now that, my dear, is literature! Our emblem of superiority over women.

VIOLETTE   "Why a slit throat, why a severed vein? Why the silly antics in the face of death? Why such wretchedness if I've already been assassinated? My book *Ravages* has been turned down. They've rejected the beginning of *Ravages*. They're not interested in the sincerity of Thérèse and Isabelle."

GENET   Not interested, not interested! They publish my work. I've become a legend in my own time. Take the bull by the horns, defend yourself! Transcend!… As for me, I give lyricism new life with a boot in the ass; muscles pumping, I draw and quarter the mythical beasts of night with my bare hands. But I don't weep, I write. I don't wipe my nose, I give dictation. I don't feel sorry for myself, I offend. I get published! We have the same publisher, you know.

VIOLETTE   Genet, I don't understand anymore. I just don't understand. "They say they fear censorship. My publisher is afraid of censorship. What is censorship? Censorship is Paris with its heart gone cold. Censorship is my hometown under frost. You cannot disturb the ways of censorship, you can't go knocking on its door or let yourself in. It cuts into your book and deletes, done and gone before you know it. Censorship is a guillotine under cover. I'd throw myself at its feet and beg for mercy if I could. I'd make myself clear."

GENET   *Bâtarde!*

VIOLETTE   *Orphelin!*

GENET   Better to be an orphan than a bastard. With a flick of the wrist and a crook of the finger, the orphan lifts up his thigh, cock on high, and writes his legend in piss. It makes them drool, they fill their heads, their lungs, with the smell of my farts, which is not the same as the smell of my shit. I hate the smell of my shit. The extraordinary sexual power of my word-flow is enough to bring my readers to ecstasy. And you call them censors!

VIOLETTE   Every day I write, every day I break into a sweat over my notebook. Is effort a hoax? Am I telling my story with the wrong words? My pen foams at the mouth, slides into a strange sentence, clings to every word. I write my life, Genet, just like you!

GENET   You're mad, woman! I don't write my life, I pimp ideas and feelings, I take pleasure from them with every inch of my tongue. You, you are on the inside, burning to death in your sickening drivel. I stand outside. I melt feelings down in my cauldron. I am the element of fire. What you call writing is the stench rising from your ovaries. Writing should be neat and clean.

VIOLETTE   "The beginning of *Ravages* is not unclean, it's the truth!"

GENET   Who cares about the truth, journalism, police reports? Who cares?

VIOLETTE   "It's about love. Thérèse and Isabelle are so brand new."

GENET   Thérèse, Isabelle… those are names for madwoman, for saints. Completely uninspired. They remind me of skirts dragging on dirty pavements, adrift in the gutter. They collapse before they get off the ground. There isn't so much as a whisper of passion in those names.

VIOLETTE   "They're schoolgirls," Genet, "they make love for three nights and three days in the dormitory. Sex is their blinding sun. Their caresses become a blessed practice. Time is their own hell, time is so short. These women are not damned, they are privileged."

GENET   From out of a bloody womb I see feminine debris… oozing, spilling… it enters the rich black earth with a rustle of bones.

VIOLETTE   "They discover the world between two legs. I describe Isabelle's dashing spirit, her elaborate flights of fancy, her recklessness; Thérèse's exalted brand of obedience."

GENET   Liturgical drama, good for drowning in the inkwell!

VIOLETTE   "I use ink for plasma; my pen is an umbilical cord. My typescript, a newborn baby."

GENET   Tarara-boom-dee-ay!

VIOLETTE   "Censorship has butchered everything."

GENET   Tarara-boom-dee-ay!

VIOLETTE   "I hear a creaking, a cracking. The vampire is on guard duty." Is there nowhere we can write in peace?

GENET   In prison, locked up, where you can waste away in seventh heaven. Where you can mate with the very substance of your actions. I write in peace because I choose to assert my essence as a thief, pimp, tough guy, drag-queen, informer, traitor, coward.

VIOLETTE   "Should I just put my two suicide victims away in the drawer?"

GENET   Your two foetuses? No, no, another publisher will take them…

VIOLETTE   Another publisher? You must be kidding, Genet. Nobody will want them. Publishers have no use for women.

GENET   Wanted: a publisher for lady dreamers. A publisher is needed for members of the weaker sex who like to explore the roots of their dreams with a fine-tooth comb.

VIOLETTE   Nobody reads my books, Genet. Your readers don't buy my books. My books are nothing but a heap of unsold merchandise tossed into basements to feed the rats, the way time feeds on painful memories. "They drove a stake through my heart. Society up in arms before my book even appears. My search through the night of memory for the magical eye of a breast, for the face, the flower, the meat of a woman's open sex. My search, an empty first-aid kit. I unbuttoned myself for more honesty in my descriptions. The freshness of a rose at three in the morning, in the summertime, that's how I thought of them. I recounted their acrobatics, their tender suckling."

GENET   *(dreamily)* The freshness of a rose… *(catching himself)* Have it out with censorship, Viollet-Le-Duc. Sort things out with the social machine once and for all. Go to it like a cow to a bull.

VIOLETTE   "Why can't I meet the publishers? Where does censorship live? Thérèse and Isabelle are not bad girls, they are my heroines. My 150 pages are not dirty. My text may not be neat and clean, but my intentions are clear."

GENET   Clean, clear! A piece of writing must awaken both the darkness and the light of constellations, imagination and fear. Your schoolgirls may not be captivating enough. What about it, architect?

VIOLETTE   But "I've lathered, laundered and rinsed out my adjectives and my metaphors."

GENET   Then write something else…

VIOLETTE   "To go on writing after such rejection?"

GENET   Motivation must come from inside, not from the realm of rejection.

VIOLETTE   "I can't do it. Dead limbs come popping out of my skin at every turn. I gave of my life to write Thérèse and Isabelle."

GENET   You're boring me…

VIOLETTE   "Without the beginning, the rest will have no impact. I'll never recover from this amputation."

GENET   You're exaggerating…

VIOLETTE   "I spent two years on that first part."

GENET   Why don't you travel then. Get away, like I do… *(He disappears.)*

VIOLETTE   Genet! Genet! "If I were a stonemason I'd rebuild the beginning of my book. I'd cement Thérèse and Isabelle together. Literature is a treacherous abyss." Orphan Genet, how old were you when your first book was published? I know: you were 32. In six years time, you'd become a famous author. Louis

Jouvet commissioned you to write *Les Bonnes* * for his theatre. Your writer friends, Sartre and Cocteau among them, petitioned the President of the Republic on your behalf, to obtain a pardon. And they succeeded, you were released from prison! I was 39 years old when my first book was published, almost forty. An old woman, slowing down and close to poverty. Nine years later, Genet, nine years, they reject my manuscript, they slice away my flesh. *(She stops.)* "Where am I coming from? From the cemetery. Thérèse and Isabelle insulted me. I didn't defend them. I'm covered in their spit. Let's get married, Violette, let's get married you and me. Let's get to our church, rotary motions will quicken. Wait, let me get the mirror. *(She goes towards her bed.)* Wait, I'll draw back the sheets. Wait, I'm spreading my thighs. Wait, I'm parting my lips. Wait, the mirror needs to be steadied. Wait, this is me I see here. How strange. How useless, this vulva…. Oh mirror, you're boring me. Down on the pillow on all fours? Why not? This bitch is ready. Despair is an animal. I am an animal. A bitch who belongs to Simone de Beauvoir, to *Les Temps Modernes*, to Gallimard, to Sartre, whom she doesn't even know. I have masters, why don't they beat me? The bitch is ready, have a sniff at her. I was only joking. I'm giving my sex some fresh air, my finger is the best. For guaranteed satisfaction, this is the one for me. Now, you dog, don't be late for the office. Thérèse and Isabelle, you will see print. How soon… I wanted to kill myself, now I want to die of pleasure. There you are, rejected manuscript. What you see here is a one-woman vertigo factory, a high-performance pleasure machine. Look at me, manuscript, I'm on my way. Grotesque, you say? I say it's great! I'm pulling it off, I'm coming, I'm coming…. Oh, this is bliss, unbearable bliss. I can't take it. *(moans)* It's all over."

> *The lighting changes, GABRIEL's voice is heard.*

GABRIEL   *(entering VIOLETTE's room with a radiant face)* Hey, pal, hey there!

SECOND TABLEAU

Être dans le ton comme le violon

GABRIEL   What're you up to, pal?

VIOLETTE   Growing old, husband dear. Ever since "I joined the herd of women a man offers things to," I've been closing in on old age.

GABRIEL   Have I hurt you, pal?

VIOLETTE   Gabriel! Gabriel! I would just love "to wake up in the morning, my spirit alive with butterfly wings; a little Tyrolean hat-feather tickling my heart. To rise and shake off yesterday's petals so as to deeply ripen the day. *Être dans le ton comme le violon*."

---

* translator's note: or *The Maids*

GABRIEL   Of course it's all my fault! You like me in a straightjacket. You'd like to hold me and feed me in the backstreets of your bed as if you had just conceived me.

VIOLETTE   We used to go to bed early, Gabriel.

GABRIEL   When I wasn't delivering…

VIOLETTE   When you weren't delivering your wedding pictures, when you weren't paying court to all your customers, when you weren't coming home with that bitter, that foreign taste of revelry in your mouth, on your tongue. The taste of all the drinks you had without me.

GABRIEL   Every job has its drawbacks…

VIOLETTE   We'd get into bed. I'd reach out for you. You'd wrap the sheets around you, your brand-new sex cradled in my hands, in my…

GABRIEL   Now listen, pal…

VIOLETTE   I am listening. My husband, clueless on how to enter his wife. My husband, always in a hurry, always cold. As soon as we'd get into bed you'd seek out my feet. Not my mouth! Not my breasts! Not my sex! You're obsessed with frozen extremities. World order, as far as you're concerned, revolves around warm feet. Humanity's highest ideal, warm feet. Never the brazier, never the glacier. I was the stranger who brought the cold as she moved closer.

GABRIEL   What did you want, a tropical island? A furnace?

VIOLETTE   A heatwave is what I wanted, husband dear. Heat, with some sun in it. Sun so hot it could melt every shell in the sea. Unlimited heat!

GABRIEL   What about my freedom?

VIOLETTE   I married a man who likes to go out alone, who likes to eat alone, walk alone, meet with his friends alone, sleep alone. I married a freedom addict!

GABRIEL   What of it?

VIOLETTE   I'm telling you our marriage reeks of mothballs. Open the windows, husband dear. Open the door! We're going to take an oxygen bath.

GABRIEL   "Look at you, poor thing! You can't go on like this. Have you seen your eyes? No, old boy, I'm not at the centre of the universe. Be reasonable."

VIOLETTE   You are the centre of the universe, for me. My eyes? What about my eyes? I'm neither wise nor reasonable, the lunatic dons a cloak of parrot feathers, she'll be "old in no time. Perhaps my inner being will have a lovely home." What's wrong with my eyes, Gabriel?

GABRIEL   Red, bloodshot, old boy. You have the eyes of a professional mourner.

VIOLETTE   "We madwomen are always weeping with far-away eyes."

GABRIEL   You are so sad. The iron mask of sadness, old boy. Well, I need a shave.

VIOLETTE   A shave?

GABRIEL   I came here to shave.

VIOLETTE   To shave! So you're going out again?

GABRIEL   I have a rendez-vous on the Left Bank.

VIOLETTE   I'm going with you.

GABRIEL   No.

VIOLETTE   I'm going with you.

GABRIEL   You're not their type. You'll be bored.

VIOLETTE   I won't be bored. I'll be with you.

GABRIEL   Go out, see some people, chase your blues away.

VIOLETTE   When you leave is when nostalgia sets in. Go on, get out, leave me to my tears!

GABRIEL   "I'll leave when I'm ready, when I've made up my mind to. I'm taking my time, I'll always take my time."

VIOLETTE   Not whose type?

GABRIEL   Not their type, that's all.

VIOLETTE   I'll wait outside if you're inside, I'll wait inside if you're outside. I'll be on the opposite side of the bridge when you cross it, turning into a turd, my heart in a shambles. I'll carry your photo-albums, your impulses, your emulsions. I'll be your watch-dog.

GABRIEL   I'm going out alone, old boy.

VIOLETTE   You hate me. You hate women. Now that Hermine is gone, you've taken over as the one who deprives me. You deny me your body, your sex, your presence.

GABRIEL   You took everything I had!

VIOLETTE   You gave me nothing!

GABRIEL   You're out of your mind, pal.

VIOLETTE   The first time we made love…

GABRIEL   Will this never end…?

VIOLETTE   I asked you to make love to me…

GABRIEL   Go on, go on, it sticks in your throat, does it, pal? You asked me to make love to you like a man makes love to another man. Isn't that right?

VIOLETTE   I had my reasons!

GABRIEL   Feeling the gloom, old boy?

VIOLETTE   I was afraid, husband dear. Afraid of living surrounded by foetuses "gone to the sewers of abortion." The calendar, Gabriel, that little cross next to D-day, to abolish distractions, to stop the wheel of fate, to arrest utter disintegration.

GABRIEL   The body of your fears looms large, old boy.

VIOLETTE   That's all you left me with, Gabriel.

GABRIEL   I never denied you a thing. It was you who didn't want me, pal. You, yelling "Take it out! Take it out!" when I was inside you.

VIOLETTE   *(mechanically)* The little cross on the calendar, next to D-day, to avoid utter disintegration in the sewers of abortion…

GABRIEL   Long live raving auto-eroticism!

VIOLETTE   The release of one's demons!

GABRIEL   Trust me. Things will be fine, just fine!

VIOLETTE   No, things won't be fine. Things will be exactly like when I try to write.

GABRIEL   What? Now what? Are you saying you can't write because of me? Your memory's awfully short, old boy. Over the years, the days, then nights of your wanton hysterics, your games of blackmail, your glorified suicides, I always encouraged you to keep writing.

VIOLETTE   Liar!

GABRIEL   Amnesiac!

VIOLETTE   You gave me your blackest looks every time you saw me open that notebook, over there on the table. I tried to write for part of the night…

GABRIEL   You could have written during the day…

VIOLETTE   During the day I was busy typing Monsieur Jules Laforgue's correspondence. During the day I worked for other people. "To begin writing at a table, in the artificial silence of a tenement courtyard, in the half-life of a cheap room, required more of a ritual than writing in the country. I'd powder my nose, rosy my cheeks, redden my lips. To perform this most awesome of ceremonies, I wore a smock of blue and white checks."

GABRIEL   Noodles, you cooked noodles every night. I was made to eat on a corner of the table while my wife wrote her second novel. How ironic, my wife writing *The Famished*, a book about the hunger in her.

VIOLETTE   I was hungry for you too!

GABRIEL   My poor boy, you were hungry for everyone and everything that came your way! As well as for her, Simone de Beauvoir. The word love…

VIOLETTE Is a nonsense word when you're talking about her. "It's so much more powerful, so much more real than a love of the mind."

GABRIEL What is it then?

VIOLETTE "It's a feeling that dares not make a move. My feeling for her reaches a climax of well-being when I deny myself so she can work."

GABRIEL I've encouraged you, pal. I've been patient!

VIOLETTE I'd be trying to write and have to talk to you at the same time, answer your questions, apologize for myself, as if this were some great death-wish obsessing my arm, driving my hand across the page.

GABRIEL I wanted you to get some sleep. In my heart I felt a mother's tender ambitions for her child…

VIOLETTE No, Gabriel! You wanted me to give up. You played the giving young husband, you snake! You baited me with your honey… my body held captive in the stream of your sperm. You never gave me any money. I had to earn my own.

GABRIEL You twist everything around! I was so miserable I spent my nights chewing the sheets. The desert, the bed, not a hair, not a thread, no sign of life, your notebooks swallowed it whole. Talk about hunger!

VIOLETTE One day I asked you if you'd be pleased to read something by me in a magazine. You said you didn't give a damn about my name in a magazine.

GABRIEL I can't stand magazines, you know that.

VIOLETTE Yes but it pays well, especially editorials.

GABRIEL Editorials! What a laugh! You need a train of thought to write an editorial, my poor boy! A seed of an idea with a concept around it. Mental structure. Ideas. Your ideas defied the laws of gravity. Pffffftt! Gone with the wind!

VIOLETTE But I did have a grain of thought, Gabriel: you! "Start your day bright and early ladies, I said to my readers. I myself rose at eleven, howling for your sex… I love to beg, I love to ask, to get, to take advantage of things. My God, oh yes my God but my quest was sublime as I wept over your bare feet in front of the sink. Get up on the right foot, I told my readers. I personally didn't give a damn about my right foot. Weak with deprivation, I'd let myself roll off our divan. My tear-soaked hair streaming down my cheeks. You'd pick me up like a bundle and toss me back onto the sheets. And so began another stormy fit of begging. You obliged me because you couldn't do away with me. No time to waste now ladies: be in a good mood the minute you get up. Learn to wrestle with everyday cares and your troubles will disappear, I said to my readers. I hid my pocketbook, you kept your money out of sight when you opened your wallet. An odd predatory duel. We lied about what we earned. Refusing to give me money was the same as refusing to give me your sex. I brought it to life with my touch while you talked to me about bronchitis, colds, woolies. Composure, *mesdames et mesdemoiselles*, composure above all! Care of the nerves. Tend your nervous system like a garden. A sound mind in a healthy body, as the saying goes. No time to waste now ladies, take a deep breath, open the windows wide as soon as you get up, I said to my readers."

GABRIEL   A fine piece of work, your composure. Fits of rage! Threats! You played the tragic little woman with the expanding, all-devouring uterus. Fucking you, my boy, was like dining with a pack of starving wild cats.

VIOLETTE   Screw off!

GABRIEL   *(about to leave, turns back)* "It's because of women that you are so deranged."

THIRD TABLEAU

Everything is Rotting, Everything is Poisoned

SACHS   Where are the letters, Violette?

VIOLETTE   Where is the trash bin?

GENET   The letters! Watch it, don't think your ugly face will escape our scrutiny.

SACHS   Where are the letters?

VIOLETTE   Where are the toilets?

GABRIEL   Your face is overcast, pal. You lie! You cheat! You deal on the black market!

SACHS   Lies are controlled by invisible threads. I'm afraid I'll never be able to figure out how to get a word of truth out of you.

GABRIEL   You should be a collaborator!

GENET   The letters!

HERMINE   Where are my letters, Violette?

THE MOTHER   Love letters from a woman to another woman. I had a dream. I had a fall. I wanted to get back into my dream, board the passing vessel, sit back comfortably, light up a Camel…

HERMINE   Where are my letters, my love?

GABRIEL   You've been exposed, pal!

SACHS   Your mother will find out!

VIOLETTE   "Everything is rotting, everything is poisoned."

SACHS   It will make her cry!

VIOLETTE "My mother is azure blue. I love her in times of tragedy, I love her after the tragedy. My mother is the offshore breeze, she'll never set foot on the threshold of a dung-heap."

SACHS It's interrogation day between four walls. You had such a talent for roaming forbidden territory without so much as batting an eye.

GENET Turn yourself in! Turn them in! Come on now, it would be a kind move on your part, Viollet-Le-Duc! One clumsy little lie won't challenge your determination to surrender to insanity!

SACHS Turn yourself in! Bit by bit, just a little at a time. Remember to mete out our rations, madame. Be nice, give us your reasons. Look, we're rolling out the red carpet, we're coming to greet you. The brotherhood of informers.

GENET She's opening her mouth!

GABRIEL She's closing her mouth!

GENET She's like a fish in a bowl!

VIOLETTE "Glub glub blub blug glub glub."

SACHS No foreign languages here, if you please.

THE MOTHER Never confess, my child, at any cost!

GABRIEL The black market of confession…

SACHS She's right: confessing requires an extreme lapse of memory…

GENET Pooh-pooh, wee-wee in her pants?

SACHS Where are the letters, Violette Leduc?

GABRIEL The letters!

SACHS Morality! A case for the vice squad, like in the newspapers. Morals, of or relating to principles of right and wrong in behaviour. Morality, the pure diamond that can cut through the ether of moral complacency.

THE MOTHER My child, if you confess, you're locking yourself out.

GABRIEL Where are the letters, old boy?

VIOLETTE "Down in the farthest reaches of my madness."

HERMINE Morals, mores, marks, mere mortals, I love you, Violette.

VIOLETTE I love you.

GABRIEL You traitor! You were caressing me…

VIOLETTE "I was paying for my security with underhanded caresses."

HERMINE You never breathed a word of this to me.

GABRIEL Liar!

VIOLETTE   Yes, I was lying. No, I wasn't lying. Violette Leduc is as mad as a hatter! *(to HERMINE)* My life depended on your letters, on the letters I expected from you. I hid Gabriel from you. I needed you. I needed him.

HERMINE   I'm afraid.

VIOLETTE   I'm afraid.

HERMINE   Just for you I'll play "Bird as Prophet," or Bach's Italian concerto.

GABRIEL   For the last time, where are those letters?

VIOLETTE   *(to HERMINE)* The letters you wrote to me on the black slate of night have all been torn up and flushed away with the pull of the chain, my love. Kiss me!

HERMINE   If you keep your ears and eyes open!

VIOLETTE   I can't kiss you and keep my eyes open!

HERMINE   You watch one side, I'll watch the other.

VIOLETTE   Kiss me! *(they kiss)*

HERMINE   *(startled, terrified)* Somebody's coming!

VIOLETTE   No, it's nothing, a bird, smoke curling out of a chimney…. Kiss me. *(They kiss.)*

HERMINE   *(getting up, covering her eyes with her hands)* There is somebody. I know it. I can see him.

VIOLETTE   Come to me. I want to rest my head in your lap.

HERMINE   Don't look at me like that.

VIOLETTE   Why not? Is it an indecent assault? If you only knew what I see in your eyes…

HERMINE   Let's go out, to a concert, to the theatre.

VIOLETTE   In your eyes, I see "a horizon of permission."

HERMINE   Gabriel?

VIOLETTE   "It's you I betray when he offers me a cigarette. My betrayal is your triumph. If you got angry I'd stop seeing him. I dread your judgment. I want to hold on to what I have: Hermine, Gabriel. What do I have? A harmless man who desires me, and I'm rarely found desirable."

HERMINE   Harmless?

VIOLETTE   "A rather small man, badly dressed, stunted."

HERMINE   A giant.

VIOLETTE   "I pacify him by caressing him with remote hands. Does he really want me? I don't think so. It's the pain he wants. The torment of what he cannot have."

HERMINE   You're lying.

VIOLETTE   Let's go to a concert, my love.

HERMINE   How did he find out we were on our way to a concert?

VIOLETTE   Who? Gabriel?

HERMINE   He's right behind us. *(We see GABRIEL.)* Don't turn around. He's been watching, waiting.

VIOLETTE   "I'm being forced to play this nasty role. He constantly worms his way into my memory, he refuses to be shut out. His audacity depresses me, fascinates me. This martyr is a crook." *(GABRIEL disappears.)*

HERMINE   You're shivering. I feel a chill, I'm shivering.

VIOLETTE   "You're shivering because of my lies."

HERMINE   My ears are sealed.

VIOLETTE   I am a whore! You are a martyr.

HERMINE   I love you as I would my very own child. I want to live with you. I'll make your dresses, I'll buy the fabric.

VIOLETTE   You're beautiful. Of the two, "you are the more feminine one, the more worthy."

HERMINE   You can ask everything of me, Violette. Pour out your demands, the long procession of your desires will light up the dark like a glittering rosary of gladness. The milky blue precious stones, the landscapes of woven textures, the twilight of hats worn by towering women…

VIOLETTE   I want a velvet powderpuff…

HERMINE   I will get you one, from the days previous to powder, from before the dawn of days, before the silkiest moss.

VIOLETTE   I'll powder my face with a cloud of golden dust when we go out. I'll wear light on my cheeks like an ancient goddess.

HERMINE   In the evening I'll give private lessons in music, and in English. We will have money my love.

VIOLETTE   We'll go to that Schumann concerto you so love.

HERMINE   Yes, we will! By day I'll be a schoolteacher; in the evening I'll give private lessons. At night I'll be your lover, and in the morning, your seamstress.

VIOLETTE   Hermine?

HERMINE   Let me get a cigarette!

VIOLETTE   My mother smokes Camels, you smoke Marylands. You have no regrets about your career, the concerts, the travelling…. Your beautiful hands were made for the piano…

HERMINE   "I'll give you raw silk, reversible satins, silk *voile*," necklaces of quartz.

VIOLETTE   I won't have to shoplift anymore. I love to wrap my two hands around your head.

HERMINE   You were shoplifting? My love, you won't have to steal anymore.

VIOLETTE   I was a thief, a common shoplifter. The shower of lights in the big department stores, Hermine! As it coursed through a thousand connecting aisles, the electricity of the big stores flooded into my body, leading me to crossroads of temptation, each one leading to another and another and another. I like myself best with red hair, a cloche hat, the tip of a bird-of-paradise feather swaying on the canary-yellow felt of a long-lost island.

HERMINE   You will have everything. I'll raise up the treasures of Atlantis for you in all the luxury shops, in the greatest couture houses.

VIOLETTE   Greedy hands crushing diamonds, weighing the bubbles of this frothy delight known as luxury for all.

HERMINE   Do you want rose-petal pink panties?

VIOLETTE   Yes, and you will get them for me. The labels confuse me. I never buy a thing, I steal, I build castles in the clouds, I take flight and spread my wings, the sure-handed manoeuvres of a thief. I steal to "rob women of the things made to feminize them."

HERMINE   Poor love, you could end up in jail.

VIOLETTE   Dearest, they caught me red-handed. "Follow me, someone says behind my back." I turn my head, I wrap my arms around my insanity and clutch it to my heart. "Follow me, says the same voice again right by my temple. And so I entered the lair of captured thieves. My escort took my briefcase, took out the objects one by one. Why do you do this, he asked. It's the first time, I said. I was crying. It's the first time, I repeated through my tears. Your first and last names, your address. I broke down, I was wailing, appealing to their mercy. My mother, it's for my mother…. It's the first time, believe me. I believe you, he said. He wanted to know my occupation: I told him about my little items in the papers, hoping to reinforce his sympathy for me. I wasn't a professional thief. I was a slug. I came out of there bruised, raw, in a state of shock."

HERMINE   You can ask anything of me, you are my child, I love you.

VIOLETTE   I want the inaccessible Paris I see in the magazines. The glamour of *Vogue*, of *Fémina*. The fragrance of *Le Jardin des Modes*.

HERMINE   You shall have them!

VIOLETTE   I want the impossible! I'm intoxicated by whatever goes beyond the regulation-size miseries of life!

HERMINE   The patterns woven into fabrics, the to-and-fro of *moiré*, of silks, are all hibernating in the Milky Way. Shall we go and pluck them?

VIOLETTE   "I was born broken. I am another woman's sorrow. A bastard, in other words!"

HERMINE   I love you, I'll comfort you.

VIOLETTE   You'll never leave me!

HERMINE   We'll live together!

VIOLETTE   Every morning I'll kiss your neck. You won't miss the conservatory? The scherzos, the adagios, the violin's echoes, the riot of trumpets…

HERMINE   I won't miss a thing.

VIOLETTE   I want the impossible: "the eyes, the complexion, the self-confidence and the arrogance of models. The nose, most of all." I want the gold sandals in Perugia's window. *Objets d'art*, suits, dresses, skirts.

HERMINE   My hands will touch the fabrics as I undress you.

VIOLETTE   You're looking over there. What do you see?

HERMINE   Couperin.

VIOLETTE   Don't be sad!

HERMINE   I'm not sad!

VIOLETTE   Play the Italian concerto for me!

HERMINE   I'm playing it!

VIOLETTE   Louder, I can hardly hear it!

HERMINE   I am playing louder.

VIOLETTE   The sun is sparkling. I choose this passage. Play it for me again!

HERMINE   I'm starting over.

VIOLETTE   Your music makes me more beautiful.

HERMINE   You are beautiful. Your eyes have a radiance all their own.

VIOLETTE   I'll read *Fémina* every day. I'll learn all about "the virtues of tonics, of astringent—enemy of enlarged pores—of cleansing milk, of nourishing creams, of orange juice,

HERMINE   of apricot powder,

VIOLETTE   crow's feet, wrinkles, dandruff, blackheads, cellulitis,

HERMINE   will all take on the urgency of Jeremiah's calamities." The rest is dross, my love.

VIOLETTE   "Clouds on open windows, away with you. Now is the time to inhale. Now is the time to exhale. Now is the time to exercise. *(HERMINE and VIOLETTE do physical exercises)* Time for rotating hips, time for taking waist measurements, time for working-off double chins. Now is the hour of the ankle, the hour of the wrist. Open window, blue skies calling for trumpets, you'll have to be patient. It's time to be more flexible, time for deep-red blood in our veins, time for better circulation. Stretched out on the floor, having touched my toes 25 times to grow 25 times young before I turn 25."

HERMINE   You will have your fill of fine meats, and vegetables. We'll drink champagne!

VIOLETTE   Mumm's Extra Dry!

HERMINE   We'll buy some every day and drink till we're delightfully delirious!

VIOLETTE   "In my mind I'll light votive candles for *Vogue*, for *Fémina*, for *Le Jardin des Modes*. I'll shed some intimacy on the mysterious realm of haute couture." I'm in love with Chiaparelli!

HERMINE   Chiaparelli? Who is that?

VIOLETTE   She is a Roman. Chanel trembles at the mention of her name. Her designs are so eccentric. She bewitches me, she seduces me. I fall to my knees at her feet. She is my queen, my sovereign, my star in the fashion constellation. The pleats of her skirts are a wonder to behold!

HERMINE   Is she the greatest designer of all?

VIOLETTE   She is the greatest. I study her designs and sketches in the magazines.

HERMINE   *(handing her a newspaper)* Look!

VIOLETTE   Where? What?

HERMINE   There, there! Chiaparelli is having a sale!

VIOLETTE   Hermine! She's having a sale! It says so right here. She's having a sale, she's having a sale!

HERMINE   We must go…

VIOLETTE   To Chiaparelli's… I'd never dare! Would you?

HERMINE   Why not, she's having a sale…

VIOLETTE   To set foot in Chiaparelli's… to set foot in Chiaparelli's…

HERMINE   We will dare!

VIOLETTE   We'll buy a scarf as a souvenir…

HERMINE   We'll buy a dress, a suit, whatever you want!

VIOLETTE   It's too expensive!

HERMINE   But she's having a sale!

VIOLETTE   Me in Chiaparelli's…. Walking in… looking around… touching things…

HERMINE   Trying on a dress… one of her works of art… buying…

VIOLETTE   Will you dare? When? When?

HERMINE   Right now. Come on my love. *(She leads VIOLETTE by the hand, leaves the kitchen moving to stage-front and immediately the magic begins, the fantasy of colours, fabrics hanging in the air, evening dresses, shawls, scarves, etc.)*

VIOLETTE   They're going to stop us, throw us out, trample and ridicule us, we'll be crushed underfoot, we'll die with our limbs neatly folded into a box.

HERMINE   Look at how beautiful everything is, Violette. Look! Look! "Can't you just imagine yourself in a Chiaparelli?"

VIOLETTE   My mother was a char-woman… my mother worked as a maid in their *châteaux*!

HERMINE   There is worse!

VIOLETTE   Worse?

HERMINE   Cleaning house for poor people!

VIOLETTE   I'm freezing, Hermine. We must leave this place! *(enter a saleslady— played by VIOLETTE's mother—she turns her head slightly, her body towards the wings.)*

THE MOTHER   Madame Guerlain's fitting, take care of Madame Guerlain's fitting. *(to HERMINE, to VIOLETTE)* Ladies?

HERMINE   The garments on sale?

THE MOTHER   *(showing the dresses, while one can hear the clatter of hangers being put back on the rack, the sound of doors)* The garments on sale? Here, and there, look at this silk…

HERMINE   Beautiful!

THE MOTHER   This dress was meant for you!

HERMINE   I don't want anything.

THE MOTHER   *(to VIOLETTE)* Something for you then! This dress will suit you, you have "a model's figure."

HERMINE   *(to VIOLETTE)* I told you so.

THE MOTHER   This suit is just exquisite. This hat is outrageous. Would you like to try this dress on? Follow me! *(She leads them to a small fitting-room with* *a three-panelled mirror. She speaks to HERMINE.)* Won't you let yourself be tempted?

HERMINE *(to VIOLETTE)* Give me your clothes, I'll hold on to them. *(VIOLETTE undresses.)*

THE MOTHER Take your time, think it over. I'll be back. *(She exits.)*

VIOLETTE Take me in your arms, Hermine. Hold me close.

HERMINE *(holding her tight)* Put the dress on, try it on, Violette.

VIOLETTE "Do you think she knows about us?"

HERMINE "I hope so. This dress is a beauty. No hem, three rows of stitching at the bottom, and thicker than wool. Is it silk, really? How do they do it?"

VIOLETTE "Do you think it's expensive?"

HERMINE Priceless. *(The saleslady returns.)* We'll take it.

THE MOTHER *(to HERMINE)* "What about you? We have some lovely things on sale you know. Why not pick something?"

HERMINE No, some other time.

VIOLETTE *(taking the dress off)* Is she here? *(to the saleslady)*

THE MOTHER Who?

VIOLETTE Madame Chiaparelli!

THE MOTHER *(correcting her)* Madame Schiaparelli will be here tomorrow. We'll put your dress in a box.

VIOLETTE *(putting the dress back on)* No.

THE MOTHER No?

VIOLETTE I'm keeping it on. I'll wear it.

THE MOTHER As you wish, madame. It looks marvelous on you. *(to HERMINE)* If you'll just come with me, we can make the final arrangements. *(She exits.)*

VIOLETTE Do you have the money? How much is it? It's too expensive. It's going to cost too much, you won't be able to afford it.

HERMINE I have everything we need right here in my pocket.

VIOLETTE You'll never leave me?

HERMINE Never. *(She exits.)*

> *VIOLETTE, alone, looking at herself in the mirror, pirouetting, walking. A man appears from the wings—the actor portraying GENET. He circles briefly around VIOLETTE and decides to approach her.*

GENET   "Allow me to approach you with all due respect and intentions. I won't mince words: I find you exciting. Shall we go? I'll caress you, you'll caress me. Goddamn your fancy airs…. Who does she think she is?"

> *He exits grumbling. Another man appears who goes up to VIOLETTE and approaches her—the actor portraying GABRIEL.*

GABRIEL   "Come with me. Don't you like me? I'll tell you a secret: I love to have my breasts tickled. I'm a man and I love it. Not interested? Get stuffed you old bag. You fell for it. Look at yourself!"

> *He exits, a third man enters—the actor playing MAURICE SACHS. He approaches VIOLETTE.*

SACHS   "Let me introduce myself. I saw everything that just happened. I've been watching you for a while. Nothing escapes me. Two fellows accosted you. I saw everything. Two of them one after the other, in broad daylight, what a nerve!… If I were you… have they no pride? I was following, observing. They are absolutely shameless. Did they introduce themselves at least? I'd have guessed it. They think they have every right. These days, propriety…. In any case, one sign from you and I'd have come running. If I say I'd like to spend some time with you, I mean it sincerely. I know a hotel not far from here, you'll see. You go in first. I'm not free, I mustn't attract attention.

> *HERMINE enters carrying a box, the man quietly withdraws, stopping a little further on to observe them.*

HERMINE   *(who doesn't see the man standing in the shadows watching them)* Do you hear it?

VIOLETTE   *(vaguely, looking towards the man)* Hmmm? Who? What?

HERMINE   That melody, the opening of the adagio from the Fifth Symphony.

VIOLETTE   Poor you, in your shabby summer coat and worn-out old shoes…

HERMINE   Get a pencil and add this up, quickly: I'll give a private lesson every day…

VIOLETTE   I'll go back to work for the publisher. They have some interesting work coming up.

HERMINE   I don't want you getting tired my love. Let's go home, shall we? I feel like undressing you, running my hands over your skin, I feel like keeping chastity at arm's length.

VIOLETTE   *(as if she were making a decision but still a bit embarrassed)* Go home without me. I'll join you shortly.

HERMINE   I don't want to leave your side, Violette. First we'll stop by the silk traders' building, I have enough money left to buy some fabric. I want to make you a blouse of ribbed lamé!

VIOLETTE   I need to walk by myself, Hermine, to hear my footsteps keeping time with my heartbeat.

HERMINE   I sew and I am not a seamstress. I love you and I don't feel guilty. I trust you, I am a true innocent. *(She is about to leave.)* See you shortly!

> She exits, and the man leaves the shadows and slowly comes to *VIOLETTE.*

FOURTH TABLEAU

The Pimp I Once Was

SACHS   *(approaching slowly, moving around VIOLETTE like one circles around a prey)* "Can I offer you something? I asked if you would like something? You must make up your mind, I haven't a lot of time."

VIOLETTE   "No, monsieur, I'm not thirsty."

SACHS   "I find you attractive, and I'm not often attracted. The woman who just left, is she your friend? If she is you can say so. Women are so needy."

VIOLETTE   I live with her.

SACHS   "How interesting. Could I arrange a meeting with you and your friend?"

VIOLETTE   "I don't know if she'll agree to it. To her, you know, men…"

SACHS   "That makes things much more interesting. Much. Ask her."

VIOLETTE   I'll ask her.

SACHS   "What would you like me to talk about? I can make conversation about anything you wish. Women need to be entertained. I can address any topic under the sun. Nothing intimidates me. I'm not an egotist. I always think of the ladies first. We must keep our little darlings happy. Are you expected somewhere? You should have said so. Time is flying, I wouldn't have talked so much, what a pity. Man is so selfish. His pleasure always comes first. What a brute! As for me, I'm thinking of your cute little puss, of that sweet little pussy under your skirt. In two hours, shall we say?"

VIOLETTE   Very well.

SACHS   "You won't stand me up?"

VIOLETTE   "I won't stand you up. *Au revoir*, monsieur."

SACHS   "You're smiling."

VIOLETTE   "I'm smiling? I didn't realize I was."

> The hustler disappears. VIOLETTE goes back to her kitchen where HERMINE is waiting for her, sewing a piece of lamé.

HERMINE   *(looking admiringly at VIOLETTE)* How beautiful you are. Do you still like your dress? I'm putting the finishing touches on this bodice, my love. "Where did you go walking?"

VIOLETTE   On the boulevards.

> *She wants to take HERMINE in her arms, lie down on the bed with her, HERMINE resists.*

HERMINE   Not now, later.

VIOLETTE   "Not now, later. You never want anything."

HERMINE   I want everything. I love you. Not now.

VIOLETTE   "That's part of loving too."

HERMINE   "You're talking like a man."

VIOLETTE   What do you know about men, Hermine!

HERMINE   I can imagine, I can imagine. Their demands, the harassment…

VIOLETTE   "They ask to have their breasts tickled. They're alone, they're lonely. They need their fantasies."

HERMINE   Were people turning around to admire you, on the boulevards? Tell me.

VIOLETTE   Distinguished old men, handsome adults, beautiful adolescents, were following me, flattering me. the Châteaubriand type, the Byron type, the Shelley type, when he was about 18. Enigmatic and beautiful." Do you believe me?

HERMINE   *(lovingly)* I believe you.

VIOLETTE   Beautiful! One of them had an intensely green reflection in his eyes, charged with darkness they were. Real darkness, more real than the dark of a crow's wing, Hermine. Every time his eyes met mine, I could hear…

HERMINE   You could hear… what?

VIOLETTE   I could hear the sound of a notch: it was a piece of my heart falling at my feet. Aren't you jealous?

HERMINE   I'm never jealous of beauty. Human beauty creates a kind of void in me, a passing rapture that leaves me breathless.

VIOLETTE   *(suddenly)* Get dressed!

HERMINE   What for? You want to go out?

VIOLETTE   I want to go out. We have a *rendez-vous*.

HERMINE   "Give me your arm while I sew." Tell me about this *rendez-vous*. I sometimes get the feeling that you stock up on *rendez-vous* the way some people stock up on canned goods, or fresh meat. With Gabriel…

VIOLETTE   You're jealous of Gabriel, aren't you?

HERMINE   I hate him. He tortures you, always in some café waiting for you, or downstairs, pacing at your door. I run into him, he looks at me but it's you he's looking for in my eyes. He hates me too. When he sees me he pounces, as swift as a squirrel, coiled like a spring, with lightning speed. Then he stops right in front of me, as if I were blocking his way, ready to obliterate me, to riddle me with arrows. Then he interrogates me: when will she be home? Where is she?

VIOLETTE   What's your answer?

HERMINE   None, I chase him off, I keep out of his way. He is my enemy, I am his enemy. He is my pain, I am his pain. We are one another's vulnerability, we exclude each other from happiness.

VIOLETTE   If we go out together, arm in arm, will it make you happy?

HERMINE   I'll feel more secure.

VIOLETTE   Well then, let's go out, to our *rendez-vous* with this fellow. It's understood that he's buying the champagne. I told him I live with you, that I love you.

HERMINE   If it's champagne you want, we can have some here.

VIOLETTE   I also want cocktails!

HERMINE   We can have them here too, my love.

VIOLETTE   "Of course we can drink here. But the ambiance, the setting, are you forgetting?" We can look in Chanel's window on the way…

HERMINE   "I hate going out. I hate being seen. Is it that important to you? How old is he? What sort is he?"

VIOLETTE   *(feeling the outcome will be in her favour)* How old? An old man, a meaningless voice, he's rich, I'm sure of it. He's invited us for drinks. Bring your friend, he said!

HERMINE   "an old fool, we'll go then."

> HERMINE *gets dressed, they leave VIOLETTE's room, move to stage-front where the third hustler awaits them—the actor portraying MAURICE SACHS.*

VIOLETTE   There he is! *Bonsoir* monsieur!

SACHS   *Bonsoir* mesdames! I was expecting you. A little champagne?

VIOLETTE   *Oui* monsieur. *(to HERMINE)* Don't be so distant, give him some encouragement!

> *He pulls some chairs together.*

HERMINE   Me? This gentlemen needs no encouragement whatsoever.

VIOLETTE   "We came here for him, no?"

HERMINE   "I'm here for you."

SACHS   *(who had gone to get the champagne, approaching)* Am I being indiscreet? I'm delighted with your presence. What powers of seduction, what beauty! *(to HERMINE)* Your friend told me all about you. I hear you are quite the virtuoso at the piano. I love the piano, I love musicians, arpeggios, the hands working in unison, fingers flying over the keys. Music is so uplifting, don't you think? Wagner! Bach! The genius of the romantics.

HERMINE   I play very badly. I don't know the first thing about music. I detest Wagner!

SACHS   I didn't mean to offend you by bringing up Wagner. Of course he's somewhat oppressive, not to say violent. I read his biography. What a womanizer he was!

HERMINE   Which one of his biographies? The one he dictated to Cosima himself?

SACHS   That one and others.

HERMINE   He is the embodiment of Pan-Germanism.

SACHS   The proclamation of the German Empire did go to his head, you're quite right. "Would it be indiscreet of me to ask your first names?"

VIOLETTE   Violette.

HERMINE   *(after hesitating)* Hermine.

SACHS   "How charming, Hermine—Violette, how absolutely charming."

HERMINE   *(to VIOLETTE, out loud)* "Tell me, is it charming, or was it fatal, this pairing of our two names?"

VIOLETTE   *(embarrassed)* I don't know. *(to the man)* Do you like this place?

SACHS   Yes, I do. Do you? It's intimate, discreet. May I offer you a drop of champagne? A gin-fizz perhaps? *(He is sweating profusely, takes out his handkerchief to mop his brow, his hands.)* Hermine—Violette, simply charming.

HERMINE   "Does your wife play the piano?"

SACHS   "No, she doesn't." Why don't we move over there, it's more intimate.

HERMINE   *(to VIOLETTE)* "Would you like that?"

VIOLETTE   Why not? *(She lights a cigarette, offers one to HERMINE.)*

HERMINE   *(to VIOLETTE)* Tell me we won't go over there? Tell me, Violette! Let's leave right now while there's still time. This fellow is pathetic!

> SACHS gets up to get more champagne.

VIOLETTE   Pathetic but nice. He has a lot of money.

HERMINE   What for? What for?

VIOLETTE   I love you Hermine. Don't think about anything else. I love you passionately.

HERMINE   "Let's leave, please. I'll pay for the champagne and that will be the end of it…. Things have a way of working out." This room is about to crush me to death, I don't want to suffer such agony!

VIOLETTE   *(with a kiss)* "You spoil-sport! What have you got against this gentleman? You're afraid of everything." *(The man comes back inside with the bottle of champagne.)* You bore me, you make my insides hurt, you drain my oxygen.

SACHS   "You are so very understanding, Violette."

HERMINE   This champagne is unbearably sweet!

VIOLETTE   "The champagne is dry, Hermine."

HERMINE   "It's warm."

VIOLETTE   "The champagne is perfectly chilled, Hermine."

SACHS   "I love to see you at each other's throats like this. Now we're getting somewhere, now we're getting somewhere."

VIOLETTE   *(to HERMINE)* Be reasonable. Understanding.

HERMINE   Very well, if you don't want to leave, I'll stay.

SACHS   Come and see your bed.

> He gets up and light falls on another space, revealing a sumptuous bed, mirrors.

HERMINE   *(shattered)* No, Violette, no. This will kill me. *(She starts crying.)*

VIOLETTE   *(taking her in her arms)* Don't cry. I love you. I want you. Together we'll map out pleasure, my love, we'll change the pulse of our blood rhythms.

SACHS   Don't leave, I beg of you.

VIOLETTE   We're staying.

HERMINE   We're staying, you're leaving!

SACHS   I'll go. I'll take my leave on tiptoe. *Vive l'amour! Vive les femmes! (He withdraws to just outside the lighted area.)*

VIOLETTE   *(to HERMINE)* I promise you everything! Everything! I adore you! We're going to travel across the skies, seduce the North Star. I'll change into a serpent, you will be fruit.

HERMINE   *(undressing)* Serpents don't talk. Serpents don't write love letters. They don't receive love letters to flush down the toilet. Will you ever stop, Violette? For one second, long enough for our happiness to catch up with us? *(They get* *into bed, SACHS is still on the outer arc of light, the light goes down. He takes a step, and another, slowly nearing the bed.)* Is he gone? Is he really gone?

VIOLETTE   He's a proper gentleman, he left.

HERMINE   Could he be dangerous? But there are two of us, aren't there?

VIOLETTE   Yes, we are two. I want to tap your deepest waters, my love. I want the universe.

HERMINE   The crystal clarity of pleasure, Violette. But it always seems to fade away into distant symmetries, out of reach…

VIOLETTE   Not another word.

SACHS   *(drawing nearer as VIOLETTE raises her head to look at him)* "Make love to her. That's all I ask." There's a lot of money in it for you.

> *The lighting fades. The man is standing at the foot of the bed, all we can see are some reflections in the mirror.*

FIFTH TABLEAU

Mister Sophocles Is Not In

> *We are in THE MOTHER's room. In her small space there is now a telephone switchboard. THE MOTHER is sitting in front of the switchboard. We see her in profile. She answers, becomes agitated, shoves some plugs into the switchboard.*

THE MOTHER   Hello, hello… *(buzz)* Hello! Yes, hold on… hello, yes, hold on monsieur, I'm trying to locate him. Ah! Monsieur Gallimard. I have André Breton on the lines. Yes, it's important…. He's in excellent humour. Hello, yes hello, ah! Monsieur Breton, here is monsieur Gallimard… yes, he's in excellent humour! *(buzz)* Hello, hello… who? Monsieur Michaux? No, I'm sorry, monsieur Michaux is away on a trip… where? In *Grande Garabagne*. Yes, it's quite far… I'm sorry?… yes, probably a French colony, monsieur *(buzz)* Hold the lines please! Hello, hello… I'm sorry, he's on another line… would you care to wait? Thank you, monsieur… very well, monsieur. Goodbye, monsieur *(buzz)* Hello, hello, yes…. Who? Monsieur Max Jacob? No, monsieur, monsieur Max Jacob is not in forever…. At Mademoiselle Chanel's? Wouldn't you be sticking around at Mademoiselle Chanel's too if she invited you, monsieur? *(buzz)* One moment… please hold the line… hello, hello… Mister Sophocles? I'm sorry, but Mister Sophocles is not in… yes… on tour… no… Mister Euripides is also out… together? I'm sure I don't know, monsieur. Would you care to leave a message?… Hello, I was telling you that monsieur Max Jacob is not in forever… no, he hasn't had a falling out with monsieur Gallimard. He is dead, monsieur… monsieur Max Jacob is dead! He died in the country, in a camp… Treblinka, Nancy… yes, monsieur Jacob was a Jew… nobody's perfect… in a camp for writers? There were writers in every camp, monsieur…

you find me rude? I find you grossly indecent, monsieur! *(She cuts the line off. Buzz.)* Hello, hello, yes… who? Monsieur Camus isn't in yet… oh, just a moment, I think I hear him coming *(She turns her head towards the back.)* monsieur Camus, you're wanted on the phone… it's monsieur Sartre, I believe… hello, who's speaking please? Monsieur Sartre… yes, just a moment, I'll put monsieur Camus on the line…. Hello, hello, yes… who? Monsieur Cocteau isn't here… he rarely comes by… yes… if you care to leave a message. I'm sorry, monsieur, but we don't give out our writers' addresses… who are you, monsieur? Oh, I see… yes… do you have a pencil? Monsieur Jean Cocteau lives at number 10, *rue d'Anjou*… with his mother? So they say… yes, yes, a bourgeois neighbourhood… Paris has many of them… *au revoir*, monsieur *(She turns her attention to the plug left hanging from the beginning.)* Hello, hello *(Her voice changes.)* Mother dear… yes… how are you? You always say that… you know very well I'm on bad terms with spelling… call you? But you don't have a telephone! You refused the telephone, mother dear… *(buzz)* Don't hang up, I'll get back to you…. Hello, hello, mother…. Do I hear you coughing? I don't like the sound of that cough. You're looking after yourself, I hope *(buzz)* I'm not hanging up, I'll get back to you…. Hello, hello, yes. Gallimard Publishing House. Who shall I say is calling? One moment. Hello, hello, monsieur Camus, it's a journalist with a funny accent…. Hello, hello, mother, are you still there? Yes… yes… she's fine… well, you know… always the same… you know her… always on the move… her trafficking… her black-marketeering… there's nothing like adversity to make my Violette blossom… you know her obsession with comestibles… me too, you say me too, this obsession with comestibles? Maybe. Hello, hello, I can hardly hear you…. It's so difficult to get through to each other… every time you call, we can barely get through to each other… it's as if this was happening on purpose! *(buzz)* Don't hang up. I said don't hang up! I'll get back to you… hello, hello, yes… hold the line, here is monsieur Jules Romains… *(buzz)* Hello, hello, mother… are you there? Yes I hear you! Do you hear me? Violette? She thinks she's the Messiah ever since Gallimard published her book…. Gallimard is a publishing house, mother. A publishing house? How can I describe it to you?… "It's a brand name, a marking at the bottom of a book cover." *(buzz)* Don't hang up, mother. Hello, hello, yes, monsieur Maurice Sachs? He's not here, monsieur…. We've not heard from Sachs… yes, a lot of rumours…. Hello, mother, are you still there? Yes, I'm tired too… I was saying that Violette thinks she's the Messiah… no I'm not being mean… she's my daughter, the fruit of my womb, mother. She exasperates me, that's all… she dresses like a beggar, she takes her knitting to public places, she sniffles, she asks to borrow money from me… no, mother, she has money, yes, I assure you she does… she's made a small fortune on the black market… I'm telling you… she has protection, some important people are looking after her… who? Simone de Beauvoir, before Maurice Sachs, Jean Cocteau…. You've never heard of them? It doesn't matter, mother, I'm telling you she has friends! Important people… oh! you know, I would have been happier if she'd become a schoolteacher… what? *(buzz)* Hello, hello, yes, monsieur Aragon? Yes, he is in, I'll put him on the line… one moment please, hold on…. Hello, mother, are you there? Yes mother, I'm angry at my daughter! I have my reasons…. If you only knew what she did to me in that book of hers, *In the prison of her skin*…. What? Certainly we discussed it… she was slightly embarrassed… you know how courageous she is! She said that she had transposed, that it was all just literature… I don't believe her! Gabriel? He asked for a divorce! It's just as well, don't you think? Hermine? I don't know… no, I don't know… I do know she left Paris… what? Violette is finding solace, of course she is… she also has Simone de Beauvoir… I'm telling you she is, mother… yes, mother… plus, she's having her menopause… yes, her menopause… I told her she should be happy about it… she'll be able to enjoy life a little… have a man, be a woman… *(buzz)* Listen, mother, there's another call coming in… yes, I've got to leave you now, call me back as soon as you can… yes… yes… I'll give her your message… trust me… you know how much she loves you… she adores you. *(buzz)* She often mentions you, mother… Fidéline this, Fidéline that… *(buzz)* I'll talk to you soon, mother. Very soon! Hello, hello, yes… yes… I'm listening… yes… I'm making a note of it… at your service, monsieur, at your service… *(the lighting fades)*…

Intermission.

SIXTH TABLEAU

The Grasshopper and the Ant

MAURICE SACHS is standing on a train-station platform, pacing, looking at his watch. Pale lighting, the sound of footsteps, the hammering of boots, orders being given in German, train whistles, the hum of activity. MAURICE SACHS is wearing a putty-coloured raincoat, a beautiful scarf around his neck. At his feet, a suitcase and in his hand a small parcel. VIOLETTE enters, running towards him.

VIOLETTE   I'm come to get you, Maurice Sachs! You're not leaving, you can't leave, tear yourself away from Paris.

SACHS   My dear, my decision is irrevocable, Paris isn't everything. There are some huge countries out there…

VIOLETTE   With fresh graves everywhere. Are you deaf? Are you mad?

SACHS   I'm leaving!

VIOLETTE   But you're a Jew!

SACHS   My dear, must you always exaggerate. Women are so dramatic about everything. I'm off to a rich country where the land is littered with bank notes and nobody there to pick them up.

VIOLETTE   Nobody there except the blood raining down. I'm going with you.

SACHS   My dear, "what do you think of love?"

VIOLETTE   "A lot of good and a lot of bad. And you?"

SACHS   "A lot of good and a lot of bad." You are on the verge of tears, my dear. It's a waste of time, I can assure you.

VIOLETTE   I'm weeping with dread. Long rusty streaks.

SACHS   I'm responsible for my life. And I want you to know that I am very attached to it.

VIOLETTE   Maurice Sachs, prodigal Maurice Sachs, my partner in seasons of insomnia, out there lies night's darkest hour, broken bodies.

SACHS   My dear, you've known me rich and you've known me poor, you've known me sad and you've known me gay, or spent with pleasure, or dead drunk, or sick and unwashed. My dear, one must channel one's worst flaws and develop one's qualities. I've never given up hope of regaining some human dignity.

VIOLETTE   Jester! Unhappy clown! Pretending to be gay! Even your raincoat is crying; and your underwear, and your scarf too are crying.

SACHS   *(holding out the small parcel he holds in his hand)* My dear, I brought you a little something! Here.

VIOLETTE   *(without taking the parcel)* I don't want to be reminded of you. I refuse! If you leave, I'll be forced to remember you.

SACHS   But I'll come back, my dear. Maurice Sachs always comes back, don't you know that? Sometimes in rags fit for a tramp, with an official stamp on his forehead. Sometimes attired like an Arabian prince, as rich as the 40 thieves.

VIOLETTE   You won't come back.

SACHS   I will come back, my dear. My papers are in order, I have at least three identities to get me past any one of the governments. I have my passport. *(He puts the parcel in her hands.)* Here, take this!

VIOLETTE   "A passport for the impossible. Your eyes are too gentle, too sad, too deep. You are a homosexual. A man who is neither a monk nor a eunuch, nor an elder. A man who is more than that, less than that."

SACHS   You're spouting like a trumpet, my dear!

VIOLETTE   My dear! My dear! Your high-society expressions break my heart.

SACHS   You Aryans, you see drama everywhere. The war, wars, they just arouse your tongue. The war of 1914, this war, all the others, Waterloo, the Napoleonic Wars, skies in flames, the French Revolution, Attila the Hun, scourge of God; but my dear, it's all a matter of money, we'll be rich and rolling in money, and spending it like crazy, riding in grand style, in a blaze of glory. You and I we'll walk together, we'll fly through the air together, take a suite at the Ritz, have champagne and caviar for breakfast. Fantasies of peace-everlasting are wrong in the female imagination. General happiness is consolidated on the Stock Exchange!

VIOLETTE   You're shivering, you're cold, you're playing with your sadness, you're eating your life alive.

SACHS   My poor child, nothing is serious, nothing is beyond change. Try to remember that. Now open this parcel!

VIOLETTE   I'm opening it. But your words are a smoke-screen, your saliva has turned to vinegar.

SACHS   Open the parcel!

VIOLETTE   *(tearing the paper)* Books! *(She reads.) Penitents in Pink Tights*, by Max Jacob, and *Ballad of Reading Gaol* by Wilde. Thank you, Maurice Sachs.

SACHS   You will read them on moonlit nights, dear child. Books are our most faithful companions: forever young, and available. Wilde is probably a familiar of yours.

VIOLETTE   I've read nothing of his. They say this is his finest book, his most moving. His suffering, just his suffering and his tears, striking the stones of his dungeon to wear them away for eternity.

SACHS   My dear, I hear salvation on the tip of your tongue. Salvation! Sheer hypocrisy, pure pettiness! You know very well there is only one form of salvation possible…. You don't? Why salvation through normalcy of course! Wilde dying in his dungeon, Verlaine in his bistrot, without Rimbaud. Rimbaud in a hospital bed, without poetry, without Verlaine, without desert.

VIOLETTE   Maurice Sachs on a train-station platform, the famous writer about to desert us.

SACHS   I was famous and quickly forgotten…

VIOLETTE   You still are! The author of *Sabbath*.

SACHS   I've just handed in my manuscript for *Chronique joyeuse et scandaleuse*. What will become of my *Decade of Illusion*, my dear? Posthumous works?

VIOLETTE   You know very well publishing is at a halt right now. It's too dangerous. Your books will soon have room to breath again. People will be talking about you and your works.

SACHS   (*laughing*) I'm a grasshopper, my dear. You are an ant. That *is* the real you, isn't it? An ant, a crumb-gatherer, a dust-eater. Your face is sagging… don't you want to be an ant? Ants are lovely! So industrious, dragging their load of memories and hopes around; masons and architects of their own world, they tunnel into the earth down to their subterranean treasure troves.

VIOLETTE   If you say so…

SACHS   The grasshopper says you…. You will write to me. I'll send you my address.

VIOLETTE   I'll write to you every day! Don't go!

SACHS   Every day? That's much too much. Your time is valuable.

VIOLETTE   What about yours? You've given me everything: kindness, enthusiasm, you've made me laugh…

SACHS   Which is not an easy thing to do.

VIOLETTE   I'll write to you every day.

SACHS   You're sinking fast, my dear. I beg of you, drop this haunted mask of yours immediately. I'm not a ghost. I'd much rather you sent me pages from your manuscript instead.

VIOLETTE   I don't want to write anymore, Sachs. I'll never be a writer.

SACHS   You're disappointing me, child.

VIOLETTE   Too bad! I don't want the isolation of writing. I can't face being so alone and shaking like a leaf, racked with amnesia, tortured by memories.

SACHS *(showing her Max Jacob's book)* Wouldn't you love to see your name in print on a romantic cover like this one? *(He reads.) In the prison of her skin*, by Violette Leduc.

VIOLETTE It's all a dream, an optical illusion, a colossal mistake.

SACHS It is a dream, and it is anguish; it is a birth, and it is pleasure; it is a gift, and it is joy.

VIOLETTE You make it sound like the easiest thing in the world.

SACHS Surely the most fascinating.

VIOLETTE My manuscript will be rejected. They're already bored stiff with my childhood memories, just like you were, and Gabriel, and Hermine. Mother will never forgive me my childhood memories.

SACHS Gabriel, dear Gabriel, that little husband of yours. Tell me, what's become of him? And your friend Hermine?

VIOLETTE Gabriel? Gone. We're getting a divorce. I was unfaithful to Hermine with Gabriel. I was unfaithful to Gabriel with Hermine. "I will always be a small-time traitor." I'm a whore.

SACHS Stop feeling sorry for yourself.

VIOLETTE "Writing is an act of prostitution. You play the vamp, you sell your charms. Every word is a come on. Come with me, adjective. Say, follow me, *chéri*. I'll show you a good time, adjective. I'll drive you wild. How much? Oh, the price of the book about to be published."

SACHS *(as if he is knocking on a door)* Knock, knock, knock!

VIOLETTE Hermine left me. I'm free. Free to lick my fingers when I eat, free to go out alone on Sundays, to spend the day in bed, to dress in rags or fish-scales, to run a blade over my wrists.

SACHS *(same game)* Knock, knock, knock!

VIOLETTE I'm not here, go away!

SACHS Knock, knock, knock!

VIOLETTE Who goes there?

SACHS It's fame, my dear. Why not open this door, make way for fame and a friend. Make way for love.

VIOLETTE Come on, do come in, love…

SACHS You will be loved…

VIOLETTE Literature leads to love?

SACHS   Literature leads to love. Love leads to literature. You'll write me your childhood memories, sitting under a tree, your pen will find the ink without thinking about it.

VIOLETTE   I'll be thinking of you. I'll write you sitting "under an apple tree laden with pink and green apples. I'll follow the path of freshly-mown wheat. Skylarks, swooping over furrowed fields in a dazzling display, where are you? The mane was in tears over the horse's eyes. He was the diligent one, the most assuming. The sow was too naked, the ewe overdressed. A hen fell in love with a cow and followed her everywhere, caged between four legs."

SACHS   You'll see your name in bookstore windows someday.

VIOLETTE   I'll write with chloroform. My prose will put readers to sleep.

SACHS   My dear child, you're such a damn nuisance!

VIOLETTE   Don't leave! I want your child.

SACHS   I've no more time. *(He looks at his watch.)* My train leaves in five minutes.

VIOLETTE   I want a child by you.

SACHS   A child by me?

VIOLETTE   Yes, you once made me the offer…

SACHS   Once upon a time, long ago… I wanted to do something for you, give you a life-line…. All your tears and despair… and you said 'No'…

VIOLETTE   That 'No' was a fake…. We were walking along the *Esplanade des Invalides*, you were telling me about your loved ones: Socrates, Elie Faure, Victor Hugo, Jacques Maritain, Henry James. Later on, in a bistrot, where you spent your last francs buying me an expensive drink, you asked me if I'd like to have your child…

SACHS   You said no and offered me money, all you had left…

VIOLETTE   I had no need of a child, Sachs. No desire to be saved in that way. A child, a parting, a farewell. A child will say goodbye too.

SACHS   I wanted to see you happy, dearest child. I'd have done anything, surely you see that.

VIOLETTE   You were my faith.

SACHS   So were you.

VIOLETTE   I loved you.

SACHS   How fortunate for you, I'm leaving!

VIOLETTE   Fortunate for me to be an Aryan while others are living in hiding, underground like animals…

SACHS   We must say goodbye, my child. *(He picks up his suitcase.)*

VIOLETTE   Why are you leaving?

SACHS   Because I've made too many enemies.

VIOLETTE   You'll be in exile.

SACHS   Do take care of yourself, of Max Jacob, of Oscar Wilde. Don't forget: Knock, knock, knock!

VIOLETTE   Who is there?

SACHS   It's fame, and love.

VIOLETTE   Why come in my friends, come in!

SACHS   Farewell, ant!

VIOLETTE   Farewell, grasshopper!

> *All the noises from the station, the German words, a train pulling out.*

SEVENTH TABLEAU

I Am An Intruder

> *The setting is a café where SIMONE de BEAUVOIR has been writing since the play began. On the table in front of her, a nearly empty glass. Around her table are three unoccupied chairs. Enter NATHALIE SARRAUTE—part played by HERMINE—and CLARA MALRAUX— role played by Violette's MOTHER. NATHALIE SARRAUTE is plainly dressed, almost severely, while CLARA MALRAUX is very chic and elegant. Simone de Beauvoir has her chignon, her turban, she too is quite plainly dressed.*

SIMONE   *(lifting her head as they enter)* Nathalie!

NATHALIE   Simone! *(They embrace while CLARA MALRAUX stays a bit behind.)* Simone de Beauvoir, you've met Clara Malraux! …

SIMONE   *(who always speaks with a rapid, clipped delivery)* Yes of course! We met at Bernard Grasset's book launch about a month ago. You were wearing that marvelous apricot-coloured dress. It was very crowded there that night, as usual, so our exchange was very brief. I was with Sartre, you were with a gentleman friend. Please sit down. I've had too much to tell you for the longest time now, forever it would seem. I'm delighted to hear that your work is being published. Indeed, the books published by my peers keep me on the alert: especially those written by women. When I woke up this morning, an idea came to me: why don't we women writers request the government to make laws guaranteeing that critics, censorship boards, and the reading committees in publishing houses, stop treating the books we women write like abnormalities—worse, like criminal offences!

CLARA   Simone de Beauvoir, you don't seriously believe that our books, our lives, could get past the inquisitors of social order merely by passing laws?

SIMONE   Sheer utopianism on my part, I know. I'm like that in the morning. Somehow everything seems possible… most of all we must appeal to friendship and intelligence.

CLARA   Forgive my skepticism, but I was born in 1900, and I was born Clara Goldschmidt, don't forget that. I myself have not been given much of a chance to forget it these past few years. In my family, a respectable family of the good Jewish bourgeoisie, we believed in friendship and intelligence. Given my many Jewish ancestors who lived through the pogroms, the Holocaust, one would think I'd have inherited an uncommon tendency to distrust, don't you? Friendship, intelligence…. Very early on, I had to learn to gauge the great gulf separating words from ideas in their speeches. Friendship! Intelligence! Somewhere between those two words, I've been stripped of freedom.

SIMONE   I understand what you're saying: to be wrenched from life, from security, to be thrown into a no-man's land where anything can happen. But now you're free.

CLARA   Free but wary, skeptical.

SIMONE   *(raising her glass)* I'd like to drink to that freedom. *Garçon! Garçon! (THE WAITER enters, played by GENET.) Garçon*, a vodka for me.

NATHALIE   Vodka!

CLARA   A glass of white wine.

THE WAITER   *(to SIMONE de BEAUVOIR)* Someone left a parcel for you with the cashier.

SIMONE   Bring it to me please.

THE WAITER   Yes *madame! (He exits.)*

CLARA   You are very much at home here!

SIMONE   I've been coming here forever, it seems. An old habit of mine, writing in cafés. I used to come here every day during the Occupation. It was too cold in my room. This is where I wrote *She Came to Stay* and *The Blood of Others*.

CLARA   I enjoyed *She Came to Stay* very much. Was it your first novel?

SIMONE   My first published novel. I'd written three more before it.

THE WAITER   Here is your book, *madame.*

SIMONE   How d'you know it's a book?

THE WAITER   By touching it, weighing it. And I see you here almost every day, writing, always writing, hours on end. So it had to be a book someone left for you with the cashier. Logical, no?

SIMONE   Yes. What about our drinks?

THE WAITER   Literature first!

NATHALIE   I prefer books to flowers, to stones, to music. Ah, sentences! Little words singing and murmuring to foil the pain of living.

SIMONE   You remind me of Sartre. Literature brings tears to his eyes.

The waiter returns with the glasses, puts them on the table and exits.

NATHALIE   What shall we drink to?

SIMONE   I'll drink to freedom, our freedom. An extraordinary word, isn't it? In my younger days, I imagined freedom as this inexhaustible force whose every appearance could enrich the world.

CLARA   *(with irony)* The great torch of freedom!

NATHALIE   You still believe in it, don't you, Simone?

SIMONE   Yes I do. It still never ceases to amaze me.

CLARA   I believe in that freedom, though it's not quite the same as yours: the freedom of the imagination. To be magically still, and always fascinated by whatever holds reality at bay. Just as in my early childhood, when I discovered that the air was full of doors and windows and walls and ceilings, all set into empty space, and that I, little Clara Goldschmidt, could open those doors and windows, push back the walls, remove the ceilings, by the sheer power of my imagination. One must take a chance on the imaginary world, take the risk of opening the door without knowing what's behind it. Who goes there? The unknown, lady in black, a fragrance of flowers, or terror?

SIMONE   *(always with her rapid delivery)* I say freedom, period. Freedom that isn't altered by being in the literal or in the imaginary world. Freedom that resembles destiny. Every encounter with destiny leaves me overwhelmed. While others feel they're victims of destiny, I say it's mine to choose. Where others believe they're in bondage to routine, I see freedom rising up.

CLARA   Things are not that black and white. I'm not interested in a kind of freedom which, more often than not, is merely vacant noise-making. The scope of your freedom is too limited, Simone de Beauvoir.

SIMONE   Freedom is my grand optimistic folly. However, psychology isn't my forte and I fear my remarks have offended you. What d'you think of me?

CLARA   *(thinking it over)* That you are monolithic. Rigid even. Unless I am confusing rigidity with strength? Perhaps I *am* confusing the two: rigid women are usually submissive, and you are not a submissive woman.

NATHALIE   Clara, when Simone says she knows nothing about psychology, I assure you it's no figure of speech. In fact, she has already applied her own type of shock treatment to Sartre…

SIMONE   Yes. He was getting interested in dreams, in drugs. He even had himself injected with mescaline to study its hallucinogenic effects. He became the prey of vulture-umbrellas, of skeleton-shoes, of swarms of crabs and octopuses on the floor, an army of rats and spiders. But that didn't last long, 24 hours, I think.

NATHALIE   But… a few weeks later, it all started up again, this time without the mescaline. He told me that when he was on the train, he saw an orangutan hanging upside down from the ceiling, and it was making faces at him!

SIMONE   *(to CLARA)* Sartre's hallucinations got worse: every clock looked to him like an owl's face, he was convinced there was a lobster trotting along behind him at all times. So when he started talking to me about 'chronic hallucinatory psychosis,' I got slightly impatient…

NATHALIE   Slightly?

SIMONE   D'you realize that in those days, 'chronic hallucinatory psychosis' could lead to insanity in 10 years? I got angry. Sartre insane, committed to an institution, how absurd. He was barely 30. Your only madness is that you think you're mad, I told him. He was betraying me. He was betraying our plans. You see I was less frightened than irritated by his hallucinations. Would I really have helped him by sharing his anguish? Loyalty does have its limits. My anger was no doubt what saved him. To my mind, we had better things to do than feel sorry for ourselves. The world was at boiling point: trials, discussions about the death penalty and its application. There was also the issue of women's voting rights, Hitler's politics, Mussolini was organizing a Fascist exhibition in Rome, then the *coup d'état* in Greece. Plus the book we wanted to write, the trips we planned. What did all of that have to do with vulture-umbrellas, spiders and clockwork owls? *(She calls for the waiter who appears immediately.)* Garçon! Garçon! A vodka. *(showing him the book)* You were right, it's a book. But there's no inscription. Try to find out who brought it here, would you? *(CLARA and NATHALIE both refuse another drink with a wave of the hand.)*

CLARA   Did you look at the wrapping? There might be a clue. What's the title…?

SIMONE   *Intruder in the Dust*, by William Faulkner. *(She checks the wrapping.)* No, nothing.

NATHALIE   It's an excellent novel. Faulkner at his best. A fragment of the Old South. It tells the story of a Black man whose unforgivable sin is to wish for himself, a slave, the same dignity as that of a white gentleman. He has been accused of murdering a white man. A youth from the town flees so as not to witness the inevitable lynching…

THE WAITER   *(entering with SIMONE's drink)* I made my enquiries.

SIMONE   And?

THE WAITER   It was a woman.

SIMONE   Does anyone here know her?

THE WAITER   She has a rather thankless face… I mean not very attractive… but impeccable style, and great legs… I've seen her here before…

SIMONE   Here?

THE WAITER   With you. She was crying while you comforted her.

SIMONE   *(to CLARA, to NATHALIE)* Violette Leduc. But that's impossible. She's in a clinic for a month… *(to THE WAITER)* Thank you. *(He exits.)* Violette, in Paris…

CLARA   The author of *In the prison of her skin* and *The Famished*?

SIMONE   Yes. *(to NATHALIE)* What've they done to her? *(optimistic)* The cure was a success and she went home sooner…

NATHALIE   I didn't know she was in a clinic. What happened?

SIMONE   She was admitted Monday… for sleep therapy.

NATHALIE   So she escaped…. Four days, sleep therapy takes longer than four days, Simone.

SIMONE   You're right. She came to my home last week… dreadful… just dreadful… I'd never seen her in such a state… haggard, sobbing her heart out… moaning… they killed it, she was saying, they killed it, they killed my child. She collapsed on the floor, drowning in her tears. I tried to calm her down so I could ask her a few questions, find out what had happened. She finally showed me a letter from her publisher. Look, she said to me, "this letter contains a corpse fresh for the communal grave… they are about to make pulp out of *In the Prison of Her Skin* and *The Famished*. They used to hide them, now they kill them. The publisher has no room. A labourer can see the result of his work. My writing was part of a demolition project. Were my little runts really taking up so much room in his basement? 'To pulp.' The expression turns my stomach. A huge bonfire would have been better. The only 'pulp' I know is the kind I get from mashing up my cooked vegetables." She was utterly humiliated, I felt her on the brink of madness…

CLARA   Couldn't she buy back the unsold copies?

SIMONE   I made her that offer. She turned me down. She showed me a piece of paper on which she'd copied out the definition of 'pulping': to reduce or send books to pulp, to tear them up in such a way that they are useful only to cardboard-makers who turn them into a mass known as paper pulp. She started tearing her hair out, screaming that she didn't want her children's flesh to be turned into the paper on which some young genius would write his bestseller.

NATHALIE   What did you do?

SIMONE   I made her some soup. She cried even harder into her soup. So I phoned a friend who knows the director of this clinic. We drove her there Monday morning. I'd planned to visit her there tomorrow, to bring her fruit, flowers…

NATHALIE   After the blow to *Ravages*…

CLARA   What blow?

NATHALIE   The publishers censored it. They refused to print the first 150 pages of her manuscript.

SIMONE   She says she's being persecuted, that she's a slime-covered louse, that the police know all about the first part of *Ravages*. 'They're going to arrest me, put me in jail, send me to the guillotine; yesterday, while I was out, they came and searched my room. I know, a chair told me,' she added. She was in genuine terror. Violette started tracing little crosses on her forehead, on the publisher's letter, on the books lying on my divan. If you only knew how helpless I felt in the face of her humiliation and suffering…

NATHALIE   You tried your absolute best for *Ravages*. You got angry, you rebelled and battled all those Parisian publishers…

SIMONE   *(as if talking to herself)* Violette in Paris…. She couldn't bear the doctors… the questions…

NATHALIE   She came back for you!

CLARA   That seems quite clear.

SIMONE   What do you know about it? Violette Leduc has friends in Paris. Family, lovers—men, women—how do I know!

NATHALIE   But Simone, she came here, she left this book for you with the cashier, like a message. She'll come back…

CLARA   "*Intruder*"? She's the intruder.

NATHALIE   She is. She's that Black slave wanting to regain his human dignity. She is the one who fled the lynching at the clinic…

SIMONE   You're probably right. But her feeling of being an intruder still puzzles me.

NATHALIE   *(after hesitating)* I sometimes feel that way when I telephone you to arrange a meeting.

SIMONE   *(surprised)* You, Natacha?

NATHALIE   Yes, me. You are so well-organized, so meticulous, your life with Sartre, your travels abroad, your books. You can account for every minute of your time, you are the mistress of your own schedule. Fine: you can give me two hours Thursday evening from 6 o'clock on. No, not this Thursday, next Thursday… and you will be there, right on time, and I will be there, an hour early so as not to waste one precious second of your time. At 8 o'clock sharp you will get up, give me a kiss and say 'Call me, Natacha' as you go out the door. *(She gets up.)*

SIMONE   You're leaving?

NATHALIE   I'm going to find Violette. I'm quite worried about her.

SIMONE   She may be on her way here, she may appear at any moment.

NATHALIE   I don't want to take that risk. If she's at home I'll bring her back here to you. If she gets here while I'm out, tell her I must speak with her. *(She shakes hands with SIMONE and CLARA, and exits.)*

CLARA   Tell me about Violette Leduc! Not to gossip, I know how you loathe gossip…. When I read the first line of *In the Prison of Her Skin*—"My mother never gave me her hand…"—I trembled for the woman assassinating her mother and prayed that this woman's mother was dead so she would never read that. If my daughter were to begin one of her books that way, I'd be shattered. My mother once said a terrible thing: my father had just died and, unaware that I was in the next room, she said to her sister: 'I would have given my three children to keep my husband.' I meant less to her than he did, my brother, my sister, meant less to her than he did. As I got older, I understood that for my mother, my father was irreplaceable, whereas we, her children, belonged to the unknown, the formless, the multiple. 'Later on, after a life thoroughly meshed with mine, I know that my mother loved me, almost as much as she loved my father." *(from* Apprendre à vivre—*Tome 1*—by Clara Malraux)

SIMONE   Our mothers! Your mother, Violette's mother, mine… let's talk about our mothers *(She turns her head a bit.)* Garçon! Garçon! *(THE WAITER enters.)* A vodka.

CLARA   A glass of white wine. *(THE WAITER exits.)*

SIMONE   *(pulling her chair up to CLARA's, leaning over to her)* I used to have this vague theoretical notion of death… *(the rest is lost, THE WAITER enters, serves the drinks and exits as the light fades)*

EIGHTH TABLEAU

A Conversation with So-Called Inanimate Objects

The setting is VIOLETTE's room. She is sitting on the floor and talking to the chair in front of her, or to her table, etc. She moves around in a crouch or on hands and knees.

VIOLETTE   *(to the chair in front of her)* What the hell are we doing here, sitting here staring at each other? I'm wasting your time, dear chair, I've got to get myself together, don't I? I can't take it anymore. *(She touches the chair, lightly, as one would touch a person's shoulder.)* And you? Does my *derrière* still attract you? As red as an apple, my ass is. The ant is going away on a trip around the world.

Shhuttt, it's a secret… I'm off to the Orient, Ethiopia, and yes, Lebanon. I get hot flashes just thinking about it. Maurice Sachs is waiting for me, sitting on a branch, squandering his money. For a song, the grasshopper will be mine for a song! *(leaning over to the chair)* I can't hear you. What? Oh, the table! *(on hands and knees, she moves to the table)* Ah! I'd eat my own shit for you. Don't look down on me, table. I like to be held in high regard. Don't you? "I want to please anyone and everyone. There are those who can say anything they please. There are those who can say nothing. There are those who are always forgiven. There are those who are never forgiven." Shall I turn out this light? Maybe it's hurting your eyes? "We're using up the light and what have you written so far?", my charming husband used to say to me. He was right, Gabriel was right, always. My books, "now you see them, now you don't. A sinking ship mysteriously lost at sea." I can't see past the end of my nose. "Good thing too, otherwise I'd be bitter, otherwise I'd have myself convinced it was all over the moment I started writing. Why am I not part of the latest crop of new publications? The publisher is ashamed. I've been swept under the carpet, I'm the rabbit who vanished into a top hat. Writing means persevering. Writing is nothing more than that." I'm hungry. What about you? *(Still on all fours, she reaches up and grabs the spinach leaves on the table.)* 'O Death, where is thy victory?' On the wings of angels, under my leaden lids. Tell me, dearest table and chair— *(She strokes them lightly with her hand.)* —am I gorgeous enough to seduce a cook? Am I irresistible? Like "the cerebral celebrities, the major secretaries?" Tell me… otherwise, what's the point of this broken-down conversation… *(All ears, she listens attentively.)* Yes…. Yes…. Yes…. "A little woman from Paris without a man in her bed." That's me. I putter with time, time putters with my face, and I get something cooking. "It's a foetus stew. I putter so as not to die after having decided to die." *(to the table, the chair, the walls)* It is me, isn't it? You do recognize me, don't you? "There's something comical about me, but I can't see it. I was blowing soap bubbles. I was going on with my life, they were going on with forgetting me. Won't they miss me? Will I disappear without leaving a trace? Will I be left to rot in the dungeons of oblivion? I'm dead. I'm weeping over a dead Violette. I'm in mourning for you, Violette." *(to the chair, to the table)* Please take care of the dear deceased. Please take me in your arms and legs. Be my widows, my heirs, my coffin, my hearse, my final journey. *(She lifts her head up and looks at the ceiling.)* You, don't you move. Your game is up, old boy. You are in my home here. Watch your buns! Don't you move! One move and I'll insult you. I want you out of the picture, vampire up above. The game is over, old boy. I told Simone de Beauvoir about you, and she told Sartre. Vampire up there in the ceiling, if you keep sucking my blood it will show, they'll see what you've done. Beware! I said beware! You leave tracks, all night long you leave tracks… I am the everlasting source, the waterfall of waterfalls, and you have nothing to say to me, nothing to teach me except the blood of blood, the death-struggle between immortals. *(screaming)* Don't move! I want you out of the picture. Stay where you belong, vampire up above. Just the slightest ripple on the skin of the ceiling is all I'll allow. *(There is a knock at the door of her room.)* Now the door is butting in! I thought it was out, or asleep. *(three knocks on the door)* A well-built door, one that never comes unhinged. *(On all fours, she moves to the door; again, three knocks.)* Who goes there? Is that you, love? Is it you, fame? *(opening the door)* Come in, my friends! *(The door is open, we see NATHALIE SARRAUTE standing on the doorstep.)*

NINTH TABLEAU

The Sperm People

NATHALIE is standing on the doorstep, very still. Then she takes a little step and VIOLETTE, on her hands and knees, moves back a bit. NATHALIE takes another step and VIOLETTE moves back again. NATHALIE enters and closes the door with careful gestures. VIOLETTE is like a hunted animal, panting. She clutches one of the legs of her chair and not once does she look up into NATHALIE's face.

VIOLETTE   *(addressing NATHALIE SARRAUTE's feet)* Who are you? Not another step. Who are you? Your first and last names won't be enough for me, I'm warning you. Don't move. I bite, I scratch, I fly off the handle. Not another step or I'll turn you in to the *gendarmes*. To the sperm people! From me they *expect* a mountain of filth. Feet, you frighten me, the pressure is frightening me. "The vampire is on guard duty at his station." Feet, don't look at the ceiling. Sleep, why don't you sleep. Yawn, like the great black Buddha by the river's edge.

NATHALIE   *(motionless, in a low voice)* Violette! Violette! It's me, Nathalie…

VIOLETTE   *(addressing her chair, the legs of her table)* Honestly now, tell me, do you know those feet? *(indicating NATHALIE's feet)* Do you recognize them? Have you seen them somewhere before? Think about it, take your time. Can you identify these feet? *(pause)* Time goes by, etched in glass. My heart could be drowning, but take your time.

NATHALIE   Violette, dear Violette, I came to get you. Look at me for just a moment.

VIOLETTE   *(looking at NATHALIE's feet)* I am looking at you. Oh you have no idea how closely I'm looking at you, Nathalie Sarraute. I'm alone here. I'm looking at you from where I am, from where I have always been. At your feet! *(She walks across the floor on all fours, slapping the floor very hard with her hands.)* At your feet! At your feet! I've laid my weapons down at your feet. I'm laying flowers at your feet.

NATHALIE   *(taking a step forward)* I came looking for you, Violette Leduc. *(She gets down on all fours and moves closer.)* Look at me, look at me, we're alone, leaning toward each other.

VIOLETTE   How do you see me? With words? With grunts and groans? With paragraphs? With a press agent?

NATHALIE   I see you in my life. Does that satisfy you?

VIOLETTE   Maybe.

NATHALIE   And you, how do you see me?

VIOLETTE   *(now looking at her)* With the eyes of the lowly, of beggars and destitute women. With the eyes of the untouchable.

NATHALIE   *(who has just sat down on the floor)* Violette, somewhere inside I'm just like you. I have a sadness…

VIOLETTE   I'm so desperate…

NATHALIE   I'm so tired…

VIOLETTE   I'm exhausted… *(Now she sits down next to NATHALIE.)*

NATHALIE   I have so little clarity…

VIOLETTE   I'm in darkness…

NATHALIE   I want to escape…

VIOLETTE   That is forbidden.

NATHALIE   No it isn't. You did it, you…

VIOLETTE   I have no respect for the rules, you know me.

NATHALIE   I admire you for it. I would never dare.

VIOLETTE   Does she know?

NATHALIE   Who?

VIOLETTE   Simone de Beauvoir.

NATHALIE   Yes, she knows. She got your message.

VIOLETTE   Is she angry? Disappointed?

NATHALIE   I don't think so. Neither angry nor disappointed. No, I think not. Ask her yourself!

VIOLETTE   She's in Paris?

NATHALIE   Yes, at the terrace of the Café de Flore, with Clara Malraux. She's waiting for you.

VIOLETTE   The sleep therapy didn't work. I escaped. Unacceptable behaviour. She paid for everything, all of it, and I ran away. Sleep therapy is expensive, the doctors, the nurses and a huge park. And a well-meaning psychoanalyst. A quiet, well-dressed gentleman, prepared to make me talk. A little voice, he had a tiny little voice which he carefully planted in my ears.

NATHALIE   And then?

VIOLETTE   And then? Then he wants to suck my blood. He uses his brain like a fishing net. He doesn't smile otherwise he'd be exposing his fangs. Essays, Nathalie! I am page number one hundred of the essay he is writing that week. I'm the third character in his plot, the mummy in the death-chamber of his latest piece of literature, his final rewrite before glory. He looks at me, he reads my thoughts, my oldest memories. This gentleman is a necrophiliac, a lover of dead letters. There's a microphone stuffed into every pore of his body. He's recording me: I will be amnesiac, surly, monosyllabic, pitiful…

NATHALIE   You didn't say anything? You refused to talk?

VIOLETTE   You must be joking! Quite the contrary, I was an avalanche under control. I have this little "sexual mechanism" that goes off in my head whenever I hear people talking. Oh, Nathalie, "it's such a calamity having ovaries in one's ears."

NATHALIE   *(laughing)* You are marvelous!

VIOLETTE   *(growing more confident)* I did my number. I had to be sneaky though, I didn't want him to think I'm smarter than I am…

NATHALIE   You are unbelievable! I would never dare put on such an act in front of a psychoanalyst.

VIOLETTE   They're not my kind of people. They're part of the riff… *(She interrupts herself, then continues.)* …of the mafia of higher learning.

NATHALIE   But I am part of the riff-raff!

VIOLETTE   So is almost everybody. The whole world is at your feet and you'll never be at mine. Whose stories are condemned in advance, yours or mine?

NATHALIE   Yours… and mine. We both write sad stories: I'm crying inside without showing tears outside. Your tears on the outside come from inside. What a mess… *(correcting herself)* Tell me about it, Violette…. Tell me what you said, what you did…

VIOLETTE   *(getting up, but NATHALIE stays on the floor)* My three-ring circus! My own personal witchcraft! All of it! My passion for homosexuals, my eternal damnation in its infinite shades. I brought out my sweet little pink babes… these would-be ladies…

TENTH TABLEAU

These Would-Be Ladies, If Only They Could Be Ladies

VIOLETTE is standing, arms open, she closes her eyes, invoking the forces, and stage-front, a man appears between two women. The man— played by GABRIEL—in bum's clothing, kisses them both in turn. The women—both transvestites—will be played by SACHS and by GENET. SACHS could be wearing a blue satin dress, blue being VIOLETTE's favourite colour, and GENET would wear white, like a bride. Also jewellery for both of them, boas, high heels. All the while VIOLETTE is talking there is tango music in the background. The three characters at stage-front will sometimes act out in pantomime what she is saying.

VIOLETTE *(opening her eyes)* They came out of my eyes, Nathalie. Out of my nights of insomnia, out of my frustrations, my despair. Can you hear them laughing? whispering? It's a conspiracy, a caste, a secret society. Each one displaying her particular charms. "These would-be ladies, if only they could be ladies, have a passion for accessorizing. They are tall and walk on stilts. High heels are said to heighten seduction. What a romance with detail and preparation. The subterfuge of martyrs." Men adore transvestites. How to be one's self, and one's other self. Clothes don't make the man. Raise your naked arms, my beautiful creatures, flaunt your arrogance, knowing I'll never dare curse you. I know your secret. Isn't it true, Nathalie, that we know the secret?

NATHALIE Parasites, blood-suckers, Violette. Sticking to our shadows, lurking behind our mirrors, avidly sucking the juice of our every movement. They let nothing go to waste, they salvage every scrap. *(drawing VIOLETTE's attention to the trio)* They are the vampires!

GENET *(dancing the tango with GABRIEL's arm around him)* You make me drool, you gorgeous beast. Eros is burning against my thigh so fair…

GABRIEL Some day I'll get a taste of you, my divine. *(They are dancing.)* Hey, where did you put it?

GENET *(innocently)* Who? What? My umbrella? My rose in a winter garden?

SACHS *(Dancing alone, he approaches the couple.)* What about me then? My dahlia is wilting, the most fabulous and funereal of flowers is dying the tango's slow death, worm-eaten in 4/4 time. *(He dances around the dancing couple.)* Am I dead? Am I forgotten? Oh, darlings, you're driving me mad!

GENET Get lost, Maurice Sachs. Your loneliness is beautiful to behold.

SACHS *(wants to slap GENET)* I don't enjoy living alone, Genet. I'm nostalgic for a man's arms around me, the heartbreaker's distracted kisses. For a man who will ravish my flesh with the spikes of his hairy body.

GENET *(still dancing with GABRIEL)* So am I, angel, so am I. Did you know the air is thicker around a gorgeous male?

SACHS Oh, the sexuous suction cups of a tongue…

GENET A density of air which only the short wavelengths of sperm can penetrate.

GABRIEL And when does this miracle occur?

GENET Why, when imagination is most vibrant: at sunset!

SACHS   When the clan's member stretches out in his love nest. Dangerous, disquieting respite…. The bull will spurt out of the man, the golden calf will stand erect, the swan—o swan's neck—your hard curves make my mouth water.

> *SACHS wants to take GENET's place in GABRIEL's arms, there is a scuffle, SACHS slaps GENET.*

GENET   Bitch!

SACHS   *(dancing with GABRIEL)* Bitch yourself, *Our Lady of the Flowers. (to GABRIEL)* Let your silken tongue spill into my mouth for eternity to unfold between my teeth.

GABRIEL   Tell me, where did you hide it?

SACHS   In the garage. *(They dance.)*

VIOLETTE   "The secret, everyone watching was aware of it. The torment, everyone watching enjoyed it. A dick between Diana's thighs. A fly in the milk. What a defeat. Utter failure, a total disaster had it been noticed. *(GABRIEL dances with the two transvestites, pulling them close, pushing them away at the same time.)* The princess-line dress, the pancake make-up, the wax treatments, the purple eye shadow, the line of pale green pencil, the precious gestures, the studied batting of the lashes, are all signs of a cock fallen into disgrace." Imitation outshines the real thing, Nathalie.

GABRIEL   I'm asking you, where did you stash it?

GENET   *(addressing MAURICE SACHS)* It's getting late, my lovely. Bearded dragons await us at heaven's door. Don't keep me waiting. I won't be reduced to tears! Come!

> *As they dance the tango, GABRIEL and SACHS glide towards the exit, preceded by GENET.*

VIOLETTE   *(just as they are about to disappear)* Doctor! Doctor!

> *The trio stops, surprised, and GABRIEL looks at VIOLETTE.*

GABRIEL   *(With one move, he chases off SACHS and GENET and moves towards VIOLETTE as she moves towards him too. GABRIEL takes a tie out of his pocket and ties it around his neck. Straightening his demeanor, the hustler is transformed into a distinguished gentleman.)* Why it's Mademoiselle Leduc! We've been looking for you everywhere at the clinic since yesterday.

VIOLETTE   I ran away, doctor.

GABRIEL   So it seems, so it seems. *(He looks around, does not see NATHALIE in the shadows, in VIOLETTE's room.)* Are we alone? *(VIOLETTE nods in the affirmative and the doctor puts on an engaging air.)* How about a short consultation then?

VIOLETTE   "I'm tramping around my room on all fours, sniffing at the tracks of my tears, gnawing on an old bone." I want to kill myself, doctor!

GABRIEL   Tut, tut, tut, now! Go on, Mademoiselle Leduc. The desire for suicide often comes pinned to the tail of sex…

VIOLETTE   I met a man…

GABRIEL   Then you must see him again, Mademoiselle Leduc. Are you still writing?

VIOLETTE   Are you, doctor?

GABRIEL   *(stunned)* Me? What a peculiar idea.

VIOLETTE   Do you feel threatened? You're blushing! You have no right to ask me if I'm writing. Not you!

GABRIEL   Let's be on friendly terms, dear…. "What are you writing at the moment?"

VIOLETTE   "Shit. Liquid shit. Diarrhea. I have the runs. It stinks of futility and incompetence. Hold your nose, doctor. I'm discouraged, it's a deadly stench."

GABRIEL   I don't believe a word of it. You're overwrought, anguished, the real woman in you will soon resurface.

VIOLETTE   If I give you my depression, what will you give me in exchange, doctor?

GABRIEL   A little unusual, this notion of exchange…. Why not tell me your life story?

VIOLETTE   If you tell me yours. Who are you? Where do you come from? Doctor, I insist on saying that you write!

GABRIEL   Nothing worth mentioning… a bit… in my spare time… a little essay here and there… I'll let you read one some day!

VIOLETTE   Me?

GABRIEL   Yes, you, Mademoiselle Leduc. Why not? Your opinion will be valuable to me. What's this, a touch of melancholy? Or is it mistrust?

VIOLETTE   I appreciate your concern, doctor.

GABRIEL   I find you very sweet.

VIOLETTE   It's a trap!

GABRIEL   Your soul is parched with loneliness, your body is aching for love…

VIOLETTE   You're puffing yourself up, parading your serene selflessness with apparent truthfulness, but I'm not a fool. You don't dare face me straight on. You'd rather pick away at me, a few bits of pain here, a string of confessions there. Every day I was at the clinic, I'd hear your footsteps in the hallway and I knew…

GABRIEL   You knew what?

VIOLETTE   That you were going to come in without knocking. Without knocking, doctor! That's why I ran away: because you entered my room without knocking. Don't ask me to feel friendly about someone who enters without knocking. You wanted me to get attached to you, didn't you?

GABRIEL   But that's part of the treatment, Mademoiselle Leduc!

VIOLETTE   "I've heard that song before. Transference here, transference there, transference everywhere. There will be no transference for me, old boy. I will love those whom I love. Why should I redirect my affections?" I'm removing you from my life, doctor. *(She moves away from him little by little.)* Your penetration of me was so insidious that I felt only a temporary pickling sensation, but now that I'm leaving you, I feel a burning spot from where the pain shoots out.

GABRIEL   What a pity, what a pity. Well, you have my address… if ever…

VIOLETTE   Yes of course, doctor, maybe some day, when old age dries up my brain… *(She turns her back to him and goes back to her room where NATHALIE is waiting, seated on the chair. GABRIEL hesitates a moment, then undoes his tie and, a bum once again, exits.)*

ELEVENTH TABLEAU

A Passion for the Impossible

At the café, just as we left them after NATHALIE's departure. CLARA MALRAUX is in the same spot, so is SIMONE de BEAUVOIR. But one must get the feeling that they have grown closer, that the ice has been broken… CLARA MALRAUX's voice is warmer when she talks to SIMONE de BEAUVOIR. Also, they call each other by their first names.

SIMONE   *(we hear the end of her sentence)* …'A very easy death.' What a lie!

CLARA   When others die…. When a mother dies, is it the death of others, Simone?

SIMONE   Death is expecting us, we have only to meet it, Clara.

CLARA   Will you fall silent as it approaches? Here it comes, inescapable, unrelenting: the fruit of 60 years, of 80 years of work is about to be snatched away from us.

> *VIOLETTE and NATHALIE can be seen in the background, then they enter the café. NATHALIE precedes VIOLETTE who is hiding behind her a bit.*

NATHALIE   *(to CLARA, to SIMONE)* Here we are!

VIOLETTE   *(showing herself, little by little, to NATHALIE)* Thank you for saying 'we.'

SIMONE   Violette Leduc, I'm pleased to see you again.

VIOLETTE   You were worried about me?

SIMONE   I did worry…

VIOLETTE   Was I in your thoughts? Now you can put me away in your briefcase and not give me another thought. You know my sorry bent, I'm old, I'm ugly, even truck drivers don't look at me!

SIMONE   Dear Violette, don't let's talk about all that anymore…

NATHALIE   Violette, I'd like to introduce you to Clara Malraux. She has read your books and thinks very highly of them.

VIOLETTE   *(pitiful)* Really? I have readers who read my vanishing books? *(to SIMONE)* "My book *The Old Maid and the Dead Man* is out. I've been looking for it in store windows. I don't see it anywhere. Another one of my children is missing."

CLARA   I'll read it. I'll write to you about it.

VIOLETTE   We've met before, haven't we? I remember your eyes, so very clear, and your big nose. I always look at people's noses.

CLARA   *(laughing)* So do I. You can't disown your face.

VIOLETTE   "We must get past the face to face to reach the soul." I've had some repair work done on my elephant's trunk, on the flesh and bone of my old geezer's beak.

CLARA   That was courageous.

VIOLETTE   Courageous? I wanted to seduce the whole world! *(still to CLARA)* You are so intelligent. Yes, I was there when Malraux said that you were more intelligent than Max Jacob. "If we're not intelligent, then the spectacle we make of our unsightly selves is a hundred times more tedious." *(to SIMONE)* I'm well aware of what you must put up with every time you look at me!

> There is a malaise, a general drifting.

NATHALIE   Clara, time is flying… our appointment is light years from here…

CLARA   *(understands, gets up)* You're right. *(to VIOLETTE as she extends her hand to her)* I will read *The Old Maid and the Dead Man*. I will write to you. *(to SIMONE, also extending her hand to her)* I would like to see you again, Simone.

SIMONE   By all means, I'd be delighted…. See you soon, I'll call you.

NATHALIE   *(shaking VIOLETTE's hand)* Au revoir, Violette. *(She kisses SIMONE.)* Au revoir, Simone. *(They exit.)*

VIOLETTE   *(after a moment's silence)* They're bored with me. She is avoiding me. "I am an inferno of despair. The ugly spectre of a toad."

SIMONE   You're an intellectual, you're a writer.

VIOLETTE   "I'm a predator. I'll have amounted to nothing but a surge of loneliness."

SIMONE   *(a bit irritated)* You're being published in *Les Temps Modernes.* My friends are talking about you, Violette Leduc. I know you're putting up a fierce struggle to write.

VIOLETTE   I resist and negotiate with my laziness, with my madness. The way they negotiate in times of war.

SIMONE   Did you work today?

VIOLETTE   Yes, I wrote to Joan of Arc, to Medea, to Phaedra, to Antigone, to Galileo. I wrote to those who share my loneliness.

SIMONE   *(inspired)* You should write your autobiography! Hermine, Gabriel, Genet, Sachs, your abortion, your despair, your nose…

VIOLETTE   Pour it all out, all of it! Even Violette Leduc the boot-legger during the French Occupation. The black-marketeering that made me rich? But if I confess everything, you'll be ashamed of me. I'll lose you.

SIMONE   *(getting up to leave)* Write. Bring me your stories. Next week, will you? Same time next Thursday?

VIOLETTE   Yes, yes, yes. At the same time. Here?

SIMONE   Yes, here. We'll find a title. I'll write the *préface*…

VIOLETTE   You are going to write a *préface* for my book…

SIMONE   I'll say who you are, what struck me about your writing. You'll find recognition yet, Violette Leduc. *(She holds her hand out.)* See you next Thursday. *(She exits.)*

> *VIOLETTE, left alone, after a moment takes SIMONE de BEAUVOIR's empty glass in her hands, sniffs it, puts it back on the table.*

VIOLETTE   *Garçon! Garçon! (THE WAITER enters, it is SACHS, still showing traces of his female disguise.)* Bring me a vodka… *(thinking twice)* A vodka and some writing paper. *(THE WAITER exits, VIOLETTE searches in her bag, takes out an old billfold and a fountain pen.)* A book, another book, I'll be worn out before it's done. A filthy hold where I can channel all my tears, my autobiography! My memories: an orange peel, an empty pack of Gauloises, an old mirror. Everything I write I take from my mother, I steal it. *(THE WAITER returns with the glass of vodka and the writing paper. VIOLETTE takes some change out of her old billfold, counts it, counts it again, hesitates, then adds a little more. THE WAITER withdraws to the back of the set but remains visible.)* My dear Fidéline, my grand-mother of innermost spaces, where are you? *(VIOLETTE prepares for writing, writes. Then we hear the voices from the opening tableau.)*

GABRIEL   Hey there, hey there, pal!

THE MOTHER   Listen to me girl!

GABRIEL   A bit of friendly advice: watch your language, pal. You're running off at the navel.

VIOLETTE   *(to herself)* Go to hell!

THE MOTHER   You're wasting your time, child. This can't be serious.

GABRIEL   You've been exposed. You're finished. You're too old to be wielding your pen like a sword. Put your paper away, stop brooding over the void, old boy.

GENET   Watch what you write, Viollet-Le-Duc. You're fondling words, you're being outrageous, *bâtarde*!

VIOLETTE   *(writing obstinately, crosses out some words, starts over)* Voices out of hollow places, voices out of the storm, thorns in my soul, be quiet.

GABRIEL   I'm a patient man. I love you.

GENET   The words you write go too far.

VIOLETTE   I'm building something. I'm a predator. I got my black style from a vulture. Go to hell…

GABRIEL   This is not the Garden of Eden, this is a state of alert, and the edge of earth is too near, they'll soon overtake the words you dared to let loose.

VIOLETTE   I'm travelling free in my feathers, in my foliage, like a bird, like the earth.

GABRIEL   You're talking gibberish, pal.

VIOLETTE   *(stubbornly continues writing)* Vampires up in the ceiling, I'm not listening to you anymore. I'm not insane, I'm not sad. I'm inventing my life with my own hand. I surprise it giving me shape, letting out my cry. *(She looks at the sheet of paper she has been writing on and reads.)* "I was born on April 7, 1907, at five in the morning. You registered me on the 8th." *(The lighting begins to fade, at the back of the café. THE WAITER wipes off a few tables and leaves. VIOLETTE continues to read what she has written.)* "I should rejoice at having spent my first 24 hours off the records. On the contrary, my 24 hours without official status poisoned my life. Always going back for more, that's my perversion. I came into the world, and I pledged myself to a passion for the impossible." *(She puts the sheet of paper down, takes up her pen, and starts writing.)*

  The end.

Night
(L'Homme gris)

by Marie Laberge

translated by Rina Fraticelli

Introduction to
Night (L'Homme gris[1])
by Marie Laberge
Introduced by Louise H. Forsyth

Night is a one-act play with two characters, a 21-year-old daughter and her 52-year-old-father. Its realistic action takes place one rainy evening in a cheap motel room on the highway between Rimouski and Sherbrooke. Roland, the father, speaks throughout the play; Christine, the daughter whom he calls Cri-Cri, does not speak until the end. Roland works hard at creating the impression of relaxed attractiveness and self-assurance, while the anorexic Christine is nervous from the start. The play is about violence, dishonesty and self-delusion. It is about father-daughter relations and how dreadfully bad they can become when fathers abuse power, lose the ability to love or even communicate, and become threatening presences. The shapes of dysfunctional families emerge in the shadows behind the central story, which, through Roland's monologue, becomes a series of flashbacks into the terrifying memory of the twenty-one years they have spent together. Roland has gone to Rimouski to remove Christine from her situation with the husband he believes to be violently abusive. Whether he is or not is never resolved in the play. In order to convince her to leave with him, Roland has told Christine that her mother is very ill in hospital and that she needs her.

Like the children in Blais's *The Ocean*, also beset with the legacy of a domineering and thoughtless father, Christine has been unable to move on and establish a family based on love and respect for herself. As well, like the mother in *The Ocean*, Christine's mother has been removed from the action of the play and is absent from the motel. We learn that she has been deceived and neglected by her husband and is apparently powerless to address the problems that are ripping Christine and the family apart. Roland's remarks about his wife in the course of the play show that he has little affection or respect for her. He is proud of the fact that he does not even listen any more to what he considers to be her meaningless chatter. In addition, he has used her and invented the lie of her heart attack in order to lure Christine to come away with him.

Night is, in essence, a monologue, with Roland going on and on in his efforts to get his daughter to speak to him and to share an interest in events in the room. Christine does not respond verbally, nor even physically in any obvious way, but her subtle mime of her reactions to her father's words leaves no doubt for the audience about her reactions and feelings. Through his monologue Roland reveals a good deal about himself, much more than he realizes, and also reveals the extent of his self-delusion regarding both himself and the nature of his relations with Christine, her mother and others. Everything throughout the play that Roland does and says seems to be entirely predictable, banal and unoriginal, from the barbecue chicken, fries and coleslaw he has bought to eat, his concerns about taxes and the price of things, to his comments on the weather. He creates the impression of being a man incapable of thinking or feeling in any way that would position him outside the box of what consumer society constructs as "normal." Nothing feels spontaneous or authentic. Everything he says is a lie, and yet he rants on about hating liars.

During the strained opening sequence, Roland begins by verifying that he has got good value for money with the motel room. From there he turns on lights, checks that the television set is in colour, wonders about the heat, and takes off his coat. Christine refuses throughout the play to remove her wet coat, and in the tense moment of silence after he first tries to take it off for her, he decides to pour himself a drink. His words and actions when he returns with a large glass of gin for himself make it clear that he is an alcoholic. Christine reveals increasing agitation with each additional drink he pours for himself.

Christine views the chicken he offers her with distaste, preferring instead to bite her nails and to smoke silently. First he tries to push food at her, then, in the end, he goes voraciously through his own chicken and hers. Gradually the revelations of his monologue raise the level of her stress more and more. The unspoken tension between them grows more intense. While the audience is aware of this, Roland dithers blithely on. First, he reveals that he has lied to her and that her mother is not at all sick. It was a mere pretext to simplify his objective of getting her away from her husband. Most disturbing, on numerous occasions as he grows increasingly uncomfortable with her resistance to all his initiatives, is his way of turning a sentence in such a way that she is made to feel guilty or that she is to blame for all her own misfortunes and any that have befallen either Roland or her mother. Such manipulation begins with the moment of her birth when, he says, his wife began to gain weight: "Yes, it was starting with you that she began to get fat." [2] Complacently affirming that he will always be there to take care of her and that he has never hurt her physically, while nevertheless acknowledging his anger and his desire to use physical violence, he fails to recognize the psychic and emotional harm he has done and the fear he is causing at the present moment: "Sometimes I understand that someone would want to take you in their two hands and to shake you until something comes out of you." [3]

Roland is particularly upset by his belief that Christine's husband beat her. This seems a reasonable belief until one realizes that he is once again blaming Christine for bringing this upon herself and that his reason for concern seems to be that he is worried about the shame and what the neighbours will think. He wonders if Christine is "normal" (27) for not having thought of the disgrace. In fact, his intense hatred for his daughter's husband seems to arise much more from an unacknowledged jealousy of him than from any kind of genuine concern for his daughter's well-being: "And all you find to do is to let yourself be slapped by a little idiot less than five foot seven inches tall! You have no pride, Cri-Cri, you have no pride, neither for yourself, nor for your parents." [4] Such accusations upset Christine so much that she must run to the bathroom to vomit. Gradually the audience realizes the very real possibility that Roland committed incest with Christine.

Their evening continues with his constant rant, projecting guilt and fear on Christine, drinking incessantly, recalling his alcoholic mother, and giving himself rationalizations about any bad behaviour he might have had, Christine taking refuge in the bathroom and seeming to shrink increasingly as time passes. In the course of his monologue, we learn that it was when she was about twelve that Christine ceased speaking and eating. After the lights go down Christine says her first hesitant words asking about Roland's father. Rather than responding to her question, Roland diminishes her yet further by commenting on her stutter and her poor prospects for future employment and happiness.

A surprising turn occurs when Roland reveals to Christine his sexual fantasies, the fantasies of a voyeur, particularly a voyeur who is also a pedophile. In a "very sensual, very troubling tone, not at all «paternal»" [5] he waxes long and eloquent about the fantasies he had about her as a pre-pubescent child, believing mistakenly that he is flattering her: "I always had an image of you in my head, when you were ten or eleven. You have no idea how pretty you were at that age. It makes no sense, but I never got tired of looking at you […] Then you started to develop a bit […] then there were your little breasts that were starting to peek through." [6] Completely unaware of the damage he is doing with his words, he adds that his attraction for her ended on her eleventh birthday, when she fell ill, quit eating, became very thin and much less beautiful. The play does not inform what happened on her eleventh birthday. Roland insists that he never touched her, only looked. Her terror may have been caused by simply feeling his salacious eyes on her. Yet he has lied consistently throughout the evening they have spent in the motel. And her fear of being alone with him in this room has grown more and more palpable, particularly as he became more drunk. In any case, he manages to twist his memory of the past so completely that he interprets his disappointment and worry at her illness and loss of fresh beauty as the reason for his drinking. Surprise! Surprise! She and the dead brother after whom she is named are responsible for his alcoholism! He has misunderstood right to the end and continued to congratulate himself on what a good father he has been and will be.

Roland's revelation provokes a complete crisis in Christine. She looks at herself in the mirror and bangs her head everywhere on her image. Roland insists that he's taking her away immediately, not knowing what else to do. But she refuses with great force, breaks the bottle of his gin, and they struggle. She must choose between killing herself or him. In desperation, she chooses to kill him. However, the final moment of the play when her body falls on his leaves little reason to hope that her desperate act can be interpreted as liberation for her.

Notes

[1]   *L'Homme gris*, suivi de *Éva et Éveline*. Montréal: VLB Éditeur, 1986. First production of *L'Homme gris* in Montréal on September 13, 1984 at the Salle Fred-Barry by Productions Marie Laberge and the Théâtre du Vieux Québec, directed by Marie Laberge, designed by Pierre Labonté with Yvon Leroux as Roland Fréchette and

Marie Michaud as Christine. This production opened in Québec City on March 26, 1985 at L'Implanthéâtre with Marc Legault as Roland Fréchette and Marie Michaud as Christine. *Night*, translation by Rina Fraticelli, had a dramatic reading by the Ubu Repertory Theater in New York in co-production with CEAD on November 19, 1986 and was produced by the Toronto Free Theatre on March 2, 1988. In *Plays by Women*, Volume Seven. London: Methuen, 1988.

[2] "Ouain, c't'à partir de toi qu'a s'est mis à engraisser." (*L'Homme gris*: 20).

[3] "J'comprends des fois qu'on aye envie d'te prendre à deux mains pis d'te brasser jusqu'à temps qui sorte queque chose de toi." (*L'Homme gris*: 24).

[4] "Pis tout c'que tu trouves à faire, c'est d'te laisser fesser par un p'tit crétin qui mesure pas cinq pieds sept! T'as pas d'fierté Cri-Cri, t'as pas d'fierté, ni pour toi, ni pour tes parents." (*L'Homme gris*: 27).

[5] "D'un ton très sensuel, très troublant, pas «paternel» pour deux cennes." (*L'Homme gris*: 49).

[6] "J'ai toujours une image de toi dans ma tête, quand t'avais dix-onze ans. Tu peux pas savoir comme t'étais belle à c't'âge-là. C'pas mêlant, j'me fatiquais pas de te r'garder [...] Pis tu commençais à t'former un peu [...] pis tes p'tits seins qui commençaient à piquer..." (*L'Homme gris*: 49).

Bibliographical Suggestions

Selected Other Works by Marie Laberge

Profession: je l'aime, unpublished. Five short plays lasting 1 1/2 hours in all, five variations on affective life, couples, desire and the difficulty of communicating (*Éva et Éveline, La Fille fuckeuse de gars, On a ben failli s'comprendre, Profession: je l'aime, T'sais veux dire*) produced by the Théâtre du Vieux Québec January 10, 1979. *Profession: je l'aime* had a dramatic reading at CEAD on March 8, 1978.

Ils étaient venus pour.... Montréal: VLB Éditeur, 1978. Dramatic reading by CEAD in Montréal on April 7, 1980, followed by a tour of several cities in France and Switzerland. First produced by the Théâtre du Bois de Coulonge in Paris in August, 1981.

C'étaient avant la guerre à L'Anse À Gilles. Montréal: VLB Éditeur, 1981. First produced by L'Atelier de la Nouvelle Compagnie Théâtrale in Montréal on January 15, 1981. *Before the War, down at l'Anse à Gilles*, tr. Alan Brown, first co-produced by CEAD and Playwrights Workshop Montréal on February 9, 1986, at the Toronto Free Theatre on February 23, 1986, and at National Arts Centre in Ottawa on March 1, 1986. Also translated the same year by John Murrell as *Before the War at l'Anse à Gilles*.

Avec l'hiver qui s'en vient. Montréal: VLB Éditeur, 1981. First produced by La Commune à Marie in Québec City on September 3, 1980. Public reading by the Nouvelle Compagnie Théâtrale in Montréal on December 9, 1985.

Jocelyne Trudelle trouvée morte dans ses larmes. Montréal: VLB Éditeur, 1983. Dramatic reading by CEAD on March 9, 1981. First produced by the Théâtre de la Commune à Marie in Québec City on October 8, 1986.

Le Banc. Montréal: VLB Éditeur, 1989. First produced by La Commune à Marie in Québec City in March, 1983.

Deux Tangos pour toute une vie. Montréal: VLB Éditeur, 1985. First produced by La Commune à Marie in Québec City on November 6, 1984.

On *L'Homme gris* and Marie Laberge

Godin, Jean-Cleo and Dominique Lafon. "Pour ne rien oublier, Marie Laberge, la parole-femme." *Dramaturgies québécoises des années quatre-vingt.* Montréal: Lémeac Éditeur, 1999: 73–197.

Moss, Jane. "Family Histories: Marie Laberge and Women's Theater in Quebec." *Postcolonial Subjects: Francophone Women Writers.* Ed. Karen Gould, Mary Jean Green, Micheline Rice-Maximin, Keith Walker, Jack Yeager. Minneapolis: University of Minnesota Press, 1996: 79–97.

———. "Québécois Theatre: Michel Tremblay and Marie Laberge." *Theatre Research International.* 21/3 (Fall 1996): 196–207.

Pocknell, Brian. "Marie Laberge," *The Oxford Companion to Canadian Theatre.* Ed. Eugene Benson & L.W. Conolly. Toronto, Oxford, New York: Oxford University Press, 1989: 287–88.

Smith, André, Ed. *Marie Laberge, dramaturge, Actes du Colloque international.* Trois-Rivières: VLB Éditeur, 1989.

About Marie Laberge

Playwright, script writer for television, actor, director, producer, teacher, and novelist Marie Laberge (born 1950 in Québec City) began as a journalism student and then enrolled at the Conservatoire d'art dramatique de Québec after joining La Troupe des Treize in 1970. She graduated from the Conservatoire in 1975. She has written more than twenty plays, all of which have had stage productions. She was the Director of the Théâtre du Trident (1977–1980), Director and President of the Centre d'Essai des Auteurs Dramatiques (1978–1981, 1987–1989), and member of the organizing committee of the Québec États généraux du Théâtre professionnel. She has received many prizes and awards, including the Governor General's Award for *C'Était avant la guerre à l'Anse à Gilles*. She received the Croix de Chevalier de l'Ordre des Arts et des Lettres de France in 1989 for *L'Homme gris* (*Night*).

She published her first novel, *Juillet*, in 1989, the same year she produced a full-length feature film for television, "Les Heures précieuses." Her novels, which have brought her many prizes and awards, have been more numerous since that time than her plays.

L'Homme Gris was first produced by Les Productions Marie Laberge and Le Thêatre du Vieux Quebec, Montreal, in September 1984, with the following company:

Roland Fréchette   Yvon Leroux
Christine   Marie Michaud

Directed by Marie Laberge
Set and lighting design by Pierre Labonté
Costumes by Carole Paré

• • •

The English-Language premiere of *L'Homme gris/Night* was produced by Toronto Free Theatre, in March 1988, with the following company:

Roland Fréchette   David Fox
Christine   Karen Woolridge

Directed by Richard Greenblatt
Set and costumes designed by Jules Tonus
Lighting designed by Jim Plaxton
Fight direction by Robert Lindsay
Stage Manager Winston Morgan

Characters

Roland Fréchette, 52. Christine's father. The very picture of a man of goodwill. Not a very large man; rather thin, well groomed and paying great attention to his physical appearance. He is a confident man, sure of himself and of his opinions. Someone who never doubts for an instant the moral rightness of his actions. Long ago he denied the world of emotion: this he considers to be a good thing, as he's felt a lot better for it. As a result, he is thoroughly incapable of appreciating what his daughter is feeling.

Christine, 21 years old. Extremely slight, thin. She is the incarnation of deeply internalized anxiety. In contrast with her father, she is thin-skinned and highly sensitive. Every minor nuance and implication of her father's words resonates loudly for her. And there are wounds…. Her very presence (without any need to overstate the acting) should help us gauge her father's words. She was once anorexic.

NIGHT

A motel. Typical conventional, boring and cheap. Twin beds separated by a night-table on which sit the telephone and a single large and ugly lamp. Stage left, a door and a window onto the outside. Stage right, the doors to the closet and to the bathroom. Downstage are a low table which will be used for the meal, and two so-called comfortable chairs, odds and ends which might have come from a living-room circa 1960, the colours all of which clash. In terms of the colours, what's most important is that they be more or less worn out while retaining a quality of harshness: carpets whose patterns are old and worn but nonetheless abrasive; garish bedspreads; lamps and curtains of extremely questionable taste. Finally, a multidirectional television set which, at the opening, is positioned toward the beds.

At the opening, the stage is lit exclusively by the glow of the motel sign, reflected through the window. As the door opens, a narrow shaft of light streaks in. We hear the rain and a terrible thunderstorm. A man enters quickly. He drops an overnight bag by the door. In his other hand, he carries very much at arm's length, two cardboard boxes tied together. He shakes the rain off himself, while taking in the room. He deposits the boxes on the table and turns back to the door. No one has followed him.

ROLAND   Chris! Hurry up! Get in here before you get soaked.

He goes to pick up the overnight bag by the door. CHRISTINE enters. She looks even younger than her age. Her hair is wet; her hands are stuck in the pockets of her navy, three-quarter-length trench coat; and she's wearing sneakers on her wet feet. She appears very uneasy. She comes in and stands stock-still in front of the window, by the TV, without showing the slightest interest in the motel room. (She ought to inspire in us the urge to gather her up, to comfort her, rock her.) ROLAND closes the door, deposits the overnight bag by the TV and switches on the overhead light which gives off a harsh, offensive glare.

Jesus! that's what you call a light! Just hang on a sec and I'll fix that up.

He springs back into action, full of cheer and somewhat strained high spirits. He turns on the bedside lamp, moving the table a little while he's at it, then the bathroom light, leaving the door ajar. The turning on of each light is punctuated by a satisfied "All right!"

CHRISTINE has not stirred. She drips quietly. ROLAND returns, turns off the overhead light and is satisfied.

All right! That's more like it. See, we just saved ourselves seven bucks, easy: it looks more like a high-class motel already. *(He goes over to the table and unties the boxes.)*

Two beds for eighteen bucks! There's even a colour TV. Is it colour? Hang on a sec. *(He goes to check.)* Darn right, it's colour, Chris, a real first-class motel. Later on, we can watch a nice movie. *(He looks at her. She hasn't moved.)* Well, sit down, Chris. Take your coat off. We'll have some supper. That'll pick you right up, you'll see. *(He goes to get her, sits her down.)* Cold? Want me to turn up the heat? There's bound to be a thermostat in here somewhere.

> *He moves behind her to help her off with her coat. She resists, silently. He pats her shoulders, but annoyed.*

All right, all right, hang on to your coat. I'm not gonna force you. You're just like Mom, hmm, always shivering just like Mom. Well, if it's all the same to you I'll just peel off a layer.

> *He takes off his trench coat and hangs it in the closet.*

You'll be doing the same thing, before you know it, just wait and see.

> *Pause. He looks at her. He is still standing behind her. He is uneasy, a little uncomfortable. The good cheer is beginning to show signs of strain. Then he finds a solution.*

Well, now, I'd say I've earned a little drink. Will you have one, Chris? With lots and lots of water.

> *CHRISTINE reacts for the first time. Alarmed, she watches him as he goes to his suitcase, opens it, taking out an unopened 26-ouncer of gin. He goes into the bathroom. We hear the glass, water. He returns with a full glass for himself and one considerably less full for her. As soon as he enters the bathroom, he starts talking louder.*

Don't get yourself into a state on Mom's account. The fact that I stopped just proves she's not dying. You know perfectly well I'd have gone straight home— I mean, to the hospital if there was really any reason to worry. Oh, it's serious, all right, but like the doctors said, she's on the road to recovery. We'll bring her through it. *(He comes back into the room.)* Here. Drink up. It'll put a little colour in your cheeks.

> *He puts her glass on the table. She doesn't touch it. Turning his back to his daughter, facing the window, he takes a long slug of his own.*

Talk about ugly weather. It hasn't let up all day. When I left Sherbrooke, I'm not kidding, I could've really used a second set of wipers. Give me snow over that kind of rain any day. First, it's nicer to look at; and secondly, it's cleaner. Rain, like this in November, gimme a break.

> *He finishes his drink in one gulp. Clicks his tongue with satisfaction.*

That's a nice little drink.

> *He turns back toward her; she hasn't moved. He catches her biting her nails.*

Are you hungry yet, Chris? We'll have ourselves a fine little feast, you'll see. *(He opens the boxes of barbecue chicken.)* Aw, look at that. The coleslaw went and spilled all over the fries. No problem. Just hand that one over to me. I'll eat it myself. There you go, kiddo, enjoy!

> *He pulls up an armchair and digs into the chicken. CHRISTINE watches him eat with considerable disgust. She returns to biting her nails without having touched her plate.*

Not bad. A little dry but the coleslaw in the fries helps a little. Maybe I should've bought you a Coke to go with, eh Chris?

> *He watches her chew her nails with some irritation. He obviously can't stand it.*

Chris! Eat your chicken instead of chewing your nails.

> *She jumps, then quickly picks up a piece of chicken, holding it gingerly in her fingers.*

That's it. Be a good girl. I'll just go and fix myself a little refill.

> *He exits to the bathroom. CHRISTINE drops the chicken and begins to dry her fingers meticulously. He returns.*

Not bad, eh? Hard to go wrong with chicken. Even Mom couldn't ruin it. I said to myself we'll get our money's worth with chicken. And you can eat it cold, no problem. Still and all. They don't give it away. Two boxes like this comes to just about $15 bucks with tax… bloody filthy tax. They get us coming and going those guys. And there's no end to it, kiddo. They bleed you all the way to the grave and then some. I give up trying to figure out how to get past those guys. I couldn't care less what the rich have to pay. But people like us, when you think how we started out, without a cent, and now, just when we can afford to relax a little, thanks to the sweat and the sacrifices we made, you know what I mean, well, it makes me sick to watch them take away the little bit extra we managed to put aside. Like we weren't even entitled to a little bit extra to make up for all the time we did without. The old money, well, they know every little trick and dodge to keep from paying taxes; it's easy for them, they're practically born knowing how to finagle their way around these things. They didn't start playing kissy face with the tax man just yesterday. But a guy like me, who's just started breathing a little easier in the last couple of years…

> *CHRISTINE takes her package of cigarettes out of her pocket and is about to take out a cigarette.*

You're not gonna smoke? You haven't eaten a thing yet. No, no, eat a bit more, then you can smoke. A person's got to eat. *(He puts her cigarettes aside, and watches her, waiting.)*

C'mon now, eat up. It's not poison, you'll see.

> She picks up the same piece of chicken again, holding it gingerly in her fingers.

That's better. *(He goes back to work on his chicken voraciously.)* Mom's been really worried, always wondering if you were getting enough to eat. Well, you gotta admit, in Mom's case enough is a lot. At least as much as you and me combined. *(He laughs.)* I'm telling you nothing's changed on that score since you left. In fact, she's put on another fifteen pounds or so, and on top of what she already had to begin with, let me tell you, it shows. To think that when I married that woman she was as thin as you are right now. Unbelievable, hmm? Well, maybe a little more… filled out more than you, but not much. That's what you might call a "distant memory." I'm telling you, if we didn't have the wedding pictures, I'd have trouble believing it myself.… It was when you arrived that she put on the great bulk of it. It's like, after you, she never lost her pot… like she stayed pregnant even after you were born. Yeah, it was with you that she started to get fat. Seems like it's pretty hard, having a baby. *(He watches her, thoughtfully.)* I wonder if it'll have the same effect on you.

> CHRISTINE drops the chicken, barely touched; it's all she can do to keep from gagging.

(angry) Not that it's likely, the way you eat. Do you eat at least? At home, I mean, with your husband, did you eat? You haven't started up that foolishness again, have you? It cost us enough, the pills and all… well, I certainly hope we've heard the last of that business.

> He looks at her. She's biting her nails again. She stops abruptly taken aback.

Is it just that you're worried about Mom? Don't be. Maybe I made it sound a little more serious than it actually is 'cause I wanted you to come back with me.… Mom too… uh, this chicken's dry…

> He finishes his drink, and gets up to get another. As soon as he is in the bathroom CHRISTINE takes out a cigarette. ROLAND enters.

I think I can allow myself this one. Especially since we're not going back on the road tonight. I'm telling you, that was a long tough haul today. Worse still, in this weather. Mom was afraid it'd turn to snow… they were calling for freezing rain… well, I'm ready for any of it: four Michelin tires.

> The "conversation" is running thin, he goes to the window.

No, it's not gonna freeze over; it's just gonna keep on raining. We won't be waking up to the first snow. Not tomorrow, anyway, so much the better or

Mom'd have a fit. (*He comes around to the table again, his glass empty.*) You're not gonna eat your fries? Well, at least yours aren't soggy. Your coleslaw didn't spill. D'you mind if I steal a couple? (*CHRISTINE pushes the box across the table to him.*) Mine were a little too wet for my taste. Here, eat this little piece. (*He holds out a piece of chicken.*) Just this one and then I'll leave you alone about it. Be a good girl.

> *She chews at the chicken slowly while continuing to smoke.*

Wouldn't you know it, your fries are better'n mine.

> *Time passes. He stops eating. Silence. He takes the wet napkin out of its pocket, wipes his finger with it, and puts it back into the box on top of the chicken. He takes out his nail clipper and gives himself a little unnecessary touch up. Such endless trimming of his fingernails is one of ROLAND's tics. A sigh.*

Yeah. Well, you're not a big talker, Chris. You never did make much noise, but this is something else again. Is this what marriage did to you? (*He laughs a little, then stops abruptly.*) Maybe it's just that you take after me—talking doesn't come easy to you. Mom doesn't have that problem—she talks. You certainly don't feel time weighing on you, like, when she's around. That's one of her good points: she's good at making conversation. I wouldn't say she's always got the most important things to say but she talks, she fills the house, like they say. And especially since you left, she never stops yakking and fussing all the time. She's always off with one of her neighbours or my sister, your aunt… cooking up something or other…. Well, it makes her happy and it doesn't bother anybody. Certainly doesn't bother me—I don't listen anymore! (*He laughs.*) It's like background noise, I mean like having a second TV going somewhere in the house… but you, now, Chris, you never did say much of anything. Except when you were just little, you hardly ever made a sound in the house. That means you were happy…. Anyhow… we did everything so you would be…. We're not the kind who'd ever hurt you. And we never scrimped either… all finished eating? Because there's something I want to talk to you about; I'd like to have a little talk with you. It's not something we've done much of, I know, but I think now… hmm… we don't have much choice… er…. Will you have another glass? Oh, no, you haven't even touched it…. Hold on a minute, I'll be right back.

> *He goes to refill his glass. CHRISTINE, extremely nervous, gnaws at her nails. He re-enters somewhat ill at ease, he doesn't know where or how to begin.*

You're thinking we could've gone straight home tonight, if I'd wanted to… I could've made it…. No. I certainly didn't stop here just to throw good money out the window. No. I stopped because I need to have a word with you before we got home, just the two of us. Not because anything bad's happened to Mom. No… uh… no… this morning, at your place when I told you about the heart attack… and the hospital… and Mom needing you with her and all—well, that wasn't exactly true. Lets say that… it was a kind of excuse I made up so I could get you out of your house and take you home. Do you understand?

She looks at him, dumbfounded, desperately chewing at a nail.

Will you please stop biting your bloody nails. It makes you look a real dummy. Do you understand what I'm saying to you? *(She indicates that she does. Trembling, she lights a cigarette. He doesn't want to look at her anymore, and begins to pace.)* Do I need to explain to you why I'm taking you home?

She stares at him, like a trapped animal.

Jesus Christ! You'd think it was me you're afraid of. You don't need to be afraid of me, Chris , and you know it. What have I ever done to you? Nothing. Have I ever laid a finger on you? Ever hit you once? Never! I always managed to get myself out of the house before I lost my temper. I always knew enough to get out of there before my hand got away from me. Same thing with Mom. Sometimes I wonder what good it did having all that control; it never stopped you from marrying a moron without even a decent trade. Anyhow, that's another story altogether. But you don't need to look at me with those big scared eyes—I never hurt you—I never touched you—and I'm not about to start now. Do you understand? Do you understand what I'm telling you? *(She nods her head, rapidly, almost violently.)* Jesus bloody Christ!—you're maddening! It's no wonder we want to grab you and shake something—a few words— anything—out of you once in a while. We wouldn't expect anything brilliant— don't worry!

He takes a swallow. Pause.

Ah… sorry. That's not what I wanted to say. I believe that you're real smart… anyway all the specialists we went to said so, you don't need to worry on that account. I even kept their written reports to prove it. It cost so much they had to give it to us in writing. At least you'll have them to make up for the diploma you never got. Don't get me wrong—I didn't say that to hurt you—I'm just telling you because someday it might be important to you. I kept all those papers just in case you need them, someday, to put your mind at ease, about yourself, like. *(pause)* But that's not what we were talking about, is it, eh, Chris? We were talking about Mom's heart attack; we were saying how it was a kind of excuse. *(pause)* I never lie, Chris, I've never told you a lie in my entire life. You know perfectly well how I feel about lying. I can't stand it. As far as I'm concerned a liar is about the worst kind of person there is. Oh, I've had to stretch the truth a little on occasion—out of human kindness—I'll admit that— and I've been known to avoid a question—to say nothing at all, I mean, rather then be forced into a lie—that's how much it disgusts me, but today, this morning, I lied to you, and the worst of it is, is that it was you who forced me to lie. It's because of you that I lied. For you. I lied to you for your own good. Because if I'd've told you the real reason, you wouldn't've come back with me, you wouldn't've wanted to. And that's why, so I could tell my little lie—that

Mom let me go alone. And that was a big deal for her, that was no small sacrifice. So now, in a little while, we'll call her, okay? We'll give her a call to put her mind at ease. And then she… can call your aunt. *(pause)* You know why I'm saying all this… don't you?

> *CHRISTINE isn't smoking anymore. Her cigarette is simply burning itself out. She is stiff, frozen there in place.*

You just don't seem to understand, Chris… when your aunt went to Rimouski to see you, three months ago, she figured out right away what was going on at your place. Seems like your idiot of a husband had no problem letting her know what he thinks about her—and us too. I don't know if he drinks—if he has any excuse at all—all I know is that your aunt found him pretty bloody violent and she thought that you were looking pretty pitiful yourself, that you looked worn right out. So—well—you know her—I mean—she doesn't waste any time—she stayed on in Rimouski two more days—in a hotel—all at her own expense—to do a little investigating. And the upshot of her investigation is that we found out all about it. Everything. Your aunt has her faults. God knows she exaggerates half the time, but with this, she even tried to hide some of the details from us— that's how shocked she was. She dug up information about him, she talked to the people who live on your block—never letting on a thing, using all sorts of real-sounding reasons for asking. You know what a good liar she is. She convinced them she was thinking of moving into the building, just wanted to find out if it was peaceful or not… there's nothing she wouldn't've said to get to the bottom of the story: and the bottom of the story is not very pretty. And when your aunt told me, well I wasn't very proud of you. She even told me— she didn't tell Mom this—but she told me that she saw you again, a little later— I guess she must've come up with another one of her lies—anyhow she saw your sprained finger—"accidentally" sprained like you told her. And that same day you were wearing a turtleneck sweater rolled practically up to your ears. And seems like everyone else was dying of heat. Did you actually think your aunt was gonna fall for it? Did you actually think she was gonna buy your story about a cupboard giving you a black eye? And what a good man your husband was? How understanding and kind he was being about your pain and all? What kind of suckers do you take us for, anyway? You're gonna have to come up with something a little better than that if you expect us to fall for it. You listen to me, Chris: there's no good reason for you to stay with him if he hits you; and there's no good reason for you to protect a guy like that. Did you ever once think of Mom? Forget about me, do you have any idea how ashamed Mom must have felt when your aunt told her? Do you have any idea how ashamed we'd be if something like this ever got out? I just don't understand how you can manage to love a guy like that—I mean, even before I knew he hit you, I couldn't understand—but now, well, I've got no choice… I've got to wonder if you're normal. Never—do you hear me—I'm never gonna let you go back to a guy that beats you. I'd rather live with the shame of divorce than risk someday somebody finding out about this. I'll never let anybody raise a hand to you.

I never did it myself—and as long as I live I'll never let anybody else do it. And that's something you can count on, Chris: if you can't look after yourself— I don't care how old you are—I'll do it for you. Someone lays a hand on you— it's me their hitting, me they're insulting, me they're cheapening. And I'm not about to be scared off by a little moron like your husband. Let him come and see me—he'll find out who he's dealing with. But he'll never lay a finger on me, that's for sure, or he'll be on the floor before he knows what hit him. But starting right now, you can just consider yourself divorced. It's not hard to plead physical cruelty in court. Never mind how much it costs, do you understand? I just don't know what you must have been thinking of to let yourself get beaten up like that for two years. I just hope it hasn't been going on for the whole two years. Because if it is two years, it's gonna take one helluva specialist to explain this one to me. You've got parents who love you. You could've come home any time, how many people can say that? We know where our duty lies—and we've never backed down from it, we always gave you the best of everything— whatever the cost—we never minded the sacrifices it meant. And all you can manage to do is get yourself beaten up by a stupid asshole who's barely five foot seven. You've got no pride, Chris, you got no pride—not for yourself and not for your parents… and don't you try telling me those lies you told your aunt, you know how…

> CHRISTINE *begins to gag. She rushes into the bathroom and closes the door. Her father goes to the door, alarmed.*

Chris? Chris? Answer me. Are you sick? Are you throwing up? Do you need any help? Open the door, now, let me in! Chris?

> *Nothing but the sound of the toilet flushing.*

Are you feeling better? Did that help? Are you feeling bad? Is that it? We won't talk about it any more, if you don't want to. I understand it's hard for you. Open the door, now, Chris. You're not sick any more, now. Is it over? Come on, come out of there, I'll take care of you. We won't talk about it anymore. Never. It's over. Dead and buried. We're gonna make a new life for you—you'll see. We'll only talk about it if you want to, if you need to. *(pause)* Are you feeling any better? Come on out here, Chris…

> CHRISTINE *comes out of the bathroom. She sits down at the edge of the bed.* ROLAND *rushes over to the table to remove boxes.*

I'll just get rid of this. You don't need to have all this chicken staring you in the face. *(He gathers it all up quickly.)* Want me to turn on the TV? Maybe there's a nice movie on. It'd take your mind off of things… just hang on one sec and I'll be right back.

> *His hands are full of boxes. He takes them to the trash can in the bathroom, he comes back, turns on the TV, puts the chairs back in place. She's still at the edge of the bed, frozen. He takes the glass he gave her.*

Good thing you didn't drink it. It wouldn't've done you any good. *(He drinks it.)* You always did have a good sensitive stomach, I mean, a kind of weakness in that area.

> *He sits in an armchair, takes out a cigarette and puts it in his mouth without lighting it.*

Oh, don't worry, I'm not gonna light it. I'm trying to quit. It's a pretty good way, actually—all you have to do is not light it. It's almost the same thing: you just don't get the smoke.

> *No response. CHRISTINE seems to have sunk into herself, beyond it all.*

Chris! Do you hear me? *(She starts, looks at him.)* Do you want one? You don't have to hold back on my account. *(She shakes her head slowly, her eyes full of tears.)* I'll stay right here… you can watch your programme, nice and peaceful. I'll finish up your drink… *(He watches the movie for a bit.)* D'you want me to turn up the sound? I'll just turn up the sound a bit, we can't hear a thing.

> *He goes to turn up the sound. She's not listening to the TV. She's just sitting there, in despair. He sits down again, gets up again, gets his slippers out of his bag and puts them on. He sits back down. He goes over to turn out the bedside lamp. The soundtrack of the movie, a dialogue about love considerably different from what we've just been hearing, continues as the lights slowly dim.*

> *The lights come up again after a little while, indicating time has passed. When they come up, CHRISTINE is in the bathroom with the door closed; ROLAND, on his way to being, but not yet, drunk, is on the telephone and nervous. He keeps a watch on the bathroom door.*

Yes. Collect, that's right… is that a problem?… Roland Frechette… uh huh…

> *He waits, drumming his fingers, fussing with the pillows on CHRISTINE's bed. There is a response at the other end of the line.*

Say "yes" Mom…. Good…. Yes, yes, it's me, it's me… no, we stopped on the way just like I said I'd do… we're at Joly, now. Well, of course she's with me…. All right, now listen, I can't talk too long but there's something I want to tell you: it's better if we don't say too much about it, d'you understand? Not a word about Frank and all that or the marriage or anything…. Well, of course! Enough to make her sick, she hasn't stopped running back and forth to the bathroom since we got here…. Stop screaming Mom, it's not that, it's just the shock.

> *CHRISTINE comes out of the bathroom without making a sound. She's still wearing her coat. She leans against the door frame. ROLAND doesn't see her.*

Let's just hold on before we start jumping to conclusions, okay? Let's just say she's feeling sick… yeah, tomorrow morning early…. It depends on Chris, if she's sick all night…

> *He turns around, sees her and pats the bed so she'll come and sit down, smiles in a discouraged sort of way as if to indicate that he's speaking to someone quite unreasonable.*

Okay… okay… I'll do that… fine… good… that's enough, now… this is long distance… that's right… goodnight, now. *(He hangs up.)* She's real worried. You know her, she always suspects the worst. If it was up to her we'd be on our way to emergency at Joly right now. And let me tell you I'm not bloody well driving you there. *(He laughs.)* You okay? Are you still cold? Come and get yourself settled in over here. Don't keep hanging around the bathroom like that, it'll just give you ideas.

> *He goes to get her, she sits on the edge of the bed.*

I've never known anyone who had such a weak stomach… you've been vomiting ever since you were twelve… Mom's not exactly wrong to worry… we figured all that vomiting was over and done with… we thought you finished with all that stuff… as far as I'm concerned you never saw the right specialist… *(pause)* Maybe it's the flu, hmmm? There's a lot of it around this time of year, and this one's a real mean bugger: one of my salesmen had it, he missed a week and a half of work and he was still green around the gills when he came back. I'm not kidding.

> *Pause. ROLAND is at a loss. He walks around her.*

Chris, if you have the flu, you know, you ought to take off that wet coat; and your shoes too. Here I'll help you.

> *He moves as if to help her. She immediately shrinks away from him, wrapping her arms around herself.*

No? You don't want to? I'm just telling you it'd help, it'd warm you up.

> *She pulls away abruptly in a protective move. He reacts as if attacked.*

No? Suit yourself. I'm certainly not gonna coax you. Not like Mom did that's for sure.

> *He gets his empty glass from the table and goes to the bathroom to refill it.*

> *CHRISTINE moves toward the very end of the bed; it's as if she is in a competition for the person who can take up the least amount of space. She draws into herself and we see her becoming more and more anxious, but without the energy to defend herself, giving her the terrified look of someone poised on alert. Nevertheless she is attuned to and registers every word that's spoken.*

> *ROLAND re-enters with his glass. He's had a lot to drink but doesn't "read" drunk in the conventional way. It's a highly internalized drunkenness that's reflected more in what he says than how he speaks.*

You okay? D'you need anything? Too bad we don't have any pills or anything with us. If Mom was here, we'd have everything we need. Mom never leaves the house without her pills—she's like a preacher with his Bible. *(He laughs. Pause. He sits on the chair.)* No, it's no joke to be stuck here like this… I just hope you can get a little sleep. If not, Mom's gonna think I've been beating up on you, too.

  He realizes abruptly what he's just said, and looks at her.

Oh, sorry, it's just an expression… *(takes out a cigarette)* D'you want one?

  She takes her own pack out of her coat pocket.

Ah! Not your brand… well, at least you're not one of those who smoke OP's…. Tons of them now saving money on our packs. The offices are full of them. Are you sure it's okay for you to smoke?… Well, I suppose you know best… it used to drive Mom crazy that you smoked. She figured it wasn't good for you—for your delicate health as she puts it… as for me… well, I don't have an opinion about it, one way or another…. A woman smoking doesn't strike me as any uglier than a man smoking. It's like they always say: you got to change with the times. A woman isn't necessarily any more vulgar just because she smokes— you've got to be pretty narrow-minded to think that these days. Of course, when I was younger it just wasn't done… only whores smoked on the street. Oh yeah, you saw a woman smoking on the street and you could go right up to her and ask her how much. Smoking and drinking… they just weren't things women did. Not that it kept them from doing it on the sly… there's a lot more of them were drinking then we'd ever thought… as for me… well, I'll tell you a secret… a big secret… my mother… my own mother drank… oh, not a drop now and again… no, no, she drank, blind drunk, like they say… an alcoholic. Yeah… well, that's why I'm so careful. *(He shows her his almost empty glass.)* I keep pretty close tabs on myself, I hold back… because I know perfectly well that I could have the tendency that way…. Tonight, now, is a different story… I'm not so drunk that I don't know that I've had more than my usual, but emotions ran pretty high today. It wasn't easy for me to do what I did. It wasn't easy, Chris. You'll understand that one day when you have kids of your own: there's some things, you might say, in life that are pretty tough going, there're things that can really knock the wind out of you. And kids… well, they're a little like parents… you might say that, finally, in the long run, they end up doing you just about as much harm as good. I'm talking in general now… about the kind of people I see… the guys at the office… *(pause)* No, it didn't take me long, let me tell you, to figure out she was a drinker. She wasn't easy to get on with, my mother, she wasn't always there…. Just a kid, I can remember, she used to sing me songs and she'd be crying and crying over them, it was unbelievable. She used to scare me something fierce. She'd talk so loud, she'd make scenes, such a big commotion that my father'd say… he took off… he flew the coop… he just couldn't take it any more—there was nothing he could do anyway…. She'd hide it everywhere: there wasn't a vinegar bottle in the house that had vinegar in it. In her perfume, in all her things—there was gin in every corner of the house. The minute she got her hands on a cent, we never had to wonder what she'd do with it—she'd take off looking for booze. Nobody knew. Not ever. My sister wasn't about to broadcast it. She took off, too. She managed to get herself married young and she never mentioned her again. Till after she was dead. Once my mother was dead, your aunt changed her tune then, it turned out, her mother was a saint who'd raised two kids all by herself, without any help from her terrible husband who'd walked out on her. I never said a thing. Never once tried to correct her... for a start it seemed like it did her some good saying that, and then it's none of my business. The only thing that's important to me is that no one knows what she's like, that she had a drinking problem.... Mom doesn't know anything about it. And not a word about it from you either, she'd never forgive me, and for sure she'd say that's where your weak stomach comes from. But it wasn't her stomach at all, it was her liver. And it killed her, too. You can't get away with that kind of drinking for long. Doesn't matter who you are. Not that it took her all that long either... I lived all alone with her from the time I was eighteen, when your sister—I mean, my sister, your aunt got married. And I stayed eleven years. Till she died. She had to be watched... so she wouldn't fall. Got to the point where she'd break an ankle or a wrist, just like that. But that was near the end.... No, it wasn't very pretty, near the end: she raved, she talked nonsense, I wonder if she even knew I was her son. Well, anyhow, I tried to forget it. I'll tell you the truth, I wish I could've forgotten her right then and there, like my sister did. She never laid eyes on her again, from the day she got married to the day she died. But I saw her. I saw her stoop lower than an animal. I saw her act like anything but a mother. And I always supplied her drink for her. For eleven years. All her drink. The stories and promises she'd make up to get her drink. I wasn't that much of a sucker. She never fooled me with her stories. Her phony excuses and her endless bloody scenes. She'd just sit there thinking I fell for it. And I'd never say a thing: I just let it pass and I'd buy her a drink for just one reason: so she'd never go out like that. I didn't want anybody to know about it or to see her like that, with her face all wild, telling them her stupid stories so they'd feel sorry for her and give her a drink. I was ashamed of her. So I went out and bought her the drink myself. I never bought the gin at the same liquor store twice in the same month. I'd go all over town if I had to, or I'd buy it in another town or I'd manage to ask someone else to pick some up for me, as a favour—not often—only when I was really stuck... yeah, well, I just didn't want anyone to get suspicious, anyone at the liquor store, any of my friends. I'd have been so ashamed. I knew—and that was plenty. I kept her supplied with everything she needed—and that's saying some—and as for her, she stayed inside, in the house. That was our arrangement. She knew if she ever stepped one foot out of the house to go begging for a drink, she'd never get another drop from me. And I never budged an inch about that. I'd never been able to stand the shame if people knew. Never. And let me tell you, she stayed in the house. A wreck... in the end, she was a real human wreck. So finally I had to get the doctor in, and he told me it wouldn't be long if she kept drinking at that rate, wouldn't take much time at all before she was dead. And he was right! I tried to get her to stop. I tried even though I knew it wouldn't do any good. Anyhow, at least I told her what the doctor said… so she'd know what she was doing. But she… she was in so much pain, she threatened me, she said she'd go out on the street screaming that she was an alcoholic and that it was her own son who was pushing her to drink. See? Y'see… I never guessed that she could've figured it out, that she'd know just exactly how to get me, that she knew that for me, the worst thing that could happen wasn't that she'd die, but that people would know. So I gave it to her. I gave as much as she wanted, and I'm not sorry. That's what she wanted, she made her own choice, all right, and that's all there was to it. *(pause)* It's funny you know, but there's times I think she hated me. Me, the only one who stayed with her, the only one who took care of her. A little while before she died she said to me, "You thought I didn't know, hmmm, you thought I didn't know that you were ashamed of your mother? Well, my little boy, when you spend your whole life being ashamed, all the time, with everybody, you learn to spot it in other people's faces. I've watched you being ashamed of me and ashamed for me since you were this tall… and it never taught you a thing, my poor ninny, it never taught you a bloody thing." That's where she was wrong because it taught me where to draw the line with the bottle. I bloody well learned how to control myself: never go over your limit. I've never been as drunk as her, and I've never needed a drink as bad as her. I like to have a drink all right—even have a tendency that way—I don't deny it—but I know it and I can handle it. No one's ever gonna be ashamed of me— I promised myself I was never gonna be ashamed again… that's why no one knows… if Mom knew about it there'd be no end to it, looking out for signs, and thinking—there, that's it, I've become an alcoholic. No. She thinks my mother died of cancer of the liver and that's just perfect. She doesn't need to know any more about it, it wouldn't make a bit of difference in her life. *(Pause. He laughs to himself.)* What she doesn't know, though, is that actually it did make a bit of a difference in her life…. A little before she died, my mother started getting worried about my future. I don't know what came over her— she must have all of a sudden remembered she'd had kids. Anyhow, near the end she wouldn't stop asking me if I was gonna get married. She'd ask me how old I was, and then right after, every time, it never failed, she'd tell me how I had to get married, absolutely, "to save myself from the drink," she'd say. As if marriage'd ever saved her from anything. Anyhow, she was wearing herself out and she was wearing me out so much with it that I finally said, yes. I was going to get married as soon as she got better. And then she started to laugh, and she said, well then, I'd be able to get married in two weeks 'cause she'd be dead and buried by then. And then, after that, she started laughing at me, saying that I wasn't any better than her and that my story about getting married wasn't even true, that I'd just said it to get a little peace. Then she said she wasn't gonna die—just to piss me off, she said—she wasn't gonna die before she'd seen this woman. That's how my mother used to talk—she was always real blunt; it was the alcohol that did that to her. Oh, there was no end to the sweet talking when she wanted something, but once she got it, she'd tell you exactly what she thought. She had such a filthy mouth on her, she'd curse the whole world. Anyhow, I ended up having to bring somebody home to her just to get a little peace. So after we agreed that she'd say that she had cancer of the liver, and not a word about the rest—so she wouldn't ruin my future—I decided to go ahead with it. In those days Mom was working as a secretary not far from my office. I'd just taken her out to a movie once, but that was it. So I asked her, as a favour, like, out of human kindness. I said. And she was willing. So I took her to see my mother, and it was my mother who planted the idea in her head that I'd be needing help after she was gone, I mean all sorts of crazy stories, her alcoholic bullshit: a big number. And Mom bought it all, the whole thing. When my mother died she even tried to find the funeral parlour and everything, but she never found it, 'cause I'd had her buried right away. But afterwards, later on, when I saw her again, after my mother was out of the picture, I started to appreciate her for herself. She was a very outgoing person, she'd never say anything out of place, she was a woman who had nothing to be ashamed of. So we got married—and you can see what a good deal it turned out to be: we get on and no arguments. Oh, we might've argued a little bit about you, back then, when you were first sick, but that's about it. If it hadn't been for you, and that sickness of yours when you were twelve, we'd've never raised our voices to each other. That's saying something, hmm?

> *CHRISTINE gets up, carefully. ROLAND assumes she's feeling sick.*

Again! You're not feeling any better? Christ, talk about a mess!

> *CHRISTINE goes to the bathroom. ROLAND stares at his glass and shakes his head.*

I think it's time to stop now. Before it starts playing tricks on me. Already, it's loosened my tongue without me even noticing. Yeah, that's enough now.

> *He empties his glass. Pause. He gets up, turns on the TV; snow, nothing else. He turns it off, goes to the window. CHRISTINE comes out of the bathroom, she looks at her father, wants to talk to him. He cuts her off.*

Okay? Feeling better now? What do you say about going to bed and getting a little sleep, hmm? We've got a big day ahead tomorrow.

> *CHRISTINE walks over and sits huddled on her bed. ROLAND goes to the bathroom, returns, turns out the light and stretches out on the bed, fully dressed.*

I'll just stretch out a bit. Don't be embarrassed to wake me up if you need anything or if you're gonna be sick.

> *He turns out the lamp between their beds. We hear the rain. A single beam of light streams in through the window—a flashing neon if possible. A little time passes, and then in the dark we hear.*

CHRISTINE   Your f-f-fa… your f-… f-ather?

> *Note: CHRISTINE is affected by a "clonic," or specific stutter. Therefore, keep strictly to those indicated, do not embellish. She stutters only on the letters 'F' and 'V'.*

ROLAND   *(surprised; still in the dark)* My father?… I don't know… I really don't know. He must be dead by now… anyhow, as far as I'm concerned he's dead. He died when I was just a kid. Anyway, don't think about that anymore, it's not important, you're better off to forget it. I don't know why I even told you about it, it's stupid. Go to sleep. Close your eyes and try to sleep. I'll do the same. Good night, now.

> *Long pause. ROLAND is restless, tosses, unable to sleep. He lights a cigarette which provides the first glimmer of light in the dark room. The flashing light continues from outside the window. ROLAND smokes. From out of the near dark, we hear CHRISTINE's small voice.*

CHRISTINE   Dad.

ROLAND   Wha? You're not asleep? You scared me…. What's wrong? Are you sick again?

CHRISTINE   Am I too heav-vy f-f-fo-for you—

> *As soon as CHRISTINE starts to stutter, ROLAND abruptly turns on the bedside lamp. CHRISTINE immediately stops talking and instinctively, in a protective move, covers her face with her hands. It's an impulse that's stronger then her. He interrupts her.*

ROLAND   Wait a minute, do you stutter like that because your embarrassed? That's just what I said! That's what I always said. *(He puts out his cigarette.)* And there wasn't a single bloody specialist who'd believe me. It was too obvious to them, they wouldn't've been able to make any more money off me… when I think how we let ourselves get taken in by people like that who just take advantage of us, who'll get us to believe anything as long as it keeps us paying. It never did much good—did it—all that running back and forth to the specialists? All it did was make Mom crazy. You're still stuttering and my guess is you're gonna be stuttering for a long time to come. And to think how fast you started talking! You were making sentences when you were two—you could say anything you wanted, not a hesitation, nothing. Your mother still has the pictures! It's school that did it to you, that ruined you—they must've embarrassed you, making you stand up and talk in front of everybody, so you started to stutter…. But you shouldn't worry about it, they say it has nothing at all to do with how smart you are. A person can be really intelligent and still stutter: they say there's no connection at all. If you could just get that through your head, I'm positive you'd stop in a second—and of course right away you'd seem smarter. I'm not saying at all that you're not already—don't get me wrong—I'm just talking about how it looks. And that's what people go by. You can't expect too much from people: they gotta go by what they see and what they hear. What can you expect, we don't always have a choice in the matter. For example, like, when I have to hire somebody for the store: now I have got to have something to go on, I've got to judge the applicant somehow. And what's gonna count most? His overall appearance. For sure if he squints or stutters, if he has any little fault like that its gonna work against him. And that doesn't mean he's not a bright person, or even an intelligent person—but we have no way of knowing that and we don't have time to do a big investigation. No. When I'm hiring it's the applicant's overall appearance I go by. *(He looks at her. Pause.)* I often ask myself what I'd do if a girl like you came into the store looking for work. I thought, well, if I wasn't biased, if you weren't my daughter, or anything. Let's say I didn't know you at all. Well, right off there's your speech defect. Because, see, you came across just fine—not a beauty or anything, but we're not running a modelling agency. No, you're pretty. A little on the skinny side, but it's the style these days, what can you do. No, the only thing that would keep me from hiring you is the way you speak. Honestly, looking at it from the outside, when I take an objective view of it, it's absolutely clear that I could never hire you the way you are. I'm not saying I'd be happy about it, but the fact is you just can't plan on a job working with the public. That, well that's an opening that's closed to you just as long as you suffer from this handicap of yours. It's not for nothing that I pushed you so hard to get rid of it. It's the kind of thing that eats away at your future. And your future is important. Especially now. *(He smiles reassuringly.)* But don't you worry about that, kiddo, we'll manage to find you something—we'll just keep on looking until we do. I've got friends and contacts all over the place—even in a depression I could find you a job, just like that. You can thank your lucky stars you've got yourself a couple of responsible parents, Chris. I'm not asking for any thanks, that's not it, but just ask yourself how many young people fall into drugs because they're left on their own… well we're not quitters, we took on our responsibilities, we've done everything we could do for you, and were gonna keep on doing it even if we don't have to any more… we're not gonna turn our backs on you just 'cause you're over eighteen. We're not that cruel. There's one thing you can always count on: you can be sure that your parents will always do their duty by you—and that's pretty rare—you'll find out soon enough. No, Mom and I always had one rule: if you have kids, look after them, make sure they've got what they need. You don't have kids just to leave them in misery. Better off to forget it.

> *He stands up, takes his glass from the table, fills it in the bathroom, returns.*

Maybe it'll help me sleep, hmmm?

> *Pause. he looks at her, thoughtfully.*

Yeah… I wonder what we're gonna do with you, Chris. It's no small thing— you've got your whole life ahead of you. You've got one helluva long haul to go yet. I used to think at least that we'd prepared you to manage a little on your own. See, Chris? You see? If you'd only been willing to finish college before getting married, you wouldn't be in such a bind right now. But no, you were in such a hurry, you were in such a hurry to throw yourself into the arms of that bum. Nineteen years old is just too young to get married. Way too young. Okay maybe I waited a bit too long, but you, Chris, well, you got married too young. Too young and—sorry to have to say it—to a real moron. Okay, okay, we said we weren't gonna talk about it. I won't say another word about it. I just want to tell you one thing: don't think I'm gonna lay any blame here, but don't think that I'm gonna blame it all on him either. A couple is a couple: and if things are bad with a couple, its pretty sure there's more then one person to blame. That's all I have to say on the subject. And you can rest assured, Chris, that I'm not the one who's gonna blame you. I just hope you've learned that you can't go throwing yourself into a marriage without thinking about it, without weighing the pros and cons. I never said anything at the time because I wanted you to be free, because it was your choice, but that guy, let's just say I'd never've hired him at the store. If he'd ever come to me looking for a job, the answer'd've been: No thanks. And yet it's not that he looks bad. But I'd still've said "no." Why? With a man, you've got to be a little more suspicious, you can't judge him the same way. With a man, I put a lot of trust in my overall impression. In a way, a woman's easier to hire. The standards are more specific, they're easier to pin down. But with a man, I don't know, it's a little more complicated, it's a little harder to know. See, in all honesty, I think I'd be more likely to make a mistake with a man, a male applicant. And also I hire a lot less of them. I'd be more inclined to be more suspicious with a guy. With a woman I know right away what I'm dealing with, if she's a featherbrain or not; I know right away if I can get her to toe the line—if I'll have control over my staff. But before you even start, it's harder with a man. Harder to size up. First of all they're gonna recognize your authority a lot less, they tend to want to impress you, to show off what they can do right in front of you. Well, that kind of stuff puts me right off. I'd rather have someone who doesn't let on how well they know the job before they do it. I'd rather see a little humility I mean. Not lying and finagling just to get the job. I've got an incredible talent, a nose for people like that, the liars and the fakes. I swear to you there's not too many of them that ever got in at the store. And if there are any there now, it just shows you they weren't the kind of liars they thought they were. *(He knocks back the last of his drink.)* One last little one and then we'll get some sleep. I won't offer you one, hmmm, all right?

> *He goes to the bathroom to fill up his glass and returns. CHRISTINE lights a cigarette nervously.*

Don't worry, hmmm, I know just where I'm at with it. I'll admit that I've had a little more then usual tonight; but you'll never see me blind drunk, don't worry.

He sits on the edge of his bed, facing her. The only indication of his advancing state might be a slight slowing down in the flow of his speech, emphasizing certain words and concepts, and in his even greater candour.

Let's just say it makes me a little more open… and I'd rather be talking to you than to Mom. With you at least I know I'm not gonna hear about any of it later. You're not about to drag up what I've said and use it as evidence against me a month from now. No, with you its almost like you never heard a word. Mom's a good woman, but she manages to finally squeeze a confession out of me, you know she's gonna make the most of it for one helluva long time to come. I don't know why she does it. You'd think she enjoyed it, you'd think she needed something to feel guilty about. Almost like she needed to keep feeding the guilt, to keep it going. Not me. Guilt, regrets—I don't know what they are. I got no use for them. I leave that to Mom. *(Pause. He laughs softly.)* The last little while, I don't know what's wrong with her, she's always going on about sex. She got it into her head that I'm not getting enough of it, that she hadn't been a good wife to me, that I could have just as easily seen others, all sorts of bullshit like that. It must be her time of life that's got her talking like that…. Because there's certainly nothing I've said or done to make her talk like that…. You know that, ah… after you… Mom couldn't have any more children. Anyhow the doctor said it was best not to. Well, I could understand that, so from that moment on… we… ah… we never touched any of that again. I won't say I didn't think about it from time to time, but it's been a while since it's crossed my mind. Well, I have to admit, I'm over fifty… but I'll tell you it's more interesting up here. *(taps his head)* You know what I think. I think people have no imagination. We don't need sex all that much in life. I mean real sex, like, actually touching, and all. I guess I'm a pure spirit that way. I like to think about it a lot: for sure, I have lots of ideas, but I'd never actually touch that sort of thing. I don't understand a man paying a woman to sleep with her. Not me. I'd just like to watch her: I'd watch her walking around, doing whatever she does, and I'd keep her inside my head and, for the rest, well that's nobody's business but mine. I have a lot of respect for women. I'm certainly not the kind of man who'd ever touch them. No, I'd be more the protector-type. I just don't like women being touched, it doesn't matter how, I just don't like it. And I gotta say that I don't like being touched either. No, I'd sooner look, dream about it, like they say—I'll never go any further than that. Another kind of control, I guess. *(pause)* It's funny, you know, there's this young girl at the store, real young, looks like a real baby—I used to like watching her fold sweaters at her counter. She had a beautiful way of moving, a very special quality… I'd think about it a lot. Well, she got the idea that I was interested in her. And she started to act nice to me, always wanting to smile at me and all. Well that was the end of it. She ruined it for me. There was nothing to do about it. It just didn't work anymore. She'd spoiled my picture of her. It was like she'd lost… well, what you'd call her innocence. Like in that movie, "Bilitis." Well I'd never seen anything that beautiful. I'd never've touched them either. Everything I like to look at was in that movie…. Those pictures turned over and over in my mind for one helluva long time. If you know what I mean. *(Pause. He laughs, embarrassed.)* It's a lucky thing your father isn't a skirt chaser, or a womanizer or anything or I'd've probably told you all about it tonight. No fear. I can even tell you about my sex life: no sweat as they say, nothing there, to shock a girl of twenty. *(He chews on a cigarette.)* Oh, I'd love a cigarette now. I'm gonna tell you something, Chris. I'm gonna pay you a compliment. And it's not just because I've gone over my limit, oh no. I'm telling you because I think it'll give you a little encouragement, because you need to hear it after what's just happened to you.

In a very sensual tone: troubling and not at all fatherly.

I always have this picture of you in my head, the way you were when you were ten, eleven. You wouldn't believe how beautiful you were at that age. It's hard to believe but I'd never get tired of looking at you. Your hair was blonder, much fairer then it is now; hardly brown at all, and curly, a real little angel face. And you were just starting to develop… you were an early bloomer that way. You grew up all at once. Overnight you had a long fine neck, and your lovely little head with your almost blonde hair, and your serious little look, and your little breasts that were just starting to bud… I'd never seen anything more beautiful. Yeah. One morning I said to Mom that you were already a beautiful young lady. I couldn't believe that you came from Mom. I couldn't believe that every day at home, in my own house, there was such a beauty for me to look at. You never realized it, but I used to look at you… that was way before I saw that film "Bilitis", well, you were my first "Bilitis." I was never so proud of you. In those days I wouldn't have traded you for a boy for anything in the world. You could've asked me for anything, you'd've had it. Lucky for me you didn't suspect the slightest thing, eh, or you could've really cleaned up. Yeah the year you were eleven—that's still what I think of when I think of you. My beautiful little eleven-year-old daughter. I never wanted time to pass. I never wanted anything to change. I would've just kept watching you like that, not saying anything, not touching, just seeing you like that was all I needed to be happy and I was. Mom was so happy that I was paying attention to you, that I was proud of you. None could've been prouder. A little angel, a little angel, pure and untouched, that's just what you were, Chris. *(pause, bitter)* That's just what you were until you fell sick and got as skinny as you did. Christ, you put one helluva scare into us. We came pretty close to thinking we were going to lose you. Skinny… talk about skinny… and stubborn and mean: never wanting to eat anything Mom made, sulking, and hiding in your room all the time, and throwing up like just now… you never got that beautiful again, I never saw my girl again, my own little girl, my innocent little angel, my untouched Chris. You were just sick too long. It was such a long time before you were all right… but at least you got your health back I guess, not real strong, but healthy. You'd lost your little girl look. That's for sure, hmmm… *(pause)* when you got out of the hospital, when I saw you again back at home—I can tell you now that you're okay—I couldn't look at you. I just couldn't, that's the truth. It was stronger than me. You looked like those pictures they used to show at the time, of Biafra, you know? And your eyes, your eyes seemed to take up your whole face…. I don't know. There's no way to say… they were eyes… like old people's eyes, no, uh… terrible eyes. I just couldn't look at you, I just couldn't bring myself, it made me feel sick. I'd be remembering you at eleven and I'd see you there, at fifteen… I'm not kidding. You'd think they'd beaten you at the hospital. You look better now than you did then just to give you some idea. No, I'll never forget it. It's like they took away my dream, took away my little girl. And the specialist said we didn't love you enough. If I didn't love you enough. I'd like to know what they think is enough. I'd like someone to come here and explain right to my face, what's enough, just exactly what love is… if I loved you… I nearly went crazy with all that business with your eyes and your sickness, and the way you came back and all. For Mom, it was while you were sick that she almost went crazy. But for me, nobody knew about it, it was after, when you came back, when you weren't you anymore. Then… if anything could've made me fall into the drink, that would've been it. It's like I couldn't get over the disappointment. I just couldn't get over it. *(pause)* Not like the other one. You see how crazy the world is: there are only two things, only two real disappointments I ever had that could've really been dangerous to me and both times I lost something. The first time was when Mom lost my boy. She was five months pregnant and she had a miscarriage. We don't know why— a question of constitution, they said. I always said Mom shouldn't have been squeezing herself into those girdles. Of course she was bigger when she was pregnant but that's only normal, isn't it? Anyhow, I lost my little boy. He was called Christopher, we had him baptized and buried. It wasn't usually done but it was important to me. He was my son. The doctors said they couldn't be sure of the sex, but I could, it'd been five months that I'd been waiting for that child, and I knew he was a boy. The first, the oldest. It seems to me that I'd've been able to handle him, to talk to him, man to man, to make something of him, to build a future for him… but no. A year later you came. We named you Christine after him, and in spite of everything, we loved you. And there isn't a damn specialist anywhere who's is gonna tell me any different. I remember you at eleven, and I'm filled with tenderness all over again for the little girl you used to be. It's not something I was always telling you, for sure, I didn't go around announcing my love, but I'd look at you and you couldn't not feel that I loved you. Then I lost my beautiful girl too. All I ever dreamed of two things in my whole life: my little boy and my little eleven-year-old girl. Well, you see, both times I was so disappointed that I nearly fell to drinking. But I ended up understanding. I understood that it's better not to dream. Count your blessings and be thankful for what you've got.

> Pause. He looks at her, discouraged, tired.

And I have a big girl now, eh Chris? And, you see, I never let you down. You never even had to call me—I just came to you. You can count on me. I'll never let you live with anyone who pushes you around, anybody who hurts you. You should learn how to defend yourself a little bit, not just give in. 'Cause, see, I might not always be there to take care of you, eh kiddo. But, we'll talk about that tomorrow in the car. We gotta lie down and get some sleep now. You okay? Not sick?

She shakes her head slowly. He doesn't see her.

Anyhow, the little bit you ate shouldn't keep you throwing up all night, hmmm? That's all done with, lie down and get some sleep, hmm? Good night.

CHRISTINE rocks herself, moaning, rocking herself harder and harder until she falls forward onto her knees. She then stands up and goes to the bathroom.

The bathroom door is ajar. There's a large mirror on the outside of the door. CHRISTINE looks at herself in the mirror, attentively, without moving. She stands before her reflection. Then she reaches for the doorknob, pulls it toward her, repeatedly slamming her face against the mirror. Harder and harder. Crying and almost mesmerized by the regular rhythm and her overwhelming despair.

ROLAND wakes up with a start.

What—what's—Chris! Are you sick?

He gets up and realizes what CHRISTINE is doing.

Are you crazy? Are you out of your mind?!

He grabs her roughly and pulls her into the room.

What the hell's got into you to make you do such a stupid thing? What's wrong with you? Haven't you had enough? 'S that it? He didn't beat you enough? You need more? You want more? Am I gonna have to lock you up to straighten you out? Am I gonna have to lock you away? Christ-all-bloody-mighty!

He slams the bathroom door. CHRISTINE is standing at the door, in terror. Furious, he tries to get a hold of himself. He can hardly look at her.

Listen to me Chris… I'm ready to believe you've been through some pretty rough times… and I'm ready to understand that you're tired and you're hurt and that you're maybe feeling bad about leaving your husband, even if he did treat you bad—I'm ready to be as understanding as you like… but you're gonna have to understand that I can't be watching you every second. You're not two years old anymore. And we're not, we're not real young anymore… you're gonna maybe have to take care of Mom more than you think. She's not at all well. She's not gonna be able to handle a girl who pulls stunts like this, that's for sure. And who spends the whole day throwing up. You can keep sucking away at us for just so long without giving anything back, Chris. You're just gonna have to grow up a little—otherwise I don't know what we're gonna do with you. We're not just gonna let you stay home, making a racket and dirtying the place up… Mom just can't handle it anymore. And I'm not sure I can take it either. Okay? Do we understand each other now? You're gonna have to be responsible, and show a little consideration 'cause we're just too old for this. Now be a good girl, and try to understand.

> *CHRISTINE starts slamming her head again, backwards this time, against the wall or door. She closes her eyes and slams, slams, as if trying to make her head and the pain explode. Her father rushes at her, grabbing her roughly to pull her away from the wall. Then, in a rush, he gets his suitcase, his coat from the closet and grabs her by the arm.*

Let's go, c'mon, we're going.

> *She pulls her arm away and backs off.*

CHRISTINE   No!

ROLAND   I said: we're going!

> *CHRISTINE is in terror. She backs away again towards the bathroom. She shakes her head rhythmically and repeats with each shake:*

CHRISTINE   No… no… no…

ROLAND   *(beside himself, screaming)* I'm not taking you to the nut house, I'm taking you home. Do you understand? HOME!

CHRISTINE   *(wild with terror, she screams too now)* N-O-O-O!

ROLAND   Jesus bloody Christ! That's enough!

> *He drops his bag and his coat, and strides over to her, utterly determined. CHRISTINE backs into the bathroom and closes the door. He rushes for the doorknob and shakes the door violently.*

Out here! Right now! Out! Or I'll break it down!

> *He shakes the doorknob and in one swift move opens the door. Immediately we hear the sound of a bottle being broken against the sink. ROLAND freezes, stunned. He backs into the room!*

Don't touch that… don't touch that… don't touch.

> *CHRISTINE comes out of the bathroom weeping, the broken gin bottle in her hands. She holds it as a weapon but we can't tell whether it's meant to be used offensively or against herself. She keeps her father at a distance. She murmurs through her tears, all the while shaking her head, no, as if overcome by the horror.*

CHRISTINE   I don't want to kill myself…. I don't want to kill myself…. I don't want to kill myself…

> *As if she were trying to find a way out of a dilemma by repeating these words. ROLAND, seeing her motionless, approaches her very cautiously.*

He holds out his hand to her and speaks softly, as if to a madwoman… he is very frightened.

ROLAND   Give, Chris… give it to Daddy… give it to Daddy… be a good girl.

Abruptly, she looks at him and slashes his arm with the bottle, missing his hand. She throws herself at him and cuts his eyes with a terrible force. They fall between the two beds, she on top of him. She lashes out, relentlessly, drawing back her arm after each blow, as if gathering strength from the building momentum. With each blow from the first to the last she shouts:

CHRISTINE   You want to kill me… you want to kill me… you want to kill me….

At the end of her strength, she propels herself away from him, still crying, her hands full of blood.

Lights fade down and out.

The end.

Marie-Antoine, Opus One
(Marie-Antoine, Opus 1)

by Lise Vaillancourt

translated by Jill MacDougall

Introduction to
Marie-Antoine, Opus One (Marie-Antoine, Opus 1 [1])
by Lise Vaillancourt
Introduced by Louise H. Forsyth

Marie-Antoine, Opus One is a play in two acts with eleven characters and choruses of mice and schoolgirls. As Vaillancourt has said, tongue in cheek, in her "Preliminary Remarks" and on the back cover of the published text, the play is a "neo-baroque tragi-comedy" and "a great opera of words." Those are her production instructions. *Marie-Antoine* is a celebration of creativity of all kinds, a celebration of life as a work of art—when vision and dreams triumph over stifling social convention. *Marie-Antoine* is a play about life as theatre. It provides a child's-eye-view on society as a strange stage constructed by adults, whereon they are players. While sometimes society's spectacles are delightful, the scripted daily routines of established, patriarchal society most often strangle the imagination. The play dramatizes the ways in which children's spontaneity is crushed while they are being trained and conditioned to take their place on their parents' formula-ridden stage. The young heroine, Marie-Antoine, does her best to remain aloof from her parents' clutches of conformity. The play's *neo-baroque* proliferation of disconnected objects, words and events resonates with her capacity for dazzling flights of play, imagination, fantasy, and onirism. Its subversion of the logic of much of what happens in the real world challenges not only social norms, but also the conventions that underlie theatrical practice in characterization, story development, and stage design. Its innovative performativity and theatricality upset received assumptions about the presumed meaning of meaningless discursive formulae. This *opera of words* has characters thoughtlessly spouting words—whether as seriously offered speeches or as parodies of musical forms such as nursery rhymes or oratorios—the insignificance of which is thus highlighted as being nothing but words! words! words!: "Once upon a nya, nya nya nya." [2] Along with the characters in the play, readers and spectators of *Marie-Antoine* are faced with the task of making sense of the formulaic words that they are hearing and that reproduce what one hears and sees regularly in the sounds, images and forms of mainstream culture.

In addition to being a wonderfully entertaining theatrical experience, *Marie-Antoine* is a subtly, yet powerfully, ironic portrait of today's society: its sexism, materialism, class inequalities, unimaginative cultural practices, and insensitivity to the needs of others.

If you wish to produce this play you must let your imagination run wild. The obviously ridiculous nature of human follies is the target of enormous laughter. The play is a festival of fantasy and untrammeled flights of madness. What might seem impossible in real life can be made possible on stage. The more incongruous the juxtapositions the better. Despite, or perhaps because of, its serious intentions, the play is an opportunity to create an enormous spoof of many theatrical and cultural conventions that seem to endure for no reason other than that that's the way things have always been done and said.

Marie-Antoine is a little girl who lives with her father, mother and maid in Saint-Blaise at the turn of the 20th century. It is her first week at school. The family goes to dinner together, carries out other daily events, and receives a series of visitors: an opera singer, a prima ballerina, the mayor's wife and her daughter, the school teacher, and the school principal. The words and actions (and even the props in the case of the maid) of all the secondary characters, however kind and amiable they are intended, contain dangerous threats of violence of which they are unaware, but by which Marie-Antoine is repelled. Marie-Antoine says nothing to the other characters through most of the play. The audience knows what she is thinking, however, through the enigmatic remarks she makes to no one in particular that none of the other characters hear. She seems to be unable to find her place in either the family or its discursive universe.

Marie-Antoine wanders through the play with her pet hen on a leash, accompanied on stage by her pale double, Lea, seen by no one but the audience until the end of the play, when the girls meet. Lea compares Marie-Antoine to Cinderella who is rescued from high society by musical mice of the forest. After she leaves the ball, the mice save her from the dreadful fate of the standard romance with the prince and his family (26–27). Later recognized by Marie-Antoine as being present and having the right to speak, Lea is finally transformed into the leading character, director and ring mistress with total control of the show. Lea may be the other part of herself that Marie-Antoine needs to determine her own identity for herself or she may be an agent of insertion for Marie-Antoine into the roles, discourse and practices of a pretentious yet meaningless world. Nothing is resolved in the end. The only apparent truth arising out of this wonderfully entertaining event derives from the recognition of the inescapable aesthetics, performativity and theatricality of all human affairs: "All the world's a stage." Each person must choose not only a role and a place, but also a vision of their own constructed reality.

The dynamics of this family, patriarchal in the extreme and entirely closed to the play of children, are established from the beginning with the family gathering for its regular, ceremonial evening meal. The father, a baron, playwright, and actor, begins the table conversation by talking about the many events during the day that have highlighted his grandeur and importance: "I have not stopped multiplying myself. Soon the whole planet will become too small to contain me. I will abound in every direction and I will be multitudes to congratulate me." [3] The mother, suitably impressed, has dutifully looked after the family's social obligations. The father's vaunting self-congratulatory statement is immediately followed by words that he tosses at Marie-Antoine to keep her silently in her place and deny her being as a child, the only kind of words he seems to be able to say to her: " Marie-Antoine, don't put your finger in your mouth." [4] In this way, Vaillancourt has situated him as the antithesis of the play's basic principle of celebration of child-like fantasy and imagination. Before the end of the play it becomes clear that the father's rejection of

Marie-Antoine as a female child seeking her own freedom and identity can be dangerous for her, can, indeed, turn to violence.

Marie-Antoine passes into the care of the bizarre, strangely Slavic maid, Jvorx, whose kind care is mitigated by her frightening stories and the violent action of using her big knife to cut off the head of a hen. The arrival of opera singer Jva Nel, who compares herself to a giant lizard, a whale and other large creatures in nature, while singing her oratorio of tribute to her mother and of lament for her state of exile, provides amusing evidence of the pretentious emptiness of high musical forms. Her dramatic and unexplained exit is immediately followed, in contrast, by Carl Orff's "Carmina Burana," music written for children and recognized for its power to stir their imagination, not repress it, and to awaken their sensitivity to music. It is music in *Marie-Antoine*, whether that of Orff or the Baroness playing the piano in a dream sequence, that conveys the longing for a life richly, fully and authentically lived. The play stirs a sense of nostalgia for such inaccessible music, like Jva Nel's oratorio, which she describes as "a familiar melody whose words are forgotten." (23)

An introduction to Marie-Antoine's new school is followed by a caricatured visit for afternoon tea by the snobbish wife of the mayor, a socially ambitious woman firmly entrenched in her patriarchal position. She is the stupidly adoring aunt of Marie-Antoine's father. She has her adolescent daughter in tow in order to show off the extravagant clothes she has just purchased for her to impress the boys. In contrast to the adult women who are grotesquely hidebound in their conformity to standard behaviour, the girls have a good time amusing themselves at their mothers' expense. The abrupt termination of the visit from the mayor's wife and daughter leads immediately to a quite long scene during which Marie-Antoine's mother tries to get close to her daughter. She invents games and tells fabulous fairy-tale-like stories that she hopes will please Marie-Antoine, draw her into action, and provoke her to respond verbally. But the mother's games and stories are dreadfully frightening and violent. Marie-Antoine remains mute and immobile. Her mother collapses alternatively into anger and sad despair, which is where the eccentric dancer Vera Crystal finds her. Sympathizing with the weeping mother and not understanding Marie-Antoine's needs, Vera Crystal gives her a lecture on her duty to love and be grateful to her parents, uttering as she goes the memorable sentence: "You have no right not to love her. She is your mother."[5] In the eyes of Vera Crystal and all the other members of this society, including the maid Jvorx, respect and affection for mothers and fathers is not a matter of spontaneity. It is a matter of duty, and it is always required, regardless of particular family circumstances. Marie-Antoine remains unmoved by such an imperative as long as Vera Crystal is there. Yet in the short monologue immediately following she acknowledges to herself that her heart has been hard and death-dealing, and she expresses her longing for an intimate relation with a mother who loves her and laughs with her: "Let me be your cheeky lover. I want to feel the laughter in your weeping cheek."[6] A scene of heavy, yet entirely phony drama played by the father is succeeded by a short scene stage-managed by Lea, trying to clear the stage, get the scenes in order, and calling for music by Orff.

The second act offers a striking scene that contrasts in every way with the nostalgia of dancing to a haunting melody. It is a scene at Marie-Antoine's school where the girls have been transformed into identical dolls learning to respond in unison to all the questions they will ever need to address. In addition to these answers, the girls are being indoctrinated into having absolute respect for "a rational, organized and hierarchical order," since "[l]iberty equals death [...] madness."[7] The children are also imbibing without question the sexist message that men are the world and that women are inferior to them, with no legitimacy as creators. Their responsibility is to preserve the established dominant culture. Marie-Antoine refuses to participate in this ritual, preferring instead to echo the teacher's words, playing humorously with them:

LAURA HOPKINS: Repeat after me: ho-me-ma-ker. Start.
LEA: Fart just like me. Sesame shaker.[8]

In the final scenes Marie-Antoine and Lea meet and speak to each other, recognizing their shared love of theatre and untrammelled imagination. Lea retains her stage manager's role to the end, while Marie-Antoine delivers a final small oratorio in which she signals her separation from the phony world of her parents and her sense of connection with the things and animals of the natural world.

Notes

[1] *Marie-Antoine, Opus 1.* Montréal: Éditions Les Herbes Rouges, 1988. First production by the Théâtre Expérimental des Femmes in Montréal on October 19, 1984 at the Salle Fred-Barry, directed by Pol Pelletier, designed by Ginette Noiseux, with Lise Vaillancourt as Marie-Antoine and Suzanne Lemoine as Lea. Its first staged reading in English as *Marie-Antoine, Opus One*, translated by Jill MacDougall, was by the New Dramatists in New York in February, 1990 in a collaboration between CEAD and New Dramatists. The English script was revised in view of production at Concordia University October 2001, directed by Robert Astle. It was translated into Italian by Titti Danese and presented at the Festival Intercity in Florence in October, 1992.

[2] "Il était une fois gna, gna, gna." (*Marie-Antoine, Opus 1*: 13).

[3] "Je n'arrête pas de me multiplier. Bientôt, je serai tellement que la terre entière ne pourra plus me contenir. J'abonderai dans tous les sens de moi-même et je serai plusieurs à me féliciter." (*Marie-Antoine, Opus 1*: 16).

[4] "Marie-Antoine, ne mets pas ton doigt dans ta bouche." (*Marie-Antoine, Opus 1*: 16–17).

[5] "Vous n'avez pas le droit de ne pas l'aimer. C'est votre mère. (*Marie-Antoine, Opus 1*: 49).

[6] "Que tu sois mon amour jugal. C'est dans ta joue pleurée que je veux sentir le rire." (*Marie-Antoine, Opus 1*: 52).

[7] "La liberté égale la mort […] La liberté égale la folie. (*Marie-Antoine, Opus 1*: 62).

[8] "Répétez après moi: ménagère […] Pétez après moi. Dans les fleurs." (*Marie-Antoine, Opus 1*: 64).

Bibliographical Suggestions

Selected Other Works by Lise Vaillancourt

Les Greseaux. bande dessinée. Montréal: Éditions Lidec, 1979.

Journal d'une obsédée. Montréal: Les Herbes rouges, 1989. (fiction)

Billy Strauss. Montréal: Les Herbes rouges, 1991. First produced at L'Espace GO in April, 1990, directed by Alice Ronfard, designed by Ginette Noiseux.

Le Petit Dragon, suivi de *La Balade pour Fannie et Carcassonne*. Brussels: Éditions Lansman, 1999. First produced by Théâtre des Confettis in Québec in 1996 and 1994.

L'Été des eiders. Montréal: Leméac, 1996. (fiction)

On *Marie-Antoine, Opus 1* and Lise Vaillancourt

Ladouceur, Louise. "*Marie-Antoine, Opus 1*." *Cahiers de théâtre. Jeu.* 34 (1985.1): 131–33.

About Lise Vaillancourt

Lise Vaillancourt (born 1954 in Montréal) studied music and composition before concentrating on theatre and film at the L'Université du Québec à Montréal and L'Université Laval. She was co-director of the Théâtre Expérimental des Femmes in Montréal between 1982 and 1987 and participated in the founding of L'Espace GO. She has been Artistic Director of the Théâtre de la Ville in Longueil. Her first play *Ballade pour trois baleines*, unpublished, was produced at the Théâtre Expérimental des Femmes in November, 1982, directed by Pol Pelletier. *Martha Jenkins*, also unpublished, was directed by Louise Laprade with Pol Pelletier and produced on the same program. The following year Vaillancourt directed *Écueil de récits dramatiques* at the T.E.F. After *Marie-Antoine* she produced and published many remarkable plays, including *Billy Strauss* and plays for children, *La Balade de Fannie et Carcassonne* and *Le Petit Dragon*, for which she was short-listed for the Governor General's Award in 2000, as she had been in 1997 for the novel *L'Été des eiders*.

Marie-Antoine, Opus 1 was first produced by Théâtre experimental des femmes, Montreal, in 1984.

• • •

Marie-Antoine, Opus One had its first staged reading by CEAD, Montreal and New Dramatists, New York, in 1990. The première production was at Concordia University, Montreal, in 2001.

Characters

GIRALDINE DE COURTEPAILLE, the mother, 34
PIERRE DE MAGNANA, the father, a baron, 48
MARIE-ANTOINE DE COURTEPAILLE, their daughter, 5
LEA, Marie-Antoine's double
JVORX, the maid, 56
JVA NEL*, the opera singer, 40
VERA CRYSTAL*, the prima ballerina, 32
MADAME DELTONGRADE*, the mayor's wife, 52
IRENE*, her daughter, 15
LAURA HOPKINS*, the school teacher, 36
ROSE-ALMA MATER*, the school principal, 52
Chorus/ pupils*

*NOTE: Actors can double to fill these roles.

Preliminary Remarks

Marie-Antoine, Opus One should be performed as a great opera of words. Music is an essential element. The excerpts indicated in the script are given as suggestions.

Marie-Antoine is always accompanied by a hen on a leash and her double, Lea. Lea is unseen and unheard by all of the characters, until she is acknowledged by Marie-Antoine in the last scenes. Lea should be the replica of Marie-Antoine, dressed as she is, but in paler colours.

The action takes place in a Victorian mansion and a school room in Saint Blaise, Quebec at the beginning of the 20th century.

MARIE-ANTOINE, OPUS ONE

PROLOGUE

MARIE-ANTOINE   *(standing centre stage with her hen on a leash)* Once upon a time there was a little girl named Marie-Antoine. Her father was a baron, her grandfather was a baron, her great-grandfather was a baron, her great-great grandfather was a baron, she was the little great-great grandchild of a great-great grandfather baron, so little that she…

Or rather:
Once upon a time there was a little blue girl with red eyes, named Marie-Antoine de Courtepaille, surnamed the child-with-the-pear-shaped-head, daughter of Pierre de Magnana, baron of High Frenzy, and of Giraldine de Courtepaille, baroness of High Frenzy since she was the wife of the baron.

Or how about like this:
Once upon a nya, nya nya nya, so the big wicked wolf thought, nya nya nya nya, and the princess in the woods, nya nya, and they celebrated their wedding happily ever after, nya.

> *Pause.*

My parents brought me into the world when I was very young. My parents were a couple united by the bonds of holy matrimony.

> *LEA appears in the orchestra pit.*

ACT I

I. 1

PIERRE, GIRALDINE, MARIE-ANTOINE, LEA.

At the mansion.

In the centre there is a large staircase leading to GIRALDINE's room, stage right, and MARIE-ANTOINE's room, stage left. At the bottom of the staircase there is a gothic pillar. JVORX's kitchen, her lair, is under the stairs. The dining room and the drawing room constitute one area with armchairs, a fireplace and a piano on one side, and, on the other, a long table. There is a large empty space in the centre of the stage. A door leads off the living room area to a patio overlooking a lake. Another door leads from the dining area to a garden. The main door through which visitors enter is situated opposite the staircase.

> *It is the evening meal. PIERRE and GIRALDINE are facing each other, standing at opposite ends of the table. MARIE-ANTOINE walks to the middle of the table, ties her chicken to the leg of her chair and sits down.*

PIERRE   *(opening his mail)* Admirers sending their greetings. Old college friends who used to praise my writings and whom I haven't seen for twenty years. Ah, what a marvel, in Paris they still remember me. They wonder about me…. How is he doing now? How old could he be, that eternal adolescent? Has his hair grown darker? They seem to think, for some odd reason, that I'm no longer young. Better that than to think I am no longer. And with this baron title no one calls me by my first name any more. Ah, I have become as mysterious as the sun itself. I rather like that. True, my plays always began and ended with that same phrase: "Take me wherever you wish, I have just killed myself." *(sitting)* Dear, pass me the salt.

GIRALDINE   *(sitting down)* Was the day prosperous?

PIERRE   The butter, please. "Prosperous" is not the word for it! I have not stopped multiplying myself. Soon the whole planet will become too small to contain me. I will abound in every direction and I will be multitudes to congratulate me. Marie-Antoine, don't put your finger in your mouth. Pass the pepper. Well, Baroness, what have we done with our day?

GIRALDINE   I went to see a friend in town.

PIERRE   Do I know her?

GIRALDINE   Oh, you must have noticed her at the Deltongrade's last week. A tall woman, the one who sang "Habanera" from *Carmen*. She had come, you recall, by foot, in the rain. The hem of her muslin dress was soaked. She had taken off her shoes. She stood barefoot on the Turkish rug, with a white rabbit in her arms. At midnight she stepped out, asking one of her grooms to prepare a wooden cage with a cushion. Saying she was going to the forest to perform an ancient ritual sacrifice, she donned an immense silver cape. Then she disappeared.

PIERRE   Ah, yes. I remember. Did you have a good time together?

GIRALDINE   I beg your pardon?

PIERRE   I asked if you enjoyed yourself this afternoon?

GIRALDINE   We talked of everything and especially nothing.

PIERRE   Marie-Antoine, stop playing with your utensils, you know how noise disturbs me.

GIRALDINE   Any plans for this evening?

PIERRE   Oh, I forgot to tell you. I asked Jva Nel to drop by. She's passing through Montreal for a few days. She should be here around nine. Marie-Antoine, go tell the maid to wipe your face off.

MARIE-ANTOINE gets up and runs into the kitchen.

You know her concert tour went very well.

I. 2

JVORX, MARIE-ANTOINE, LEA.

The kitchen: JVORX's lair opens up. Smoke. Long knives, dead poultry hanging on the walls or lying on the counter. Over her black dress JVORX wears a starched white apron. Her cap has a peak jutting out, making her appear as if she has a horn in the middle of her forehead.

JVORX *(mumbling under her breath)* Crerar jirstoff makall la ma micha! Berstk vla tol bern. Zou la daltoff ke re tour. Zaki. Toloff makal la ma micha. *(in a normal voice)* And scrub! And rub! And scrub! And scour the bottom to get to the black iron, make spotless the black iron. Ahk, I did not put enough oil on it. Such a nice roast that I stuck with cloves and seasoned with crushed garlic. I took it out just in time. The *ma micha* was right, yes, always put more oil, start the fire very very high so it sears the meat, then let it simmer very, very slowly. *(She wipes her hands.)* Come Mam'zelle Antoine, climb up here on the counter and let me wash you up. So! What colour are your knees today? And your hands? Look at that, will you? You would think you had been digging all day in the ground, trying to find old bones. Lucky your father did not notice that. Ahk, such a face you make. Look at this hair, so many knots. Perhaps soon I must go in with a pair of scissors. *(She undresses MARIE-ANTOINE.)* You know, when I was a little girl, grandmother, my *ma micha*, used to comb my hair. My hair was like a bird's nest, just like yours, I do not know how many combs got stuck in the tangles. Since *ma micha* was blind besides, and I had as much hair on my head as hay in a bundle, the combs became like needles. So, she could not find them anymore. The more she lost, the harder it was. She did not dare touch me for fear of sticking herself. *(combing MARIE-ANTOINE who starts to scream)* The *ma micha* used to say she combed my hair because screaming is good for little children, to develop their lungs. *(washing MARIE-ANTOINE)* Scrub, scrub, scrub to get to the flesh. Then massage, rub her well. Then splash water on her body until she is wet down to the bones. Here, dry yourself while I prepare a little ointment for your eyes. There. Now the nightgown. Ahk, the head in bad position, there, come on, push, push the head through or you will smother in the flannel. Come on Mam'zelle Antoine, a little effort, push, da, push, here it comes, yaaa, there we are. Open your eyes now. The ointment always sticks to the eyelids, but it smells good. Stand near the stove to warm up before you go back into the living room.

JVORX takes an enormous knife and cuts the head off a chicken. Startled, MARIE-ANTOINE jumps up and runs away as fast as she can. Huge laughter from JVORX. The lair closes.

I. 3

JVORX, GIRALDINE, PIERRE, MARIE-ANTOINE, LEA, JVA NEL.

MARIE-ANTOINE runs into the dining room. She unties her hen, takes it in her arms, goes upstairs, sets the hen on the pillar, sits on the steps and stays very straight, watching her parents. She appears angry or worried. GIRALDINE is sitting in an armchair with a closed book dangling from her hand. Seated near the fireplace, PIERRE is reading his paper. MARIE-ANTOINE's gaze follows the noises in the house: the pendulum, the rustling of the baron's newspaper, the wind that whistles under the door, the baron's little cough. During this time, the light begins to fade slowly. The pendulum slows down to the same tempo. MARIE-ANTOINE merely observes. Her gaze comes to rest on her mother.

The doorbell rings. JVORX rushes by wiping her hands on her apron.

JVA NEL *(from the vestibule)* It smells wonderful here! Good evening, Jvorx.

JVORX Madame Jva Nel, it is my roast.

JVA NEL And mine is a perfume from Paris.

JVORX If you would please follow me. *(entering the drawing room and announcing)* Madame Jva Nel.

JVA NEL Pierre, darling, kiss this ancient saurian hand.

PIERRE Dearest Jva Nel, how are you?

JVORX exits.

JVA NEL Giraldine.

GIRALDINE Hello, Jva Nel.

PIERRE So, how was this tour?

JVA NEL A torrent, darling. A veritable tidal wave. *(turning to MARIE-ANTOINE)* So, Marie-Antoine, I see you have grown another step.

PIERRE I saw the New York papers. Rave reviews. America is at your feet.

JVA NEL And I am this lost continent that moves forward to accept flowers.

PIERRE It's fame and glory, divine Jva Nel, simple fame and glory.

JVA NEL But let's not talk of that anymore. This evening, I have abandoned the universe. It's too much to be thinking about day in and day out.

PIERRE Can I offer you something to drink?

GIRALDINE You look wonderful, Jva Nel.

PIERRE Some sherry? Some brandy? A delicious little liqueur?

JVA NEL It's the fresh air, love. There's nothing like the fresh air, the *aria fresca*!

JVORX   Did you ring, Monsieur?

PIERRE   Yes, Jvorx. Bring some champagne to celebrate our friend's homecoming. *(full of charm)* Would the ladies care to accompany me? Why don't I play something on the piano? What aria were you speaking of, dearest?

JVA NEL   I just got back from the shore. I walked for hours among the fluttering seagulls. And I thought about you, Giraldine. I had this incessant oratorio in my head that I would like to compose for you. It would begin like this.

JVA NEL'S ORATORIO

Partially sung and partially spoken. The lyrical and dramatic quality resembles seventeenth-century sacred opera.

Let me be that wounded animal. With my blood, leave streaks across the blond desert. I do not know why this uncontrolled flow, this escape of myself to another language, and why this quest for people to hear me. *(moving toward the audience)* People of a country that is not mine, here I am. Alone on this stage, your face inspires me, dare me to stay until I find the words to reach you. I am dying here before you. This elegance that speaks, dressed in black satin and silk, is not me. It is another, many others who are trying to say something, trying to interpret a well-known song whose words are forgotten. My mother was beautiful at a time when the rains fell without stopping. Then came the drought and her face lost its colour. No more water. Not enough. Does anyone here have some flowers, that I might taste the temperature of your country? *(pause)* My bones are covered with the skins of all the mothers who bore me. A black skin from Africa, an ochre skin from Nepal, a white skin from French lands. My hands are the remnants of the great palm-fingered saurian lizards. My ears are the size of Quaternary elephants. My right leg is that of a very great and very ancient bird that lived in the swamps of my history. You see this red foot, this long foot that dangles behind in a perpetual curtsy, that is my mother's foot, dead on the tomb that she had dug up to find her own body. I have my mother's nails, which have dug down to the heart of the earth. I have her hair, which smells of algae and wrack. And her eyes that have seen only tears all life long. I have her mouth with lips rippling continuously like the veils of the medusa. On my left foot I wear a patent leather shoe, the very one she wore when she went to the opera one evening just to hear the prima donna's finale death solo. Nomad since birth, my brow is swept by trade winds and sand storms. My brow has touched soils of marvelous, brilliant light. My brow has rubbed against others. My brow has bent over many things, over my thoughts. Today, my muscles snap like sails in high seas. My arms flap to the frantic beat of a century that never tires of goading us on. My shoulders bear the weight of all the white dawns I have awoken to. I speak only of myself, but whatever is left me belongs to others, to my ascendancy, to this race I carry on my back, that sticks to me, that will never leave. I have crossed all winds, all rains, devastated landscapes and dusts of ruin. Different lights have tinted my cheeks. I move forward on fragile grounds like a lost continent. Here, at the end of my journey, I offer you the years of silence that inhabit me. I have come to give birth to a familiar melody whose words are forgotten. I have come to sing this air like wind pushing clouds. I have come with no other baggage than these clothes, in the skins of time that are left me. From the Quaternary to today, now I wish to move in the beauty of a transformed path. Does anyone here recognize that the voice which trembles is that of a volcano erupting? Do others recognize the monsters of beauty that bore me? Swept ashore like the song of a whale, yesterday, I heard a call, a few words of this aria. I opened my eyes. I stood up. I walked all the way here. And here I am. Kiss this ancient saurian hand, Madame. I have come to make my exit. *(exiting, dramatically)* Yes, dear Madame. Fresh air, there's nothing like it.

> *JVA NEL's exit is punctuated by the music. The lights go down on the baron, standing with his back to the audience, and the baroness who has remained in her chair facing the audience.*

MARIE-ANTOINE   Once again, Jva Nel was swept away in the great airs that characterized her. I took notes in my diary. Later, I would write a short piece on our origins. Afterwards, when Jva Nel had finished singing, I started writing. The only thing I was sure of was that I loved her. Oh, how I loved her.

> *All light has faded except on MARIE-ANTOINE.*

Outside of these evening visits, there was nothing, less than nothing. That was 1912. I was five and a half and I still wasn't talking. The town was called Saint Blaise and my chicken's name was Caesar.

> *Blackout.*

I. 4

> *LEA.*

> *The twelve strokes of midnight are heard.*

LEA   *(running to the top of the stairs)* It is midnight. Cinderella must run as fast as she can before the clock strikes twelve, because if she doesn't get to her carriage and back home in time, she is lost, finished, annihilated. Her good fairy warned her. She runs so fast, her heart is so filled with anxiety, that she stumbles and falls dead of a dreadful faint at the bottom of the palace steps. She ran for nothing. On the damp ground where she lies, thousands of little mice who had watched her from a distance during the ball come to fetch her. All together, in one collective movement, they lift her body and carry her off to their grotto in the flank of the blue mountain. The prince who watched her run away a while ago has gone back to the party without giving her a second thought. The little mice carry her proudly along the path that leads to their cave, singing the ode to Cinderella that they compose as they strut along in measured time.

LEA begins to sing and invites the audience to follow. She designates certain spectators to sing a mouse or two or more, constituting the chorus of mice.

SONG OF THE LITTLE MICE

A sing-along, a cappella.

(refrain)
Fearless, fearless, we are marching through the forest,
With Cinderella in our arms.
Fearless, fearless, we've left the palace of the king,
With our song, we know no wrong.

(couplet)
The night is clear, the forests are our lands,
Along the paths where we have danced 'til dawn
Many a step, many a laugh, many a life,
We've come away, here to stay, we mice.

> *Refrain. LEA alone.*

(LEA leading two "mice.")
Along the paths where we have danced 'til dawn
We'll find the cave that will be her home.

(LEA leading all.)
And may she rest in peace!
And may she grow in peace!
And may she heal in peace!
Fulfill herself in peace!

TWO MICE   And we'll watch over her, sitting in the trees,
Watching all the people, asking silly questions.

ONE MOUSE   And by the thousands we will sing.

> *All repeat couplet.*

> *LEA runs out through the patio doors.*

I. 5

MARIE-ANTOINE.

MARIE-ANTOINE's bedroom: She is alone, sitting on her bed.

MARIE-ANTOINE   I'm lonely in my room. The walls have nothing to say, my bed doesn't fly, the door doesn't creak, the floor stays under my feet, and that's just their tough luck. The window is too high. I only see sky, the moon and the stars, only that. No horizon, no movement, no Jack or Jill tumbling down the hill. I flutter my eyelashes very quickly to tickle the tummy of the night. Not one laugh. No reaction at all. I keep my eyes closed. I'm waiting for an image, something, someone. I fall asleep, sucking my thumb. Tomorrow is my first day of school. Tomorrow, I'll leave this place.

> *A roar of thunder and then a bolt of lightning. Blackout.*

I. 6

> *ROSE-ALMA MATER, GIRALDINE, MARIE-ANTOINE, LEA.*
>
> *At the school.*
>
> *Ringing of school bell. Then rain is heard. It will continue to fall until MARIE-ANTOINE's last speech in ACT II.*
>
> *ROSE-ALMA MATER, the school principal is seated with GIRALDINE. MARIE-ANTOINE stands stiffly next to her mother. LEA is hiding under the principal's desk, chanting nursery-rhyme ditties. Throughout this scene, GIRALDINE mouths her words as if in a silent film.*

ROSE-ALMA MATER   Ah! Madame de Courtepaille! Delighted to meet you. Please have a seat. Good morning, little girl. So, today's the big day! I am Rose-Alma Mater, the school principal. And what is your name?

LEA   One potato, two potato, three potato, four,
Mama has locked the kitchen door.
Five potato, six potato, seven potato, eight
Papa's gone out the garden gate.

ROSE-ALMA   Oh, now don't be so shy. Come, tell me your name. I beg your pardon, Madame, you were saying? What! This child can't talk yet? Well, I'm sorry but we don't accept the deaf and dumb in our establishment.

LEA   And he'll huff and he'll puff
And he'll blow your house down.
The wolf and my daddy
Have come back to town.

ROSE-ALMA   …has no physiological disorder? Then what on earth is wrong with her?

LEA   Eeny, meeny, miney, moe,
On the road to Borneo,
If I holler let me go,
Eeny, meeny, miney, moe,

ROSE-ALMA   …Yes, that is hard to understand. You say she ceased speaking after the words "daddy" and "mommy"? Is she an only child?

LEA   Hey diddle, diddle, fiddliayo,
The cow jumped over the doodliayo,

Kiddlido, do, do major domo,
And add whatever you want here.

ROSE-ALMA   …Yes, yes, I see your point. I suppose if she were in contact with other children, she would begin to speak.

LEA   Mischievous marvels, free for me
Gyroscopes and isotopes
Juliar dyee meyor canal
Viler dyee jie cri
Pantometric diagnostic
Jus' leave me alone. I c'n do it all by myself.

ROSE-ALMA   …Very well then. I am willing to take her at least this year. Your husband, the baron, is a very influential man. I'll make an exception in your case.

LEA   Rub a dub dub
Three cats in a tub,
But they can't jump over the moon.

ROSE-ALMA   Well, that's done. She's enrolled in our school. We'll see what happens. She does seem to understand what's going on, don't you Marie-Antoine? You see, I've written your name down.

LEA   There are spiders and there are squeeders,
There are diapoletical washaspleeders
Sprawling on their naked stomachs.

ROSE-ALMA   …Yes, that's right, Madame de Courtepaille, I'll just show her around and introduce her to her teacher, Miss Laura Hopkins, a rare pearl, take my word for it. Simply send someone around to fetch her in an hour…. Fine. *(shaking GIRALDINE's hand)* Good day, Madame.

> *GIRALDINE exits.*

LEA   Adventuracible squirts of black mass and flat hearts.

ROSE-ALMA   Come along with me, Marie-Antoine. I'll show you our lovely school and introduce you to Miss Laura Hopkins, your teacher. *(dragging her out the door)* You'll see, she's very nice.

LEA   One, two, buckle my shoe,
Three, four…
Where'd my mother go?
What are you doing, you?

> *Blackout.*

I. 7

GIRALDINE, JVORX, MME DELTONGRADE, IRENE, MARIE-ANTOINE, LEA, PIERRE.

At the mansion.

GIRALDINE *(calling into the kitchen)* Jvorx, can I do anything to help?

JVORX Ahk, so nice to offer me help, yes, I have my hands very full. If you could help bring in the poultry. Set them on the counter, I'll take care of them later. *(They pass crates from the door to the counter.)* Emile came a while ago, at the same time as the iceman, and the priest stopped by to talk. I had no time to straighten up. I sent the gardener to fetch Mam'zelle at the school as you asked me. Ahk, they should be back already, but with this rain, it must be hard to get through. *(The doorbell rings.)* Here is the doorbell again. Are you expecting someone, Madame?

GIRALDINE No…

JVORX Excuse me if I am impatient, but if they do not stop I will never get through the day's work.

GIRALDINE Never mind, Jvorx. I'll go.

> *GIRALDINE goes to the vestibule. MME DELTONGRADE and her daughter enter suddenly. They are laden down with shopping bags and boxes of clothes.*

MME DELTONGRADE Peek-a-boo! It's me. I was just walking by the gate and I thought to myself, why not drop in and say hello to the wife of my favourite nephew. *(She kisses GIRALDINE on the cheek.)*

GIRALDINE Good afternoon, Auntie. Hello, Irene.

MME DELTONGRADE Is Jvorx off?

GIRALDINE No, she's in the kitchen. It's delivery day for the season.

MME DELTONGRADE And where is Pierre?

GIRALDINE He's been out fishing since early this morning.

MME DELTONGRADE The dear child. What an angel. He doesn't change. Even as a little boy, he would trot off with his father to fish in the very deep lakes near the very high mountains. What do you think of my hat? I designed the pattern myself, as best I could. Fashion demands daring, my dear, and I thought I might innovate. I find you very pale, Giraldine. You should get out more. Of course, with this wretched weather, it isn't easy. I've just come from the dressmaker's. Irene has grown so much over the summer that we have to change her entire wardrobe.

> *MARIE-ANTOINE enters with her hen on a leash. LEA appears at the garden doors.*

GIRALDINE   Let me take your things. May I offer you something?

MME DELTONGRADE   What might you offer me? Are you speaking of the adorable little monster who's staring at me over there? I'll just help myself to some, thanks. Come, Marie-Antoine, come kiss your dear old auntie.

     MARIE-ANTOINE doesn't budge.

GIRALDINE   *(trying to keep the situation in hand)* A cup of tea perhaps?

MME DELTONGRADE   I simply dropped by to say hello but if you insist, and only if you insist, I'll dry off a bit before I'm on my way. I'll tell you about the renovation plans I've been concocting for our town.

GIRALDINE   Wait till I give Jvorx some instructions. I'll be right back. *(She goes to the kitchen.)*

MME DELTONGRADE   *(speaking in a loud voice)* What exquisite taste! These drapes are new, aren't they? I must confess I stepped in because I was attracted by the new colours I saw in your window. These are from Italy, right?

GIRALDINE   *(returning to the drawing room)* No, from Norway.

MME DELTONGRADE   Oh, Italy or Norway, Norway or Italy, these drapes have obviously come from across the Atlantic. You can tell that at first glance. Irene, show Marie-Antoine what I bought you while I chat with Giraldine. My little girl has become so coquettish, you know. It was time to get her some new clothes. She's constantly trying on my things and admiring herself in the mirror, especially since she met the Harrington boy. I have to tell you about it. *(She pulls GIRALDINE aside.)*

     IRENE takes MARIE-ANTOINE over to the dining room table.

IRENE   I don't need to tell you that I'm bored to death whenever we go to the country house. My parents invite all kinds of people every evening for bridge, and the Harringtons bring their son to keep me company. They're planning on marrying us off, you know. Harry is, in the words of my father, a prize catch. He's going to inherit a big factory that makes ladies' undergarments. Can you imagine? If I marry him I'm likely to die smothered in his corsets. That's what I dreamt last night. He underweared me from head to toe and I died of general strangulation. This may sound absurd but it's no more absurd than this marriage idea. Besides, Harry is American. He doesn't understand a word I say. Look, I'll show you something. The latest rage in fashion. Yes, yes, that's what they call it. Rage. And this is the latest one. I've got an idea. Come here and help me. We'll have some fun. Bring the chair over near the pillar.

     She pulls a hat out of one of the boxes while MARIE-ANTOINE drags the chair over next to the pillar. IRENE steps up on the chair and then the pillar. IRENE begins a striptease for MARIE-ANTOINE. Her face contorts in a furious but silent rage as she rips off each article of clothing.

Admire my new hat. My new veil. *(Silent scream of rage as she sends her hat sailing.)* My new petticoats. *(same action)* My new bodice. *(She unhooks her dress and exposes her bodice, another scream.)* My new silk stockings. *(same action)* My new way of sitting down, of turning my head, of averting my gaze, of blushing a bit, and also my new smile for young men with a future.

> *MARIE-ANTOINE giggles.*

MME DELTONGRADE   As the mayor's wife, the restoration of the church is a project particularly dear to my heart. Gaston only speaks of sewer pipes and such, but exterior appearances are most important. I'll deal with the post office and town hall afterward. The church is in such a pitiful state, and so austere looking! The priest certainly doesn't make it more colourful. Always dressed in black with his eternal Roman collar. Yes, I suppose you'd say, as a priest, he must dress like that, but there's no reason to impose his dingy clothes and stuffy ways on an entire building. I want to make Saint Blaise into a place of renown, as famous as any other village, as famous as… well, you know those little Austrian villages that you see in history books. To do this we have to change the look of our buildings and I'm going to tackle the church first. With audacity! We are in a modern era. I will begin with the statues. I want them draped in sumptuous fabrics. That will be a change from the dreadful grey they're wearing now, all washed-out and flaking. How does that strike you? Oh, and that's not all. I've thought of planting fruit trees in the cemetery and painting the tombstones. And I'm going to offer the priest a nice silk scarf to replace his Roman collar. Rome's glory is a thing of the past, but Saint Blaise is just beginning! Gaston thinks my ideas are pure madness and that, in any case, it will take donations. But I tell him that with my artistic gifts, I will accomplish whatever I set out to do.

> *Holding a tray of tea and fruit salad, JVORX has been standing in the centre observing the scene.*

JVORX   If you allow me, Madame, I must say that your daughter would go very well in your church.

MME DELTONGRADE   *(turning around suddenly)* Irene, what on earth are you doing? What is this sudden craze for heights? Get down from there immediately. Irene, obey your mother.

IRENE   I can't get down. I feel dizzy.

JVORX   Madame, I have made some tea and some fruit salad.

MME DELTONGRADE   *(In her exasperation, she has thrown her hat off. It lands in the fruit salad.)* What ridiculous idea got into your head? Whatever prompted you to perch up there? This certainly isn't the way I raised you. *(kneeling, imploring)* Irene, I beg of you, come down immediately.

IRENE   Give me your hand. I'm scared. The pillar is moving.

MME DELTONGRADE *(extending her arm but not reaching IRENE)* Oh, darling, don't make any sudden movements, above all avoid any sudden movements.

> *PIERRE enters.*

PIERRE Ladies…

MME DELTONGRADE *(Still kneeling, she turns toward him.)* My nephew, almost my son!

PIERRE My aunt, almost my mother!

> *He goes to her, kneels, and kisses her knee, then lays over her legs, his head in her lap. Together they form a* pietà *tableau. All are frozen. Then suddenly PIERRE rises.*

I'm just rushing through. I have to go back to the lake. It's a positive orgy of fishing today. Do send my best to Uncle.

> *He exits.*

MME DELTONGRADE What an angel. So handsome. The spitting image of his father. Always away and about. Always busy.

JVORX Madame, should I serve the tea?

MME DELTONGRADE *(cutting in as GIRALDINE is about to answer)* No, Giraldine, don't bother. With all this, I'm behind schedule now. Come, Irene, just put your foot on this chair. There, now. Put your clothes on and we're off. Where is my hat?

JVORX In the fruit salad, Madame.

MME DELTONGRADE Oh, now look what you made me do. Come along. Giraldine, take good care of Pierre. I found him a bit disturbed, poor boy. *(She puts on her hat.)*

GIRALDINE Madame, remove your hat.

MME DELTONGRADE I beg your pardon?

GIRALDINE Take off that hat.

MME DELTONGRADE *(staring a moment at GIRALDINE, then briskly)* Come along, Irene.

> *They exit.*

I. 8

JVORX, GIRALDINE, MARIE-ANTOINE, LEA.

JVORX Should I take this back to the kitchen, Madame?

GIRALDINE   *(turning sharply toward MARIE-ANTOINE)* No, leave it there, Jvorx. Marie-Antoine might get hungry? Bring us some wine.

JVORX   Wine, Madame?

GIRALDINE   Yes. Some white wine, Jvorx.

> *Pause. JVORX exits.*

Did you have a nice conversation with Irene?

> *MARIE-ANTOINE picks up her hen and walks it around, plays with it and strokes it.*

At any rate, you had a good time, didn't you?

> *JVORX enters, sets a bottle of wine and two glasses on the table, and then exits.*

Why don't we play a game together? Would you like that? *(She takes an explorer's helmet from the wall.)* Here, put this on.

> *Indifferent, MARIE-ANTOINE continues to play with her hen.*

(shoving the helmet on the girl's head) There you are! *(She pours a glass of wine and drinks.)* I'll play the panting she-wolf, caught in a trap. Like this. You'll be the poacher who's come to check her traps. You're coming to kill me, all right? But just as you're about to shoot, the wolf speaks. This is what she says: "If you kill me, I will be transformed into a very little girl, and when you grow up, the little girl I've become will nest inside your hips. And try as you might to get your teeth into a slice of life, her presence will haunt you. Then one day, in spite of yourself, you will start howling at the moon, and your eyes will cloud over, until you can see nothing, until you become a she-wolf in the night. You will disappear into this deep forest and you will fall in the trap where I am now. And then, a little girl will come, a little poacher checking her traps. And then, you'll find you are face to face with your own self." *(pause)* Would you like to play the game?… Unless the story bores you.

> *MARIE-ANTOINE stands staring at her mother and, visibly shaken, stiffens. During the rest of the scene GIRALDINE takes frequent, nervous gulps of wine.*

All right, let's change the story. *(She pours a glass of wine and hands it to MARIE-ANTOINE.)* Here. This is for you. Sit down there.

> *Slowly, MARIE-ANTOINE sits at the end of the table.*

You are a blue princess with red eyes. You live in the forest. The forest is your kingdom. Take off the hat and your shoes.

> *MARIE-ANTOINE doesn't move. Violently, GIRALDINE rips off the helmet and the girl's shoes.*

You don't look wild enough, you see, with that dress. Take it off.

> *MARIE-ANTOINE doesn't move.*

Very well, leave your dress on. After all, you are a princess. Where was I? Oh, yes. One day, a day like all the others since you were born, a very tall and very handsome woman appears to you and asks to sit at your table. Impressed by her beauty, you accept. She eats *(eating some grapes)*, and she laughs *(exaggerated laughter)*, drinks *(drinking some wine)*, and speaks like this: "In my tender youth, I lived in a kingdom just like yours. One day, I decided to leave and to wander the four corners of the earth. I explored all the countries of the sun. I partook of all the feasts and I danced in all the villages I passed through. Then, tired of being in foreign lands, I returned to my kingdom. But oh, misfortune, when I arrived home, I found everything had burned to the ground. I was totally discouraged. It was then that an old woman appeared and said, 'If you go into the forest, on the other side of the mountain, you will find a kingdom exactly like the one you once owned. There lives a princess with red eyes, named the child-with-the-pear-shaped-head. Go to her and ask if you can share the kingdom with her. If she refuses or says nothing, seduce her. Then she might agree since she knows nothing of beauty or sensual pleasure.' I decided to go into the forest. I met the young princess. She looked very wild indeed. I asked her for some wine and grapes. Impressed by my great beauty, she accepted. I told her my story. She stared at me without uttering a word. There was lightning in her eyes. Lightning and fire. I approached her gently with my perfumes. I danced the dances of all countries. I seduced her as the old woman had advised me. When evening came, there near the fire, she killed me with an arrow forever." I am bored. I am bored. I am bored. *(She paces up and down like a wounded animal, goes to look out the window, suddenly sits at the piano and plays, then sends the music sheets flying.)* Take off your clothes. I have never seen you. Who are you? Where did you come from? Why such severity in that little body? Be my little monkey, my little clown. Make me laugh. Make me laugh. Make me laugh. *(She runs to her room and slams the door.)*

> *MARIE-ANTOINE opens her school bag, sits on the floor, and pulls out her books and notebooks. GIRALDINE enters again wearing a different dress and calmly sits in an armchair to read. MARIE-ANTOINE writes in her notebook. GIRALDINE suddenly leaves her book, stands quietly, moves behind her daughter, kneels, starts to touch her, stops, and then violently grabs the girl in her arms.*

Why do you refuse to speak to me?

> *MARIE-ANTOINE jumps up with a start, escaping the embrace. She runs to the safety of JVORX's lair. GIRALDINE bursts into tears.*

I. 9

VERA CRYSTAL, JVORX, GIRALDINE, MARIE-ANTOINE, LEA.

> *The doorbell rings. Muttering, JVORX hurries to open the door. VERA CRYSTAL rushes in. She is a most eccentric woman. Dressed in a cape over a tutu, she is covered with jewellery. She wears a wide-brimmed hat.*

VERA CRYSTAL   Lord, what wretched weather!

JVORX   Good afternoon, Madame Vera Crystal.

VERA CRYSTAL   Hello, Jvorx. Here I am again, unannounced, barging in like a bull in an ointment shop. Here, take these flowers and try to save them. They've been through the deluge.

JVORX   Yes, Madame.

VERA CRYSTAL   Oh, and take these too. They're presents I brought from New York for Madame. Is she here?

JVORX   Yes, but…

VERA CRYSTAL   Don't bother then. You can take them to her later.

JVORX   Yes, Madame.

VERA CRYSTAL   *(removing her hat)* My hat is all wet. See that it's dried.

JVORX   Yes, Madame.

VERA CRYSTAL   Where is my dear old friend?

JVORX   In the drawing room… but wait a minute. I will announce you.

VERA CRYSTAL   No, don't. I want to surprise her.

JVORX   Madame Vera Crystal, it is best to wait.

> *VERA enters the drawing room and finds GIRALDINE lying in the middle of the rug.*

VERA CRYSTAL   Oh, what a heart-wrenching sight. Look how I find you. Fallen on the ground, spread out like a lake. *(She picks her up.)* What tragic scenery you make. Nature has indeed gratified you. What can this end of the earth be? *(drawing GIRALDINE to her room)* Come, darling, talk to me. Tell your old childhood friend. Here. I will draw a veil of silence between the world and us.

> *She throws the corner of her cape around GIRALDINE's shoulders. Enveloped in the cape, the two women move up the staircase.*

I. 10

JVORX, MARIE-ANTOINE, LEA, VERA CRYSTAL.

JVORX   *(gathering VERA's things)* Ahk, these artists. All the same. What am I doing in such a house, loaded down like a donkey? *(noticing MARIE-ANTOINE)* So, you are here. Come with me. I have made you a bowl of soup with some nice warm bread. And go fetch your hen. It is not a good time for such an animal. Night is about to fall on our heads. Who knows what can happen at this hour? Bring her in here. She must be hungry too.

> *MARIE-ANTOINE finds her hen and follows JVORX into the kitchen.*

Here, eat now. Ahk, such a day. How is it possible to have a hard head of wood like you, a heart of stone like you and those eyes like hot iron? Why do you never speak to her, huh? Why do you keep words only for yourself, selfish girl? Such a shame, making your mother cry. Your soul must be one very dark place, Mam'zelle Antoine, blacker than my iron pots. Ahk, maybe you think I do not understand, huh? I understand you, yes, I know. I know you are plotting something with that hen. I know like I myself laid it. She thinks that if by chance you drop your bread, she is in luck and those noodles in your bowl, if by accident you throw them her way, she will have a feast tonight.

> *MARIE-ANTOINE throws her dish on the floor and runs out of the kitchen.*

Mam'zelle Antoine! Is this any way for a young lady to behave? What would your father say if he saw you?

> *MARIE-ANTOINE runs to the stairs and climbs up and down, four steps at a time.*

MARIE-ANTOINE METE RAYSAC
RETON KATEL
ZARULY ZARULY
MOORTEA NAVEL

> *These phrases are repeated rapidly, with fury and distress, until VERA CRYSTAL appears suddenly at the top of the stairs.*

VERA CRYSTAL Hey, little girl. Hey, Antoine-Marie, come here. I need to talk to you.

> *MARIE-ANTOINE runs back down the stairs and plops on the sofa. LEA follows, propping up pillows for herself and sitting with her arms extended in queenly fashion. Throughout the following sequence, MARIE-ANTOINE is still and silent. LEA is not heard by the other characters.*

LEA Come now, Vera darling. Don't stand there all agape. I pray you, sit down there between two stools and just throw away your troubles here at my feet. Revel in your frazzle, reveal your razzle-dazzle. Let's have a ball. Crystal, Crystal Ball. I want to see the world and read the future.

VERA CRYSTAL *(moving to the sofa)* But why are you always running? I thought you might escape me, but you are sitting exactly where I wanted you.

LEA Serve me a red sermon in a toreador cape. Come on. Ole-oley!

VERA CRYSTAL Antoine-Marie, I won't beat around the bush. The last time I talked to you up on the mountain, I thought you had understood. You do recall, I hope. That day you ran off into the forest and we hunted for twenty-four hours straight while your mother was dying of worry… proof enough of how much she loves you. She loves you more than herself. You are the essence of her life. And still you dare to treat her so wickedly. Why? Tell me why? Antoine-Marie, look at me.

LEA   I am looking at you, Crystal Glass.

VERA CRYSTAL   Why can't you give back some of the affection she lavishes on you? You have no right to refuse her that. You have no right not to love her. She is your mother, Antoine-Marie, your mother who gave you life, the greatest gift on earth. Because of that, you must show respect and be grateful, and even then, you will never, never do you hear, be able to pay back what she has given you. And I, better than another, can tell you… about the generosity of a mother, her tender love, her constant attention, her self-sacrifice. I, better than any other, can tell you what it means to be a mother.

LEA   Yes, Vera Crystal, you who are not one.

VERA CRYSTAL   Yes, Antoine-Marie, I who had no mother. And who suffered so because of that. You don't know how lucky you are. A warm house full of toys, all the dolls you want, good food. You have everything without even asking for it. You should respect your parents. Is that clear?

LEA   Crystal clear, Baccarat Crystal.

VERA CRYSTAL   Have you ever wondered what you might do without them? A tiny, fragile little girl with no means whatsoever, yes, alone with no parents to take care of you? Well, I'll tell you. *(Macabre music is heard. VERA CRYSTAL mimes her narrative.)* You would wander, half dead of hunger and thirst, along dark and treacherous paths, forever seeking a haven to shield you from the merciless storm, the cold and implacable world, and, after a short while, you would doubtless die, frozen or devoured by the wolves that relentlessly stalk you. I can tell you this because you are a big girl now. You must take care of your dear little mother, comfort her, protect her. *(The music rises toward a crescendo during the following.)* Yes, Vera is telling you this. Vera-goddess, Vera-star, Vera-prima-ballerina, who is acclaimed and manipulated in the hands of greedy producers, who is nourished by the letters of adoring admirers, who died two hundred and three times on the stage like a swan, and who is always, in the midst of raving mobs and exhausting tours, always alone, without a husband to lean on, without children for company, without a warm, peaceful home. Vera is alone and unhappy on the mountain peak of her glory, alone with herself and her tragic fate. Oh, solitude. Oh, misfortune. What are all these jewels compared to the smile of a child? *(The music begins to fade.)* Go, repent now. May these words have touched your wicked heart like a magic potion that filters through the darkness, soothing the wrath in that pear-shaped head of yours.

> *GIRALDINE's loud sobs are heard.*

What? Do you hear that? Is it possible? Or am I hallucinating? Do I hear Giraldine sobbing in her room? Inconsolable mother, inconsolable child. Listen, Antoine-Marie, listen to your mother's heart swelling like a… *(Abruptly, the music stops in the middle of a phrase.)* Antoine-Marie… Antoine-Marie, come back, I haven't finished…

> *MARIE-ANTOINE jumps up and runs to the door leading to the garden, slams it, and runs back to hide near the stairs. Hearing the door slam, VERA CRYSTAL lets out an "Oh, my God" and rushes out to the garden.*

> *MARIE-ANTOINE, at centre stage, launches into a sort of pow-wow, flailing her arms about as if calling for help. Spinning until dizzy, she eventually falls down. GIRALDINE's sobs are still heard.*

MARIE-ANTOINE *(alone)* When my mother cries, her dress squints, her eyelids get wrinkled, her great height falls apart and topples on to me. I stay in her shadow. I stay in the trembling waters of her shadow. It is hot and salty. My rock heart sinks me to the bottom, where white birds lie keeled over, not flying anymore. Giraldine de Courtepaille, keep me here at the bottom. If I come out, let it be in a line along your cheek. Let me be your cheeky lover. I want to feel the laughter in your weeping cheek.

> *Blackout.*

I. 11

> *PIERRE, GIRALDINE, JVORX.*

> *It is the middle of the night. The baron enters the drawing room. He is wearing a long white nightshirt that falls open over his bare torso and flows about his ankles. He is drenched by the rain. The following monologue is exalted and melodramatic.*

PIERRE *(alone in the drawing room)* Tonight I played the role of my life. I've just come from my father's theatre. *(with a little laugh)* I still have lipstick on. It tastes like raspberries. *(increasingly melodramatic)* My brother Abakanovitch was there, that emerald-green hound of my nights, come to eat my penis and to lick my invisible wounds. What a magnificent beast! Such grandeur, my brother Abakanovitch! What was I saying? My temple, my hand trembles. I have played the role of a lifetime, the one I wrote for myself when my brother had just come into the world. Abakanovitch, that's how I named him. There is a lake behind my theatre. When he was little, Abakanovitch was afraid to come at night. He preferred to romp during the day, when the sunlight ran through the ruins. I taught him the gentle wish for life, the troubling bursts of laughter. Slowly, I tamed him. Never was he a problem for me. He played marvelously; he abandoned himself completely. Our gestures were the softest and the most innocent in the world. He loved the colour of my skin. We spent many long years in that open-air theatre. I have just come from there. Oh, happy sun of my breast. One night, my breast opened and I brought you into the world. On a rainy night, me, your brother, in the ruins of our father's theatre. No others but us were alive at that moment, there on the cliffs of High Frenzy. We had the world to ourselves. I could have loved you till the end of my days, but you left our lands, you left me alone, one evening when I had brought you some flowers and delicious liqueurs. You announced that you were leaving for Vienna to study psychoanalysis. Did Freud fall in love with you? Could he have taken you under his wing? For you never returned. And then, today, after fifteen long years away, I receive this letter saying you're coming back. Since this morning, my life has been swept away in mad visions of us together. I am not certain where I am anymore, except that I am bound to this woman by the absurd ties of marriage. And that I have, who knows by what magic, a daught…. No, it's not true. It's all a dream. You're coming tomorrow. How will you find me now? Will you believe me if I tell you the woman you'll see tomorrow is dead, that she died some hundred years ago? And that the little girl is self-generated? Will you believe me, darling brother? Above all, will you recognize me? Am I still handsome enough to seduce you? Oh, brother of my rippling senses… I am ardently in wait. Take me, take me wherever you wish. I have just killed myself. Slip, as you used to not so long ago, into the warm folds of my robes. Deign to caress my naked shoulders with your divine gaze. Brother Abakanovitch, I went this night to implore your hound soul. Love me. This is the end. This night I have played the role of my life. I hear a hound howling in the theatre. A dog.

> *He collapses, sobbing.*

GIRALDINE *(from the top of the stairs)* What is that? Pierre? Pierre, is that you? What's that dog howling? Jvorx. Jvorx.

> *JVORX emerges from her lair.*

JVORX Madame, you called me?

GIRALDINE Yes, Jvorx. I heard some animal moaning. See what it is.

> *Carrying a candle, JVORX moves to the baron.*

JVORX *(calling up)* Madame, it is your husband.

GIRALDINE My husband! My husband? My husband. Thank you, Jvorx. You may go now. *(She stops midway down the stairs.)* Pierre, what's wrong?

PIERRE I am so terribly unhappy, so unhappy, if you only knew.

GIRALDINE Come to bed, dear. It's late. Very late.

PIERRE Yes, I'm coming. I was on my way.

> *PIERRE climbs the stairs to the bedroom. They exit.*
>
> *Blackout.*

I. 12

LEA.

LEA appears with a sword and a long quill pen. She is wearing mud-stained boots.

LEA   I ran all the way from garden to courtyard, from ballroom to greenroom, evicting several gallant knights along my way.

> *She sits on the edge of the stage and speaks directly to the audience.*

The story must go on and I don't know what to tell you except that my soul is restless at this hour of the night. Is it the moon in her last quarter? Is it my stomach that's been empty all day? Where does this come from, this anxious fear of never seeing dawn again? And what of this stopping of everything, waiting tensely for this outcome? I ask you. My mind jumps around and plays with imaginary lights. I am waiting. I look up. Nothing on the roofs. Only the eaves groaning. No cries on the roofs. No one calls, nor speaks, nor says anything at all. The solitude of the roofs. I will never grow up but I will reach greater heights because I have little time left. You'd better believe it. Nobody believes it but me. *(She rises.)* Hey, there, you. Yes, you. You seem to be tired of this musical instrument. Why don't you play something for me. Aw, come on, play something. Isn't the night worth it? I want to think tonight and to find something.

> *A flute is heard playing an excerpt from Carl Orff's "Uf dem Anger"* (Carmina Burana).

ACT II

II. 1

GIRALDINE, MARIE-ANTOINE, LEA, PIERRE.

At the mansion.

It is early the following morning. It is still raining, but there are occasional rays of sun. The stage is empty for a moment and then GIRALDINE appears. She seems sad and worried. She goes to the kitchen, takes some fruit and bread into the dining room, moves feverishly back and forth between the china cupboard and the table, and sets the breakfast table as best she can.

MARIE-ANTOINE comes down the stairs carrying her hen in her arms. She goes to the kitchen to find JVORX who is not there. LEA appears in MARIE-ANTOINE's room.

GIRALDINE   Jvorx left early this morning for Saint Luc to see an old friend who died. She left in a hurry, at dawn. She wanted to get a close look at death. That's life.

> *Sullen, MARIE-ANTOINE sits at the table, swings her legs, and pets her hen. GIRALDINE continues setting the table. She is trembling; her eyes fill with tears. She begins to hum a song.*

MARIE-ANTOINE   *(to herself)* That's life, that's life. Am I living or dying, damn it?

> *In a brisk gesture, she drops her hen. GIRALDINE drops her cup. PIERRE enters.*

PIERRE   Good morning, my little gazelles. And how are we today? I say that the mayor fell off his horse yesterday. That you should have been there to see. That he was so funny, sitting there in a mud hole. Ah, ha, I'm still laughing about it now! I stop laughing, sit at the table, look for my paper, shoo away that cursed chicken, put on my glasses, mumble in an absent voice that I must go to town for the day to take care of some urgent business. And how is gold trading today? And what odd sunlight we're having this morning. Where are my glasses? Ah! Ha! On my nose. Where is my napkin? Where is my fork? What is that lint on my trousers? Is the coffee ready? Ah, but you know I like it strong. Whatever are we going to do without Jvorx? My dear, you're looking very pale. I think you should go see Gerard and take Marie-Antoine along. Too frail, that child; it borders on infirmity. I can't stand sickly-looking children. Your faces are so white. Go for a walk around the house, dear. Or… I don't know. Hey, why don't I tell Gerard to stop by and see you? Ah, I feel fit as a fiddle this morning. I'm in wonderful shape. What time is it? Eight o'clock already. I've got to be off. I'll catch Emile on my way out and tell him to take Marie-Antoine to school. About tomorrow's reception, tell Jvorx that I want to see her as soon as she comes back. Rotten luck, a death just before our party. Frankly, we could have been spared that. Oh, and I forgot to tell you. I received a letter from my brother yesterday. Remember, I've told you about him. He's arriving tomorrow. Perhaps he'll get here just in time for our celebration? He'll send a telegram. I thought we might put him up for a few days, what do you say? It's been fifteen years. Perhaps you'll get his message today. Do keep me informed. I'll be back for dinner. Fine, well they're waiting for me at the stables. See you tonight, my gazelles. Blah… this coffee is cold, Giraldine, very cold.

> *He exits. GIRALDINE brushes her hand slowly across her temple, several times, staring at the doors closing behind the baron. Then she takes a cup of coffee and moves slowly to the drawing room. MARIE-ANTOINE follows discreetly, puts her hen up on the pillar, and remains hidden, watching.*

> *GIRALDINE sits at the piano.*

GIRALDINE   One day I went to the theatre to hear a pianist perform a Mozart concerto, and the curtain came up on the piano, and we heard a shot. Everyone was startled, then someone appeared on stage and, very awkwardly, announced that the pianist had been assassinated just before her entrance. Today, I am playing the same concerto with the Great Philharmonic Orchestra of Vienna. My hands slide voluptuously over the ivory keys. Intense pleasures lace the corners of my mouth. As I reach the crescendo, from my boldness and verve is born a new and totally unexpected force. I discover myself, loving, confident, and beautiful. Snow is falling on the entire orchestra, on the entire Viennese Opera, on the entire city of Vienna, offering herself, magnificent and magic. It is no longer this room, no longer even a concert hall. It is a team of four black horses galloping at incredible speed, carrying me away in the music. All the violins and the cymbals resound through the leaves of the trees. I turn my head back, in the sunny wind, in the clearing that looms at the end of the road, coming closer, arriving. My carriage stops. I get out quickly and spring lightly into the vast field where someone jumps up, opening his arms, his mind, and his heart. Then in one swift instant, everything stops. Before the end of the piece. Before the ovation, before the consummation. Is it possible that all this air is smothering me? Is it possible that all this space is paralyzing me? Farther than this house. Farther than this country. I wanted to go farther than that. I am weeping but I am no longer here, because death has come to take me. One night, very long ago, without even realizing it, I crossed over. One night I died in the company of people laughing and talking, in the company of people who laughed and talked a great deal.

> *MARIE-ANTOINE feeds her hen and then leaves for school. GIRALDINE is frozen at the piano and will remain so until the final scene of the play.*

> *Blackout.*

II. 2

LAURA HOPKINS, MARIE-ANTOINE, LEA, PUPILS.

At the school.

A deafening toll of bells. The light comes up slowly on the classroom. LAURA HOPKINS marches to her position in front of the class that is composed of four life-size dolls, which may be played by four actors. MARIE-ANTOINE arrives late. LEA appears at the back of the class.

LAURA HOPKINS   Girls…. Who discovered America and in what year? Yes, Catherine? *(The mechanical whine of a doll is heard.)* Very good. How much is one plus two? Jeanne? *(again a whine)* Good, very good. What colour is my skirt? Madeleine? *(a whine)* That's right. What is your father's profession? Isabelle? Oh, a lawyer! Very interesting. Take out your music books and turn to the first page. Let's hear your scales. *(The dolls sing, running continually up and down the scale from* do *to* sol *and back during the following speech.)* According to Rameau's laws of harmony, the diatonic scale is a musical system where all the tones are given unequal force to express human life, to give it meaning and make it bearable within a rational, organized and hierarchical order. All together please. Josephine, stay with the others. Every musical piece must end in order. This is called cadence, which is the ultimate goal of harmony, both in theory and practice. Stop! *(All the voices cease except one.)* All together class, at the same time. I said the same time, Josephine! Let's do a little arithmetic. Liberty equals death. Continual change equals the dissolution of this world. How much is one plus four? Isabelle, dear? *(a whine)* Very very good. For homework I want you to prepare a short oral composition on autumn the trees and the leaves. Poetry must be supported by an ontological hierarchy. The purpose of an ontological argument is to prove the existence of any given being solely by the analysis of its definition, for example: He is perfect therefore He exists. This is the very foundation of history. Liberty equals madness. How much is two plus four? Jeanne? *(a whine)* Fine. Open your history books to page one. Do your scales. *(The dolls begin singing their scales as before.)* Two great inventions mark the beginning of our civilization: gun powder and the printing press. Wars and books. Devastation and imagination. Man does not have to seek his place in the world. He is himself the world, as vast and unique. Here, woman must find shelter. The idealistic life cannot run the risk of spontaneity. It feeds from the works of the dead. That is solid ground. And girls, don't forget that you must acquire all this culture not for creation but for conservation. Stop! *(All the voices cease except one.)* Josephine, I told you, all together at the same time! What does your father do for a living? A farmer. Then go to the corner and repeat: " I am an ass and I want some grass." *(A doll's whine that mimics the rhythm of the phrase, but with little conviction.)* Come, come, repeat: "I am an ass and I want some grass." *(The doll's whine becomes more convincing; the phrase is repeated throughout the scene.)* To wind up, a few questions about the future. What would you like to be when you grow up? A nurse, a missionary, a seamstress, a teacher, or a homemaker? Come now. Marie-Antoine, try to answer.

> *MARIE-ANTOINE is silent.*

Come on, give it a try.

> *The girl remains silent. As usual, LEA is unheard by the rest of the characters.*

Marie-Antoine!

LEA   Laura Hopkins!

LAURA HOPKINS   Make an effort, for heaven's sake! What would you like to be when you grow up?

LEA   Mistake a forceps, rof venhey cakes! Twat dould ouy kyle ot eb nhew ouy worg pu?

LAURA HOPKINS   I can wait.

LEA   I nac taiw.

LAURA HOPKINS   Well?

LEA   Lew?

LAURA HOPKINS   Repeat after me: ho-me-ma-ker. Start.

LEA   Fart just like me. Sesame shaker.

LAURA HOPKINS   Hou-se-wi-fe.

LEA   Mou-se-li-fe.

LAURA HOPKINS *(emphatically)* Housewife! So…?

LEA   How come you get to ask all the questions?

LAURA HOPKINS   *(very loud)* I'll give you a minute to think about it.

MARIE-ANTOINE   *(to herself)* Do you understand what ties me to my mother, me to the sea, the sea to the river, the river to the well, the well to the earth, the earth to my mother, my mother to me, me to the sea?

LAURA HOPKINS   Start your scales again, class. And all together this time! *(shrilly)* Marie-Antoine, I order you to answer!

> *All—except MARIE-ANTOINE who remains silent and JOSEPHINE who chants "ass… grass"—repeat their scales.*

LEA   Stand up.

> *The scales become higher pitched.*

LAURA HOPKINS   Keep repeating, Josephine.

LEA   Stand up.

LAURA HOPKINS   "I am an ass and I want some grass."

MARIE-ANTOINE   Stand up.

LAURA HOPKINS   Come on girls, all together.

LEA   Stand up.

LAURA HOPKINS   What do you, Marie-Antoine, want to be when you grow up?

> *The scales and JOSEPHINE's lamentation reach a simultaneous climax.*

LEA & MARIE-ANTOINE   *(together)* Stand up on the chair, stand up on the desk, stand up right in the middle of the room, stand in front of the blackboard, stand in the corner. *(They run to the staircase in the mansion.)* Stand up on the first step, march up to the third step, march to the Fifth Symphony by Beethoven, stand up on the tablecloth and play the conductor. *(MARIE-ANTOINE runs to the table.)* Stand up and march!

II. 3

> *PIERRE, MARIE-ANTOINE, LEA, JVORX, GIRALDINE.*
>
> *At the mansion.*
>
> *MARIE-ANTOINE has climbed on the table and is marching to the beat of Beethoven's "Fifth Symphony." Immobile, GIRALDINE is still sitting at the piano. LEA observes the following scene from the top of the stairs.*

PIERRE   *(rushing in suddenly)* Marie-Antoine, sit down! *(screaming)* My God, this child is intolerable. Giraldine, what have you done with your daughter? Haven't you raised her? Marie-Antoine, for the last time, sit down!

> *MARIE-ANTOINE plops down suddenly on the table.*

Ah ha! Her footprints on the tablecloth. Jvorx. Jvorx!

> *JVORX comes rushing in.*

Jvorx, take her away and shut her up in her room. Double lock the door. I don't want to see her again. From now on, she will eat alone and you will check her homework. Hurry up, get her out of my sight.

> *JVORX tries to take the girl in her arms, but MARIE-ANTOINE struggles.*

So, you don't want to answer Laura Hopkins's questions, heh? You persist in your little pig-headed game. We'll see which of us is more pig-headed. I'm sick of your capricious silence. I will teach you to behave with thrashings, with the whip, with whipped cream pies, with blank bullets and no sugar on the strawberries. Go on, take her away.

JVORX tries to pick her up again, but MARIE-ANTOINE escapes her. The girl jumps off the table and stands, arms akimbo, confronting her father.

What a disgrace! I am leaving!

MARIE-ANTOINE and JVORX follow the baron's exit with their gaze. Then JVORX drags MARIE-ANTOINE to her room.

Blackout.

II. 4

MARIE-ANTOINE, LEA.

Lights rise on MARIE-ANTOINE's room. She has set up five dolls in front of her and uses the bed as a stage. LEA is hiding under the bed.

MARIE-ANTOINE   *(speaking to the dolls)* We're going to play mother. I'll be the big girl, and you'll be my little mothers. The first one who cries gets a kick in the shins. *(to one of the dolls)* You there, Sleeping Beauty, you're going to wake up and stay standing for a hundred years. *(shaking the doll)* Come on. Wake up. Come on.

LEA, holding one hand to her brow, her eyes closed, emerges from under the bed. Her voice is high-pitched and resembles that of a Punch and Judy character.

LEA   Where am I? What am I doing? Do I hear a voice? What is it saying?

MARIE-ANTOINE   *(amazed)* It's you! Sleeping Beauty! *(She begins shaking LEA.)* Wake up. Wake up.

LEA   Why would I wake up, sweetheart? Look, I can do a lot of things with my eyes closed. I can stand up, sit in front of the mirror, comb my hair, put on lipstick, dress, undress…

MARIE-ANTOINE   If you keep this up, I'm going to sock you in the nose.

LEA   Oh, I feel weak again. I'd best go back to sleep.

MARIE-ANTOINE   No, I want you to wake up.

LEA   Then you must kiss me. It is the only way to wake me, you know.

Irritated, MARIE-ANTOINE obliges by kissing her quickly on the forehead.

(offended) That's a girl peck. It has absolutely no effect.

MARIE-ANTOINE   I'm not your Prince Charming.

LEA   Kiss me again. Perhaps I'll wake up this time… unless I change into a frog. *(She offers her mouth to MARIE-ANTOINE who kisses her.)* Oh… ah… wha… where… where am I? Who are you?

MARIE-ANTOINE   I am Marie-Antoine de Courtepaille and you are in my house. And here are my mothers: Cinderella, Snow White, Fountain of Youth, and Skin-of-a-Thousand-Animals.

LEA   Pleased to meet you. Oh, that little speech made me tired. I think I'll go back to bed.

MARIE-ANTOINE   No, sit down here. *(seating her with the dolls)*

LEA   Kiss me.

MARIE-ANTOINE   We're not here to play romance.

LEA   Then what are we playing?

MARIE-ANTOINE   Theatre.

LEA   *(excited)* First rate! I adore the theatre. *(posing on the bed)* Like this? How do I look? Am I catching the light? Perhaps I need more makeup?

MARIE-ANTOINE   *(reseating her with the dolls)* You are not an actress. You are the audience.

LEA   Then where are they? Where are your actresses?

MARIE-ANTOINE   There will be neither actresses nor actors. I will perform alone.

LEA   Very well then, I am leaving. I prefer romance to this sort of theatre. What do you say, Cinderella? How about you, Fountain? Wouldn't we be better off in a good café, sitting around a bottle of wine, laughing and talking?

MARIE-ANTOINE   *(furiously)* Stay where you are!

LEA   Oh, very well, since you insist, I'll stay.

> *MARIE-ANTOINE is setting up a puppet theatre.*

Oh, look. A tiny little theatre. Isn't that charming? Don't you think it's charming, Snow White? That is your name, isn't it? Delighted to meet you.

> *MARIE-ANTOINE announces the curtain with three knocks.*

Oh, the curtain is going up!

MARIE-ANTOINE   Over here is a baron. And here is a baroness.

> *The following is spoken in a loud voice like a child reciting.*

Go, baron,
Go to your dressing room,
You can take off your makeup now.
No use, I don't believe you anymore.

Go, baroness,
Go to unite in the bonds of holy matrimony
With your husband, and weep.
No use, I don't give a damn anymore.
Go play the props,
That would suit you much better.
I do not despise you.
I wish you no harm.
I do not wish your house to burn.
I do not want to give you a thrashing.
I simply do not love you, and that's all there is to it.

LEA   Bravo! What a beautiful play. Would you like to change roles now? You will play Sleeping Beauty so lie down. *(She puts MARIE-ANTOINE to bed and tucks her in.)* In the meantime, I'm going to chat with these ladies.

> *MARIE-ANTOINE falls asleep.*

Ah, wasn't it a lovely evening? Let's drink to the occasion. I just happen to have a bottle of Puys de Vauchy on me, vintage 1809, that I stole from… uh, no, that I took…. Never mind. What does it matter? Let's raise our glasses to a lovely evening and to the future…. No, that's a little vague, don't you think? Oh, I've got it. Let's drink to our questions about the future. That's more precise. Cheers! Dear friends, do you think it is possible to change the course of our lives, our destiny? What is this inertia that keeps us nailed to our seats? How far could we go? And what did you want to be when you were little? Fountain of Youth? But Fountain… you're crying? *(The dolls cry out and intone musical scales in unison.)* Fountain, darling, what is it? What's wrong with you? What's wrong…?

> *The music and the wails rise. LEA runs away. MARIE-ANTOINE wakes up abruptly.*

II. 5

LAURA HOPKINS, MARIE-ANTOINE, LEA, PUPILS.

At school and at the mansion.

The music and the crying stop suddenly. Lights come up on the entire space, erasing the boundaries. MARIE-ANTOINE is sitting in her bed as if she were sitting at her desk.

LAURA HOPKINS   It is forbidden to speak or open your desks. You have half an hour to fill up the page. The first one who breaks the rules will be sent out. I have warned you.

MARIE-ANTOINE   I am looking at the world upside-down. I see pairs of feet stomping the floor, getting impatient, twisting, rubbing against each other. It smells like burned erasers. Josephine is short of breath. Catherine has eaten her pencil. Isabelle is finishing off her eraser. We are having a test.

LAURA HOPKINS   Josephine, keep your eyes on your paper. Don't look at your neighbour, I have warned you.

MARIE-ANTOINE   Far away, ideas drift towards me like the arms of hula dancers wearing multicoloured veils. My clenched fists are black. My wide-open eyes are red.

LAURA HOPKINS   Jeanne, why did you drop your eraser on the floor? To pick it up and catch a glimpse of your neighbour's paper, heh? I have warned you.

MARIE-ANTOINE   The ideas come closer; they are here. They have arrived from the ocean. Their lips are moving, but I can't hear what they're saying, like you hear the light, but you can't hear the mountain. Wind blows through my head. I open up.

LAURA HOPKINS   Just two more minutes.

MARIE-ANTOINE   Silence.

LAURA HOPKINS   One more minute.

MARIE-ANTOINE   Words.

LAURA HOPKINS   Pass your papers to the front of the row.

MARIE-ANTOINE   My paper is blank.

LAURA HOPKINS   Take out your reading books.

MARIE-ANTOINE   Inside my desk there's a duck pond. All my pencils float about like rotten wood. My reading book is a mess.

LAURA HOPKINS   Open your books to page one.

She freezes. There is a sudden gust of wind that makes her hair fly about as if electrified.

II. 6

MARIE-ANTOINE, LEA.

"Tanz" from Carmina Burana *is heard. LEA gallops across the stage as if she were riding a horse through the classroom. Until she notices and acknowledges LEA, MARIE-ANTOINE is totally absorbed in her reading.*

MARIE-ANTOINE   *(reading)* On page one, "Lea has a pretty dress."

LEA   *(bursting in)* At last, they're talking about me. Looks like I'm just in time. Enough talk, we must run and dance now.

MARIE-ANTOINE   On page thirty-one, "Lea plays with her dolls."

LEA Balderdash, dolls!

MARIE-ANTOINE On page fifty-one, "Lea is a sweet little girl."

LEA Hurrah for the sweet little girl! (*She has crossed the stage and is climbing the stairs.*) On page one hundred and one, Lea has blond hair and a mocking smile, a clear eye, a lively tongue, a taste for risk, a taste for action, a taste for playing with wind and tornados. (*She reaches the top of the stairs.*) On page one thousand one hundred and one, Lea jumps out of the book, up on the desk, down on the chair, and into the room. (*She appears before MARIE-ANTOINE.*) On page two thousand and one, Lea spins around in the thick mass of her hair. On page five thousand and one, Lea-the-filly, Lea-the-free-mare, Lea-the-female gallops to the top of the mound of Venus, swept away in her desire for alpine conquests. There is no end in sight. The end was on page one.

> She grabs MARIE-ANTOINE and brings her to the top of the stairs. Then she claps her hands, commanding:

ACTION!

II. 7

JVORX, MME DELTONGRADE, IRENE, LAURA HOPKINS, VERA CRYSTAL, GIRALDINE, PIERRE, MARIE-ANTOINE, LEA.

JVORX, MME DELTONGRADE, her daughter IRENE, LAURA HOPKINS, and VERA CRYSTAL enter and stand in a semi-circle at the foot of the stairs. PIERRE enters abruptly, goes to the piano where GIRALDINE has remained seated, takes her hand and leads her to the staircase. Midway up the stairs, the couple turns to face the guests.

PIERRE My dear friends, you can't imagine how delighted I am to welcome you to our anniversary celebration. I don't want to make a long speech. I just want to say that our life is fulfilled, our happiness complete, and our accord… common. Giraldine, I love you. Thank you.

MME DELTONGRADE It's as touching as they day they were married. I think I'm going to cry.

LAURA HOPKINS Bravo, Monsieur de Magnana! I can see you are a great master. Congratulations, Madame de Courtepaille.

VERA CRYSTAL What a picture they make! Such a handsome couple. The pinnacle of art. And how sumptuous, how mysterious.

PIERRE (*moving down the stairs*) Pardon me, I must see what Abakanovitch is doing in the garden.

MME DELTONGRADE Pierre, come now. Abakanovitch has been dead for two years. Get a hold of yourself.

IRENE   Maman, could I have a glass of champagne?

LEA   MUSIC!

> *The rain stops. Pause. MARIE-ANTOINE moves slowly down the stairs followed by LEA.*

Short Oratorio of Marie-Antoine

MARIE-ANTOINE   *(spoken very simply)* My mother has the rough skin of stone statues. I press my ten fingers on the walls of her tomb. My imprints are like little prehistoric animals. I love her secretly because it's bad. I bury my secret next to her, my dirty desire, my filthy feet, my grimy fingers, and I wait for the bomb in the mountain. Night is a long time coming. When it's dark, I give birth to thousands of little animals. I pull out, I spit out, I rip out of my bowels all the crooked animals. They come out with picks and shovels. Together we dig a tunnel to the mountain. I want to offer my mud, my throat, my death to the mountain, my life to the bomb in the mountain. I hear my mother crying in the boiling night. The forest is on fire. One day I will come back here where I was born, I will return to see her absence in the sand. That is my own mirage, my waterless oasis. We have come close to the mountain. On my arm I write a message: "I am the child of the child. I am the baby of the baby. I am the secret of my drool." On my stomach I write: "Away with little pot-bellies." Drums beating like a heart, triumphantly I enter the mountain. All my animals let out prehistoric screams. On my forehead I write: "I am a rock that speaks in the fire." Outside I hear a march of young boys singing like girls. They march on like war. The goatsuckers sing at night, and yet, this is not a sign of death. I write again, on my legs, my feet, my chest, my forehead: "Lea is alone and unarmed." We are at the centre of the boiling night. All my crooked animals are singing. It must be very beautiful out tonight…. One last time I write on my body: "Do not shoot her."

> *MARIE-ANTOINE and LEA have reached the bottom steps. LEA moves between the two parents. MARIE-ANTOINE exits.*

LEA   CURTAIN!

> *The end.*

Bibliography

Anon. *Chansonnières québécoises II. Angèle Arsenault, 1975–1982; Édith Butler, 1975–1985; Clémence Desrochers, 1963–1985; Louise Forestier, 1974–1984.* Sherbrooke, Bibliothèque du Séminaire de Sherbrooke, 1986

Barrette, Michèle. "Dire aux éclats," *Cahiers de théâtre. Jeu.* [numéro spécial "Théâtre-Femmes" dirs: Michèle Barrette, Hélène Beauchamp, Émile Bessette, Gilbert David, Joceline Hardy, Lorraine Hébert, Pierre Lavoie, Francine Noël, Michel Vaïs] 16 (1980.3): 79–94.

Beauchamp-Rank, Hélène. "La Vie théâtrale à Montréal de 1950–1970: théâtres, troupes, saisons, répertoires," *Le Théâtre canadien-français.* Archives des Lettres Canadiennes, Tome V. Montréal: Fides, 1976. 267–90.

Beauchamp, Hélène & Judith Renaud. "Justement! oui, encore! Entretien avec le théâtre des Cuisines." *Cahiers de théâtre. Jeu.* 16 (1980.3): 97–115.

Beauchamp, Hélène & Gilbert David, Ed. *Théâtres québécois et canadiens-français au XXe Siècle.* Sainte-Foy: Presses de l'Universite du Québec, 2003.

Beauchamp, Hélène & Ric Knowles, Ed. "Theatre and Translation," "A Servant of Two Masters: an Interview with Linda Gaboriau," *Canadian Theatre Review.* 102 (Spring 2000): 41–47.

Belzil, Patricia & Solange Lévesque, Ed. *L'Album du Théâtre du Nouveau Monde.* Montréal: Éditions Jeu, 1997.

Bird, Kym. *Redressing the Past. The Politics of Early English-Canadian Women's Drama, 1880–1920.* Montréal & Kingston: McGill-Queen's Press, 2004.

Bishop, Neil B. "Enfance de l'oeuvre, enfance à l'oeuvre," *Nouveaux regards sur le théâtre québécois.* Ed. Betty Bednarski & Irene Oore. Montréal: XYZ, 1997: 59–70.

Boisclair, Isabelle. "Les Femmes et le fait littéraire (1900–1959)." *Ouvrir la voie/x. Le Processus constitutif d'un sous-champ littéraire féministe au Québec (1960–1990).* Québec: Nota bene, 2004: 71–111.

Borduas, Paul-Émile et al. *Refus global.* [Saint-Hilaire: Maurice Perron, 1948] Montréal: Anatole Brochu Éditeur, 1972.

Bourassa, André. "Premières Modernités 1930–1965," *Le Théâtre au Québec 1825–1980.* Ed. Renée Legris, Jean-Marc Larrue, André-G. Bourassa, Gilbert David. Montréal: VLB Éditeur, 1988: 89–110.

Brisset, Annie. *Sociocritique de la traduction: Théâtre et altérité au Québec (1968–1988).* Longueil: Préambule, 1990.

Burgoyne, Lynda. "Théâtre et homosexualité féminine," *Cahiers de théâtre. Jeu.* 54 (mars 1990): 114.

———. "Critique théâtrale et pouvoir androcentrique. Réception critique de «Leçon d'Anatomie» et de «Joie»," *Cahiers de théâtre. Jeu*, 65 (décembre 1992): 46–52.

———. "D'une sorcière à l'autre," *Cahiers de théâtre. Jeu*. 66 (mars 1993). Special issue on *Théâtre-femmes*: 29–37.

Butler, Judith. "Performative Acts and Gender Constitution: An Essay in Phenomenology and Feminist Theory," *Performing Feminisms. Feminist Critical Theory and Theatre*. Ed. Sue-Ellen Case. Baltimore & London, Johns Hopkins University Press, 1990: 270–82.

Camerlain, Lorraine. "L'Écriture dramatique des femmes, Prise 1: Un Festival en Mémoire," *Cahiers de théâtre. Jeu*. 32 (1984): 8–11.

———. "En de multiples scènes," *Canadian Theatre Review*. Special Issue on "Feminism and Canadian Theatre," Ed. Robert Wallace. 43 (Summer 1985). 73–90.

———. "O.K. On Change!," *Cahiers de théâtre. Jeu*. 45 (1987): 83–97.

———. "Un Mouvement irréversible," *Cahiers de théâtre. Jeu*. 66 (mars 1993). Special issue on *Théâtre-femmes*: 9–12.

Camerlain, Lorraine & Carole Fréchette. "Le Théâtre expérimental des femmes: essai en trois mouvements." *Cahiers de théâtre. Jeu*. 36 (1985.3): 59–66.

Carrière, Louise. *Femmes et cinéma québécois*. Montréal: Boréal Express, 1983.

Chartier, Daniel. "L'Oeuvre théâtrale d'Yvette Ollivier Mercier-Gouin devant la critique des années trente au Québec," *Nouveaux Regards sur le théâtre québécois*. Ed. Betty Bednarski & Irene Oore. Montréal: XYZ, 1997: 37–46.

———. "Le Théâtre d'Yvette Ollivier Mercier-Gouin: Égarement et désorganisation du système de réception," *L'Émergence des classiques. La Réception de la littérature québécoise des années 1930*. Montréal: Éditions Fides, 2000: 41–279.

Coll. "Les Automatistes," *La Barre du Jour*. 17-18-19-10 (janvier-août 1969).

Coll. *La Vraie Vie des masquées*. Montréal: Éditions du Remue-Ménage, 1977. [First production in 1977 in St-Bruno.]

Collectif Clio. *L'Histoire des femmes au Québec depuis quatre siècles*, nouvelle édition. Montréal: Le Jour, 1992.

Collin, Solange. "…Le Théâtre des Cuisines 1," *La Nouvelle Barre du Jour*. 196 (mars 1987). Special issue on "*Femmes scandales 1965–1985*": 27–32.

Cotnoir, Louise. "Woman/ Women on Stage." *A Mazing Space. Writing Canadian Women Writing*. Ed. Shirley Neuman & Smaro Kamboureli. Edmonton: Longspoon/ NeWest, 1986: 307–11.

Cotnoir, Louise & Louise Dupré. "La Traversée des miroirs," [About *Si Cendrillon pouvait mourir*] *La Nouvelle Barre du Jour*. 196 (mars 1987): 19–25. Special issue on "*Femmes scandales 1965–1985*."

Daoust, Jean-Paul. "3 et 7 le numéro magique," *Cahiers de théâtre. Jeu.* 9. (automne 1978): 56–58. [First produced at the CEGEP Édouard-Montpetit in Longueil April 15, 1978.]

David, Gilbert. "Un nouveau territoire théâtral, 1965–1980," *Le Théâtre au Québec 1925–1980*. Ed. Renée Legris, Jean-Marc Larrue, André-G. Bourassa, Gilbert David. Montréal: VLB Éditeur, 1988. 141–69

————. "Un Théâtre à vif: Écritures dramatiques et pratiques scéniques au Québec, de 1930 à 1990," Thèse de doctorat, 1995. Université de Montréal.

Delisle, Jeanne-Mance. *Un Reel ben beau, ben triste*. Montréal: Éditions de la Pleine Lune, 1980. [First produced by the Théâtre de Coppe (Rouyn) in May 1978.]

Donohoe, Joseph I. & Jonathan M. Weiss. *Essays on Modern Quebec Theater*. East Lansing: Michigan State University Press, 1995.

Doucette, L.E. "Drama in French." *The Oxford Companion to Canadian Theatre*. Ed. Eugene Benson & L.W. Conolly. Toronto, Oxford, New York: Oxford University Press, 1989: 169–82.

Dumont, Micheline & Louise Toupin. *La Pensée féministe au Québec. Anthologie (1900–1985)*. Montréal: Éditions du Remue-Ménage, 2003.

Du Sablon, Claire. *Chronologie historique des femmes du Québec*. http://www.pages.infinit.net/histoire/femmes.html.

Eddie, Christine. *Le 20e Siècle de la culture québécoise: la quête d'une identité*. 2002. http://www.stat.gouv.qc.ca/observatoire/publicat_obs/pdf/IVCulture.pdf.

Féral, Josette. "Écriture et déplacement: la femme au théâtre," *The French Review*. 56.2 (December 1982): 281–92.

————. "«Enfin de véritables serviteurs du théâtre!»." [Interview with Françoise Berd, March 15, *Solitude rompue*. Ed. Cécile Cloutier-Wojciechowska & Réjean Robidoux. Ottawa: Éditions de l'Université d'Ottawa, 1986: 103–12.

————. "La Place des femmes dans les théories actuelles du jeu théâtral: l'exemple de Pol Pelletier," *Nouveaux Regards sur le théâtre québécois*. Ed. Betty Bednarski & Irene Oore. Montréal & Halifax: XYZ Éditeur & Dalhousie French Studies, 1997: 105–16.

————, ed. *Theatricality*. Special Issue of *SubStance*. 31.2/3 (98/99), (2002). http://muse.jhu.edu/journals/substance/toc/sub31.2.html.

————. "Arrêter le mental. Entretien avec Pol Pelletier," *Cahiers de théâtre. Jeu*, 65 (décembre 1992): 35–45.

Forsyth, Louise H. "First Person Feminine Singular: Monologues by Women in Several Modern Quebec Plays," *Canadian Drama/L'Art Dramatique Canadien*. 5.2 (1979).

————. "Feminist Theatre," *The Oxford Companion to Canadian Theatre*. Ed. Eugene Benson & L.W. Conolly. Toronto, Oxford, New York: Oxford University Press, 1989: 203–06.

————. "L'Acte théâtral au féminin: la transgression de la représentation théâtrale par la répétition et le spectacle," *Les Discours féminins dans la littérature postmoderne au Québec*. Ed. Raija Koski, Kathleen Kells, Louise H. Forsyth. San Francisco: Edwin Mellen Press, 1993: 185–202.

————. "Relire le théâtre-femmes. *Encore cinq minutes* de Françoise Loranger," *L'Annuaire théâtral*, 21 (printemps 1997): 43–61.

————. "*A Clash of Symbols*: When I Put on What I Want to Put On," *Canadian Theatre Review*. [Special Issue on "Solo Performance, Ed. Ric Knowles & Harry Lane] 92 (Fall 1997): 27.

Forte, Jeannie. "Women's Performance Art: Feminism and Postmodernism." *Performing Feminisms. Feminist Critical Theory and Theatre*. Ed. Sue-Ellen Case. Baltimore & London, Johns Hopkins University Press, 1990: 251–69.

Fréchette, Carole. "Deux ou trois choses à propos de mon parcours d'auteure." *Théâtre. Les Cahiers de la Maîtrise*. 7 (2002): 93–95.

Gaboriau, Linda. "Jovette Marchessault. A Luminous Wake in Space." *Canadian Theatre Review*. 43 (Summer 1985): 91–99.

————. "Traduire le génie de l'auteur." *Cahiers de théâtre. Jeu*. 56 (sept. 1990): 43–48. [Special Issue on «Traduction théâtrale», Ed. Pierre Lavoie.]

————. "The Cultures of Theatre." *Culture in Transit: Translating the Literature of Quebec*. Ed. Sherry Simon. Montréal: Véhicule, 1995: 83–90.

Gagnon, Dominique, Louise Laprade, Nicole Lecavalier & Pol Pelletier. *À ma mère, à ma mère, à ma mère, à ma voisine*. Montréal: Éditions du Remue-Ménage, 1979. [First produced at the Théâtre Expérimental de Montréal May 16–June 11, 1978.]

Gagnon, Lise. "Que sont les féministes devenues?" *Cahiers de théâtre. Jeu*. 117 (décembre 2005): 29–33.

Gauvin, Lise. "Conversation avec Thérèse Renaud." *Entretiens avec Fernand Leduc, suivis de Conversation avec Thérèse Renaud*. Saint-Laurent: Liber, 1995: 149–73.

Godard, Barbara. "Between Repetition and Rehearsal: Conditions of (Women's) Theatre in Canada in a Space of Reproduction," *Theatre Research in Canada/Recherches Théâtrales au Canada* (1992): 18–33.

Godin, Jean-Cléo & Dominique Lafon. "Pour ne rien oublier, Marie Laberge, La parole-femme," "Chronologie 1980–1990." *Dramaturgies québécoises des années quatre-vingt*. Montréal: Leméac, 1999. 173–97, 217.

Godin, Jean-Cléo & Laurent Mailhot. *Le Théâtre québécois. Introduction à dix dramaturges contemporains*. Montréal: Hurtubise HMH, 1970.

————. *Le Théâtre québécois II. Nouveaux auteurs, autres spectacles.* Montréal: Hurtubise HMH, 1980.

Greffard, Madeleine. "Le Théâtre à la radio: Un facteur de légitimation et de redéfinition." *L'Annuaire théâtral.* 23 (été/automne 1998): 53–73.

Greffard, Madeleine & Jean-Guy Sabourin. *Le Théâtre québécois.* Éditions Boréal Express, 1997.

Haentjens, Brigitte, Catherine Caron & Sylvie Trudel. *Strip.* Ottawa: Éditions Prise de Parole, 1983.

Hébert, Chantal. *Le Burlesque au Québec. Un Divertissement populaire.* Montréal: Hurtubise HMH, 1981.

Hébert, Lorraine. "Pour une définition de la création collective," *Cahiers de théâtre. Jeu.* 6 (été/ automne 1977): 38–46.

————. "Réquisitoires," *Cahiers de Théâtre. Jeu.* 16 (1980.3): 57–78.

Jasmin, Judith. "Problèmes du spectacle au Canada I et II." *La Nouvelle Revue Canadienne.* 1. 1 & 2. (fév.-mars 1951): 72–80.

Jean, Michèle. *Québécoises du 20e Siècle.* Montréal: Éditions du Jour, 1974.

Knowles, Ric and Harry Lane. "Editorial: Solo Performance." *Canadian Theatre Review.* 92 (Fall 1997): 3–4.

Kolodny, Annette. "Dancing through the Minefield: Some Observations on the Theory, Practice, and Politics of a Feminist Literary Criticism." *Feminisms, an Anthology.* Ed. Robyn R. Warhol. New Brunswick: Rutgers University Press, 1997.

Koustas, Jane. "Traduire ou ne pas traduire le théâtre? L'Approche sémiotique," *Traduction, Terminologie, Rédaction.* 1.1 (1988): 127–38.

————. "From Gélinas to Carrier: Critical Response to Translated Quebec Theatre in Toronto." *Studies in Canadian Literature.* 17:2 (1992).

————. "From Homespun to Awesome: Translated Theatre in Toronto," *Essays on Modern Quebec Theatre.* Ed. Joseph Donohue Jr. & Jonathan M. Weiss. East Lansing: Michigan State University Press, 1995. 81–109.

Ladouceur, Louise. "Separate Stages: La Traduction du théâtre dans le contexte Canada/Québec," Diss. University of British Columbia, Vancouver, 1997.

————. "A Version of Quebec: le théâtre québécois au Canada anglais," *L'Annuaire théâtral.* 27 (printemps 2000): 108–19.

————. Making the Scene: la traduction du théâtre d'une langue officielle à l'autre au Canada. Québec: Éditions Nota bene, 2005.

Lafon, Dominique. "L'Image de la femme dans le théâtre québécois." *Revue de l'Université d'Ottawa.* 50.1 (1980). 148–52.

————. "Entre Cassandre et Clytemnestre: le théâtre québécois, 1970–1990." *Theatre Research International*. 17.3 (automne1992): 236–45.

————, Ed. *Le Théâtre québécois 1975–1995*. Montréal: Fides, 2001 Archives des Lettres Canadiennes, Tome X.

Lamonde, Yvan. "La Modernité au Québec: pour une histoire des brèches (1895–1950)." *Territoires de la culture québécoise*. Sainte-Foy: Presses de l'Université Laval, 1991. 259–74.

Lamy, Suzanne. D'*Elles*. Montréal: Éditions de l'Hexagone, 1979.

Laplante-L'Héraut, Juliette. "Le Théâtre de Femmes au Québec (1966–1982): Contexte et Textes." MA, Université Concordia, 1987.

Laprade, Louise. "Autour du Théâtre Expérimental des Femmes." *La Nouvelle Barre du Jour*. 196 (mars 1987): 81–86. "*Femmes scandales 1965–1985*"

Larrue, Jean-Marc. "Le Théâtre au Québec entre 1930 et 1950: les années charnières." *L'Annuaire Théâtral*. 23 (printemps 1998): 19–37.

Lavoie, Pierre. "«L'Espoir est une poire»," *Cahiers de théâtre. Jeu*, 65 (décembre 1992): 24–29.

Leblanc, Alonzo. "Femmes en solo." "Le Théâtre," *Revue d'histoire littéraire du Québec et du Canada français*. Dir. René Dionne. 5 (hiver-printemps 1983): 89–98.

Legris, Renée. "Radio Drama in Québec." "Television Drama in Québec." *The Oxford Companion to Canadian Theatre*. Ed. Eugene Benson & L.W. Conolly. Toronto, Oxford, New York: Oxford University Press, 1989: 456–58, 522–24.

————. "Les Dramatiques à la télévision 1969–1996," *Panorama de la littérature québécoise contemporaine*. Ed. Réginald Hamel. Montréal: Guérin, 1997: 64–97.

Legris, Renée & Louise Blouin. "Les Écritures fonctionnelles de la radio 1969–1996," *Panorama de la littérature québécoise contemporaine*. Ed. Réginald Hamel. Montréal: Guérin, 1997: 35–63.

Legris, Renée & Pierre Pagé. "Le Théâtre à la radio et à la télévision au Québec," *Le Théâtre canadien-français*. Archives des Lettres Canadiennes, Tome V. Montréal: Fides, 1976: 291–318.

MacDougall, Jill. *Performing Identities on the Stages of Québec*. New York: New York University, 1993.

MacDougall, Jill & P. Stanley Yoder, Ed. *Contaminating Theatre. Intersections of Theatre, Therapy, and Public Health*. Evanston, Ill. Northwestern University Press, 1998.

Maheux-Forcier, Louise. *Arioso*, suivi de *Papiers d'Arménie*. Montréal: Pierre Tisseyre, 1981. [Produced and broadcast on Radio-Canada, January 1982. In order to avoid "scandal," this representation of love between two women had been refused in 1973.]

Mailhot, Laurent. "Orientation récentes du théâtre québécois." *Le Théâtre canadien-français*. Archives des Lettres Canadiennes, Tome V. Montréal: Fides, 1976. 319–40.

Mailhot, Laurent & Doris-Michel Montpetit. *Monologues québécois 1890–1980*. Montréal: Leméac, 1980.

Mercier-Gouin, Yvette. *Cocktail*. Montréal: Éditions Albert Lévesque, 1935. [First produced at the Théâtre Stella in Montréal on March 22, 1935 and at the Palais Montcalm in Québec on May 23, 1935.]

Moss, Jane. "Les Folles du Québec: The Theme of Madness in Quebec Women's Theater." *The French Review*. 57.5 (April 1984): 617–24.

———. "Women's Theater in Quebec.," *Traditionalism, Nationalism, and Feminism: Women Writers of Quebec*. Ed. Paula Gilbert Lewis. Westport, Conn.: Greenwood Press, 1985: 241–54.

———. "Creation Reenacted: The Woman Artist as Dramatic Figure." *The American Review of Canadian Studies*. 15.3 (Autumn 1985): 263–72.

———. "Giants and Fat Ladies: Carnival Themes in Contemporary Quebec Theater." *Québec Studies*. 3 (1985): 160–68.

———. "Bingo, Zorro and Nashville: Popular Culture and Recent Quebec Drama." *Journal of Canadian Culture*: 51–59.

———. "The Body as Spectacle: Women's Theater in Quebec." *Women & Performance: A Journal of Feminist Theory*. 3.1 (1986): 56–64.

———. "Living with Liberation: Quebec Drama in the Feminist Age." *Atlantis*. 14.1 (Fall 1988): 32–37.

———. "In Search of Lost Intimacy: Mothers and Daughters in Women's Theatre." *Modern Language Studies* (1989): 45–52.

———. "Fillial (Im)pieties: Mothers and Daughters in Quebec Women's Theater." *American Review of Canadian Studies*. 19.2 (1989): 177–85.

———. "Women's Theater in Quebec: Choruses, Monologues and Dialogues." *Feminist Voices*. 276.

———. "Dramatizing Sexual Difference: Gay and Lesbian Theater in Quebec." *American Review of Canadian Studies*. 22.4 (Winter 1992): 489–98.

———. "'All in the Family': Québec Family Drama in the 1980s." *Journal of Canadian Studies*. 27.2 (Summer 1992): 97–106.

———. "Hysterical Pregnancies and Post-Partum Blues: Staging the Maternal Body in Recent Quebec Plays," *Essays on Modern Quebec Theater*. Ed. Joseph I. Donohoe Jr. & Jonathan M. Weiss. East Lansing: Michigan State University Press, 1995: 47–59.

———. "Family Histories: Marie Laberge and Women's Theater in Quebec." *Postcolonial Subjects: Francophone Women Writers.* Ed. Karen Gould, Mary Jean Green, Micheline Rice-Maximin, Keith Walker, Jack Yeager. Minneapolis: University of Minnesota Press, 1996: 79–97.

———. "Dramatizing the Discourse of Female Desire." *Women by Women. The Treatment of Female Characters by Women Writers of Fiction in Quebec since 1980.* Ed. Roseanna Lewis Dufault. Madison & Teaneck: Fairleigh Dickinson University Press & Associated University Presses, 1997: 17–28.

———. "Québécois Theatre: Michel Tremblay and Marie Laberge." *Theatre Research International.* 21/3 (Fall 1996): 196–207.

Nardocchio, Elaine F. "1958–1968: Ten Formative Years in Quebec's Theatre History." *Canadian Drama/L'Art Dramatique Canadien.* 9:1 (1983): 165–94.

Nichols, Glen, ed. "Translation/Traduction," *Theatre Research in Canada/ Recherches Théâtrales au Canada.* 24.1–2 (2003).

Noël, Francine. "Plaidoyer pour mon image," *Cahiers de Théâtre. Jeu.* 16 (1980.3): 23–56.

Noiseux, Ginette. "De Quoi j'me mêle?" *Cahiers de Théâtre. Jeu.* 34 (1984.3): 13–24.

———. "Du Théâtre Expérimental des Femmes à l'Espace GO: Entretien avec Ginette Noiseux." *Cahiers de théâtre. Jeu.* 57 (1990): 196–207.

———. "Du Théâtre Expérimental des Femmes à l'Espace GO [1985]: Une Autre Manière de Dire," *Théâtre. Les Cahiers de la Maîtrise,* 7 (2002): 44–55.

O'Leary, Véronique. "…Le Théâtre des Cuisines 2." *La Nouvelle Barre du Jour.* 196 (mars 1987): 33–50. *"Femmes scandales 1965–1985"*

O'Neill-Karch, Mariel & Pierre Paul Karch. "Le Théâtre québécois à Toronto," "Le Théâtre." *Revue d'histoire littéraire du Québec et du Canada français.* Dir. René Dionne . 5 (hiver-printemps 1983): 99–105.

Oore, Irene. "Les Couples de voix dans le théâtre radiophonique de Marie-Claire Blais." *Nouveaux Regards sur le Théâtre Québécois.* Ed. Betty Bednarski & Irene Oore. Montréal: XYZ, 1997: 71–82.

Pedneault, Hélène. *Notre Clémence. Tout l'Humour du Vrai Monde.* Montréal: Éditions de l'Homme, 1989.

Pelletier, Francine. "3 femmes, un théâtre." *Femme du Québec* (nov.-déc. 1979): 5–6.

———. "Cinq Pièces de femmes." *Cahiers de théâtre. Jeu.* 16 (1980): 219–24.

Pelletier, Pol. "Histoire d'une Féministe." *Trac. Cahier de théâtre expérimental* (déc. 1978): 92–113.

———. "Petite Histoire du théâtre de femmes au Québec." *Canadian Woman Studies/ Cahiers de la Femme.* 2.2 (1980): 85–87.

———. *La Lumière blanche*. Montréal: Les Herbes Rouges, 1989: [First produced at the TEF April 9, 1981.]

———. *Joie*. Montréal: Éditions du Remue-Ménage, 1995.

———. "Réflexions autour de «Joie»," *Cahiers de théâtre. Jeu*, 65 (décembre 1992): 29–34.

Perrault, Katherine. "Beyond the Patriarchy: Feminism and the Chaos of Creativity." *Journal of Dramatic Theory and Criticism*. 17.1 (Fall 2002): 45–67.

Portal, Louise & Marie-Louise Dion. *Où en est le miroir?* Montréal: Éditions du Remue-Ménage, 1979. [First produced on April 12, 1978 at the Centre d'essai of L'Université de Montréal, by Le Théâtre de la Manufacture.]

Raymond, Yves & Gilbert David. "Autour de *La Cathédrale…* (1949) de Jean Despréz. Une Création à l'ombre de *Tit-Coq*." *L'Annuaire théâtral*. 23 (printemps 1998): 109–30.

Renaud, Thérèse. *Une Mémoire déchirée*. Montréal: L'Arbre HMH, 1978.

Riendeau, Pascal & Bernard Andrès. "La Dramaturgie depuis 1980." *Panorama de la littérature québécoise contemporaine*. Ed. Réginald Hamel. Montréal: Guérin, 1997: 208.

Robert, Lucie. "Réflexions sur trois lieux communs concernant les femmes et le théâtre," *Revue d'Histoire Littéraire du Québec et du Canada français*. 5.2 (hiver 1983): 75–88.

———. "Pour une histoire de la dramaturgie québécoise." *L'Annuaire théâtral*. 5–6: 163–69.

———. "The New Quebec Theater." *Canadian Canons: Essays in Literary Value*. Ed. Robert Lecker. Toronto: University of Toronto Press, 1991: 112–23.

———. "Changing the Subject: A Reading of Contemporary Feminist Drama." *Women on the Canadian Stage: The Legacy of Hrotsvit*. Ed. Rita Much. Winnipeg: Blizzard Publishing, 1992.

———. "Les Revues," *Panorama de la littérature québécoise contemporaine*. Ed. Réginald Hamel. Montréal: Guérin, 1997: 141–85.

———. "Une Carrière impossible: la dramaturgie au féminin." *Trajectoires au féminin dans la littérature québécoise (1960–1990)*. Ed. Lucie Joubert. Québec: Éditions Nota Bene, 2000: 141–55.

———. "Le Grand Récit féminin ou de quelques usages de la narrativité dans les textes dramatiques de femmes." *Le Théâtre et ses nouvelles dynamiques narratives*. Ed. Chantal Hébert & Irène Perelli-Contos. Sainte-Foy: Presses de l'Université Laval, 2004: 61–85.

Rubess, Bañuta. "Montreal Pol Pelletier, March 1985." *CTR*, 43 (Summer 1985): 179–84.

Show des Femmes de Thetford Mines. *Si Cendrillon Pouvait Mourir!* Montréal: Éditions du Remue Ménage, 1980. [First produced at Thetford Mines on March 8, 1975]

Simard, François-Xavier & André La Rose. *Jean Despréz (1960–1965). Une Femme de tête, de courage et de coeur.* Ottawa: Éditions du Vermillon, 2002.

Smart, Patricia. *Les Femmes du Refus Global.* Montréal: Éditions du Boréal, 1998.

Sullivan, Françoise. "La Danse et l'espoir," *Refus global.* Montréal: Anatole Brochu Éditeur, 1772: 95–106.

Théâtre des Cuisines. *Môman travaille pas, a trop d'ouvrage.* Montréal: Éditions du Remue-Ménage, 1976. [Founded in 1973 par Solange Collin, Carole Fréchette, Véronique O'Leary, *Nous Aurons les Enfants que Nous Voulons* first produced on March 8, 1974 in the Saint-Édouard parish hall in Montréal, another show in 1975, and *Môman* in 1976.]

———. "Manifeste du Théâtre des Cuisines (1975)." *Cahiers de théâtre. Jeu.* 7 (hiver 1978): 69–78.

———. *As-Tu Vu? Les Maisons s'emportent!* Montréal: Éditions du Remue-Ménage, 1980. [First produced May 10, 1980 in the Auditorium of the CEGEP Rosemont.]

Thibault, Gérard & Chantal Hébert. "Une 'Star' est née chez Gérard." *Chez Gérard. La Petite Scène des Grandes Vedettes. 1938–1978.* Sainte-Foy: Éditions Spectaculaires, 1988: 281–94.

Tremblay-Matte, Cécile. *La Chanson écrite au féminin. 1730–1990 de Madeleine de Verchères à Mitsou.* Laval: Éditions Trois, 1990.

Vaillancourt, Lise. "Montrer l'ensemble d'un monde vu et réalisé par des femmes." *Cahiers de théâtre. Jeu.* 36 (1985.3): 67–69.

Villemaire, Yolande. *Belles de nuit.* Montréal: Les Herbes Rouges, 1983. ["Belles de nuit" was broadcast by Radio-Canada FM on May 27, 1983.]

Wallace, Robert. "D'où cela vient-il? Réflexions sur la réception critique du théâtre francophone récent à Toronto." Tr. Michel Vaïs. *Cahiers de théâtre. Jeu.* 49 (1988): 9–21.

Wilson, Ann, Ed. "Publishing Canadian Theatre." Special Issue of *Canadian Theatre Review.* 98 (Spring 1999).

Zimmerman, Cynthia. *Playwriting Women. Female Voices in English Canada.* Toronto: Simon & Pierre, 1994.

About the Translators *

Louise H. Forsyth is professor emerita at the University of Saskatchewan, where she combined teaching and graduate supervision among the departments of Women's and Gender Studies, Languages and Linguistics, and Drama. She worked for many years at the University of Western Ontario. She published translations of three early Québec plays in *Canada's Lost Plays*, Vol. IV, of Marie Savard's *Bien à moi*, and of various texts in connection to her research on Québec writer Nicole Brossard. Her previously unpublished translations include Margaret Hollingsworth's *War Babies* into French (student production at the University of Western Ontario 1990) and Françoise Loranger's *Double jeu* (in this volume).

Rina Fraticelli. As a dramaturge and writer in the theatre and as a filmmaker, Rina Fraticelli has worked since the early 70s to strengthen the presence of women in Canadian society. In 1982, she authored *The Status of Women in the Canadian Theatre*, which described in detail, and for the first time, the extent and mechanics of women's systematic marginalization. Later, as Executive Producer of Studio D, the groundbreaking women's studio of the National Film Board of Canada, she oversaw the production of such works as *A Company of Strangers* and *Forbidden Love*; and extended the mandate of the studio to ensure the full participation of First Nations and visible minority women. As an independent filmmaker, she wrote "Women: A True Story" directed by Lea Pool and narrated by Susan Sarandon; as well as writing, directing and producing a number of films on a range of social issues and arts subjects. She was awarded a Genie for producing "Fiction and Other Truths: A Film about Jane Rule". Rina Fraticelli first encountered the work of Marie Laberge through Transmissions, a programme she developed while director of Playwrights Workshop in Montreal to foster translations of Canadian plays, commissioning John Murrell to translate Laberge's chef d'oeuvre *C'était avant la guerre à l'Anse à L'Ance à Gilles* [*Before the War at L'Anse à Gilles*]. In addition to *L'Homme gris*, Fraticelli has translated two other plays by Laberge, *Oublier* [*Take Care*] and *Aurélie ma soeur* [*My Sister Aurelie*]. Rina Fraticelli is currently executive producer of the Pacific and Yukon Studio of the National Film Board of Canada.

Linda Gaboriau is a Montreal-based dramaturg and literary translator. Born in Boston, Massachusetts, Gaboriau moved to Montreal, Quebec in 1963 to pursue education in French Language and Literature at McGill University. She has worked as a freelance journalist for the CBC as well as the Montreal *Gazette*, and worked in Canadian and Quebecois theatre. Gaboriau has won awards for her translations of more than 70 plays and novels by Quebec writers, including many of the Quebec plays best known to English Canadian audiences.

Pamela Grant is a professor and head of English Studies in the *Département des lettres et communications* at the *Université de Sherbrooke*, where she teaches courses in professional writing, editing, translation, and translation theory. She holds a PhD in Linguistics from the *Université de Montréal*. She was the Quebec English specialist for the *Canadian Oxford Dictionary* and is on the Advisory Committee for the revised edition of the *Guide to Canadian English Usage*. She is a co-editor of the *Bibliography of Comparative Studies in Canadian, Québec, and Foreign Literatures* and has published her research in a variety of scholarly publications in Canada, Europe, and the United States. She is an accredited professional translator (OTTIAQ).

Susanne de Lotbinière-Harwood lives and teaches in Montréal. She published "Re-belle et infidèle: la traduction comme pratique de ré-écriture au féminin/The Body Bilingual: translation as a rewriting in the feminine" (Remue-ménage/Women's Press, 1991), as well as numerous texts about her practice of both literary and art-text translation. Her work in these fields led to years of "performative lecturing" in North America and Europe, and to an exhibition of her art-text translation artifacts at La Centrale, Montréal, 2001.

Jill MacDougall. Translator of Francophone plays, cultural politics critic, and director, facilitator and teacher of theatre, Jill MacDougall has worked in France, Congo, Ivory Coast, Quebec, and the United States. Her publications include numerous articles and translations of African and Québécois playwrights as well as two books: *Contaminating Theatre: Intersections of Theatre, Therapy, and Public Health* co-edited with P. Stanley Yoder and *Performing Identities on the Stages of Quebec*. She is currently co-director of Theatre Dynamics, workshops using theatre for personal and social change.

Gregory J. Reid is a professor of English and Comparative Literature and Drama in the *Département des lettres et communications* of the *Université de Sherbrooke*. He is the author of *The Cunning to Be Strange* (a collection of short stories) and *A Re-examination of Tragedy and Madness in Eight Selected Plays from the Greeks to the 20th Century*, and a co-editor of the *Bibliography of Comparative Studies in Canadian, Québec and Foreign Literatures*. His recent articles "Mapping *Jouissance*: Insights from a Case Study in the Schizophrenia of Canadian Drama" in *Comparative Drama* and (with Christine Famula) "Catachresis in Antonine Maillet's *La Sagouine* and the Luis De Céspedes Translation" in *Theatre Research in Canada* are reflections on the process of translating drama.

[*] Despite my best efforts, I was unable to obtain bio notes for Alan Brown, R. Chamberlain, and Luis de Céspedes. (LHF)

About the Editor

Louise H. Forsyth has always loved performance and theatre. As an amateur lover of the stage, she has acted, sung, danced, written, directed, produced, translated, stage managed, served as props manager, and hung out as much as she could as spectator. Woven into an amateur obsession with theatre has been her professional life, where she wrote two theses on the French classic writer of theatrical comedy, Molière, taught courses and supervised theses in theatre, drama, and dramatic literature, wrote scholarly studies about French and Québec playwrights, and theorized about acting and dramatic writing. Her areas of academic specialization are feminist performance and dramaturgy in Québec. Along with her passion for what the women of Québec have written for theatre, she has been engaged for quite some time with developing theories of dramaturgy and acting *au féminin*, along with revealing the sources of tenacious sexism in the practices and conventions for doing theatre, for studying and evaluating it, and for recounting its history. In short, she has been wondering for quite some time why women's roles have tended to remain stereotypical in works for stage, TV and film, why theatre done by women—when its perspective is explicitly derived from a woman's point of view—is still easily dismissed with a summary shrug as deserving only condescending scorn, why women's theatrical experimentation is so rarely discussed by scholars as serious theoretical work or used by them in their own theoretical reflections, and why the silence of critics on women and their richly creative activities has not yet been overcome when it comes to their accounts of theatre history.